Joseph A. DeVito
Hunter College of the City

Dawne Clark
Mount Royal College

D0902774

Messages

Building
Interpersonal
Communication
Skills

**Third
Canadian
Edition**

PEARSON
and

Toronto

ICE

CANADIAN IN-CLASS EDITION

Library and Archives Canada Cataloguing in Publication

DeVito, Joseph A., 1938–
    Messages : building interpersonal communication skills / Joseph A.
DeVito, Rena Shimoni, Dawne E. Clark.—3rd Canadian ed.

Includes bibliographical references and index.
ISBN 978-0-205-50230-1

    1. Interpersonal communication—Textbooks. I. Shimoni, Rena, 1948–
II. Clark, Dawne, 1952– III. Title.

BF637.C45D48 2008   158.2   C2006-906338-9

Copyright © 2008, 2005, 2001 Pearson Education Canada, a division of Pearson Canada Inc.,
Toronto, Ontario.
Pearson Allyn and Bacon. All rights reserved. This publication is protected by copyright and
permission should be obtained from the publisher prior to any prohibited reproduction, stor-
age in a retrieval system, or transmission in any form or by any means, electronic, mechan-
ical, photocopying, recording, or likewise. For information regarding permission, write to the
Permissions Department.

Original edition published by Pearson Education, Inc., Upper Saddle River, New Jersey, USA.
Copyright © 2005 Pearson Education, Inc. This edition is authorized for sale only in Canada.

ISBN-13: 978-0-205-50230-1
ISBN-10: 0-205-50230-X

Editor-in-Chief, Vice-President of Sales: Kelly Shaw
Acquisitions Editor: Chris Helsby
Sponsoring Editor: Carolin Sweig
Marketing Manager: Leigh-Anne Graham
Supervising Developmental Editor: Suzanne Schaan
Production Editor: Amanda Wesson
Copy Editor: Julie Fletcher
Proofreader: Valerie Adams
Production Coordinator: Janis Raisen
Composition: Christine Velakis
Photo Research: Bree Seeley
Permissions Research: Bree Seeley
Art Director: Julia Hall
Cover Design: David Cheung
Interior Design: Anthony Leung
Cover Image: Getty Images/Stockbyte

For permission to reproduce copyrighted material, the publisher gratefully acknowledges the
copyright holders listed on page 332, which is considered an extension of this copyright page.

Statistics Canada information is used with the permission of Statistics Canada. Users are forbidden to copy the data and redisseminate them, in an original or modified form, for commercial purposes, without permission from Statistics Canada. Information on the availability
of the wide range of data from Statistics Canada can be obtained from Statistics Canada's
Regional Offices, its World Wide Web site at http://www.statcan.ca, and its toll-free access
number 1-800-263-1136.

1 2 3 4 5   12 11 10 09 08

Printed and bound in the United States of America.

Brief Contents

Contents

Part Three

Messages in Context   193

Specialized Contents

Preface

This book was written in response to the need for a text that emphasizes **critical thinking** by integrating it into all aspects of interpersonal communication, encourages the development of **interpersonal skills** (the practical skills for personal, social, and professional success), explains the influence of **culture** and **gender** on just about every aspect of interpersonal communication, and stresses **listening** as an essential (but too often neglected) part of interpersonal communication. *Messages* answers these needs by providing thorough coverage of each of these major elements, which are introduced in Chapter 1 as integral components of interpersonal competence and then reinforced throughout the book through discussion and real-life examples and exercises.

This edition of *Messages* also responds to the specific needs of Canadian students. Although there are many similarities between Canadians and Americans, there are also clear demographic differences in our countries that affect communication. Therefore, we have included Canadian examples, told Canadian stories, and where possible, quoted Canadian research. Our students need to be aware of the fact that Canadians haven't been as prolific in communication research. If they want more Canadian research, we encourage them to go on to graduate studies and add more original Canadian research to the existing knowledge bank.

New to This Edition

Key changes in this third Canadian edition include the following:

- This In-Class edition is aimed at ensuring student success through new **pedagogical features** that help students develop better study techniques and strategies (see detailed descriptions below).

- Chapter 12 has been revised to provide a new focus on **workplace communication**. Effective communication in the workplace is crucial for career success and for the success of the organization in today's highly competitive world. Many workplaces are extremely diverse—people from different cultures, different ages, and life stages, as well as people with different abilities and diverse professional orientations. Accompanying all these differences are very different styles and norms of communication. This chapter will help students gain an understanding of the barriers to effective communication that result from these differences and provide helpful strategies to effective communication in the workplace. We consider verbal, written, and electronic communication in the workplace as a way of creating effective teams and promoting leadership throughout the organization.

- **New technologies**—such as cell phones and text messaging—and the implications of **computer-mediated communications** for interpersonal communication are considered throughout the text, especially in Chapters 8 and 10. Technology is changing both the way we communicate and the substance of our interpersonal relationships. While most young people have simply accepted the new technology as the way they live, very few of them have considered how it is changing the world of interpersonal communication in some very deep and meaningful ways that may isolate them from other generations in both their personal and professional lives.

- The coverage of **intercultural communication** has been updated throughout the text, especially in Chapter 9.
- New material has been incorporated on topics such as **ageism** (Chapter 5), **nonverbal communication** (Chapter 6), **anger** (Chapter 7), and **conflict management** (Chapter 11).
- New research had been added throughout.
- A new Canadian **Companion Website** is tied directly to this edition, offering practice quizzes and other resources.

In-Class Features

A number of new features have been added to the book to create an In-Class edition. These features are designed to help students get the most out of the course, both in class and out:

- **What Kind of Learner Are You?** The self-assessment quiz on page xix will show students how they learn. Icons representing five key learning styles mark the **Study Tips** that appear throughout the text in the margin. This feature will help students develop a variety of study skills and tactics to improve their chance of success.

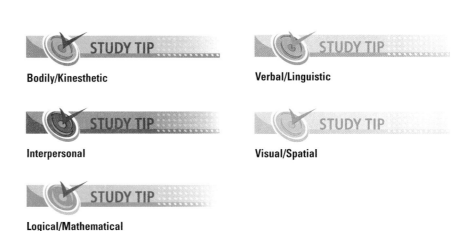

Bodily/Kinesthetic

Verbal/Linguistic

Interpersonal

Visual/Spatial

Logical/Mathematical

- **In-Class Notes.** Each chapter has several **In-Class Notes** correlated to instructors' PowerPoint slides containing key information, with space for students to make notes while in class or while reading after class. Making good notes is one of the keys to being a successful student. When students refer back to the notes in the original context as they prepare for tests or exams, they will find that they can recall the information more easily.

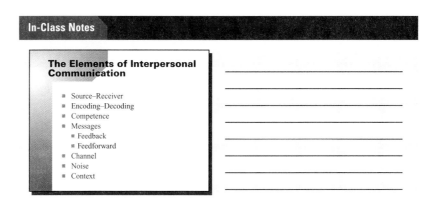

In-Class Notes

The Elements of Interpersonal Communication

- Source–Receiver
- Encoding–Decoding
- Competence
- Messages
  - Feedback
  - Feedforward
- Channel
- Noise
- Context

- **Embedded Study Guide.** A **vocabulary quiz**, **multiple choice questions**, and **true–false questions** at the end of each chapter offer students a good way to practise for tests; they can check their answers in the answer key at the back of the text.

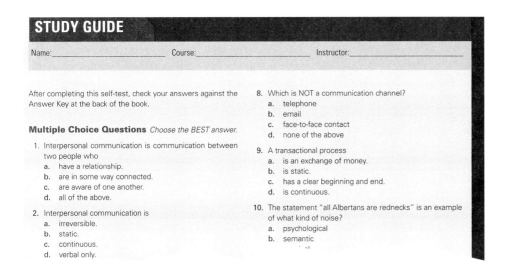

- **Introduction to Interpersonal Communication: A Study Chart with Research Navigator™.** Packaged with every new copy of the text is a handy laminated chart with key concepts and important terms described and defined in note form for easy reference. The chart also contains an access code for Research Navigator™, an online research tool that provides research tips as well as access to a database of journal articles. The Study Guide at the end of each chapter includes questions for further study using Research Navigator™.

Interactive Pedagogy

In addition to the special in-class features noted above, the text includes a variety of features that ask students to respond to and get personally involved with the material presented:

- **Test Yourself** offers self-tests that encourage students to assess themselves on a wide variety of interpersonal issues discussed throughout the text—for example, willingness to self-disclose, conversational satisfaction, ethnocentricity, and

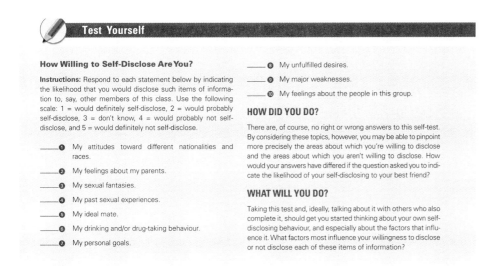

tendency to be aggressive and argumentative in conflict situations. At the end of each self-test are two types of questions. The first asks, "How did you do?" and contains scoring instructions so that students can compute their own score for the self-test. The second asks, "What will you do?" and invites students to consider the changes (if any) they might make in their interpersonal communication behaviour in light of their responses on the test. A complete list of these self-tests appears in the Specialized Contents on page ix.

- **Skill Building Exercises** appear in the Study Guide at the end of the chapters. These exercises are designed to encourage students to interact with and personalize the concepts discussed in the text. These exercises are discussed in more detail under "Themes" below.

Skill Building Exercises

2.1 To Disclose or Not to Disclose?

Whether you should self-disclose is one of the most difficult decisions you have to make in interpersonal communication. Here are several instances of impending self-disclosure. For each, indicate whether you think the self-disclosure would be appropriate and why.

1. A mother of two teenage children (one boy, one girl) has been feeling guilty for the past year over a romantic affair she had with her brother-in-law while her husband was in prison. A few months ago, she and her husband divorced. She wants to self-disclose her affair and her guilt to her children.

2. Tom wants to break off his engagement to Cathy because he has fallen in love with another woman. Tom wants to call Cathy on the phone, break his engagement, and disclose his new relationship.

3. Sam has been living in a romantic relationship with another man for the past several years. Sam wants to tell his parents, with whom he has been very close throughout his life, but can't get up ‸‸‸ courage to do ⁘ ‸‸‸‸‸‸ to tell them ⁙

2.2 Times for Self-Disclosure

Self-disclosures occur throughout a relationship, but not always at what you may think is the right time. Some disclosures seem to occur too early and signal an intimacy that is not echoed in the relationship; the disclosures seem prematurely and inappropriately intimate. Some disclosures, on the other hand, occur too late; we feel we should have been told something earlier and may resent learning about it so late in the day. And, of course, some disclosures seem to occur at exactly the right time. This exercise explores the timeliness of self-disclosures.

Another way of looking at this exercise is from an ethical perspective: from the standpoint of your right to know certain information about a person with whom you become relationally involved. At what point in the relationship do you have a right to know this type of information?

Listed below are 10 items of personal information. Next to each item indicate the stage at which you would expect someone with whom you are in a relationship to disclose this type of information. Use X for any item you feel ‸‸ be disclosed ‸‸‸‸‸ ‸‸‸ following

- **Summaries of Concepts and Skills** discussed in each chapter appear at the end of the chapter as checklists, allowing students to review their own mastery of the relevant skills covered in each chapter.

Summary of Concepts and Skills

This chapter explored the self in interpersonal communication. We looked at the four selves of the Johari model and at how to increase self-awareness. Next we looked at self-disclosure, the process of revealing ourselves to others, and at some of the advantages and disadvantages of doing so. We then explored apprehension, what causes it, and how it can be managed effectively.

1. Self-concept is the image that you have of yourself. It is developed from the images of you that others have and that they reveal to you, the comparisons you make between yourself and others, and the way you interpret and evaluate your own thoughts and behaviours.

2. The four selves are the open self (what we and others know about us); the blind self (what others know but we do not know about ourselves); the hidden self (what we know but keep hidden from others); and the unknown self (what neither we nor others know).

3. We may increase self-awareness by asking ourselves about ourselves, listening to others, actively seeking information about ourselves, seeing ourselves from different perspectives, and increasing our open selves.

4. Self-disclosure is a type of communication in which we reveal information about ourselves to others.

5. Self-disclosure is generally recipro‸‸ ‸‸e self-
di‸‸‸ ‸ ‸‸‸ person stim‸‸

10. People with high apprehension behave differently from people with low apprehension. Highly apprehensive people communicate less and avoid situations and occupations that demand a lot of communication. They are less likely than other people to be seen as leaders, have more negative attitudes toward school, and are more likely to drop out of university. Highly apprehensive people are also less satisfied with their jobs and engage more in steady dating.

11. Techniques for managing communication apprehension include acquiring communication skills and experience, focusing on success, reducing unpredictability, and being familiar with the situation.

Check Your Ability

Check your ability to apply the following skills. You will gain most from this brief exercise if you think carefully about each skill and try to identify instances from your recent communication experiences in which you did or did not act on the basis of the specific skill. Use a rating scale such as the following: 1 = almost always, 2 = often, 3 = sometimes, 4 = rarely, and 5 = almost never.

‸‸ ‸‸ your ‸‸‸ ‸ ‸‸ek to

- **Critical Thinking Questions** and provocative **Quotations** in the margins invite active involvement and analysis.

> **"** If your lips would keep from slips,
> Five things observe with care;
> To whom you speak, of whom you speak,
> And how, and when, and where. **"**
>
> —W. E. Norris

What role does directness play in other forms of online communication—for example, in chat groups or newsgroups?

Themes

Several themes highlight the skills of interpersonal communication and—taken together—define the unique perspective of this text:

- an emphasis on **skill building,** with guidelines and experiences to help students master crucial skills and an emphasis on these skills as they operate in the workplace
- an integration of **listening** skills with the various topics of interpersonal communication
- a consideration of **critical thinking** principles and techniques to help students think more logically about interpersonal communication (or about anything else)
- an emphasis on **culture** and cultural sensitivity as it influences all forms of interpersonal interaction
- a focus on **ethical issues** as they relate to a wide range of interpersonal communication situations
- **power and empowerment** skills for increasing interpersonal effectiveness
- an **interactive presentation** to make learning about interpersonal communication more exciting and more personal

Skill Building

This text emphasizes the development of interpersonal communication skills such as accuracy in interpersonal perception, the use of active listening skills, and constructive approaches to interpersonal conflict. These skills are written into the text discussions and appear in all chapters.

Each chapter contains **Skill Building Exercises** that apply the material in the chapter to specific situations. Some of these exercises are designed to increase awareness of the ways in which interpersonal communication actually works so that messages will be more effective. These "awareness" exercises include those focusing on the role of ethics in interpersonal communication, explaining interpersonal difficulties, and exploring the sources of cultural beliefs. Other exercises are practice experiences aimed at increasing the ability to formulate more effective messages. These exercises focus on skills such as paraphrasing to ensure understanding, confronting intercultural difficulties, and generating win–win solutions in interpersonal conflict.

Although this is not a textbook on business communication, it does highlight **workplace interpersonal skills**, not only in Chapter 12, "Interpersonal Communication and the Workplace," but also throughout the text. The workplace context gives a concreteness that will help students understand and apply those skills in any situation. A series of **Skills Toolboxes** identify a specific skill relevant to a particular chapter and apply it to the workplace—for example, dealing with difficult listeners or networking. Each toolbox ends with a section entitled "Then and Now" that asks students to recall a situation and the way they communicated in it and to consider how they would communicate in that same situation now, based on the insights in the chapter and in the toolbox. A complete list of these boxes appears in the Specialized Contents on page ix.

Listening

This edition covers listening in two ways. Chapter 4 focuses exclusively on listening: It covers the listening process from receiving to responding, examines the role of culture and gender in listening, and provides guidelines for increasing listening effectiveness.

In addition, many chapters include a **Listen to This** box. These boxes discuss listening skills as they relate to the chapter content—for example, listening to the emotions of others is presented in the chapter on emotions (Chapter 7); listening and technology is presented in the chapter on conversation messages (Chapter 8); and sexist, heterosexist, and racist listening is presented in the chapter on culture (Chapter 9). In this way, students can appreciate listening as a fundamental skill that is crucial at each stage in the interpersonal communication experience and in all interpersonal contexts. At the end of each box is a case for analysis that asks students to offer listening suggestions in a variety of situations. A complete list of these boxes is given in the Specialized Contents on page ix.

Critical Thinking

Messages emphasizes critical thinking—thinking logically about interpersonal communication or about anything else—in numerous sections throughout the text, asking students to analyze and evaluate a variety of interpersonal messages, techniques, and conclusions.

Critical thinking is also emphasized in three features. First, **Critical Thinking** boxes appear throughout the text. These boxes discuss specific applications of critical thinking to the chapter topic; for example, they explore thinking critically about listening, attitudes, and biases. Each of these boxes concludes with a brief section that asks students to recall specific examples of the types of issues raised in the boxes. A complete list of these boxes is given in the Specialized Contents on page xi.

Second, **Critical Thinking Questions** appear in the margins. These questions encourage students to question what they read and to apply the insights to other areas of communication. These questions may be discussed as they come up in the text or reviewed after completing the chapter.

Third, the **Research Navigator**™ questions will guide students in examining published research and evaluating and synthesizing what they read there.

Culture and Intercultural Communication

The text presents interpersonal communication as taking place in a context that is becoming increasingly intercultural. Chapter 9, "Interpersonal Communication and Culture," covers intercultural communication in depth, focusing on the nature of culture and of intercultural communication, the ways in which cultures differ (for example, in individualism and collectivism, high and low context, and masculinity and femininity), and the ways to improve intercultural communication.

In addition, integrated discussions of culture appear throughout the text. These discussions include

- culture and human communication, including cultural awareness, the relevance of culture, and the aim of a cultural perspective (Chapter 1)
- culture's influence on self-disclosure and on apprehension (Chapter 2)
- stereotypes versus cultural awareness in perceptual accuracy (Chapter 3)
- listening, culture, and gender (Chapter 4)
- gender and cultural differences in verbal directness; language as a cultural institution and cultural maxims; sexism, heterosexism, and racism in language; and cultural identifiers (Chapter 5)
- culture and nonverbal communication; for example, in touching, time, and colour perception (Chapter 6)
- the influence of culture on emotions; societal rules and customs (Chapter 7)
- conversational taboos; cultural sensitivity as a metaskill (Chapter 8)
- interpersonal communication and culture: culture and intercultural communication, how cultures differ, and ways to improve intercultural communication (Chapter 9)
- culture and gender differences in relationships (Chapter 10)
- conflict and culture (Chapter 11)
- cultural diversity at work; the cultural dimension of power (Chapter 12)

Ethics

A series of **Talking Ethics** boxes highlight a variety of ethical issues in interpersonal communication—for example, outing, motivational appeals, lying, and silence. These boxes will serve as frequent reminders that ethical considerations are an integral part of every interpersonal communication decision. At the end of each box, students are asked, "What would you do?" in response to a real-life situation. In this way, they are encouraged to interact with the material contained in the box and to apply it to ethical questions they will encounter every day. A complete list of these boxes is provided in the Specialized Contents on page ix.

Power and Empowerment

Because power permeates all forms of interpersonal communication, the themes of **personal empowerment** and empowering others are integral to this text. The aim of *Messages* is to provide students with the skills and experiences to become more effective, more empowered, and more empowering individuals. This orientation underlies the book's emphasis on building skills useful at home and at work, and it comes into sharp focus in the final chapter, Chapter 12, "Interpersonal Communication and the Workplace." Here, issues such as increasing personal power through self-esteem, speaking with power, and communicating with greater assertiveness are discussed.

Instructor's Resources

- **MyTest.** MyTest, for Pearson Education Canada, is a powerful assessment generation program that helps instructors easily create and print quizzes, tests, and exams, as well as homework or practice handouts. Questions and tests can all be authored online, allowing instructors ultimate flexibility and the ability to efficiently manage assessments at any time, from anywhere. The MyTest for *Messages*, Third Canadian Edition, contains about 600 multiple choice, true/false, short answer, and essay test questions. See your local sales representative for details and access.

The Instructor's Resource CD-ROM (0-205-51677-7) includes the following resources:

- **Test Item File.** This testbank, provided in Microsoft Word format, contains all the questions from the MyTest for *Messages*, Third Canadian Edition.

- **Instructor's Manual.** The Instructor's Manual provides chapter overviews and learning and skill objectives for each chapter. It also offers ideas to activate class discussions and contains exercises to illustrate the concepts, principles, and skills of interpersonal communication.

- **PowerPoints.** New in this edition, chapter-by-chapter PowerPoint presentations highlight the key concepts from the text. Several slides from each chapter have been reproduced and integrated within the text itself as In-Class Notes.

Some of these instructor supplements are also available for download from a password protected section of Pearson Education Canada's online catalogue (vig.pearsoned.ca). Navigate to your book's catalogue page to view a list of supplements that are available. See your local sales representative for details and access.

Student Resources

Companion Website (www.pearsoned.ca/devito). New to this edition, this Canadian version of the *Messages* site provides chapter-by-chapter quizzes to help students test their knowledge, as well as additional self-tests and skill-building exercises. Other resources include Ask Yourself exercises that offer practice in making communication decisions, flashcards to test students' knowledge of key terms, and links to other useful sites.

Allyn & Bacon Communication Studies Website. This site includes modules on interpersonal and small group communication and public speaking and includes web links, enrichment materials, and interactive activities to enhance students' understanding of key concepts. Access this site at **www.ablongman.com/commstudies**.

Acknowledgments

The publishers and authors would like to thank Danica Lavoie of Centennial College, who provided the study tips that appear in the margins. We also want to thank the people who contributed to the third Canadian edition by reviewing the previous edition and/or manuscript for the new edition, including the following:

Bruce Bennett, College of New Caledonia
Jean Brown, Cambrian College
Patricia Campbell, Red Deer College
Rachel Devins, Concordia University
Carole E. Harlow, University College of the Fraser Valley
Ann Kenney-Lee, British Columbia Institute of Technology
Shannon MacRae, Niagara College
David E. Reagan, Camosun College
Brian Seville, Cape Breton University

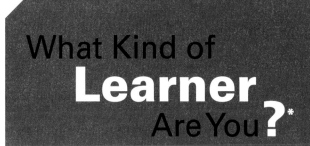

What Kind of Learner Are You?*

AN INTRODUCTION TO LEARNING STYLES

It happens in nearly every college and university course: Students listen to lectures throughout the semester. Each student hears the same words at the same time and completes the same assignments. However, after finals, student experiences will range from fulfillment and high grades to complete disconnection and low grades or withdrawals.

Many causes may be involved in this scenario—different levels of interest and effort, for example, or outside stresses. Another major factor is learning style (any of many particular ways to receive and process information). Say, for example, that a group of students is taking a first-year composition class that is often broken up into study groups. Students who are comfortable working with words or happy when engaged in discussion may do well in the course. Students who are more mathematical than verbal, or who prefer to work alone, might not do as well. Learning styles play a role.

There are many different and equally valuable ways to learn. The way each person learns is a unique blend of styles resulting from distinctive abilities, challenges, experiences, and training. In addition, how one learns isn't set in stone; particular styles may develop or recede as responsibilities and experiences lead someone to work on different skills and tasks. The following assessment and study strategies will help you explore how you learn, understand how particular strategies may heighten your strengths and boost your weaknesses, and know when to use them.

MULTIPLE INTELLIGENCES THEORY

There is a saying, "It is not how smart you are, but how you are smart." In 1983, Howard Gardner, a Harvard University professor, changed the way people perceive intelligence and learning with his theory of multiple intelligences. This theory holds

Intelligences and Characteristic Skills		
INTELLIGENCES	**DESCRIPTION**	**CHARACTERISTIC SKILLS**
Verbal/Linguistic	Ability to communicate through language through listening, reading, writing, speaking	• Analyzing own use of language • Remembering terms easily • Explaining, teaching, learning, & using humour • Understanding syntax and meaning of words • Convincing someone to do something

continued

*This material originally created by Sarah Kravits.

INTELLIGENCES	DESCRIPTION	CHARACTERISTIC SKILLS
Logical/Mathematical	Ability to understand logical reasoning and problem solving, particularly in math and science	• Recognizing abstract patterns and sequences • Reasoning inductively and deductively • Discerning relationships and connections • Performing complex calculations • Reasoning scientifically
Visual/Spatial	Ability to understand spatial relationships and to perceive and create images	• Perceiving and forming objects accurately • Manipulating images for visual art or graphic design • Finding one's way in space (using charts and maps) • Representing something graphically • Recognizing relationships between objects
Bodily/Kinesthetic	Ability to use the physical body skillfully and to take in knowledge through bodily sensation	• Connecting mind and body • Controlling movement • Improving body functions • Working with hands • Expanding body awareness to all senses • Coordinating body movement
Intrapersonal	Ability to understand one's own behaviour and feelings	• Evaluating own thinking • Being aware of and expressing feelings • Taking independent action • Understanding self in relationship to others • Thinking and reasoning on higher levels
Interpersonal	Ability to relate to others, noticing their moods, motivations, and feelings	• Seeing things from others' perspectives • Cooperating within a group • Achieving goals with a team • Communicating verbally and non-verbally • Creating and maintaining relationships
Musical/Rhythmic	Ability to comprehend and create meaningful sound and recognize patterns	• Sensing tonal qualities • Creating or enjoying melodies and rhythms • Being sensitive to sounds and rhythms • Using "schemas" to hear music • Understanding the structure of music and other patterns
Naturalistic	Ability to understand features of the environment	• Deep understanding of nature, environmental balance, ecosystem • Appreciation of the delicate balance in nature • Feeling most comfortable when in nature • Ability to use nature to lower stress

that there are at least eight distinct *intelligences* possessed by all people, and that every person has developed some intelligences more fully than others. (Gardner defines an "intelligence" as an ability to solve problems or fashion products that are useful in a particular cultural setting or community.) According to the multiple intelligences theory, when encountering an easy task or subject, you are probably using a more fully developed intelligence; when having more trouble, you may be using a less developed intelligence.

In the following table are descriptions of each of the intelligences, along with characteristic skills. The *Multiple Pathways to Learning* assessment, based on Gardner's work, will help you determine the levels to which your intelligences are developed.

PUTTING ASSESSMENTS IN PERSPECTIVE

Before you complete *Multiple Pathways to Learning*, remember: No assessment has the final word on who you are and what you can and cannot do. An intriguing but imperfect tool, its results are affected by your ability to answer objectively, your mood that day, and other factors. Here's how to best use what this assessment, or any other, tells you:

Use assessments for reference. Approach any assessment as a tool with which you can expand your ideas of yourself. There are no "right" answers, no "best" set of scores. Think of it in the same way you would a set of eyeglasses for a person with blurred vision. The glasses will not create new paths and possibilities but will help you see more clearly the ones that already exist.

Multiple Pathways to Learning

Rate each statement: rarely = 1,   sometimes = 2,   often = 3,   almost always = 4

Write the number of your response on the line next to the statement and total each set of 6 questions.

1. I enjoy physical activities.	19. I like math.
2. I am uncomfortable sitting still.	20. _____ I like science.
3. I prefer to learn through doing rather than listening.	21. _____ I problem-solve well.
4. I tend to move my legs or hands when I'm sitting.	22. _____ I question why things happen or how things work.
5. I enjoy working with my hands.	23. I enjoy planning or designing something new.
6. I like to pace when I'm thinking or studying.	24. I am able to fix things.
TOTAL for Bodily-Kinesthetic (B-K)	**TOTAL for Logical-Mathematical (L-M)**

7. I use maps easily.	25. I listen to music.
8. I draw pictures or diagrams when explaining ideas.	26. I move my fingers or feet when I hear music.
9. I can assemble items easily from diagrams.	27. I have good rhythm.
10. I enjoy drawing or taking photographs.	28. I like to sing along with music.
11. I do not like to read long paragraphs.	29. People have said I have musical talent.
12. I prefer a drawn map over written directions.	30. I like to express my ideas through music.
TOTAL for Visual-Spatial (V-S)	**TOTAL for Musical (M)**

13. I enjoy telling stories.	31. I like doing a project with other people.
14. I like to write.	32. People come to me to help them settle conflicts.
15. I like to read.	33. I like to spend time with friends.
16. I express myself clearly.	34. I am good at understanding people.
17. I am good at negotiating.	35. I am good at making people feel comfortable.
18. I like to discuss topics that interest me.	36. I enjoy helping others.
TOTAL for Verbal-Linguistic (V-L)	**TOTAL for Interpersonal (Inter)**

continued

Rate each statement: rarely = 1,   sometimes = 2,   often = 3,   almost always = 4

Write the number of your response on the line next to the statement and total each set of 6 questions.

37.	I need quiet time to think.
38.	When I need to make a decision, I prefer to think about it before I talk about it.
39.	I am interested in self-improvement.
40.	I understand my thoughts, feelings, and behaviour.
41.	I know what I want out of life.
42.	I prefer to work on projects alone.

TOTAL for Intrapersonal (Intra)

43.	I enjoy being in nature whenever possible.
44.	I would enjoy a career involving nature.
45.	I enjoy studying plants, animals, forests, or oceans.
46.	I prefer to be outside whenever possible.
47.	When I was a child I liked bugs, ants, and leaves.
48.	When I experience stress I want to be out in nature.

TOTAL for Naturalist (N)

Use assessments for understanding. Understanding the level to which your intelligences seem to be developed will help prevent you from boxing yourself into limiting categories. Instead of saying "I'm no good in math," someone who is not a natural in math can make the subject easier by using appropriate strategies. For example, learners who respond to visuals can learn better by drawing diagrams of math problems. The more they know of themselves, the more they will be able to assess and adapt to any situation—in school, work, and life.

Face challenges realistically. Any assessment reveals areas of challenge as well as ability. Rather than dwelling on limitations (which often results in a negative self-image) or ignoring them (which often leads to unproductive choices), use what you know from the assessment to look at where you are and set goals that will help you reach where you want to be.

Following the assessment, you will see information about the typical traits of each intelligence, and more detailed study strategies geared toward the five intelligences most relevant for studying this text. During this course, make a point of exploring a large number of new study techniques; consider all the different strategies presented here, not just the ones that apply to your strengths. Why?

Change. Because you have abilities in all areas, though some are more developed than others, you may encounter useful suggestions under any of the headings. Furthermore, your abilities and learning styles change as you learn, so you never know what might work for you.

Strategies help overcome weaknesses as well as build strengths. Knowing learning styles is not only about guiding your life toward your strongest abilities; it is also about choosing strategies to use when facing life's challenges. Strategies for your weaker areas may help when what is required of you involves tasks and academic areas that you find difficult. For example, if you are not strong in logical-mathematical intelligence and have to take a math course, the suggestions geared toward logical-mathematical learners may help you build what skill you have.

As you complete the assessment, try to answer the questions objectively—in other words, answer the questions to best indicate who you are, not who you want to be (or who your parents or instructors want you to be). Don't be concerned if some of your scores are low—that is true for almost everyone.

SCORING THE ASSESSMENT

Indicate your scores by completing the table below. A score of 20–24 indicates a high level of development in that particular type of intelligence, 14–19 a moderate level, and below 14 an underdeveloped intelligence.

	20–24 (Highly Developed)	14–19 (Moderately Developed)	Below 14 (Underdeveloped)
Bodily-Kinesthetic			
Visual-Spatial			
Verbal-Linguistic			
Logical-Mathematical			
Musical			
Interpersonal			
Intrapersonal			
Naturalist			

STUDY TIPS FOR DIFFERENT LEARNING STYLES

Finding out what study strategies work best for you is almost always a long process of trial and error, often because there is no rhyme or reason to the search. If you explore strategies in the context of learning style, however, you give yourselves a head start. Now that you have completed the *Multiple Pathways to Learning* assessment, you will be able to look at the following material with a more informed view of what may help you most.

The five intelligences that have the most relevance to study in this course are bodily/kinesthetic, interpersonal, logical/mathematical, verbal/linguistic, and visual/spatial. Study tips based on these five intelligences can be found throughout the text, identified with coloured icons.

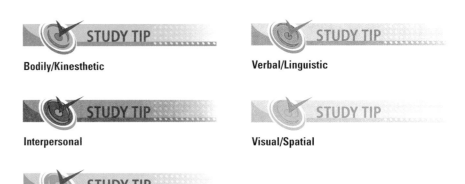

Bodily/Kinesthetic

Interpersonal

Logical/Mathematical

Verbal/Linguistic

Visual/Spatial

We hope this self-assessment and the accompanying study tips help you become a more satisfied and effective learner.

Chapter 1

Interpersonal Communication

Chapter Topics

This chapter introduces the nature and principles of interpersonal communication and the role of culture.

What Is Interpersonal Communication?

Principles of Interpersonal Communication

Culture and Interpersonal Communication

Chapter Skills

After completing this chapter, you should be able to:

- interact interpersonally, recognizing all significant elements.

- engage in interpersonal communication, recognizing its essential principles.

- interact interpersonally, recognizing cultural differences.

Grace and Mark have been dating for the last three years. Although they're deeply in love, there are some problems facing their relationship. Grace wants to continue her education and become an accountant; Mark wants to continue working at the local gas station. Grace wants to wait to have children; Mark wants lots of children as soon as possible. Grace wants to have her mother live with them; Mark is opposed. Whenever one of them brings up one of these problems, they get into an argument and often stay angry for days at a time. Both Grace and Mark feel that once they get married, they will work out these and any other problems that arise. Love, they feel, will conquer all.

Reno has five children—two preteens, and three teenagers. For most of his life, Reno has worked as a maintenance worker for the Saskatoon School Board. Although he's deeply interested in the lives of his wife and children, he feels he's often ignored. His children rarely confide in him; whenever they have important news, they go to their mother. Reno feels left out of the family. He feels his only function is to earn money, and he has seriously considered leaving his family and starting a new life in another city.

For the last 14 years, Karla has worked in a toy factory in Vancouver that was recently purchased by a Hong Kong investment firm. The production department, which Karla headed for the last four years, has been reorganized and is now run by three people—two managers from Hong Kong and Karla. Although production is up, morale is down. Karla used to handle most problems informally by talking with the crew over lunch or at company parties. Now, however, the managers handle all problems at formal business meetings. Karla feels that the new owners have virtually eliminated her job and that she is being kept on just because the union contract protects her. She's thinking of asking for a transfer or seeking a position with another company.

Each of these situations revolves around problems in communication, and the people in them would profit from learning the principles and skills of interpersonal communication. Whether in a romantic or friendly relationship, a large family, or a work environment, the principles of interpersonal communication are powerful tools for dealing with problems such as those described above. Mark and Grace, for example, don't seem to know how to resolve their differences, and the way they talk about their problems only aggravates the situation. Their belief that love will conquer all prevents them from seeing the difficulties that confront their relationship now—and that will not go away with marriage. The guidelines for conflict resolution discussed in Chapter 11 would help Mark and Grace considerably.

Reno feels left out and doesn't know how to get his wife and children to confide in him—or to self-disclose—nor does he know how to communicate his own feelings. So it's not surprising that his children have learned that their father is not the parent to go to with feelings. Reno wants involvement, but he doesn't know how to get it. The suggestions for facilitating self-disclosure and for communicating empathy and support discussed in Chapter 2 would prove helpful to Reno.

Karla is having trouble communicating in this new intercultural setting. The new owners of the plant are unaware that morale is down, largely because no one has voiced concern. Karla's self-esteem has been damaged; she feels she is no longer important and she doesn't know how to deal with the new situation. Karla would profit from the material on self-esteem in Chapter 12, as well as from the discussions of culture throughout this text, especially suggestions in Chapter 9 for improving intercultural communication.

In every realm of life, people can understand and improve situations like these by mastering the skills of interpersonal communication. This book will help teach those skills. So important have they become that the Conference Board of Canada (2003) has identified interpersonal communication skills and the ability to work effectively with others as critical to successful employment. Many recent university graduates, however, lack these skills (Robbins & Hunsaker, 2003). In an attempt to address this deficit, a number of Canadian universities now require good written and oral communication skills as learning outcomes for all students.

This book will help you improve your interpersonal skills in order to become more effective in a wide variety of interpersonal communication situations in your

What other problems might Grace and Mark, Reno, and Karla be experiencing? What suggestions might you make to help them deal with their communication problems?

personal and professional life. Research resources are available at www. researchnavigator.com. A very useful blog site that is frequently updated with useful information related to topics covered in the different chapters can be found at http://tcbdevito.blogspot.com.

Before you begin studying this exciting and practical area, examine your own beliefs about interpersonal communication by taking the self-test below.

Test Yourself

What Do You Believe About Interpersonal Communication?

Instructions: Respond to each of the following statements with T (true) if you think the statement is always or usually true, or F (false) if you believe the statement is always or usually false.

_____ ❶ Good communicators are born, not made.

_____ ❷ The more you communicate, the better your communication will be.

_____ ❸ Unlike effective speaking, effective listening really cannot be taught.

_____ ❹ Opening lines such as "Hello, how are you?" or "Fine weather today" serve no useful communication purpose.

_____ ❺ The best way to communicate with someone from a different culture is exactly as you would with someone from your own culture.

_____ ❻ When verbal and nonverbal messages contradict each other, people believe the verbal message.

_____ ❼ Complete openness should be the goal of any meaningful interpersonal relationship.

_____ ❽ Interpersonal conflict is a reliable sign that your relationship is in trouble.

_____ ❾ Like good communicators, small-group leaders are born, not made.

_____ ❿ Fear of speaking is detrimental, and the effective speaker must learn to eliminate it.

HOW DID YOU DO?

If you're like most people, you probably have been told a lot of things about communication that—like the statements above—are simply not true. In fact, not one of the above statements is true. As you read this book, you'll discover why these statements are false, and you'll learn more about the problems that can arise when you act on the basis of such misconceptions.

WHAT WILL YOU DO?

This is perhaps a good place to start practising the critical thinking skill of questioning commonly held assumptions about communication and about thinking of yourself as a communicator. What other beliefs do you hold about communication and about yourself as a communicator? How do these beliefs influence your communication behaviour?

WHAT IS INTERPERSONAL COMMUNICATION?

Interpersonal communication occurs between two people who share a relationship. **Communication** occurs when you send or receive messages and when you assign meaning to such messages. Interpersonal communication is always distorted by "noise," occurs within a context, and involves some opportunity for feedback.

Interpersonal communicators are conscious of one another and of their connection with one another. They're interdependent: what one person thinks and says impacts on what the other thinks and says. Interpersonal communication includes the conversations that take place between an interviewer and a potential employee, between a son and his father, between two sisters, between a teacher and a student, or between two lovers or two friends. Even the stranger asking for directions from a local resident has a relationship with that person.

Communication is a *transactional* process in which each person serves simultaneously as speaker and listener. According to the **transactional view**, at the same

> ❝ If your lips would keep from slips,
> Five things observe with care;
> To whom you speak, of whom you speak,
> And how, and when, and where. ❞
> —W. E. Norris

Interpersonal Communication

- Communication that takes place between two people who share a relationship.

time that you send messages, you're also receiving messages from your own communications and from the reactions of the other person (Figure 1.1). And at the same time that you're listening, you're also sending messages. In a transactional view, each person is seen as speaker and listener, simultaneously communicating and receiving messages (Watzlawick et al., 1967; Barnlund, 1970; Watzlawick, 1977, 1978; Harris, 2002).

In a transactional view, the elements of communication are seen as *inter*dependent (never *in*dependent). Each element exists in relation to the others, and a change in any one element of this **process** produces changes in the other elements. For example, suppose you're talking with a group of your friends and your mother enters the group. This change in "audience" will lead to other changes; perhaps you'll change what you say or how you say it. Regardless of what change is introduced, other changes will be produced as a result.

Of course, interpersonal communication often takes place face-to-face, and this is the type of interaction that probably comes to mind when you think of conversation. But today, much conversation takes place online (Hanke, 2005; Shtern, 2005). Online communication is part of people's experience throughout the world and is important personally, socially, and professionally. The major types of online conversation that differ from one another and from face-to-face interaction are email, mailing list groups, chat groups, and blogs (Keren, 2004).

In face-to-face conversation you're expected to contribute to the ongoing discussion. In chat groups you can simply observe; in fact, you're encouraged to "lurk"—to observe the participants' interaction before you say anything yourself. In this way, you'll be able to learn the cultural rules and norms of the group.

Another obvious difference between face-to-face and computer communication is that in face-to-face interaction, the individuals are usually clearly identified. In computer-mediated communication, however, you may remain anonymous (Shtern, 2005). You may also pose as someone you're not—as a person of another sex or race, for example, or even as someone who is significantly older or younger than you really are, or of significantly different status (Saunders et al., 1994). Numerous examples exist of predators who conceal their true identity in order to lure unsuspecting

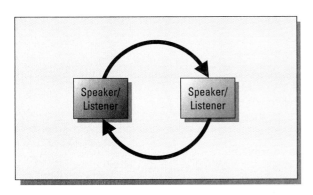

Figure 1.1

The Transactional View

In this view, a complex ball game is underway in which each player could send and receive any number of balls at any time. Players would be able to throw and catch balls at the very same time (Pearson et al., 2003). Can you think of any other analogies for this transactional view of communication?

victims. In face-to-face communication, your physical self—the way you look, the way you're dressed—greatly influences the way your messages will be interpreted. In computer-mediated communication, you reveal your physical self through your own descriptions. Although you may send photos of yourself via computer, you can also send photos of other people and claim they're photos of you. There is, in short, much greater opportunity for presenting yourself as you would like to be seen when communicating via computer.

"I loved your E-mail, but I thought you'd be older."

© The New Yorker Collection 1998 Robert Weber from cartoonbank.com. All Rights Reserved.

Interpersonal Communication Involves at Least Two People

Each person functions as a **source** (formulating and sending messages) and as a **receiver** (receiving and understanding messages). The linked term *source–receiver* emphasizes that each person is both source and receiver.

By putting your meanings into sound waves (or gestures, facial expressions, or postural adjustments), you're putting your thoughts and feelings into a **code**, or a set of symbols—a process called *en*coding. By translating sound and light waves into ideas, you're taking them out of the code they're in—a process called *de*coding. So you can call speakers (or, more generally, *senders*) **encoders**: those who put their meanings *into* a code. And you can call *listeners* (or, more generally, receivers) **decoders**: those who take meanings *out of* a code. Since encoding and decoding activities are combined in each person, the term *encoding–decoding* is used to emphasize this inevitable dual function.

Usually, you encode an idea into a code that the other person understands; for example, you use words and gestures for which both you and the other person have similar meanings. At times, however, you may want to exclude others; for example, you might speak in a language that only one of your listeners knows or use jargon to prevent others from understanding. At other times, you may assume incorrectly that the other person knows your code and unknowingly use words or gestures the other person simply doesn't understand.

For interpersonal communication to occur, meanings must be encoded and decoded. If Jamie has his eyes closed and is wearing stereo headphones as his dad is speaking to him, interpersonal communication is not taking place—simply because the messages, both verbal and nonverbal, are not being received.

Messages

For interpersonal communication to exist, **messages** that express your thoughts and feelings must be sent and received. Interpersonal communication may be verbal or nonverbal, but it's usually a combination of both. You communicate interpersonally with words as well as with gestures and touch, for example. Even the clothes you wear communicate, as do the way you walk and the way you shake hands, comb your hair, sit, smile, or frown. Everything about you has the potential to send interpersonal messages, and every message has an **effect**, or outcome.

In face-to-face communication, your messages are both verbal and nonverbal; you supplement your words with facial expressions, body movements, and variations in vocal volume and rate, for example. When you communicate through a keyboard, your message is communicated primarily with words. This does not mean that you cannot communicate emotional meanings; in fact, some researchers have argued that diagrams, pictures, and varied typefaces enable you to communicate messages that are rich in emotional meaning (Lea & Spears, 1995). Similarly, you can use emoticons (see the discussion in Chapter 7). Basically, however, a keyboarded or written message is communicated with words, and so sarcasm, for example, is difficult to

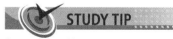

STUDY TIP

Communicate with a classmate using only facial expressions and body movements. Afterwards, discuss whether your messages were fully understood.

In a small group, discuss the nonverbal messages that we communicate through the clothing we wear.

convey unambiguously—whereas in face-to-face communication you might wink or smile to indicate that your message should not be taken seriously or literally.

Message Overload Message overload (often called information overload in business) is one of the greatest obstacles to efficient communication and may even lead to health problems among corporate managers (Lee, 2000). The ease with which people can copy or forward email and internet messages has obviously contributed to message overload, as has the volume of junk email and spam that seems to increase every day. Invariably, you must select certain messages to attend to and other messages to ignore. Today, for example, the North American worker is exposed to more messages in one year than a person living in 1900 was in his or her entire life. The average employee now receives more than 50 emails daily, and in one day the average manager sends and receives more than 100 documents.

Message overload absorbs an enormous amount of time. The more messages you have to deal with, the less time you have for the most important messages or tasks. Similarly, errors are more often made under conditions of message overload, simply because you cannot devote the time necessary to address any one item. The more rushed you are, the more likely you are to make mistakes.

How does feedback work in conversation between people with impaired hearing? Between a person with impaired hearing and a person with normal hearing? Between people who are blind? Between a person who is blind and a person who has normal vision?

Feedback **Feedback** is a special type of message. When you send a spoken or written message to another person, you get feedback from your own message: You hear what you say; you feel the way you move; you see what you write. On the basis of this information, you may correct yourself, rephrase something, or perhaps smile at a clever turn of phrase. This is self-feedback.

You also get feedback from others. The person with whom you're communicating is constantly sending you messages that indicate how he or she is receiving and responding to your messages. Nods of agreement, smiles, puzzled looks, and questions asking for clarification are all examples of feedback.

Notice that in face-to-face communication you can monitor the feedback of the other person as you're speaking. In computer-mediated communication, that feedback will come much later and thus is likely to be more clearly thought out and perhaps more closely monitored.

Feedforward Much as feedback contains information about messages already sent, **feedforward** is information about messages before they're sent. Opening comments such as "Wait until you hear this" or "I'm not sure of this, but..." or "Don't get me wrong, but..." are examples of feedforward. These messages tell the listener something about the messages to come or about the way you'd like the listener to respond. Nonverbally, for example, you give feedforward by your facial expressions, eye contact, and physical posture; with these nonverbal messages you tell the other person something about the messages you'll be sending. A smile may signal a pleasant message; eye avoidance may signal that the message to come is difficult and perhaps uncomfortable to express. A book's table of contents, its preface, and (usually) its first chapter are also examples of feedforward.

Channel

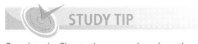

Complete the Chapter 1 crossword puzzle on the textbook website.

The communication **channel** is the medium through which message signals pass. The channel works like a bridge connecting source and receiver. Normally two, three, or four channels are used simultaneously. Thus, for example, in face-to-face **speech** interactions, you speak and listen, using the vocal–auditory channel. However, you also make gestures and receive these signals visually, using the visual channel. Similarly, you emit odours and smell the odours of others through the chemical channel. Often you touch one another, and communicate through the tactile channel.

Another way to classify channels is by the means of communication. Face-to-face contact, telephones, email, movies, television, smoke signals, and telegraph

are all examples of channels. Of most relevance today, of course, is the difference between computer-mediated interpersonal communication—interaction through email, chat lines, and usenet groups—and face-to-face communication.

Noise

Noise is anything that interferes with your receiving the message someone is sending or with their receiving your message. Noise may be physical (loud talking, honking cars, illegible handwriting, or "garbage" on your computer screen), physiological (hearing or visual impairment, articulation disorders), psychological (preconceived ideas, wandering thoughts), or semantic (misunderstood meanings). Technically, noise is anything that distorts or gets in the way of the message.

Because messages may be visual as well as spoken, noise may also be visual. Thus, sunglasses that prevent someone from seeing the nonverbal messages sent by your eyes are considered noise, as is blurred type on a printed page. Table 1.1 identifies the four major types of noise in more detail.

All communications contain noise. Noise cannot be totally eliminated, but its effects can be reduced. Making your language more precise, sharpening your skills for sending and receiving nonverbal messages, and improving your listening and feedback skills are some ways to combat the influence of noise.

Context

Communication always takes place within a context: an environment that influences the form and the content of communication. At times the context is so natural that you ignore it, like street noise. At other times the context stands out and the ways in which it restricts or stimulates your communications are obvious. Think, for example, of the different ways you'd talk at a funeral, in a quiet restaurant, and at a rock concert.

The **context of communication** has at least four dimensions: physical, cultural, social–psychological, and temporal. The tangible or concrete environment, such as the room, workplace, or outdoor space in which communication takes place, makes up the *physical dimension*. When you communicate with someone face-to-face, you're both in essentially the same physical environment. In computer-mediated communication, you may be in drastically different environments—one of you may be on a beach in San Juan while the other is in a Bay Street office.

Cellphone communication adds complexity to the notion of physical and social–psychological contexts. We often hear very intimate cellphone conversations

TABLE 1.1	**Four Types of Noise**

One of the most important skills in communication is to recognize the four types of noise and develop ways to combat them. For example, what kinds of noise occur in the classroom? What kinds of noise occur in your family communications? What kinds occur at work? What can you do to combat these kinds of noise?

TYPE OF NOISE	DEFINITION	EXAMPLE
Physical	Interference that is external to both speaker and listener; interferes with the physical transmission of the signal or message	Screeching of passing cars, hum of computer, sunglasses
Physiological	Physical barriers within the speaker or listener	Visual impairments, hearing loss, articulation problems, memory loss
Psychological	Cognitive or mental interference	Biases and prejudices in senders and receivers, closed-mindedness, inaccurate expectations, extreme emotionalism (anger, hate, love, grief)
Semantic	Different meanings assigned by speaker and listener	Language differences, use of jargon or overly complex terms not understood by listener

The Elements of Interpersonal Communication

- Source–Receiver
- Encoding–Decoding
- Competence
- Messages
  - Feedback
  - Feedforward
- Channel
- Noise
- Context

in very public places such as waiting rooms and airports. Thus, the norms of a private sphere seem to be invading public and personal context. This invasion may cause discomfort to some unwitting participants who happen to be seated nearby.

The *cultural dimension* consists of the rules, norms, beliefs, and attitudes of the people who are communicating, which are passed from one generation to another. For example, talking to strangers is considered polite in some cultures, while in others it is not.

The *social–psychological dimension* includes, for example, the status relationships among the participants: distinctions such as those between employer and employee, and salesperson and store owner. Formality or informality, friendliness or hostility, and cooperativeness or competitiveness of the interaction are also part of the social–psychological dimension.

The *temporal* or *time dimension* has to do with where a particular message fits into a sequence of communication events. For example, if you tell a joke about sickness immediately after your friend tells you she is sick, the joke will be perceived differently than the same joke told to your friends in the locker room.

Given the basic definition of interpersonal communication, the transactional perspective, and an understanding that interpersonal communication occurs in many different forms, let's expand our model as in Figure 1.2 and look at each of the essential elements in interpersonal communication: source–receiver, messages, feedback, feedforward, channels, noise, and context. Along with this discussion you may wish to visit www.acc-cca.ca, the website of the Canadian Communication Association. This national organization brings together members of academic, government, and business communities to promote the investigation of communication issues.

In face-to-face communication, both people interact in real time. In computer communication, this real time interaction occurs only sometimes. In email, "snail mail," and newsgroup communication, for example, the sending and receiving may be separated by several days or much longer. In chat groups, on the other hand, communication takes place in real time; the sending and receiving take place (almost) simultaneously.

Interpersonal Competence

Your ability to communicate effectively is your **interpersonal competence** (Spitzberg & Cupach, 1989). Your **competence** includes the knowledge that in certain contexts and with certain listeners, one topic is appropriate and another is not. It includes your understanding of the rules of nonverbal communication—such as the appropriateness of touching, vocal volume, and physical closeness (see Figure 1.3 on page 10).

A major goal of this text (and your course) is to expand your competence so that you'll have a greater arsenal of communication choices at your disposal. It's much like learning vocabulary: The more words you know, the more ways you'll have to express yourself. The greater your interpersonal competence, the more options you'll have for communicating with friends, lovers, and family, with colleagues on the job, and in just about any situation where you'll talk with another person. The greater your competence, the greater your own power to accomplish what you want to accomplish—to ask for a raise or a date; to establish temporary work relationships, long-term friendships, or romantic relationships; to communicate empathy and support; or to gain compliance or resist the compliance tactics of others. Whatever your interpersonal goal, increased competence will help you accomplish it more effectively.

In short, interpersonal competence includes knowing how interpersonal communication works and how to best achieve your purposes by adjusting your messages according to the context of the interaction, the person with whom you're interacting, and a host of other factors discussed throughout this text. The process goes like this: Knowledge of interpersonal communication *leads to* greater interpersonal ability, which *leads to* a greater number of available choices or options for interacting, which *leads to* greater likelihood of interpersonal effectiveness.

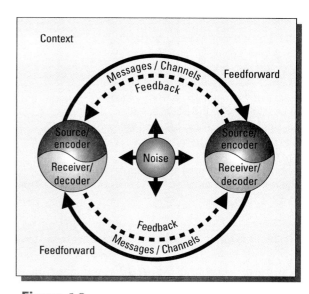

Figure 1.2

The Process of Interpersonal Communication
This model puts into visual form the various elements of the interpersonal communication process. How would you diagram the interpersonal communication process?

Competence and Interpersonal Skills This text explains the theory and research in interpersonal communication in order to provide you with a firm foundation for understanding how interpersonal communication works. With that understanding as a foundation, you'll be better able to develop and master the very practical skills of interpersonal communication. To help you achieve this goal, this text highlights the skills of interpersonal communication in a variety of ways. Skills are discussed *throughout the text* along with the relevant theory and research on which they are based. We include skill-building exercises, information, and self-assessment exercises to help build your competence.

Competence and Listening Competence in interpersonal communication is often viewed as "speaking effectiveness," with little attention paid to listening. But as demonstrated throughout the text, listening is an integral part of interpersonal communication; you cannot be a competent communicator if you're a poor listener. Both

Thinking Critically About Interpersonal Communication

Think critically about interpersonal communication, recognizing that:

- The study of interpersonal communication involves both theory and research, *and* practical skills for increasing interpersonal effectiveness. A knowledge of theory will help you better understand the skills, and a knowledge of skills will help you better understand theory.

- The principles discussed throughout this book relate directly to your everyday interactions. To help make this material easier to assimilate, try to recall examples

from your own communications to illustrate the ideas considered here.

- Be willing to change your ways of communicating and even your ways of thinking about interpersonal communication. Carefully assess what you should strengthen or revise and what you should leave as is.

EXAMPLES?

Can you give an example of a situation in which you experimented with ways of communicating different from your usual?

Figure 1.3

The Competent Interpersonal Communicator

Indicate how competent you feel in each of these six areas right now and give yourself scores from 1 (little competence) to 10 (a great deal of competence). Return to this figure periodically to re-rate yourself. By the end of the course, you should have increased all of your scores significantly.

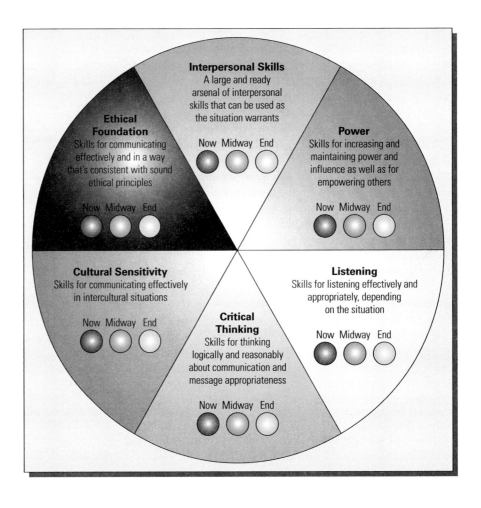

> ❝ If people knew how hard I worked to get my mastery, it wouldn't seem so wonderful after all. ❞
>
> —Michelangelo

speaking and listening skills are crucial to interpersonal competence. Listening, therefore, is emphasized in this text in two major ways.

Chapter 4 is devoted to listening. Discussions cover the nature and importance of listening, the steps you go through in listening, the role of culture and gender in listening, and ways to increase your listening effectiveness.

Listen to This boxes are positioned throughout the text to illustrate how listening relates to the topic of the chapter and to provide a variety of specific listening skills. Among the topics these boxes address are the importance of listening to yourself; the role of gender differences; sexist, heterosexist, and racist listening; ways to listen during conflict; and how to listen to empower others. Each of the listening boxes ends with a case that asks you to offer listening suggestions for a wide variety of interpersonal communication situations. These cases underscore a basic principle of listening—that listening is a process requiring action by the listener, not a passive process that simply happens when you open your ears. A complete list of all *Listen to This* boxes appears in the Specialized Contents on page xi.

Competence and Critical Thinking Competence in interpersonal communication depends on **critical thinking**, which is a "process of examining information and reaching a judgment or decision" (Wade & Tavris, 1990). Critical thinking is logical thinking; it's thinking that is well reasoned, unbiased, and clear. It's a way of thinking intelligently, carefully, and with as much clarity as possible. It's the opposite of what you'd call sloppy, illogical, or careless thinking.

Without critical thinking there can be no competent exchange of ideas, no competent communication. And these skills, according to one study of corporate executives, are essential for effective management (Robbins & Hunsaker, 2003). Because of its central importance, critical thinking is given special prominence in this text.

Adults, when speaking of things they don't want a child to understand, often spell out key words, thus speaking in a code that young children can't yet break. Computer communication enables you to do a similar thing. For example, when sending your credit card number to a vendor, you might send it in encrypted form, coded into a symbol system that others will not be able to understand (decode). Similarly, in chat groups you might write in a language that only certain of your readers will understand. In what other types of situations would you use a code that certain others cannot understand?

Thinking Critically About boxes are presented throughout the text. In the early chapters these boxes explain what critical thinking is; in later chapters they identify specific skills that will help you become a more critical, reasoned, and careful thinker. In addition, frequent questions appear in the margins, requiring you to exercise and apply your critical thinking to a wide variety of interpersonal communication issues discussed in the text.

Throughout this text, you'll find numerous recommendations for communicating more effectively. As you read, keep in mind that the description of these skills is almost always too general; they are rarely specific enough for automatic application to any given situation. So ask yourself: What is there about your unique and specific situation that you need to take into account in deciding what to do? What are your communication options? Which seem the most promising? Can you play these through in your mind? Also, recognize that, although great effort has been made to indicate cultural differences and variation and to adapt this textbook for a Canadian audience, most of the research on communication available today comes from the United States. So before using your skill, it's always appropriate to ask if there are cultural differences that might bear on the skill and its successful application.

Critical thinking enables you to ask and answer questions of clarification or challenge, to draw and evaluate conclusions, and to organize your thoughts and speak or write them coherently. Critical thinking also allows you to distinguish between logical and illogical inferences, to weigh the truth of arguments instead of simply accepting them on faith, and to make connections between new knowledge and what you already know.

Competence and Culture The term *culture* refers to the lifestyle of a group of people. A group's culture consists of its values, beliefs, artifacts, ways of behaving, and ways of communicating. Culture includes all that members of a social group have produced and developed—their language, ways of thinking, art, laws, and religion. Culture is transmitted from one generation to another not through genes but through communication and learning, especially through teaching by parents, peer groups, schools, religious institutions, and government agencies. Because most cultures teach women and men different attitudes and ways of communicating, many of the gender differences we observe may be considered cultural—although, of course, the biological differences between men and women also play a part.

Competence is sometimes culture specific; communications that prove effective in one culture will not necessarily prove effective in another. For example, giving a birthday gift to a close friend would be appreciated by members of many cultures and in some cases would be expected. But birthday gifts are frowned upon by Jehovah's Witnesses because they don't celebrate birthdays (Dresser, 1996). Because of the vast range of cultural differences that impact on interpersonal communication, the role of culture is discussed in every chapter of this book.

Competence and Ethics Interpersonal communication also involves questions of **ethics**. A moral dimension exists in any interpersonal communication act (Jaksa & Pritchard, 1994; Bok, 1978). For example, while it might be effective to lie in order to sell a product, doing so would not be ethical. The decisions you make concerning communication are guided not only by what you consider effective but also by what you consider right. The relatively recent proliferation of electronic forms of communication, such as the internet, brings with it new moral choices and the need for new frameworks for ethical decision making (Frost, 2003).

Ethical dimensions of interpersonal communication are presented throughout the text in *Talking Ethics* boxes and include, for example, the ethics of outing, lying, interpersonal silence, motivational appeals, and gossiping about secrets. Each of these ethics boxes presents a case calling for a decision and asks what you would do in the situation described. These cases are designed to illustrate the fact that ethics is not some abstract concept studied in philosophy; ethical principles underlie day-to-day decisions we all have to make. A complete list of all *Talking Ethics* boxes appears in the Specialized Contents on page xi.

As you read this text, you'll see that these five themes of competence are not separate and distinct from one another but rather interact and overlap. For example, as already noted, critical thinking pervades the entire interpersonal communication process and also serves as a foundation for your cultural awareness, listening effectiveness, and skill development. Similarly, an awareness of cultural differences will make you a more effective listener, a more discerning user of skills, and more conscious of the ethical dimension of interpersonal communication. So as you read the text and work actively with the concepts, remember that everything—the regular text, the boxed features, the material in the margins, the summaries, and the vocabulary tests at the end of the chapters—is designed to contribute to one overarching aim: to increase your interpersonal communication competence.

Talking Ethics The Ethics of Communicating in Cyberspace

Because of the explosion in computer communication, "nethics" (the ethics of internet communication) has become an important part of ethical communication generally. Of course, the same principles that govern ethical face-to-face interaction should also prevail when you communicate online. Here, however, are a few principles with special relevance to computer communication. It's unethical to

1. Invade the privacy of others. Reading the files of another person or breaking into files that you're not authorized to read is unethical, just as it would be to read a person's diary or personal letters.

2. Harm others or their property. Creating computer viruses, publishing instructions for making bombs, or creating websites that promote sexism, racism, heterosexism, or ageism is unethical.

3. Spread falsehoods. Lying on the internet—about other people, about the powers of medical or herbal treatments,

or about yourself (in, say, misrepresenting yourself in chat groups)—is unethical.

4. Plagiarize. Appropriating the work of another as your own—whether the original work appeared on the internet or in a book or journal—is unethical.

5. Steal passwords, PINs, or authorization codes that belong to others. Theft of these private codes is similar to stealing and using another person's credit card.

6. Copy software programs that you haven't paid for.

WHAT WOULD YOU DO?

As an experiment, you develop a computer virus that can destroy websites. Recently, you've come across various websites that you feel promote child pornography. You wonder if you can ethically destroy these websites. And, further, you wonder if not destroying them can actually be more unethical than using your newly developed virus.

Ethics

Communication is ethical when it facilitates an individual's freedom of choice and unethical when it interferes with freedom of choice.

_____
_____
_____
_____
_____
_____
_____
_____
_____

PRINCIPLES OF INTERPERSONAL COMMUNICATION

Another way to define interpersonal communication is to consider its major principles. These principles, although significant in terms of explaining theory, also have very practical applications and will provide insight into such practical issues as

- why disagreements so often centre on trivial issues and yet seem so difficult to resolve.
- why you'll never be able to mind-read to know just what another person is thinking.
- how communication expresses power relationships.
- why you and your partner often see the causes of arguments very differently.

Interpersonal Communication Is a Package of Signals

Communication behaviours, whether they involve verbal messages, gestures, or some combination thereof, usually occur in "packages" (Pittenger et al., 1960). Usually, verbal and nonverbal behaviours reinforce or support each other. Normally, all parts of a message system work together to communicate a particular meaning. You don't express fear with words while the rest of your body is relaxed. You don't express anger through your posture while your face smiles. Your entire body works together—verbally and nonverbally—to express your thoughts and feelings.

> ❝ All generalizations are false, including this one. ❞
> —Alexander Chase

Contradictory Messages With any form of communication, whether interpersonal messages, small group communication, public speaking, or mass media, you probably pay little or no attention to its "packaged" nature. But when there's an incongruity—when the chilly handshake belies the verbal greeting, when the nervous posture belies the focused stare, when the constant preening belies the expressions of being comfortable and at ease—you take notice. Invariably you begin to question the

Look at the photos of Peter Mansbridge from *The National* and George Stroumboulopoulos from *The Hour*—two Canadian television personalities who present the evening news. Which of these two personalities looks more formal and serious? Which looks more relaxed? What conveys these messages in the photos?

credibility, the sincerity, and the honesty of the individual.

Contradictory messages are particularly damaging when children are involved. Children can neither escape from such situations nor communicate about the communications. They can't talk about the lack of correspondence between one set of messages and another set. They can't ask their parents, for example, why they don't hold them or hug them when they say they love them.

Contradictory messages may be the result of the desire to communicate two different emotions or feelings. For example, you may like a person and want to communicate a positive feeling, but you may also feel resentment toward this person and want to communicate a negative feeling as well. The result is that you communicate both feelings; for example, you say that you're happy to see the person, but your facial expression and body posture communicate your negative feelings (Beier, 1974). In this example, and in many similar cases, the socially acceptable message is usually communicated verbally, whereas the less socially acceptable message is communicated nonverbally.

Interpersonal Communication Involves Content and Relationship Messages

Interpersonal messages combine **content and relationship dimensions**—that is, they refer to the real world, to something external to both speaker and listener. At the same time, they also refer to the relationship between the parties. For example, a supervisor may say to a trainee, "See me after the meeting." This simple message has a content message that tells the trainee to see the supervisor after the meeting. It also contains a **relationship message** that says something about the connection between the supervisor and the trainee. Even the use of the simple command shows there is a status difference that allows the supervisor to command the trainee. You can appreciate this most clearly if you visualize this command being made by the trainee to the supervisor. It appears awkward and out of place, because it violates the normal relationship between supervisor and trainee.

Many conflicts arise because people misunderstand relationship messages and cannot clarify them. Other problems arise when people fail to see the difference between content messages and relationship messages. A good example occurred when my mother came to stay for a week at a summer place I had. On the first day she swept the kitchen floor six times. I repeatedly told her that it did not need sweeping and that I would be tracking in dirt and mud from the outside. She persisted in sweeping, however, saying that the floor was dirty. On the content level, we were talking about the value of sweeping the kitchen floor. On the relationship level, however, we were talking about something quite different. We were each saying, "This is my house." When I realized this, I stopped complaining about the relative usefulness of sweeping a floor that did not need sweeping. Not surprisingly, she stopped sweeping.

Ignoring Relationship Messages   Examine the following interchange and note how relationship considerations are ignored.

MESSAGES	COMMENTS
Paul: I'm going bowling tomorrow. The guys at the plant are starting a team.	He focuses on the content and ignores any relationship implications of the message.
Judy: Why can't we ever do anything together?	She responds primarily on a relationship level, ignoring the content implications of the message and expressing her displeasure at being ignored in his decision.
Paul: We can do something together any time; tomorrow's the day they're organizing the team.	Again, he focuses almost exclusively on the content.

This example reflects research findings that show that men focus more on content messages, whereas women focus more on relationship messages (Wood, 1994). Once you recognize this gender difference, you can increase your sensitivity to the opposite sex.

Acknowledging Relationship Messages   Here is essentially the same situation but with added sensitivity to relationship messages and to gender differences.

MESSAGES	COMMENTS
Paul: The guys at the plant are organizing a bowling team. I'd sure like to be on the team. I'd like to go to the organizational meeting tomorrow. Okay?	Although he focuses on content, he shows awareness of the relationship dimensions by asking if this would be okay and by expressing his desire rather than his decision to attend this meeting.
Judy: That sounds great, but I'd really like to do something together tomorrow.	She focuses on the relationship dimension but also acknowledges his content orientation. Note too that she does not respond defensively, as if she has to defend herself or her emphasis on relationship aspects.
Paul: How about you meeting me at Luigi's and we can have dinner after the organizational meeting?	He responds to the relationship aspect—without abandoning his desire to join the bowling team—and seeks to incorporate it into his communications. He tries to negotiate a solution that will meet both Judy's and his needs.
Judy: That sounds great. I'm dying for spaghetti and meatballs.	She responds to both messages, approving of both his joining the team and their meeting for dinner.

Arguments over the content dimension—such as what happened in a movie—are relatively easy to resolve. You may, for example, simply ask a third person what took place or see the movie again. Arguments on the relationship level, however, are much more difficult to resolve, in part because people seldom recognize that the argument is a relationship one.

In what ways might you misread the meanings of another person by focusing only on the content and neglecting the relationship messages?

Interpersonal Communication Is a Process of Adjustment

The principle of **adjustment** states that interpersonal communication can take place only to the extent that the people who are talking share the same communication system. We can easily understand this when dealing with speakers of two different languages; much miscommunication is likely to occur. The principle, however, takes on particular relevance when you realize that no two people share identical communication systems. Parents and children, for example, not only have very different vocabularies but, more important, have different meanings for some of the terms they have in common. Consider, for example, the differences between parents' and children's understanding of such terms as *music*, *success*, and *family*. Different cultures and social groups, even when they share a common language, also have different nonverbal communication systems. To the extent that these systems differ, communication will be hindered.

The principle of adjustment is especially important in intercultural communication, largely because people from different cultures use different signals. Sometimes the same signals signify quite different things. In North America, for example, focused eye contact tends to mean honesty and openness. But in Japan and in many Hispanic cultures, that same behaviour may signify arrogance or disrespect if engaged in by, say, a youngster who is communicating with someone significantly older.

Interpersonal Communication Is Ambiguous

All messages are ambiguous to some degree. An ambiguous message is one that can be interpreted as having more than one meaning. Sometimes ambiguity results when we use words that can be interpreted differently. Informal time terms offer good examples; different people may interpret terms such as *soon*, *right away*, *in a minute*, *early*, and *late* very differently. The terms themselves are ambiguous.

Interpersonal Communication Is Inevitable, Irreversible, and Unrepeatable

Three characteristics often considered together are interpersonal communication's **inevitability**, **irreversibility**, and unrepeatability.

Communication Is Inevitable   You cannot *not* communicate. Often communication is intentional, purposeful, and consciously motivated. Sometimes, however, you are communicating even though you may think you are not, or may not even want to. A dramatic example of the truthfulness of this statement was seen when Stephen Harper, prime minister of Canada, first came to office. Those who knew him considered his avoidance of the media a thoughtful strategy to limit exposure until he had clarity on the issues. But this approach was interpreted more negatively by journalists, who saw it as an effort to restrict and control, as was clearly illustrated in the cartoon shown to the left (*Time*, April 10, 2006).

In the same way that you cannot *not* communicate, you also cannot *not* influence the person you interact with (Watzlawick, 1978). Persuasion, like communication, is also inevitable. Recent research suggests that the influencing power of communication extends to electronic as well as face-to-face communication. For example, website content is manipulated to draw users to visit particular sites, and to make specific choices during their visit (Knobloch et al., 2003). The issue, then, is not whether you will or will not persuade or influence another; rather, it's *how* you'll exert your influence.

An example of the impossibility of not communicating.

Communication Is Irreversible Notice that only some processes can be reversed. For example, you can turn water into ice and then reverse the process by turning the ice back into water. Other processes, however, are irreversible. You can, for example, turn grapes into wine, but you cannot reverse the process and turn wine into grapes. Interpersonal communication is an irreversible process. Although you may try to qualify, deny, or somehow reduce the effects of your message, you cannot withdraw the message you have conveyed. Similarly, once you press the send key, your email is in cyberspace and impossible to retrieve. Because of irreversibility, be careful not to say things you may wish to withdraw later. Carefully monitor messages of commitment, messages sent in anger, or messages of insult or derision. Otherwise, you run the risk of saying something you'll be uncomfortable with later.

> 66 Once a word has been allowed to escape, it can never be recalled. 99
>
> —Horace

Communication Is Unrepeatable The reason that communication is unrepeatable is simple: Everyone and everything is constantly changing. As a result, you never can recapture the exact same situation, frame of mind, or relationship dynamics that defined a previous interpersonal act. For example, you never can repeat meeting someone for the first time, comforting a grieving friend, or resolving a specific conflict.

You can, of course, try again; you can say, "I'm sorry I came off so pushy—can we try again?" Notice, however, that even when you say this, you have not erased the initial (and perhaps negative) impression. Instead, you try to counteract this impression by going through the motions again. In doing so, you hope to create a more positive impact that will lessen the original negative effect.

Face-to-face communication fades after you have spoken. There is no trace of your communication outside of the memories of the parties involved or of those who overheard your conversation. In computer-mediated communication, however, the messages are written and may be saved, stored, and printed. Both face-to-face and computer-mediated messages may be kept confidential or revealed publicly. But computer messages can be made public more easily and spread more quickly than face-to-face messages. And in the case of written messages, clear evidence exists of what you said and when you said it.

In-Class Notes

The Purposes of Communication

- Relate
- Learn
- Influence
- Help
- Play

_____

_____

_____

_____

_____

_____

_____

_____

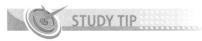

Interpersonal Communication Serves a Variety of Purposes

Interpersonal communication can be used to accomplish a variety of purposes. Understanding how it serves these purposes will help you more effectively achieve your own interpersonal purposes. Interpersonal communication enables you to *learn*, to better understand the external world of objects, events, and other people. Although a great deal of information comes from the media, you probably discuss and ultimately "learn" or internalize information through interpersonal interactions. In fact, your beliefs, attitudes, and values are probably influenced more by interpersonal encounters than by the media or even by formal education. Through interpersonal communication you also learn about yourself. By talking about yourself with others, you gain valuable feedback on your feelings, thoughts, and behaviours. Through these communications you also learn how you appear to others—for example, who likes or dislikes you, and why.

Interpersonal communication helps you *relate*. One of the greatest needs people have is to establish and maintain close relationships. You want to feel loved and liked, and in turn you want to love and like others. Such relationships help to alleviate loneliness and depression, enable you to share and heighten your pleasures, and generally make you feel more positive about yourself.

Very likely, you *influence* the attitudes and behaviours of others in your interpersonal encounters. You may wish another person to vote a particular way, try a new diet, buy a new book, listen to a record, see a movie, take a specific course, think in a particular way, believe that something is true or false, or value some idea—the list is endless. A good deal of your time is probably spent in interpersonal persuasion.

Talking with friends about your weekend activities, discussing sports or dates, telling stories and jokes, and, in general, just passing the time are all activities that fulfill a *play* function. Far from being frivolous, this function is an extremely important one that gives our activities a necessary balance and our minds a needed break from all the seriousness around us. Everyone has an inner child, and that child needs time to play.

Therapists of various kinds serve a helping function by offering guidance through interpersonal interaction. But everyone interacts to *help* in everyday life: You console a friend who has broken off a love affair, counsel another student about what courses to take, or offer advice to a colleague about work. Success in accomplishing this helping function, professionally or otherwise, depends on your knowledge of and skill in interpersonal communication.

In-Class Notes

Principles of Interpersonal Communication

Interpersonal Communication

- is a package of signals.
- involves both content and relationship messages.
- is a process of adjustment.
- is ambiguous
- is inevitable, irreversible, and unrepeatable.
- serves a variety of purposes.

_____

_____

_____

_____

_____

_____

_____

_____

CULTURE AND INTERPERSONAL COMMUNICATION

As noted earlier, the word *culture* refers to the **beliefs** (convictions), ways of behaving, and artifacts of a group that are transmitted through communication and learning rather than through genes. Different cultures teach men and women different attitudes, beliefs, values, and ways of communicating and relating to one another (Macgeorge et al., 2003). This does not deny that biological factors also play a role in the differences between male and female behaviour. In fact, recent research continues to uncover biological roots for traits—such as happiness and shyness—that were once thought entirely learned (McCroskey, 1998).

How relevant do you think cultural differences are to your own current interpersonal interactions? How relevant will cultural differences be to you in the next 10 or 15 years?

The Importance of Culture

Because your interpersonal communications are heavily influenced by the culture in which you were raised (Burleson & Mortenson, 2003), culture is given a prominent place in this text. This section explains the relevance of culture to interpersonal communication, and the aims and benefits of a cultural perspective.

Vast demographic changes are taking place throughout Canada. A walk through any large city, many small towns, or just about any college or university campus reinforces the fact that Canada is largely a collection of many different cultures. Many cultural groups have been successful in preserving their uniqueness and special traditions while contributing to Canadian society as a whole. In fact, the Canadian identity is considered to be a multicultural mosaic, with different cultural groups within the mosaic influencing each other in a multitude of ways. The composition of this mosaic is also dynamic, since immigration patterns can change rapidly. For example, the number of immigrants to Canada from African countries in 1997–1998 was 6.9 percent of total immigrants, increasing to 9.3 percent in 2001–2002. Similarly, the proportion of immigrants to Canada from India went up to 12.1 percent from 9.0 percent. In contrast, the proportion of immigrants to Canada from all European countries in the same years went down to 16.8 percent, from 20.6 percent (Statistics Canada, at www.statcan.ca/english/Pgdb/population/demo08.htm, June 20, 2003).

With immigration patterns changing so rapidly, Canada is likely to look different in the coming years. Do any of these patterns surprise you? What might your own province, city, or town look like 30 years from now, and how might this future cultural landscape affect your own intercultural communication?

As a result of these changes, Canadians have become increasingly respectful of cultural differences. Rather than wanting everyone to be the same, we are coming to see that diversity enriches our society and that it's possible for a united Canada to embrace a broad range of traditions, beliefs, and ways of living. And with some notable exceptions—hate speech, racism, sexism, and homophobia come quickly to mind—we're more concerned with saying the right thing and ultimately with developing a society in which all cultures can coexist and enrich one another. At the same time, the ability to interact effectively with members of other cultures often translates into financial gain, increased employment opportunities, and better advancement prospects.

Today, most countries are economically dependent on one another. Our economic lives depend on our ability to communicate effectively across cultures. Similarly, our political well-being depends in great part on that of other cultures. Political unrest in any part of the world—in the Middle East or in Eastern Europe, to take just two examples—affects our own security. Intercultural communication and understanding now seem more crucial than ever.

The rapid spread of communication technology has brought foreign and sometimes very different cultures right into our living rooms. News from foreign countries is commonplace. We see nightly—in vivid colour—what is going on in remote countries. Technology has made intercultural communication easy, practical, and inevitable. Daily, the media bombard us with evidence of racial tensions, religious disagreements, and sexual bias. These problems are generally caused when intercultural

In the photo on the left, Wayne Gretzky is depicted as a hockey superstar; in the photo on the right he appears with Jean Chrétien and Catriona LeMay Doan following Vancouver's successful bid to host the 2010 Winter Olympics. Do you think Gretzky's interpersonal communication style has evolved as his role has grown from athlete to include that of manager and spokesperson? In what ways?

Do you agree that the media and the internet are fostering an Americanization of different cultures? Some people find this an unpleasant prospect and see it as the loss of diversity; others see it as inevitable and as the result of a democratic process whereby people select the values and customs they wish to adopt. How do you feel about this Americanization?

communication fails. The internet has made intercultural communication as easy as writing a note on your computer. We can now communicate by email with someone in Europe or Asia just as easily as with someone in another Canadian city or province.

Still another reason for the importance of cultural awareness is that interpersonal competence is specific to a given culture; what proves effective in one culture may prove ineffective in another. For example, in North America, corporate executives get down to business during the first several minutes of a meeting. In Japan, however, business executives interact socially for an extended period and try to find out something about one another. Thus, the communication principle influenced by North American culture would advise participants to tackle the meeting's agenda during the first five minutes. The principle influenced by Japanese culture would advise participants to avoid dealing with business until everyone has socialized sufficiently and feels well enough acquainted to begin negotiations. Neither principle is right or wrong. Each is effective within its own culture, and ineffective outside its own culture.

A cultural emphasis helps distinguish what is *universal* (true for all people) from what is *relative* (true for people in one culture and not true for people in other cultures) (Matsumoto, 1994). The principles for communicating information and for changing listeners' attitudes, for example, will vary from one culture to another. If you're to understand communication, you need to know how its principles vary and how the principles must be qualified and adjusted on the basis of cultural differences.

And, of course, you need cultural understanding in order to communicate effectively in a wide variety of intercultural situations. Success in interpersonal communication—on your job and in your social life—will depend on your ability to communicate effectively with people who are culturally different from you. Respecting the values and beliefs of others does not necessarily mean that you agree with them. What you are respecting is the right of others to be different from you.

Summary of Concepts and Skills

This chapter explored the nature of interpersonal communication, described several principles of interpersonal communication, and stressed the centrality of culture.

1. Interpersonal communication is a transactional process that takes place between two people who have a relationship.

2. Essential to an understanding of interpersonal communication are the following elements: source–receiver, encoding–decoding, messages (including feedback and feedforward), channels, noise (physical, physiological, psychological, and semantic), context (physical, cultural, social–psychological, and temporal), and competence.

3. Interpersonal communication
   - is a package of signals that usually reinforce but may also contradict one another.
   - consists of both content and relationship messages; we communicate about objects and events in the world but also about the relationship between source and receiver.
   - is a process by which we each adjust to the specialized communication system of the other.
   - is ambiguous and can be interpreted as having more than one meaning.
   - is inevitable (communication will occur whether we want it to or not); irreversible (once something is received, it remains communicated and cannot be erased from a listener's memory); and unrepeatable (no communication act can ever be repeated exactly).
   - is purposeful; through interpersonal communication we learn, relate, influence, play, and help.

4. Interpersonal communication is heavily influenced by culture—by the beliefs, attitudes, and values taught and practised by cultural members.

Check Your Ability

Several interpersonal skills were noted in this chapter. Evaluate your own ability to do the following, using this rating scale: 1 = almost always, 2 = often, 3 = sometimes, 4 = rarely, and 5 = almost never.

_____ ❶ Interact interpersonally, recognizing that all the elements of communication are in a constant state of transaction, with each element influencing every other element.

_____ ❷ Communicate with an understanding that meaning is derived from the entire package of signals, both verbal and nonverbal.

_____ ❸ Distinguish between content and relationship messages and respond to both.

_____ ❹ Adjust your messages to the unique communication system of the other participant.

_____ ❺ Communicate *after* thinking, especially in light of the inevitability, unrepeatability, and irreversibility of interpersonal communication.

_____ ❻ Communicate while recognizing the variety of purposes that interpersonal interaction may serve.

_____ ❼ Use the principles of interpersonal communication while recognizing its cultural context.

After completing this self-test, check your answers against the Answer Key at the back of the book.

Multiple Choice Questions *Choose the BEST answer.*

1. Interpersonal communication is communication between two people who
   a. have a relationship.
   b. are in some way connected.
   c. are aware of one another.
   d. all of the above.

2. Interpersonal communication is
   a. irreversible.
   b. static.
   c. continuous.
   d. verbal only.

3. The elements of interpersonal communication include source–receiver and a(n)
   a. channel.
   b. play.
   c. adjustment.
   d. monitor.

4. Interpersonal communication serves several purposes, including
   a. channelling, joking, loving.
   b. constructing, ruling, reaching.
   c. learning, helping, playing.
   d. helping, learning, channelling.

5. The objective of this text is
   a. to provide a formula for all behaviour.
   b. to enhance your competence.
   c. to provide you with relevant theory.
   d. to explain observable behaviour.

6. Which is NOT an element of interpersonal communication?
   a. source–receiver
   b. context
   c. feedback
   d. empathy

7. Which of the following is an encoder?
   a. writer
   b. listener
   c. reader
   d. audience

8. Which is NOT a communication channel?
   a. telephone
   b. email
   c. face-to-face contact
   d. none of the above

9. A transactional process
   a. is an exchange of money.
   b. is static.
   c. has a clear beginning and end.
   d. is continuous.

10. The statement "all Albertans are rednecks" is an example of what kind of noise?
    a. psychological
    b. semantic
    c. physical
    d. paranoia

True–False Questions *Write a T or F in the blank next to the statement.*

_T_ Feedforward is information about a message before you send it.

_F_ Only one channel is used while encoding.

_T_ Noise is anything that distorts a message or prevents its being received.

_T_ Extreme anger can be a type of noise.

_F_ The cultural dimension of communication has to do with status.

_T_ Critical thinking can enhance your competence.

_T_ Usually, verbal and nonverbal communication support each other.

_F_ Contradictory messages are a part of competence.

_F_ Communication competence has nothing to do with ethics.

_T_ One of the problems with message overload is that it absorbs a lot of time.

Vocabulary Quiz
The Language of Interpersonal Communication

Match the terms of interpersonal communication with their definitions. Record the number of the definition next to the appropriate term.

a. _7_ interpersonal communication

b. _10_ encoding

c. _1_ feedback

d. _4_ semantic noise

e. _5_ cultural context

f. _3_ feedforward

g. _8_ relationship messages

h. _2_ source–receiver

i. _9_ signal-to-noise ratio

j. _6_ communication as a transactional process

1. Messages sent back to the source in response to the source's messages.

2. Each person in the interpersonal communication act.

3. Information about messages that are yet to be sent.

4. Interference that occurs when the receiver does not understand the meanings intended by the sender.

5. The rules and norms, beliefs and attitudes of the people communicating.

6. Communication as an ongoing process in which each part depends on each other part.

7. Communication that takes place between two people who have a relationship between them.

8. Messages referring to the connection between the two people in communication.

9. A measure of meaningful message compared with interference.

10. The process of sending messages; for example, in speaking or writing.

Skill Building Exercises

1.1 Giving Effective Feedback

How would you give feedback in these varied situations? You may wish to read a bit more about feedback before completing this exercise. Write one or two sentences of feedback for each of these situations:

■ A friend you like but don't have romantic feelings for asks you for a date.

■ Your instructor asks you to evaluate the course.

■ An interviewer asks if you want a credit card.

■ A homeless person smiles at you on the street.

■ A colleague at work tells a homophobic joke.

1.2 Giving Effective Feedforward

For each of the following situations, you may feel there's a need to preface your remarks with some kind of feedforward—some kind of prefatory comment before stating your main or primary message. For each situation (a) identify the specific purpose you hope to achieve with your feedforward, and (b) write a brief feedforward message that helps you achieve the purposes you identified in (a).

1. You see an attractive person in one of your classes and would like to get to know the person a bit more with the possible objective of a date.

2. You just saw the posted grades for the midterm; your close friend failed, but you did extremely well. In the cafeteria, you meet your friend, who asks, "How'd I do on the midterm?"

3. You have a reputation for injecting outlandish ideas into otherwise formal and boring discussions. This time, however, you want to offer a proposal that you fear will seem to be one of your standard outlandish comments but is actually an idea that you think could work. You want to assure your group that this idea is worthy of their undivided attention.

Feedforward can help set a favourable mood or give listeners needed information, paving the way for greater interpersonal effectiveness.

1.3 Explaining Interpersonal Difficulties

Using the principles of interpersonal communication discussed in this chapter, try *describing* what is going on in the following cases. These scenarios are extremely brief and are written only as aids to stimulate you to think more concretely about the axioms.

1. Grace feels that her fiancé, Tom, by not defending her proposal at a company where both work, created a negative attitude and encouraged others to reject her ideas. Tom says that he felt he could not defend her proposal because others in the room would have felt his defence was motivated by their relationship. So he felt it was best to say nothing.

2. A couple together for 20 years argues about the most seemingly insignificant things—who takes out the garbage, who does the dishes, who decides where to eat, and on and on. The arguments are so frequent and so unsettling that the two people are seriously considering separating.

3. In the heat of a big argument, Harry said he didn't want to see Peggy's family ever again: "They don't like me and I don't like them." Peggy reciprocated and said she felt the same way about his family. Now, weeks later,

there is still a great deal of tension between them, especially when they're with one or both families.

4. Pat and Chris have been online friends for the last two years, communicating with each other at least once a day. Recently, Pat wrote several things that Chris interpreted as insulting and as ridiculing Chris's feelings and dreams. Chris wrote back expressing resentment over these last messages, and then stopped writing. Pat has written every day for the last two weeks to try to patch things up, but Chris won't respond.

Thinking Critically About Interpersonal Difficulties.

Although the instructions asked you to describe what is going on in these situations, did you also think of recommendations for reducing the communication problems? What advice would you give these people? What principle would you find especially useful in explaining to each of the people involved what is going on?

1.4 Exploring Cultural Beliefs

Review the following cultural maxims. Select any one that seems especially interesting and identify:

a. the meaning of the maxim

b. the cultural value(s) it embodies and speaks to

c. the similarity or difference between it and what your own culture teaches

1. A penny saved is a penny earned.
2. All is not gold that glitters.
3. All things come to those who wait.
4. Blessed are the meek.
5. Blood is thicker than water.
6. Children should be seen and not heard.
7. Do unto others as you would have others do unto you.
8. Don't put off 'til tomorrow what you can do today.
9. God is just.
10. Honesty is the best policy.
11. If you've got it, flaunt it. Blow your own horn.
12. It's better to light a candle than to curse the darkness.
13. Love thy neighbour.
14. Never give a sucker an even break.
15. No one likes a sore loser.
16. Nothing succeeds like success.
17. Patience is a virtue.
18. Real men don't cry.
19. Respect your elders.
20. Self-praise smells bad.
21. Smile though your heart is breaking.
22. Stick with your own kind.
23. Tell it like it is.
24. The apple doesn't fall far from the tree.
25. There's no defence like a good offence.
26. Throw caution to the wind.
27. Time is money.
28. Time waits for no one.
29. Tomorrow will take care of itself.
30. What goes around comes around.

Have you ever applied your chosen maxim (or any of the maxims listed here) to specific interpersonal situations? What effect did the maxim's application have on the interaction?

Web Explorations

Companion Website

Visit the Companion Website at www.pearsoned.ca/devito for student resources related to this chapter, including self-grading quizzes, additional skill-building exercises, and links to other online resources.

Research Navigator

Explore our research resources at www.researchnavigator.com

- Find and read an article on the nature, elements, or principles of interpersonal communication. On the basis of this article, what can you add to the discussion presented here?

- Use this site to investigate one of the key terms discussed in this chapter (for example, encoding, decoding, competence, messages, feedback, feedforward, channel, noise, context, purpose, or ethics). What additional insights can you provide?

- Try using the research resources to find answers to any one of the following questions. If you can't find answers (after all, research hasn't provided answers to all interesting questions), try designing a research study that would help you answer the question.

1. Are interpersonal communication skills related to success as a friend, lover, or parent?

2. How is interpersonal communication applicable to your own profession?

3. How do men and women differ in their interpersonal communication patterns?

Chapter 2
The Self in Interpersonal Communication

Chapter Topics

This chapter explores the nature and role of the self in interpersonal communication.

Self-Concept and Self-Awareness

Self-Disclosure

Interpersonal Apprehension

Chapter Skills

After completing this chapter, you should be able to:

- analyze your self-concept and increase self-awareness.

- self-disclose and respond to the disclosures of others appropriately.

- manage your fear of communicating; communicate with confidence in a variety of contexts.

Aesop, the great writer of fables, tells the story of Mercury, one of the gods of Ancient Rome. Although a lesser god, Mercury aspired to be more. So one day, disguised as an ordinary man, he entered a sculptor's studio where he saw statues of the gods and goddesses for sale. Eyeing a statue of Jupiter, one of the major gods, Mercury asked the price. "A crown," the sculptor said. Mercury laughed, for he thought that was such a low price; maybe Jupiter was not so important after all. Then he asked the price of a statue of Juno, a major goddess. "Half a crown," said the sculptor. This seemed to please Mercury, who thought that surely his likeness would command a much higher price. So, pointing to a statue of himself, he proudly asked its price. "Oh, that: I'll give you that one free if you buy the other two."

Mercury was engaging in **social comparison**, a way of gaining insight into his own self-concept; he was comparing his reputation with the reputations of others. By doing so, Mercury got a good idea of his own relative importance. In this chapter we look at self-concept and self-awareness, and particularly at how we develop an image of ourselves and how we can increase our own self-awareness. With this information as a foundation, we then look at self-disclosure—the process of revealing ourselves to another person—and we consider speaker apprehension and some ways to reduce fear of communication.

SELF-CONCEPT AND SELF-AWARENESS

What sense of self do members of the Royal Family project? How much of their self-concept do you think comes from the extensive "grooming" they have received for their role as royals? How might a person develop a positive sense of self without such a privileged background?

Central to all forms of interpersonal communication is your self-concept—the image you have of yourself—and how that image is formed. Equally significant is your self-awareness, the degree to which you know yourself. Let's look first at self-concept.

Self-Concept

Your **self-concept** is your image of who you are. It's how you perceive yourself: your feelings and thoughts about your strengths and weaknesses, and your abilities and limitations. Self-concept develops from the image that others have of you; the comparisons you draw between yourself and others; your cultural experiences in the realms of race, ethnicity, gender, and gender roles; and your evaluation of your own thoughts and behaviours (Figure 2.1).

Others' Images of You If you wanted to see the way your hair looked, you'd probably look in a mirror. But what would you do if you wanted to see how friendly or how assertive you are? According to the concept of the *looking-glass self* (Cooley, 1922), you would look at the image of yourself that others reveal to you through their behaviours, and especially through the way they treat you and react to you.

Of course, you would not look to just anyone. Rather, you would look to those who are most significant in your life—to your *significant others*. As a child, for example, you would look to your parents and then to your elementary school teachers. As an adult you might look to your friends and romantic partners. If these significant others think highly of you, you will see a positive self-image reflected in their behaviours; if they think little of you, you will see a more negative image.

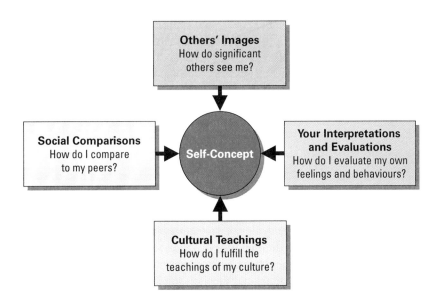

Figure 2.1

The Sources of Self-Concept
This diagram depicts the four sources of self-concept, the four contributors to how you see yourself. As you read about self-concept, consider the influence of each factor throughout your life. Which factor influenced you most as a preteen? Which influences you the most now? Which will influence you the most 25 or 30 years from now?

Social Comparisons Another way you develop self-concept is to compare yourself with others, to engage in what are called social comparisons (Festinger, 1954; Chin & McConnell, 2003; Guimond et al., 2006). Again, you don't choose just anyone. Rather, when you want to gain insight into who you are and how effective or competent you are, you look to your peers. For example, after an exam you probably want to know how you performed relative to the other students in your class. This gives you a clearer idea of how effectively you performed. If you play on a baseball team, it's important to know your batting average in comparison with the batting averages of others on the team. Your absolute score on the exam or your batting average may be helpful in telling you something about your performance, but you gain a different perspective when you see your scores in comparison with those of your peers.

Cultural Teachings Through your parents, teachers, and the media, your culture instills in you a variety of beliefs, values, and attitudes about matters such as success (how you should define and achieve it); the relevance of religion, race, or nationality; and the ethical principles you should follow in your business and personal life. These teachings provide benchmarks against which you can measure yourself. For example, your ability to achieve what your culture defines as success will contribute to a positive self-concept. Your failure to achieve what your culture values (for example, not being married by the time you're 30) may contribute to a negative self-concept.

When you demonstrate the qualities that your culture or organization (because organizations are much like cultures) teaches, you will see yourself as a cultural success and will be rewarded by other members of the culture or organization. Seeing yourself as culturally successful and being rewarded by others will

What kinds of information about yourself do you seek from social comparisons? With whom do you compare yourself?

contribute positively to your self-concept. When you fail to demonstrate such qualities, you're more likely to see yourself as a cultural failure and to be punished by other members of the culture, contributing to a more negative self-concept.

Your Own Observations, Interpretations, and Evaluations You also observe, interpret, and evaluate your own behaviour. For example, let's say you believe that lying is wrong. If you lie, you will probably evaluate this behaviour in terms of your internalized beliefs about lying and will react negatively to your own behaviour. You may, for example, experience guilt as a result of your own behaviour that contradicts your beliefs. On the other hand, let's say that you pull someone out of a burning building at great personal risk. You will probably evaluate this behaviour positively; you will feel good about this behaviour and, as a result, about yourself.

The better you understand why you view yourself as you do, the better you'll understand who you are. You can gain additional insight into yourself by looking more closely at self-awareness—and especially at the Johari model of the self.

Self-Awareness

Because you control your thoughts and behaviours largely to the extent that you understand who you are, it's crucial to increase your self-awareness. **Self-awareness** also helps you identify your strengths and weaknesses so that you can capitalize on your strengths and direct your energies to correcting your weaknesses. The **Johari window**, a model of the four selves, is particularly helpful in explaining the self and in offering suggestions on how to increase self-awareness (Figure 2.2).

Your Four Selves Assume that the model in Figure 2.2 represents you. The model is divided into quadrants, each of which contains a different self. Visualize the entire model as constant in size, but with each section as variable: sometimes small, sometimes large. Changes in one quadrant will cause changes in the other quadrants; for example, if you enlarge the open self, then another self must get smaller.

The Johari model emphasizes that the several aspects of the self are not separate and distinct pieces. Rather, they're parts of a whole that interact with one another. Like the model of interpersonal communication, this model of the self is transactional: Each part is dependent on each other part.

Your *open self* represents all the information, behaviours, attitudes, feelings, desires, motivations, and ideas that characterize you. The type of information included here might vary from your name and sex to your age, religious affiliation, and batting average. The size of your open self changes, depending on the situation and the individuals you're interacting with. Some people probably make you feel comfortable and support you. To them, you may open yourself wide. With others, you might prefer to leave most of yourself closed or unknown.

Your *blind self* represents all the things about yourself that others know but that you do not. These include, for example, your habit of rubbing your nose when you

Of the four sources of self-concept, which most influences the way you see yourself? Which gives you the most positive feedback? Which gives you the most negative feedback?

 **STUDY TIP**

Draw a Johari window. In the appropriate window, list five characteristics of your *open self*, and five characteristics of your *hidden self*.

Figure 2.2

The Johari Window

This diagram is a tool commonly used for examining what you know and don't know about yourself. It is also an effective way of explaining the nature of self-disclosure, covered later in this chapter. The window gets its name from its inventors, **Jo**seph Luft and **Ha**rry Ingham. When interacting with your peers, which self is your largest? Your smallest?

Source: From *Group Processes: An Introduction to Group Dynamics*, 3rd ed., by Joseph Luft. Copyright © 1984 by Mayfield Publishing. Reprinted by permission.

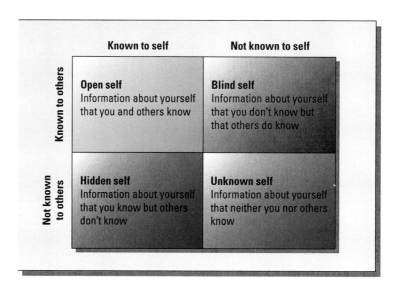

get angry, your defence mechanisms, and your repressed experiences. Interpersonal communication depends on both parties' sharing the same basic information about each other. Where blind areas exist, communication will be more difficult. Yet blind areas always exist. You can shrink your blind area, but you can never totally eliminate it.

Your *hidden self* contains all that you know of yourself but that you keep to yourself. This area includes all your successfully kept secrets. In any interaction, this area includes everything you have not revealed and perhaps seek actively to conceal. When you move information from this area to the open area—as in, say, telling someone a secret—you're self-disclosing, a process examined later in this chapter.

Your *unknown self* represents truths that exist but that neither you nor others know. We infer the existence of this unknown self from dreams, psychological tests, or therapy. For example, through therapy you might become aware of your high need for acceptance and how this influences the way you allow people to take advantage of you. With this insight, this information moves from the unknown self to the hidden self and perhaps to the open self.

Increasing Self-Awareness Embedded in the discussion of the Johari window were suggestions on how to increase your own self-awareness; these suggestions are discussed more fully below.

Listen to Others. You can learn a great deal about yourself from listening to others and seeing yourself as others do. Conveniently, others are constantly giving you the very feedback you need to increase self-awareness. In every interpersonal interaction, people comment on you in some way—on what you do, what you say, how you look. Sometimes these comments are explicit: "Loosen up," "Don't take things so hard," "You seem angry." Often, however, they're hidden in the way others look at you or in what they talk about. Pay close attention to this kind of information (both explicit and hidden) and use it to increase your own self-awareness. The discussion of verbal and nonverbal communication in Chapters 5 and 6 offers suggestions and insights that will assist you in reading hidden messages.

Increase Your Open Self. Revealing yourself to others will help increase your self-awareness. At the very least, you will bring into focus what you may have buried within. As you discuss yourself, you may see connections that you had previously missed. With feedback from others, you may gain still more insight. Also, by increasing your open self, you increase the chances that others will reveal what they know about you. We must remember that our cultural background will influence our approach to the open and hidden self, and even to the blind and unknown self. Canadians tend to be less prone to avid self-disclosure than our American counterparts. Compare, for example, Canadian television talk show hosts (such as Vicki Gabereau) with popular American talk show hosts (such as Oprah Winfrey or Jerry Springer), whose shows often focus on the disclosure of highly personal and private matters.

Seek Out Information to Reduce Your Blind Self. Encouraging people to reveal what they know about you will help to increase your awareness. You need not be so blatant as to say, "Tell me about myself" or "What do you think of me?" You can, however, use some situations that arise every day to gain self-information. "Do you think I came down too hard on the kids today?" "Do you think I was assertive enough when asking for a raise?" But use this route to self-awareness in moderation. If you do it too often, your friends will soon look for someone else to talk with.

Another way to seek out information about yourself is to visualize how your parents, teachers, friends, the stranger on the bus, or your neighbour's child see you. Recognize that each of these people sees you differently; to each you're a different person. Yet you're really *all* those people. This visualization experience will surely

66 The worst of all deceptions is self-deception. 99

—Plato

Very likely you talk to yourself, sometimes silently and sometimes, perhaps, out loud. This self-talk is important because it influences your self-concept—the way you feel about yourself. By listening carefully to what you tell yourself, you'll gain both self-awareness and self-esteem. Listen especially to two types of statements: self-destructive statements and self-affirming statements.

Self-destructive statements damage your self-esteem and prevent you from building meaningful and productive relationships. They may be about yourself ("I'm not creative," "I'm boring"), your world ("The world is an unhappy place," "They'll never offer me this job"), or your relationships ("All the good people are already in relationships," "If I ever fall in love, I know I'll be hurt"). Recognizing that you may have internalized such beliefs is a first step toward eliminating them. A second step involves recognizing that these beliefs are unrealistic and self-defeating, and that you must substitute more realistic ones. For example, you might try replacing the unrealistic belief that you always have to please others with the more realistic belief that although it would be nice if others were pleased with you, it certainly isn't essential (Ellis, 1988).

Self-affirming statements, on the other hand, are positive and self-supportive. They remind you of your successes and focus on your good deeds, positive qualities, strengths, and virtues. These statements concentrate on your potential, not your limitations (Brody, 1991; Spencer et al., 2001). Here is just a small sampling of self-affirmations that you may wish to try saying to yourself and—most important—listening to:

1. I'm a competent person.
2. I'm worth loving and having as a friend.
3. I'm a good team player.
4. I'm empathic and supportive.
5. I facilitate open communication.
6. I can accept my past but can also let it go.
7. I'm an effective and valuable worker.
8. I'm open-minded and listen fairly to others.
9. I can apologize.
10. I'm flexible and can adjust to different situations.

SUGGESTIONS?

Sindra's 10-year-old son has such low self-esteem that it prevents him from trying to do things that he is probably very capable of doing. For example, he refuses to play baseball because he thinks he can't; he refuses to answer questions in class because he thinks he'll be wrong. What advice would you give Sindra to help her help her son?

give you new and valuable perspectives on yourself. It will convince you that you're actually a different person with every person you interact with. For example, my colleagues see me as serious and always doing a hundred things at the same time. My students, however, see me as humorous and laid back.

In-Class Notes

Increasing Self-Awareness

- Listen to others.
- Increase your open self.
- Seek information about yourself.

_____

_____

_____

_____

_____

_____

_____

_____

_____

SELF-DISCLOSURE

When you move information from the hidden self into the open self, you're self-disclosing; you're revealing information about yourself to others. You can self-disclose through overt statements as well as through slips of the tongue and unconscious nonverbal movements. **Self-disclosure** may involve communicating information that you tell others freely, or information that you normally keep hidden. It may supply information ("I earn $45 000 annually") or reveal feelings ("I'm feeling really depressed"). Self-disclosure can vary from the insignificant ("I'm a Sagittarius") to the highly revealing ("I'm currently in an abusive relationship," or "I'm always depressed").

Only new knowledge represents "disclosure." To tell someone something about yourself that he or she already knows is not self-disclosure. And self-disclosure involves at least one other individual. It cannot be *intra*personal communication (communication with yourself). Nor may you disclose in a way that makes the message impossible for another person to understand. For a communication to be self-disclosure, someone must receive and understand the information.

Factors Influencing Self-Disclosure

Many factors influence whether or not you disclose, what you disclose, and to whom you disclose. Among the most important factors are who you are, your culture, your gender, who your listeners are, and what your topic is.

Who You Are Highly sociable and extroverted people self-disclose more than those who are less sociable and more introverted. People who are apprehensive about talking in general also self-disclose less than those who are more comfortable communicating.

People who are viewed in our society as competent communicators tend to engage in self-disclosure more than less competent communicators (Rubin et al., 2000). Perhaps competent communicators have greater self-confidence and more positive things to reveal. Similarly, their self-confidence may make them more willing to risk possible negative reactions to their disclosures (Crocker, 2002).

Your Culture Different cultures view self-disclosure differently. People in the United States, for example, disclose more than those in Great Britain, Germany, Japan, or Puerto Rico (Abrams et al., 2002; Kito, 2005). South Americans are more likely to self-disclose than (U.S.) North Americans (Horenstein & Downey, 2003). Similarly, American students self-disclose more about controversial issues and to different types of people than do Chinese students (Chen, 1992). Chinese Singaporean students consider more topics to be taboo and inappropriate for self-disclosure than their British peers (Goodwin & Lee, 1994). Among the Kabre of Togo, secrecy is a major part of everyday interaction (Piot, 1993).

Some cultures view disclosing one's inner feelings as a weakness. Among some groups, for example, it would be considered out of place for a man to cry at a happy occasion such as a wedding, whereas that same display of emotion would go unnoticed in some Latin cultures. Similarly, in Japan it's considered undesirable for colleagues to reveal personal information, whereas in much of North America it's expected (Hall & Hall, 1987).

Would this photo seem strange to you if instead of six women it featured six men? What has your culture taught you about self-disclosure? Does it provide different "rules" for men and for women?

In some cultures—for example, Mexican culture—there's a strong emphasis on discussing all matters in a positive mode, and this undoubtedly influences the way Mexicans approach self-disclosure as well. Negative self-disclosures, for example, are usually made only to close intimates and then only after considerable time has elapsed in a relationship. This reluctance to disclose negative information extends to revealing HIV-positive status and is thus creating serious problems in Mexico's efforts to prevent and treat HIV infection (Szapocznik, 1995).

These differences aside, there are also important similarities across cultures. For example, people from Great Britain, Germany, the United States, and Puerto Rico are all more apt to disclose certain kinds of personal information—such as details about hobbies, interests, attitudes, and opinions on politics and religion—than to discuss finances, sex, personality, and interpersonal relationships (Jourard, 1971). Similarly, one study showed self-disclosure patterns between American males to be virtually identical to those between Korean males (Won-Doornink, 1991).

How might failing to understand cultural or gender differences in self-disclosure distort your evaluation of a person's disclosure messages?

Your Gender The popular stereotype of gender differences in self-disclosure emphasizes the male's reluctance to speak about himself. For the most part, research supports this view and shows that women disclose more than men. This is especially true in same-sex dyads (two-person groups); women disclose more intimately (and with more emotion) when talking with other women than with men (Dindia, 2000). Men and women, however, make negative disclosures nearly equally (Naifeh & Smith, 1984), and recent studies suggest that gender differences may be receding (Sprecher & Hendrick, 2004).

More specifically, women disclose more than men about their previous romantic relationships, their feelings about their closest same-sex friends, their greatest fears, and what they don't like about their partners (Sprecher, 1987). Women also seem to increase the depth of their self-disclosures as a relationship becomes more intimate, while men seem not to change their self-disclosure levels. Men, for example, have more taboo topics on which they will not disclose information to their friends than do women (Goodwin & Lee, 1994). Finally, women even self-disclose more to members of the extended family than men do (Argyle & Henderson, 1985; Moghaddam et al., 1993). One notable exception occurs in initial encounters. Here men will disclose more intimately than women, perhaps "in order to control the relationship's development" (Derlega et al., 1985). Interestingly, a recent study in Taiwan found that sexual self-disclosure in cyberspace is greater for males than for females (Chiou & Wan, 2006).

Talking Ethics   Outing

An interesting variation on self-disclosure occurs when someone takes information from someone else's hidden self and makes it public. Although this third-party disclosure can concern any aspect of a person's hidden self—for example, an athlete's prison record or drug habit, a movie star's ill health or alcoholism, or a politician's criminal associates or financial dealings—the media have paid special attention to revealing a person's affectional orientation; the process is called **outing** (Signorile, 1993; Johansson & Percy, 1994).

Those against outing argue that people have a right to privacy and that no one else should take that right from them. Because outing can lead to severe consequences—for example, loss of job, expulsion from the military, or social and physical harassment—no one but the individual in question has the right to reveal such information. Those in favour of outing argue that it's an expedient political and social weapon to silence those gay men and lesbians who, in an effort to keep their own orientation secret, support or refuse to protest homophobic policies.

WHAT WOULD YOU DO?

An excellent staff reporter and regular contributor to the university newspaper brings to the editor a story revealing that a particular professor is a lesbian. This professor has repeatedly voted against adding any courses on gay or lesbian topics to the curriculum. She is also an advisor to an exclusive sorority that has repeatedly refused admission to lesbian students. What would be the ethically responsible thing for this editor to do? What would you do in this situation if you were the editor and final judge of whether the article was published?

Your Listeners Self-disclosure occurs more readily in small groups than in large groups. Dyads are the most hospitable setting for self-disclosure. With one listener, you can attend to the responses carefully. You can monitor the disclosures, continuing if there is support from your listener and stopping if there is not. With more than one listener, such monitoring becomes difficult, because the listeners' responses are sure to vary.

Sometimes self-disclosure takes place in group and public speaking situations. In consciousness-raising groups and in meetings like those of Alcoholics Anonymous, members may disclose their most intimate problems to tens or perhaps hundreds of people at one time. In these situations, group members are pledged to be totally supportive. These and similar groups are devoted specifically to encouraging self-disclosure and to providing mutual support for the disclosures.

At times, self-disclosure occurs more in temporary than in permanent relationships—for example, between strangers on a train or plane—in a kind of "in-flight intimacy" (McGill, 1985). In this kind of situation, two people set up an intimate self-disclosing relationship during a brief travel period, but they don't pursue it beyond that point. In a similar way, you might set up a relationship with one or several people on the internet and engage in significant disclosure. Perhaps knowing that you'll never see these other people and that they will never know where you live or work or what you look like makes it a bit easier. You're also more likely to disclose information you received from a low-level intimate (say a casual acquaintance) to a higher-level intimate (say a best friend) than you are to disclose information you received from a high-level intimate to a low-level intimate. This is a specific instance of the more general principle that you're more likely to communicate important information upward (to those of greater intimacy) than downward (to those of less intimacy) (Yovetich & Drigotas, 1999).

You're more likely to disclose when the person you're with discloses. This **dyadic effect** (what one person does, the other person does likewise) probably leads you to feel more secure and reinforces your own self-disclosing behaviour. Disclosures are also more intimate when they're made in response to the disclosures of others (Berg & Archer, 1983). Research finds too that reciprocal self-disclosure occurs more quickly and at higher levels online than it does in face-to-face interactions (Levine, 2000; Joinson, 2001).

Your Topic You're also more likely to disclose about some topics than others. For example, as mentioned earlier, you're probably more likely to self-disclose information about your job or hobbies than about your sex life or financial situation (Jourard, 1968, 1971). You're also more likely to disclose favourable information than unfavourable information. Dating couples are more likely to disclose information about nonsexual topics than about sexual ones (Byers & Demmons, 1999). Generally, the more personal and negative the topic, the less likely people are to self-disclose. However, Canadians also seem to be hesitant to share information about their accomplishments and achievements. Considerations of modesty and humility may inhibit disclosures of this nature.

The self-test on disclosure (page 36) focuses on the influences of the five factors just discussed: you, your culture, your gender, your listeners, and your topic.

The Rewards and Dangers of Self-Disclosure

Like other forms of interpersonal communication, self-disclosure entails both potential rewards and potential dangers. Let's look first at the rewards.

Rewards of Self-Disclosure Research shows that self-disclosure helps to increase self-knowledge, communication and relationship effectiveness, and physiological well-being.

STUDY TIP

With a classmate, debate the merits of parents' revealing financial worries to their children.

STUDY TIP

Create a list of the pros and cons of self-disclosure. From your perspective, do the pros outweigh the cons?

How Willing to Self-Disclose Are You?

Instructions: Respond to each statement below by indicating the likelihood that you would disclose such items of information to, say, other members of this class. Use the following scale: 1 = would definitely self-disclose, 2 = would probably self-disclose, 3 = don't know, 4 = would probably not self-disclose, and 5 = would definitely not self-disclose.

_____ ❶ My attitudes toward different nationalities and races.

_____ ❷ My feelings about my parents.

_____ ❸ My sexual fantasies.

_____ ❹ My past sexual experiences.

_____ ❺ My ideal mate.

_____ ❻ My drinking and/or drug-taking behaviour.

_____ ❼ My personal goals.

_____ ❽ My unfulfilled desires.

_____ ❾ My major weaknesses.

_____ ❿ My feelings about the people in this group.

HOW DID YOU DO?

There are, of course, no right or wrong answers to this self-test. By considering these topics, however, you may be able to pinpoint more precisely the areas about which you're willing to disclose and the areas about which you aren't willing to disclose. How would your answers have differed if the question asked you to indicate the likelihood of your self-disclosing to your best friend?

WHAT WILL YOU DO?

Taking this test and, ideally, talking about it with others who also complete it, should get you started thinking about your own self-disclosing behaviour, and especially about the factors that influence it. What factors most influence your willingness to disclose or not disclose each of these items of information?

Self-Knowledge. One reward of self-disclosure is that you gain a new perspective on yourself and a deeper understanding of your own behaviour. Through self-disclosure you may bring to consciousness a great deal that you might otherwise keep from conscious analysis. For example, as Tony talks about the difficulties he had living with an alcoholic father, he may remember details of his early life or entertain new feelings.

Even **self-acceptance** is difficult without self-disclosure. You accept yourself largely through the eyes of others. Through self-disclosure and subsequent support, you may be in a better position to see the positive responses to you. And you're more likely to respond by developing a more positive self-concept.

Communication and Relationship Effectiveness. You understand the messages of another person largely to the extent that you understand the person. For example, you can tell when a friend is serious or joking, when someone you know well is being sarcastic out of fear and when out of resentment. Self-disclosure is an essential condition for getting to know another individual.

Couples who engage in significant self-disclosure are found to remain together longer than couples who do not (Sprecher, 1987). Self-disclosure helps us achieve a closer relationship with the person to whom we self-disclose (Schmidt & Cornelius, 1987). Within a sexual relationship, self-disclosure increases sexual rewards and general relationship satisfaction. These two benefits in turn increase sexual satisfaction (Byers & Demmons, 1999). Without self-disclosure, meaningful relationships seem impossible to develop.

Physiological Health. People who self-disclose are less vulnerable to illnesses and less likely to feel depressed (Pennebacker, 1991). For example, bereavement over the death of someone very close is linked to physical illness for those who bear this alone and in silence. But it's unrelated to any physical problems for those who share their grief with others. Similarly, women who suffer sexual trauma normally experience a variety of illnesses (among them headaches and stomach problems). Women who keep these experiences to themselves, however, suffer illnesses to a much greater extent than those who talk with others about these traumas. The physiological effort required to keep your burdens to yourself seems to interact with the effects of the trauma to create a combined stress that can lead to physical illness.

In-Class Notes

Rewards of Self-Disclosure

- Greater self-knowledge
- Increased communication effectiveness
- Better physiological health

Dangers of Self-Disclosure   As is usually the case, when the potential rewards are great, so are the risks. Self-disclosure is no exception: The risks can be considerable and can be personal, relational, and professional.

Personal Risks.   If you self-disclose certain aspects of your life, you may face rejection from even the closest friends and family members. Those who disclose that they have AIDS, for example, may find that their friends and family no longer want to be quite as close as before.

Relationship Risks.   Even in close and long-lasting relationships, self-disclosure can cause problems. Total self-disclosure may prove threatening to a relationship by decreasing trust. Self-disclosures concerning infidelity, romantic fantasies, past indiscretions or crimes, lies, or hidden weaknesses and fears could easily have such negative effects.

Professional Risks.   The extensive media coverage of gays and lesbians in the U.S. military who are coming out in protest of the "don't ask, don't tell" policy illustrates the professional dangers that self-disclosure may entail. Similarly, politicians who disclose that they have been in therapy may lose party and voter support. Revealing political views or attitudes toward different religious or racial groups may create problems on the job, as may disclosing health problems such as HIV-positive status (Fesko, 2001). Teachers who disclose former or current drug use, for example, may find themselves denied tenure and may eventually fall victim to "budget cuts."

> ❝ Confiding a secret to an unworthy person is like carrying grain in a bag with a hole. ❞
>
> —Ethiopian proverb

Guidelines for Self-Disclosure

Because self-disclosure is an important type of interpersonal communication with the potential for great rewards and great dangers, here are some guidelines—first, for making self-disclosures and, second, for responding to the disclosures of others.

Guidelines for Making Self-Disclosures In trying to answer the question, "Should I disclose?" consider the following questions.

What Is Your Motivation for Self-Disclosing? Self-disclose out of concern for the relationship, for the others involved, and for yourself. Some people self-disclose out of a desire to hurt the listener rather than from a desire to improve the relationship—as when children tell their parents that they never loved them, or when a person informs a relationship partner that he or she stifled emotional development. But what if you feel ignored and unimportant because your partner devotes all available time to professional advancement? Instead of letting these feelings smoulder and turn into resentment, it might be helpful to the relationship to disclose them.

Is This Self-Disclosure Appropriate? Appropriate self-disclosures include honest expressions of feelings ("I feel uncomfortable when you criticize me in front of my friends"); past behaviours that another has a right to know about ("I was married when I was 17; we divorced two years later"); or personal abilities or lack of them that affect others ("I've never hung wallpaper before but I'll do my best"). Self-disclose in an atmosphere in which your listener can give open and honest responses. Don't wait until you're boarding the bus to say to your friend, "I got some really bad news today. I'll tell you about it later."

> ❝ Never reveal all of yourself to other people; hold back something in reserve so that people are never quite sure if they really know you. ❞
>
> —Michael Korda

Is the Other Person Also Disclosing? During your disclosures, give the other person a chance to reciprocate with his or her own disclosures. If the other person does not do so, then reassess your own self-disclosures. The lack of reciprocity may signal that this person, at this time and in this context, does not welcome your disclosures. Therefore, disclose gradually and in small increments so that you can retreat if the responses are not positive enough. Lack of reciprocity may also be due to cultural differences; in some cultures, significant self-disclosure takes place only after an extremely long acquaintanceship or may be considered inappropriate among, say, opposite-sex friends.

Will This Self-Disclosure Impose Burdens? Carefully weigh the potential problems that the self-disclosure may cause. Could you, if you were to disclose your previous prison record, afford to lose your job? If you were to disclose your previous failed romantic relationships, would you be willing to risk discouraging your present relational partner?

Ask yourself whether you're making unreasonable demands on the listener. For example, consider the person who discloses in confidence to his or her own mother-in-law an affair with a neighbour. This type of situation places an unfair burden on the mother-in-law. She is now in a bind: Should she break her promise of secrecy or allow her own child to believe a lie? Parents often place unreasonable burdens on their children by self-disclosing marital problems or infidelities or self-doubts. They fail to realize that the children may be too young or too emotionally involved to deal effectively with this information. Often such disclosures do not make the relationship a better one. Instead they may simply add tension and friction.

In making the choice between disclosing and not disclosing, keep in mind—besides the advantages and dangers already noted—the irreversible nature of communication discussed in Chapter 1. No matter how many times you may try to qualify something or take it back, once you have said it, you cannot withdraw it. You cannot erase the conclusions and inferences listeners have made on the basis of your disclosures. This is not to suggest that you therefore refrain from self-disclosing, but only that it's especially important here to recognize the irreversible nature of communication.

In-Class Notes

Guidelines for Making Self-Disclosures

- Understand your motivation.
- Judge the appropriateness.
- Assess whether the self-disclosure is reciprocal.
- Weigh the potential problems that disclosure may cause.

_____
_____
_____
_____
_____
_____
_____
_____

Guidelines for Responding to Disclosures   When someone discloses to you, it's usually a sign of trust and affection. In serving this most important receiver function, keep the following in mind.

Practise the Skills of Effective and Active Listening.   The skills of effective listening are discussed in detail in Chapter 4. These are especially important when listening to self-disclosures. Listen with empathy. Listen with an open mind. Repeat in your own words what you think the speaker has said so you can be sure you understand both the thoughts and the feelings. Express an understanding of the speaker's feelings to allow the speaker the opportunity to see these through the eyes of another individual. Ask questions to ensure your own understanding and to signal your own interest and attention.

Support the Discloser.   Express support for the person during and after the disclosures. Try to avoid making judgments. Concentrate on **affirmation**—understanding and empathizing with the discloser. Make your supportiveness clear to the discloser through your verbal and nonverbal responses. Nod your head to show you understand and echo the person's feelings and thoughts. Maintain eye contact and otherwise show your positive attitudes toward the discloser and the act of disclosing.

Keep the Disclosures Confidential.   When a person discloses to you, it's because she wants you to know her feelings and thoughts. If the discloser wishes these feelings and thoughts to be shared, then it's up to her to disclose them. If you reveal these disclosures to others, it will probably inhibit this person's future disclosures, and as a result, your relationship will suffer. In addition to keeping disclosures confidential, avoid using them against the person at some later time. Many self-disclosures expose a vulnerability or weakness. If you later turn around and use these against the person, you betray the confidence and trust invested in you.

One response that is seldom mentioned in discussions of disclosure is to tell someone that you simply do not want to hear his disclosure. Have you ever said this? Has anyone ever responded to your attempted self-disclosure with a refusal to listen? Under what conditions would such refusals be appropriate? Under what conditions would they be inappropriate?

It's interesting to note that one of the netiquette rules of email is that you shouldn't forward mail to third parties without the writer's permission. This rule is a useful one for self-disclosure generally: Maintain confidentiality; without permission, don't pass on to others disclosures made to you.

In-Class Notes

Guidelines for Responding to Self-Disclosures

- Listen with empathy and an open mind.
- Express support verbally and nonverbally.
- Do not be judgmental.
- Keep disclosures confidential.
- Remember that self-disclosure is usually a sign of trust and affection.

_____

_____

_____

_____

_____

_____

_____

_____

INTERPERSONAL APPREHENSION

After taking the test "How Apprehensive Are You?" (below), pair up with a classmate whose score is either much higher or much lower than yours. Share tips and techniques for reducing apprehension.

The term **communication apprehension** refers to a feeling of fear or anxiety about a situation in which a person must communicate. Some people develop negative feelings about communication and therefore expect the worst of themselves when they're called on to speak. To those who feel high anxiety in such circumstances, it just doesn't seem worthwhile to try. This is not to say that apprehensive people are ineffective or unhappy. Most of them have learned or can learn to deal with their communication anxiety or fear.

"Communication apprehension," researchers note, "is probably the most common handicap . . . suffered by people in contemporary American society" (McCroskey &

 Test Yourself

How Apprehensive Are You?

Instructions: This questionnaire consists of six statements concerning your feelings about communication with other people. Please indicate in the space provided the degree to which each statement applies to you by marking whether you (1) strongly agree, (2) agree, (3) are undecided, (4) disagree, or (5) strongly disagree with each statement. There are no right or wrong answers. Work quickly; record your first impression.

_____ ❶ While participating in a conversation with a new acquaintance, I feel very nervous.

_____ ❷ I have no fear of speaking up in conversations.

_____ ❸ Ordinarily I am very tense and nervous in conversations.

_____ ❹ Ordinarily I am very calm and relaxed in conversations.

_____ ❺ While conversing with a new acquaintance, I feel very relaxed.

_____ ❻ I'm afraid to speak up in conversations.

HOW DID YOU DO?

Compute your score as follows:

_____ **1** Begin with the number 18; it's used as a base so that you won't wind up with negative numbers.

_____ **2** To 18, add your scores for items 2, 4, and 5.

_____ **3** Subtract your scores for items 1, 3, and 6 from your step 2 total.

_____ **4** The result (which should be somewhere between 6 and 30) is your apprehension score for interpersonal conversations. The higher the score, the greater your apprehension. A score above 18 indicates some degree of apprehension.

WHAT WILL YOU DO?

Try first to identify those interpersonal situations that create the greatest apprehension for you. What factors can you identify that contribute to apprehension? What can you do to reduce the impact of those factors?

Source: From James C. McCroskey, *Introduction to Rhetorical Communication*, 7th ed. (Englewood Cliffs, NJ: Prentice-Hall, 1997).

Wheeless, 1976). According to surveys of university students, between 10 and 20 percent suffer "severe, debilitating communication apprehension"; another 20 percent suffer from "communication apprehension to a degree substantial enough to interfere to some extent with their normal functioning."

Culture and Apprehension

Interacting with members of cultures different from your own can create uncertainty, fear, and anxiety, all of which contribute to speaker apprehension (Anderson et al., 2002).

When you're speaking with people from cultures very different from your own, you're likely to be more uncertain about the situation and about your listeners' possible responses (Gudykunst & Nishida, 1984; Gudykunst et al., 1985). When you're sure of a situation and can predict what will happen, you're more likely to feel comfortable and at ease. But when you cannot predict what will happen, you're likely to become more apprehensive (Gudykunst, 2002).

Such situations can also engender fear. You might, for example, have a greater fear of saying something that might prove offensive or of revealing your own prejudices. The fear is easily transformed into apprehension. These situations can also create anxiety. For example, if your prior relationships with members of a culturally different group were few or if they were unpleasant, then you're likely to experience greater anxiety when dealing with other members of that group than if your prior experiences were numerous and positive (Stephan & Stephan, 1992).

How fearful are you of communicating? In what situations do you have greatest apprehension? How does communication apprehension figure into your social life? Into your professional life? How can it hurt you?

Skills Toolbox | Revealing Yourself in Interpersonal Relationships

At what stage in a relationship—if any—do you have an obligation to reveal the information listed in the first column? Record your answers for romantic relationships in the second column and for friendship relationships in the third column. Use numbers from 1 to 10, visualizing relationships on a continuum on which 1 is initial contact and 10 is extreme intimacy. If you feel you would never have an obligation to reveal this information, use 0.

In which type of relationship—romantic or friendship—do you incur the greater obligation to reveal yourself? In which type of relationship do you have less of an obligation to reveal such

INFORMATION	ROMANTIC RELATIONSHIP	FRIENDSHIP RELATIONSHIP
HIV status		
Past sexual experiences		
Annual salary and net worth		
Affectional orientation		
Race, nationality, and religious beliefs		
Social and political beliefs and attitudes		

information (the 0s in your responses)? In which type of relationship does the obligation to reveal yourself come earlier? Try formulating in one sentence the obligation you have as a friend or as a romantic partner to reveal information about yourself.

You don't have to reveal everything about yourself, but there may be obligations to reveal some information to certain relationship partners.

THEN AND NOW

Have you ever been in an interpersonal situation where you revealed more about yourself than you should have? Why did you feel that you had revealed too much? What happened to the relationship as a result? How have you changed your habits of self-disclosure? Have the changes made your relationships stronger?

Some research suggests that people respond more negatively to those they perceive as apprehensive than to those they perceive as more confident and less fearful (Richmond & McCroskey, 1996). Do you respond more negatively to those you see as apprehensive than to those you see as less fearful? Would you prefer to work with one type rather than the other? Would you rather date one type than the other?

Your thoughts and feelings about other people will also influence your apprehension. For example, if you hold stereotypes and prejudices, or if you feel that you're very different from these other people, you're likely to experience more apprehension than if you saw them as similar to you.

Managing Apprehension

Although most of us suffer from some communication apprehension, we can successfully manage it and control it—at least to some degree. Here are some suggestions (Beatty, 1988; McCroskey, 1997; Richmond & McCroskey, 1996).

Acquire Communication Skills and Experience   If we lack typing skills, we can hardly expect to type very well. Yet we rarely assume that a lack of interpersonal skills and experience can cause difficulty with communication and create apprehension. It can. After all, if you have never asked for a date and have no idea how to do it, it will be natural to feel apprehensive doing so. In this course, you're gaining the skills of effective interpersonal interaction. Engage in experiences—even if they prove difficult at first—to help you acquire the skills you need most. The more preparation and practice you put into something, the more comfortable you will feel with it.

Focus on Success   The more you perceive a situation as one in which others will evaluate you, the greater your apprehension will be (Beatty, 1988). Employment interviews and asking for a date, for example, are anxiety provoking, largely because they're highly evaluative. Your prior history in similar situations also influences the way you respond to new ones. Prior success generally (though not always) reduces apprehension. Prior failure generally (though not always) increases apprehension. If you see yourself succeeding, you'll stand a good chance of doing just that. So think positively. Visualize others giving you positive evaluations. Concentrate your energies on doing the best job you can in any situation you find yourself. You now have new skills and new experiences, and these will increase your chances for success. Do be careful, however, that your focus on success does not translate into the need to appear perfect, an attitude that is likely to increase your interpersonal apprehension (Saboonchi et al., 1999).

Reduce Unpredictability   The more unpredictable the situation, the greater your apprehension is likely to be. New and ambiguous situations are unpredictable; therefore, you naturally become anxious. In managing apprehension, therefore, try to reduce any unpredictability. When you're familiar with the situation and with what is expected of you, you're better able to predict what will happen. This will reduce the ambiguity and perceived newness of the situation. So, for example, if you're going to ask the boss for a raise, become familiar with the situation to the greatest extent you can. If possible, sit in the chair you will sit in; then rehearse your statement of the reasons you deserve the raise and the way in which you'll present them.

Put Apprehension in Perspective   Whenever you engage in a communication experience, remember that the world won't end if you don't succeed. Also remember that other people are not able to perceive your apprehension as sharply as you do. You may feel dryness in your throat and a rapid heartbeat; however, no one will know this but you.

Summary of Concepts and Skills

This chapter explored the self in interpersonal communication. We looked at the four selves of the Johari model and at how to increase self-awareness. Next we looked at self-disclosure, the process of revealing ourselves to others, and at some of the advantages and disadvantages of doing so. We then explored apprehension, what causes it, and how it can be managed effectively.

1. Self-concept is the image that you have of yourself. It is developed from the images of you that others have and that they reveal to you, the comparisons you make between yourself and others, and the way you interpret and evaluate your own thoughts and behaviours.

2. The four selves are the open self (what we and others know about us); the blind self (what others know but we do not know about ourselves); the hidden self (what we know but keep hidden from others); and the unknown self (what neither we nor others know).

3. We may increase self-awareness by asking ourselves about ourselves, listening to others, actively seeking information about ourselves, seeing ourselves from different perspectives, and increasing our open selves.

4. Self-disclosure is a type of communication in which we reveal information about ourselves to others.

5. Self-disclosure is generally reciprocal; the self-disclosures of one person stimulate the self-disclosures of the other person.

6. Both men and women avoid self-disclosure for fear of projecting a negative image. Men also avoid self-disclosure so they can maintain control; women also avoid self-disclosure to avoid personal hurt and problems in relationships.

7. Through self-disclosure you may gain self-knowledge, increase communication effectiveness, enhance the meaningfulness of your interpersonal relationships, and promote physical health.

8. Serious dangers exist in self-disclosing. Your interpersonal, social, and business relationships may be severely damaged if your self-disclosures are not positively received.

9. Communication apprehension is a feeling of fear or anxiety about communication situations.

10. People with high apprehension behave differently from people with low apprehension. Highly apprehensive people communicate less and avoid situations and occupations that demand a lot of communication. They are less likely than other people to be seen as leaders, have more negative attitudes toward school, and are more likely to drop out of university. Highly apprehensive people are also less satisfied with their jobs and engage more in steady dating.

11. Techniques for managing communication apprehension include acquiring communication skills and experience, focusing on success, reducing unpredictability, and being familiar with the situation.

Check Your Ability

Check your ability to apply the following skills. You will gain most from this brief exercise if you think carefully about each skill and try to identify instances from your recent communication experiences in which you did or did not act on the basis of the specific skill. Use a rating scale such as the following: 1 = almost always, 2 = often, 3 = sometimes, 4 = rarely, and 5 = almost never.

_____ **1** Analyze your own self-concept and seek to discover the sources that influenced it.

_____ **2** Become aware of your own communication patterns, especially as they relate to self-disclosing messages.

_____ **3** Engage in activities that increase self-awareness.

_____ **4** Regulate self-disclosures on the basis of the topic, listener, purposes, and so on.

_____ **5** Critically weigh the potential rewards and costs of self-disclosure before disclosing.

_____ **6** Self-disclose appropriately.

_____ **7** Respond to the self-disclosures of others as appropriate.

_____ **8** Manage the fear of communicating in interpersonal situations.

_____ **9** Communicate in interpersonal encounters with confidence.

After completing this self-test, check your answers against the Answer Key at the back of the book.

Multiple Choice Questions *Choose the BEST answer.*

1. The Johari window has four quadrants, which are
   a. unknown, social, blind, aware.
   b. hidden, social, open, blind.
   c. unknown, hidden, open, blind.
   d. hidden, social, open, closed.

2. Which self represents all that you know of yourself but that you keep to yourself?
   a. unknown
   b. known
   c. hidden
   d. blind

3. Communication apprehension
   a. is no big deal.
   b. is probably the most common fear of Canadians.
   c. comes from too much exercise.
   d. diminishes with increased conspicuousness.

4. Through self-disclosure you will NOT
   a. gain self-knowledge.
   b. achieve closer relationships.
   c. discourage others' self-disclosure.
   d. promote physical health.

5. Social comparisons
   a. involve comparisons of yourself with your peers.
   b. are done with significant others.
   c. are a sign of social inadequacy.
   d. use the "looking-glass self."

6. Asking about yourself is
   a. egocentric.
   b. a way to increase your open self.
   c. a way to increase self-awareness.
   d. counterproductive.

7. We are likely to self-disclose EXCEPT when
   a. we are with people we like.
   b. others self-disclose.
   c. we are in small groups.
   d. we are feeling less competent.

8. You should self-disclose only if
   a. it is appropriate.
   b. there is a desire to improve the relationship.
   c. it imposes no burdens.
   d. all of the above.

9. Lack of reciprocity in self-disclosure is
   a. deferring to the one who wishes to disclose.
   b. a natural balance.
   c. important feedback from the other person.
   d. a desire to hurt or punish.

10. The more unpredictable the situation
   a. the less time to get apprehensive.
   b. the greater the apprehension.
   c. the more conspicuous you are.
   d. all of the above.

True–False Questions *Write a T or F in the blank next to the statement.*

1. _T_ Self-disclosure is inevitable.
2. _T_ The Johari window has four quadrants.
3. _F_ Your unknown self is known to others.
4. _F_ Your blind self is known to you.
5. _T_ Reciprocity encourages more disclosure.
6. _F_ Self-disclosure should be burdensome.
7. _T_ Significant others increase our self-awareness.
8. _F_ Communication apprehension is quite rare.
9. _F_ Highly apprehensive people are socially charming and adept.
10. _F_ Females disclose less than males.

Vocabulary Quiz
The Language of the Self

Match the terms listed here with their definitions. Record the number of the definition next to the name of the concept.

a. _6_ Johari model
b. _4_ the open self
c. _2_ the blind self
d. _5_ the hidden self
e. _9_ the unknown self
f. _7_ self-awareness
g. _8_ self-disclosure
h. _3_ the dyadic effect
i. _1_ communication apprehension
j. _10_ gender and culture

1. Fear or anxiety over communicating.

2. The part of the self that contains information about the self that is known to others but unknown to oneself.

3. The tendency for the behaviours of one person to stimulate behaviours in the other person, usually used to refer to the tendency for one person's self-disclosures to stimulate the listener to self-disclose also.

4. The part of the self that contains information about the self that is known to oneself and to others.

5. The part of the self that contains information about the self that is known to oneself but unknown to (hidden from) others.

6. A diagram of the four selves.

7. A knowledge of oneself.

8. The process of revealing something significant about oneself to another individual or to a group, something that would not normally be known by them.

9. The part of the self that contains information about the self that is unknown to oneself and to others.

10. Two of the factors that influence self-disclosure.

Skill Building Exercises

2.1 To Disclose or Not to Disclose?

Whether you should self-disclose is one of the most difficult decisions you have to make in interpersonal communication. Here are several instances of impending self-disclosure. For each, indicate whether you think the self-disclosure would be appropriate and why.

1. A mother of two teenage children (one boy, one girl) has been feeling guilty for the past year over a romantic affair she had with her brother-in-law while her husband was in prison. A few months ago, she and her husband divorced. She wants to self-disclose her affair and her guilt to her children.

2. Tom wants to break off his engagement to Cathy because he has fallen in love with another woman. Tom wants to call Cathy on the phone, break his engagement, and disclose his new relationship.

3. Sam has been living in a romantic relationship with another man for the past several years. Sam wants to tell his parents, with whom he has been very close throughout his life, but can't get up the courage to do so. He decides to tell them in a long letter.

4. Mary and Jim have been married for 12 years. Mary has been honest about most things and has self-disclosed a great deal to Jim—about her past romantic encounters, her fears, her ambitions, and so on. Yet Jim doesn't reciprocate. He almost never shares his feelings and has told Mary almost nothing about his life before they met. Mary wonders if she should continue her pattern of self-disclosure.

Thinking Critically About Self-Disclosure.

What are your reasons for your judgments? Which self-disclosure do you think will prove most effective? Least effective? Which disclosures seem appropriate to the receiver? Are the intended methods (phone call or letter) likely to prove effective? Will the self-disclosure help accomplish what the person wishes to accomplish?

2.2 Times for Self-Disclosure

Self-disclosures occur throughout a relationship, but not always at what you may think is the right time. Some disclosures seem to occur too early and signal an intimacy that is not echoed in the relationship; the disclosures seem prematurely and inappropriately intimate. Some disclosures, on the other hand, occur too late; we feel we should have been told something earlier and may resent learning about it so late in the day. And, of course, some disclosures seem to occur at exactly the right time. This exercise explores the timeliness of self-disclosures.

Another way of looking at this exercise is from an ethical perspective: from the standpoint of your right to know certain information about a person with whom you become relationally involved. At what point in the relationship do you have a right to know this type of information?

Listed below are 10 items of personal information. Next to each item indicate the stage at which you would expect someone with whom you are in a relationship to disclose this type of information. Use X for any item you feel should not be disclosed at any time. Use the following shorthand for the stages appropriate for those items you feel should be disclosed.

Cp = Contact (perceptual)
Ci = Contact (interactional)
It = Involvement (testing)
Ii = Involvement (intensifying)
Iic = Intimacy (interpersonal commitment)
Isb = Intimacy (social bonding)

_____ 1. correct age

_____ 2. history of family mental illness or genetic disorders

_____ 3. relationship history (previous involvements, children)

_____ 4. annual income, assets, and debts

_____ 5. cultural background (race and nationality) and beliefs (for example, prejudices, ethnocentrism)

_____ 6. sexual orientation and inclinations

_____ 7. religion and religious beliefs

_____ 8. HIV status

_____ 9. attitudes toward commitment and fidelity; relationship expectations

_____ 10. political beliefs and attitudes

Thinking Critically About Times for Self-Disclosure.

After you have labelled all 10 items, consider some or all of the following questions. Work alone, in groups, or with the class as a whole.

- Does age influence appropriateness? For example, are certain items important at 18 but unimportant at 50? Important at 50 but unimportant at 18?

- Do men and women expect the same level of self-disclosure from their partners? If you have the opportunity, you may wish to compare your responses to the 10 items with the responses of others in your group or class. Are there noticeable gender differences?

- Do men and women follow different norms or rules in self-disclosing? How would you state these rules?

- In what kinds of relationships would you expect self-disclosure to be highest and lowest? Heterosexual? Gay male? Lesbian? What reasons can you advance to support your prediction? How would you go about testing your prediction?

- Does the future of the relationship (as envisioned by each person) influence the timing of self-disclosures?

- Do cultures vary in the way their members disclose? What implications might these differences have for intercultural communication? For example, can you identify potential problems that different cultural time schedules for self-disclosure might create?

2.3 Using Performance Visualization to Reduce Apprehension

Performance visualization is a technique designed specifically to reduce the outward manifestations of speaker apprehension and to reduce negative thinking (Ayres & Hopf, 1993). Try reducing your own communication apprehension by following these two simple suggestions.

1. The first step in performance visualization is to develop a positive attitude and a positive self-perception. Visualize yourself as being an effective speaker. Visualize yourself communicating as a fully and totally confident individual. Look at your listeners and speak. Throughout your conversation see yourself as fully in control of the situation. See your listeners paying rapt attention from the time you begin to the time you stop. Throughout this visualization, avoid all negative thoughts. As you visualize yourself as an effective speaker, take special note of how you walk, look at your listeners, respond to questions, and especially how you feel about the whole experience.

2. The second step in performance visualization is to model your performance on that of an especially effective speaker. View a particularly competent speaker and make a mental movie of him or her. Try selecting a presentation that's on video so you can replay it several times. As you review the actual and mental movie, begin to shift yourself into the role of speaker. Become this effective speaker.

Thinking Critically About Performance Visualization.

How did you feel as you were visualizing yourself as a successful and effective speaker? What actions did you see yourself performing? What person did you select to model your performance on? What is there about this person that led you to select him or her as your model? In what ways might you improve your next experience of performance visualization?

Web Explorations

Companion Website

Visit the Companion Website at www.pearsoned.ca/devito for student resources related to this chapter, including self-grading quizzes, additional skill-building exercises, and links to other online resources.

Research Navigator

Explore our research resources at www.researchnavigator.com

- Find and read an article on the self (for example, self-concept, self-esteem, self-awareness, self-disclosure, or communication apprehension). On the basis of this article, what can you add to the discussion presented here?

- You can use this or other articles to investigate one of the key terms discussed in this chapter (for example, self-concept, self-awareness, social comparison, self-disclosure, communication apprehension, dyadic effect). What additional insights can you provide?

- Try finding answers to one of the following questions or designing a research study to answer it.

1. Do people change their self-concept as they age?
2. How do children and adults differ in self-disclosure to friends?

3. Are shyness and communication apprehension hereditary? Learned?

Chapter 3
Interpersonal Perception

Chapter Topics

This chapter introduces interpersonal perception—the ways you see and evaluate other people.

The Stages of Perception

The Processes of Perception

Increasing Accuracy in Interpersonal Perception

Chapter Skills

After completing this chapter, you should be able to:

- perceive others with the knowledge that perceptions are influenced by who you are and by external stimuli.

- avoid common perceptual barriers while perceiving others.

- perceive others more accurately, using a variety of strategies.

These photographs show two different images of Canadian singer Céline Dion. If you didn't know who she was, what meaning might you assign to each image? For example, would you guess that the photo on the left depicts a popular entertainer? What would you think of the woman shown in the photo on the right?

Appearances are often deceiving, and what you think you see may not be the entire story. This lesson will prove useful to anyone engaged in perceptions of other people—the topic of this chapter.

What should a popular singer look like?

STUDY TIP

Create a diagram that outlines the five stages of interpersonal perception.

❝ We must always tell what we see. Above all, and this is more difficult, we must always see what we see. ❞

—Charles Peguy

THE STAGES OF PERCEPTION

Perception is the process by which you become aware of objects, events, and especially people through your senses: sight, smell, taste, touch, and hearing. Perception is an active, not a passive process. Your perceptions result from what exists in the outside world *and* from your own experiences, desires, needs and wants, loves, and hatreds. One of the reasons perception is so important in interpersonal communication is that it influences your communication choices. The messages you send and listen to will depend on how you see the world, on how you size up specific situations, and on what you think of the people with whom you interact.

Interpersonal perception is a continuous series of processes that blend into one another. *For convenience of discussion* we can separate these processes into five stages: (1) You sense or pick up some kind of stimulation; (2) you organize the stimuli in some way; (3) you interpret and evaluate what you perceive; (4) you store your perception in memory; and (5) you retrieve it when needed.

Stage One: Stimulation

At this first stage, your senses encounter a **stimulus**—you hear a new CD, you see a friend, you smell someone's perfume, you taste an orange, you feel another's sweaty palm. Naturally, you don't perceive everything; rather, you engage in *selective perception*. This general term includes *selective attention* and *selective exposure*. In **selective attention**, you attend to those things that you anticipate will fulfill your needs or will prove enjoyable. For example, when daydreaming in class, you don't hear what the instructor is saying until your name is called. Your selective attention mechanism focuses your senses on your name.

Through **selective exposure** you expose yourself to people or messages that will confirm your existing beliefs, contribute to your objectives, or prove satisfying in some way. For example, after you buy a car, you're more apt to read and listen to advertisements for the car you just bought, because these messages tell you that you made the right decision. At the same time, you will tend to avoid ads for the cars that you considered but eventually rejected, because these messages tell you that you made the wrong decision.

You're also more likely to perceive stimuli that are greater in intensity than surrounding stimuli and those that have novelty value (Kagan, 2002). For example, television commercials normally play at a greater intensity than regular programming to ensure that you take special notice. You're also more likely to notice the coworker who dresses in a novel way than you are to notice the one who dresses like everyone else. You will quickly perceive someone who shows up in class wearing a tuxedo or at a formal party in shorts. A recent study has shown that communication on the internet is perceived more positively when messages are more personalized (Sriram & Shyam, 2006).

Stage Two: Organization

At the second stage, you organize the information your senses pick up. Three interesting ways in which people organize their perceptions are by rules, schemata, and scripts. Let's look at each briefly.

Organization by Rules   One frequently used rule is that of *proximity* or physical closeness. The rule, simply stated, is that things that are physically close together constitute a unit. Thus, using this rule, you would perceive people who are often together, or messages spoken one immediately after the other, as units—as belonging together. You also assume that verbal and nonverbal signals sent at about the same time are related and constitute a unified whole; you assume they follow a *temporal rule*, which says that things occurring together in time belong together.

Another rule is *similarity*—things that are physically similar or that look alike belong together and form a unit. This principle of similarity would lead you to see people who dress alike as belonging together. Or you might assume that people who work at the same jobs, who are of the same religion, who live in the same building, or who talk with the same accent belong together.

You use the principle of *contrast* when you note that some items (people or messages, for example) don't belong together—that they are too different from each other to be part of the same perceptual organization. So, for example, in a conversation or a public speech, listeners will focus their attention on changes in intensity or rate because these contrast with the rest of the message.

Organization by Schemata   Another way you organize material is by creating **schemata**, mental templates or structures that help you organize the millions of items of information you come into contact with every day as well as those you already have in memory. Schemata may thus be viewed as general ideas about people (Torontonians, children, Americans); yourself (your qualities, abilities, and even liabilities); or social roles (what a police officer, professor, or multibillionaire CEO is like). (The word *schemata* is the plural of *schema* and is preferred to the alternative plural *schemas*.)

> ❝ It's not whether you really cry. It's whether the audience thinks you are crying. ❞
>
> —Ingrid Bergman

Organization by Scripts   A script is really a type of schema, but because it's a special type of schema, it's given a different name. A **script** is an organized body of information about some action, event, or procedure. It's a general idea of how some event should play out or unfold; it's the rules governing events and their sequence. For example, you probably have a script for eating in a restaurant, with the actions organized into a pattern something like this: Enter, take a seat, review the menu, order from the menu, eat your food, ask for the bill, leave a tip, pay the bill, exit the restaurant. Similarly, you probably have scripts for how you do laundry, conduct an interview, introduce someone to someone else, or ask for a date.

What shortcuts do you use in helping yourself to understand, remember, and recall information about people and events? Can you give specific examples of rules, schemata, and scripts that you maintain and that influence your perceptions?

Stage Three: Interpretation–Evaluation

The interpretation–evaluation stage of perception (the two processes cannot be separated) is inevitably subjective (Mohr & Kenny, 2006) and is greatly influenced by your experiences, needs, wants, values, beliefs about the way things are or should be, expectations, physical and emotional state, and so on. Your interpretation–evaluation will be influenced by your rules, schemata, and scripts as well as by your gender. For example, women have been found to view others more positively than men do (Winquist, Mohr, & Kenny, 1998). A recent study shows that gender differences in perceptions also affect learning (Ong & Lai, 2006).

In addition to mastering specific communication skills, you—as a critical thinker—need to be willing to examine your own **attitudes** about critical thinking and about yourself as a critical thinker.

- Analyze yourself as a critically thinking communicator. Self-analysis is essential if you're to use this material in any meaningful sense. Be open-minded to new ideas, even those that contradict your existing beliefs.

- Observe the behaviours of those around you as well as your own. See in real life what you read about here; it will then have clearer application to your own day-to-day interactions.

- Delay conclusions until you have collected sufficient information. But do realize that eventually you need to make a decision; at some point, thinking needs to give way to action.

- Analyze and evaluate ideas instead of accepting them just because they appear in a textbook or are mentioned by an instructor.

EXAMPLES?

Can you find examples of ideas, suggestions, or conclusions discussed in this textbook that you disagree with or that you'd like more evidence for before you accept them? How would you go about investigating the evidence for these ideas, suggestions, or conclusions?

You develop schemata from your own experience—from actual experiences as well as from television, reading, and hearsay. Thus, for example, you might have a schema for college athletes; it might include perceptions that athletes are physically strong, ambitious, academically weak, and egocentric. And, of course, you've probably developed schemata for different religious, racial, and national groups; for men and women; and for people of different affectional orientations. Each group with which you have some familiarity will be represented in your mind in some kind of schema. Schemata help you organize your perceptions by allowing you to classify millions of people into a manageable number of categories or classes. As we'll see, however, schemata can also create problems—they can lead you to see what is not there or to miss seeing what is there.

How accurate is your interpersonal perception? What cues do you look for when judging other people after first meeting them?

For example, upon meeting a new person who is introduced to you as a university hockey player, you will tend to apply your schema to this person and view him as physically strong, ambitious, academically weak, and egocentric. You will, in other words, see this person through the filter of your schema and evaluate him according to your schema for university athletes. Similarly, when viewing someone performing some series of actions (say, eating in a restaurant), you apply your script to this event and view the event through the script. You interpret the actions of the diner as appropriate or inappropriate, depending on your script for this behaviour and the ways in which the diner performs the sequence of actions.

Stage Four: Memory

Your perceptions and their interpretations–evaluations are put into memory; they're stored so that you may ultimately retrieve them at some later time. For example, you have in memory your schema for university athletes and the fact that Ben Williams is a hockey player. Ben Williams is then stored in memory with "cognitive tags" that tell you that he's strong, ambitious, academically weak, and egocentric. Now, despite the fact that you've not witnessed Ben's strength or ambitions and have no idea of his academic record or his psychological profile, you still may store your memory of Ben along with the qualities that make up your schema for "university athletes."

Now let's say that at different times you hear that Ben failed Spanish I (normally an A or B course at your school), that he got an A in chemistry (normally a tough course), and that he is transferring to Queen's University as a theoretical physics major. Schemata act as filters or gatekeepers; they allow certain information to get stored in relatively objective form, much as you heard or read it. But schemata may distort or prevent other information from getting stored. As a result, these three items of information about Ben may get stored very differently in your memory along with your schema for university athletes.

For example, you may readily store the information that Ben failed Spanish, because it's consistent with your schema; it fits neatly into the template you have for university athletes. Information that's consistent with your schema—as in this example—will strengthen your schema and make it more resistant to change (Aronson et al., 1994). Depending on the strength of your schema, you may also store in memory, even though you didn't hear it, a perception that Ben did poorly in other courses as well. The information that Ben got an A in chemistry, because it contradicts your schema (it just doesn't seem right), may easily be distorted or lost. The information that Ben is transferring to Queen's, however, is a bit different. This information is also inconsistent with your schema, but it is so drastically inconsistent that you may begin to look at this mindfully and may even begin to question your schema, or perhaps view Ben as an exception to the general rule. In either case, you're going to etch Ben's transferring to Queen's very clearly in your mind.

Stage Five: Recall

At some later date, you may want to recall or access the information you have stored in memory. Let's say you want to retrieve your information about Ben because he's a topic of conversation among you and a few friends. As we'll see in our discussion of listening in Chapter 4, memory isn't reproductive; you don't simply reproduce what you've heard or seen. Rather, you reconstruct what you've heard or seen into a whole that is meaningful to you—depending in great part on your schemata and scripts—and it's this reconstruction that you store in memory. Now, when you want to retrieve this information from memory, you may recall it with a variety of inaccuracies. You're likely to

> 66 Tact is the ability to describe others as they see themselves. 99
>
> —Eleanor Chaffee

- recall information that is consistent with your schema; in fact, you may not even be recalling the specific information (say, about Ben), but may actually be recalling your schema (which contains the information about university athletes and, because of this, also about Ben).
- fail to recall information that is inconsistent with your schema; you have no place to put that information and so you easily lose it or forget it.
- recall information that drastically contradicts your schema, because it forces you to think (and perhaps rethink) about your schema and its accuracy; it may even force you to revise your schema for university athletes in general.

Reflections on the Model of Perception

Before moving on to the more specific processes involved in interpersonal perception, let's spell out some of the implications of this five-stage model for your own interpersonal perceptions:

1. Everyone relies heavily on shortcuts. Rules, schemata, and scripts, for example, are all useful shortcuts that simplify your understanding, remembering, and recalling information about people and events. If you didn't have these shortcuts, then you'd have to treat every person, role, or action differently from each other person, role, or action. This would make every experience a new one, totally unrelated to anything you already know. If you didn't use these shortcuts, you'd be unable to generalize, draw connections, or otherwise profit from previously acquired knowledge.

2. Shortcuts, however, may mislead you; they may contribute to your remembering things that are consistent with your schemata, even if they didn't occur, and to your distorting or forgetting information that is inconsistent.

3. What you remember about a person or an event isn't an objective recollection but is more likely heavily influenced by your preconceptions or your schemata about what belongs and what doesn't belong, what fits neatly into the templates in your brain and what doesn't fit. Your reconstruction of an event or person contains a lot of information that was not in the original sensory experience—and may omit a lot that was in the experience.

4. Memory is especially unreliable when the information is ambiguous—when it can be interpreted in different ways. For example, consider the statement, "Ben didn't do as well in his other courses as he would have liked." If your schema of Ben was "brilliant," then you might "remember" that Ben got Bs. But if, as in our example, your schema was of the academically weak athlete, you might "remember" that Ben got Ds. Conveniently, but unreliably, schemata reduce ambiguity.

5. Judgments about others are invariably ethnocentric: Because your schemata and scripts are created on the basis of your own cultural experiences, you invariably apply these to members of other cultures. From there it's easy to infer that when members of other cultures do things that conform to your scripts, they're right, and when they do things that contradict your scripts, they're wrong—a classic example of ethnocentric thinking. As you can appreciate, this tendency can easily contribute to intercultural misunderstandings.

6. A similar problem arises when you base your scripts for different cultural groups on stereotypes you may have derived from television or movies. For example, you may have scripts for religious Muslims that you derived from stereotypes presented in the media, and which you then apply to all Muslims, seeing what conforms to your script and failing to see or distorting what does not conform to your script.

STIVERS

©1991 Stivers

WHAT DO YOU LIKE IN A MAN?

© 1991 Mark Stivers. Reprinted by permission.

THE PROCESSES OF PERCEPTION

Before reading about the specific processes that you use in perceiving other people, examine your own perception strategies by taking the self-test below.

Test Yourself

How Accurate Are You at People Perception?

Instructions: Respond to each of the following statements with T (true) if the statement is usually or generally accurate in describing your behaviour, and with F (false) if the statement is usually or generally inaccurate in describing your behaviour. Try to avoid the tendency to give what you feel is the desirable answer; just be truthful.

_____ ❶ I base most of my impressions of people on the first few minutes of our meeting.

_____ ❷ When I know some things about another person, I can fill in what I don't know.

_____ ❸ I make predictions about people's behaviours that generally prove true.

_____ ❹ I have clear ideas of what people of different national, racial, and religious groups are really like.

_____ ❺ I generally look for lots of cues about a person's attitudes and behaviours, not just their most obvious physical or psychological characteristics.

_____ ❻ I avoid making assumptions about what is going on in someone else's head on the basis of their behaviours.

_____ **7** I pay special attention to behaviours of people that might contradict my initial impressions.

_____ **8** On the basis of my observations of people, I formulate guesses about them (which I am willing to revise) rather than firmly held conclusions.

_____ **9** I avoid making judgments about people until I learn a great deal about them and see them in a variety of situations.

_____ **10** After I formulate an initial impression, I check my perceptions by, for example, asking questions or by gathering more evidence.

HOW DID YOU DO?

This brief perception test was designed to raise questions to be considered in this chapter, not to provide you with a specific perception score. The first four questions refer to tendencies to judge others on the basis of first impressions (question 1); implicit personality theories (question 2; see discussion below); prophecies (3); and stereotypes (4). Ideally you would have answered "false" to these four questions because they represent sources of distortion. Questions 5 through 10 suggest specific guidelines for increasing accuracy in people perception: looking for a variety of cues (5); avoiding the tendency to mind read (6); being especially alert to contradictory cues (7); formulating hypotheses rather than conclusions (8); recognizing the diversity in people (9); and delaying conclusions until more evidence is in (10). Ideally you would have answered "true" to these six questions, because they represent suggestions for increased accuracy in perception.

WHAT WILL YOU DO?

As you read this chapter, think about these guidelines and consider how you might use them for more accurate and reasonable people perception. At the same time, recognize that situations vary widely; these suggestions will prove useful most of the time but not all of the time. In fact, you may want to identify situations in which you shouldn't follow these suggestions.

In-Class Notes

The Processes of Perception

- Implicit Personality Theories
- Self-Fulfilling Prophecies
- Primacy–Recency
- Consistency
- Stereotypes
- Attributions

_____

_____

_____

_____

_____

_____

_____

_____

_____

Implicit Personality Theories

Each person has a subconscious or implicit system of rules—an **implicit personality theory**—that says which characteristics of an individual go with other characteristics. Consider, for example, the following brief statements. Note the word in parentheses that you think best completes each sentence:

- Carlo is energetic, eager, and (intelligent, stupid).
- Kim is bold, defiant, and (extroverted, introverted).
- Joe is bright, lively, and (thin, heavy).
- Ava is attractive, intelligent, and (likeable, unlikeable).
- Susan is cheerful, positive, and (outgoing, shy).
- Angel is handsome, tall, and (friendly, unfriendly).

We make self-fulfilling prophecies about ourselves as well as about others. For example, you predict that you'll do poorly in an examination, so you don't read the questions carefully and don't make any great effort to organize your thoughts or support your statements. Or you predict that people won't like you, so you don't extend yourself to others. You can also make positive predictions about yourself, and these too will influence your behaviour. For example, you can assume that others will like you and so approach them with a positive attitude and demeanour. Generally, how do your predictions influence your achieving your personal and professional goals?

What makes some of these choices seem right and others wrong is your implicit personality theory. Your theory may, for example, have told you that a person who is energetic and eager is also intelligent, not stupid—even though there is no logical reason why a stupid person could not be energetic and eager.

The widely documented **halo effect** is a function of the implicit personality theory (Beebe et al., 2000). If you believe a person has some positive qualities, you're likely to infer that she also possesses other positive qualities. For example, it has recently been shown that women who rated their partners as physically attractive also attributed more positive qualities to them, although men did so less (Levesque et al., 2006). There is also a *reverse halo effect*: If you know a person possesses several negative qualities, you're more likely to infer that the person also has other negative qualities.

As might be expected, the implicit personality theories that people hold differ from culture to culture, from group to group, and even from person to person. For example, consider the different personality theories that graduate students and high school dropouts might have for university students. Likewise, an individual may have had great experiences with doctors and so may have a very positive personality theory of doctors, whereas another person may have had negative experiences with doctors and may thus have developed a very negative personality theory.

The Self-Fulfilling Prophecy

A **self-fulfilling prophecy** occurs when you make a prediction that comes true because you act on it as if it were true (Beebe et al., 2000). Put differently, a self-fulfilling prophecy occurs when you act on your schema as if it were true and, in doing so, you make it true. There are four basic steps in the self-fulfilling prophecy:

1. You make a prediction or formulate a belief about a person or a situation. For example, you predict that Shafiq is friendly in interpersonal encounters.

2. You act toward that person or situation as if that prediction or belief were true. For example, you act as if Shafiq were a friendly person.

3. Because you act as if the belief were true, it becomes true. For example, because of the way you act toward Shafiq, he becomes comfortable and friendly.

4. You observe *your* effect on the person or the resulting situation, and what you see strengthens your beliefs. For example, you observe Shafiq's friendliness, and this reinforces your belief that he is in fact friendly.

The self-fulfilling prophecy can also be seen when you make predictions about yourself and fulfill them. For example, perhaps you enter a group situation convinced that the other members will dislike you. Almost invariably you'll be proved right; the other members will appear to you to dislike you. What you may be doing is acting in a way that encourages the group to respond to you negatively. In this way you fulfill your prophecies about yourself.

A widely known example of the self-fulfilling prophecy is the **Pygmalion effect**. In a well-known study, teachers were told that certain pupils were expected to do exceptionally well, although they were late bloomers. The names of these students were actually selected at random by the experimenters. The results, however, were not random. The students whose names were given to the teachers actually performed at a higher level than others. In fact, these students' IQ scores even improved more than did the other students'. The teachers' expectations probably prompted them to give extra attention to the selected students, thereby positively affecting their performance (Rosenthal & Jacobson, 1968; Insel & Jacobson, 1975). Studies have found the same general effect in military training and business settings:

Trainees and workers performed better when their supervisors were given positive information about them (McNatt, 2001). In fact, researchers have identified the Pygmalion effect in contexts as varied as leadership, athletic coaching, and effective stepfamilies (Eden, 1992; Solomon et al., 1996; Einstein, 1995; McNatt, 2001).

Self-fulfilling prophecies can short-circuit critical thinking and influence another person's behaviour (or your own) so that it conforms to your prophecy. As a result, these prophecies can lead you to see what you predicted rather than what is really there—for example, to perceive yourself as a failure because you have predicted it rather than because of any actual failures.

In-Class Notes

Self-Fulfilling Prophecy

- You make a prediction about a person.
- You act as if the prediction is true.
- Your behaviour causes the prediction to come true.
- What you see then strengthens your belief.

Primacy–Recency

Assume for a moment that you're enrolled in a course in which half the classes are extremely dull and half extremely exciting. At the end of the semester, you evaluate the course and the instructor. Will your evaluation be more favourable if the dull classes occurred in the first half of the semester and the exciting classes in the second? Or will it be more favourable if the order were reversed? If what comes first exerts the most influence, you have a *primacy effect*. If what comes last, or most recently, exerts the most influence, you have a *recency effect*.

In the classic study on the effects of **primacy** and **recency** in interpersonal perception, college students perceived a person who was described as "intelligent, industrious, impulsive, critical, stubborn, and envious" more positively than a person described as "envious, stubborn, critical, impulsive, industrious, and intelligent" (Asch, 1946). Clearly, there's a tendency to use early information to get a general idea about a person and to use later information to make this impression more specific. The initial information helps you form a schema for the person. Once that schema is formed, you're likely to resist information that contradicts it.

One interesting practical implication of primacy–recency is that the first impression you make on others is likely to be the most important. The reason for this is that the schema that others form of you functions as a filter to admit or block additional information about you. If the initial impression or schema is positive, others are likely to remember additional positive information because it confirms this original positive image or schema, and to forget or distort negative information because it contradicts this original positive schema. Others are also more likely to interpret information that is really ambiguous as positive. If the initial impression is positive, then you win all three ways.

 **STUDY TIP**

Discuss how the primacy–recency effect might influence your selection of a time slot for on-campus job interviews.

❝ Manage every second of a first meeting. Do not delude yourself that a bad impression can be easily corrected. Putting things right is a lot harder than getting them right first time. ❞

—David Lewis

❝ I make up my mind about people in the first 10 seconds, and I very rarely change it. **❞**

—Margaret Thatcher, former British prime minister

STUDY TIP

With a friend or classmate, debate the merits of Margaret Thatcher's approach to sizing people up.

The tendency to give greater weight to early information and to interpret later information in light of early impressions can lead you to formulate a total picture of an individual based on initial impressions that may not be typical or accurate. For example, if you judge a job applicant as generally nervous when he or she may simply be showing normal nervousness at being interviewed for a much-needed job, you will have misperceived this individual.

Similarly, this tendency can lead you to discount or distort subsequent perceptions so as not to disrupt your initial impression or upset your original schema. For example, you may fail to see signs of deceitfulness in someone you like because of your early impression that this person is a good and honest individual.

Consistency

The tendency to maintain balance among perceptions or attitudes is called **consistency** (McBroom & Reed, 1992). You expect certain things to go together and other things not to go together. On a purely intuitive basis, for example, respond to the following sentences by noting your *expected* response:

1. I expect a person I like to (like, dislike) me.
2. I expect a person I dislike to (like, dislike) me.
3. I expect my friend to (like, dislike) my friend.
4. I expect my friend to (like, dislike) my enemy.
5. I expect my enemy to (like, dislike) my friend.
6. I expect my enemy to (like, dislike) my enemy.

According to most consistency theories, your expectations would be as follows: You would expect a person you like to like you (1) and one you dislike to dislike you (2). You would expect your friend to like your other friend (3) and to dislike your enemy (4). You would expect your enemy to dislike your friend (5) and to like your other enemy (6). All these expectations are intuitively satisfying.

Further, you would expect someone you like to possess characteristics you like or admire, and you would not expect your enemies to possess characteristics you like or admire. Conversely, you would expect people you like to lack unpleasant characteristics and people you dislike to possess unpleasant characteristics.

Uncritically assuming that an individual is consistent can lead you to ignore or distort your perceptions of behaviours that are inconsistent with your picture of the whole person. For example, you may misinterpret Kim's basic shyness because your image of Kim is "bold, defiant, and extroverted." Consistency can also lead you to see certain behaviours as positive if you interpret other behaviours positively (the halo effect), or as negative if you interpret other behaviours negatively (the reverse halo effect).

Stereotyping

One of the most common shortcuts in interpersonal perception is stereotyping. A sociological or psychological **stereotype** is a fixed impression of a group of people; it's a schema. We all have attitudinal stereotypes—of national, religious, sexual, or racial groups, or perhaps of criminals, prostitutes, teachers, or plumbers. Regarding recent concerns about weight and obesity, it has been shown that weight plays a considerable role in perceptions of women (Wade & DiMaria, 2003). Overweight women are stereotyped as lazy, greedy, and selfish, leading to discrimination against them in employment contexts. Interestingly, this stereotyping is less prominent for black women (Wade & DiMaria, 2003). If you have some of these predetermined fixed impressions, upon meeting a member of a particular group, you will often see that person primarily as a member of that group and apply to him all the characteristics you assign to that group. If you meet

How would you describe the first impression that people form of you? What specific cues do you communicate to give them this impression?

someone who is a prostitute, for example, you may apply a host of characteristics for prostitutes to this one person. To complicate matters further, you will often "see" in this person's behaviour the manifestation of characteristics that you would not "see" if you didn't know that this person was a prostitute. Because there are few visual and auditory cues in online communication, it's not surprising to find that people rely heavily on stereotypes in forming impressions of online communication partners (Jacobson, 1999).

Stereotypes can easily distort accurate perception and prevent you from seeing an individual as an individual rather than as a member of a group.

The tendency to group people and to respond to individuals primarily as members of a group can lead you to perceive that an individual possesses those qualities (usually negative) that you believe characterize her group—for example, "All Mexicans are..." or "All Baptists are..."—and therefore to fail to appreciate the multifaceted nature of all individuals and groups. Stereotyping can also lead you to ignore each person's unique characteristics and to therefore fail to benefit from the special contributions each individual can bring to an encounter.

What stereotypes, if any, would your family or friends have of the people depicted in this photograph? What stereotypes, if any, do you have?

STUDY TIP

In a small group, identify stereotypes associated with people who have physical disabilities, and discuss the impact these stereotypes have on how able-bodied people interact with people who have physical disabilities.

Attribution

Attribution is the process by which we try to explain the motivation for a person's behaviour. Perhaps the major way we do this is to ask ourselves if the person was in control of the behaviour. If people are in control of their own behaviour, then we feel justified in praising them for positive behaviours and blaming them for negative behaviours. You probably make similar judgments based on controllability in many situations. Consider, for example, how you would respond to a situation in which an acquaintance failed her history exam or had her car repossessed.

Very likely you would be sympathetic if you felt she was *not* in control of what happened; for example, if the examination was unfair or if she couldn't make her car payments because she lost her job as a result of discrimination. On the other hand, you probably would not be sympathetic or might blame her for her problems if you

In-Class Notes

Stereotypes

- are a fixed impression of a group of people
- may be influenced by nationality, religion, sexual orientation, or any other characteristic that defines a group
- distort accurate perceptions
- prevent seeing someone as an individual

_____

_____

_____

_____

_____

_____

_____

_____

_____

> ❝ To see ourselves as others see us is a most salutary gift. Hardly less important is the capacity to see others as they see themselves. ❞
>
> —Aldous Huxley

felt that she was in control of what happened; for example, if she went to a party instead of studying, or if she gambled her car payments away.

Generally, research shows that if we feel people are in control of negative behaviours, we will come to dislike them. If we feel people are not in control of negative behaviours, we will come to feel sorry for them and not blame them for their negative circumstances. Attribution of causality can lead to several major barriers. Three such barriers (the self-serving bias, overattribution, and the fundamental attribution error) are examined in the Skills Toolbox below.

INCREASING ACCURACY IN INTERPERSONAL PERCEPTION

Successful interpersonal communication depends largely on the accuracy of your interpersonal perception. As you will see, potential barriers can arise with each of the perceptual processes. These barriers include the self-serving bias, overattribution, and the fundamental attribution error.

Skills Toolbox   3 Ways to Avoid Attribution Errors

Three major attribution problems can interfere with the accuracy of your interpersonal perceptions whether on or off the job.

1. After getting a poor performance evaluation, you're more likely to attribute it to the difficulty of the job or the unfairness of the supervisor—that is, to uncontrollable factors. After getting an extremely positive evaluation, however, you're more likely to attribute it to your ability or hard work—that is, to controllable factors. This tendency is called the **self-serving bias**, or the inclination to take credit for the positive and deny responsibility for the negative (Hogg, 2002). To prevent this bias from distorting your attributions, consider the potential influences of both internal and external factors on your positive *and* negative behaviours. Ask yourself to what extent your negative behaviours may be due to internal (controllable) factors and your positive behaviours to external (uncontrollable) factors. Just asking the question will prevent you from mindlessly falling into the self-serving bias trap.

2. If someone you work with had alcoholic parents or is blind or was born into great wealth, you might attribute everything that person does to such factors. For example, "Sally has difficulty working on a team because she grew up in a home of alcoholics," "Alex overeats because he's blind," "Lillian lacks ambition because she always got whatever she wanted without working for it." This is called **overattribution,** which is the tendency to single out one or two obvious characteristics and attribute everything a person does to these one or two characteristics. To prevent overattribution, recognize that most behaviours result from a lot of factors and that you almost always make a mistake when you select one factor and attribute everything to it. So when you make a judgment, ask yourself if other factors might be influencing behaviours that seem at first glance to stem solely from one factor.

3. When Nila is late for a meeting, you're more likely to conclude that she is inconsiderate or irresponsible than to attribute her lateness to a bus breakdown or to a traffic accident. This tendency to conclude that people do what they do because that's the kind of people they are rather than because of the situation they're in is called the **fundamental attribution error**. When you commit this error, you overvalue the contribution of internal factors and undervalue the influence of external factors. To avoid making this error, ask yourself if you're giving too much emphasis to internal factors and too little emphasis to external factors. Interestingly, this tendency may be culture specific and not universal as previously thought (Goode, 2000). For example, in one study, U.S. and Korean students were presented with a speech endorsing a particular position and told that the writer had been instructed to write this and really had no choice. The American students were more likely to conclude that the speaker believed in the position endorsed; they believed that what the speaker said reflected what the speaker believed, not the external circumstances of being forced to write the speech. Korean students, on the other hand, were less likely to believe in the sincerity of the speaker and gave greater weight to the external factor that the speaker was forced to write the speech.

THEN AND NOW

Have you ever fallen into one of these three errors in perceiving another person? What happened? What would you do differently now?

There are, however, additional ways to think more critically about your perceptions and thereby to increase your perceptual accuracy. Some of these are considered in the following discussion.

Analyze Your Perceptions

When you become aware of your perceptions, you'll be able to subject them to logical analysis—to critical thinking. Here are a few suggestions.

- Recognize your own role in perception. Your emotional and physiological state will influence the meaning you give to your perceptions. A movie may seem hysterically funny when you're in a good mood but just plain stupid when you're in a bad mood or when you're preoccupied with family problems. Be aware of your own biases. Know when your perceptual evaluations are unduly influenced by your own biases—for example, by a tendency to perceive only the positive in people you like and only the negative in people you don't like. Even your gender will influence your perceptions. Women consistently evaluate other people more positively than do men on such factors as agreeableness, conscientiousness, and emotional stability (Winquist et al., 1998).

- Avoid early conclusions. On the basis of your observations of behaviours, formulate hypotheses to test against additional information and evidence rather than drawing conclusions you then look to confirm. Delay formulating conclusions until you have had a chance to process a wide variety of cues. Similarly, avoid the one-cue conclusion. Look for a variety of cues pointing in the same direction. The more cues pointing to the same conclusion, the more likely your conclusion will be correct. Be especially alert to contradictory cues, ones that refute your initial hypotheses. It's relatively easy to perceive cues that confirm your hypotheses but more difficult to acknowledge contradictory evidence. At the same time, seek validation from others. Do others see things the same way you do? If not, ask yourself if your perceptions may be in some way distorted.

- Avoid mind reading—that is, don't try to read the thoughts and feelings of other people merely from observing their behaviours.

Regardless of how many behaviours you observe and how carefully you examine them, you can only *guess* what is going on in someone's mind. A person's motives are not open to outside inspection; you can only make assumptions based on overt behaviours.

Check Your Perceptions

Perception checking is another way to reduce uncertainty and to make your perceptions more accurate. The goal of perception checking is not to prove that your initial perception is correct but to further explore the thoughts and feelings of the other person. With this simple technique, you lessen your chances of misinterpreting another's feelings. At the same time, you give the other person an opportunity to elaborate on his or her thoughts and feelings.

In its most basic form, perception checking consists of two steps. First, describe what you see or hear, recognizing that even descriptions are not really objective but are heavily influenced by who you are, your emotional state, and so on. At the same time, you may wish to describe what you think is happening. Again, try to do this as descriptively (not evaluatively) as you can. Sometimes you may wish to offer several possibilities:

- You've called me from work a lot this week. You seem concerned that everything is all right at home.
- You've not wanted to talk with me all week. You say that my work is fine, but you don't seem to want to give me the same responsibilities that other editorial assistants have.

Altercasting is a technique that encourages you to put yourself into the frame of mind of someone else. It helps provide you with a different perspective—an alternative vision. For example, if you were a real estate sales representative, altercasting would help if you placed yourself in the role of the home buyer and perhaps even went through the process of looking for a home as a would-be buyer. Altercasting is also useful when two people want to understand each other's perspective; each might altercast and play the role of the other. In this *role reversal* you and your romantic partner, for example, might each play the part of the other in a mock argument. The reverse role playing allows *you* to see how your partner sees you and allows *your partner* to see how you see him or her.

EXAMPLES?

Give an example of how you might use altercasting in one of the following situations:

- An advertiser is developing a package for a new cereal, toothpaste, or detergent.
- A designer for a food store wants to increase sales, despite the arrival of two new supermarkets in the area.
- A new teacher wants to be a great teacher.
- A company manager supervises 20 culturally diverse men and women.
- A parent has a child who is often truant.

Second, ask the other person for confirmation. Do be careful that your request for confirmation doesn't sound as if you already knew the answer, and avoid phrasing your questions defensively. Avoid saying, for example, "You really don't want to go out, do you; I knew you didn't when you turned on that lousy television." Instead, ask for confirmation in as supportive a way as possible: "Would you rather watch TV?" Other examples:

- Are you worried about me or the kids?
- Are you pleased with my work? Is there anything I can do to improve my job performance?

Reduce Your Uncertainty

Consider how you would use perception checking in such situations as these: (a) Your friend says he wants to drop out of college; (b) your cousin hasn't called you in several months, though you have called her at least six times; (c) another student seems totally detached from everything that happens in class.

We all tend to try to reduce uncertainty, a process that enables us to achieve greater accuracy in perception. In large part we learn about uncertainty and how to deal with it from our culture.

Culture and Uncertainty People from different cultures differ greatly in their attitudes toward uncertainty and how to deal with it, and these attitudes have an impact on perceptual accuracy. In some cultures people do little to avoid uncertainty and have little anxiety about not knowing what will happen next. Uncertainty in these cultures is a normal part of life and is accepted as it comes; members don't feel threatened by unknown situations. Examples of such low-anxiety cultures include Singapore, Jamaica, Denmark, Sweden, Hong Kong, Ireland, Great Britain, Malaysia, India, the Philippines, and the United States. Other cultures do much to avoid uncertainty and have a great deal of anxiety about not knowing what will happen next; uncertainty is seen as threatening and something that must be counteracted. Examples of such high-anxiety cultures include Greece, Portugal, Guatemala, Uruguay, Belgium, El Salvador, Japan, Yugoslavia, Peru, France, Chile, Spain, and Costa Rica (Hofstede, 1997). Interestingly, cultures that differ in their acceptance of uncertainty also differ in the way they relate to situations of limited information and ambiguity (Vishwanath, 2003).

The potential for communication problems can be great when people come from cultures with different attitudes toward uncertainty. For example, managers from cultures with weak uncertainty avoidance will not get too upset when workers are late and will accept workers who work only when they have to. Managers from cultures with strong uncertainty avoidance will expect workers to be busy at all times and will have little tolerance for lateness.

Because weak uncertainty avoidance cultures have great tolerance for ambiguity and uncertainty, they minimize the rules governing communication and relationships (Hofstede, 1997; Lustig & Koester, 1999). People who don't follow the same rules as the cultural majority are readily tolerated. Different approaches and perspectives may even be encouraged in cultures with weak uncertainty avoidance. In contrast, strong uncertainty avoidance cultures create very clear-cut rules for communication. It's considered unacceptable for people to break these rules.

Students from cultures with weak uncertainty avoidance appreciate freedom in education and prefer vague assignments without specific timetables. These students will want to be rewarded for creativity and will easily accept the instructor's occasional lack of knowledge. Students from strong uncertainty avoidance cultures prefer highly structured experiences where there is little ambiguity; they prefer specific objectives, detailed instructions, and definite timetables. These students expect to be judged on the basis of the right answers and expect the instructor to have all the answers all the time (Hofstede, 1997).

Ways to Reduce Uncertainty   A variety of strategies can help reduce uncertainty (Gudykunst, 1994). Observing another person who is engaged in an active task, preferably interacting with others in more informal social situations, will often reveal a great deal about the person. This is because in informal situations, people are less apt to monitor their behaviours and more likely to reveal their true selves.

You can also manipulate the situation in order to observe the person in more specific and more revealing contexts. Employment interviews, theatrical auditions, and student teaching are some situations people create to observe how a person acts and reacts and, hence, to reduce uncertainty about the person.

When you log on to an internet chat group for the first time and you lurk, reading exchanges between other group members before saying anything yourself, you're learning about the people in the group and about the group itself and thus reducing uncertainty. When uncertainty is reduced, you're more likely to make contributions that will be appropriate to the group and less likely to violate any of the group's norms; in short, you're more likely to communicate effectively.

Another way to reduce uncertainty is to collect information about a person through asking others. You might ask a colleague whether a third person finds you interesting and might like to have dinner with you.

And, of course, you can interact with the individual. For example, you can ask questions such as "Do you enjoy sports?" "What did you think of that computer science course?" "What would you do if you got fired?" You also learn about others by disclosing information about yourself. Your disclosures help create an environment that encourages disclosures from the person about whom you wish to learn more.

Increase Your Cultural Sensitivity

Recognizing and being sensitive to cultural differences will help increase your accuracy in perception. For example, Russian or Chinese artists, such as ballet dancers, will often applaud their audience, but Canadian audiences may interpret this applause as egotistical. Similarly, a German man will enter a restaurant before a woman in order to see if the place is respectable enough for her to enter. This custom is easily misinterpreted in cultures where courtesy dictates that a woman should enter first (Axtell, 1993).

Cultural sensitivity helps counteract the considerable difficulty most people have in understanding the nonverbal messages of people from other cultures. For example, it is easier to read the facial expressions and decode the emotions expressed by members of your own culture than to read facial expressions in members of other cultures

Here are three theorems, paraphrased from the *theory of uncertainty reduction*, which is concerned with how communication reduces the uncertainty you have about another person (Berger & Calabrese, 1975): (1) The more people communicate, the more they like each other; (2) the more people communicate, the more intimate their communications will be; and (3) the more nonverbally expressive people are, the more they like each other. Do your own experiences support these statements? Can you give a specific example for one of the propositions?

Increasing Accuracy in Perception

- Analyze your perceptions.
- Check your perceptions.
- Reduce uncertainty.
- Be culturally sensitive.

_____
_____
_____
_____
_____
_____
_____
_____
_____

(Weathers et al., 2002). This "in-group advantage" can assist your perceptional accuracy with members of your own culture but will often hinder your accuracy with members of other cultures (Elfenbein & Ambady, 2002).

Summary of Concepts and Skills

This chapter discussed the way we receive messages through perception and explained how perception works, the processes that influence it, and how to make our perceptions more accurate.

1. Perception is the process by which you become aware of the many stimuli impinging on your senses. Perception occurs in five stages: (1) sensory stimulation occurs; (2) sensory stimulation is organized; (3) sensory stimulation is interpreted–evaluated; (4) sensory stimulation is held in memory; (5) and sensory stimulation is recalled.

2. The following processes influence perception: (1) implicit personality theory; (2) self-fulfilling prophecy; (3) primacy–recency; (4) consistency; (5) stereotyping; and (6) attribution.

3. The term _implicit personality theory_ refers to the private personality theory that you hold and that influences how you perceive other people.

4. A self-fulfilling prophecy occurs when you make a prediction or formulate a belief that comes true because you have made the prediction and acted as if it were true.

5. Primacy–recency effects have to do with the relative influence of stimuli as a result of their order. If what occurs first exerts greater influence, you have a primacy effect. If what occurs last exerts greater influence, you have a recency effect.

6. Consistency influences you to see what is consistent and to not see what is inconsistent with your expectations.

7. Stereotyping is our tendency to develop and maintain fixed, unchanging perceptions of groups of people and to use these perceptions to evaluate individual members, ignoring their individual, unique characteristics.

8. Attribution is the process through which you try to understand the behaviours of others (and your own, in self-attribution)—particularly the reasons or motivations for these behaviours. Many attributions are made on the basis of controllability. Errors of attribution include the self-serving bias, overattribution, and the fundamental attribution error.

9. You can increase the accuracy of your interpersonal perceptions in several ways. (1) Analyze your perceptions; for example, recognize your role in perception,

formulate hypotheses rather than conclusions, look for a variety of cues (especially contradictory ones), avoid mind reading, and beware of your own biases. (2) Check your perceptions, describing what you see or hear and asking for confirmation. (3) Reduce uncertainty by, for example, lurking before joining a group, gathering information about the person or situation, or interacting and observing the interaction. (4) Be culturally sensitive, recognizing the differences between you and others and also the differences among members of any cultural group.

Check Your Ability

Throughout this discussion of perception, a variety of skills were identified and are presented here in summary. Check your ability to apply these skills: 1 = almost always, 2 = often, 3 = sometimes, 4 = rarely, 5 = hardly ever.

_____ **❶** I think mindfully when I use perceptual shortcuts so that they don't mislead and result in inaccurate perceptions.

_____ **❷** I guard against ethnocentric thinking by viewing the behaviour and customs of others from a multicultural view rather than from just my cultural view.

_____ **❸** I bring to consciousness my implicit personality theories.

_____ **❹** To guard against the self-fulfilling prophecy, I take a second look at my perceptions when they conform too closely to my expectations.

_____ **❺** Recognizing how primacy–recency works, I actively guard against first impressions that might prevent accurate perceptions of future events; I formulate hypotheses rather than conclusions.

_____ **❻** Understanding that assumptions about consistency may lead to inaccurate perceptions, I recognize that people may be inconsistent from one situation to another.

_____ **❼** I recognize stereotyping in the messages of others and avoid it in my own.

_____ **❽** I am aware of and am careful to avoid the self-serving bias, overattribution, and the fundamental attribution error in trying to account for another person's behaviour.

_____ **❾** I think critically about perception by analyzing my perceptions, checking perceptions for accuracy, using uncertainty reduction strategies, and acting with cultural sensitivity.

Name:_____ Course:_____ Instructor:_____

After completing this self-test, check your answers against the Answer Key at the back of the book.

Multiple Choice Questions *Choose the BEST answer.*

1. Perception involves
   a. sensing, organizing, interpreting–evaluating.
   b. intensifying, organizing, evaluating.
   c. novelty, selectivity, intensity.
   d. semantics, bombardment, interpretation.

2. Primacy effect is a part of the theory referred to as
   a. assimilation.
   b. first impressions.
   c. stereotyping.
   d. evolution.

3. Implicit personality theories are
   a. subconscious rules of group communication.
   b. rules telling us which characteristics go with other characteristics.
   c. printing terms used in communication.
   d. police category for perpetrators.

4. Attribution is a process of
   a. selecting a strategy for accurate people perception.
   b. interpreting–evaluating excuses.
   c. self-fulfilling prophecy.
   d. explaining motivation for behaviour.

5. An important rule to increase your accuracy in people perception is to
   a. check your perceptions.
   b. act on your assumptions.
   c. rely on implicit personality theories.
   d. none of the above.

6. We make judgments about others based on each of the following EXCEPT
   a. stereotypes.
   b. first impressions.
   c. seeing from the other's point of view.
   d. implicit theories.

7. Acting as if a prediction were true is
   a. recency effect.
   b. primacy effect.
   c. stereotyping.
   d. self-fulfilling prophecy.

8. Assumptions about personality traits that go with other traits is called
   a. implicit theories.

   b. misperceptions.
   c. prophecies.
   d. perspective taking.

9. Believing a person has *all* positive qualities because he or she has *some* positive qualities is called
   a. the Vulcan Mind Meld.
   b. stereotyping.
   c. first impression.
   d. the halo effect.

10. The tendency to maintain balance among perceptions or attitudes is called
    a. attribution.
    b. prophecies.
    c. stereotyping.
    d. consistency.

True–False Questions *Write a T or F in the blank next to the statement.*

1. __F__ Perception is one easy step.

2. __F__ The primacy effect refers to the most important thing we perceive.

3. __T__ A self-fulfilling prophecy occurs when you predict and act as if something is true.

4. __F__ It is important to form conclusions quickly about people.

5. __T__ We tend to perceive things that are physically similar as belonging together.

6. __T__ First impressions exert the most influence on perception.

7. __T__ Attribution is the process of explaining the reason for someone's behaviour.

8. __F__ Ignoring your biases will increase accuracy in perception.

9. __F__ You should never delay conclusions when making critical perceptions.

10. __F__ Perception is reality.

Vocabulary Quiz
The Language of Interpersonal Perception

Match the terms dealing with interpersonal perception listed here with their definitions. Record the number of the definition next to the name of the appropriate concept.

a. _5_ script

b. _3_ implicit personality theory

c. _6_ stereotype

d. _4_ proximity

e. _1_ the fundamental attribution error

f. _8_ self-fulfilling prophecy

g. _10_ mind reading

h. _2_ perception checking

i. _9_ self-serving bias

j. _7_ schemata

1. A process that overvalues the contribution of internal factors and undervalues the influence of external factors in explaining behaviour.

2. A way of increasing accuracy in perception that focuses on describing what you think is going on and then asking for confirmation.

3. A theory of personality that each individual maintains, complete with rules or systems, and through which the individual perceives others.

4. The tendency to see things that are physically close to each other as belonging together, as forming a unit.

5. An organization of information about some action, event, or procedure.

6. A fixed impression of a group of people.

7. The mental templates or structures that help you organize new information as well as the information you already have in memory.

8. The situation in which you make a prediction and then act in a way to make that prediction come true.

9. A tendency to take credit for positive things and deny responsibility for negative things.

10. Drawing conclusions about what is going on in the mind of another person, such as the person's motives or intentions.

Skill Building Exercises

3.1 Perspective Taking

Assuming the perspective of another person and looking at the world through this point of view, rather than through your own, is crucial in achieving mutual understanding. For each of the behaviours listed below, identify specific circumstances that would lead to a *positive perception* and specific circumstances that might lead to a *negative perception*. The first one is done for you.

1. A woman gives a homeless person a $20 bill.
   Positive perception: The woman once had to beg to get money for food. She now shares all she has with those who are in that situation.
   Negative perception: The woman is a first-class snob. She just wants to impress her friends, to show them that she has so much money she can afford to give $20 to a total stranger.

2. A passerby ignores a homeless person who asks for money.

3. A middle-aged man walks down the street with his arm around a teenage girl.

4. A mother refuses to let her teenage son back into her house.

Thinking Critically About Perspective Taking.

The following should be clear: Often, in perceiving a person, you may assume a specific set of circumstances and, on this basis, evaluate specific behaviours as positive or negative. You may also evaluate the very same specific behaviour positively or negatively, depending on the circum-

stances that you infer to be related to the behaviour. Clearly, if you're to understand the perspective of other people, you need to understand the reasons for their behaviours and need to resist defining circumstances from your own perspective.

3.2 Perceptual Differences

Examine each of the following situations and indicate how each of the people identified might view the situation.

Lily, a single parent, has two small children, ages 7 and 12, who often lack some of the important things children their age should have (e.g., school supplies, sneakers, and toys) because Lily can't afford them. Yet Lily smokes two packs of cigarettes a day.

Lily sees...

Lily's 12-year-old daughter sees...

Lily's parents (who also smoke two packs a day) see...

The children's teachers see....

Lily has extremely high standards, feels that getting all As in university is an absolute necessity, and would be devastated with even one B. Fearing that first B (after three and a half years of university), Lily cheats on an exam in a Family Communication course and gets caught by the instructor.

Lily sees...

The instructor sees...

The average B− student sees...

Lily, a supervisor in an automobile factory, has been ordered to increase production or be fired. In desperation, Lily gives a really tough lecture to the workers, many of whom are insulted and, as a result, slow down rather than increase their efforts.

Lily sees...

The average worker sees...

Lily's supervisor sees...

Thinking Critically About Perceptual Differences.

Which principle of perception can you derive from this brief experience? Can you recall a situation in which this principle was ignored or violated? What happened?

Web Explorations

Companion Website

Visit the Companion Website at www.pearsoned.ca/devito for student resources related to this chapter, including self-grading quizzes, additional skill-building exercises, and links to other online resources.

Research Navigator

Explore our research resources at www.researchnavigator.com

■ Find and read an article on perception, how it works, or how it can be made more effective. On the basis of this article, what can you add to the discussion presented here?

■ Use an article you find to investigate one of the key terms discussed in this chapter (for example, perception, self-fulfilling prophecy, primacy and recency, script, schemata, stereotype, or attribution). What additional insights can you provide?

■ Try finding answers to one of the following questions, or design a research study to answer it.

1. Are people who attribute controllability to the homeless more negative in their evaluation of homelessness than those who attribute a lack of controllability?

2. Are men and women equally accurate in interpersonal perception?

3. What is the current status of research on the halo effect?

Chapter 4

Interpersonal Listening

Chapter Topics

This chapter introduces the process of listening and offers suggestions for increasing your own listening effectiveness.

The Stages of Listening

Listening, Culture, and Gender

Increasing Listening Effectiveness

Chapter Skills

After completing this chapter, you should be able to:

- listen more effectively at each of the five stages of listening.

- interact with a clear understanding of cultural and gender listening differences.

- regulate your listening on the basis of empathy, judgment, depth, and active interaction.

Example 1

Foreman: Hey, Al, I don't get this production order. We can't handle this run today. What do they think we are?

Supervisor: But that's the order. So get it out as soon as you can. We're under terrific pressure this week.

Foreman: Don't they know we're behind schedule already because of that press breakdown?

Supervisor: Look, Kelly, I don't decide what goes on upstairs. I just have to see that the work gets out and that's what I'm gonna do.

Foreman: The guys aren't gonna like this.

Supervisor: That's something you'll have to work out with them, not me.

Example 2

Foreman: Hey, Ross, I don't get this production order. We can't handle this run today. What do they think we are?

Supervisor: Sounds like you're pretty sore about it, Kelly.

Foreman: I sure am. We were just about getting back to schedule after that press breakdown. Now this comes along.

Supervisor: As if you didn't have enough work to do, huh?

Foreman: Yeah. I don't know how I'm gonna tell the guys about this.

Supervisor: Hate to face 'em with it now, is that it?

Foreman: I really do. They're under a real strain today. Seems like everything we do around here is rush, rush.

Supervisor: I guess you feel like it's unfair to load anything more on them.

Foreman: Well, yeah. I know there must be plenty of pressure on everybody up the line, but—well, if that's the way it is . . . guess I'd better get the word to 'em.

> " Big people monopolize the listening. Small people monopolize the talking. "
>
> —David Schwartz

These examples, supplied by Carl Rogers and Richard Farson (1981), reflect an essential difference in listening techniques. In Example 1 the supervisor uses common but ineffective listening. In Example 2 the supervisor uses effective listening techniques. As you read this chapter, think about what the supervisor does in Example 2 but not in Example 1. Why do the supervisor's responses in Example 1 create problems? Why do the supervisor's responses in Example 2 prove more effective?

In interpersonal communication, listening is the activity to which we devote most of our time (Janusik, 2002).

It is important to realize that the pattern of listening behaviours show considerable variability, depending both on individual personality and on the context of the communication taking place (Bommelje et al., 2003; Imhof, 2004).

In-Class Notes

The Purposes of Listening: The Same as the Purposes of Communication

- Relate
- Learn
- Influence
- Help
- Play

_____

_____

_____

_____

_____

_____

_____

Throughout this chapter we will explore the differences between ineffective and effective listening. More specifically, this chapter examines the listening process and some of the reasons we listen. It focuses on some of the cultural and gender differences observed in listening and the implications of these differences for effective interpersonal listening. The chapter's major emphasis is on the principles of effective listening and on how you can listen more effectively. (You may want to check out the International Listening Association to get an overview of a professional academic organization devoted to listening. Visit www.listen.org.)

Listening serves a variety of purposes: it helps you to learn, relate, influence, play, and help. Table 4.1 summarizes these purposes, along with potential benefits you might derive from accomplishing them.

THE STAGES OF LISTENING

Listening can be described as a series of five steps: *receiving*, *understanding*, *remembering*, *evaluating*, and *responding*. The process is visualized in Figure 4.1. This model, and the suggestions throughout this chapter for improving listening, draws on theories and models that numerous listening researchers have developed (e.g., Nichols, 1961; Steil et al., 1983; Brownell, 1987; Alessandra, 1986; Nichols, 1995). Note that the listening process is a circular one. The responses of Person A serve as the stimuli for Person B, whose responses, in turn, serve as the stimuli for Person A, and so on.

Each of these stages involves dangers or barriers that need to be avoided as you make your way from receiving to responding.

Receiving

Listening is a much more extensive process than hearing. Hearing is simply receiving—essentially the first stage of listening. Listening begins, but does not end, with receiving the messages the speaker sends. These messages are both verbal and nonverbal; they consist not only of words but also of gestures, facial expressions, and the like. At this stage, you note what is said (verbally and nonverbally) and also what is omitted. For example, you receive not only your friend's request for a loan, but also the omission of any stated intention to pay you back in a reasonable time. The following suggestions should help you receive messages more effectively:

- Focus your attention on the speaker, not on what you'll say next.
- Focus your attention on the speaker's verbal and nonverbal messages—on what is said and not said.
- Avoid distractions in the environment. For example, shut off the stereo or tell your assistant to hold all calls.
- Maintain your role as listener; avoid interrupting until the speaker is finished.

Understanding

Understanding occurs when you learn what the speaker means. Understanding includes both the thoughts that are expressed and the emotional tone that accompanies them; for example, the urgency or the joy or sorrow expressed in the message.

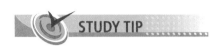
STUDY TIP

Sit in a circle with 10 of your classmates. Have one person in the circle whisper a message to the next person, and so on, until the message makes its way to the end of the circle. Compare the original message to the final message. At what stage did the message get distorted and why?

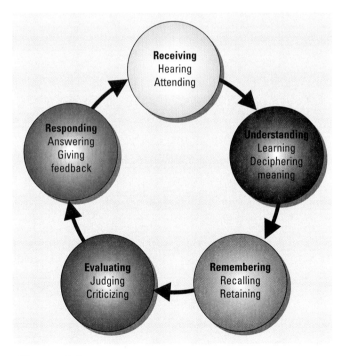

Figure 4.1

The Five Stages of Listening

This model depicts the stages involved in listening. Note that receiving or hearing is not the same thing as listening but is, in fact, only the first step in a five-step process. How would you further distinguish between hearing and listening? Can you identify people you know who "hear" but don't "listen"?

TABLE 4.1

TABLE 4.1   The Purposes and Benefits of Effective Listening

These purposes are, of course, the same as the purposes of interpersonal communication discussed in Chapter 1.

EFFECTIVE LISTENING WILL RESULT IN INCREASING YOUR ABILITY TO	BECAUSE YOU WILL	FOR EXAMPLE
learn: to acquire knowledge of others, the world, and yourself, so as to make more reasonable decisions and avoid problems.	profit from the insights of others and acquire more information relevant to decisions you'll be called upon to make in business or in personal life.	Listening to Peter talk about his travels to Cuba will help you learn more about Peter and about life in another country; listening to the difficulties of your sales staff may help you improve sales training.
relate: to gain social acceptance and popularity.	find that people come to like others who are attentive and supportive.	Others will like you more, once they feel you have genuine concern for them.
influence the attitudes and behaviours of others.	find that people are more likely to respect and follow those they feel have listened to them.	Workers are more likely to follow your advice once they feel you have listened to their insights and concerns.
play.	know when to suspend evaluative thinking and when to engage in supportive and accepting listening.	Listening to your coworkers' anecdotes will enable you to appreciate the relationships between the worlds of work and play.
help others.	hear more, empathize more, and come to understand others more deeply.	Listening to your child's complaints about her teacher will put you in a better position to help your child with school.

> " Listen to information on subjects you are unacquainted with, instead of always striving to lead the conversation to some favourite one of your own. By the last method you will shine, but will not improve. "
>
> —William Hazlitt

To achieve understanding:

- Relate the speaker's new information to what you already know. (How will this new proposal change our present health care?)
- See the speaker's messages from the speaker's point of view; avoid judging the message until it's fully understood as the speaker intended it.
- Ask questions for clarification, if necessary; ask for additional details or examples if needed.
- Rephrase (paraphrase) the speaker's ideas to check on your understanding of the speaker's thoughts and feelings.

Remembering

Messages that you receive and understand need to be retained for at least some period of time. In some small group and public speaking situations you can augment your memory by taking notes or by taping the messages. In most interpersonal communication situations, however, such note taking would be considered inappropriate—although you often do write down a phone number or an appointment or directions.

What you remember is not what was actually said, but what you think (or remember) was said. Memory for speech is reconstructive, not reproductive. In other words, you don't simply reproduce in your memory what the speaker said; rather, you reconstruct the messages you hear into a system that makes sense to you—a concept noted in the discussion of perception in Chapter 3. To illustrate this important concept, try to memorize the list of 12 words presented below (Glucksberg & Danks, 1975). Don't worry about the order; only the number you remember counts. Take about 20 seconds to memorize as many words as possible. Don't read any further until you have tried to memorize the list.

Word List

BED	AWAKE
DREAM	NIGHT

COMFORT	SLUMBER
REST	TIRED
WAKE	EAT
SOUND	SNORE

Now close the book and write down as many words from the list as you can remember. Don't read any further until you have tested your own memory. If you're like my students, you not only remembered most of the words, but also added at least one word: *sleep*. Most people recall that *sleep* was on the list; but, as you can see, it isn't. What happened was that you didn't reproduce the list; you reconstructed it. In this case you gave the list meaning by including the word *sleep*. This happens with all types of messages; they are reconstructed into a meaningful whole—and in the process, a distorted version is often remembered.

To ensure more accurate remembering:

- Identify the central ideas and the major support advanced.

- Summarize the message in an easier-to-retain form, but do not ignore crucial details or qualifications.

- Repeat names and key concepts to yourself silently or, if appropriate, aloud.

- If this is a formal talk with a recognizable organizational structure, identify the structure and use it (see it in your mind) to organize what the speaker is saying.

Some people, when they get older, lose some memory ability. But this happens far less than most people's stereotypes would suggest. What are your stereotypes of older people's listening abilities and habits?

Evaluating

Evaluating consists of judging messages. At times you may try to evaluate the speaker's underlying intent, often without much conscious awareness. For example, Elaine tells you she is up for a promotion and is really excited about it. You may then try to judge her intention. Does she want you to use your influence with the company president? Is she preoccupied with the possible promotion, thus telling everyone? Is she looking for a pat on the back? Generally, if you know the person well, you will be able to identify the intention and respond appropriately.

In other situations, **evaluation** is more in the nature of a critical analysis. For example, while listening to proposals advanced in a business meeting, you evaluate them. Are they practical? Will they increase productivity? What is the evidence? Are there more practical alternative proposals? Some suggestions for this stage of listening:

- Resist evaluation until you fully understand the speaker's point of view.

- Assume that the speaker is a person of goodwill, and give the speaker the benefit of any doubt by asking for clarification on issues you object to. (For example, are there any other reasons for accepting this new proposal?)

- Distinguish facts from inferences (see Chapter 5), opinions, and personal interpretations by the speaker.

- Identify any biases, self-interests, or prejudices that may lead the speaker to slant information unfairly.

How can hearing what you expect to hear (a rather natural tendency) prevent you from listening openly to what is being said? Have you ever "heard" what you expected to hear, only to find out later that what you heard was different from what was said?

How does listening work in gossip?

Responding

Responding occurs in two phases: (1) the responses you make while the speaker is talking, and (2) the responses you make after the speaker has stopped talking. Responses made while the speaker is talking should be supportive and should acknowledge that you're listening. These include what nonverbal researchers call *backchannelling cues*—responses such as "I see," "yes," and "uh-huh"—which let the speaker know you're paying attention.

Listening critically depends in part on assessing the truth and accuracy of the information and the honesty and motivation of the speaker. Thus, in addition to keeping an open mind and delaying judgments, it's necessary to focus on other issues as well:

- Is what the speaker says the truth as far as you understand it? For example, is this car really that great? Are there any disadvantages to this particular car?

- Has the speaker presented the information in enough detail? Have crucial parts been left out? For example, has the speaker identified all the costs?

- Is the speaker being honest? Is the speaker's motivation merely self-gain? For example, might this speaker be distorting the facts merely to make a sale and earn a commission?

- Does the speaker use fallacious reasoning, such as stating that X causes Y when the evidence merely confirms that X and Y occur together? Are conclusions about "all" or "most" people based on a sample that is both large and representative of the population?

- Does the speaker rely too heavily on emotional appeals? Are these appeals legitimate?

- Does the speaker have the credibility you want and expect? For example, is the speaker competent and knowledgeable about the topic?

EXAMPLES?

Can you give an example of a situation in which you got into trouble because you didn't listen critically?

Listen to This   Listening Ethically

As a listener you have certain ethical obligations. First, you owe the speaker an *honest hearing*. Avoid prejudging the speaker. Try to put aside prejudices and preconceptions so that you can evaluate the speaker's message fairly. At the same time, try to empathize with the speaker. You don't have to agree with the speaker, but try to understand emotionally as well as intellectually what the speaker means. Then accept or reject the speaker's ideas on the basis of the information offered, not on the basis of some bias or incomplete understanding.

Second, you owe the speaker *honest responses*. Just as you should be honest with the listener when speaking, you should be honest with the speaker when listening. This means giving open and honest feedback. It also means reflecting honestly on the questions that the speaker raises. Much as the listener has a right to expect an active speaker, the speaker has the right to expect an active listener. The speaker has a right to expect a listener who will actively deal with, rather than just passively hear, the message.

SUGGESTIONS?

Helen, a good friend of yours, has been having difficulty with her friend Sara—who, Helen says, constantly criticizes her and makes her feel inadequate. It's gotten to the point that Helen just tunes Sara out and ignores her. But this, according to Helen, has only made Sara more critical. What advice would you give Helen?

Responses made after the speaker has stopped talking are generally more elaborate. Examples include expressing empathy ("I know how you must feel"); asking for clarification ("Do you mean this new health plan will replace the old one? Or will it be just a supplement?"); challenging ("I think your evidence is weak"); and agreeing ("You're absolutely right, and I'll support your proposal when it comes up for a vote"). In responding:

- Be supportive of the speaker throughout the talk by using varied backchannelling cues; using only one—for example, saying "uh-huh" throughout—will make it appear that you're not listening but are merely on automatic pilot.

- Express support for the speaker in your final responses.

- Own your own responses; state your thoughts and feelings as your own, using I-messages. For example, say "I think the new proposal will entail greater expense than you outlined" rather than "everyone will object to the plan's cost."

STUDY TIP

Use the flash cards for Chapter 4 on the textbook website to see how well you can remember the concepts discussed in this chapter.

Before reading about the principles of effective listening, examine your own listening habits and tendencies by taking the self-test "How Do You Listen?" that follows. The "desirable" answers may seem obvious, but try to give responses that are true for you in most of your listening experiences.

> **❝** Listening, not imitation, may be the sincerest form of flattery. **❞**
>
> —Joyce Brothers

Test Yourself

How Do You Listen?

Instructions: Respond to each statement using the following scale: 1 = always, 2 = frequently, 3 = sometimes, 4 = seldom, and 5 = never.

_____ **❶** I listen actively, communicate acceptance of the speaker, and prompt the speaker to further explore his or her thoughts.

_____ **❷** I listen to what the speaker is saying and feeling; I try to feel what the speaker feels.

_____ **❸** I listen without judging the speaker.

_____ **❹** I listen to the literal meanings that a speaker communicates; I don't look too deeply into hidden meanings.

_____ **❺** I listen without active involvement; I generally remain silent and take in what the other person is saying.

_____ **❻** I listen objectively; I focus on the logic of the ideas rather than on the emotional meaning of the message.

_____ **❼** I listen critically, evaluating the speaker and what the speaker is saying.

_____ **❽** I look for the hidden meanings—the meanings that are revealed by subtle verbal or nonverbal cues.

HOW DID YOU DO?

These statements focus on the ways of listening discussed in this chapter. All of these ways are appropriate at some times but not at other times. The only responses that are inappropriate are "always" and "never." Effective listening is listening that is tailored to the specific communication situation.

WHAT WILL YOU DO?

Consider how you might use these statements to begin to improve your listening effectiveness. A good way to begin doing this is to review these statements, trying to identify situations in which each statement would be appropriate and situations in which each statement would be inappropriate.

LISTENING, CULTURE, AND GENDER

Listening is difficult in part because of the inevitable differences in communication systems between speaker and listener. To listen effectively, it is important to be aware of both the speaker's communication competence and the listener's expectations (Imhoff, 2002). Because each person has had a unique set of experiences, each person's communication and meaning system is going to be different from the other person's. When speaker and listener come from different cultures or are of different genders, the differences and their effects are naturally much greater. Let's look first at culture.

Listening and Culture

The culture in which you were raised will influence your listening in a variety of ways (Kiewitz et al., 1997), including language and speech, direct and indirect styles, nonverbal differences, and feedback.

Even when speaker and listener speak the same language, they speak it with different meanings and different accents. No two speakers speak exactly the same language. Every speaker speaks an *idiolect*: a unique variation of the language (King & DiMichael, 1992). Speakers of the same language will, at the very least, have different meanings for the same terms because they have had different experiences.

Significant differences in expressions and idioms may be found regionally; for example, a Prince Edward Islander will talk about having a "strunt on today," referring to being sulky or in ill humour. Differences in meaning also occur between countries: in Canada, an invitation to "Come to tea" may mean dipping a teabag in a cup of hot water, but in Britain it can refer to enjoying a full meal.

Speakers and listeners who have different native languages and who may have learned English as a second language will have even greater differences in meaning. Translations are never precise and never fully capture the meaning in the other language. If you learned your meaning for *house* in a culture in which everyone lived in their own house with lots of land around it, then communicating with someone whose meaning was learned in a neighbourhood of high-rise tenements is going to be difficult. Although each of you will hear the word *house*, the meanings you'll develop will be drastically different. In adjusting your listening—especially in an intercultural setting—understand that the speaker's meanings may be very different from yours, even though you're speaking the same language.

Some cultures—those of Western Europe, Canada, and the United States, for example—favour **direct speech** in communication; they advise us to "say what you mean and mean what you say." This directness is relative. For example, Canadian visitors to Israel would find that a typical Israeli style is even more direct and could wrongly be perceived as harsh or rude. Many Asian cultures, on the other hand, favour **indirect speech**, emphasizing politeness and maintaining a positive public image rather than literal truth. Listen carefully to people with different styles of directness. Consider the possibility that the meaning the speaker wishes to communicate with indirectness may be very different from the meaning you would communicate with indirectness.

Speakers from different cultures also have different *display rules*—cultural rules that govern which nonverbal behaviours are appropriate and which are inappropriate in a public setting. As you listen to other people, you also "listen" to their nonverbal messages. If these are drastically different from what you expect on the basis of the verbal message, you may perceive a kind of noise or interference or even contradictory messages. Also, of course, different cultures may give very different meanings to the same nonverbal gesture. This topic is considered in detail in Chapter 6.

Members of some cultures tend to give direct and honest feedback. Speakers from these cultures expect feedback to be an honest reflection of what their listeners are feeling. In other cultures—Japan and Korea are good examples—it's more important to be positive than to be truthful; listeners may respond with positive feedback (say, in commenting on a business colleague's proposal) even though they don't feel positive. Listen to feedback, as you would to all messages, with a full recognition that various cultures view feedback very differently.

Listening and Gender

Recently, Canadian researchers have clearly established significant gender differences in listening skills (Hunter et al., 2005). This continues earlier work, such as that done by Deborah Tannen (1990; Tannen & Alatis, 2003), who illustrated that when men and women talk, men lecture and women listen. The lecturer is positioned as the superior—as the teacher, the expert. The listener is positioned as the inferior—as the student, the non-expert.

Women, according to Tannen, seek to build rapport and establish a closer relationship, and so use a "people-oriented" listening style (Worthington, 2001) to achieve these ends. For example, women use more listening cues that let the other person know they are paying attention and are interested. Not only do men use fewer listening cues, but they also interrupt more, and they will often change the topic to one they know more about. Their primary goal in a given interaction is to play up their expertise, emphasize it, and use it in dominating the conversation. When doing so, their listening style tends to be more "time-oriented" (Worthington, 2001).

> " Listen long enough and the person will generally come up with an adequate solution. "
>
> —Mary Kay Ash

You might be tempted to conclude from this that women play fair in conversation and that men don't; for example, that men consistently seek to put themselves in a position superior to women. But that may be too simple an explanation. Research shows that men communicate this way not only with women but also with other men. Men are not showing disrespect for their female conversational partners but are simply communicating as they normally do. Women, too, communicate with other women the same way they do with men.

Tannen argues that a man's goal in conversation is to be accorded respect, so a man seeks to display his knowledge and expertise even if he has to change the topic to one he knows a great deal about. Women, on the other hand, seek to be liked, so a woman expresses interest, rarely interrupts a man to take her turn as speaker, and gives lots of cues (verbally and nonverbally) to indicate that she is listening.

Men and women also show that they are listening in different ways. A woman is more apt to give lots of listening cues, such as interjecting "yeah" or "uh-huh," nodding in agreement, and smiling. A man is more likely to listen quietly without giving lots of listening cues as feedback. Women also make more eye contact when listening than do men, who are more apt to look around and often away from the speaker (Brownell, 2002). Tannen also argues, however, that men do listen less to women than women listen to men. The reason, says Tannen, is that listening places the person in an inferior position, whereas speaking places the person in a superior position.

There is no evidence to show that these differences represent any negative motives—a desire on the part of men to prove themselves superior or on the part of women to ingratiate themselves. Rather, these differences in listening are largely the result of the way in which men and women have been socialized. Can men and women change these habitual ways of listening (and speaking)?

STUDY TIP

Write a paragraph that presents your views on whether men and women should change their habitual ways of listening and speaking.

| **Skills Toolbox** | **6 Ways to Deal with Difficult Listeners** |

Walt Whitman once said, "To have great poets, there must be great audiences too." The same is true of interpersonal interaction: To have great interpersonal communication, there must be great listeners as well as great talkers. Here are a few types of difficult listeners and brief suggestions for dealing with them.

1. The *static listener* gives no feedback, remains relatively motionless, reveals no expression. *Ask questions. Pause to allow the person to say something. Ask for agreement with your facial expressions.*

2. The *monotonous feedback giver* seems responsive, but the responses never vary; regardless of what you say, the response is the same. *Comment on the feedback, saying, for example, "So, do you agree?" or "Am I making sense?"*

3. The *overly expressive listener* reacts to just about everything with extreme responses. Even though you're saying nothing provocative, the reaction is intense. *Some people are just more expressive than others; take pleasure in the fact that you're having such an effect.*

4. The *eye avoider* looks all around the room and at others but never at you. *Maintain eye contact as much as possible, and*

ask questions; try to involve the other person in what you're saying.

5. The *preoccupied listener* listens to other things at the same time, perhaps even with headphones turned up so loud that it interferes with your own thinking. *If what you're saying requires total concentration, then ask for it, saying something like "This is really important" or "I need your total concentration."*

6. The *thought-completing listener* listens a little and then finishes your thought. You wonder if you're really that predictable. *This behaviour often isn't as bad as it seems and may occur simply because the person knows you very well. It does create problems, however, when someone completes your thoughts incorrectly. When this happens, just say so: "No, that's not what I was going to say. Actually, what I was going to say was..."*

THEN AND NOW

Have you ever been confronted by one of these listeners? What did you do to get the person to listen more effectively? What would you do if this happened today?

INCREASING LISTENING EFFECTIVENESS

Because you listen for different purposes, the principles of effective listening should vary from one situation to another. The following four dimensions of listening illustrate the appropriateness of different listening modes for different communication situations.

Empathy and Objective Listening

If you want to understand what a person means and what a person is feeling, you need to listen empathically: to feel with them, see the world as they see it, feel what they feel. Yet although empathy is beneficial in most situations, there are also times when you need to go beyond empathy and look at the situation more objectively. It's important to listen to a friend tell you how the entire world hates him or her and to understand how your friend feels and why. But at times you may need to stand back from the situation and perhaps see beyond what your friend sees. Sometimes you have to put your empathic responses aside and listen in a more detached or analytical way.

In adjusting your empathic and objective listening focus, see the sequence of events as punctuated from the speaker's point of view, and see how this can influence what the speaker says and does (Chapter 1). View the speaker as an equal. Seek to understand both thoughts and feelings. Don't consider your listening task finished until you have understood what the speaker is feeling as well as thinking.

To encourage openness and empathy, try to eliminate any physical or psychological barriers to equality; for example, step from behind the large desk separating you from an employee. Avoid interrupting—a sign that you feel what you have to say is more important.

Avoid "offensive listening," the tendency to listen to bits and pieces of information that will help you attack the speaker or find fault with something the speaker has said.

Would it be more difficult to empathize with someone who was overjoyed because of winning $7 million in the lottery or with someone who was overcome with sadness because of the death of a loved one? How easy or difficult would it be for you to empathize with someone who was depressed because an expected raise of $40 000 turned out to be only $25 000? In general, do you find it more difficult to empathize with negative or with positive feelings?

Talking Ethics | ## A Question of Choice

Your 90-year-old aunt has been diagnosed with terminal cancer. The physicians tell you that there is no need to tell her about this; it will only depress her and hasten her death. But they leave the decision up to you. If you tell your aunt the truth, you may hurt her emotionally and physically. If you choose not to tell her, you may deny her the option of making choices she might want to make if she knew of her true physical condition. What do you do?

This situation raises the issue of choice in interpersonal communication, an interesting way to look at a person's ethical obligations. The assumption underlying the concept of choice is that people have a right to make their own choices and, consequently, have a right to hear information that has a bearing on these choices. Thus, interpersonal communications are ethical to the extent that they present a person with this information and thereby facilitate the person's freedom of choice. Communications are unethical to the extent that they prevent an individual from hearing information relevant to the choices he or she will make.

In sum, you have the right to hear information about yourself that others possess and that influences the choices you'll make. For example, you have the right to face your accusers, to know what witnesses will be called to testify against you, to see your credit ratings, and to know what employment insurance payments you'll receive.

At the same time, you also have the obligation to allow others to hear information that you possess that bears on their choices or on choices of society generally. Thus, for example, you have an obligation to identify wrongdoing that you witness, to identify someone in a police lineup, to report criminal activity, and to testify at a trial when you possess pertinent information.

WHAT WOULD YOU DO?

You're heading a five-person team charged with writing your company's annual report. Two of the people on the team do absolutely no work, and this only adds to the burden borne by you and the other two members. Your supervisor has asked how things are going. You feel you have an obligation to the company to report the two negligent workers; yet you've established a friendship with them. You feel that to report them would violate the friendship and also make you extremely unpopular with the other workers. You also wonder if, after telling your supervisor, you then have the obligation to inform the two members that you have reported to the supervisor that they're not doing their job. Efforts to get the two members to do their share of the work have failed repeatedly. What would you do in this situation?

Non-judgmental and Critical Listening

Effective listening involves listening both non-judgmentally in order to understand, and listening critically in order to make an evaluation or judgment. Listen first with an open mind; this will help you better understand the messages. Then supplement your understanding with critical listening, which will help you better analyze and evaluate the messages. Effective listening requires that you exercise both levels.

Avoid distorting messages through oversimplification, or **levelling**—the tendency to eliminate details and to simplify complex messages so that they're easier to remember. Also avoid filtering out unpleasant or undesirable messages; you may miss the very information you need to change your assumptions or your behaviours.

Recognize your own ethnic, national, or religious biases. Everyone has them, and they can easily interfere with accurate listening. Biases cause you to distort messages by leading you to hear meanings that conform to your own prejudices and expectations. They may lead you to give increased importance to something because it confirms your biases or to minimize it because it contradicts them.

Which of the suggestions for adjusting between non-judgmental and critical listening do you regularly follow? What one suggestion do you follow least often?

Surface and Depth Listening

In most messages, there is an obvious surface meaning that a literal reading of the words and sentences reveals. But messages also often contain a deeper level of meaning. Sometimes it's the opposite of the expressed literal meaning; sometimes it seems totally unrelated. In reality, few messages have only one level of meaning. Most function on two or three levels at the same time. Consider some frequently heard messages. For example, a friend asks you how you like his new haircut. Another friend asks you how you like her painting. On one level the meaning is clear: Do you like the haircut? Do you like the painting? It's reasonable to assume, however, that on another level your friends are asking you to say something positive—he's asking about his appearance, and she's asking about her artistic ability. The parent who seems at first to be complaining about working hard at the office or in the home may be asking for appreciation. The child who talks about the unfairness of the other children in the playground may be asking for some expression of caring. To appreciate these other meanings, you need to engage in in-depth listening.

When listening interpersonally, be particularly sensitive to different levels of meaning. If you respond only to the surface-level communication (the literal meaning), you may miss the opportunity to make meaningful contact with the other person's feelings and real needs. For example, if you say to your parent, "You're always complaining. I bet you really love working so hard," you may be failing to answer a very real call for understanding and appreciation.

In regulating your surface and depth listening, focus on both verbal and nonverbal messages. Recognize both consistent and inconsistent "packages" of messages, and take these cues as guides to the meaning the speaker is trying to communicate. Ask questions when in doubt. Listen also to what is omitted.

Listen for both content and relational messages. The student who constantly challenges the teacher is, on one level, communicating disagreement over content. However, on another level—the relationship level—the student may be voicing objections to the instructor's authority or authoritarianism. If the instructor is to deal effectively with the student, he or she must listen and respond to both types of messages.

In your classroom listening, do you ever tend to filter out unpleasant or difficult messages? What effects might this have?

Can you identify an example from your own experience in which messages were communicated on two different levels but either you or the other person listened to and responded to only one level?

"I can't get off the phone, he won't stop listening!"

Reprinted by permission of Jerry Marcus.

Don't disregard the literal (surface) meaning of interpersonal messages in your attempt to uncover the more hidden (underlying) meanings. If you do, you'll quickly find that your listening problems disappear: No one will talk to you any more. Balance your attention between the surface and the underlying meanings. Respond to the various levels of meaning in the messages of others as you would like others to respond to yours—sensitively but not obsessively, readily but not over-ambitiously.

One listening expert advises that you use your two ears to hear what the person is saying, but use your third ear to listen to why they're saying what they're saying (Rosen, 1998).

Active and Inactive Listening

Active listening is one of the most important communication skills you can learn (Gordon, 1975). Consider the following brief statement from Julia, and some possible responses:

Julia: That creep gave me a C on the paper. I really worked on that project, and all I get is a lousy C.

Robert: That's not so bad; most people got around the same mark. I got a C, too.

Michael: So what? This is your last semester. Who cares about marks anyway?

Hana: You should be pleased with a C. Misha and Michael both failed, and John and Haruki got Ds.

Diana: You got a C on that paper you were working on for the last three weeks? You sound really angry and hurt.

All four listeners are probably eager to make Julia feel better, but they go about it in very different ways and—you can be sure—with very different outcomes. The first three listeners give fairly typical responses. Robert and Michael both try to minimize the significance of a C grade. Minimizing is a common response to someone who has expressed displeasure or disappointment; usually, it's also inappropriate. Although well-intentioned, this response does little to promote meaningful communication and understanding. Hana tries to give the C grade a more positive meaning. Note, however, that all three listeners also say a great deal more: that Julia should not

In-Class Notes

Listening Dimensions

- Empathic vs. Objective
- Non-judgmental vs. Critical
- Surface vs. Depth
- Active vs. Inactive

_____

_____

_____

_____

_____

_____

_____

_____

_____

be feeling unhappy, that her feelings are not legitimate. These responses deny the validity of Julia's feelings and put her in the position of having to defend them.

Diana, however, is different. Diana uses **active listening**, a process of sending back to the speaker what the listener thinks the speaker meant, both literally and emotionally. Active listening does not mean simply repeating the speaker's exact words. It's rather a process of putting into some meaningful whole your understanding of the speaker's total message—the verbal and the nonverbal, the content and the feelings.

In Canada, there are cultural differences in the process of active listening. French Canadians, for example, tend to be very expressive, whereas Aboriginal people would likely attend to the conversation in a more subdued fashion. It is important to pay attention to the different forms active listening can take.

Purposes of Active Listening   Active listening serves a number of important purposes. First, it *shows that you're listening.* Often that is the only thing the speaker really wants—to know that someone cares enough to listen.

Second, it helps you *check how accurately you have understood* what the speaker said and meant. By reflecting back what you perceive to be the speaker's meaning, you give the speaker an opportunity to confirm, clarify, or amend your perceptions. In this way, future messages have a better chance of being relevant and purposeful.

Third, through active listening, you *express acceptance of the speaker's feelings.* Note that in the sample responses given, the first three listeners challenge the speaker; they refuse to give legitimacy to Julia's expressed feelings. The active listener accepts the speaker. The speaker's feelings are not challenged; rather, they're echoed in a sympathetic and empathic manner. Not surprisingly, training in active listening helps to increase a person's empathy (Ikemi & Kubota, 1996). Note, too, that in the first three responses, the feelings of the speaker are denied without ever actually being identified. Diana, however, not only accepts Julia's feelings but also identifies them explicitly, again allowing the opportunity for correction.

Interestingly enough, when confronted by a person in distress, those listeners who try to solve the person's problem or who veer off the issue by engaging in chit-chat come away significantly more depressed than those listeners who show acceptance of the distressed person's problems or who use supportive listening techniques (Notarius & Herrick, 1988).

Fourth, in active listening you *prompt the speaker to further explore his or her feelings and thoughts.* The active listening response gives the speaker a chance to elaborate on these feelings without having to defend them. Active listening sets the stage for meaningful dialogue, a dialogue of mutual understanding. In stimulating this further exploration, active listening also encourages the speaker to resolve his or her own conflicts.

These advantages should not be taken to mean that active listening is always desirable; it isn't. For example, sometimes **passive listening**—listening that is attentive and supportive but less involved—is a better approach.

Techniques of Active Listening   Three techniques will help you master active listening. At first, these principles may seem awkward and unnatural. With practice, however, they will flow and blend into a meaningful and effective dialogue.

Paraphrase the Speaker's Meaning.   State in your own words what you think the speaker meant. This paraphrasing helps to ensure understanding because the speaker can correct or modify your

Do you notice differences in the ways men and women engage in active listening? Can you offer specific examples to bolster your conclusions?

Purposes of Active Listening

- Show you are listening.
- Check understanding.
- Express acceptance.
- Explore feelings and thoughts.

_____

_____

_____

_____

_____

_____

_____

_____

STUDY TIP

With each of you taking a turn, practise the components of active listening with a classmate, focusing on the topic of how you feel about this course so far.

> Listening is not merely not talking, though even that is beyond most of our powers; it means taking a vigorous, human interest in what is being told us.
>
> —Alice Duer Miller

Do you engage in much active listening? For example, of the four responses given in the dialogue that opened this discussion of active listening, which would you be most likely to give? Do your close friends practise active listening when they listen to you? Can you give a specific example of active listening that you were recently involved in?

restatement. It also communicates your interest and your attention. Everyone wants to feel attended to, especially when angry or depressed. The active listening paraphrase confirms this.

When you paraphrase the speaker's meanings, you give the speaker a kind of green light to go into more detail, to elaborate. Thus, when you echo the thought about the C grade, the speaker can elaborate on why that mark was important. Make your paraphrases objective; be careful not to lead the speaker in the direction you think best. Also, be careful that you don't maximize or minimize the speaker's emotions; try to echo these feelings as accurately as you can.

Express Understanding of the Speaker's Feelings. In addition to paraphrasing the content, echo the feelings you believe the speaker expressed or implied. This enables you to check your perception of the speaker's feelings and provides the speaker with the opportunity to see his or her feelings more objectively.

Expressing understanding is especially helpful when someone is angry, hurt, or depressed. Hearing these feelings objectively and seeing them from a less impassioned perspective will help the person deal effectively with them.

Most of us hold back our feelings until we are certain that others will be accepting. We need to hear statements such as "I understand" and "I see how you feel." When we feel that our emotions are accepted, we then feel free to go into more detail. Active listening provides the speaker with this important opportunity.

Ask Questions. Ask questions to make sure that you understand the speaker's thoughts and feelings and to secure additional helpful information. Design your questions to provide just enough stimulation and support for the speaker to express the thoughts and feelings he wants to express. Avoid questions that pry into irrelevant areas or that challenge the speaker in any way.

Note the active listening techniques used throughout this dialogue:

Petra: That creep demoted me. He told me I wasn't an effective manager. I can't believe he did that, after all I've done for this company.

Saul: I can understand your anger. You've been manager for three or four months now, haven't you?

Petra: A little over three months. I know I was on trial, but I thought I was doing a good job.

Saul: Can you get another trial?

Petra: Yes, he said I could try again in a few months. But I feel like a failure.

Saul: I know what you mean. It's not a pleasant feeling. What else did he say?

Petra: He said I had trouble getting the paperwork done on time.

Saul: You've been late filing the reports?

Petra: A few times.

Saul: Is there a way to delegate the paperwork?

Petra: No, but I think I know now what needs to be done.

Saul: You sound as though you're ready to give that manager's position another try.

Petra: Yes, I think I am, and I'm going to let him know that I intend to apply in the next few months.

Even in this brief interaction, Petra has moved from unproductive anger with the supervisor, as well as a feeling of failure, to a determination to correct an unpleasant situation. Note, too, that Saul didn't offer solutions but "simply" listened actively.

As stressed throughout this discussion, listening is situational; the type of listening that is appropriate varies with the situation. You can visualize a listening situation as one in which you have to make choices among at least the dimensions of listening just discussed (see Figure 4.2). Each listening situation should call for a somewhat different configuration of listening responses; the art of effective listening is largely one of making appropriate choices along these dimensions.

Empathic ____:____:____:____:____:____ Objective

Non-judgmental ____:____:____:____:____:____ Critical

Surface ____:____:____:____:____:____ Deep

Active ____:____:____:____:____:____ Inactive

Figure 4.2

Listening Choices

Effective listening is largely a matter of adjusting your behaviour along such dimensions as these. Can you identify an interpersonal situation that would call for listening that is empathic, non-judgmental, surface, and active; and another situation that would call for listening that is objective, critical, in-depth, and inactive?

In-Class Notes

Techniques for Active Listening

- Paraphrase the speaker's thoughts.
- Express understanding of the speaker's feelings.
- Ask questions.

_____

_____

_____

_____

_____

_____

_____

_____

Summary of Concepts and Skills

This chapter defined listening, explored its five stages, and identified some of the reasons we listen. We also looked at the wide cultural and gender differences in listening. Finally, we looked at the types of listening and how best to adjust our listening to achieve maximum effectiveness.

1. Listening may be viewed as a five-step process: receiving, understanding, remembering, evaluating, and responding. Listening difficulties and obstacles exist at each of these stages.

2. We listen for a variety of reasons: to learn, to relate, to influence, to play, and to help.

3. Cultural differences in accents, in the directness of people's style of communicating, in nonverbal behaviours, and in the feedback people give and expect may create listening difficulties.

4. Men and women seem to listen with different purposes in mind and with different behaviours.

5. Effective listening depends on varying your listening behaviour appropriately between empathic and objective, non-judgmental and critical, surface and depth, and active and inactive listening.

Check Your Ability

Check your ability to apply the skills described at the right. You will gain most from this brief experience if you think carefully about each skill and try to identify recent instances in which you did or did not act on the basis of the specific skill. Use a rating scale such as the following: 1 = almost always, 2 = often, 3 = sometimes, 4 = rarely, and 5 = almost never.

_____ ❶ In receiving messages, focus attention on the speaker's verbal and nonverbal messages, and avoid interrupting.

_____ ❷ In understanding messages, relate the new information to what you already know; ask questions and paraphrase to ensure understanding.

_____ ❸ In remembering messages, identify the central ideas, summarize the message in an easier-to-retain form, and use repetition (aloud or to yourself) to help with key terms and names.

_____ ❹ In evaluating messages, try first to understand fully what the speaker means; also try to identify any biases and self-interests that may lead to an unfair presentation of material.

_____ ❺ In responding to messages, express support and own your own responses.

_____ ❻ In listening and in speaking, recognize the cultural differences that can create barriers to mutual understanding.

_____ ❼ In listening, recognize that women and men may listen with different purposes in mind and that they may act differently but mean the same thing—or act similarly but mean different things.

_____ ❽ Regulate and adjust your listening between empathic and objective, non-judgmental and critical, surface and depth, and active and inactive listening.

After completing this self-test, check your answers against the Answer Key at the back of the book.

Multiple Choice Questions   *Choose the BEST answer.*

1. The listening stage of understanding
   a. occurs when you learn what the speaker means.
   b. judges the speaker's message immediately.
   c. allows the listener to regulate the topics.
   d. avoids the use of questions.

2. The stages of listening are receiving, understanding, evaluating and
   a. judging.
   b. resisting.
   c. responding.
   d. realizing.

3. In evaluating, you should
   a. identify biases or self-interests of the speaker.
   b. combine facts with inferences.
   c. regard the speaker with suspicion.
   d. use your own prejudices.

4. Which of the following is not a good reason for us to listen?
   a. to help
   b. for enjoyment
   c. for information
   d. to reinforce personal biases

5. Which of the following is a female listening style?
   a. using listening cues often, such as "yeah" or "uh-huh"
   b. putting oneself in a superior position
   c. dominating the conversation
   d. changing the topic to one of her own expertise

6. Which of the following is a male listening style?
   a. interrupting
   b. topic control
   c. dominating the conversation
   d. all of the above

7. Listening with empathy involves
   a. speaking your feelings clearly.
   b. understanding the speaker's feelings clearly.
   c. judging the speaker's feelings.
   d. judging your feelings.

8. Objective listening involves
   a. withholding judgment.
   b. not interrupting.
   c. recognizing your biases.
   d. all of the above.

9. Active listening techniques include
   a. interrupting.
   b. judging.
   c. domination.
   d. paraphrasing.

10. When listening in different cultures, understand that
    a. differences should be ignored.
    b. differences do not affect meaning.
    c. language meanings differ in different cultures.
    d. language meaning is the same in different cultures.

True–False Questions   *Write a T or F in the blank next to the statement.*

1. __T__ Listening is a process.
2. __F__ Hearing and listening are the same.
3. __F__ Remembering is the same as retention.
4. __T__ Responding is a part of feedback.
5. __F__ Evaluating is a poor listening technique.
6. __T__ Language meanings vary based on culture.
7. __F__ Directness in all cultures is the same.
8. __T__ Men interrupt more than women.
9. __T__ Women use more listening cues than men.
10. __F__ Active listening is a poor listening technique.

Vocabulary Quiz
The Language of Listening

Match these terms about listening with their definitions. Record the number of the definition next to the term.

a. __7__ listening
b. __6__ levelling
c. __5__ receiving
d. __8__ empathic listening
e. __9__ supportive listening
f. __2__ active listening
g. __1__ memory
h. __4__ paraphrasing
i. __3__ evaluating

1. A reconstructive, not a reproductive process.

2. A process of sending back to the speaker what the listener thinks the speaker meant, literally and emotionally.

3. An essential stage in the listening process in which we make judgments about a message.

4. A restatement of something said in your own words.

5. Only the first stage in listening; similar to hearing.

6. The reduction of the number of details that we remember about something we have heard.

7. A process of receiving, understanding, remembering, evaluating, and responding to messages.

8. Placing ourselves into the position of the speaker so that we feel as the speaker feels.

9. Listening by giving the speaker positive feedback.

Skill Building Exercises

4.1 Reducing Barriers to Listening

Visualize yourself ready to talk with the following people on the topics noted. What barriers to listening (at any stage: receiving, understanding, remembering, evaluating, or responding) might arise in each encounter? What would you do to prevent these barriers from interfering with effective listening?

1. A friend tells you he's HIV positive.

2. An instructor argues that the feminist movement is dead.

3. A coalition of homeless people claims the right to use public spaces.

4. A politician says that relationships between different races will never be better.

5. A Catholic priest argues that people should remain virgins until marriage.

6. A relative argues that abortion, regardless of the circumstances, is murder.

7. A telephone company representative asks that you switch to their new long-distance system.

Thinking Critically About Barriers to Listening.

In thinking about these situations, consider how your initial expectations would influence your listening. How would you assess the person's credibility (even before you began to talk)? How would this influence your listening? Would you begin listening with a positive, a negative, or a neutral attitude? How might these attitudes influence your listening?

4.2 Making Decisions About Active Listening

Here are several situations in which active listening responses seem appropriate. How would you respond to these situations?

1. Your friend Karla has been married for the last three years and has two small children, one who is two years old and one who is six months old. Recently, Karla has been having an affair with a colleague at work. Her husband discovered this and is now suing for divorce. She confides this to you and says, *I really don't know what I'm going to do. I may lose the kids. I could never support myself and live the way we do now. I sure love that BMW. I wish these last two months had never happened and that I had never started up with Taylor.*

2. Your boss, Ruth, has been an especially hard supervisor to work for. She is a perfectionist who doesn't understand that people make mistakes. On several occasions she has filed negative evaluation reports on you and other members of your department. This has prevented you and others from getting merit raises in at least three instances. During lunch, Ruth comes over to your table and tells you that she has been fired and has to clean out her desk by 3:00 p.m. She says: *I can't believe they did this to me; I was the best supervisor they had. Our production level was always the highest in the company. They're idiots. Now I don't know what I'm going to do. Where will I get another job?*

3. Your mother has been having a difficult time at work. She was recently passed up for promotion and has received one of the lowest merit raises given in the company. She says, *I'm not sure what I did wrong. I do my work, mind my own business, don't take my sick days like everyone else. How could they give that promotion to Manuela, who's only been with the company for two years? I've given them seven years. Maybe I should just quit and try to find something else.*

Thinking Critically About Active Listening.

What is the single most important value to be achieved through active listening? What is the single most important suggestion to remember when listening actively?

4.3 Paraphrasing to Ensure Understanding

One of the most important skills in effective listening is paraphrasing. For each of the following messages, write a paraphrase that you think would be appropriate. After you complete the paraphrases, ask another person if he or she would accept them as objective restatements of the thoughts and feelings expressed. Rework the paraphrases until the other person agrees that they are accurate. A sample paraphrase is provided for number 1.

1. I can't deal with my parents' constant fighting. I've seen it for the last 10 years and I really can't stand it any more.

   Paraphrase: *You have trouble dealing with their fighting. You seem really upset by this last fight.*

2. Did you hear I got engaged to Jerry? Our racial and religious differences are really going to cause difficulties for both of us. But we love each other—we'll work it through.

3. I got a C on that paper. That's the worst mark I've ever received. I just can't believe that I got a C. This is my major. What am I going to do?

4. I can't understand why I didn't get that promotion. I was here longer and did better work than Thompson. Even my two supervisors said I was the next in line for the promotion. And now it looks like another one won't come along for at least a year.

5. That rotten, inconsiderate pig just up and left. He never even said goodbye. We were together for six months and after one small argument he leaves without a word. And he even took my bathrobe—that expensive one he bought for my last birthday.

6. I'm just not sure what to do. I really love Helen. She's the sweetest kid I've ever known. I mean she'd do anything for me. But she really wants to get married. I do too, and yet I don't want to make such a commitment. I mean that's a long-term thing. And, much as I hate to admit it, I don't want the responsibility of a wife, a family, a house. I really don't need that kind of pressure.

Thinking Critically About Paraphrasing.

How might paraphrasing be of value in interpersonal conflict situations? In intercultural communication situations? Can you identify situations where paraphrasing would be inappropriate?

Web Explorations

Companion Website

Visit the Companion Website at www.pearsoned.ca/devito for student resources related to this chapter, including self-grading quizzes, additional skill-building exercises, and links to other online resources.

Research Navigator

Explore our research resources at www.researchnavigator.com

- Find and read an article on listening, styles or types of listening, or culture or gender differences in listening. On the basis of this article, what can you add to the discussion presented here?

- Use such an article to investigate one of the key terms discussed in this chapter (for example, listening, direct and indirect styles, critical listening, feedback, empathy, or active listening). What additional insights can you provide?

- Try finding answers to one of the following questions, or design a research study to answer it.

  1. Do women and men listen equally effectively?
  2. What do experts in your own field say about listening?
  3. Do men or women differ in their empathic abilities? In their empathic behaviours?

Chapter 5

Verbal Messages

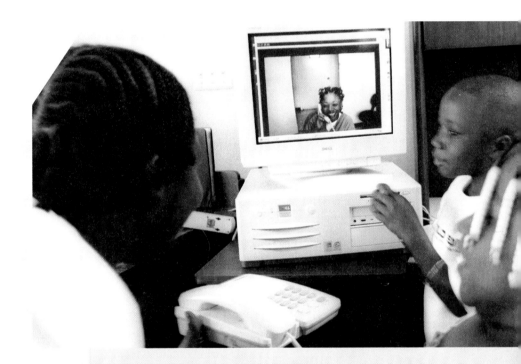

Chapter Topics

This chapter introduces verbal messages and offers suggestions for making your own messages more effective.

The Nature of Verbal Messages

Confirmation and Disconfirmation

Using Verbal Messages Effectively and Critically

Chapter Skills

After completing this chapter, you should be able to:

- communicate, recognizing that meanings are in people; are context based; have both denotative and connotative meanings; vary in directness; are culturally based; and vary in abstraction.

- regulate your confirmations as appropriate, especially avoiding sexist, heterosexist, and racist language, and, in general, language that puts down other groups.

- identify conceptual distortions in your own and others' language and avoid those distortions in your own messages.

On the second night of their honeymoon, a couple is sitting in a hotel lounge. The woman strikes up a conversation with the couple next to her. The husband refuses to communicate with the couple and becomes antagonistic toward his wife and the couple. The wife then grows angry because he has created such an awkward and unpleasant situation. Each becomes increasingly disturbed, and the evening ends in a bitter conflict, each spouse convinced of the other's lack of consideration. Eight years later, the couple analyze this argument.

Apparently, the word "honeymoon" meant different things to each of them. To the husband it meant a golden opportunity to ignore the rest of the world and simply explore each other. He felt his wife's interaction with the other couple implied there was something lacking in him. To the wife, her honeymoon meant an opportunity to try out her new role as wife. "I had never had a conversation with another couple as a wife before," she says. "Previous to this I had always been a 'girlfriend' or 'fiancée' or 'daughter' or 'sister.'"

This example—taken from Ronald D. Laing, H. Phillipson, and A. Russell Lee in *Interpersonal Perception* (1966; also Watzlawick, 1977)—illustrates the confusion that can result when you look for meaning in the words and not in the person. This confusion is one of the ways that verbal messages—the topic of this chapter—can fail to communicate their intended meaning.

THE NATURE OF VERBAL MESSAGES

In communication you use two major signal systems—the verbal and the nonverbal. This chapter focuses on the *verbal* system: how spoken and written **language** serves as a system for communicating meaning, how it can be used effectively, and how it creates problems when it isn't. Keep in mind that "the world in language is half someone else's" (Salamensky, 2001). Before words are passed along to the receiver, they exist in the mind of the transmitter. Successful verbal communication, then, will occur if the two sides can arrive at a mutually agreed-upon meaning.

Messages Are Denotative and Connotative

Verbal communication is sometimes referred to as symbolic because it uses a learned, socially shared language system in which words or symbols are used to describe reality (Buck & Van Lear, 2002). Within this system, two general types of meaning are essential to identify: denotation and connotation. The term **denotation** refers to the meaning you'd find in a dictionary; it's the meaning that members of the culture assign to a word. **Connotation** is the emotional meaning that specific speakers/listeners give to a word. Take as an example the word "death." To a doctor this word might mean (denote) the time when the heart stops. This is an objective description of a particular event. On the other hand, to a mother who is informed of her son's death, the word means (connotes) much more. It recalls her son's youth, ambitions, family, illness, and so on. To her, "death" is a highly emotional, subjective, and personal word. These emotional, subjective, or personal associations comprise the word's connotative meaning. The denotation of a word is its objective definition. The connotation of a word is its subjective or emotional meaning.

Messages Vary in Directness

Think about how you'd respond to the following verbal messages:

1a. I'm so bored; I have nothing to do tonight.

2a. I'd like to go to the movies. Would you like to come?

1b. Do you feel like hamburgers tonight?

2b. I'd like hamburgers tonight. How about you?

Statements 1a and 1b are relatively indirect; they're attempts to get the listener to say or do something without committing the speaker. Statements 2a and 2b are more direct—they state more clearly the speaker's preferences and then ask if the listener agrees.

Here we focus on the advantages and disadvantages of directness. For the most part, the advantages of indirect messages are the disadvantages of direct messages, and the disadvantages of indirect messages are the advantages of direct messages.

Advantages of Indirect Messages   Indirect messages allow you to express a thought without insulting or offending anyone; they allow you to observe the rules of polite interaction. So instead of saying, "I'm bored with this group," you say, "It's getting late, and I have to get up early tomorrow." Instead of saying, "This food tastes like cardboard," you say, "I just started my diet" or "I just ate." In each instance you're stating a preference indirectly so as to avoid offending someone. Not all direct messages, however, should be considered impolite. In one study of Spanish and English speakers, for example, no evidence was found to support the assumption that politeness and directness were incompatible (Mir, 1993).

> ❝ One great use of words is to hide our thoughts. ❞
>
> —Voltaire

Sometimes indirect messages allow us to ask for compliments in a socially acceptable manner. A person who says, "I was thinking of getting a nose job" may hope to get the response "A nose job? You? Your nose is perfect."

Disadvantages of Indirect Messages   Indirect messages, however, can also create problems. Consider the following dialogue:

Alexis: You wouldn't like to have my parents over for dinner this weekend, would you?

Sam: I really wanted to go to the beach and just relax.

Alexis: Well, if you feel you have to go, I'll make the dinner myself. You go to the beach. I really hate having them over and doing all the work myself. It's such a drag shopping, cooking, and cleaning all by myself.

Given this situation, Sam has two basic alternatives. One is to stick with the plans to go to the beach and relax. In this case Alexis is going to be upset and Sam is going to feel guilty for not helping with the dinner. A second alternative is to give in to Alexis, help with the dinner, and not go to the beach. In that case, Sam is going to have to give up a much desired plan and is likely to resent Alexis's "manipulative" tactics. Regardless of which decision is made, this "win–lose" strategy creates resentment, competition, and often an "I'll get even" attitude. With direct requests, this type of situation is much less likely to develop. Consider:

Alexis: I'd like to have my parents over for dinner this weekend. What do you think?

Sam: Well, I really wanted to go to the beach and just relax.

Regardless of what develops next, both individuals are starting out on relatively equal footing. Each has clearly and directly stated a preference. Although at first these preferences seem mutually exclusive, it may be possible to meet both people's needs. For example, Sam might say, "How about going to the beach this weekend and having your parents over next weekend? I'm really exhausted; I could use the rest."

How would you describe this dinner scene in denotative terms? In connotative terms?

What role does directness play in other forms of online communication—for example, in chat groups or news groups?

Here is a direct response to a direct request. Unless there is some pressing need to have Alexis's parents over for dinner this weekend, this response may enable each to meet the other's needs.

Gender and Cultural Differences in Directness   A popular stereotype in much of North America holds that women are indirect in making requests and in giving orders—and that this indirectness communicates powerlessness, a discomfort with authority. Men, the stereotype continues, are direct, sometimes to the point of being blunt or rude. This directness communicates men's power and comfort with their own authority.

Deborah Tannen (1994b) provides an interesting perspective on these stereotypes. Women are, it seems, more indirect in giving orders; they are more likely to say, for example, "It would be great if these letters could go out today" rather than "Have these letters out by three." But Tannen (1994b) argues that "issuing orders indirectly can be the prerogative of those in power" and in no way shows powerlessness. Power, to Tannen, is the ability to choose your own style of communication.

According to Tannen, men are more likely to use indirectness when they express weakness, reveal a problem, or admit an error—that is, when they're saying something that goes against the masculine stereotype.

Many Asian and Latin American cultures stress the values of indirectness, largely because indirectness enables a person to avoid appearing criticized or contradicted and thereby losing face (Tae-Seop, 2002). An example of a somewhat different kind of indirectness is the greater use of intermediaries to resolve conflict among the Chinese than among North Americans (Ma, 1992). In most of the United States, however, people are taught that directness is the preferred style. "Be upfront" and "Tell it like it is" are commonly heard communication guidelines. In Canada, while being direct might conflict with the common expectation of "being nice and polite," it is still the preferred mode of communication in many business and personal settings. Contrast this North American preference with the following two Japanese principles of indirectness (Tannen, 1994b):

- *omoiyari*, a concept close to empathy, says that a listener needs to understand the speaker without the speaker's being specific or direct. This style obviously places a much greater demand on the listener than a direct speaking style would.
- *sassuru* advises listeners to anticipate a speaker's meanings and use subtle cues from the speaker to infer his or her total meaning.

In thinking about direct and indirect messages, it's important to be aware of the ease with which misunderstandings can occur. For example, a person who uses an indirect style of speech may be doing so to be polite and may have been taught this style by his or her culture. If you assume, because of your own culture, that the person is using indirectness to be manipulative, then miscommunication is inevitable.

> There you have it. The blandest adjective in the English language, and we have claimed it as our own. Canadians are nice.
>
> —Will Ferguson

Messages Vary in Abstraction

Consider the following list of terms:

- entertainment
- TV show
- Canadian TV show
- recent Canadian TV show
- *Royal Canadian Air Farce*

At the top is the general or abstract word "entertainment." Note that entertainment includes all the other items on the list, plus various other items—films, novels,

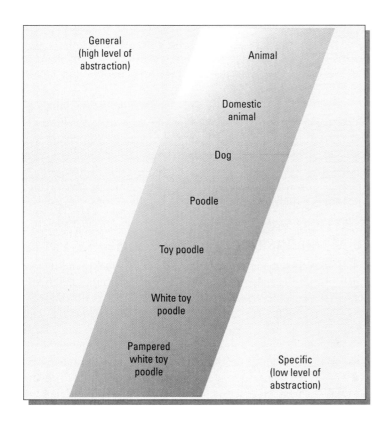

Figure 5.1

The Abstraction Ladder

As you go up in abstraction, you get more general; as you go down in abstraction, you get more specific. How would you arrange the following terms in order of abstraction, from most specific to most general: vegetation, tree, elm tree, thing, organic thing, blooming elm tree?

STUDY TIP

Create an abstraction ladder, using the word "internet" as the concept with the highest level of abstraction. Create a hierarchy of four terms below it that illustrate lower levels of abstraction, with the bottom term being the least abstract.

drama, comics, and so on. "TV show" is more specific and concrete. It includes all of the items below it as well as various other items such as Indian TV shows or Russian TV shows. It excludes, however, all entertainment that is not TV. "Canadian TV show" is again more specific than TV show and excludes all shows that are not Canadian. "Recent Canadian TV show" further limits Canadian TV shows to a time period. "*Royal Canadian Air Farce*" specifies concretely the one item to which reference is made.

The most general term—in this case, "entertainment"—conjures up many different images. One person may focus on television, another on music, another on comic books, and still another on radio. To some, "television" may bring to mind documentaries or newscasts. To others, it brings to mind the proliferation of so-called reality shows. *Royal Canadian Air Farce* guides the listener still further—in this case, to one TV program. But note that even though the name identifies one program, different listeners are likely to focus on different aspects of the show: perhaps its theme, perhaps its specific characters, perhaps the political context of a given episode. As you get more specific—less abstract—you more effectively guide the images that come to your listeners' minds.

Effective verbal messages include words that range widely in abstractness (see Figure 5.1). At times, a general term may suit your needs best; at other times a more specific term may serve better. The general suggestion for effective communication is to use abstractions sparingly and to express your meanings specifically with words that are low in abstraction. However, are there situations when terms high in abstraction would be more effective than specific terms? How would you describe advertisements for cosmetics in terms of high and low abstraction? Advertisements for cereals? Advertisements for cat and dog food? How would you describe political campaign speeches in terms of abstraction?

Message Meanings Are in People

If you wanted to know the meaning of the word "love," you'd probably turn to a dictionary. There you'd find that love is, according to the *Canadian Oxford*, "an intense feeling of deep affection or fondness for a person or thing; great liking." This is the denotative meaning. But where would you turn if you wanted to know what Pedro means when he says, "I'm in love"? Of course, you'd turn to Pedro to discover his meaning. It's in this sense that meanings are in people, not in words. Consequently, to uncover meaning, you need to look into people and not merely into words.

Also recognize that as you change, you also change the meanings you created out of past messages. Thus, although the message sent may not have changed, the meanings you created from it yesterday and the meanings you create today may be quite different. Yesterday, when a special someone said, "I love you," you created certain meanings. But today, when you learn that the same "I love you" was said to three other people—or when you fall in love with someone else—you drastically change the meanings you draw from those three words.

Message Meanings Depend on Context

Both verbal and nonverbal communications exist in a context, and that context to a large extent determines the meaning of any verbal or nonverbal behaviour. In terms of verbal messages, the same words may have totally different meanings when they occur in different contexts. For example, the greeting "How are you?" means "Hello" to someone you pass regularly on the street, but means "Is your health improving?" when said to a friend in the hospital. The Canadian "eh" can be a question or confirmation, depending on the context. Similarly, the meaning of a given message depends on the behaviour it accompanies or is close to in time. Saying "This stinks to high heaven" in reaction to the behaviour of a politician means something quite different than when said in reaction to a piece of overripe cheese. Divorced from the context, it's often impossible to tell what meaning words are intended to convey. Of course, even if you know the context in detail, you still may not be able to decipher the meaning of some messages, because the same words will never have an identical meaning to different people (Harris, 2002).

Especially important is the cultural context, which is emphasized throughout this text. The cultural context will influence not only the meaning assigned to speech but also whether your meaning is friendly, offensive, disrespectful, condescending, sensitive, and so on. Some researchers suggest not focusing exclusively on the cultural context because verbal communication is multidimensional, and in order to decode its meanings, other factors need to be examined as well (Tzanne, 2000).

"Eh" isn't the only Canadian expression that derives its meaning from its cultural context. If you're unemployed you might be on pogey; if you're going 10 clicks an hour you're probably driving too slow; and if you're cold you might need to put on your toque. And depending on where you are in the country and how old you are, you'll be sitting on either a chesterfield or a couch. Can you think of other expressions that are particular to Canada or to your region?

Source: *Sault Star*, June 30, 2003.

In-Class Notes

The Nature of Language

- Messages are denotative and connotative.
- Messages vary in directness.
- Messages vary in abstraction.
- Meanings are in people.
- Meanings depend on context.

_____

_____

_____

_____

_____

_____

_____

_____

_____

Messages Vary in Inclusion

Some messages are inclusive; they include all people present and they acknowledge the relevance of others. Other messages exclude specific people and, in some cases, entire cultural groups.

You see messages of exclusion when in-group language is used in the presence of an out-group member. When doctors get together and discuss medicine, there's no problem. But when they get together with someone who isn't a doctor, they often fail to adjust to this new person. Instead, they simply continue with discussions of anatomy, symptoms, medication, and other topics that exclude others present. When those others are patients, serious communication problems can result.

Another form of excluding talk is using the terms of one's own cultural group as universal, as applying to everyone. The problem in doing so is that the use of such terms excludes others. For example, "church" refers to a place of worship for specific religions but not for all religions. Similarly, "Bible" refers to Christian religious scriptures and is not a general term for "religious scriptures." Nor does "Judeo–Christian tradition" include the religious traditions of everyone. Similarly, the terms "marriage," "husband," and "wife" refer to some heterosexual relationships and exclude others; they also exclude gay and lesbian relationships.

When you're in a group, instead of using language that excludes one or more members, consider the principle of **inclusion**. Regardless of the type of communication situation you're in, try to find ways to include everyone in the interaction. Even if job-related issues have to be discussed in the presence of someone who is not a fellow employee, you can include that person by, for example, seeking his or her perspective or drawing an analogy from his or her field.

Another way to practise inclusion in a group discussion is to fill in relevant details for those who may be unaware of them. When people, places, or events are mentioned, briefly identify them, as in "Margo—she's Jeff's daughter—loved Simon Fraser."

Also, consider the vast array of alternative terms that are inclusive rather than exclusive. For example, one could use "place of worship" instead of "church," "temple," or "mosque" when talking about religious houses of worship in general. Similarly, "committed relationship" is more inclusive than "marriage"; "couples therapy" is more inclusive than "marriage counselling"; and "life partner" is more inclusive than "husband" or "wife." Referring to "religious scriptures" is more inclusive than "Bible." Of course, if you're referring to a specific Baptist church or specific married heterosexual couples, then the terms "church" and "marriage" are appropriate.

For a related but somewhat different perspective on inclusion and exclusion, let's turn to the communication behaviours known as confirmation and disconfirmation.

CONFIRMATION AND DISCONFIRMATION

Before reading about confirmation and disconfirmation, take the self-test on page 98 to examine your own communication behaviour.

A useful way to introduce disconfirmation and its alternatives—confirmation and rejection—is to consider a specific situation: Jessica arrives home late one night. Justin is angry and complains about Jessica's coming home so late. Consider some responses Jessica might make:

1. Stop screaming. I'm not interested in what you're babbling about. I'll do what I want, when I want. I'm going to bed.

2. What are you so angry about? Didn't you get in three hours late last Thursday? When you went to that office party? So knock it off.

3. You have a right to be angry. I should have called when I was going to be late, but I got involved in a serious discussion at work and I couldn't leave until it was resolved.

STUDY TIP

Either from memory or using an internet search engine, identify a situation where a public figure claimed his or her words were taken out of context. Research the original context and determine how the message's meaning changed as a result of being taken out of context.

How Confirming Are You?

Instructions: In your typical communications, how likely are you to display the following behaviours? Use the following scale in responding to each statement: 5 = always, 4 = often, 3 = sometimes, 2 = rarely, and 1 = never.

_____ **1** I acknowledge the presence of another person both verbally and nonverbally.

_____ **2** I acknowledge the contributions of the other person by, for example, supporting or taking issue with what the person says.

_____ **3** During conversation, I make nonverbal contact by maintaining direct eye contact, touching, hugging, kissing, or otherwise demonstrating acknowledgment of the other person.

_____ **4** I communicate as both speaker and listener, with involvement, and with a concern and respect for the other person.

_____ **5** I signal my understanding of the other person both verbally and nonverbally.

_____ **6** I reflect back the other person's feelings as a way of showing that I understand these feelings.

_____ **7** I ask questions, as appropriate, concerning the other person's thoughts and feelings.

_____ **8** I respond to the other person's requests by, for example, returning phone calls and answering letters within a reasonable time.

_____ **9** I encourage the other person to express his or her thoughts and feelings.

_____ **10** I respond directly and exclusively to what the other person says.

HOW DID YOU DO?

All 10 statements are phrased so that they express confirming behaviours. Therefore, high scores (say, above 35) reflect a strong tendency to engage in confirmation. Low scores (say, below 25) reflect a strong tendency to engage in disconfirmation. Don't assume, however, that all situations call for confirmation and that only insensitive people are disconfirming. You may wish to consider kinds of situations in which disconfirmation would be, if not an effective response, at least a legitimate one.

WHAT WILL YOU DO?

Because most people want to become more confirming, the text offers suggestions for increasing your own confirming tendencies. Treating the statements in the self-test as suggestions for increasing confirmation is a good way to start increasing your own confirming behaviour.

In response 1, Jessica dismisses Justin's anger and even indicates a dismissal of Justin as a person. In response 2, Jessica rejects the validity of Justin's reasons for being angry but does not dismiss Justin's feelings of anger or Justin as a person. In response 3, Jessica acknowledges Justin's anger and the reasons for being angry. In addition, Jessica provides some kind of explanation and in doing so shows that Justin's feelings matter and that Justin as a person is important and deserves to know what happened. The first response is an example of disconfirmation, the second of rejection, and the third of confirmation.

Psychologist William James once observed that "No more fiendish punishment could be devised, even were such a thing physically possible, than that one should be turned loose in society and remain absolutely unnoticed by all the members thereof." In this often quoted observation, James identifies the essence of disconfirmation (Watzlawick et al., 1967; Veenendall & Feinstein, 1995).

Disconfirmation is a communication pattern in which you ignore someone's presence as well as that person's communications. You say, in effect, that this person and what this person has to say are not worth serious attention or effort; that this person and this person's contributions are so unimportant or insignificant that there is no reason to concern yourself with them.

Note that disconfirmation is not the same as **rejection**. In rejection you disagree with the person; you indicate your unwillingness to accept something the other person says or does. In disconfirming someone, however, you deny that person's significance; you claim that what this person says or does simply does not count.

Confirmation is the opposite communication pattern. In confirmation you not only acknowledge the presence of the other person but also indicate your acceptance of this person, of this person's definition of self, and of your relationship as defined or viewed by this other person.

Disconfirmation and confirmation may be communicated in numerous ways. Table 5.1 shows just a few.

You can gain insight into a wide variety of offensive language practices by viewing them as types of disconfirmation, as language that alienates and separates. Three obvious practices are sexism, heterosexism, and racism.

Sexism

One widespread expression of sexism is **sexist language** (Kleinman, 2002; Swim et al., 2004). Sexist language puts down someone because of his or her gender and the term usually refers to language that is derogatory toward women. The National Council of Teachers of English (www.ncte.org) has proposed guidelines for nonsexist (gender-free, gender-neutral, or sex-fair) language. These guidelines concern the use of the generic word "man," the use of generic "he" and "his," and sex-role stereotyping.

Generic *Man* The word "man" refers most clearly to an adult male. To use the term to refer to both men and women emphasizes maleness at the expense of femaleness. Similarly, the terms "mankind" or "the common man" or even "cavemen" imply a primary focus on adult males. Gender-neutral terms can easily be substituted. Instead of "mankind," you can say "humanity," "people," or "human beings." Instead of "the common man," you can say "the average person" or "ordinary people." Instead of "cavemen," you can say "prehistoric people" or "cave dwellers."

Similarly, the use of terms such as "policeman" or "fireman," and other terms that presume maleness as the norm and femaleness as a deviation from this norm, are clear and common examples of sexist language. Consider using nonsexist alternatives

Self-concept is influenced by the way in which you hear yourself talked about. For example, it's been argued that sexist language will influence a woman's self-concept (Kleinman, 2002). Do you find this logical? Do you find it true to your own experiences?

TABLE 5.1	**Confirmation and Disconfirmation**

This table parallels the self-test presented on page 98 so that you can see clearly not only the confirming but also the opposite, disconfirming behaviours. As you review this table, try to imagine a specific illustration for each of the ways of communicating disconfirmation and confirmation (Pearson et al., 2003; Galvin & Brommel, 2000).

CONFIRMATION

1. Acknowledge the presence and the contributions of the other person by either supporting or taking issue with what the other says (self-test items 1 and 2).

2. Make nonverbal contact by maintaining direct eye contact, touching, hugging, kissing, or otherwise demonstrating acknowledgment of the other person. Engage in dialogue—communication in which both people are speakers and listeners, both are involved, and both are concerned with each other (items 3 and 4).

3. Demonstrate understanding of what the other person says and means and reflect these feelings to demonstrate your understanding (items 5 and 6).

4. Ask questions of the other person concerning both thoughts and feelings; acknowledge the questions of the other person; return phone calls, answer letters (items 7 and 8).

5. Encourage the other person to express thoughts and feelings, and respond directly and exclusively to what the other person says (items 9 and 10).

DISCONFIRMATION

1. Ignore the presence and the messages of the other person; express (nonverbally and verbally) indifference to anything the other says.

2. Make no nonverbal contact; avoid direct eye contact; avoid touching the other person. Engage in monologue—communication in which one person speaks and one person listens, and in which there is no real interaction, concern, or respect for the other person.

3. Jump to interpretation or evaluation rather than working at understanding what the other person means; express your own feelings, ignore feelings of the other, or give abstract intellectualized responses.

4. Make statements about yourself; ignore any lack of clarity in the other's remarks; ignore the other's requests; fail to answer questions, return phone calls, or answer letters.

5. Interrupt or otherwise make it difficult for the other to express him or herself; respond only tangentially or by shifting the focus in another direction.

for these and similar terms; make these alternatives (for example, "police officer" and "firefighter") a part of your active vocabulary. Offer alternatives for each of these terms: "man," "countryman," "manmade," "manpower," "repairman," "doorman," "fireman," "stewardess," "waitress," "salesman," "mailman," and "actress."

When asked what they would like to change about the communication style of the opposite sex, men said they wanted women to be more direct and women said they wanted men to stop interrupting and offering advice (Noble, 1994). What one change would you like to see in the communication style of the opposite sex? Of your own sex?

Generic *He* and *His*   The use of the masculine pronoun to refer to any individual regardless of sex is certainly declining. But only as recently as 1975, for example, all university textbooks used the masculine pronoun as generic. There seems to be no legitimate reason why the feminine pronoun cannot alternate with the masculine pronoun to refer to hypothetical individuals, or why phrases such as "he and she" or "her and him" cannot be used instead of just "he" or "him." Alternatively, sentences can be restructured to eliminate any reference to gender. For example, instead of saying, "The average student is worried about his marks," you may say "The average student is worried about marks."

Sex Role Stereotyping   The words you use often reflect a sex role bias—the assumption that certain roles or professions belong to men and others belong to women. To eliminate sex role stereotyping from verbal communication, avoid, for example, making the hypothetical elementary school teacher female and the college professor male. Avoid referring to doctors as male and nurses as female. Avoid noting the sex of a professional with terms such as "female doctor" or "male nurse." When you're referring to a specific doctor or nurse, the person's gender will become clear when you use the appropriate pronoun: "Dr. Smith wrote the prescription for her new patient" or "The nurse recorded the patient's temperature himself."

Heterosexism

A close relative of sexism is heterosexism—a relatively new addition to the list of linguistic prejudices. As the term implies, *heterosexism* refers to attitudes, behaviours, and language that disparage gay men and lesbians. As with racist language, **heterosexist language** includes derogatory terms used for lesbians and gay men. For example, recent surveys in the American military show that 80 percent of those surveyed heard "offensive speech, derogatory names, jokes or remarks about gays" and that 85 percent believed that such derogatory speech was "tolerated" (*New York Times*, March 25, 2000, p. A12). You also see heterosexism in more subtle forms of language usage; for example, when you qualify a professional as a "gay athlete" or "lesbian doctor," and in effect say that athletes and doctors are not normally gay or lesbian. Further, this kind of expression highlights the affectional orientation of the athlete or the doctor in a context where it may have no relevance, and doing so is the same as qualifying by gender, as already noted.

Still another instance of heterosexism—and perhaps the most difficult to deal with—is the presumption of heterosexuality. Usually, people assume that the person they're talking to or about is heterosexual—and usually they're correct, because most people are heterosexual. At the same time, however, this presumption denies the lesbian or gay identity legitimacy. The practice is very similar to the presumption of whiteness and maleness that we have made significant inroads in eliminating. For example, when a man and a woman appear together at a business meeting, it will surprise some people to learn that the woman is the boss. Here are a few additional suggestions for avoiding heterosexist, or what some would call homophobic, language.

What specialized verbal skills do politicians such as federal minister Rona Ambrose need to have? Given that so few Canadian women occupy high-level political positions, do you think Ambrose has changed her verbal communication style to increase her likelihood of success? In what ways?

- When talking about gay men and lesbians, avoid offensive nonverbal mannerisms that parody stereotypes.
- Avoid "complimenting" gay men and lesbians by saying that they "don't look it." To gay men and lesbians, this is not a compliment. Similarly, expressing disappointment that a person is gay with comments such as "What a waste!" is not really a compliment, although they're sometimes meant as such.
- Avoid making the assumption that every gay or lesbian knows what every other gay or lesbian is thinking. Such an assumption is very similar to asking a Japanese person why Sony is investing heavily in Canada, or asking an African American, "How long do you think Shaquille O'Neal will continue playing in the NBA?"
- Avoid denying individual differences. Saying things like "Lesbians are so loyal" or "Gay men are so open with their feelings," ignores the reality of wide differences within any group and is potentially insulting to all groups.

In what ways does this photo comment on sex role stereotyping? What interpersonal communication problems (if any) would you anticipate that these firefighters might have?

- Avoid overattribution, the tendency to attribute just about everything a person does, says, and believes to the fact that the person is gay or lesbian. This tendency helps to recall and perpetuate stereotypes (see Chapter 3).
- Remember that relationship milestones are important to all people. Ignoring anniversaries or the birthday of a relative's partner is resented by everyone.

Racism

According to Andrea Rich (1974), "any language that, through a conscious or unconscious attempt by the user, places a particular racial or ethnic group in an inferior position is racist." **Racist language** expresses racist attitudes. It also, however, contributes to the development of racist attitudes in those who use or hear the language. Even when racism is subtle, unintentional, or even unconscious, its effects are systematically damaging (Dovidio et al., 2002).

Members of one culture use racist terms to disparage members of other cultures, their customs, or their accomplishments. Racist language emphasizes differences rather than similarities and separates rather than unites members of different cultures. Generally, the dominant group uses racist language to establish and maintain power over other groups. The social consequences of racist language in terms of employment, education, housing opportunities, and general community acceptance are well known.

Many people feel that it's permissible for members of a culture to refer to themselves in racist terms. That is, Asians may use negative terms referring to Asians, Italians may use negative terms referring to Italians, and so on. This practice is seen clearly in rap music, in which performers use derogatory racial terms (*New York Times*, January 24, 1993, pp. 1, 31). The reasoning seems to be that groups should be able to laugh at themselves.

It's interesting to note that terms denoting some of the major movements in art—for example, "impressionism" and "cubism"—were originally applied negatively. The terms were then adopted by the artists themselves and eventually became positive. A parallel can be seen in the use of the word "queer" by some lesbian and gay organizations that use the term in an effort to diminish its negative connotation.

❝ Many interviewers, when they come to talk to me, think they're being progressive by not mentioning in their stories any longer that I'm black. I tell them, "Don't stop now. If I shot somebody you'd mention it." ❞

—Colin Powell

Consider this situation: An instructor at your school persists in calling the female students "girls," refers to gay men and lesbians as "queers," and refers to various racial groups with terms that most people would consider inappropriate. When told that these terms are offensive, the instructor claims the right to free speech and argues that to prevent instructors from using such terms would be a restriction on free speech, which would be a far greater wrong than being culturally or politically incorrect. How would you comment on this argument?

One possible problem, though, is that such terms may not lose their negative connotations and may simply reinforce the negative stereotypes that society has already assigned to certain groups. By using these terms, members may come to accept the labels with their negative connotations and thus contribute to their own stereotyping.

The point has often been made that there are aspects of language that may be inherently racist (Davis, 1973; Bosmajian, 1974). For example, one examination of English found 134 synonyms for "white." Of these, 44 had positive connotations (for example, "clean," "chaste," and "unblemished"), and only 10 had negative connotations (for example, "whitewash" and "pale"). The remaining synonyms were relatively neutral. Of the 120 synonyms for "black," 60 had unfavourable connotations ("unclean," "foreboding," and "deadly"), and none had positive connotations.

Ageism

Ageism is discrimination based on age. One researcher offers a more comprehensive definition: "any attitude, action, or institutional structure which subordinates a person or group because of age or any assignment of roles in society purely on the basis of age" (Traxler, 1980). In North America and throughout much of the industrialized world, ageism signifies discrimination against the old and against aging in general. But ageism can also refer to prejudice against other age groups. For example, if you describe all teenagers as selfish and undependable, you're discriminating against a group purely because of their age and, thus, you are ageist in your statements. In some cultures—some Asian and some African cultures, for example—the old are revered and respected. Younger people seek them out for advice on economic, ethical, and relationship issues.

Popular language is replete with examples of ageist phrases: "little old lady," "old hag," "old-timer," "over the hill," "old coot," and "old fogy" are just some examples. As with sexism, qualifying a description of someone in terms of his or her age demonstrates ageism. For example, if you refer to "a quick-witted 75-year-old" or "an agile 65-year-old" or "a responsible teenager," you are implying that these qualities are unusual in people of these ages and thus need special mention. You're saying that "quick-wittedness" and "being 75" do not normally go together; you imply the same abnormality for "agility" and "being 65," and for "responsibility" and "being a teenager." The problem with this kind of stereotyping is that it's simply wrong. There are many 75-year-olds who are extremely quick-witted—and many 30-year-olds who aren't.

You also communicate ageism when you speak to older people in overly simple words or explain things that don't need explaining. Nonverbally, you demonstrate ageist communication when, for example, you avoid touching an older person but touch others, or when you avoid making direct eye contact with the older person but readily do so with others. Also, it's a mistake to speak to an older person at an overly high volume; this suggests that all older people have hearing difficulties, and it tends to draw attention to the fact that you are talking down to the older person.

Of course, the media perpetuate ageist stereotypes by depicting older people as unproductive, complaining, and unromantic. Rarely, for example, do television or films show older people working productively, being cooperative and pleasant, and engaging in romantic and sexual relationships.

One useful way to avoid ageism is to recognize and avoid the illogical stereotypes that ageist language is based on. Do you

- avoid talking down to a person because he or she is older? Older people are not mentally slow; most people remain mentally alert well into old age.
- refrain from refreshing an older person's memory each time you see the person? Older people can and do remember things.
- avoid implying that relationships are no longer important? Older people continue to be interested in relationships.

STUDY TIP

In a small group, identify some of the popular stereotypes that older people use to characterize younger people. How might some of these stereotypes be dispelled?

Disconfirmation: Denying Others' Significance

- Sexism: derogatory behaviour or language toward one sex (usually women)
- Heterosexism: assuming that all people are heterosexual
- Racism: conscious or unconscious attempt to place a racial or ethnic group in an inferior position
- Ageism: discrimination based on age

- speak at a normal volume and maintain a normal physical distance? Being older does not mean being hard of hearing or being unable to see; most older people hear and see quite well, sometimes with hearing aids or glasses.
- engage older people in conversation as you would wish to be engaged? Older people are interested in the world around them.

Even though you want to avoid ageist communication, there are times when you may wish to make adjustments when talking with someone who does have language or communication difficulties. The American Speech and Hearing Association offers several useful suggestions (www.asha.org, accessed January 31, 2003):

- Reduce as much background noise as you can.
- Ease into the conversation by beginning with casual topics and then moving into more familiar topics. Stay with each topic for a while; avoid jumping too quickly from one topic to another.
- Speak in relatively short sentences and questions.
- Give the person added time to respond. Some older people react more slowly and need extra time.
- Listen actively. Practise the skills of active listening discussed in the previous chapter.

Cultural Identifiers

Perhaps the best way to avoid sexism, heterosexism, and racism in language is to examine the preferred cultural identifiers to use (and not to use) in talking about members of different cultures. As always, when in doubt, find out. The preferences and many of the specific examples identified here are drawn largely from the findings of the Task Force on Bias-Free Language of the Association of American University Presses (Schwartz, 1995). Realize that not everyone would agree with these recommendations; they're presented here—in the words of the Task Force—"to encourage sensitivity to usages that may be imprecise, misleading, and needlessly offensive" (Schwartz, 1995). They're not presented so that you can "catch" someone being politically incorrect or label someone culturally insensitive.

Generally: The term "girl" is equivalent to "boy" and should be used only to refer to a very young female. Neither term should be used for people older than, say, 13 or 14. "Girl" is never used to refer to a grown woman, nor is "boy" used to refer to people in blue-collar positions, as it once was. Many people evaluate the term "lady" negatively, because it connotes the stereotype of the prim and proper woman. "Woman" or "young woman" is preferred. "Older person" is preferred to "elder," "elderly," "senior," or "senior citizen" (technically, someone older than 65). However, some cultures use "elder" to describe respected or revered members of their communities, and the term often connotes a position of influence or prestige.

Generally: "Gay" is the preferred term for a man who has an affectional preference for other men, and "lesbian" is the preferred term for a woman who has an affectional preference for other women. ("Lesbian" means "homosexual woman," so the phrase "lesbian woman" is redundant.) This preference for the term "lesbian" is not universal among homosexual women, however; in one survey, for example, 58 percent preferred "lesbian," but 34 percent preferred "gay" (Lever, 1995). "Homosexual" refers to both gay men and lesbians, but more often merely denotes an affectional orientation to members of one's own sex. "Gay" and "lesbian" refer to a lifestyle and not simply to sexual orientation. "Gay" as a noun, although widely used, may prove offensive in some contexts; for example, "We have two gays on the team." And the term "queer," although used within the gay community in an effort to remove the negative stigma through frequent usage—as in "queer power"—is often resented in the gay community when used by outsiders. Because most scientific thinking holds that one's sexuality is genetically determined rather than a matter of choice, the term "sexual orientation" rather than "sexual preference" or "sexual status" (which is also vague) is preferred.

Generally: Most African Americans prefer "African American" to "black" (Hecht et al., 1993), though "black" is often used with "white" and is often used in a variety of other contexts (for example, Department of Black and Puerto Rican Studies, *Journal of Black History*, and Black History Month). In Canada, the term "black" is considered acceptable by members of those communities.

Generally: "White" is used to refer to people whose roots are in European cultures. Some Canadians prefer their national origins to be emphasized, such as "German Canadian" or "Greek Canadian."

"Inuk" (plural, "Inuit") was officially adopted at the Inuit Circumpolar Conference to refer to the indigenous peoples of Alaska, Northern Canada, Greenland, and Eastern Siberia. These terms have been preferred to "Eskimo" in Canada for several years. "Eskimo" was applied to the indigenous peoples of the north by Europeans and derives from a word that means "raw meat eaters" (Maggio, 1997). "Inuk" is also preferred in the United States, although the term "Eskimo" or "Native Alaskan" is still used by the U.S. Census Bureau.

"Indian" refers to someone from India and is incorrectly used when applied to members of other Asian countries. In general, "Indian" is no longer an appropriate term for the indigenous or native peoples of the Americas. "Aboriginal" or the name of the specific tribe or band is preferred; in Canada, "First Nations" is the most commonly accepted term for non-Inuit and non-Métis peoples (Métis are a distinct group descended from both Natives and Europeans). Note that many Native people self-identify as "Indians," and in Canada, "Indian" is a legal term for Native peoples in regards to government status and treaties.

"Muslim" is the preferred form (rather than the older "Moslem") to refer to a person who adheres to the religious teachings of Islam. The terms "Mohammedan" or "Mohammedanism" are not considered appropriate; they imply worship of Muhammad, the prophet, which is "considered by Muslims to be a blasphemy against the absolute oneness of God" (Maggio, 1997).

Although there is no universal agreement, "Jewish people" is thought to be preferable to "Jews"; and "Jewess" (to refer to a Jewish female) is considered derogatory. However, this preference may be due to anti-Jewish propaganda that gave the term "Jew" a negative association. In fact, calling someone "a Jew" should be no different than calling someone "a Christian" or "a Muslim."

Visit www.statcan.ca. Look up your own city and cities you've visited or hope to visit, and examine their cultural makeup. What labels are used for the various cultural groups? Are these labels consistent or at variance with the cultural identifiers suggested in this chapter?

What cultural identifiers do you prefer? Have these preferences changed over time? How can you let other people know the designations that you want or don't want to be used to refer to you? An interesting exercise—especially in a large and multicultural class—is for each student to write anonymously his or her preferred cultural identification on an index card and have the cards read aloud.

The Active Living Alliance for Canadians with a Disability (www.ala.ca) suggests the use of the following principle when referring to a person who has a disability: Describe the person first, then the impairment, but only if it is relevant to the conversation. (When discussing that Aileen has won the lottery, it may not be necessary to indicate that Aileen is a person with a disability.) Instead of "handicapped," use "person with a disability"; replace "deaf and dumb" with "person with a hearing impairment"; and avoid "retarded" or "mentally retarded" and substitute "person with an intellectual impairment." Can you think of other examples?

Since history was written from a European perspective, Europe was taken as the focal point, and the rest of the world was defined in terms of its location relative to that continent. Thus, Asia became "the East" or "the Orient," and Asians became "Orientals"—a term that is today considered inappropriate and "Eurocentric." People from Asia are "Asians," just as people from Africa are "Africans" and people from Europe are "Europeans."

USING VERBAL MESSAGES EFFECTIVELY AND CRITICALLY

A chief concern when using verbal messages is to recognize what critical thinking theorists call "conceptual distortions": mental mistakes, misinterpretations, or reasoning fallacies. Avoiding these distortions and substituting a more critical, more realistic analysis is probably the best way to improve your own use of verbal messages.

Messages Symbolize Reality (Partially)

Language symbolizes reality; it's not the reality itself. Of course, this is obvious. But consider: Have you ever reacted to the way something was labelled or described rather than to the actual item? Have you ever bought something because of its name rather than because of the actual object? If so, you were probably responding as if language were reality, a distortion called intensional orientation (the "s" in "intensional" is intentional).

Orientation **Intensional orientation** refers to our tendency to view people, objects, and events in the way they're talked about—the way they're labelled. For example, if Nila were labelled "uninteresting," you would, responding intensionally, evaluate her as uninteresting even before listening to what she had to say. You'd see Nila through a filter imposed by the label "uninteresting." **Extensional orientation**, on the other hand, is the tendency to look first at the actual people, objects, and events, and only afterwards at their labels. In Nila's case, it would mean looking at her without any preconceived labels, guided by what she says and does, not by the words used to label her.

Remember that language symbolizes only a part of reality, never the whole. Whatever someone says—regardless of what it is or how extensive it is—is only part of the story.

> " It is not only true that the language we use puts words in our mouths; it also puts notions in our heads. "
>
> —Wendell Johnson

Skills Toolbox | Using Your Vocal Qualities

"Don't speak to me in that tone of voice!" is a familiar comment in interpersonal conflict. Your tone of voice often has more impact than your actual words, communicating an important part of you and your personality to others.

Language can be interpreted in different ways, but through the use of vocal qualities you can clarify the intent of your message and communicate your feelings, likes, and dislikes. By varying tone, you can reinforce what you are saying verbally.

Below are some tips for effective use of tone:

1. Speak naturally and at ease, rather than adopting vocal qualities that do not fit who you are.
2. Show enthusiasm by using the appropriate pitch, volume, and inflection.
3. Project strong, full, but not overwhelming resonance.
4. Use your mouth and lips to enunciate clearly and distinctly.
5. Be interesting by varying your vocal qualities—avoid speaking in a monotone voice.
6. Watch for signals from those who are listening, and adapt your volume, speed, and tone accordingly.

THEN AND NOW

Have you ever found yourself communicating one message with your words and an entirely different message with your tone of voice? Which message was the one you really meant—the one said with your words or with the tone of your voice? How was your message received? How do you use your voice now to more effectively communicate what you mean?

A weasel is a slippery beast: just when you think you're going to catch it, it slips away. Weasel words are words whose meanings are difficult to pin down, words that allow the speaker to weasel out of an implied commitment or agreement (Larson, 1998; Wrighter, 1972). For example, a medicine that claims to work better than Brand X doesn't specify how much better or in what respect it performs better. Is it possible that it is better in one respect and less effective on nine other measures? "Better" is a weasel word. "Like" is another word often used for weaselling, as when a claim is made that "Brand X will make you feel like a new man" or—with the "like" only

implied—that "Brand X makes you feel young again." Exactly what these claims mean in specific terms would be impossible to pin down. Other weasel words are "helped," "virtually," "as much as," and "more economical." Try looking for weasel words; you'll often find them lurking in the promises of advertisers and politicians.

EXAMPLES?

Choose an advertisement in a recent newspaper or magazine or on the net that uses weasel words. What effect does the advertiser hope these words will have on the reader?

Lying occurs when "one person intends to mislead another, doing so deliberately, without prior notification of this purpose, and without having been explicitly asked to do so by the target [the person the liar intends to mislead]" (Ekman, 1985b). Lying and deception occur on a daily basis (Scholl & O'Hair, 2005), yet research shows that most individuals are very poor lie detectors (Lock, 2004). Although lying usually involves overt statements, it may also be committed by omission: When you omit something relevant, leading others to draw incorrect inferences, you're lying just as surely as if you had stated an untruth. Similarly, although most lies are verbal, some are nonverbal. Both the innocent facial expression— despite the commission of some wrong—and the knowing nod instead of the honest expression of ignorance are common examples of nonverbal lying (O'Hair et al., 1981). Lies may range from the "white lie" in which you "just stretch the truth" to lies that form the basis of relationship infidelity, libel, and perjury. And, not surprisingly, lies have ethical implications.

Some lies are considered innocent, acceptable, and generally ethical (for example, lying to a child to protect a

belief in Santa Claus or the Tooth Fairy; telling people who look terrible that they look great; or publicly agreeing with someone just to enable the person to save face). Other lies are considered unacceptable and generally unethical (for example, lying to defraud investors, to falsely accuse someone of a crime, or to get out of paying your fair share of income tax). Still other lies, however, aren't so easy to classify as ethical or unethical.

WHAT WOULD YOU DO?

You've been called for jury duty but really don't want to serve. You've served before and have never been empanelled for a trial—you suspect it's because you teach critical thinking courses. So rather than spend two weeks in a jury room for no reason, you wonder if it would be ethical to lie and say that your invalid mother can't do without you (even though, in fact, your sister could easily fill in for you). Would it be ethical to lie under these circumstances? What would you do in this situation?

Messages Express Facts and Inferences

You can construct statements of both fact and inference without making any linguistic distinction between the two. Similarly, when you articulate or listen to such statements, you often don't make a clear distinction between statements of fact and statements of inference. Yet there are great differences between the two. Barriers to clear thinking can be created when inferences are treated as facts, a tendency called **fact–inference confusion**.

For example, you can say, "She's wearing a blue jacket," and you can say, "He's harbouring an illogical hatred." Although the sentences have similar structures, they're different. You can observe the jacket and the blue colour, but how do you observe "illogical hatred"? Obviously, this is not a **factual statement** but rather an **inferential statement**, one made on the basis not only of what you observed but also what you inferred. For a statement to be considered factual, it must be made by the observer after observation and must be limited to what is observed (Weinberg, 1959).

There is nothing wrong with making inferential statements. You must make them to talk about much that is meaningful to you. Problems arise when you act as if those inferential statements are factual. You may test your ability to distinguish facts from inferences by taking the self-test below (based on tests constructed by Haney, 1973).

Test Yourself

Can You Distinguish Facts from Inferences?

Instructions: Carefully read the following report and the observations based on it. Indicate whether you think, on the basis of the information presented in the report, that the observations are true, false, or doubtful. Write T if the observation is definitely true, F if the observation is definitely false, and "?" if the observation may be either true or false. Judge the observations in order. Do not reread the observations after you have indicated your judgment, and do not change any of your answers.

A well-liked college teacher had just completed making up the final examinations and had turned off the lights in the office. Just then a tall, broad figure with dark glasses appeared and demanded the examination. The professor opened the drawer. Everything in the drawer was picked up and the individual ran down the corridor. The dean was notified immediately.

_____ ❶ The thief was tall and broad and wore dark glasses.

_____ ❷ The professor turned off the lights.

_____ ❸ A tall figure demanded the examination.

_____ ❹ The examination was picked up by someone.

_____ ❺ The examination was picked up by the professor.

_____ ❻ A tall, broad figure appeared after the professor turned off the lights in the office.

_____ ❼ The man who opened the drawer was the professor.

_____ ❽ The professor ran down the corridor.

_____ ❾ The drawer was never actually opened.

_____ ❿ Three persons are referred to in this report.

HOW DID YOU DO?

After you answer all 10 questions, form small groups of five or six and discuss the answers. Look at each statement from each member's point of view. For each statement, ask yourself, "How can you be absolutely certain that the statement is true or false?" You should find that only one statement can be clearly identified as true and only one as false; eight should be marked "?"

WHAT WILL YOU DO?

As you read this chapter, try to formulate specific guidelines that will help you distinguish facts from inferences.

To avoid fact–inference confusion, phrase inferential statements not as factual but as tentative. Recognize that they may prove to be wrong. Inferential statements should leave open the possibility of alternatives. If, for example, you treat the statement "Our biology teacher was fired for poor teaching" as factual, you eliminate any alternatives. When making inferential statements, be psychologically prepared to be proved wrong. If you're prepared to be wrong, you will be less hurt if you're shown to be wrong. Be especially sensitive to this distinction when you're listening. Most talk is inferential. Beware of the speaker who presents everything as fact. Analyze closely and you'll uncover a world of inferences.

Messages Are Relatively Static

Language changes only very slowly, especially when compared with the rapid changes in people and things. **Static evaluation** is the tendency to retain evaluations without change, even if the reality to which they refer is changing. Often a verbal statement you make about an event or person remains static ("That's the way he is; he's always been that way") while the event or person may change enormously.

> 66 A word is not a crystal, transparent and unchanged, it is the skin of a living thought and may vary greatly in color and content according to the circumstances and the time in which it is used. 99
>
> —Oliver Wendell Holmes

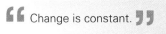

> **"** Change is constant. **"**
>
> —Benjamin Disraeli

While you'd probably agree that everything is in a constant state of flux, do you act as if you know this? Do you act in accordance with the notion of change or just accept it intellectually? Do you realize, for example, that even if you've failed at something once, you need not fail again? Your evaluations of yourself and of others must keep pace with the rapidly changing real world; otherwise your attitudes and beliefs will be about a world that no longer exists.

Messages Can Obscure Distinctions

Messages can obscure distinctions, both by generalizing about people or events that are covered by the same label but are really quite different (indiscrimination), and by making it easy to focus on extremes rather than on the vast middle ground (polarization).

How does indiscrimination operate in intercultural communication? Can you provide specific examples you've witnessed?

Indiscrimination   Each word in the language can refer to a lot of things; words such as "teacher" or "textbook" or "computer program" refer to a wide variety of specific people and things. When you allow the general term to obscure the specific differences (say, among teachers or among textbooks), you're into a pattern called indiscrimination.

Indiscrimination refers to the failure to distinguish between similar but different people, objects, or events. It occurs when you focus on classes and fail to see that each phenomenon is unique and needs to be looked at individually.

Everything is unlike everything else. Our language, however, provides you with common nouns such as "teacher," "student," "friend," "enemy," "war," "politician," and "liberal." These words lead you to focus on similarities—to group together all teachers, all students, all politicians. At the same time, the terms divert attention away from the uniqueness of each person, each object, and each event.

Misevaluation is at the heart of stereotyping on the basis of nationality, race, religion, gender, and affectional orientation. A stereotype, you'll remember from Chapter 3, is a fixed mental picture of a group that is applied to each individual in the group without regard to his or her unique qualities.

Most stereotypes are negative and denigrate the group to which they refer. Some, however, are positive. A particularly popular example is the stereotype of Asian Canadian students as successful, intelligent, and hardworking.

Whether stereotypes are positive or negative, they create the same problem: They provide you with shortcuts that are often inappropriate. For instance, when you meet a particular person, your first reaction may be to pigeonhole her into some category—perhaps religious, national, or academic ("She's a typical academic: never

In-Class Notes

Fact–Inference Confusion Occurs When

- inferences are treated as fact.
- statements are made based on observation and inferences.
- factual statements are not based on observed facts only.
- inferential statements are not recognized as important to establish what is meaningful.

_____

_____

_____

_____

_____

_____

_____

_____

thinks of the real world"). Then you assign to this person all the qualities that are part of your stereotype. Regardless of the category you use or the specific qualities you're ready to assign, you fail to give sufficient attention to the individual's unique characteristics. Two people may both be Christian, Asian, and lesbian, for example, but each will be different from the other. Indiscrimination is a denial of another's uniqueness.

A useful antidote to indiscrimination (and stereotyping) is the **index**. This mental subscript identifies each individual as an individual, even though each may be covered by the same label. Thus, politician$_1$ is not politician$_2$; teacher$_1$ is not teacher$_2$. The index helps you to discriminate among without *discriminating against*. Although the label "politician," for example, covers all politicians, the index makes sure that each politician is thought about as an individual.

Polarization   Another way in which language can obscure differences is in the predominance of extreme terms and the relative lack of middle terms, a situation that often leads to **polarization**. You can appreciate the role language plays in fostering polarization by identifying the opposites of the following terms: "happy," "long," "wealth," "life," "healthy," "up," "left," "legal," "heavy," "strong." This should have been relatively easy; you probably identified the opposites very quickly. Now identify the middle terms, the terms referring to the middle ground between the terms and the opposites you supplied. These terms are likely more difficult to come up with and took more time and effort. Further, if you compare your responses with those of others, you'll find that most people agree on the opposites; most people would have said "unhappy," "short," "poverty," and so on. But when it comes to the middle terms, the degree of agreement will be much less. Thus, language makes it easy to focus on opposites and relatively difficult to talk about the middle areas.

Polarization, then, is the tendency to look at the world in terms of opposites and to describe it in extremes—good or bad, positive or negative, healthy or sick, intelligent or stupid. Polarization is often referred to as the fallacy of "either/or" or "black and white." Most of life exists somewhere between the extremes. Yet there's a strong tendency to view only the extremes and to categorize people, objects, and events in terms of these polar opposites.

Problems are created when opposites are used in inappropriate situations. For example, "The politician is either for us or against us." These options do not include all possibilities. The politician may be for us in some things and against us in other things, or may be neutral. When relating to the Gulf War in Iraq, people were categorized as

STUDY TIP

Draw a horizontal line with the word "young" at one end, and "old" at the other. Identify and write down the middle terms that you feel belong between these poles. Compare the middle terms you use with those of a classmate. What do you notice?

In-Class Notes

Polarization

- the tendency to look at the word in terms of opposites and extremes
- the fallacy of either/or and black/white statements
- inappropriate use of opposites
- implying that there are only two sides to a problem—failure to look for middle ground

either hawks or doves. But clearly many people were neither, and many were hawks on certain issues and doves on others.

To correct this tendency to polarize, beware of implying (and believing) that two extreme classes include all possible classes—that an individual must be one or the other, with no alternatives ("Are you pro-choice or pro-life?"). Most people, most events, and most qualities exist between polar extremes. When others imply that there are only two sides or two alternatives, look for the middle ground.

Summary of Concepts and Skills

In this chapter we considered verbal messages: the nature of language and the ways in which language works; the concept of disconfirmation and how it relates to sexist, heterosexist, and racist language; and the ways in which language can be used more effectively.

1. Language meanings are in people, not in things.

2. Meanings are context based; the same message in a different context will likely mean something different.

3. Language is both denotative (conveying meanings that are objective and generally agreed upon) and connotative (conveying meanings that are subjective and generally highly individual).

4. Language varies in directness; you can use language to state exactly what you mean or to hedge and state your meaning very indirectly.

5. Language is a cultural institution; each culture has its own rules identifying the ways in which language should be used.

6. Language varies in abstraction; words can vary from extremely general to extremely specific.

7. Disconfirmation is the process of ignoring the presence and the communications of others. Confirmation is accepting, supporting, and acknowledging the importance of the other person.

8. Sexist, heterosexist, and racist language puts down and negatively evaluates various cultural groups.

9. Using language effectively involves eliminating conceptual distortions and substituting more accurate assumptions about language, the most important of which are:

   ■ Language symbolizes reality; it's not the reality itself.

   ■ Language can express both facts and inferences, and distinctions need to be made between them.

   ■ Language is relatively static, and because reality changes so rapidly, you need to constantly revise the way you talk about people and things.

■ Language can obscure distinctions in its use of general terms and in its emphasis on extreme rather than middle terms.

Check Your Ability

The nature of language, disconfirmation, and popular conceptual distortions has important implications for effective communication skills. Check your ability to apply these skills. Use a rating scale such as the following: 1 = almost always, 2 = often, 3 = sometimes, 4 = rarely, and 5 = hardly ever.

_____ ❶ I recognize that meaning is in people and not in things and I therefore focus on what the person means as well as what the words mean.

_____ ❷ I look for both the connotative and the denotative meanings when listening.

_____ ❸ I recognize cultural and gender differences in the rules for using language; each culture has its own rules, which must be recognized and taken into consideration if communication is to be effective.

_____ ❹ I am generally confirming in my communications and acknowledge others and their contributions.

_____ ❺ I avoid disconfirmation through sexist, heterosexist, and racist language.

_____ ❻ I avoid responding (intensionally) to labels as if they're objects; instead, I respond extensionally and look first at the reality and only then at the words.

_____ ❼ I distinguish facts from inferences and respond to inferences with tentativeness.

_____ ❽ I avoid indiscrimination by treating each person and situation as unique.

_____ ❾ I avoid polarization by using "middle ground" terms and qualifiers in describing the world and especially people.

After completing this self-test, check your answers against the Answer Key at the back of the book.

Multiple Choice Questions *Choose the BEST answer.*

1. Looking at the world in extremes (good and bad, rich or poor, etc.) is
   a. prejudicial.
   b. magnetism.
   c. polarization.
   d. intensional orientation.

2. Inferences
   a. should be separated from facts.
   b. are generally not helpful.
   c. seldom occur.
   d. do not involve conclusions.

3. An example of tentative language is
   a. "the only effective way."
   b. "so far as I know."
   c. "everyone knows."
   d. "it's obvious."

4. Static evaluation is
   a. the denial of change.
   b. a member of the clergy.
   c. clothes dryer cling.
   d. an electrical discharge.

5. Meanings may include
   a. ideas.
   b. attitudes.
   c. feelings.
   d. all of the above.

6. Connotation is
   a. the feelings or emotions evoked by a word.
   b. the dictionary meaning of a word.
   c. the perception of meaning.
   d. none of the above.

7. Denotation is
   a. the feelings evoked by a word.
   b. the dictionary meaning of a word.
   c. the perception of meaning.
   d. all of the above.

8. A pattern in which you ignore someone's presence as well as their communication is
   a. abstraction.
   b. direct communication.
   c. indirect communication.
   d. disconfirmation.

9. Ignoring or denying change in communication and meaning is
   a. abstraction.
   b. static communication.
   c. indirect communication.
   d. direct communication.

10. Racism
    a. is a common language perception.
    b. has denotative power.
    c. places a racial or ethnic group in an inferior position.
    d. implies polarization.

True–False Questions *Write a T or F in the blank next to the statement.*

1. _____ Meanings are in people, not words.

2. _____ Meanings depend on denotation.

3. _____ Language is both connotative and demonstrative.

4. _____ Polarization describes the world in terms of intensity.

5. _____ Labels encourage intensional orientation.

6. _____ Indiscrimination groups people or things without seeing uniqueness.

7. _____ Abstract language is a form of indirectness.

8. _____ Denotative language is the dictionary meaning of language.

9. _____ Communication is the process in which you reconstruct in someone else's mind what is in your mind.

10. _____ Meanings are in words, not people.

Vocabulary Quiz
The Language of Language

Match these terms about language with their definitions. Record the number of the definition next to the term.

a. _____ polarization

b. _____ intensional orientation

c. _____ connotative meaning

d. _____ fact–inference confusion

e. _____ confirmation

f. _____ static evaluation

g. _____ indiscrimination

h. _____ sexist language

i. _____ level of abstraction

j. _____ netiquette

1. Treating inferences as if they were facts.

2. The denial of change in language and in thinking.

3. The emotional, subjective aspect of meaning.

4. A communication pattern in which we acknowledge the

presence of and signal the acceptance of another person.

5. The rules for polite communication on the internet.

6. The degree of generality or specificity of a term.

7. Language derogatory to one sex, generally to women.

8. The failure to see the differences among people or things covered by the same label.

9. A focus on the way things are talked about rather than on the way they exist in the world.

10. An almost exclusive focus on extremes, often to the neglect or omission of the vast middle ground.

Skill Building Exercises

5.1 Climbing the Abstraction Ladder

The abstraction ladder is a device used to illustrate the different levels of abstraction on which different terms exist. In Figure 5.1 (see page 95), notice that as you go from "animal" to "pampered white toy poodle," your meaning is becoming less abstract—you're getting more and more specific. As you get more specific, you more clearly communicate your own meanings and more easily direct the listener's attention to what you wish. For each of the general terms listed below, provide at least four possible terms that indicate increasing specificity. The first example is done for you.

Level 1	Level 2 *more specific than 1*	Level 3 *more specific than 2*	Level 4 *more specific than 3*	Level 5 *more specific than 4*
house	mansion	brick mansion	large brick mansion	CEO's mansion
desire	_____	_____	_____	_____
car	_____	_____	_____	_____
toy	_____	_____	_____	_____
magazine	_____	_____	_____	_____
sports	_____	_____	_____	_____

Thinking Critically About Abstractions.

The general suggestion for effective communication is to use abstractions sparingly and to express your meanings specifically. However, are there situations in which terms high in abstraction would be more effective than specific terms? How would you describe advertisements for cosmetics in terms of high and low abstraction? Ads for cereals? Ads for cat and dog food? How would you describe political campaign speaking in terms of abstraction?

5.2 Confirming, Rejecting, and Disconfirming

Classify the various responses to the following scenarios as confirmation, rejection, or disconfirmation. Then develop original scenarios and examples of all three types of responses.

1. Enrique receives this semester's marks in the mail; they're a lot better than previous semesters' marks, but they're still not great. After opening the letter, Enrique says: "I really tried hard to get my marks up this semester." Enrique's parents respond:

_____ Going out every night hardly seems like trying very hard.

_____ What should we have for dinner?

_____ Keep up the good work.

_____ I can't believe you've really tried your best; how can you study with the stereo blasting in your ears?

_____ I'm sure you've tried really hard.

_____ That's great.

_____ What a rotten day I had at the office.

_____ I can remember when I was in school; I got all Bs without ever opening a book.

2. Pat, who has been out of work for the past several weeks, says: "I feel like such a failure; I just can't seem to find a job. I've been pounding the pavement for the last five weeks and still nothing." Pat's friend responds:

_____ I know you've been trying really hard.

_____ You really should get more training so you'd be able to sell yourself more effectively.

_____ I told you a hundred times you need that university degree.

_____ I've got to go to the dentist on Friday. Boy, do I hate that.

_____ The employment picture is bleak at this time of the year, but your qualifications are really impressive. Something will come up soon.

_____ You're not a failure. You just can't find a job.

_____ What do you need a job for? Stay home and keep house. After all, Chris makes more than enough money for you to live in style.

_____ What's five weeks?

_____ Well, you'll just have to try harder.

Thinking Critically About Confirmation, Rejection, and Disconfirmation.

Generally, communication experts would advise you to be more confirming than disconfirming. Can you identify situations where disconfirmation would be a more effective response than confirmation? Are there situations when confirmation would be inappropriate?

Provide examples of a confirmatory, rejecting, and disconfirmatory response to your friend's statement: "I haven't had a date in the last four months. I'm getting really depressed over this." Another example: Your friend tells you of relationship problems: "Rani and I just can't seem to get along any more. Every day is a hassle. Every day there's another conflict, another battle. I feel like walking away from the whole mess."

5.3 "Must Lie" Situations

In an episode of _Seinfeld,_ the group visits a friend who has just had a baby—the ugliest baby anyone has ever seen. But everyone, of course, tells the parents the baby is beautiful, even "breathtaking." It's a "must lie" situation, the group agrees; and anyway, the parents will never know that their baby is not only not beautiful but also downright ugly. Can you identify other "must lie" situations—situations in which lying seems the only socially acceptable response? Try recording these, using the following chart:

Liar: Who must lie?	Situation: What is the occasion that prompts the "must lie" situation?	Target: Who is the person who must be lied to?	Pupose: What is the purpose of the lie? What would happen if the truth were told? What does the liar hope to achieve by lying?
1. _____	_____	_____	_____
2. _____	_____	_____	_____
3. _____	_____	_____	_____
4. _____	_____	_____	_____
5. _____	_____	_____	_____

Thinking Critically About "Must Lie" Situations.

What ethical issues are involved in such situations? That is, can any of these lies be considered unethical? Can the failure to lie in any of these situations be considered unethical?

Web Explorations

Companion Website

Visit the Companion Website at www.pearsoned.ca/devito for student resources related to this chapter, including self-grading quizzes, additional skill-building exercises, and links to other on-line resources.

Research Navigator

Explore our research resources at www.researchnavigator.com:

■ Find and read an article on meaning or messages (for example, on message directness, language, confirmation or disconfirmation, sexism, heterosexism, ageism, racism, hate speech, or the relationship of language and culture). On the basis of this article, what can you add to the discussion presented here?

■ Use the article you find to investigate one of the key terms discussed in this chapter (for example, meaning, message, abstraction, denotation and connotation, directness, intensional orientation, polarization, language, symbols, disconfirmation, racism, sexism, or heterosexism. What additional insights can you provide?

■ Try finding answers to one of the following questions, or design a research study to answer it.

1. Do men and women follow different rules for politeness in, say, conversation? In business?

2. How is politically incorrect language dealt with in the workplace?

3. How is disconfirmation used in internet communication?

4. What are the effects of using racist, sexist, heterosexist, and ageist language on campus?

Chapter 6
Nonverbal Messages

Chapter Topics

This chapter introduces the nonverbal message system: the way you communicate without words.

The Functions of Nonverbal Messages

The Channels of Nonverbal Messages

Culture and Nonverbal Messages

Chapter Skills

After completing this chapter, you should be able to:

- use nonverbal messages in conjunction with verbal messages to serve a variety of functions.

- use a wide variety of nonverbal communication forms to encode and decode meanings.

- use nonverbal behaviours with an awareness of cultural differences and influences.

In a communications class at the University of Guelph, the instructor asks, "Would anyone like to respond to the question in Chapter 9?" Mohammed, sitting in the front row, energetically puts up his hand. Dana, sitting in the back, slides down in her seat and looks at the floor.

In this example, you see the powerful messages communicated without words. In this chapter we look at these nonverbal messages—the ways they function in conjunction with verbal messages, the types or channels of nonverbal messages, and the cultural variations in nonverbal communication.

Nonverbal communication is communication without words. You communicate nonverbally when you gesture, smile or frown, widen your eyes, move your chair closer to someone, wear jewellery, touch someone, raise your vocal volume, or even say nothing. The crucial aspect is that the message you send is in some way received by at least one other person. Most theorists would argue that if you gesture while you are alone in your room and no one is there to see you, then communication has not taken place. The same is true of verbal messages, of course; if you recite a speech and no one hears it, then communication has not taken place.

Competence in nonverbal communication can yield two principal benefits (Guerrero et al., 1999; Burgoon & Hoobler, 2002). First, the greater your ability to encode and decode nonverbal signals, the higher your popularity and psychosocial well-being are likely to be. (Not surprisingly, encoding and decoding abilities are highly correlated; if you're good at expressing yourself nonverbally, then you're likely to also be good at reading the nonverbal cues of others.) This relationship is likely part of a more general relationship: Research indicates that people who are high in interpersonal skills generally are perceived to be high on such positive qualities as expressiveness, self-esteem, outgoingness, social comfort, sociability, and gregariousness. Interpersonal skills really do matter. Second, the greater your nonverbal skills, the more successful you're likely to be at influencing and deceiving others. Skilled nonverbal communicators are highly persuasive. This persuasive power can be used to help or support another, or it can be used to deceive and fool.

Directly related to these advantages are research findings showing that women are the better encoders and decoders of nonverbal messages (Hall, 1998; Burgoon & Hoobler, 2002). Although this superiority does not hold in all contexts, it does apply in most. For example, in a review of 21 research studies on encoding, 71 percent found women to be superior senders of nonverbal messages. And in a review of 61 studies on decoding, 84 percent found women to be superior receivers (Hall, 1998).

THE FUNCTIONS OF NONVERBAL MESSAGES

To appreciate the many functions of nonverbal communication, let's look at two things: the ways in which nonverbal communication messages are integrated with verbal messages, and the functions that researchers have focused on most extensively (Burgoon & Hoobler, 2002; Burgoon & Bacue, 2003).

Integrating Nonverbal and Verbal Messages

In face-to-face communication you blend verbal and nonverbal messages to best convey your meanings. Here are six ways in which nonverbal messages are used with verbal messages; these will help to highlight this important verbal–nonverbal interaction (Knapp & Hall, 1996).

Nonverbal communication is often used to *accent* or emphasize some part of a verbal message. You might, for example, raise your voice to underscore a particular word or phrase, bang your fist on the desk to stress your commitment, or look longingly into someone's eyes when saying, "I love you."

You may deliberately *contradict* your verbal messages with nonverbal movements—for example, by crossing your fingers or winking to indicate that you're lying.

When verbal and nonverbal messages contradict each other, do you believe the nonverbal? Under what conditions would you believe the verbal? When would you believe the nonverbal?

Begin your reading of nonverbal communication with the following suggestions in mind:

- Analyze your own nonverbal communication patterns. If you're to use this material in any meaningful way—for example, to change some of your behaviours—then self-analysis is essential.
- Observe. Observe. Observe. Observe both your own behaviours and the behaviours of those around you. See in everyday behaviour what you read about here and discuss in class.
- Resist the temptation to draw conclusions from nonverbal behaviours. Instead, develop hypotheses (educated guesses) about what is going on, and test your hypotheses on the basis of other evidence.
- Connect and relate. Although the channels of nonverbal communication are presented separately in textbooks, in actual communication situations they all work together.

EXAMPLES?

Think of an example of someone you know who uses nonverbal behaviour ineffectively—and an example of someone who uses nonverbal behaviour effectively. What specific nonverbal behaviours do you find effective? Ineffective?

Nonverbal communication may *complement* or add nuances of meaning not communicated by your verbal message. Thus, you might smile when telling a story (to suggest that you find it humorous) or frown and shake your head when recounting someone's deceit (to suggest your disapproval).

Movements may be used to *regulate*, control, or indicate your desire to control the flow of verbal messages, as when you purse your lips, lean forward, or make hand gestures to indicate that you want to speak. You might also put up your hand or vocalize your **pauses** (for example, with "um" or "ah") to indicate that you have not finished and are not ready to relinquish the floor to the next speaker.

You can *repeat* or restate the verbal message nonverbally. You can, for example, follow your verbal "Is that all right?" with raised eyebrows and a questioning look, or motion with your head or hand to repeat your verbal "Let's go."

You may also use nonverbal communication to *substitute* or take the place of verbal messages. For instance, you can signal "okay" with a hand gesture. You can nod your head to indicate Yes or shake your head to indicate No. Or you can glance at your watch to communicate your concern with time.

In-Class Notes

Verbal–Nonverbal Interaction

- Accenting
- Contradicting
- Complementing
- Regulating
- Repeating
- Substituting

_____

_____

_____

_____

_____

_____

_____

STUDY TIP

With a classmate, debate the pros and cons of using email and/or internet chat to communicate provocative or confrontational messages.

Researching Nonverbal Communication Functions

Although nonverbal communication serves the same functions as verbal communication, nonverbal researchers have singled out several functions in which nonverbal messages play particularly important roles (Burgoon et al., 1995; Burgoon & Hoobler, 2002).

Forming and Managing Impressions   You form impressions of others largely through their nonverbal communications. Based on a person's body size, skin colour, and dress, as well as on the way the person smiles, maintains eye contact, and expresses himself facially, you form impressions—you judge who the person is. One nonverbal researcher groups these impressions into four categories (Leathers, 1997): credibility (how competent and believable you find the person); likeability (how much you like or dislike the person); attractiveness (how attractive you find the person); and dominance (how dominant the individual is).

Of course, you reveal yourself to others largely through the same nonverbal signals you use to size up others. But not only do you communicate your true self nonverbally, you also manage the impression that you give to others. Impression management may, for example, mean appearing brave when you're really scared, or appearing happy when you're really sad.

Forming and Defining Relationships   Much of your relationship life is lived nonverbally. Largely through nonverbal signals, you communicate the nature of your relationship to another person, and you and that person communicate nonverbally with each other. Holding hands, looking longingly into each other's eyes, and even dressing alike are ways in which you communicate closeness in your interpersonal relationships.

You also use nonverbal signals to communicate your relationship dominance and status (Knapp & Hall, 1996). The large corner office with the huge desk communicates high status just as the basement cubicle communicates low status.

Structuring Conversation and Social Interaction   When you're in conversation, you give and receive cues—signals that you're ready to speak, to listen, to comment on what the speaker just said—that regulate and structure the interaction. These turn-taking cues may be verbal (as when you say, "What do you think?"), but most often they're nonverbal: A nod of the head in the direction of someone else signals that you're ready to give up your speaking turn and want this other person to say something. You also show that you're listening and that you want the conversation to continue (or that you're not listening and want the conversation to end) largely through nonverbal signals.

Influence and Deception   You can influence others not only through what you say but also through your nonverbal signals. A focused glance that says you're committed; gestures that further explain what you're saying; appropriate dress that says, "I'll easily fit in with this organization"—these are a few examples of ways in which you can exert nonverbal influence.

And with the ability to influence, of course, comes the ability to deceive—to lie, to mislead another person into thinking something is true when it's false or that something is false when it's true. One common example of nonverbal deception is using your eyes and facial expressions to communicate a liking for other people when you're really interested only in gaining their support in some endeavour. Not surprisingly, you also use nonverbal signals to detect deception in others. For example, you may well suspect a person of lying if she avoids eye contact, fidgets, and conveys verbal and nonverbal messages that are inconsistent.

Emotional Expression   Although people often explain and reveal emotions verbally, nonverbal expressions probably communicate more about emotional experience. For example, you reveal your level of happiness or sadness or confusion largely through facial expressions. Of course, you also reveal your feelings by posture (for example, whether tense or relaxed), gestures, eye movements, and even the dilation of your pupils.

THE CHANNELS OF NONVERBAL MESSAGES

Nonverbal communication is probably most easily explained in terms of the various channels through which messages pass. Here we'll survey 10 channels: body, face, eye, space, artifactual, touch, paralanguage, silence, time, and smell.

Body Messages

Two aspects of the body are especially important in communicating messages. First, the movements you make with your body communicate; second, the general appearance of your body communicates. According to Pease (2006), the way we stand, sit, and tilt our heads, where we put our hands, what our eyes look like and where they wander give cues that help us get a handle on what our boss and colleagues are telling us with every gesture and pose.

What is the purpose of the traditional photo shoot? What is the politician or celebrity trying to say to the public with such a photo opportunity? What is important about the body language that the individual portrays in these types of opportunities?

Body Movements   Nonverbal researchers identify five major types of body movements: emblems, illustrators, affect displays, regulators, and adaptors (Ekman & Friesen, 1969; Knapp & Hall, 1996).

   Emblems are body gestures that directly translate into words or phrases, for example, the okay sign, the thumbs-up for "good job," and the V for victory. You use these gestures consciously and purposely to communicate the same meaning as the words. But emblems are culture specific, so be careful when using your culture's emblems in other cultures.

Research shows that women are perceived to be—and are in reality—more skilled at both encoding and decoding nonverbal messages (Briton & Hall, 1995). Do you notice this in your own interactions?

In-Class Notes

Channels of Nonverbal Communication

- Body
- Eyes
- Paralanguage
- Silence
- Space
- Smell
- Face
- Time
- Artifacts
- Touch

_____

_____

_____

_____

_____

_____

_____

_____

- In North America, you wave with your whole hand moving from side to side to say hello, but in a large part of Europe that same signal means "no." In Greece such a gesture would be considered insulting to the person to whom you're waving.
- The V for victory is common throughout much of the world; but if you make this gesture in England with the palm facing your face, it's as insulting as the raised middle finger is in North America.
- In North America and in much of Asia, hugs are rarely exchanged among acquaintances, but among Latinos and Southern Europeans, hugging is a common greeting gesture, and failing to hug someone may communicate unfriendliness.

> **ff** The body says what words cannot. **JJ**
>
> —Martha Graham

Illustrators enhance (literally "illustrate") the verbal messages they accompany. For example, when referring to something to the left, you might gesture toward the left. Most often you illustrate with your hands, but you can also illustrate with head and general body movements. You might, for example, turn your head or your entire body toward the left. You might also use illustrators to communicate the shape or size of objects you're talking about.

Research points to still another advantage of illustrators—namely, that they increase your ability to remember. In one study, people who illustrated their verbal messages with gestures remembered some 20 percent more than those who didn't gesture (Goldin-Meadow et al., 2001).

Affect displays include movements of the face (smiling or frowning, for example) and of the hands and general body (body tension or relaxation, for example). These communicate emotional meaning. You use affect displays to accompany and reinforce your verbal messages but also as substitutes for words. For example, you might smile while saying how happy you are to see your friend, or you might simply smile. Or you might rush to greet someone with open arms. (Because affect displays are centred primarily in the facial area, we'll consider these in more detail in the "Facial Messages" section on the next page.) Affect displays are often unconscious; you smile or frown, for example, without awareness. At other times, however, you may smile with awareness, consciously trying to convey pleasure or friendliness.

Regulators are behaviours that monitor, control, coordinate, or maintain the speaking of another individual. When you nod your head, for example, you tell the speaker to keep on speaking; when you lean forward and open your mouth, you tell the speaker that you would like to say something.

In-Class Notes

Five Types of Body Messages

- Emblems are gestures that directly translate into words.
- Illustrators enhance the verbal message they accompany.
- Affect displays communicate emotional meaning.
- Regulators are behaviours that monitor, control, coordinate, or maintain the speaking of others.
- Adaptors are gestures that satisfy a personal need.

_____

_____

_____

_____

_____

_____

_____

_____

Adaptors are gestures that satisfy some personal need. **Self-adaptors** are self-touching movements; for example, rubbing your nose, scratching to relieve an itch, or moving your hair out of your eyes. **Alter-adaptors** are movements directed at the person with whom you're speaking; for example, removing lint from a person's jacket, straightening a person's tie, or folding your arms in front of you to keep others a comfortable distance from you. **Object-adaptors** are gestures focused on objects; for example, doodling on or shredding a Styrofoam coffee cup.

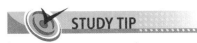

STUDY TIP

Communicate a message to a classmate or a family member using a combination of body movements, emblems, and regulators.

Body Appearance Your general body appearance also communicates (Ehrlich, 2000). Height, for example, has been shown to be significant in a wide variety of situations. In the U.S., tall presidential candidates have a much better record of being elected than do their shorter opponents. Tall people seem to be paid more and are favoured by interviewers over shorter applicants (DeVito & Hecht, 1990; Knapp & Hall, 1996; Harris, 2002).

Your body also reveals your race (through skin colour and tone) and may give clues as to your specific nationality. Your weight in proportion to your height will also communicate messages to others, as will the length, colour, and style of your hair.

Your general **attractiveness** is also a part of body communication. Attractive people have the advantage in just about every activity you can name (Horton, 2003). They get better grades in school, are more valued as friends and lovers, and are preferred as coworkers (Burgoon et al., 1995). Although we normally think that attractiveness is culturally determined—and to some degree it is—recent research seems to show that definitions of attractiveness are becoming universal (Brody, 1994; Chin & McConnell, 2003). A person rated as attractive in one culture is likely to be rated as attractive in other cultures—even in cultures whose people are widely different in appearance.

Facial Messages

Throughout your interpersonal interactions, your face communicates many things, especially your emotions. Facial movements alone seem to communicate the degree of pleasantness, agreement, and sympathy you feel; the rest of your body doesn't provide any additional information. But for other emotional messages—for example, the intensity with which an emotion is felt—both facial and bodily cues are used (Graham et al., 1975; Graham & Argyle, 1975).

Try to express surprise using only facial movements. Do this in front of a mirror and try to describe in as much detail as possible the specific movements of the face that make up a look of surprise. If you signal surprise like most people, you probably use raised and curved eyebrows, long horizontal forehead wrinkles, wide-open eyes, a dropped-open mouth, and lips parted with no tension. Even if there were differences from one person to another—and clearly there would be—you probably could recognize the movements listed here as indicative of surprise.

Of course, some emotions are easier to communicate and to decode than others. For example, in one study, participants judged happiness with 55 to 100 percent accuracy, surprise with 38 to 86 percent accuracy, and sadness with 19 to 88 percent accuracy (Ekman et al., 1972). Research finds that women and girls are more accurate judges of facial emotional expression than men and boys (Argyle, 1988; Lewin & Herlitz, 2002).

Facial Management As you grew up, you learned your culture's nonverbal system of communication. You also learned certain **facial management techniques**; for example, to hide certain emotions and to emphasize others. Table 6.1 identifies four types of facial management techniques that you will quickly recognize (Malandro et al., 1989).

You learn these facial management techniques along with display rules that tell you what emotions to express when; these are the rules of appropriateness. For example, when someone gets bad news in which you may secretly take pleasure, the display rule dictates that you frown and otherwise nonverbally signal your displeasure. If you violate these display rules, you will be judged insensitive.

TABLE 6.1 Facial Management Techniques

Can you identify a specific situation in which you or someone with whom you interacted used one of these techniques?

TECHNIQUE	FUNCTION	EXAMPLE
Intensifying	To exaggerate a feeling	Exaggerating surprise when friends throw you a party, to make your friends feel better
De-intensifying	To underplay a feeling	Covering up your own joy in the presence of a friend who didn't receive such good news
Neutralizing	To hide a feeling	Covering up your sadness so as not to depress others
Masking	To replace or substitute the expression of one emotion for another	Expressing happiness in order to cover up your disappointment at not receiving the gift you had expected

> **❝** Without wearing any mask we are conscious of, we have a special face for each friend. **❞**
>
> —Oliver Wendell Holmes

Some intervention programs for children with autism attempt to increase eye contact to a rate of 50 percent of the time or better. However, one study found that while playing with games in small groups, typical 5- to 10-year-olds look at each other's faces, on average, less than 20 percent of the time. This suggests that while some eye contact is important in social interactions ... too much eye contact could make individuals stand out from their peers. During a typical conversation with a friend, what percentage of time do you think *you* spend making eye contact?

Source: *Bridges*, "Bringing Together Albertans on Developmental Disability," Spring 2001, p. 13.

Further support for this hypothesis comes from a study that compared two groups of participants: those who felt emotions such as happiness and anger, and those who both felt and expressed these emotions. In support of the facial feedback hypothesis, subjects who felt and expressed the emotions became emotionally aroused faster than those who only felt the emotion (Hess et al., 1992).

Generally, research finds that facial expressions can produce or heighten feelings of sadness, fear, disgust, and anger. But this effect does not occur with all emotions; smiling, for example, doesn't seem to make us feel happier (Burgoon et al., 1995). This could be because smiling is not always associated with positive emotions. It is sometimes used in response to perceived social status, with those in power smiling less than their subordinates, and women smiling more than men regardless of their level of power (LaFrance, 2002). Further, it has not been demonstrated that facial expressions can eliminate one feeling and replace it with another. So if you're feeling sad, smiling will not eliminate the sadness and replace it with gladness. A reasonable conclusion seems to be that your facial expressions can influence some feelings but not all (Burgoon et al., 1995; Cappella, 1993).

Eye Messages

The eyes have long been regarded as the most important nonverbal message system. Recent research has also highlighted the importance of eyebrows in nonverbal communication, a finding with potential implications for the design of computerized facial recognition systems (Sadr et al., 2003).

Research on communication via the eyes shows that messages vary depending on the duration, direction, and quality of the eye behaviour. For example, in every culture there are strict, though unstated, rules for the proper duration of eye contact. When eye contact falls short of this amount, you may think the other person is uninterested, shy, or preoccupied. When the appropriate amount of time is exceeded, you may perceive the person as showing unusually high interest.

The direction of the eye glance also communicates. Among many Canadians, you're expected to glance alternately at the other person's face, then away, then again at the face, and so on. The rule for the public speaker is to scan the entire audience, not focusing for too long on or ignoring any one area of the audience. When you break these directional rules, you communicate different meanings—abnormally high or low interest, self-consciousness, nervousness over the interaction, and so on. The quality of eye behaviour—how wide or how narrow your eyes get during interaction—also communicates meaning, especially interest level and such emotions as surprise, fear, and disgust.

Eye Contact   With eye contact you send a variety of messages, one of which is a request for feedback. In talking with someone, you look at her or him intently, as if to say, "Well, what do you think?" As you might predict, listeners gaze at speakers more than speakers gaze at listeners. In public speaking, you may scan hundreds of people to secure this feedback.

Another type of message informs the other person that the channel of communication is open and that he or she should now speak. You see this regularly in conversation, when one person asks a question or finishes a thought and then looks to you for a response.

Eye contact may also send messages about the nature of a relationship. For example, if you engage in prolonged eye contact, coupled with a smile, you'll signal a positive relationship. If you stare or glare at the person while frowning, you'll signal a negative relationship.

Eye contact messages enable you to psychologically lessen the physical distance between you and another person. When you catch someone's eye at a party, for example, you become psychologically close, though you may be physically far apart.

Eye Avoidance   When you avoid eye contact or avert your glance, you help others to maintain their privacy. You may do this when you see a couple arguing in public: You turn your eyes away (though your eyes may be wide open) as if to say, "I don't mean to intrude; I respect your privacy." Eye avoidance can also signal lack of interest in a person, a conversation, or some visual stimulus. At times you may hide your eyes to block off unpleasant stimuli (a particularly gory or violent scene in a movie, for example) or close your eyes to block out visual stimuli and thus heighten other senses. For example, you may listen to music with your eyes closed. Lovers often close their eyes while kissing, and many prefer to make love in a dark or dimly lit room.

Space Messages

Your use of space to communicate—an area of study known technically as **proxemics**—speaks as surely and as loudly as words and sentences. Speakers who stand close to their listener, with their hands on the listener's shoulders and their eyes focused directly on those of the listener, communicate something very different from speakers who stand in a corner with arms folded and eyes downcast. Similarly, **territoriality**—the territory you occupy or own and the way you protect this territory—also communicates. The executive office suite on the top floor, with huge windows, private bar, and plush carpeting, communicates something totally different from the two-by-two-metre cubicle. There is some evidence that suggests men tend to display firmer boundaries around their territory, yet personalize this space less than women do (Kaya & Weber, 2003).

Spatial Distance Messages   Edward Hall (1959, 1966) distinguishes four distances that define the type of relationship between people and the type of communication in which they're likely to engage (see Table 6.2). In **intimate distance**, ranging from actual touching to 46 centimetres, the presence of the other individual is unmistakable. Each person experiences the sound, smell, and feel of the other's breath. You use intimate distance for lovemaking, comforting, and protecting. This distance is so short that most people do not consider it proper in public.

Personal distance refers to the protective "bubble" that defines your personal space, ranging from 46 centimetres to 1.2 metres. This imaginary bubble keeps you protected and untouched by others. You can still hold or grasp another person at this distance, but only by extending your arms; this allows you to take certain individuals, such as loved ones, into your protective bubble. At the outer limit of personal distance, you can touch another person only if both of you extend your arms. At this distance you conduct much of your interpersonal interactions; for example, talking with friends and family.

STUDY TIP

As you make your way through the day, take note of the protective "bubble" that defines your personal space. How and why does it differ, depending on whom you are speaking with?

In judging whether someone likes you, what nonverbal cues should you look for? List them in the order of their importance, using 1 for the cue that is of most value to you as you make your judgment, 2 for the cue that is next most valuable, and so on, right down to perhaps 10 or 12. Do you really need two lists—one for judging a woman's liking and one for a man's?

At **social distance**, ranging from 1.2 to 3.7 metres, you lose the visual detail you have at personal distance. You conduct impersonal business and interact at a social gathering at this social distance. The more distance you maintain in your interactions, the more formal they appear. In the offices of high officials, desks are positioned so that the official is assured of at least this distance from clients.

Public distance, from 3.6 to more than 7.6 metres, protects you. At this distance you could take defensive action if threatened. On a public bus or train, for example, you might try to keep at least this distance from a drunken passenger. Although at this distance you lose fine details of the face and eyes, you're still close enough to see what is happening.

Influences on Spatial Distances   Several factors influence the way you relate to and use space in communicating. Here are a few examples of how status, culture, subject matter, gender, and age influence space communication (Burgoon et al., 1995).

People of equal *status* maintain shorter distances between themselves than do people of unequal status. When status is unequal, the higher-status person may approach the lower-status person more closely than the lower-status person would approach the higher-status person.

Members of different *cultures* treat space differently. For example, people from northern European cultures and many North Americans stand fairly far apart when conversing; people from southern European and Middle Eastern cultures tend to stand much closer. It's easy to see how those who normally stand far apart may interpret the close distances of others as pushy and overly intimate. It's equally easy to appreciate how those who normally stand close may interpret the far distances of others as cold and unfriendly.

When discussing personal *subjects* you maintain shorter distances than when discussing impersonal subjects. Also, you stand closer to someone who is praising you than to someone criticizing you.

TABLE 6.2	Relationships and Proxemic Distances

Note that these four distances can be further divided into close and far phases and that the far phase of one level (say, personal) blends into the close phase of the next level (social). Do your relationships also blend into one another? Or are your personal relationships totally separated from your social relationships?

RELATIONSHIP	DISTANCE
Intimate Relationship	Intimate Distance 0 ——————— 46 centimetres close phase — far phase
Personal Relationship	Personal Distance 46 centimetres ——————— 1.2 metres close phase — far phase
Social Relationship	Social Distance 1.2 ——————— 3.6 metres close phase — far phase
Public Relationship	Public Distance 6 ——————— 7.6 + metres close phase — far phase

Your *gender* also influences your spatial relationships. Women generally stand closer to each other than men. Similarly, when someone approaches another person, he or she will come closer to a woman than to a man. With increasing *age* there is a tendency for the spaces to become larger. Children stand much closer than do adults. These findings provide some evidence that these distances are learned behaviours.

Territoriality Messages Territoriality, a term from ethology (the study of animals in their natural habitat), is an ownership-like reaction toward a particular space or object. The size and location of human territories also say something about **status**. An apartment or office in midtown Manhattan or downtown Tokyo is extremely high-status territory since the cost restricts it to the wealthy.

Status is also indicated by the unwritten law granting the right of invasion. In some cultures and in some organizations, for example, higher-status individuals have more of a right to invade the territory of others than vice versa. The president of a large company can invade the territory of a junior executive by barging into her office, but the reverse would be unthinkable.

Like animals, humans also mark their territory (Hickson & Stacks, 1993). For example, you might place an item of clothing or a book at a table in the cafeteria to claim this place as your territory. Or you might have initials on your briefcase. Other types of **markers** are used to separate one territory from another; for example, the bar used at the supermarket checkout to separate your groceries from those of the person behind you, or the armrest used in a theatre to separate your seat from those beside you.

Artifactual Messages

Artifactual messages are those made by human hands. Thus, colour, clothing, jewellery, and the decoration of space are considered artifactual. Let's look at each of these briefly.

Colour There is some evidence that colours affect us physiologically. For example, respiratory movements increase with red light and decrease with blue light. Similarly, eye blinks increase in frequency when eyes are exposed to red light and decrease when exposed to blue. This seems consistent with our intuitive feelings that blue is more soothing and red more arousing. When a school changed the colour of its walls from orange and white to blue, the blood pressure of the students decreased and their academic performance increased (Malandro et al., 1989).

Colour communication also influences perceptions and behaviours (Kanner, 1989). People's acceptance of a product, for example, can be largely determined by its packaging, especially its colour. In one study, the very same coffee taken from a yellow can was described as weak, from a dark brown can as too strong, from a red can as rich, and from a blue can as mild. Even your acceptance of a person may depend on the colours worn. Consider, for example, the comments of one colour expert (Kanner, 1989): "If you have to pick the wardrobe for your defence lawyer heading into court and choose anything but blue, you deserve to lose the case...." Black is so powerful it could work against the lawyer with the jury. Brown lacks sufficient authority. Green would probably elicit a negative response. Recent research, however, suggests that our responses to colour may be more complex than what was previously thought, and may depend on such factors as our education and our knowledge about the world (Jacobsen, 2003).

Clothing and Body Adornment People make inferences about who you are—at least in part—from the way you dress. Whether these inferences are accurate or not, they will influence what people think of you and how they react to you. Your socioeconomic class, your seriousness, your attitudes (for example, whether you're conservative or liberal), your concern for convention, your sense of style, and perhaps

STUDY TIP

With a classmate, discuss how you use adornment (e.g., colour, clothing, piercing, tattoos) to communicate artifactual messages.

even your creativity will all be judged in part by the way you dress (Molloy, 1977; Burgoon et al., 1995; Knapp & Hall, 1996). Similarly, college students will perceive an instructor dressed informally as friendly, fair, enthusiastic, and flexible, and the same instructor dressed formally as prepared, knowledgeable, and organized (Malandro et al., 1989).

The way you wear your hair also communicates aspects of who you are—from a concern about being up to date, to a desire to shock, to perhaps a lack of interest in appearances. Your jewellery, too, sends messages about you. Some jewellery is a form of **cultural display**, indicating a particular cultural or religious affiliation. Wedding and engagement rings are obvious examples that communicate specific messages. What judgments are made will depend, of course, on who the receiver is, the communication context, and all the factors identified throughout this text.

Body piercing has become increasingly popular, especially among the young. Nose and nipple rings, and tongue and belly button jewellery send a variety of messages. Although people wearing such jewellery may wish to communicate different meanings, those interpreting the messages of body piercing seem to infer that the wearers are communicating an unwillingness to conform to social norms and a willingness to take greater risks than those without such piercing (Forbes, 2001). It's worth noting that in a study of employers' perceptions, employers rated and ranked applicants with eyebrow piercing significantly lower than those without such piercing (Acor, 2001).

Tattoos—whether temporary or permanent—likewise communicate a variety of messages, often the name of a loved one or some symbol of allegiance or affiliation. Tattoos also communicate to the wearers themselves. For example, tattooed students see themselves (and perhaps others do as well) as more adventurous, creative, individualistic, and risk prone than those without tattoos (Drews et al., 2000).

Space Decoration   The way you decorate your private spaces also speaks about you. The office with a mahogany desk and bookcases and oriental rugs communicates your importance and status within the organization, just as a metal desk and bare floor indicate that you are much farther down in the hierarchy.

Similarly, people will make inferences about you based on the way you decorate your home. The expensiveness of the furnishings may communicate your status and wealth; their coordination your sense of style. The magazines you choose may reflect your interests, and the arrangement of chairs around a television set may reveal how important watching television is to you. The contents of bookcases lining the walls

A popular tactic of American defence lawyers in sex crimes against women, gay men, and lesbians is to blame the victim by, among other things, implying that the way the victim was dressed provoked the attack. New York and Florida prohibit defence attorneys from referring to the way a sex-crime victim was dressed at the time of the attack (*New York Times,* July 30, 1994, p. 22). What do you think of this?

What inferences would you make about the occupant of this office, solely on the basis of what appears in this photo?

reveal the importance of reading in your life. Even the food and beverages you serve or display in your home can send out messages about your lifestyle and priorities (Bourque, 2001). In fact, there is probably little in your home that would not send messages from which others would draw inferences about you.

Similarly, the absence of certain items will communicate something about you. Consider what messages you would get from a home where no television, phone, or books could be seen. In recent years, it has become popular to follow the design principles of feng shui, the ancient Chinese art of object placement in decoration and arrangement of space (Chamberlain, 2005). Following feng shui will send messages to others about you. Can you think what some of these messages might be?

Touch Messages

Touch communication, or **tactile communication**, is perhaps the most primitive form of communication (Montagu, 1971). Touch develops before the other senses; even in the womb the child is stimulated by touch. Soon after birth the child is fondled, caressed, patted, and stroked. In turn, the child explores his or her world and quickly learns to communicate a variety of meanings through touch.

The Meanings of Touch   Researchers in the field of **haptics**—the study of touch—have identified the major meanings of touch (Jones & Yarbrough, 1985; Jones, 1999):

- *Positive emotion.* Touch may communicate positive feelings such as support, appreciation, inclusion, sexual interest or intent, and affection.
- *Playfulness.* Touch often communicates our intention to play, either affectionately or aggressively.
- *Control.* Touch may direct the behaviours, attitudes, or feelings of the other person. To get attention, for example, you may touch a person as if to say, "Look at me" or "Look over here."
- *Ritual.* Ritualistic touching revolves around greetings and departures; for example, shaking hands to say hello or goodbye, or hugging, kissing, or putting your arm around another's shoulder when greeting or saying farewell.
- *Task-relatedness.* Task-related touching occurs while you're performing some function, such as removing a speck of dust from another person's face or helping someone out of a car.

Recognize that different cultures will view these types of touching differently. For example, some task-related touching, viewed as acceptable in much of North America, would be viewed negatively in some cultures. Among Koreans, for example, it's considered disrespectful for a storekeeper to touch a customer in, say, handing back change; it's considered too intimate a gesture. But members of other cultures, who expect some touching, may consider the Koreans' behaviour cold and insulting.

Touch Avoidance   Much as we touch and are touched, we also avoid touch from certain people and in certain circumstances. Researchers in nonverbal communication have found some interesting relationships between **touch avoidance** and other significant communication variables (Andersen & Leibowitz, 1978; Hall, 1996).

Among research findings, for example, is the fact that touch avoidance is positively related to communication apprehension; those who fear oral communication also score high on touch avoidance. Touch avoidance is also high with those who self-disclose little. Both touch and self-disclosure are intimate forms of communication; thus, people who are reluctant to get close to another person by self-disclosing also seem reluctant to get close by touching.

> " There is a very simple rule about touching," the manager continued. "*When you touch, don't take.* Touch the people you manage only when you are *giving* them something—reassurance, support, encouragement, whatever. "
>
> —Kenneth Blanchard and Spencer Johnson

How would you describe the rules of touch avoidance for passengers on a commuter train? For students at a football stadium? For members of your family at dinner? For students in a residence hall?

Today, there is growing recognition in Canada that touching can be highly disrespectful. Employers, for example, are much more careful not to touch their employees, as are college instructors with their students.

Paralanguage Messages

The term **paralanguage** refers to the vocal but nonverbal dimensions of speech—how you say something, not what you say. A traditional exercise used by students to increase their ability to express different emotions, feelings, and attitudes is to repeat a sentence while stressing different words. Significant differences in meaning are easily communicated, depending on where the speaker places the stress. Consider the following variations:

1. What *have* you done?
2. *What* have you done?
3. What have *you* done?

Each sentence communicates something different; in fact, each asks a different question, although the words are the same. All that distinguishes the sentences is stress—one aspect of paralanguage. In addition to stress and **pitch** (highness or lowness), paralanguage includes such **voice qualities** or characteristics as **rate** (speed), **volume** (loudness), and rhythm as well as the vocalizations you make in crying, whispering, moaning, belching, yawning, and yelling (Trager, 1961; Argyle, 1988). A variation in any of these features communicates. When you speak quickly, for example, you communicate something different from when you speak slowly. Even though the words may be the same, if the speed (or volume, rhythm, or pitch) differs, the meanings people receive will also differ.

Might drawing conclusions (rather than making hypotheses) about personality from someone's nonverbal behaviours prevent you from seeking further information and hinder you from seeing evidence contrary to your conclusion? Have you ever drawn conclusions about another person and then acted as if these conclusions were accurate when they weren't? Has anyone ever drawn conclusions in this way about you?

Judgments about People   Paralanguage cues are often used as a basis for judgments about people—for example, evaluations of their emotional state or even their personality. A listener can accurately judge the emotional state of a speaker from vocal expression alone, if both speaker and listener speak the same language. Paralanguage cues are not so accurate when used to communicate emotions to those who speak a different language (Albas et al., 1976).

Less reliable are judgments made about personality. Some people, for example, may conclude that a person who speaks softly must feel inferior or believe that no one wants to listen or that nothing he or she says is significant. Some people might also believe that someone who speaks loudly has an over-inflated ego and thinks everyone in the world wants to hear him or her.

Silence Messages

Like words and gestures, **silence** can also communicate important meanings and serve important functions (Johannesen, 1974; Jaworski, 1993). Silence allows the speaker *time to think*, time to formulate and organize verbal communications. Before messages of intense conflict, as well as before those confessing undying love, there is often silence. Again, silence seems to prepare the receiver for the importance of these messages.

Some people use silence as a *weapon* to hurt others. We often speak of giving someone "the silent treatment." After a conflict, for example, one or both individuals may remain silent as a kind of punishment. Silence may also be used to hurt others by a refusal to acknowledge the presence of another person, as in disconfirmation (see Chapter 5). In that case, silence is a dramatic demonstration of the total indifference one person feels toward the other.

Sometimes silence is used as a *response to personal anxiety*, shyness, or threats. You may feel anxious or shy among new people and prefer to remain silent. By remaining silent you preclude the chance of rejection. Only when you break your silence and make an attempt to communicate with another person do you risk rejection.

Silence may be used to *prevent communication* of certain messages. In conflict situations, silence is sometimes used to prevent certain topics from surfacing and to prevent one or both parties from saying things they may later regret. In such situations, silence often allows us time to cool off before expressing hatred, severe criticism, or personal attacks—which, as we know, are irreversible.

Silence can also be used to encourage others to communicate. Often, students, particularly those for whom English is a second language, need time and silence after a question is asked in order to formulate a response.

Of course, you may also use silence when you simply have *nothing to say*, when nothing occurs to you, or when you don't want to say anything. James Russell Lowell expressed this best: "Blessed are they who have nothing to say, and who cannot be persuaded to say it." Silence may also be used to avoid responsibility for wrongdoing (Beach, 1990–1991).

> **""** Speaking is silver, silence is gold. **""**
>
> —German proverb

In-Class Notes

Silence

- allows time to think.
- can hurt others.
- might indicate anxiety.
- may prevent communication.
- can communicate emotions.
- may indicate nothing to say.

_____

_____

_____

_____

_____

_____

_____

_____

Often, but not always, you have the right to remain silent, to preserve your privacy, and to withhold information that has no bearing on the matter at hand. In most job-related situations, your previous relationship history, affectional orientation, or religion is usually irrelevant to your ability to function as, say, a doctor or police officer. This information may thus be kept private. If this kind of information becomes relevant—if, for example, you're about to enter a new relationship—then there *may be* an obligation to reveal your relationship history, affectional orientation, or religion.

In a court, of course, you have the right to refuse to incriminate yourself: to reveal information about yourself that could be used against you. But you don't have the right to refuse to reveal information about the criminal activities of others, although in some situations, psychiatrists, clergy, and lawyers may be exempt from this general rule.

WHAT WOULD YOU DO?

As you walk by a house, you witness a mother shaking and hitting her two- or three-year-old child in the backyard. You worry that the mother might harm the child, and your first impulse is to report the incident to the police. At the same time, you don't want to interfere with a mother's right to discipline her child, nor to make trouble for someone who may be an excellent parent generally but is perhaps having a particularly bad time today. What is your ethical obligation in this case? What would you do in this situation?

Time Messages

> ❝ Seize the day, and put the least possible trust in tomorrow. ❞
>
> —Horace

The study of **temporal communication**, known as **chronemics**, concerns the use of time—how you organize it, react to it, and communicate messages through it (Bruneau, 1990; Harris, 2002). Consider, for example, **psychological time**—the emphasis you place on the past, present, and future. If you embrace a past orientation, you have special reverence for the past. You relive old times and regard old methods as the best. You see events as circular and recurring, so the wisdom of yesterday is applicable today and tomorrow. In a present orientation, however, you live in the present: for now, not tomorrow. With a future orientation, you look toward and live for the future. You save today, work hard in university, and deny yourself luxuries because you're preparing for the future.

Different time perspectives also account for much intercultural misunderstanding, since different cultures often teach their members drastically different time orientations. For example, people from some Latin cultures would rather be late for an upcoming appointment than end a current conversation abruptly or before it has come to a natural end. So the Latino may see lateness as a result of politeness, while others see it as impolite to the person waiting at the upcoming appointment (Hall & Hall, 1987).

> ❝ Those who live to the future must always appear selfish to those who live to the present. ❞
>
> —Ralph Waldo Emerson

Similarly, the future-oriented person who works for tomorrow's goals will frequently look down on the present-oriented person as lazy and poorly motivated for enjoying today and not planning for tomorrow. In turn, the present-oriented person may see those with strong future orientations as obsessed with amassing wealth or rising in status.

Another time-related topic is the theory of biorhythms: the idea that our bodies operate on physical, intellectual, and emotional time cycles, each of which lasts for different periods of time.

Smell Messages

Smell communication, or **olfactory communication**, is extremely important in a wide variety of situations and has become big business (Kleinfeld, 1992). For example, there is some evidence (though clearly not very conclusive evidence) that the smell of lemon contributes to a perception of health, the smells of lavender and eucalyptus seem to increase alertness, and the smell of rose oil seems to reduce blood pressure. The smell of chocolate seems to reduce theta brain waves and thus produce a sense of relaxation and a reduced level of attention (Martin, 1998). Findings such as these have contributed to the growth of aromatherapy and an increase in the number of aromatherapists (Furlow, 1996). Because humans possess "denser skin concentrations of scent glands than almost any other mammal," the argument has been made that we need only discover how we use scent to communicate a wide variety of messages (Furlow, 1996). Here are some of the most important messages scent seems to communicate:

- *Attraction messages.* Humans use perfumes, colognes, aftershave lotions, powders, and the like to enhance their attractiveness to others and to themselves. After all, you also smell yourself, and when the smells are pleasant, you feel better about yourself. Women, research finds, prefer the scent of men who bear a close genetic similarity to themselves—a finding that may account, in part, for humans' attraction to people much like themselves (Ober et al., 1997; Wade, 2002).

- *Taste messages.* Without smell, taste would be severely impaired. For example, without smell, it would be extremely difficult to taste the difference between a raw potato and an apple. Street vendors selling hot dogs, sausages, and similar foods are aided greatly by the smells that stimulate the appetites of passersby.

- *Memory messages.* Smell is a powerful memory aid; you often recall situations from months and even years ago when you happen upon a similar smell.

- *Identification messages.* Smell is often used to create an image or an identity for a product. Advertisers and manufacturers spend millions of dollars each year creating scents for cleaning products and toothpastes, for example. These scents have nothing to do with the products' cleaning power; instead, they function solely to help create an image. There is also evidence that we can identify our "significant others" by smell. For example, young children were able to identify the T-shirts of their brothers and sisters solely on the basis of smell (Porter & Moore, 1981). And one researcher goes so far as to advise: "If your man's odor reminds you of Dad or your brother, you may want genetic tests before trying to conceive a child" (Furlow, 1996).

CULTURE AND NONVERBAL MESSAGES

Not surprisingly, nonverbal communication is heavily influenced by culture. Consider a variety of differences. At the sight of unpleasant pictures, members of some cultures (Canadian and European, for example) will express disgust facially. Members of other cultures (Japanese, for example) will avoid facially expressing disgust (Ekman, 1985b; Matsumoto, 1991). See Table 6.3 for more cultural differences in communication.

How many of the cultural differences in nonverbal signals discussed here have you witnessed? Have you seen cultural differences not discussed here?

TABLE 6.3 A Few Cultural Differences in Nonverbal Messages

Can you identify other behaviours that can create cultural problems?

Communication Behaviour	May Be Considered
Blinking your eyes	impolite in Taiwan
Folding your arms over your chest	disrespectful in Fiji
Waving your hand	insulting in Nigeria and Greece
Gesturing with the thumb up	rude in Australia
Tapping your two index fingers together	an invitation to sleep together in Egypt
Pointing with the index finger	impolite in many Middle Eastern countries
Bowing to a lesser degree than your host	a statement of superiority in Japan
With a clenched fist, inserting your thumb between your index and middle finger	obscene in some southern European countries
Pointing at someone with your index and third fingers	a wish that evil will fall on the person in some African countries
Resting your feet on a table or chair	insulting in some Middle Eastern countries

Another aspect of artifactual communication that varies greatly from one culture to another is the meaning that gifts have. In some cultures, a set of knives for the kitchen would be an appropriate house gift; in other cultures (for example, Chinese) a gift of knives would be considered inappropriate and offensive.

Touching also varies greatly across cultures. For example, African Americans touch one another more than whites do. Similarly, touching declines from kindergarten to grade 6 for white but not for African American children (Burgoon et al., 1995). Similarly, Japanese touch one another much less than do Anglo-Saxons, who in turn touch one another much less than do southern Europeans (Morris, 1977; Burgoon et al., 1995).

Not surprisingly, the role of silence is seen differently in different cultures (Basso, 1972). Among the Apache, for example, mutual friends do not feel the need to introduce strangers who may be working in the same area or on the same project. The strangers may remain silent for several days. During this time the individuals look each other over, trying to determine if the other person is all right. Only after this period do the individuals talk. When courting, especially during the initial stages, the Apache remain silent for hours; if they do talk, they generally talk very little. Only after a couple has been dating for several months will they have lengthy conversations. These periods of silence are generally attributed to shyness or self-consciousness, but the use of silence is explicitly taught to Apache women, who are especially discouraged from engaging in long discussions with their dates. Silence during courtship is a sign of modesty to many Apache.

Time is another communication channel with great cultural differences. Two types of cultural time are especially important in nonverbal communication: formal and informal. In North American culture, *formal time* is divided into seconds, minutes, hours, days, weeks, months, and years. Other cultures may use seasons or phases of the moon to delineate time periods. In some universities, courses are divided into 50- or 75-minute periods that meet two or three times a week for 14-week periods called semesters: eight semesters of fifteen or sixteen 50-minute periods per week equal a university education. Other universities use quarters or trimesters. As these examples illustrate, formal time units are arbitrary. The culture establishes them for convenience.

Informal time terms such as "forever," "immediately," "soon," "right away," and "as soon as possible" are more general. Informal time creates the most communication problems, because the terms have different meanings for different people.

Attitudes toward time vary from one culture to another. One study measured the accuracy of clocks in six cultures—Japan, Indonesia, Italy, England, Taiwan, and the United States. Japan had the most accurate clocks, Indonesia the least accurate. And a measure of the speed at which people in these six cultures walked found that the Japanese walked the fastest, the Indonesians the slowest (LeVine & Bartlett, 1984).

Summary of Concepts and Skills

In this chapter we explored nonverbal communication—communication without words—and considered such topics as body movements, facial and eye movements, spatial and territorial communication, artifactual communication, touch communication, paralanguage, silence, and time communication.

1. The five body movements are emblems (nonverbal behaviours that rather directly translate words or phrases); illustrators (nonverbal behaviours that accompany and literally illustrate the verbal messages); affect displays (nonverbal behaviours that communicate emotional meaning); regulators (nonverbal behaviours that coordinate, monitor, maintain, or control the speaking of another individual); and adaptors (nonverbal behaviours that usually serve some kind of need, as in scratching an itch).

2. Facial movements may communicate a variety of emotions. The most frequently studied facial movements are happiness, surprise, fear, anger, sadness, and disgust/contempt. Facial management techniques enable you to control revealing the emotions you feel.

3. The facial feedback hypothesis claims that facial display of an emotion can lead to physiological and psychological changes.

4. Eye movements may seek feedback, signal others to speak, signal the nature of a relationship, and compensate for increased physical distance.

5. Pupil size shows your interest and level of emotional arousal. Pupils enlarge when you are interested in something or emotionally aroused in a positive way.

6. Proxemics is the study of the communicative function of space and spatial relationships. Four important proxemic distances are intimate distance, ranging from actual touching to 46 centimetres; personal distance, ranging from 46 centimetres to 1.2 metres; social distance, ranging from 1.2 to 3.6 metres; and public distance, ranging from 3.6 to more than 7.6 metres.

7. Your treatment of space is influenced by such factors as status, culture, context, subject matter, sex, age, and positive or negative evaluation of the other person.

8. Territoriality has to do with your possessive reaction to an area of space or to particular objects.

9. Artifactual communication consists of messages that are human-made; for example, messages conveyed by colour, clothing and body adornment, or space decoration.

10. Touch (haptics) may communicate a variety of meanings, the most important being positive affect, playfulness, control, ritual, and task-relatedness. Touch avoidance is the desire to avoid touching and being touched by others.

11. Paralanguage consists of the vocal but nonverbal dimensions of speech. It includes rate, pitch, volume, resonance, and vocal quality as well as pauses and hesitations. Based on paralanguage, we make judgments about people and their communication effectiveness.

12. Silence communicates in a variety of ways, from hurting another with the "silent treatment" to communicating deep emotional responses.

13. Time can be used to communicate, and chronemics is the study of the messages communicated by our treatment of time.

14. Smell can communicate messages that enhance attraction, taste, memory, and identification.

15. Cultural variations in nonverbal communication are great. Different cultures, for example, assign different meanings to facial expressions and to colours, have different spatial rules, and treat time very differently.

Check Your Ability

This chapter has covered a variety of communication skills. Check your ability to apply these skills by indicating how often the following statements apply to you. Use the following rating scale: 1 = almost always, 2 = often, 3 = sometimes, 4 = rarely, and 5 = almost never.

_____ ❶ You recognize messages communicated by body gestures, and facial and eye movements.

_____ ❷ You take into consideration the interaction of emotional feelings and nonverbal expressions of the emotion; each influences the other.

_____ ❸ You recognize that what you perceive is only a part of the total nonverbal expression.

_____ ④ You use eye movements to seek feedback, to inform others to speak, to signal the nature of your relationship with others, and to compensate for increased physical distance.

_____ ⑤ You give others the space they need—for example, giving more space to those who are angry or disturbed.

_____ ⑥ You use artifacts to communicate the desired messages.

_____ ⑦ You are sensitive to the touching behaviours of others and distinguish between touches that communicate positive emotion, playfulness, control, ritual, and task-relatedness.

_____ ⑧ You recognize and respect each person's touch-avoidance tendency; you pay special attention to cultural and gender differences in touching preferences and in touch-avoidance tendencies.

_____ ⑨ You vary paralinguistic features (such as rate, pausing, pitch, and volume) to communicate intended meanings.

_____ ⑩ You use silence to communicate intended meanings and are sensitive to the meanings communicated by the silence of others.

_____ ⑪ You are specific when using normally informal time terms.

_____ ⑫ You interpret time cues from the cultural perspective of the person with whom you're interacting.

After completing this self-test, check your answers against the Answer Key at the back of the book.

Multiple Choice Questions *Choose the BEST answer.*

1. Nonverbal communication does not include
   a. vocal characteristics.
   b. body movement.
   c. words.
   d. odours.

2. The principal benefits of competency in nonverbal communication are
   a. greater encoding–decoding skills and increased ability to influence.
   b. better ability to listen to a message and better decoding skills.
   c. greater ability at masking and desensitizing.
   d. all of the above.

3. Which of the following are classes of nonverbal movement?
   a. affect displays and armour
   b. adoptions and illustrators
   c. stress and self-touch
   d. emblems and affect displays

4. Proxemics is the study of
   a. accidental gestures.
   b. eye behaviour.
   c. spatial distances.
   d. intimacy.

5. Paralanguage
   a. includes the vocal and verbal aspects of speech.
   b. studies the things we do while we are speaking.
   c. presents the legalities of kinesics.
   d. refers to how we say something rather than what we say.

6. Haptics has several meanings, one of which is
   a. positive emotion.
   b. adaptation.
   c. neutralizing.
   d. all of the above.

7. A meaning or purpose of touch is
   a. control.
   b. ritual.
   c. task-related.
   d. all of the above.

8. Silence is a communication tool used
   a. to increase effectiveness.
   b. instead of nonverbal communication.
   c. to prevent communication.
   d. all of the above.

9. The tone of your voice is a nonverbal dimension known as
   a. kinesics.
   b. emblems.
   c. paralanguage.
   d. affect displays.

10. Neutralizing is a nonverbal technique which manages
    a. facial expression.
    b. emblems.
    c. kinesics.
    d. none of the above.

True–False Questions *Write a T or F in the blank next to the statement.*

1. _____ Nonverbal communication occurs in a context.

2. _____ Nonverbal communication does not interact with verbal communication.

3. _____ Nonverbal communication has a very small role in impression formation.

4. _____ Regulators control your own speaking rate.

5. _____ Adaptors are a form of self-touching.

6. _____ Women smile more than men.

7. _____ Women are touched more by others.

8. _____ Masking exaggerates hidden feelings.

9. _____ Space equals status.

10. _____ Silence can hurt others.

Vocabulary Quiz
The Language of Nonverbal Communication

Match the terms of nonverbal communication with their definitions on the next page. Record the number of the appropriate definition next to each term.

a. _____ emblems

b. _____ affect displays

c. _____ proxemics

d. _____ territoriality

e. _____ haptics

f. ____ paralanguage

g. ____ chronemics

h. ____ artifactual communication

i. ____ informal time

j. ____ psychological time

1. Movements of the facial area that convey emotional meaning—for example, anger, fear, or surprise.

2. The study of the communicative nature of time—how we treat time and how we use it to communicate.

3. Culturally dependent general terms denoting time periods.

4. Nonverbal behaviours that directly translate words or phrases—for example, the signs for "okay" and "peace."

5. Touch or tactile communication.

6. One's orientation to the past, present, or future.

7. Communication that takes place through various artifacts—for example, clothing, jewellery, buttons, or the furniture in your house and its arrangement.

8. The study of the communicative function of space; the study of how people unconsciously structure their space—the distance between people in their interactions, the organization of space in homes and offices, and even the design of cities.

9. A possessive or ownership reaction to an area of space or to particular objects.

10. The vocal but nonverbal aspect of speech; for example, the rate, volume, pitch, and stress variations that communicate different meanings.

Skill Building Exercises

6.1 Integrating Verbal and Nonverbal Messages

Think about how you integrate verbal and nonverbal messages in your own everyday communications. Try reading each of the following statements and describing (rather than acting out) the nonverbal messages that you would use in making these statements in normal conversation.

1. I couldn't agree with you more.
2. Absolutely not. I don't agree.
3. Hurry up; we're an hour late already.
4. You look really depressed. What happened?
5. I'm so depressed I can't stand it.
6. Life is great, isn't it? I just got the job of a lifetime.
7. I feel so relaxed and satisfied.
8. I'm feeling sick; I think I have to throw up.
9. You look fantastic; what did you do to yourself?
10. Did you see that accident yesterday?

Thinking Critically About Verbal and Nonverbal Messages.

This experience was probably a lot more difficult than it seemed at first. The reason is that we're generally unaware of the nonverbal movements we make; often they function below the level of conscious awareness. What value might there be in bringing these processes to consciousness? Can you identify any problems with this?

6.2 Facial Expressions

The objective of this exercise is to gain a greater understanding of the role of facial features in communicating different emotions. Draw faces, depicting only eyebrows, eyes, and mouth, to illustrate the primary emotions: happiness (provided as an

Happiness	Mouth upturned, eyes opened, eyebrows arched.
Surprise	
Fear	
Anger	
Sadness	
Disgust	
Contempt	
Interest	

example), surprise, fear, anger, sadness, disgust, contempt, and interest. In the space provided, write a verbal description of how one would facially express each of these emotions. Follow the format provided in the Happiness example.

Thinking Critically About Facial Expressions.

Compare your faces and descriptions with those done by others. What do the several faces for each emotion have in common? How do they differ? What do the verbal descriptions have in common? How do they differ?

6.3 Communicating Nonverbally

This exercise has several parts and asks you to explore the various channels of nonverbal communication discussed in this chapter in different ways.

1. The objective of this first exercise is to gain a greater understanding of the role of nonverbal channels in communicating emotions. Using any nonverbal channels you wish, communicate these primary emotions: happiness, surprise, fear, anger, sadness, disgust, contempt, and interest. In a small group discussion, brief talk, email, or brief paper, describe the nonverbal channels you would use in communicating any one of these emotions. Consider as many as possible of the 10 channels discussed in this chapter.

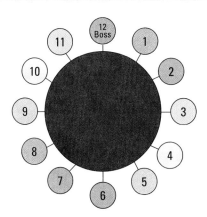

2. **Sitting at the Company Meeting** Where would you sit in each of the four situations identified below? What would be your first choice? Your second choice?

   a. You want to polish the apple and ingratiate yourself with your boss.
   b. You aren't prepared and want to be ignored.
   c. You want to challenge your boss on a certain policy that will come up for a vote.
   d. You want to be accepted as a new (but important) member of the company.

Why did you make the choices you made? Do you normally make choices based on such factors as these? What inter-

personal factors—for example, the desire to talk to or the desire to get a closer look at someone—influence your day-to-day seating behaviour?

3. Consider the meanings colours communicate. The colour spectrum is presented with numbers from 1 to 25 to facilitate identifying the colours. Assume that you're working for an advertising agency and that your task is to select colours for the following products: an herbal tea made from basil, a candy-flavoured toothpaste for children, and a low-calorie ice cream. What major colours would you use? What colours would serve as accents?

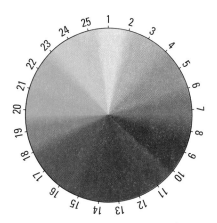

4. Paralanguage variations can communicate praise and criticism. Read aloud each of the following 10 sentences, first to communicate praise and second, criticism. Then consider which paralanguage cues you used to communicate the praise and criticism.

   a. Now that looks good on you.
   b. You lost weight.
   c. You look younger than that.
   d. You're gonna make it.
   e. That was some meal.
   f. You really know yourself.
   g. You're an expert.
   h. You're so sensitive. I'm amazed.
   i. Your parents are really something.
   j. Are you ready? Already?

Although this exercise focused on paralanguage (vocal variations), did you also read the statements with different facial expressions, eye movements, and body postures?

Thinking Critically About Communicating Nonverbally.

How effective would you consider yourself as a nonverbal message sender? A nonverbal message receiver? With which channels are you most effective? Least effective?

Web Explorations

Companion Website

Visit the Companion Website at www.pearsoned.ca/devito for student resources related to this chapter, including self-grading quizzes, additional skill-building exercises, and links to other online resources.

Research Navigator

Explore our research resources at www.researchnavigator.com

- Find and read an article on one of the channels of nonverbal communication discussed in this chapter (for example, body, face, eyes, space, artifacts, touch, paralanguage, silence, or time). On the basis of this article, what can you add to the discussion presented here?

- Investigate one of the key terms discussed in this chapter (for example, body movements, facial management, facial feedback, eye contact, touch, paralanguage, silence, space, distance, territoriality, artifactual communication, time communication, social clock). What additional insights can you provide?

- Try finding answers to one of the following questions, or design a research study to answer it.

  1. How do men and women in different cultures express romantic interest?
  2. Are concepts of body attractiveness universal across all cultures?
  3. How are status and touching related?
  4. In what ways do children born blind express themselves nonverbally?

Chapter 7
Emotional Messages

Chapter Topics

This chapter explores the nature of emotions, discusses problems in communicating emotions, and offers suggestions for more effective emotional communication.

Emotions and Emotional Messages

Obstacles in Communicating Emotions

Guidelines for Communicating Emotions

Chapter Skills

After completing this chapter, you should be able to:

- communicate your positive and negative emotions more appropriately.

- combat the common obstacles in communicating emotions.

- communicate emotions and respond to the emotions of others more effectively.

A young wife leaves her house one morning to draw water from the local well; her husband watches from the porch. As she walks back from the well, a stranger stops her and asks for some water. She gives him a cupful, then invites him home to dinner. He accepts. The husband, wife, and guest have a pleasant meal together. The husband, in a gesture of hospitality, invites the guest to spend the night—with his wife. The guest accepts. In the morning the husband leaves early to bring home breakfast. When he returns, he finds his wife again in bed with the visitor.

The question is: At what point in this story does the husband feel angry?

The answer is: It depends on the culture to which you belong (Hupka, 1981). In Canada or the United States, a husband would likely feel angry at a wife who slept with a stranger, and a wife would likely feel angry at being offered to a guest as if she were a lamb chop. But these reactions are not universal.

- A Pawnee husband of the nineteenth century would have been enraged at any man who dared ask his wife for water.
- An Ammassalik husband finds it perfectly honourable to offer his wife to a stranger, but only once. He would be angry to find his wife and the guest having a second encounter.
- A Toda husband at the turn of the last century in India would not have been angry at all. The Todas allowed both husband and wife to take lovers, and women were even allowed to have several husbands. Both spouses might feel angry, though, if one of them had a sneaky affair without announcing it publicly.

This report by Carole Wade and Carol Tavris (1998) illustrates that the emotions you feel depend, at least in part, on your culture. In this chapter we look at emotions and especially at the communication of emotions. What are emotions? What makes you experience emotion? Why do you find it difficult to express emotions? How can you learn to better communicate your emotions? How can you better deal with the emotions of others? These are some of the questions we'll consider.

EMOTIONS AND EMOTIONAL MESSAGES

Communicating emotions is both difficult and important. It's difficult because our thinking often gets confused when we are intensely emotional. It's also difficult because we were not taught how to communicate emotions and we have few effective models we might imitate. Communicating emotions is important because feelings represent a great part of your meanings. If you don't convey your feelings or if you communicate these feelings inadequately, you will fail to communicate a great part of your meaning. Consider what your communications would be like if you left out your feelings when talking about flunking a recent test, winning the lottery, becoming a parent, getting engaged, driving a car for the first time, becoming a citizen, or being promoted to supervisor. Emotional expression is so much a part of communication that even in the cryptic email message style, emoticons have become popular. (Two excellent websites contain extensive examples of smileys, emoticons, acronyms, and shorthand abbreviations: www.netlingo.com/smiley.cfm and www.netlingo.com/emailsh.cfm.) Let's look at several general principles of emotions and emotional expression.

The Body, Mind, and Culture in Emotions

Emotion involves at least three parts: bodily reactions (such as blushing when you're embarrassed); mental evaluations and interpretations (as in calculating the odds of drawing an inside straight at poker); and cultural rules and beliefs (for example, feeling proud when your child graduates from college).

Bodily reactions are the most obvious aspect of our emotional experience, because we can observe them easily. Such reactions span a wide range. They include, for example, the dilated pupils of attraction, the sweating palms that accompany nervousness, and the self-touching that goes with discomfort. When you judge people's emotions, you probably look to these nonverbal behaviours. You conclude

> *" When dealing with people, remember you are not dealing with creatures of logic, but with creatures of emotion, creatures bristling with prejudice, and motivated by pride and vanity. "*
>
> —Dale Carnegie

> *" Emotion is not something shameful, subordinate, second-rate; it is a supremely valid phase of humanity at its noblest and most mature. "*
>
> —Joshua Loth Liebman

Generally speaking, how accurate do you think you are in judging the emotions of others from only their facial expressions? What specific facial cues do you use most in making your judgments?

that Ramon is happy to see you because of his smile and his open body posture. You conclude that Lisa is nervous from her tense posture, vocal hesitations, and awkward movements.

The mental part of emotional experience involves the evaluations and interpretations you make on the basis of your behaviours. For example, leading psychotherapist Albert Ellis (1988; Ellis & Harper, 1975), whose insights are used throughout this chapter, claims that your evaluations of what happens have a greater influence on your feelings than what actually happens. Let's say, for example, that your best friend, Ling, ignores you in the college cafeteria. The emotions you feel will depend on what you think this behaviour means. You may feel pity if you figure that Ling is depressed because her father died. You may feel anger if you believe that Ling is simply rude and insensitive and snubbed you on purpose. Or you may feel sadness if you believe that Ling is no longer interested in being friends with you.

In an interesting study that illustrates the influence that our interpretations have on the emotions we experience, students were asked how they felt when they failed or did well on a university examination (Weiner et al., 1979). Students who did poorly felt *anger* or *hostility* if they believed that others were responsible for their failure—for example, if they felt the instructor gave an unfair examination. Those who believed that they themselves were responsible for the failure felt *guilt* or *regret.* Students who did very well felt *pride* and *satisfaction* if they believed their success was due to their own efforts, or felt *gratitude* and *surprise* (or even felt *guilt*) if they believed that their success was due to luck or chance. Have your own interpretations ever influenced the emotions you experienced? Have they ever not influenced the emotions you felt?

The culture you were raised in and live in gives you a framework both for interpreting emotions in others and for expressing emotions. Stephan, Stephan, and De Vargas (1996) examined the different ways people expressed their emotions, depending upon whether they were from a collectivist or an individualistic culture, using participants from Costa Rica and the United States. (See Chapter 9 for descriptions of these types of cultures.) Participants from Costa Rica, a collectivist culture, were careful to express emotions in ways that did not negatively affect others, whereas participants from the United States were more concerned about revealing their true feelings, regardless of the impact on others.

A colleague gave a lecture in Beijing to a group of Chinese university students. The students listened politely, but they made no comments and asked no questions after her lecture. At first, she concluded that the students were bored and uninterested. Later, she learned that Chinese students show respect by being quiet and seemingly passive. They think that asking questions would imply that she was not clear in her lecture. In other words, the culture—whether Canadian or Chinese—influenced the interpretation of the students' feelings.

Emotions, Arousal, and Expression

How would you feel in each of the following situations?

1. You have just heard that you won the lottery.
2. You were just told you got the job you applied for.
3. Your best friend just died.
4. Your parents just told you they are getting divorced.

You would obviously feel very differently in each of these situations. In fact, each feeling is unique and unrepeatable. Yet amid the differences, there is some similarity. For example, most people would argue that the feelings in the first two examples are more similar to each other than they are to the last two. Similarly, the last two are more similar to each other than they are to the first two.

Your Basic Emotions To capture the similarities among emotions, many researchers have tried to identify basic or primary emotions. Robert Plutchik (1980; Havlena et al., 1989) developed a most helpful model. In this model, as shown in Figure 7.1, the eight pieces of the pie represent the eight basic emotions: joy, acceptance, fear, surprise, sadness, disgust, anger, and anticipation. Emotions that are close to each other on this wheel are also close to each other in meaning. For example, joy and anticipation are more closely related than are joy and sadness, or acceptance and disgust. Emotions that are opposite each other on the wheel are also opposite in their meaning. For example, joy is the opposite of sadness; anger is the opposite of fear.

In this model there are also blends. These are emotions that are combinations of the primary emotions. These are noted outside the emotion wheel. For example, according to this model, love is a blend of joy and acceptance. Remorse is a blend of disgust and sadness.

STUDY TIP

Examine photos of celebrities in a magazine. Can you identify the emotions they are expressing, before reading the captions?

In-Class Notes

Emotions

Emotions	Expression	Behaviour
■ Happiness	■ Talking about it	■ Feel anger: act angry—or not
■ Sadness	■ Refusing to speak	■ Feel love: act lovesick—or not
■ Depression	■ Fighting	■ Feel pride: act proud—or not
■ Joy	■ Crying	

Emotional Arousal If you were to describe the events leading up to emotional arousal, you would probably describe three stages: (1) an event occurs, (2) you experience an emotion—you feel surprise, joy, anger, and (3) you respond physiologically—your heart beats faster, your face flushes, and so on. Figure 7.2 (A) depicts this commonsense view of emotions.

Psychologist William James and physiologist Carl Lange offered a different explanation. Their theory places physiological arousal before the experience of the emotion. The James–Lange sequence is: (1) an event occurs, (2) you respond physiologically, and (3) you experience an emotion—for example, you feel joy or sadness. Figure 7.2 (B) depicts the James–Lange view of emotions.

Psychologist Stanley Schachter (1964) has presented evidence for a **cognitive labelling theory** of emotional arousal. According to Schachter you interpret the physiological arousal and, on the basis of this interpretation, experience the emotions of joy, sadness, or whatever. The sequence of events goes like this: (1) an event occurs, (2) you respond physiologically, (3) *you interpret this arousal—that is, you decide what emotion you're experiencing*, and (4) you experience the emotion. Your interpretation of your arousal will depend on the situation you're in. For example, if you experience an increased pulse rate after someone you've been admiring smiles at you, you may interpret this as joy. You may, however, interpret that same increased heartbeat as fear when three suspicious-looking strangers approach you on a dark street. It's only after you make the interpretation that you experience the emotion; for example, the joy or the fear. This sequence of events is pictured in Figure 7.2 (C).

Emotional Expression Emotions are the feelings you have—your feelings of anger, sorrow, guilt, depression, happiness, and so on. Emotional expression, on the other hand, is the way you communicate these feelings. Theorists do not agree over whether you can choose the emotions you *feel*. Some argue that you can, others argue that you cannot. You are, however, clearly in some control of the ways in which you *express* your emotions. You do not have to express what you feel.

Whether you choose to express your emotions will depend on your own attitudes about emotional expression, which you may wish to explore by taking the self-test on page 144. For example, if you feel anger, you may choose to express or not express it.

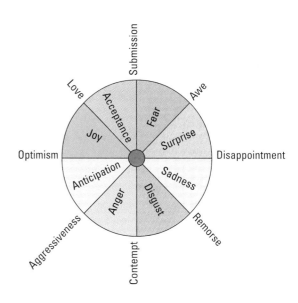

Figure 7.1

A Model of the Emotions
Do you agree with the basic assumptions of this model? For example, do you see love as a combination of joy and acceptance, and optimism as a combination of joy and anticipation?

Source: From *Emotion: A Psychoevolutionary Synthesis* by Robert Plutchik. Copyright © 1980. Reprinted by permission of Allyn & Bacon.

A popular belief about relationships is that if a relationship is not characterized by strong emotions and emotional expression, then there must be something wrong with it. Would you agree with this?

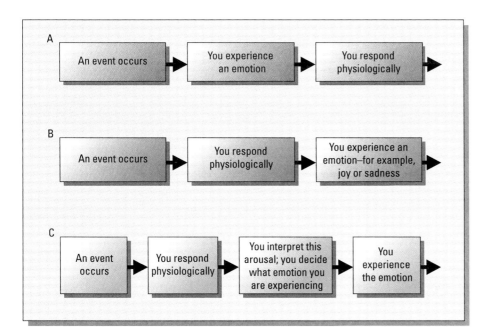

Figure 7.2

Three Views of Emotion
Discuss these three sequences. Can you think of examples to illustrate each sequence? Which sequence seems to illustrate your experience?

Theories of Emotions

You come across a bear on the hiking trail:

1. Are you scared because you see the bear? (commonsense theory)

2. Are you scared because your knees are shaking, your heart is pounding, and you can hardly breathe? (James–Lange theory)

3. Are you scared because you have decided that shaky knees, pounding hearts, and inability to breathe are logical responses to a threat? (cognitive labelling theory)

_____

_____

_____

_____

_____

_____

_____

_____

You do not have to express anger just because you feel angry. In fact, you may feel angry but outwardly act calmly, dispassionately, and lovingly. For example, if there are several promotions to be made in your office and you don't get the first one, you may feel anger. But you may decide that to show your anger could hurt your chances for getting one of the other promotions. You may, therefore, decide to respond calmly, on the assumption that this will help your advancement more than an expression of anger will.

Before taking the test below, realize that people are more likely to receive expressions of positive affect positively and with approval, whereas negative affect is more likely to meet negative reactions (Sommers, 1984; Monahan, 1998; Metts & Planalp, 2002). But it's not always easy to determine how others will perceive an emotion; for example, jealousy, although a negative emotion, may be perceived positively, as a sign that you really care (Metts & Planalp, 2002).

If you decide to communicate your feelings, you need to make several decisions. For example, you have to choose how to do so—face-to-face or by letter, phone, email, or office memo. And you have to choose the specific emotions you will and will not reveal. And third, you have to choose the language in which you express your emotions.

 ## Test Yourself

How Do You Feel About Communicating Emotions?

Instructions: Respond to each of the following statements with T if you feel the statement is a generally true description of your attitudes about expressing emotions, or with F if you feel the statement is generally a false description of your attitudes.

_____ **1** Expressing feelings is healthy; it reduces stress and prevents wasting energy on concealment.

_____ **2** Expressing feelings can lead to interpersonal relationship problems.

_____ **3** Expressing feelings can assist others in understanding you.

_____ **4** Emotional expression is often an effective means of persuading others to do as you wish.

_____ **5** Expressing emotions may lead others to perceive you negatively.

_____ ⑥ Emotional expression can lead to greater and not less stress; expressing anger, for example, may actually increase your feelings of anger.

HOW DID YOU DO?

These statements are arguments that are often made for and against expressing emotions. Statements 1, 3, and 4 are arguments made in favour of expressing emotions; 2, 5, and 6 are arguments made against expressing emotions. You can look at your responses as revealing (in part) your attitude favouring or opposing the expression of feelings. "True" responses to statements 1, 3, and 4, and "False" responses to statements 2, 5,

and 6 indicate a favourable attitude to expressing feelings. "False" responses to statements 1, 3, and 4 and "True" responses to statements 2, 5, and 6 indicate a negative attitude.

WHAT WILL YOU DO?

There is evidence suggesting that expressing emotions can lead to all six outcomes—the positives and the negatives—so general suggestions for increasing your willingness to express your emotions are not offered. These attitudes and their consequences underscore the importance of critically assessing your options for emotional expression. Be flexible, remembering that what will work in one situation will not work in another.

Here is a list of terms for describing your emotions. It's adapted from the model of emotions developed by Plutchik (1980). Notice that the terms included for each basic emotion provide you with lots of choices for expressing the intensity level you're feeling. For example, if you're extremely happy, then *bliss, ecstasy,* or *enchantment* may be an appropriate description. If you're mildly happy, then perhaps *contentment, satisfaction,* or *well-being* may be more descriptive. Look over the list and try grouping the terms into three levels of intensity: high, middle, and low. Before doing that, however, look up the meanings of any words that are unfamiliar to you.

> ❝ We know too much and feel too little. At least, we feel too little of those creative emotions from which a good life springs. ❞
>
> —Bertrand Russell

Happiness: bliss, cheer, contentment, delight, ecstasy, enchantment, enjoyment, felicity, joy, rapture, gratification, pleasure, satisfaction, well-being
Surprise: amazement, astonishment, awe, eye-opening, incredulity, jolt, revelation, shock, unexpectedness, wonder, startle, catch off-guard, unforeseen
Fear: anxiety, apprehension, awe, concern, consternation, dread, fright, misgiving, phobia, terror, trepidation, worry, qualm, terror
Anger: acrimony, annoyance, bitterness, displeasure, exasperation, fury, ire, irritation, outrage, rage, resentment, tantrum, umbrage, wrath, hostility
Sadness: dejected, depressed, dismal, distressed, grief, lonely, melancholy, miserable, sorrowful, unhappy
Disgust: abhorrence, aversion, loathing, repugnance, repulsion, revulsion, sickness, nausea, offensiveness
Contempt: abhorrence, aversion, derision, disdain, disgust, distaste, indignity, insolence, ridicule, scorn, snobbery, revulsion, disrespect
Interest: attention, appeal, concern, curiosity, fascination, notice, spice, zest, absorb, engage, engross

Emotions and Culture   The chapter-opening vignette provided an excellent example of the influence of culture on emotional expression and illustrated the role of **cultural display rules**. These are cultural teachings that advise members of a society about which emotions are permissible to express as well as the circumstances or contexts in which emotional expression is considered appropriate. For example, in one study, Japanese and American students watched a particularly unpleasant film of an operation (Ekman, 1985b). The students were videotaped both in an interview situation about the film and alone while watching the film. When alone, both American and Japanese students showed very similar reactions. But in the interview, American and Japanese students followed different rules for the display of emotions: The American students readily displayed facial expressions indicating displeasure, whereas the Japanese students did not display any great emotion. Similarly, cultural display rules influence what is and what is not considered appropriate emotional expression in a romantic relationship, depending on the stage your relationship is at. You're more likely to inhibit any expression of negative emotions in the early stages of a relationship than after you've achieved some level of involvement or intimacy (Aune et al., 1996).

Cultural differences also exist in decoding the meaning of a facial expression. For example, American and Japanese students were asked to judge the meaning of a smiling and a neutral facial expression. The American rated the smiling face as more attractive, more intelligent, and more sociable than the neutral face. The Japanese, however, rated the smiling face as more sociable but not as more attractive. The Japanese, in fact, rated the neutral face as the more intelligent (Matsumoto & Kudoh, 1993).

Similarly, Japanese women are not supposed to reveal broad smiles and so will hide their smile, sometimes with their hands (Ma, 1996). Women in North America, on the other hand, have no such restrictions and so are more likely to smile openly.

In-Class Notes

Cultural Display Rules

- Which emotions are permissible to express?
- In which context is expression appropriate?

_____

_____

_____

_____

_____

_____

_____

_____

Thinking Critically About   Emotional Appeals

Part of thinking critically about messages involves identifying and analyzing emotional appeals and realizing that these appeals do not constitute logical proof.

One popular emotional appeal is aimed at pity. Organizations use this strategy in seeking support for aid to needy children. You're shown the hungry and sad children—and you feel pity. The objective, of course, is to get you to experience so much pity that you'll contribute to finance the aid efforts. People who beg for money often emphasize their difficulties in an effort to evoke pity and donations.

Another popular appeal is to guilt. A person who does something for you may make you feel guilty unless you do something in return. Or someone may present herself as being in desperate need and make you feel guilty for having what you have and not sharing it.

Listen to a message's emotional dimension critically:

- Realize that emotional appeal does not constitute proof. No matter how passionate the speaker is, remember that passion does not prove the case.
- Realize that, as a listener, you really can't tell with certainty what the speaker is actually feeling. The speaker may, in fact, be using a wide variety of facial management techniques to communicate emotions without actually feeling them.
- Realize that some speakers may use emotional appeals instead of evidence and logical arguments. Some, in fact, may try to use emotional appeals to divert attention away from a lack of evidence.

EXAMPLES?

Give an example of emotional appeals you witnessed or used recently. Were they effective in achieving their aim?

North Americans are also more apt to express negative emotions to their friends and positive emotions to relative strangers. In contrast, Poles and Hungarians are more likely to express negative emotions to strangers and positive emotions to friends (Matsumoto, 1996).

Canadians, by and large, tend to be more reluctant to openly express emotions than are their American neighbours. The popularity of talk shows where people openly cry, yell, and scream in front of millions of viewers suggests the acceptability of emotional expression in American culture.

STUDY TIP

Examine 10 advertisements in a magazine and categorize them by the type of appeal they use to influence consumers. How many rely on emotion versus logic?

Emotions and Gender   Researchers agree that men and women experience emotions similarly (Oatley & Duncan, 1994; Cherulnik, 1979; Wade & Tavris, 1998). The differences that are observed between men and women are differences in emotional expression. Men and women seem to have different **gender display rules**, much as different cultures have different cultural display rules. Gray and Heatherington (2003) examined the effect of social context on the extent to which young men express sadness. They induced sadness in 87 college men and then invited them into a room with two others (either two men or two women) to talk about their feelings. In general, participants expressed significantly more sadness when the others in the room were expressive and accepting. To a lesser extent, the male college students were more able to talk about their feelings of sadness to other men than to women.

Some societies permit and even expect men to show strong emotions. They expect men to cry, to show fear, to express anger openly. Other societies—and many groups within general Canadian culture—criticize men for experiencing and expressing such emotions. Plant et al. (2000) conducted three separate studies to determine the relationship between gender and the interpretation of emotionally expressive behaviour. Participants believed that women experienced and expressed emotions more often than men. What did your culture teach you about gender and the expression of emotions, particularly strongly felt emotions and emotions that show weakness (such as fear, discomfort, or uncertainty)?

Women talk about feelings and emotions and use communication for emotional expression more than men (Barbato & Perse, 1992). Perhaps because of this they also express themselves facially more than men. Even junior and senior high school students show this gender difference. Recent research has found that this difference may well be due to differences in the brains of men and women; women's brains have a significantly larger inferior parietal lobe, which seems to account for their greater awareness of feelings (Barta, 1999).

What has your experience revealed about the ways different cultures express emotions? What similarities and differences have you observed?

Women are also more likely to express socially acceptable emotions than are men (Brody, 1985). For example, women smile significantly more than men. In fact, women smile even when smiling is not appropriate—for example, when reprimanding a subordinate. Men, on the other hand, are more likely than women to express anger and aggression (Fischer, 1993; DePaulo, 1992; Wade & Tavris, 1998). Similarly, women are more effective at communicating happiness and men are more effective at communicating anger (Coats & Feldman, 1996). Women also cry more than men (Metts & Planalp, 2002).

Some research has also looked at the reactions to emotional expression of men and women. In one study, participants watching a video of a courtroom trial rated women most guilty when they displayed either extremely high or extremely little emotion. Women were rated least guilty when they expressed moderate levels of emotion. Men, on the other hand, were rated similarly, regardless of the level of emotions they displayed (Salekin et al., 1995).

Other research suggests that women respond well to men who express emotions (Werrbach et al., 1990). While watching a movie, a confederate of the experimenter in one study displayed a variety of emotions; participants were then asked what they thought of this person. Results showed that men were liked best when they cried, whereas women were liked best when they did not cry (Labott et al., 1991).

Principles of Emotional Communication

Identifying several major principles of **emotional communication** should further explain how emotions work in communication.

Emotions Are Always Important   Although emotions are especially salient in conflict situations and in relationship development and dissolution, they are actually a part of all messages. Emotions are always present—sometimes very strongly, sometimes only mildly—and they must be recognized as a part of the communication experience. This is not to say that emotions should always be talked about or that all emotions you feel should be expressed. In some instances, as we've already seen, you may want to avoid revealing your emotions; for example, you might not want to show your frustration over a customer's indecision or reveal to your children your doubts about finding a job.

Emotional Feelings and Emotional Expression Are Not the Same   Recall from our earlier discussion of facial management techniques (Chapter 6) that emotions are frequently disguised. Remember that you can intensify, de-intensify, neutralize, and mask your emotions so that others will think you're feeling something different from what you really are feeling. From this simple principle two useful corollaries can be derived:

- You cannot tell what other people are feeling simply from observing them, so don't assume you can. It's far better to ask the person to clarify what he or she is feeling.
- Others cannot always tell what you're feeling from the way you act. So if you want others to know how you feel, it's probably a good idea to tell them.

Emotions Are Communicated Verbally *and* Nonverbally   As with most meanings, emotions are encoded both verbally and nonverbally. Your words, the emphasis you give them, and the gestures and facial expressions that accompany them all help to communicate your feelings. Conversely, emotions are decoded on the basis of both verbal and nonverbal cues. And of course emotions, like all messages, are most effectively communicated when verbal and nonverbal messages reinforce and complement each other.

Can you think of a specific instance when failing to appreciate the cultural and gender differences in emotional expression led you to miss another's meaning?

How might confusing emotional expression with feelings lead you to make inferential leaps from, say, a person's facial expression to his or her feelings of depression? Can you recall an instance in which someone confused your emotional expression with your feelings?

There is some evidence that it's actually more difficult to judge when an intimate is lying than when a stranger is lying (Metts, 1989). Do you find this generally true?

Emotional Expression Can Be Good *and* Bad In a relationship, expressing emotions can be cathartic and may even benefit the relationship. Expressing emotions can help you air dissatisfactions and perhaps reduce or even eliminate them. Through emotional expression you can come to understand each other better, which may lead to a closer and more meaningful relationship.

On the other hand, expressing emotions may cause relationship difficulties. Expressing your irritation with a worker's customary way of answering the phone, for example, may generate hostility. Expressing jealousy when your partner spends time with friends may lead your partner to fear being controlled and losing autonomy.

Emotions Are Often Contagious If you've ever watched an infant and mother interacting, you have seen how quickly the infant mimics the emotional expressions of the mother. If the mother smiles, the infant smiles; if the mother frowns, the infant frowns. As a child gets older, he or she begins to pick up more subtle expressions of emotions. A parent's anxiety or fear or anger, for example, are quickly identified and often mimicked by the child. In a study of university roommates, the depression of one roommate spread to the other over a period of just three weeks (Joiner, 1994). In short, through **emotional contagion**, emotions are passed from one person to another. In conversation and in small groups, the strong emotions of one person can easily prove contagious to others present; this can be productive when the emotions are productive, and unproductive when the emotions are unproductive.

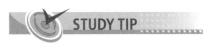
STUDY TIP

Test the notion of emotional contagion by smiling at a teacher or store clerk and noting their reaction.

Listen to This | ## Listening to the Emotions of Others

Expressing your own feelings is only half of the process of emotional communication; the other half is listening. Sometimes you may feel awkward listening to the feelings of others, almost as if you're eavesdropping and overhearing matters that are really too personal. At other times you may feel awkward because you don't quite know what to say. Here are a few guidelines for making an often difficult process a little easier.

- Provide a supportive atmosphere. Avoid equating responding to another's feelings with solving the person's problems. It's usually more productive to view your task in more limited terms—as encouraging the person to express and perhaps clarify his or her feelings and as providing a supportive atmosphere.
- Empathize with the person. Try to see the situation from the point of view of the speaker, to put yourself into the position of the other person. Be especially careful to avoid evaluating the other person's feelings. For example, saying "Don't cry; (s)he wasn't worth it" or "You'll get promoted next year" can easily be interpreted as meaning "Your feelings are wrong or inappropriate."

- Focus on the other person. Avoid responding with your own problems. It's very easy, listening to a friend talk of a broken love affair, to interject with your own similar past situations. And although this can be a useful technique for showing your understanding, it creates problems if it refocuses the conversation on you and away from the person who needs to talk.
- Show your interest. Encourage the person to explore his or her feelings. You might, for example, use simple encouragers like "I see" or "I understand." Or ask questions that let the speaker know that you're listening and that you're interested in hearing more.

SUGGESTIONS?

Your best friend tells you that he suspects his girlfriend is seeing someone else. He's extremely upset and tells you that he wants to confront her with his suspicions but is afraid of what he'll hear. What listening guidelines would you suggest he use if he does confront his girlfriend?

OBSTACLES IN COMMUNICATING EMOTIONS

The expression of feelings is a part of most meaningful relationships, yet is often very difficult. For that reason we need to examine the obstacles to effective emotional expression and to consider some guidelines. Three major obstacles stand in the way of effective emotional communication: (1) society's rules and customs, (2) fear, and (3) inadequate interpersonal skills.

As noted in the text, men have an especially hard time expressing grief. Why do you think this is so?

Societal Rules and Customs

"Cowboy syndrome" is a pattern of behaviour seen in the old cowboy movies from which the syndrome gets its name (Balswick & Peck, 1971), and it is still prevalent in rural areas of western Canada. The cowboy syndrome describes the closed and non-expressive male. This man is strong but silent. He never feels any of the softer emotions (such as compassion, love, or contentment). He never ever cries, experiences fear, or feels sorry for himself. Unfortunately, many men grow up trying to live up to this unrealistic image. It's a syndrome that prevents open and honest expression. Researcher Ronald Levant (*Time*, January 20, 1992, p. 44) has argued that men's inability to deal with emotions as effectively as women is a "trained incompetence." Such training begins early in life when boys are taught not to cry and to ignore pain. This does not necessarily suggest, however, that men should communicate their emotions more openly. Unfortunately, there are many who will negatively evaluate men who express emotions openly and often; such men may be judged ineffective, insecure, or unmanly.

Nor are women exempt from the difficulties of emotional expression. At one time, our society permitted and encouraged women to express emotions openly. The tide now is turning, especially for women in executive and managerial positions. Today the executive woman is being forced into the same cowboy syndrome. She is not allowed to cry or to show any of the once acceptable "soft" emotions. She is especially denied these feelings while she is on the job.

For both men and women, the best advice (as with self-disclosure or any of the characteristics of communication effectiveness discussed in this book) is to express your emotions selectively. Carefully weigh the arguments for and against expressing your emotions. Consider the situation, the people you're with, the emotions themselves, and all the elements that make up the communication act. And, most important, consider your options for communicating—not only what you'll say but also how you'll say it.

STUDY TIP

Discuss the impact of "cowboy syndrome" on society. Consider the impact on areas such as politics, mental and physical health, and relationships.

> By starving emotions we become humorless, rigid and stereotyped; by repressing them we become literal, reformatory and holier-than-thou; encouraged, they perform life; discouraged, they poison it.
>
> —Joseph Collins

Fear

A variety of types of fear stand in the way of emotional expression. Emotional expression exposes a part of you that makes you vulnerable to attack. For example, if you express your love for another person, you risk being rejected. That is, by exposing a "weakness," you can now easily be hurt by the uncaring and the insensitive. Or you may be angry and want to say something, but fear that you might hurt the person and then feel guilty yourself.

In addition, you may not reveal your emotions for fear of causing a conflict. Expressing your dislike for your partner's friends, for example, may create difficulties for the two of you, and you may not be willing to risk the argument and its aftermath.

Because of fears such as these, you may deny to others and perhaps even to yourself that you have certain feelings. In fact, this kind of **denial** is the way many people were taught to deal with emotions.

Inadequate Interpersonal Skills

Perhaps the most important obstacle to effective emotional communication is lack of interpersonal skills. Many people simply don't know how to express their feelings. Some people, for example, can express anger only through violence or avoidance. Others can deal with anger only by blaming and accusing others. And many people cannot express love. They literally cannot say, "I love you."

Obstacles in Communicating Emotions

- Social rules: cowboy syndrome
- Fear of exposing weakness
- Inadequate interpersonal skills

Expressing negative feelings is doubly difficult. Many of us suppress or fail to communicate negative feelings for fear of offending the other person or making matters worse. But failing to express negative feelings will probably not help the relationship, especially if these feelings are concealed frequently and over a long time.

GUIDELINES FOR COMMUNICATING EMOTIONS

Communicating your emotions and responding appropriately to the emotional expressions of others is as important as it is difficult (Burleson, 2003). Your first task, or series of tasks, is intrapersonal: understanding your emotions, deciding if you wish to express them, and assessing your communication options should you decide to express your emotions. Let's focus on these tasks first; then we'll consider some guidelines for their actual expression.

- *Understand your emotions.* Consider how you would feel if your best friend just got the promotion that you wanted or if your brother, a police officer, was shot while breaking up a street riot. Think about your emotions as objectively as possible. Think about

  1. the antecedent conditions that may be influencing your feelings.

  2. the bodily reactions you'd be experiencing.

  3. the interpretations and evaluations you'd be giving to those reactions.

  Try to answer the questions "Why am I feeling this way?" or "What happened to lead me to feel as I do?"

- *Decide if, in fact, you want to express your emotions.* It will not always be possible to stop and think about whether you wish to express your emotions—at times you may respond almost automatically. When you do have this choice, remember that it isn't always necessary or wise to give vent to every feeling you have. Consider also whether your emotional communication will be a truthful expression of your feelings. When emotional expressions are faked—when, for example, you smile though feeling angry—you may actually be creating emotional and physical stress (Grandey, 2000). Remember, too, the irreversibility of communication discussed in Chapter 1: Once you communicate something, you cannot take it back.

> People *can* change their feelings. No matter what happens to them, they *can* creatively decide to feel one way or another about it. And they have quite a range of possible feelings to choose from!
>
> —Albert Ellis

- *Evaluate your communication options.* Evaluate in terms of both effectiveness (what will work best and help you achieve your goal) and ethics (what is right or morally justified).

Now that you understand your emotions, have decided that you want to express them, and have carefully assessed the effectiveness and ethics of your available options, consider the following guidelines for emotional expression.

Describe Your Feelings

Be as specific as possible. Consider, for example, the frequently heard "I feel bad." Does it mean "I feel guilty" (because I lied to my best friend)? Does it mean "I feel

Guidelines for Communicating Emotions

Intra-personal tasks:
- Understand your emotions.
- Decide if you wish to express your feelings.
- Assess your communication options.

Tasks for expression:
- Describe your feelings.
- Identify the reasons for your feelings.
- Anchor your feelings to the present.
- Own your own feelings.

_____

_____

_____

_____

_____

_____

_____

_____

Talking Ethics — Motivational Appeals

Appeals to motives are commonplace. For example, if you want a friend to take a vacation with you, you're likely to appeal to motives such as the desire for fun and excitement, the financial advantage of taking the trip now rather than at the height of the season, and perhaps the possibility that you or your friend might find romance on the vacation. If you look at the advertisements for cruises and vacation packages, you'll see very similar motives being appealed to. And there can be no doubt that such motivational appeals are effective. But are they ethical? Or would you say they are ethical under certain conditions but unethical under other conditions?

When thinking in terms of ethics, consider the legitimacy of appeals based on emotions. As a parent, for example, is it ethical to use appeals to fear to dissuade your teenage children from engaging in sexual relationships? From smoking? From taking drugs? From associating with people of another race or affectional orientation? Is your motive relevant to the question

of whether such appeals are ethical or unethical? Is it ethical to use emotional appeals (say, to guilt, fear, or sympathy) to get a friend to lend you money? To take a vacation with you? To have sex with you?

WHAT WOULD YOU DO?

You're a car dealer and your job is to sell cars. A potential customer comes into the showroom. After a brief interview, you know that this person should logically buy a moderately priced car rather than going into debt to buy the higher-priced fancy sports model. Would it be ethical for you to appeal to the customer's desire for status and sexual gratification to ensure the sale of the expensive sports car? Would it be ethical for you to appeal to the same status and sex motives with a customer who could easily afford the most expensive car on the lot? What would you do in each of these situations?

lonely" (because I haven't had a date in the last two months)? Or does it mean "I feel depressed" (because I failed that last exam)? Specificity helps. Describe also the intensity with which you feel the emotion: "I feel so angry I'm thinking of quitting the job." "I feel so hurt I want to cry." Learn the vocabulary to describe your emotions and feelings in specific and concrete terms.

Identify the Reasons for Your Feelings

Describe the reasons you're feeling as you are. "I'm feeling guilty because I lied to my best friend." "I feel lonely; I haven't had a date for the last two months." "I'm really depressed after failing that last exam." If your feelings were influenced by something the person you're talking to did or said, describe this also. For example, "I felt so angry when you said you wouldn't help me" or "I felt hurt when you didn't invite me to the party."

Anchor Your Feelings to the Present

In expressing feelings—inwardly or outwardly—try to link your emotions to the present. Coupled with a specific description and the identification of the reasons for your feelings, such statements might look like this: "I feel like a failure right now; I've erased this computer file three times today." "I felt foolish when I couldn't think of that formula." "I feel stupid when you point out my grammatical errors."

Own Your Own Feelings

Perhaps the most important guideline for effective emotional communication is this: Own your feelings; take personal responsibility for your feelings (Proctor, 1991). Consider the following statements:

"You make me angry."

"You make me feel like a loser."

"You make me feel stupid."

"You make me feel like I don't belong here."

Note that in these statements the speaker is blaming the other person for the way he is feeling. Of course, you know—on more sober reflection—that no one can make anyone feel anything. Others may do things or say things to us, but we interpret those things. We develop feelings as a result of the interaction between, for example, what people say and our own interpretations. **Owning feelings** means taking responsibility for them. It means acknowledging that our feelings are our feelings. The best way to own our statements is to use **I-messages**, rather than **you-messages**. With this acknowledgment of responsibility, the above statements would look like these:

"I get angry when you come home late without calling."

"I begin to think of myself as a loser when you criticize me in front of my friends."

"I feel so stupid when you use medical terms that I don't understand."

"When you ignore me in public, I feel like I don't belong here."

Note that these rephrased statements do not attack the other person and demand that she change certain behaviours. They merely identify and describe your feelings about those behaviours. The rephrased statements do not encourage defensiveness. With I-message statements, it's easier for other people to acknowledge their behaviours and to offer to change them.

Also use I-messages to describe what, if anything, you want the listener to do: "I'm feeling sorry for myself right now; just give me some space. I'll give you a call in a few days." Or, more directly: "I'd prefer to be alone right now."

> **"** You can handle people more successfully by enlisting their feelings than by convincing their reason. **"**
>
> —Paul P. Parker

> **"** One of the greatest gifts you can give the people you love is to hear their anger and frustration without judging or contradicting them. **"**
>
> —Harold H. Bloomfield

Most examples of how we fail to own our own feelings express negative judgments. But we can also fail to own our own feelings when expressing positive evaluation, as in "The class seemed to enjoy the presentation" (instead of "I gave a really good speech") or "Everyone seems to think I know what I'm doing" (instead of "I finally mastered this business"). Do you own both positive and negative feelings equally?

Handle Your Anger: A Special Case

As a kind of summary of emotional communication, this section looks at anger. Anger is one of the eight basic emotions identified in Plutchik's model (Figure 7.1, page 143). It's also an emotion that can create considerable problems if not managed properly. Anger varies from mild annoyance to intense rage; increases in pulse rate and blood pressure usually accompany these feelings.

Anger is not always necessarily bad. In fact, anger may help you protect yourself, energizing you to fight or flee. Often, however, anger does prove destructive—as when, for example, you allow it to obscure reality or to become an obsession.

Anger doesn't just happen; you make it happen by your interpretation of events. Yet life events can contribute mightily. There are the road repairs that force you to detour so you wind up late for an important appointment. There are the moths that attack your favourite sweater. There's the water leak that ruins your carpet. People, too, can contribute to your anger: the driver who tailgates, the clerk who overcharges you, the supervisor who ignores your contributions to the company. But it is you who interpret these events and people in ways that stimulate you to generate anger.

Anger Communication

Anger communication is not angry communication. In fact, it might be argued that the communication of anger ought to be especially calm and dispassionate. Here, then, are a few suggestions for communicating your anger in a non-angry way:

1. Get ready to communicate calmly and logically. First, relax. Try to breathe deeply; think pleasant thoughts; perhaps tell yourself to "take it easy," "think rationally," and "calm down." Try to get rid of any unrealistic ideas you may have that might contribute to anger; for example, is what this person did so reprehensible, or was it perhaps just a selfish act of a frightened individual?

2. Examine your communication options. In most situations there are many different ways to express yourself, so don't jump to the first possibility that comes to mind. Assess your options for the form of the communication—should you communicate face-to-face? By email? By telephone? Similarly, assess your options for the timing of your communication, for the specific words and gestures you might use, for the physical setting, and so on.

3. Consider the advantages of delaying the expression of anger. For example, consider writing the email but sending it to yourself, at least until the next morning. Then the options of revising it or not sending it at all will still be open to you.

4. Remember that different cultures have different display rules—norms for what is and what is not appropriate to display. Assess the culture you're in as well as the cultures of the other people involved, especially the other cultures' display rules for communicating anger.

5. Apply the relevant skills of interpersonal communication. For example, be specific, use I-messages, avoid "allness"—or generalities—avoid polarized terms, and in general communicate with all the competence you can muster.

6. Recall the irreversibility of communication. Once you say something, you'll not be able to erase or delete it from the mind of the other person.

These suggestions are not going to solve the problems of road rage, gang warfare, or domestic violence. Yet they may help—a bit—in reducing some of the negative consequences of anger and perhaps even some of the anger itself.

Summary of Concepts and Skills

In this chapter we explored the nature and role of emotions in interpersonal communication. We examined the role of the body, mind, and culture in defining emotions, and we looked at some basic or primary emotions. More important, we looked at the obstacles to meaningful emotional communication and some guidelines that might help us communicate our feelings more effectively and also respond to the feelings of others.

1. Emotions consist of a physical part (our physiological reactions); a cognitive part (our interpretations of our feelings); and a cultural part (the influence of our cultural traditions on our emotional evaluations and expressions).

2. Our primary emotions, according to Robert Plutchik (1980), are joy, acceptance, fear, surprise, sadness, disgust, anger, and anticipation.

3. Psychologists have proposed different explanations of how emotions are aroused. One reasonable sequence is this: An event occurs, we respond physiologically, we interpret this arousal, and we experience the emotion.

4. Emotional expression is largely a matter of choice, though it is heavily influenced by culture and gender.

5. Useful principles of emotional communication include the following: emotions are always important; emotional expression and emotional feeling are not the same thing; emotions are communicated both verbally and nonverbally; emotional expression can be both good and bad; and emotions are contagious.

6. Among the obstacles to effective communication of feelings are societal rules and customs, fear of making oneself vulnerable, denial, and inadequate communication skills.

7. The following guidelines should help make your emotional expression more meaningful: Understand your feelings; decide if you wish to express your feelings (not all feelings need be or should be expressed); assess your communication options; describe your feelings as accurately as possible; identify the reasons for your feelings; anchor your feelings and their expression to the present time; and own your own feelings.

8. In responding to the emotions of others, try to see the situation from the perspective of the other person. Avoid refocusing the conversation on yourself. Show interest and provide the speaker with the opportunity to talk and explore his feelings. Avoid evaluating the feelings of the other person.

Check Your Ability

Check your ability to apply the following skills. You will gain most from this brief exercise if you think carefully about each skill and try to identify instances from your recent communication experiences in which you did or did not act on the basis of the specific skill. Use a rating scale such as the following: 1 = almost always, 2 = often, 3 = sometimes, 4 = rarely, and 5 = almost never.

_____ ❶ Identify destructive and constructive beliefs about emotions.

_____ ❷ Identify and be able to describe emotions (both positive and negative) more clearly.

_____ ❸ Use I-messages when communicating your feelings.

_____ ❹ Communicate more effectively with the grief stricken.

_____ ❺ Communicate emotions more effectively.

_____ ❻ Respond to the emotions of others more appropriately by using, for example, active listening skills.

_____ ❼ Evaluate the arguments for and against expressing emotions for each specific situation.

Name:_____ Course:_____ Instructor:_____

After completing this self-test, check your answers against the Answer Key at the back of the book.

Multiple Choice Questions *Choose the BEST answer.*

1. The components of emotions are
   a. bodily reactions, attitudes, and responses.
   b. bodily reactions, mental evaluations and interpretations, and cultural rules and beliefs.
   c. sense data, interpretation–evaluation, and feedback.
   d. physiology, psychology, and gerontology.

2. Which is the most skillful expression of emotion?
   a. "I feel betrayed when you share my secrets."
   b. "You infuriate me by your lack of consideration."
   c. "Are you sure this is safe to do?"
   d. "I feel like you hate me."

3. Of these theories, the one that includes four steps is the
   a. James–Lange theory of emotions.
   b. cognitive labelling theory of emotions.
   c. commonsense view of emotions.
   d. Troy Aikman theory of affects.

4. The cowboy syndrome illustrates
   a. the male inability to reveal emotions.
   b. the female ability to not reveal emotions.
   c. the male ability to tame animals.
   d. the male ability to complete passes.

5. The process of taking responsibility for your feelings is called
   a. response flexibility.
   b. emotional expression.
   c. owning feelings.
   d. display rules.

6. Emotions consist of a physical, a cognitive, and a _____ part.
   a. contextual
   b. cultural
   c. critical
   d. communication

7. The following are obstacles to effective communication of feelings EXCEPT for
   a. the fear of being vulnerable.
   b. denial.
   c. inadequate skills.
   d. emotional expression.

8. Which of these is NOT a primary emotion?
   a. joy
   b. acceptance
   c. trembling
   d. surprise

9. Which of these statements about anger is false?
   a. Anger doesn't just happen.
   b. Anger is the result of actions which you cannot control.
   c. Anger results from the way you interpret events.
   d. Anger is not necessarily bad.

True–False Questions *Write a T or F in the blank next to the statement.*

1. _____ Whatever your emotional state, share the thought immediately with others.

2. _____ What actually happens has a greater influence on your feelings than your interpretations of the event.

3. _____ Emotional expression makes you vulnerable to attack.

4. _____ Your emotions depend a great deal on your culture.

5. _____ I-messages encourage owning your feelings.

6. _____ All feelings should be freely expressed.

7. _____ Disgust is a primary emotion.

8. _____ There are several different views about exactly how emotions are experienced.

9. _____ Emotions are experienced in only one way.

10. _____ You should tell your instructor in no uncertain terms how you feel about this text.

Vocabulary Quiz
The Language of Emotions

Match the terms concerning the communication of emotions with their definitions. Record the number of the definition next to the appropriate term.

a. _____ emotion

b. _____ James–Lange theory

c. _____ cognitive labelling theory

d. _____ emotional expression

e. _____ cowboy syndrome

f. _____ owning feelings

g. _____ I-messages

h. _____ emotional appeals

i. _____ gender display rules

j. _____ cultural display rules

1. The male's lack of ability to reveal the emotions he is feeling because of the belief that men should be strong and silent.

2. The process by which we take responsibility for our own feelings instead of attributing them to others.

3. Messages that explicitly claim responsibility for one's own feelings.

4. Rules for expressing and not expressing various emotions that different cultures teach their members.

5. The sequence of events in emotions as follows: An event occurs; we respond physiologically; we experience the emotion.

6. The feelings we have; for example, our feelings of guilt, anger, or sorrow.

7. Conventional ideas about what emotional expressions are appropriate for one gender or the other.

8. Non-logical means of persuasion.

9. The sequence of events in emotions as follows: An event occurs; we respond physiologically; we interpret this arousal (that is, we decide what emotion we are experiencing); we experience the emotion.

10. The way one chooses to communicate one's feelings.

Skill Building Exercises

7.1 Communicating Your Emotions

Communicating emotions is one of the most difficult of all communication tasks. Here are some situations to practise on. Visualize yourself in each of the following situations, and respond as you think an effective communicator would respond.

1. A colleague at work has revealed some things you did while you were in university, many of which you would rather others on the job did not know about. You told your colleague these things in confidence and now just about everyone knows. You're angry and decide to confront her.

2. A close friend comes to your apartment in deep depression and tells you that his spouse of 22 years has fallen in love with another person and wants a divorce. Your friend is at a total loss as to what to do and comes to you for comfort and guidance.

3. A neighbour who has lived next door to you for the last 10 years and who has had many difficult financial times has just won several million dollars in the lottery. You meet in the hallway of your apartment house.

4. Your grandmother knows she is dying and calls you to spend some time with her. She wants you to know how much she has always loved you and that her only regret in dying is not being able to see you anymore.

Thinking Critically About Communicating Your Emotions.

If you have the opportunity, compare your responses with those of others. Can you derive two or three general principles for effectively communicating emotions from this experience?

7.2 Emotional Advice

For each of the following situations, identify (1) the nature of the problem—what is going wrong, (2) two or three possible solutions that might correct or at least lessen the problem, and (3) the one solution you would recommend to the parties involved.

1. Joe is extremely honest and open, maybe a bit too honest; he regularly says everything he feels without self-censorship or self-monitoring. Not surprisingly, he often offends people. Joe is entering a new work environment and worries that his total honesty may not be the best way to win friends and influence people.

2. Marie and Tom have been married for several years. Marie is extremely expressive—yelling one minute, crying the next. Tom, on the other hand, is the stereotypically non-expressive male; rarely can anyone tell what he's thinking or feeling. Recently, this difference has been causing interpersonal problems. Tom feels Marie doesn't think through her feelings but just reacts impulsively; Marie feels that Tom is unwilling to share his inner life with her.

3. Alex and Deirdre have dated steadily for the last four years. Deirdre is extremely non-expressive but believes that, because of their long and close relationship, Alex should know how she's feeling without her having to spell it out. When Alex doesn't respond appropriately, Deirdre becomes angry and says that Alex doesn't understand her because he doesn't really love her. If he did, she says, he would know what she's feeling without her being explicit. Alex says this is crazy; he's no mind reader and never claimed to be. If Deirdre wants something, he says, she ought to say so; he doesn't feel he has the obligation to guess what is going on in Deirdre's head.

4. Tobin has recently been put in charge of a group of blue-collar workers at a small printer repair firm. Tobin is extremely reserved and rarely reveals any extreme emotion. He gives instructions, praises the workers, and offers criticisms all with the same tone of voice and facial expressions. This has led the workers to feel he's insincere and isn't really feeling what he says.

5. Shasta always smiles, no matter what she says, and she expresses herself in a lilting tone that leads most people to feel she is pleased. In her work as a high school history teacher, this tendency seems to have created problems. When the students don't do their homework or when they otherwise violate established rules, her criticism seems to carry no weight. The students never feel Shasta is disturbed or really chastising them. It has gotten to the point where she has lost all control and authority in the classroom.

Thinking Critically About Emotional Advice.

Discuss these situations and your recommended solutions for lessening the problems with others in your class. Do men and women offer different types of advice? Can you identify typical male solutions and typical female solutions?

7.3 Communicating Emotions Effectively

The 10 statements in the right-hand column are all ineffective expressions of feelings. For each statement, (1) identify why the statement is ineffective (for example, what problem or distortion the statement creates), and (2) rephrase the statement into a more effective message in which you:

- describe your feelings and their intensity as accurately as possible.

- identify the reasons for your feelings and what influenced or stimulated you to feel as you do.

- anchor your feelings to the present.

- use I-messages to own your own feelings and claim responsibility for these feelings.

- use I-messages to describe what (if anything) you want the other person to do because of your feelings.

1. Your lack of consideration makes me so angry I can't stand it anymore.

2. You hurt me when you ignore me. Don't ever do that again.

3. I'll never forgive that louse. The hatred and resentment will never leave me.

4. I hate you. I'll always hate you. I never want to see you again. Never.

5. Look, I really can't bear to hear about your problems of deciding who to date tomorrow and who to date the next day and the next. Give me a break. It's boring. Boring.

6. You did that just to upset me. You enjoy seeing me get upset, don't you?

7. Don't talk to me in that tone of voice. Don't you dare insult me with that attitude.

8. You make me look like an idiot just so you can act like a know-it-all. You always have to be superior, always the damn teacher.

9. I just can't think straight. That assignment frightens me to death. I know I'll fail.

10. When I left the interview, I let the door slam behind me. I made a fool of myself, a real fool. I'll never get that job. Why can't I ever do anything right? Why must I always make a fool of myself?

Thinking Critically About Communicating Emotions Effectively.

Which of the five guidelines listed above do you see violated most often in these statements? With which guideline do you have the most difficulty? In one sentence, how would you describe the difference between the ineffective and effective communication of feelings?

Web Explorations

Companion Website
Visit the Companion Website at
www.pearsoned.ca/devito for student resources related to this chapter, including self-grading quizzes, additional skill-building exercises, and links to other online resources.

Research Navigator

Explore our research resources at
www.researchnavigator.com

- Find and read an article on one of the topics covered in this chapter (for example, emotions, emotional commu-

nication, anger management, or grief). On the basis of this article, what can you add to the discussion presented here?

- Investigate one of the key terms discussed in this chapter (for example, emotion, display rules, emotional appeals, emotional expression, grief, emotional contagion). What additional insights can you provide?

- Try finding answers to one of the following questions, or design a research study to answer it.

1. How do children and adults differ in the way they deal with anger?

2. How do men and women differ in their emotional expression?

3. What motivational appeals are used to appeal to 18- to 35-year-olds? To 55- to 70-year-olds?

Chapter 8
Conversation Messages

Chapter Topics

This chapter discusses the process of conversation, what it is, how it's managed, and how you can make it more effective.

The Process of Conversation

Managing Conversation

Effective Conversation

Technology and Conversation

Computer Mediated Communications

Chapter Skills

After completing this chapter, you should be able to:

- follow the basic structure for conversation.

- initiate, maintain, and close conversations more effectively.

- use the principles of conversational effectiveness with mindfulness, flexibility, cultural sensitivity, and metacommunication.

- be aware of the influence of technology on conversations.

A letter to Ann Landers

Dear Ann: Can you stand one more letter about parents who are "boring and repetitious"? I found solutions. May I share them?

Show interest. My father-in-law (74) brings up his World War II service every time we see him. So I ask questions. What part of the South Pacific? What were your duties? Do you still hear from people you served with? I ask him to pull out his maps and show me exactly where he was. It turns into a fascinating story and, of course, he loves it.

Your first Plymouth only cost $800? What colour was it? Was it automatic? How many miles did you get on a gallon of gas? Do you have pictures of it? Where were you living then? I mention the car I'm driving and laugh about the contrasts and comparisons.

When Mom wants to talk about the past, I encourage her to tell us again about how she met Dad. She loves that story. Another favourite topic is the day I was born. Her eyes shine with delight every time she tells us how "babies come when they are ready—doctor or no doctor."

Our parents made room for us in their lives, whether they wanted to or not. So now it's our turn to make room for them.

_____

"Seeing Myself in 40 Years"

> " Conversation is the socializing instrument par excellence, and in its style one can see reflected the capacities of a race. "
>
> —José Ortega y Gasset

This letter to Ann, "Seeing Myself in 40 Years," shows unusual insight into the topic of this chapter—conversational effectiveness. All of us engage in conversations daily, more or less effectively.

In this chapter we look at the conversation process—what the process is; the principles you follow in conversing; how you manage a conversation (for example, opening, maintaining, and closing); and how you try to prevent and repair conversational problems.

Before reading about the process of conversation, think about some of your own conversations—both satisfactory and unsatisfactory interactions. You may find it helpful to think of a specific recent conversation as you respond to the conversation self-test below. Before taking the test, have a short conversation with your neighbour about a specific topic: the next assignment, your part-time job, and so forth.

Test Yourself

How Satisfying Is Your Conversation?

Instructions: Respond to each of the following statements by recording the number best representing your experience. Use the following scale: 1 = strongly agree, 2 = moderately agree, 3 = slightly agree, 4 = neutral, 5 = slightly disagree, 6 = moderately disagree, and 7 = strongly disagree.

_____ ❶ The other person let me know that I was communicating effectively.

_____ ❷ Nothing was accomplished.

_____ ❸ I would like to have another conversation like this one.

_____ ❹ The other person genuinely wanted to get to know me.

_____ ❺ I was very dissatisfied with the conversation.

_____ ❻ I felt that during the conversation I was able to present myself as I wanted the other person to view me.

_____ ❼ I was very satisfied with the conversation.

_____ ❽ The other person expressed a lot of interest in what I had to say.

_____ ❾ I did NOT enjoy the conversation.

_____ ❿ The other person did NOT provide support for what she was saying.

_____ ⓫ I felt I could talk about anything with the other person.

_____ ⓬ We each got to say what we wanted.

_____ ⓭ I felt that we could laugh easily together.

_____ ⓮ The conversation flowed smoothly.

_____ ⓯ The other person frequently said things that added little to the conversation.

_____ ⓰ We talked about something I was NOT interested in.

HOW DID YOU DO?

To score your test:

1. Add the scores for items 1, 3, 4, 6, 7, 8, 11, 12, 13, and 14. This is your Step 1 total.

2. Reverse the scores for items 2, 5, 9, 10, 15, and 16. For example, if you responded to Question 2 with a 7, reverse this to 1; reverse 6 to 2; reverse 5 to 3; keep 4 as 4; reverse 3 to 5; reverse 2 to 6; and reverse 1 to 7. Add these reversed scores. This is your Step 2 total.

3. Add the totals from Steps 1 and 2 to get your communication satisfaction score.

You may interpret your score along the following scale:

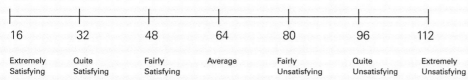

16	32	48	64	80	96	112
Extremely Satisfying	Quite Satisfying	Fairly Satisfying	Average	Fairly Unsatisfying	Quite Unsatisfying	Extremely Unsatisfying

Source: This test was developed by Michael Hecht. It appeared in Michael Hecht, "The Conceptualization and Measurement of Interpersonal Communication Satisfaction," *Human Communication Research* 4 (1978): 253–264 and is reprinted by permission of the author.

WHAT WILL YOU DO?

More important than locating your score on this continuum is identifying the qualities that make a conversation satisfying for you. How will these qualities vary depending on the type of conversation you're engaged in—say, a business meeting with your supervisor or an intimate talk with a close friend? To increase your conversational satisfaction, as this chapter will explain, the best advice is to try to incorporate qualities of interpersonal effectiveness into your own conversations: Be positive, empathic, other-oriented, and so on.

THE PROCESS OF CONVERSATION

Most often, of course, conversation takes place face-to-face, and this is the type of interaction that probably comes to mind when you think of conversation. But today much conversation also takes place online. Online communication is becoming a part of people's experience worldwide. Such communications are important personally, socially, and professionally.

With the understanding that conversation can take place in a wide variety of channels, let's look at the way conversation works. Conversation takes place in five steps: opening, feedforward, business, feedback, and closing (see Figure 8.1).

Step One: Opening

The first step is to open the conversation, usually with some verbal greeting—"Hi," "How are you?" "Hello, this is Joe"; or nonverbal greeting—a smile, or a wave.

You can accomplish a great deal in your opening (Krivonos & Knapp, 1975). First, your greeting can tell others that you're accessible, that you're available to them

Log on to an international Internet Relay Chat channel (for example, #brazil, #finland, #italia, #polska). What can you learn about the conversational practices of other cultures from simply lurking on this channel?

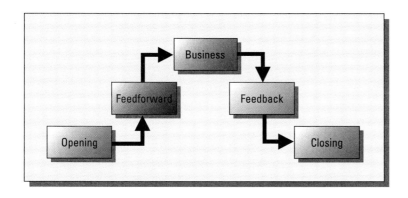

Figure 8.1

The Conversation Process
The conversation process occurs in five basic steps: opening, feed forward, business, feedback, and closing. Can you break down the conversation process into steps or stages that are significantly different from those identified here?

❝ The time has come, the Walrus said,
To talk of many things:
Of shoes—and ships—and sealing wax—
Of cabbages—and kings—
And why the sea is boiling hot—
And whether pigs have wings. ❞

—Lewis Carroll

What other methods seem to work for opening a conversation? Do you use similar or different methods when opening a conversation with a man and with a woman? Would you use similar or different methods depending on whether you wanted to establish a friendship or a business relationship?

for conversation. You can also reveal important information about the relationship between yourself and the other person. For example, a big smile and a warm "Hi, it's been a long time" may signal that your relationship is still a friendly one, that you aren't angry any longer, or any of numerous other messages. Your greeting also helps maintain the relationship. You see this function served between workers who pass each other frequently. This greeting-in-passing assures both people that even though they don't stop and talk for an extended period, they still have access to each other.

In normal conversation, the other person returns your greeting with a greeting that is similar in its formality and intensity. When it isn't—when the other person turns away or responds coldly to your friendly "Good morning"—you know that something is wrong. Similarly, openings are generally consistent in tone with the main part of the conversation; you would not normally follow a cheery "How ya doing today, big guy?" with news of a family death.

Step Two: Feedforward

At the second step in conversation there is usually some kind of feedforward (see Chapter 1). Here you give the other person a general idea of what the conversation will focus on: "I have to tell you about Jack," or "Did you hear what happened in class yesterday?" or "We need to talk about our vacation plans." When feedforwards are misused—for example, when they are overly long or insensitive—they can create conversational problems.

As with the greeting, you can accomplish a great deal with feedforward. For example, you can (1) open the channels of communication; (2) preview the message; (3) altercast; and (4) disclaim. Let's look at each possibility in more detail.

Open the Channels of Communication   Opening the channels of communication informs us that another person is willing to communicate.

Preview Future Messages   Feedforward messages frequently preview other messages. Feedforward may, for example, preview the content ("I'm afraid I have bad news for you"); the importance ("Listen to this before you make a move"); the form or style ("I'll tell you all the gory details"); and the positive or negative quality ("You're not going to like this, but here's what I heard") of subsequent messages.

In-Class Notes

The Conversation Process: Conversation Methods

1. Opening: "Hi! What's going on?"
2. Feedforward: "I hate to bother you, but…"
3. Business: "I've just found a new way to import a file."
4. Feedback: "So, you may want to try it."
5. Closing: "Gotta go…"

_____

_____

_____

_____

_____

_____

_____

_____

Altercast   Feedforward is often used to place the receiver in a specific role and to request that the receiver respond to you in terms of this assumed role. For example, you might ask a friend, "As an advertising executive, what would you think of corrective advertising?" This question casts your friend in the role of advertising executive to answer from a particular point of view.

Disclaim   The **disclaimer** is a statement that aims to ensure that your message will be understood and will not reflect negatively on you (Hewitt & Stokes, 1975; McLaughlin, 1984). Suppose, for example, you fear that your listeners will think your comment is inappropriate, or that they may rush to judge you without hearing your full account, or that they may think you're not in full possession of your faculties. In such cases you may use some form of disclaimer and say, for example, "This may not be the place to say this, but..." or "Just hear me out before you hang up."

Step Three: Business

The third step in the conversational process is the "business," the substance or focus of the conversation.

Business is a good word to use for this stage, because the term emphasizes that most conversations are goal-directed. You converse to fulfill one or several of the purposes of interpersonal communication: to learn, relate, influence, play, or help (see Chapter 1). The term is also general enough to include all kinds of interactions. During the business stage you talk about Jack, what happened in class, or your vacation plans. This is obviously the longest part of the conversation and the reason for both the opening and the feedforward. Not surprisingly, each culture has its own conversational **taboos**—topics or language that should be avoided, especially by visitors from other cultures.

Step Four: Feedback

The feedback step is the reverse of the feedforward step. Here you reflect back on the conversation to signal that the business is completed: "So, you may want to send Jack a get-well card," or "Wasn't that the craziest class you ever heard of?" or "I'll call for reservations while you shop for what we need." In another sense, as described in Chapter 1, feedback takes place throughout the interpersonal communication process. Speakers and listeners constantly exchange feedback—messages sent back to the speaker concerning reactions to what is said (Clement & Frandsen, 1976). Feedback tells the speaker what effect she is having on listeners. On the basis of this feedback, she may adjust, modify, strengthen, de-emphasize, or change the content or form of the messages.

Feedback can take many forms. A frown or a smile, a yea or a nay, a pat on the back or a punch in the mouth are all types of feedback.

Positive feedback (applause, smiles, heads nodding in approval) tells the speaker that his message is being well received. **Negative feedback** (boos, frowns, and puzzled looks, gestures signifying disapproval) tells the speaker that something is wrong and that some adjustment needs to be made.

Feedback may be *person focused* ("You're sweet," or "You have a great smile") or *message focused* ("Can you repeat that phone number?" or "Your argument is a good one").

Feedback can be *immediate* or *delayed.* Generally, the most effective feedback is that which is most immediate. In interpersonal situations, feedback is most often, though not always, sent immediately after the message is received.

Feedback varies from the spontaneous and totally honest reaction (*low-monitored* feedback) to the carefully constructed response designed to serve a specific purpose (*high-monitored* feedback).

Feedback is *supportive* when you console another person, when you simply encourage the other to talk, or when you affirm another's self-definition. *Critical* feedback, on the other hand, is evaluative, as in when you judge another's performance.

Step Five: Closing

The fifth and last step in conversation, the opposite of the first step, is the closing, or goodbye (Knapp et al., 1973; Knapp & Vangelisti, 2000). This step signals the end of accessibility. Just as the opening signalled access, the closing signals the end of access. The closing may also signal some degree of supportiveness; for example, you might express your pleasure in interacting through a comment such as "Well, it was good talking with you." In some conversations the closing summarizes the interaction. Like the opening, the closing may be verbal or nonverbal but it is usually a combination of both. Examples of verbal closings include expressions of appreciation, concern for the other's welfare, or reinforcement as well as leave-taking phrases. Nonverbal closings include breaking eye contact, positioning your legs or feet toward the door and away from the person you're talking with, leaning forward, or placing your hands on your knees or legs (often accompanied by forward leaning) to signal the intention to stand up. As with openings, usually the verbal and the nonverbal are combined; for example, you might say "It was good seeing you again" while leaning forward with hands on your knees.

Reflections on the Steps of Conversation

Not all conversations will be neatly divided into these five steps. Often the opening and the feedforward are combined—as when you see someone on campus, for example, and say "Hey, listen to this"; or when, in a work situation, someone says, "Well, folks, let's get the meeting going." In a similar way, the feedback and the closing might be combined: "Look, I've got to think more about this commitment, okay?"

This conversational process model can help us identify conversational skill deficits and distinguish effective and satisfying from ineffective and unsatisfying conversations. Consider, for example, how people can damage entire conversations through the following violations:

- using openings that are insensitive; for example, "Wow, you've gained some weight."
- using openers that fail to acknowledge the listener; for example, never asking "How are you?"
- using overly long feedforwards that make you wonder if the speaker will ever get to the business
- omitting feedforward before a truly shocking message (for example, the death or illness of a friend or relative), which leads you to see the other person as insensitive or uncaring
- doing business without the normally expected greeting; as when, for example, your doctor begins the conversation with "Well, what's wrong?"
- omitting feedback, which leads you to wonder if the listener heard what you said or cared
- omitting an appropriate closing, which makes you wonder if the other person is disturbed or angry with you
- not giving clear closure (say, on the phone) so it's not clear if the person wants to hang up or continue talking

Of course, each culture will alter the five basic steps in different ways. In some cultures the openings are especially short; in others the openings are elaborate, lengthy, and sometimes highly ritualized. It's easy in intercultural communication situations to violate another culture's conversational rules. Being overly friendly, too formal, or too forward may easily hinder the remainder of the conversation. We may see the rule violator as too aggressive, too stuffy, or too pushy—almost immediately we dislike the person and put a negative cast on the future conversation.

MANAGING CONVERSATION

Speakers and listeners have to work together to make conversation an effective and satisfying experience. We can look at **conversational management** in terms of opening, maintaining, repairing, and closing conversations.

Opening Conversations

Opening a conversation is especially difficult. At times you may not be sure of what to say or how to say it. You may fear being rejected or having someone not understand your meaning. One way to develop opening approaches is to focus on the elements of the interpersonal communication process we discussed in Chapter 1.

Keep in mind two general rules. First, be positive. Lead off with something positive rather than something negative. Say, for example, "I really enjoy coming here" instead of "Don't you just hate this place?" Second, do not be too revealing; don't self-disclose too much early in an interaction. If you do, people will think it strange.

The Opening Line Another way of looking at the process of initiating conversations is to examine the infamous "opening line."

The opening lines most preferred by both men and women are generally those that are direct ("Would you like to have a drink after dinner?") or innocuous ("What do you think of the band?") (Kleinke, 1986). The lines least preferred by both men and women are those that are cute–flippant ("Bet I can out-drink you")—and women dislike these openers even more than men. Men, who generally underestimate how much women dislike the cute–flippant openers, probably continue to use these lines because they are indirect enough to cushion any rejection. Men also underestimate how much women actually like innocuous openers. Women prefer men to use openers that are modest and avoid coming on too strong. Women, in contrast, tend to also overestimate how much men like innocuous lines. And women generally underestimate how much men like direct openers. Most men prefer openers that are very clear in meaning, which may be because men are not used to having a woman initiate a meeting.

STUDY TIP

It's your first day in class and you're asked to introduce yourself. Write an introduction that includes a self-reference and a context reference.

Does your experience agree or disagree with Chris Kleinke's conclusions about how men and women use and respond to opening lines?

In what types of situations do you have the most difficulty opening a conversation? What can you do to make it easier to open a conversation with friends? With those who have just met?

Opening a Conversation

Make references to
- self
- others
- relationship
- context

Two general rules:
1. Be positive.
2. Disclose appropriately.

Maintaining Conversations

In maintaining conversations you follow a variety of principles and rules. Let's consider one key general principle and its several rules; then we'll look at the ways in which the speaker and listener turns are exchanged in conversation.

The Principle of Cooperation During conversation you probably follow the **principle of cooperation**, agreeing with the other person that you will both cooperate in trying to understand each other (Grice, 1975). If you didn't agree on **cooperation**, then communication would be extremely difficult, if not impossible. You cooperate largely by adhering to four **conversational rules**—rules that speakers and listeners in Canada and in many other cultures follow in conversation. Although the names for these rules may be new, the principles themselves will be easily recognized from your own experiences.

1. You follow the **quantity rule** when you're only as informative as necessary to communicate the intended meaning. Thus, you include information that makes the meaning clear, but you omit what does not.

2. You follow the **quality rule** by saying what you know or believe to be true and by not saying what you know to be false. When you're in conversation, you assume that the other person's information is true—at least as far as she knows.

3. You follow the **relation rule** when you talk about what is relevant to the conversation.

4. You follow the **manner rule** by being clear, by avoiding ambiguities, by being relatively brief, and by organizing your thoughts into a meaningful sequence. Thus, you use terms that the listener understands and omit or clarify terms that you suspect the listener will not understand.

Conversational Rules, Culture, and Gender The four rules just discussed aptly describe most conversations as they take place in much of Canada. Recognize, however, that these rules may not apply

What kinds of openers do you prefer to hear?
What kind do you use?

in all cultures; also, other cultures may have other rules. Some of these other rules may contradict the advice generally given to persons communicating in Canada or in other cultures (Keenan, 1976). Here are a few rules appropriate in countries other than Canada, but also appropriate to some degree throughout Canada.

Researchers who study Japanese conversations and group discussions have noted a rule of preserving peaceful relationships with others (Midooka, 1990). The ways to maintain such peaceful relationships will vary with the person with whom you're interacting. For example, in Japan your status or position in the hierarchy will influence the amount of self-expression you're expected to engage in. Similarly, there is a great distinction made between public and private conversations. The rule of peaceful relationships is much more important in public than in private conversations in which the rule may be and often is violated.

The rule of self-denigration, observed in the conversations of Chinese speakers, may require that you avoid taking credit for some accomplishment or make less of some ability or talent you have (Gu, 1990). To put yourself down in this way is a form of politeness that seeks to elevate the person to whom you're speaking.

The rule of politeness is probably universal across all cultures (Brown & Levinson, 1987). Cultures differ, however, in how they define politeness and in how important politeness is compared to, say, openness and honesty. People in Asian cultures, especially the Chinese and Japanese, are often singled out because they emphasize politeness more and mete out harsher social punishments for violators of courtesy norms than most people would in North America or western Europe. This pattern has led some to propose that a rule of politeness operates in Asian cultures (Fraser, 1990). When this rule operates, it may actually conflict with other rules. For example, the rule of politeness may require that you not tell the truth—a situation that would violate the rule of quality.

Canadians are known internationally for being polite. On the other hand, in New York City, the low level of politeness between cab drivers and riders has elicited a great deal of criticism. In an attempt to combat this negative attitude, cab drivers have been given 50 polite phrases and instructions to use them frequently. The phrases include "May I open (close) the window for you?" "Madam (Sir), is the temperature OK for you?" and "I'm sorry, I made a wrong turn. I'll take care of it, and we can deduct it from the fare" (*New York Times*, May 6, 1996, p. B1).

You may wish to take the self-test below to help you think about your own level of politeness.

What types of conversation do you find stressful? Can you identify how you might reduce such stress?

> ❝ You're a real Canadian if somebody steps on your toe and you say, 'Oh, I'm sorry!' ❞
>
> —Will Ferguson

Test Yourself

How Polite Is Your Conversation?

Instructions: This is an approach to a conversational politeness scale—a device for measuring politeness in conversation. Try estimating your own level of politeness. For each item below indicate how closely the statement describes your *typical* behaviour in conversations with peers. Avoid giving responses that you feel might be considered "socially acceptable"; instead, give responses that accurately represent your typical conversa-

tional behaviours. Use a 10-point scale, with 10 being "very accurate description of my typical communications in conversations" and 1 being "very inaccurate description of my typical communications in conversations."

_____ ❶ I make jokes at the expense of another nationality, race, religion, or affectional orientation.

_____ ❷ I say "please" when asking someone to do something.

_____ **3** When talking with guests in my home, I leave the television on.

_____ **4** I make an effort to make sure that other people are not embarrassed.

_____ **5** I use body adaptors when in conversation—for example, touching my hair or face, playing with a pen or Styrofoam cup, or touching the clothing of the other person.

_____ **6** I ask people I call if it's a good time to talk.

_____ **7** I will raise my voice to take charge of the conversation.

_____ **8** I give the speaker cues to show that I'm listening and interested.

_____ **9** I avoid using terms that might prove offensive to people with whom I'm talking, such as terms that might be considered sexist, racist, or heterosexist.

_____ **10** I interrupt the speaker when I think I have something important to say.

HOW DID YOU DO?

This scale was developed to encourage you to consider some of the ways in which politeness is signalled in conversations, and to encourage you to examine your own politeness behaviours.

Nevertheless, you may want to compile a general politeness score that you can compare with those of others. To compile your politeness score, follow these steps:

- Step 1. Add up your scores for items 2, 4, 6, 8, and 9.
- Step 2. Reverse your scores for items 1, 3, 5, 7, and 10. For example, if you ranked a statement 10, it becomes 1; if you ranked a statement 9, it becomes 2; 8 becomes 3, 7 becomes 4, 6 becomes 5, 5 becomes 6, 4 becomes 7, 3 becomes 8, 2 becomes 9, and 1 becomes 10.
- Step 3. Add the scores for Steps 1 and 2 (using the reversed scores for the items noted in Step 2).
- Your score should fall somewhere between 10 (extremely impolite) to 100 (extremely polite).

WHAT WILL YOU DO?

Realize that this "scale" is only a pedagogical tool; it's not a scientifically valid research instrument, so use it to stimulate thinking about your own interpersonal politeness behaviours rather than to give yourself a label. Notice that your score indicates your evaluation of your own conversational behaviours, so this score may be very different from the scores others would assign to you. Generally, do you think you see yourself as more (or less) polite than your peers see you? What might you do to increase your level of perceived politeness?

In internet communication, politeness is covered very specifically by the rules of netiquette, which are very clearly stated in most computer books. For example, find out what a group is talking about before breaking in with your own comment, be tolerant of newbies (those who are new to newsgroups or chat groups), don't send duplicate messages, and don't attack other people.

There are also large gender differences (as well as some similarities) in the expression of politeness (Holmes, 1995). Generally, studies from several different cultures show that women use more polite forms than men (Brown, 1980; Wetzel, 1988; Holmes, 1995). For example, in both informal conversation and in conflict situations, women tend to seek areas of agreement more than do men. Young girls are more apt to try modifying expressions of disagreements, whereas young boys are more apt to express "bald disagreements" (Holmes, 1995). Similarities also exist. For example, men and women in the United States and New Zealand seem to pay compliments in similar ways (Manes & Wolfson, 1981; Holmes, 1986, 1995), and both use politeness strategies when communicating bad news in an organization (Lee, 1993).

Politeness also varies with the type of relationship. One researcher, for example, has proposed that politeness is considerably greater with friends than with either strangers or intimates (Wolfson, 1988; Holmes, 1995). Wolfson (1988) depicts this relationship as in Figure 8.2.

The Principle of Dialogue Think about your own conversational tendencies. Which of the following paired statements *generally* characterize your interpersonal interactions?

- You frequently use negative criticism ("I didn't like that explanation.") and negative personal judgments ("You're not a very good listener, are you?").

- You frequently use dysfunctional communication, such as expressing unwillingness to talk or using messages that are unrelated to the topic of discussion ("There's no sense discussing this; I can see you're not rational.").

- You rarely demonstrate (by paraphrasing or summarizing) that you understand the other person's meaning.

- You rarely request clarification of the other person's perspectives or ideas.

- You frequently request personal positive statements or statements of approval ("How did you like the way I told that guy off? Clever, no?").

- You avoid negative criticism and negative personal judgments; you practise using positive criticism ("I liked those first two explanations best; they were really well reasoned.").

- You keep the channels of communication open ("I really don't know what I did that offended you; please tell me, because I don't want to hurt you again.").

- You frequently paraphrase or summarize what the other person has said to ensure accurate understanding.

- You request clarification as necessary, and you ask for the other person's point of view because of a genuine interest in the other person's perspective.

- You avoid requesting personal endorsement or approval statements.

The conversational behaviours described in the left column are examples of monologue; statements on the right are examples of dialogue. **Monologue** is communication in which one person speaks and the other listens—there's no real interaction between participants. A person engaged in monologue is focused only on her own goals and has no concern for the listener's feelings or attitudes; this speaker is interested in the other person only insofar as that person can serve the speaker's purposes.

Not surprisingly, effective communication is based not on monologue but on its opposite: **dialogue** (Buber, 1958; Yaufair Ho et al., 2001; McNamee & Gergen, 1999). In dialogue there is two-way interaction. Each person is speaker and listener, and sender and receiver, and there is deep concern for the other person and for the relationship between the two people. The objective of dialogue is mutual understanding and empathy. Each person respects the other, not because of the other can do or give but simply because he is a human being and therefore deserves to be treated honestly and sincerely.

The Principle of Turn-Taking   The defining feature of conversation is that the roles of speaker and listener are exchanged throughout the interaction. We use a wide variety of verbal and nonverbal cues to signal **conversational turns**—the changing (or maintaining) of the speaker or listener roles during the conversation. Combining the insights of a variety of communication researchers (Duncan, 1972; Burgoon et al., 1995; Pearson & Spitzberg, 1990), let's examine conversational turns in terms of speaker cues and listener cues.

Speaker Cues.   As a speaker, you regulate conversation through two major types of cues. *Turn-maintaining cues* enable you to maintain the role of speaker. You communicate these cues by, for example, audibly inhaling breath to show that you have more to

> **"** Most conversations are monologues delivered in the presence of witnesses. **"**
>
> —Margaret Millar

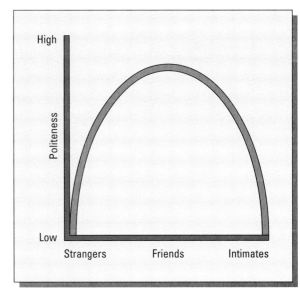

Figure 8.2
Wolfson's Bulge Model of Politeness
Do you find this model a generally accurate representation of your own level of politeness in different types of relationships? Can you build a case for an inverted U theory, in which politeness would be high with both strangers and intimates and low with friends?

Dialogue

- Two-way interaction takes place.

- Each person is speaker and listener.

- Each person feels deep concern for the other person and the relationship.

- Both share the goal of mutual understanding and empathy.

_____

_____

_____

_____

_____

_____

_____

> **"** There is no such thing as conversation. It is an illusion. There are intersecting monologues, that is all. **"**
>
> —Rebecca West

> **"** Two monologues do not make a dialogue. **"**
>
> —Jeff Daly

say; continuing a gesture to show that your thought is not yet complete; avoiding eye contact with the listener to indicate that you're not yet passing the speaking turn on to the listener; or vocalizing pauses ("er," or "umm") to prevent the listener from speaking and to show that you're still talking.

Turn-yielding cues tell the listener that you're finished and wish to exchange the role of speaker for the role of listener. You may communicate these cues by dropping your intonation; by a prolonged silence; by making direct eye contact with a listener; by asking a question; or by nodding in the direction of a particular listener.

Listener Cues. As a listener you can regulate conversation by using three types of cues. First, *turn-requesting cues* tell the speaker that you would like to take a turn as speaker. Second, through *turn-denying cues* you indicate your reluctance to assume the role of speaker. Third, through *backchannelling cues* you communicate various meanings back to the speaker—but without assuming the role of the speaker. You convey your *involvement* with the speaker through attentive posture, forward leaning, and focused eye contact; or *boredom* through an inattentive posture, backward leaning, and avoidance of eye contact. You can also request that the speaker *pace* the conversation differently, or you can signal the speaker to give you *clarification*.

Some backchannelling cues are actually *interruptions*. Backchannelling interruptions, however, are generally confirming rather than disconfirming. They tell the speaker that you're listening and are involved (Kennedy & Camden, 1988). Other interruptions are not as confirming and simply take the speaking turn away from the speaker, either temporarily or permanently. Sometimes the interrupter may apologize for breaking in; at other times the interrupter may not even seem aware of interrupting.

Interruptions can, of course, serve a variety of specific functions. For example, interruptions may be used to change the topic, to correct the speaker, to seek information or clarification, or to introduce essential information. And, of course, you can interrupt to end the conversation.

Not surprisingly, research finds that superiors (bosses, supervisors) and those in positions of authority (police officers, interviewers) interrupt those in inferior positions more than the other way around (Ashcraft, 1998; Carroll, 1994). In fact, it would probably strike you as strange to see a worker repeatedly interrupting a supervisor or a student repeatedly interrupting a professor.

Repairing Conversations

At times you may say the wrong thing, but you can't erase the message—communication really is irreversible. So you may try to account for it. Perhaps the most common way of doing this is with the excuse (Snyder, 1984; Snyder et al., 1983).

You learn early in life that when you do something that others will view negatively, an **excuse** is in order to justify your performance. You're especially likely to offer an excuse when you say or are accused of saying something that runs counter to what is expected, sanctioned, or considered right by your listeners. Ideally, the excuse lessens the negative impact of the message.

Motives for Excuse Making   The major motive for excuse making seems to be maintaining self-esteem—projecting a positive image to yourself and to others. You also may offer an excuse to reduce the stress that results from a bad performance. In other words, you may feel that if you can offer an excuse—especially a good one that is accepted by those around you—it will reduce the negative reaction to your performance and the subsequent stress.

Excuses also enable you to maintain effective interpersonal relationships, even after some negative behaviour. For example, after criticizing a friend's behaviour and observing the friend's negative reaction to your criticism, you might offer an excuse such as "Please forgive me; I'm really exhausted. I'm just not thinking straight." Excuses place your messages—even your failures—in a more favourable light.

Types of Excuses   One categorization describes three basic classes of excuses (Snyder, 1984). Think of recent excuses you have used or heard. Did they fall into any of these classes?

- I didn't do it: *You deny that you did what you're accused of. "I never said that." "I wasn't even near the place when it happened." "She did it, not me."*

- It wasn't so bad: *You admit to doing it, but you claim the offence was not really so bad or perhaps that there was justification for it. "I only padded the expense account by a few dollars." "Sure, I hit him, but he was asking for it."*

- Yes, but...: *You claim that extenuating circumstances account for your behaviour. "It was the liquor talking." "I was too upset to think clearly."*

After reviewing the research on the empathic and listening abilities of men and women, Pearson, West, and Turner (1995) conclude: "Men and women do not differ as much as conventional wisdom would have us believe. In many instances, she thinks like a man and he thinks like a woman because they both think alike." Does your experience support or contradict this observation?

In-Class Notes

The Best Excuses

- I understand the problem.

- I acknowledge my responsibility.

- I am upset with myself for doing this.

- Please forgive me for _____.

- I will never _____ again.

_____

_____

_____

_____

_____

_____

_____

_____

Have you heard (or used) any excuses lately? What functions did these excuses serve? Were they effective? How might they have been made more effective? In what types of situations do you find that excuses only aggravate the problems they were meant to solve? If you were compiling a book on *The World's Worst Excuses,* which one(s) would you include? Which would you include in *The World's Best Excuses?*

ff To make excuses before they are needed is to blame one's self. **JJ**

—Spanish proverb

Good Excuses   The most important question to most people is, What makes a good excuse (Snyder, 1984; Slade, 1995)? Bad excuses only make matters worse—so how can you make good excuses and thus get out of problems?

The best excuses contain five elements (Slade, 1995; Coleman, 2002):

1. You demonstrate that you really see the problem and that your partner's feelings are legitimate and justified. Avoid minimizing the issue or your partner's feelings ("You're overreacting," or "I was only two hours late.").

2. You acknowledge responsibility for doing what you did. Avoid qualifying responsibility ("I'm sorry *if* I did anything wrong") or expressing a lack of sincerity ("OK, I'm sorry; it's obviously my fault—*again*").

3. You say that you regret what you did; you make it clear that you're not happy with yourself for doing what you did.

4. You request forgiveness for what you did. It's important to be specific.

5. You make it clear that this will never happen again.

Closing Conversations

Closing a conversation is almost as difficult as opening a conversation. It's frequently an awkward and uncomfortable part of interpersonal interaction. Here are a few **leave-taking cues** you might consider for closing a conversation:

- Reflect back on the conversation and briefly summarize it to bring it to a close. For example, "I'm glad I ran into you and found out what happened at that union meeting. I'll probably be seeing you at the workshops."

- State the desire to end the conversation directly and to get on with other things. For example, "I'd like to continue talking but I really have to run. I'll see you around."

- Refer to future interaction. For example, "Why don't we get together next week sometime and continue this discussion?"

- Ask for closure. For example, "Have I covered what you wanted to know?"

- Say that you enjoyed the interaction. For example, "I really enjoyed talking with you."

With any of these closings, it should be clear to the other person that you're attempting to end the conversation. Obviously, you will have to use more direct methods with individuals who don't take these subtle hints—who don't realize that *both* people are responsible for the interpersonal interaction and for bringing it to a satisfying closing.

EFFECTIVE CONVERSATION

Because each conversation is unique, **interpersonal effectiveness** skills cannot be applied indiscriminately. Shortly we'll consider specific conversational skills, but you'll need to apply these skills selectively. For example, although openness is a generally positive quality in romantic relationships, it may be quite inappropriate with your supervisor or postal worker. Fortunately, there are general skills to help you regulate your more specific skills.

General Conversational Skills

Four general skills will prove especially valuable in helping you decide how to apply your specific skills. These general skills are mindfulness, flexibility, cultural sensitivity, and metalinguistic abilities.

Mindfulness Mindfulness is a state of awareness in which you're conscious of your reasons for thinking or behaving. In its opposite, **mindlessness**, you lack conscious awareness of what or how you're thinking (Langer, 1989). To apply interpersonal skills effectively in conversation, you need to be mindful of the unique communication situation you're in, of your available communication options, and of the reasons why one option is likely to be better than the others (Elmes & Gemmill, 1990; Burgoon et al., 2000).

Langer (1989) offers several suggestions for increasing mindfulness:

- Create and re-create categories. See an object, event, or person as belonging to a variety of categories. Avoid storing in memory an image of a person with, for example, only one specific label; it will be difficult to re-categorize that image later.
- Be open to new information, even if it contradicts your most firmly held stereotypes.
- Be willing to see your own and others' behaviours from a variety of perspectives.
- Be careful of relying too heavily on first impressions; treat first impressions as tentative, as hypotheses.

Flexibility Flexibility is a quality of thinking and behaving in which you vary your messages based on the unique situation. One test of flexibility asks you how true you believe certain statements are; for example, "People should be frank and spontaneous in conversation" or "When angry, a person should say nothing rather than say something she will be sorry for later." The "preferred" answer to all such questions is "sometimes true," underscoring the importance of flexibility in all interpersonal situations (Hart et al., 1980).

Increasing Flexibility. Here are a few ways to cultivate flexibility:

- Realize that no two situations or people are exactly alike. Ask yourself what is different about this situation or person, and take these differences into consideration as you construct your messages.
- Realize that communication always takes place in a context; ask yourself what is unique about this specific context and how this should influence your messages.
- Realize that everything is in a state of flux. Maybe the way you communicated last month was effective, but that doesn't necessarily mean it will be effective today or tomorrow. Realize too that sudden changes (a breakup with a partner or a fatal illness) will influence what are and are not appropriate messages.
- Realize that every situation offers you different options for communicating. Think about these options, and try to predict the effects each option might have.

Cultural Sensitivity Cultural sensitivity is an attitude and way of behaving in which you're aware of and acknowledge cultural differences. Cultural sensitivity is crucial on a global scale, as in efforts toward world peace and economic growth; it's also essential for effective interpersonal communication and for general success in life (Franklin & Mizell, 1995). Without cultural sensitivity there can be no effective interpersonal communication between people who differ in gender, race, nationality, or affectional orientation. So be mindful of the cultural differences between yourself and the other person. The close physical distance that is normal in Arab cultures may prove too familiar or too intrusive in much of Canada, the United States, and northern Europe. The empathy that most Canadians welcome may make most Koreans uncomfortable (Yun, 1976).

Increasing Cultural Sensitivity. Here are a few guidelines to follow for achieving greater cultural sensitivity.

- Prepare yourself. Read about and listen carefully for culturally influenced behaviours.
- Recognize and face your own and others' fears of acting inappropriately with members of different cultures.
- Recognize differences between yourself and culturally different groups.
- At the same time, recognize that there are often enormous differences within any given cultural group.
- Recognize differences in meaning; words rarely mean the same thing to members of different cultures.
- Be conscious of the cultural rules and customs of others.

Metacommunication **Metacommunication** is communication that refers to other communications; it's communication about communication. Both verbal and nonverbal messages can be metacommunicational. Verbally, you can convey metamessages such as "Do you understand what I'm trying to say?" Nonverbally, you can lean forward in an exaggerated conspiratorial fashion when confiding some dubious tidbit of gossip. Interpersonal effectiveness often hinges on the ability to metacommunicate. For example, in conflict situations it's often helpful to talk about the way you fight. In interpersonal relationships, it's often helpful to talk about what each of you means by "steady" or "really care." On the job, it's often necessary to talk about the ways people delegate orders or express criticism.

Here are a few suggestions for using metacommunication:

- Give clear feedforward. This will help the other person get a general picture of the message that will follow and make understanding easier.
- Confront contradictory or inconsistent messages. At the same time, explain any message of your own that may appear inconsistent to your listener.
- Explain the feelings that go with your thoughts. Often people communicate only the thinking part of their message, with the result that listeners are not able to appreciate the other parts of their meaning.
- Paraphrase your own complex messages. Similarly, to check on your own understanding of another's message, paraphrase what you think the other person means and ask if you are accurate.

What potential barriers (cultural, status, age, etc.) seem to have been overcome in this photograph of a professor and her students?

- Ask questions. If you have doubts about another's meaning, don't assume; instead, ask.
- When you do talk about talk, do so only to enhance clarity or to gain an understanding of the other person's thoughts and feelings. Avoid substituting talk about talk for talk about a specific problem.

Specific Conversational Skills

The skills of conversational effectiveness we discuss here are (1) openness; (2) empathy; (3) positiveness; (4) immediacy; (5) interaction management; (6) expressiveness; and (7) other-orientation. These qualities are derived from a wide spectrum of ongoing research (Bochner & Kelly, 1974; Rubin & Martin, 1994; Spitzberg & Hecht, 1984; Spitzberg & Cupach, 1989; Whalen-Bell, 2003). As you read about these concepts, keep the general skills in mind.

Openness   **Openness** involves your willingness to self-disclose—to reveal information about yourself that might normally be kept hidden. Openness also includes your willingness to listen openly and to react honestly to the messages of others.

Communicating Openness.   Consider these few ideas:

- Self-disclose when appropriate. Be mindful about your self-disclosures, remembering that this form of intimate communication has both benefits and dangers.
- Respond to those with whom you're interacting with spontaneity and with appropriate honesty—but also with an awareness of what you're saying and what the possible outcomes of your messages might be.
- Own your own feelings and thoughts. Take responsibility for what you say. Use I-messages instead of you-messages. For example, instead of saying, "You make me feel stupid when you don't ask my opinion," say, "I feel stupid when you ask everyone else what they think but don't ask me." When you use I-messages, you say, in effect, "This is how *I* feel," "This is how *I* see the situation," and "This is what *I* think."

In-Class Notes

Skills for Conversational Effectiveness

- openness
- empathy
- positiveness
- immediacy
- interaction management
- expressiveness
- other-orientation

_____

_____

_____

_____

_____

_____

_____

Empathy   To empathize with someone is to feel as that person feels. When you feel **empathy** for another, you're able to understand what the other is experiencing from that person's point of view. Empathy does *not* necessarily mean that you agree with what the other person says or does. You never lose your own identity or your own attitudes and beliefs. To *sympathize,* on the other hand, is to feel *for* the individual—to feel sorry for the person, for example.

Empathy, then, enables you to understand, emotionally and intellectually, what another person is experiencing. Not surprisingly, empathy can have significant effects. For example, a study of physician empathy found that patients with empathic physicians experienced significantly less depression and were less likely to consider euthanasia than those with nonempathic physicians (Emanuel et al., 2000).

***Communicating Empathy*.**   Here are a few suggestions to help you communicate empathy effectively (Authier & Gustafson, 1982).

- Self-disclose. Express the similarities between your experiences and the experiences of the other person. At the same time, however, acknowledge that you're aware of the differences. For example, "I never failed a course, but I got enough Ds to understand why you feel so down."
- Avoid judgmental and evaluative (nonempathic) responses. Avoid *should* and *ought* statements that try to tell the other person how he or she *should* feel. For example, avoid expressions such as "Don't feel so bad," "Don't cry," "Cheer up," or "In time you'll forget all about this."

Skills Toolbox   7 Ways to Avoid Being Conversationally Difficult

At work meetings or at the water cooler, some people make conversation extremely difficult. Here's a brief list of conversationally difficult people and some suggestions to avoid becoming one of them.

1. *The detour taker* begins to talk about a topic; but then a key word or idea suggests another topic, and off this person goes pursuing the new topic. *Follow a logical pattern in conversation; avoid long and/or frequent detours.*
2. *The moralist* seems to have an inside track on what's right and what's wrong. The moralist's business is judgment, and this individual frequently interjects moral judgments into even the most mundane conversations: "You really shouldn't have said that" or "You know, you should...." *Avoid evaluation and judgment; see the world through the eyes of the other person and (perhaps) the other culture.*
3. *The storyteller* has difficulty talking about the here and now and so tells stories. Mention a topic and the storyteller has a ready tale that makes you sorry you ever brought the subject up in the first place. This is especially problematic at company meetings, in which you want to accomplish a certain amount of work in the allotted time. *Talk about yourself in moderation; be other-oriented.*
4. *The interrogator* is a mixture of police officer, lawyer, and teacher and seems to do nothing but ask questions. No sooner have you answered one question than you are peppered with another and another and another. *Ask questions in moderation—to secure needed information, not to get every detail imaginable.*

5. *The egotist* is interested only in herself and shows this by connecting even the most wide-ranging topics to self-related concerns. Often this gets in the way of effective team conferences, and invariably it wastes everyone's time. *Be other-oriented; focus on the other person as an individual; listen as much as you speak, and speak about the listener at least as much as you speak about yourself.*
6. *The doomsayer* is the ultimate negative thinker. No matter what you say, the doomsayer will read something negative into it. To the doomsayer, the past was a problem, the present is unsatisfying, and the future is bleak. *Be positive.*
7. *The advisor* assumes, whenever you express a doubt or mention a decision, that you want advice; this person proceeds to analyze the pros and cons of each alternative and then provides the solution. The idea that you simply wanted to express a doubt never occurs to the conversational advisor. *Avoid giving unsolicited advice. Don't assume that discussing a problem is the same as asking for a solution.*

THEN AND NOW

Have you ever been in a conversation in which you acted the role of one or more of these conversationally difficult people? What specifically did you do to make the conversation difficult? If you were having the same conversation today, what would you do differently?

- Use reinforcing comments. Let the speaker know that you understand what he is saying, and encourage him to continue talking about the issue. For example, use comments such as "I see," "I get it," "I understand," "Yes," and "Right."
- Demonstrate interest by maintaining eye contact (avoid scanning the room or focusing on objects or persons other than the person with whom you're interacting); maintaining physical closeness (avoid large spaces between yourself and the other person); leaning toward (not away from) the other person; and showing your attentiveness with your facial expressions, nods, and eye movements.
- To foster more open and honest communication, address mixed messages. When your friend verbally expresses contentment but shows nonverbal signs of depression it may be prudent to question the possible discrepancy.

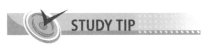

STUDY TIP

Role play a conversation with a classmate, using a style from the seven styles of conversationally difficult people. After a few minutes, see if your classmate can identify your style. Then reverse roles.

Positiveness **Positiveness** in interpersonal communication involves the use of positive rather than negative messages. For example, instead of the negative "I wish you wouldn't ignore my opinions," consider the positive alternative: "I feel good when you ask my opinions." Instead of the negative "You look horrible in stripes," consider the positive "I think you look great in solid colours."

Communicating Positiveness. Here are a few suggestions for communicating positiveness. Following these tips may be a bit easier for women than for men, because women generally are more apt to express positiveness in their evaluations in both face-to-face and computer-mediated communication (Adrianson, 2001).

- Look for the positive in the person or in the person's work and compliment it. Compliment specifics; overly general compliments ("Your project was interesting") are rarely as effective as those that are specific and concrete ("Your proposal will produce a great financial saving").
- Express satisfaction when communicating with others by, for example, using positive facial expressions, maintaining a reasonably close but appropriate distance, focusing eye contact, and avoiding glancing away from the other person for long periods of time.
- Recognize cultural differences in expressing positive messages or compliments (Dresser, 1996). For example, in Canada it would be considered appropriate for a teacher to compliment a student for doing well on an exam or for a supervisor to compliment a worker for doing an exceptional job on some project. But in other cultures (collectivist cultures, for example) compliments like these would be considered inappropriate, because they single out the individual and separate that person from the group. Similarly, the responses to compliments will vary from one culture to another (Chen, 1993). While many Canadians often have difficulty accepting compliments, a compliment is generally supposed to be accepted graciously; you did a good job and have a right to have that acknowledged. In more collectivist cultures, however, you're expected to deny your right to the compliment and instead to credit the group or the situation.

> ❝ There is nothing you can say in answer to a compliment. I have been complimented myself a great many times, and they always embarrass me—I always feel that they have not said enough. ❞
>
> —Mark Twain

Immediacy **Immediacy** has to do with the joining of speaker and listener; it's the creation of a sense of togetherness, of oneness. When you communicate immediacy you convey a sense of interest and attention, a linking with the other person. People respond to communication that is immediate more favourably than to communication that is not. In various studies, for example, students of instructors who communicated immediacy felt that the instruction was better and the course more valuable than students of instructors who did not communicate immediacy (Moore et al., 1996; Witt & Wheeless, 2001).

Communicating Immediacy.   Here are a few suggestions for communicating immediacy:

- Maintain appropriate eye contact and limit looking around at others; smile and otherwise express your interest.
- Maintain a physical closeness, which suggests a psychological closeness; maintain a direct and open body posture.
- Focus on the other person's remarks. Let the speaker know that you heard and understood what was said and will base your feedback on it.
- Reinforce, reward, or compliment the other person. Use expressions such as "I like your new outfit" or "Your comments were really to the point."
- Use the other person's name; for example, say, "Yasmin, what do you think?" instead of "What do you think?"
- Express immediacy with cultural sensitivity. In Canada, immediacy is generally seen as friendly and appropriate. In other cultures, however, the same behaviours may be viewed as overly familiar, as presuming that relationship is close when it's only one of acquaintanceship (Axtell, 1993).

Interaction Management   **Interaction management** consists of the techniques and strategies by which you regulate and carry on an interpersonal interaction. Effective interaction management results in an interaction that's satisfying to both parties. Neither person feels ignored or on stage; each contributes to and benefits from the interpersonal exchange.

Managing Communication Interactions.   Of course, this entire text is devoted to the effective management of interpersonal interactions—but here are a few specific suggestions:

- Maintain your role as speaker or listener—and pass the opportunity to speak back and forth—through appropriate eye movements, vocal expressions, and body and facial gestures.
- Keep the conversation fluent, avoiding long and awkward pauses. For example, researchers have found that patients are less satisfied with their interaction with their doctor when the silences between their comments and the doctor's responses are overly long (Rowland-Morin & Carroll, 1990).
- Communicate by means of verbal and nonverbal messages that are consistent and reinforce one another. Avoid sending contradictory signals—for example, a nonverbal message that contradicts the verbal message.

Expressiveness   **Expressiveness** is the skill of communicating genuine involvement and includes, for example, taking responsibility for your thoughts and feelings, encouraging expressiveness or openness in others, and providing appropriate feedback.

Communicating Expressiveness.   Here are a few suggestions for communicating expressiveness:

- Use appropriate variations in vocal rate, pitch, volume, and rhythm to convey involvement and interest. Use appropriate variations in verbal language, avoiding clichés and trite expressions—which can signal a lack of originality and personal involvement.

> ❝ If you can't say anything good about someone, sit right here by me. ❞
>
> —Alice Roosevelt Longworth

STUDY TIP

Watch a seasoned journalist interview someone on your local newscast or entertainment news show. Identify the techniques used by the journalist to convey expressiveness and to encourage the interviewee to self-disclose.

- Use appropriate gestures, especially those that focus on the other person rather than on yourself. For example, maintain eye contact and lean toward the person; at the same time, avoid making self-touching gestures or directing your eyes to others in the room.
- Be conscious of different cultures' approaches to expressiveness. Some cultures (Italian, for example) encourage expressiveness and teach children to be expressive. Other cultures (Japanese and Thai, for example) encourage a more reserved response style (Matsumoto, 1996). Some cultures (Arab and many Asian cultures, for example) consider expressiveness by women in business settings to be generally inappropriate (Lustig & Koester, 1999; Axtell, 1993; Hall & Hall, 1987).
- Give verbal and nonverbal feedback to show that you're listening. Such feedback—called "conversational pitchback" by one researcher—promotes relationship satisfaction (Ross, 1995).

Other-Orientation   Other-orientation is the ability to adapt interpersonal messages to the other person; it involves communicating attentiveness and interest in the other person and in what the person says.

Communicating Other-Orientation.   You'll recognize the following behaviours in those with whom you enjoy talking:

- Show consideration and respect. For example, ask if it's all right to dump your troubles on someone before doing so; ask if your phone call comes at a good time before launching into your conversation.
- Acknowledge the other person's feelings as legitimate: "You're right" or "I can understand why you're so angry; I would be, too." Such responses help focus the interaction on the other person and assure the person that you're listening.
- Acknowledge the importance of the other person. Ask the other person for suggestions and opinions. Similarly, ask for clarification as appropriate to make sure that you understand what the other person means.
- Focus your messages on the other person. Verbally, use open-ended questions (as opposed to questions that merely ask for a yes or no answer) to involve the other person in the interaction, and make statements that directly address the person. Nonverbally, use focused eye contact and appropriate facial expressions; smile, nod, and lean toward the other person.
- Grant the other person permission to express (or to not express) feelings. A simple statement such as "I know how difficult it is to talk about feelings" opens up the topic of feelings and gives the person permission to pursue such a discussion or to say nothing.

What one quality of conversational effectiveness do you think is the most important in establishing a romantic relationship? In dealing effectively with interpersonal conflict? In employer–employee communication? Why?

TECHNOLOGY AND CONVERSATION

Cellphones

The year 2002 was a landmark year—the year that the number of cell or mobile phone subscribers exceeded the number of landline subscribers across the globe (Srivastava, 2005). When first introduced, the cellphone was a useful technological device. Now, with its huge computational power, and photo and video capacity, it has become a key social object that plays a role in almost every aspect of the user's life.

Lin Chu, originally from Hong Kong, was introduced at a party shortly after her arrival in Vancouver. The hostess, anxious to make her feel welcome, spoke to her in "English Made Easy." Using expressive gestures and speaking in a loud, clearly articulated voice, she asked, "Would you (pointing to Chu) like something to eat (pointing to her mouth and making chewing motions)?" Chu responded, "I'd love a sherry." She had spent the last four years earning her PhD at Oxford University in England.

Our good intentions to assist new Canadians can be insulting if we make assumptions that are unfounded.

Consider the following list of "don'ts."
Don't assume that you have to:

- speak in elementary English.
- gesture more than normal.
- speak slower than normal.
- speak louder than normal.
- explain everything in great detail.

EXAMPLES?

Many new Canadians do need time to develop proficiency in English. Have you had the experience of trying to communicate in an unfamiliar language? What assistance would you have appreciated? What assumptions would you hope others would avoid making?

Not too long ago, cellphones were tools that the workplace used to ensure business was being conducted efficiently. Now, only the rare person over the age of 12 does not own and carry a cellphone. A great deal of work is conducted using cellphones from many places other than the office. Parents often require their children to keep their cellphones handy so that they can be reached whenever parents feel the need to check in. And, of course, cellphones are essential for friends to keep in touch. As a result, cellphones have radically impacted the number and form of conversations in which people are engaging.

Building a Communications Network

Face-to-face conversations are often dependent upon place. People meet in coffee shops, around the water cooler at work, or around the dinner table at home, and engage in face-to-face conversations to catch up on the day, to gossip, to ask advice, and to plan future activities. Place is often a key element in the type of conversation and the sense of collective identity of a family, a group of friends, or a team of employees. With the increasing use of cellphones, Srivastava (2005) suggests that the sense of belonging to a place (such as a family home, a school, or a workplace) may be slowly giving way to a sense of belonging to a communications network.

For example, merely a few years ago, if you wished to call a friend, you usually called him at home on a landline. You may have chatted to his mom first before being passed over to him. Parents usually were aware of who was calling their children and how long their children were spending on the phone, and felt a connection with their children's friends and classmates. Now, family members may each have individual cellphones and can receive calls from their friends wherever they may be. Phone calls become much more private and family members' social lives become separated from that of the family as a whole.

This can have both positive and negative effects. Srivastava (2005) suggests that cellphones may be contributing to the fragmentation of the family unit because the family home is no longer the location or place to reach a person. A person's social network is no longer primarily based through family connections but can be completely individualized and separate from those of the rest of the family members. However, on the positive side, cellphones also provide external support for individual family members, especially in situations of abused children or spouses.

No other technological device has become so personal and closely connected to our sense of self. Many people use their cellphones at all times of the day and night, decorate them to suit their personalities, and often sleep with them close at night to use as an alarm clock or in case of emergency. Srivastava (2005) suggests that the cellphone helps people feel connected at all times to their outside world so that they feel less alone. A 2003 UK survey (Harkin, 2003) found that people said that they worried about leaving home without their cellphones in case they missed important calls, and that 46 percent of cellphone users described the loss of their cellphone as a form of bereavement.

Conversational Privacy

Arguably, one of the most challenging issues of increasing cellphone use is the question of conversational privacy. Face-to-face conversations are held with the acknow-ledgement that those who are close by will be able to hear what is being said. However, cellphone conversations often take place in very public places—restaurants, elevators, and even public washrooms; and at often inappropriate times—during meetings, concerts, even weddings and funerals. While some people are becoming more conscious of the etiquette of holding a private conversation in a public place, many users still need frequent reminders to turn off their phones or to silence the ring. This still leaves those who are within hearing but outside of the conversation in the uncomfortable position of eavesdropping, especially if the phone call is of a private nature. An even more uncomfortable situation occurs when the person you are talking to suddenly interrupts your conversation to take a phone call on a cell, or worse, on a tiny wireless headset. Etiquette problems will become increasingly complex as this nearly invisible technology advances.

Text Messaging

Despite its growing popularity, or perhaps because of it, the cost of maintaining and using a cellphone is often quite prohibitive. Young people have become wise in the ways of using their cellphones to maximize potential use while minimizing costs. One way is through text messaging, which requires an entirely different mode of conversation from that discussed earlier. Text messages are short and to the point, with no attention given to the traditional conventions of opening, feedforward, business, feedback, and closing, instead often jumping straight to the business portion. As well, a very abbreviated form of language is used in text messaging to speed up the process and facilitate keying on a phone pad.

While providing a less expensive way to communicate, text messaging appears to have impacted the conversational abilities of some young people. Parents note that their children often struggle with traditional phone conversations, preferring to respond with single words, and rarely offering information to move a conversation along. As well, text messages are often about more mundane topics such as the score in the hockey game on TV or what clothes will be worn to school. Both parents and teachers have commented that young people are becoming experts at skimming along the surface of many topics at once but are often reluctant or unable to delve more deeply into a topic. These parents and teachers wonder if such reluctance—or inability—is related to abbreviated text messaging conversational skills (Wallis, 2006).

Text messaging also appears to have some major social and political implications when used on a mass scale. Rheingold (2002) explores the power of motivating the masses using text messaging rather than more traditional communication methods. For example, he describes cellphone users in Stockholm who use text messages to alert riders to the location of transit inspectors in order to avoid fines. Rheingold has also cited text messaging as being partly responsible for the overthrow of Joseph Estrada in the Philippines. More recently, text messaging has been implicated in encouraging mass protests against a series of cartoons of the Prophet Mohammed published by several newspaper chains.

Britain's Prince William is faced with frequent onslaughts from "star-struck" students. A sophisticated text-messaging network has materialized, automatically distributing information about the Prince's whereabouts. Whenever he is seen about town, messages are sent out about his location to a small group. The text messages are then forwarded to an ever-growing number of young girls, meaning that information about Prince William's activities can take just seconds to reach over a hundred royal-watchers. Poor Prince William is most likely dreaming of better days when mobile phones were only in the hands of the chosen few.

(*Guardian Unlimited*, 2003, as cited in Srivastava, 2005)

Srivastava (2005) discusses the phenomenon of "flash mobs," the assembly of unrelated people on a moment's notice through mass text messaging. These are described as a "large group of people who gather in a usually predetermined location, perform some brief action and then quickly disburse." Flash mobs are generally peaceful, with their objective being to maximize surprise and fun in the minimum time.

The faithful can also offer prayers through text messaging. Srivastava (2005) describes how Hindus in India can text the word "puja," meaning "prayer," to a mobile cell operator to have prayers said for them. The Vatican sends out "thoughts for the day" to subscribers, and in Morocco, incoming text messages are free during the Haj, or pilgrimage, to Mecca.

COMPUTER MEDIATED COMMUNICATIONS

Look around at any group of young people, whether in school, at the mall, or in their homes, and you will see them plugged in to iPods, cellphones, and computers. They are busy conversing with others in a technologically enhanced way. A study conducted by the Kaiser Family Foundation and Stanford University, entitled *Generation M: Media in the Lives of 8–18 Year Olds* (cited in Azzam, 2006) sampled more than 2000 students in grades 3 through 12 in the United States. The researchers found that young people continue to spend about 6.5 hours per day devoted to media use, an amount that has remained relatively steady in the past few years. However, their increasing use of a number of different media simultaneously translates to about 8.5 hours of media exposure daily. In addition, nearly one-third of the respondents indicated that they talk on their cellphone, instant message, watch TV, listen to music, or surf the web for fun for most of the time that they are doing their homework. The respondents indicated that their bedrooms are increasingly becoming media centres that include TVs, computers with webcams, video games, and phones. The students also reported that, as they get older, their parents become increasingly lax about supervising how they engage with media, for how long, and with whom.

Computer mediated communications (CMC) has become an area of increased interest due to the pervasiveness of technologies such as electronic mail (email), and other online environments such as electronic bulletin boards, chat rooms, instant messaging (IM), user groups, and so on. Because conversations are not face-to-face when using CMC, these technologies are altering what we have come to understand as the traditional rules of conversation. When communication is mediated through computer technology, people engaged in conversations can alter how they present themselves, avoid the use of nonverbal cues, make use of radically different verbal codes and feedback patterns, and change the process by which they form intimate relationships (Tidwell & Walther, 2002). As Spears and Lea state (1994, as cited in Soukup, 1999), "CMC introduces the possibility of revolutionary social and structural changes in the ways people communicate and relate to each other."

Email

When email was first introduced, it was supposed to eventually result in a paperless office. Through email, messages could be sent out to recipients without the need for the physical circulation or posting of a paper memo. In reality, email may be providing an additional communication burden for many. It is not uncommon for professionals to receive several hundred emails a day—not including spam or junk mail. Often, those messages are forwards or replies to everyone on the address list and, therefore, of little interest. Other emails, though, require a quick or immediate response.

In many offices, email is replacing the quick face-to-face conversations or questions that could occur by walking down the hall or making a phone call. Because email is often used to ask a question which requires a fairly quick response, many people will interrupt other work to respond quickly if a new e-mail has arrived in their inbox. Others become quite addicted to regularly checking their email for new messages, even during family meals, throughout the night, or first thing in the morning before leaving for school or work.

On the other hand, email is a wonderful way to connect people wherever they may be. Internet cafés help travelling young people keep in contact with family and friends back home. Business centres in hotels enable professionals to keep up to date with affairs back at the office, to direct further work, and to be involved in business decisions. Email, in this sense, provides a quick and reliable communication channel.

While email doesn't follow the same conversational patterns discussed in the first part of the chapter, it does have its own form of etiquette and pattern. Each message usually begins with a form of conversation opener, moves to the business portion of the conversation, followed by a closing. The recipient will often respond with the feedforward or feedback portions of the conversation process. Emoticons are used by both the initiator and the respondent to provide feedback in lieu of facial expressions, tone of voice, or body language. However, since email is essentially devoid of these tone indicators, it is notorious for sending messages in which meanings are misread or misinterpreted. It is important to reread email messages before sending them, to determine if your choice of words sends the message you intend.

Online Environments

"There's an extraordinary fit between the medium and the moment, a heady giddy fit in terms of social needs. [The online environment] is less risky if you are lonely and afraid of intimacy, which is almost a definition of adolescence.

Skills Toolbox   6 Ways to Effective Business Email

Netiquette is the system of rules for communicating politely over the internet or over an intranet. These rules, as you'll see, are especially applicable to business email; but they apply generally to all computer-mediated communication.

1. Don't shout. WRITING IN CAPS IS PERCEIVED AS SHOUTING. It's okay to use caps occasionally to achieve emphasis. If you wish to give emphasis, underline, _like this_, or use asterisks *like this*.
2. If your email system has a spell-checker or grammar checker, use it. There's little sense in sending emails that may be read by those making decisions about promotions and work assignments, only to show that you're careless in spelling or grammar.
3. Respond to emails promptly. Even if you have to give a more extended response than you now have time for, reply as soon as possible; for example, "Thanks for your email. I'll need a few days to track down the information you want. I'll be back to you asap." It takes almost no time to

do this but assures the sender that his or her message reached the right person and will get a response.
4. Be brief. Follow the maxim of quantity by communicating only the information that is needed; follow the maxim of manner by communicating clearly, briefly, and in an organized way.
5. When sending email to a group of people, consider the value of not disclosing each person's email address and instead consider addressing it to "undisclosed recipients" or to "colleagues."
6. Resist the tendency to clog the email systems of colleagues with baby photos, long drawn-out stories, or attachments that they probably don't want.

THEN AND NOW

Have you ever communicated impolitely over the net? What specifically did you do? What would you do differently now?

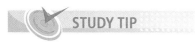

STUDY TIP

Use the flash cards for Chapter 8 on this textbook's website to see how well you can remember the concepts discussed in this chapter.

Things get too hot, you log off, while in real time and space, you have consequences.... Online life is like an identity workshop and that's the job of adolescents—to experiment with identity" (Turkle, as cited in Wallis, 2006).

Face-to-face social situations, such as school or work, require that we learn how to hold conversations with a variety of people, some who will become friends but most who will never move beyond the acquaintance stage. For some people, this need to engage in positive social interaction is extremely difficult. Online environments, on the other hand, allow for the development of much broader and less restrictive social networking systems. Imagine connecting to a chat room to create an instant network of friends, all of who know only what you choose to tell them about yourself.

The increasing involvement of young people in online networks is raising a number of concerns. Today people of all ages lead tightly scheduled lives that often leave little time for socializing over a cup of coffee or at a family meal. Technology offers a convenient way to continue to socialize. However, involvement in online social networks is becoming a compulsion for many users and can reduce the amount of time spent in the actual physical company of others. Many educators and psychologists are now talking of ways to actively break free of online compulsions that drive people to get up in the middle of the night to check their email or carry their cellphones with them constantly.

Many young people claim that they are involved in online networks with a limited amount of parental supervision. Without reinforced rules, young people run the risk of wandering into unsavoury online neighbourhoods and communicating with the "wrong crowd." Newspapers are full of stories about young people being lured into compromising situations by people posing as their online friends.

Cyberbullying—using electronic messaging to ostracize, threaten, and harass an individual—is on the rise. Bullies use camera phones and chat rooms to target victims through text messaging and blog sites, with little possibility of evasion by the victims or identification of the bullies. Cyberbullying incidents have included students creating a website dedicated to the harassment of a fellow student, and posting on a website photos taken in a locker room through a camera phone. Internet service providers have long resisted being censors, and the police cannot become involved until the abuse reaches the level of death threats or criminal harassment (Gillis, 2006).

A Note on Computer Conversation Skills

Research has just begun to focus on computer communication skills. Some research evidence suggests, for example, that small computer-communicating groups function better in some ways than face-to-face groups (Harris, 1995; Kiesler & Sproull, 1992; Olaniran, 1994). Compared to face-to-face groups, computer groups generated a greater number of unique ideas, proposed more unconventional or risky decisions, took longer to reach agreement, engaged in more explicit and outspoken advocacy, and had more equal participation among members.

Here are some guidelines for making your own online communication more effective:

- Watch your spelling. If you have a spellchecker, use it.
- Remember that what you write can easily be made public. So, to quote Sidney Biddle Barrows, "Never say anything on the [internet] that you wouldn't want your mother to hear at your trial."
- Follow the rules of netiquette and avoid potential sources of conflict such as spamming and flaming.
- Clean up your writing—consider your choices for communicating mindfully.

- Be explicit as to your good intentions; avoid the possibility of being misunderstood. If, for example, you think your sarcasm may not be interpreted as humour, then use the smiling emoticon :-).
- Follow the suggestions and guidelines for interpersonal communication generally; after all, they aren't that different.

In-Class Notes

Computer Conversation

- Watch your spelling.
- Remember that what you write may become public.
- Follow the rules of netiquette.
- Clean up your writing.
- Be explicit in your good intentions.
- Follow the general rules for interpersonal communication.

_____

_____

_____

_____

_____

_____

_____

_____

Summary of Concepts and Skills

In this chapter we looked at conversation and identified five stages that are especially important in conversation. We also looked at conversational management (issues involved in initiating, maintaining, repairing, and closing conversations) and at the skills of conversational effectiveness.

1. Conversation consists of five general stages: opening, feedforward, business, feedback, and closing.

2. The disclaimer (a statement that helps ensure that your message will be understood as you wish and will not reflect negatively on you) is often used to prevent conversational problems.

3. Conversations can be initiated in various ways; for example, with self, other, relational, and context references.

4. People maintain conversations by taking turns at speaking and listening. Turn-maintaining and turn-yielding cues are used by the speaker; turn-requesting, turn-denying, and backchannelling cues are used by the listener.

5. You can close a conversation using a variety of methods. For example: Reflect back on conversation as

in summarizing; directly state your desire to end the conversation; refer to future interaction; ask for closure; and/or state your pleasure with the interaction.

6. Conversational repair is frequently undertaken through excuses (statements of explanation designed to lessen the negative impact of a speaker's messages). "I didn't do it," "It wasn't so bad," and "Yes, but..." are major types of excuses.

7. The skills of conversational effectiveness need to be applied with mindfulness, flexibility, cultural sensitivity, and metacommunication (as appropriate). Conversational effectiveness skills comprise openness, empathy, positiveness, immediacy, interaction management, expressiveness, and other-orientation.

Check Your Ability

Check your ability to apply the following skills. You will gain most from this brief exercise if you think carefully about each skill and try to identify instances from your recent communication experiences in which you did or did not act on the basis of the specific skill. Use a rating scale such as the following: 1 = almost always, 2 = often, 3 = sometimes, 4 = rarely, and 5 = almost never.

_____ **1** Follow the basic structure of conversations but deviate with good reason.

_____ **2** Regulate feedback in terms of positiveness, person and message focus, immediacy, self-monitoring, and supportiveness, as appropriate to the situation.

_____ **3** Initiate conversations with a variety of people with comfort and relative ease.

_____ **4** Maintain conversations by smoothly passing the speaker turn back and forth.

_____ **5** Recognize when conversational repair is necessary and make the appropriate repairs in a timely fashion.

_____ **6** Close conversations with comfort and relative ease.

_____ **7** Apply the specific skills of interpersonal communication mindfully, flexibly, and with cultural sensitivity, and metacommunicate as appropriate.

_____ **8** Use the skills of conversational effectiveness (openness, empathy, positiveness, immediacy, interaction management, expressiveness, and other-orientation).

Name:_____ Course:_____ Instructor:_____

After completing this self-test, check your answers against the Answer Key at the back of the book.

Multiple Choice Questions *Choose the BEST answer.*

1. Two parts of the conversational process are
   a. opening and closing.
   b. maintaining and feedback.
   c. opening and maintaining.
   d. all of the above.

2. Previewing your message is called
   a. feedforward.
   b. feedback.
   c. feedlot.
   d. feed me.

3. The substance or focus of the conversation is
   a. opening.
   b. closing.
   c. business.
   d. pleasure.

4. An example of feedback is
   a. a nod.
   b. a smile.
   c. a frown.
   d. all of the above.

5. When you only say what is necessary, you're obeying the rule of
   a. relation.
   b. quality.
   c. quantity.
   d. manner.

6. People who digress in their conversations are breaking the rule of
   a. manner.
   b. quality.
   c. quantity.
   d. relation.

7. All of the following are motives for excuse making EXCEPT
   a. maintaining self-esteem.
   b. reducing stress.
   c. reducing negative reaction.
   d. reinforcing negative reaction.

8. When closing a conversation
   a. state the desire to end the conversation.
   b. stare off into space.
   c. maintain silence.
   d. focus on nonverbal messages.

9. All of the following are guidelines for achieving greater cultural sensitivity in conversation EXCEPT
   a. recognizing and facing your own and others' fears.
   b. recognizing differences between yourself and other culturally different groups.
   c. preparing yourself.
   d. recognizing that everyone is really just the same.

10. Which of the following is NOT true about computer mediated communications (CMC)?
    a. The disadvantages of CMC far outweigh the advantages.
    b. CMC involves the use of technology to communicate with others.
    c. There is a risk that CMC can be addictive for some people.
    d. CMC has many advantages for those who are shy, struggle with face-to-face interactions, or are in abusive situations.

True–False Questions *Write a T or F in the blank next to the statement*

1. _____ Good excuses are used in moderation.

2. _____ Feedforward previews upcoming messages.

3. _____ The purpose of disclaimers is to keep the speaker from looking bad.

4. _____ Business is the focus or substance of the conversation.

5. _____ The expressive speaker communicates genuine involvement.

6. _____ Other-orientation shows consideration and respect.

7. _____ Excuses are a form of conversational repair.

8. _____ One aspect of positiveness is complimenting.

9. _____ All of the above statements are true.

Vocabulary Quiz
The Language of Conversation

Match the terms listed here with their definitions. Record the number of the definition next to the term.

a. _____ excuse

b. _____ disclaimer

c. _____ business

d. _____ turn-yielding cues

e. _____ feedforward

f. _____ backchannelling cues

g. _____ conversation

h. _____ immediacy

1. An interaction in which speaker and listener exchange their roles non-automatically.

2. A form of conversation repair.

3. Information that tells the listener about the messages that will follow.

4. A statement that aims to ensure that your message will be understood and will not reflect negatively on you.

5. A conversation stage during which the major purpose of the interaction is accomplished.

6. Cues that tell the listener that the speaker is finished and wishes to exchange the role of speaker for the role of listener.

7. Cues through which the listener communicates information back to the speaker without assuming the role of speaker.

8. The joining of speaker and listener.

Skill Building Exercises

8.1 Gender and the Topics of Conversation

Below is a chart for recording topics of conversation that you think would be extremely comfortable to talk about (and therefore highly likely to occur) and extremely uncomfortable to talk about (and therefore highly unlikely to occur), for men talking to men, women talking to women, and men and women talking to each other. Fill in each section with at least three topics. After you have completed the chart, you can compare your responses with those of others in a small group or with those of the entire class. One interesting way to do this is for one person to read out a topic (without revealing the particular section he or she put it in) and see if others can identify the appropriate section. This exercise will give you a general idea of how widely held are our beliefs about the topics on which men and women can talk. General discussion may centre on a variety of issues; for example:

1. Why did certain topics seem more appropriately positioned in one section rather than another? For example, what evidence did you use for classifying some topics as comfortable for men or for women?

2. What communication problems might arise because of these differences in the likelihood of certain topics being discussed?

3. How would you go about testing the accuracy of your predictions about which topics go in which sections?

	Man to Man	Woman to Woman	Man to Woman or Woman to Man
Comfortable/highly likely to occur	1.	1.	1.
	2.	2.	2.
	3.	3.	3.
Uncomfortable/highly unlikely to occur	1.	1.	1.
	2.	2.	2.
	3.	3.	3.

Thinking Critically About Gender and Conversation.

Why did certain topics seem more appropriately positioned in one box than in another? What evidence did you use for classifying some topics as comfortable for men or for women? Can you identify potential communication problems that might arise because of these differences in the likelihood of certain topics being discussed? How would you go about testing the accuracy of your predictions for which topics go in which boxes?

8.2 Opening and Closing a Conversation

Think about how you might open a conversation with the people described in the following scenarios. What general approaches would meet with a favourable response? What general approaches would be frowned on?

1. On the first day of class, you and another student are the first to come into the classroom and are seated in the room alone.

2. You are a guest at a friend's party. You are one of the first guests to arrive and are now there with several other people to whom you have only just been introduced. Your friend, the host, is busy with other matters.

3. You have just started a new job in a large office where you are one of several computer operators. It seems as if most of the other people know one another.

4. You are in the college cafeteria eating alone. You see another student who is also eating alone and whom you recognize from your English literature class. But you're not sure if this person has noticed you in class.

Now think about how you might go about closing each of the following conversations. What types of closing seem most effective? Which seem least effective?

1. You and a friend have been talking on the phone for the last hour, but not much new is being said. You have a great deal of work to get to and would like to close the conversation. Your friend just doesn't seem to hear your subtle cues.

2. You are at a party and are anxious to meet a person with whom you have exchanged eye contact for the last 10 minutes. The problem is that a friendly and talkative former teacher of yours is demanding all your attention. You don't want to insult the instructor, but at the same time you want to make contact with this other person.

3. You have had a conference with a supervisor and learned what you needed to know. The supervisor, however, doesn't seem to know how to end the conversation, seems very ill at ease, and continues to go over what has already been said. You have to get back to your desk and must close the conversation.

4. You are at a party and notice a person you would like to get to know. You initiate a conversation, but after a few minutes you realize that this person is not someone with whom you wish to spend any more time. You want to close the conversation as soon as possible.

Thinking Critically About Opening and Concluding Conversations.

What kinds of conversational openers and closers do you find particularly ineffective, offensive, or annoying? In what situations do you find these types of openers and closers occur most often?

8.3 Formulating Excuses

Although excuses are not necessarily appropriate in every situation, there are many instances in which an excuse can help to lessen the possible negative effects of a mishap. For each of the five situations listed above, try formulating a suitable excuse and a justification explaining why this excuse will lessen any negative consequences. Three general types of excuses that you might use as starting points are:

- I didn't do what I'm accused of doing, or I *did* do what I'm accused of *not* doing ("I didn't say that." "I wasn't even near the place." "I did try to get in touch with you to tell you I'd be late.")

- It wasn't so bad. ("Sure I pushed him, but I didn't kill him.")

- Yes, but... ("It was just my jealousy making those accusations.")

1. Because of an email glitch, colleagues at work all receive a recent personal letter you sent to a friend in which you admitted to having racist feelings. You even gave several examples. As you enter work, you see a group of colleagues discussing your letter. They are not pleased.

2. Your boss accuses you of making a lot of long-distance personal phone calls from work, a practice that is explicitly forbidden.

3. In a discussion with your supervisor, you tell a joke that puts down lesbians and gay men. Your supervisor tells you she finds the joke homophobic and offensive to everyone; she adds that she has a gay son and is proud of him. Because you just started the job, you are still on probation—and this supervisor's recommendation will count heavily.

4. Your friend tells you that he thinks you hurt Joe's feelings when you criticized his presentation.

5. Your history instructor is walking behind you and hears you and another student discussing your class. Your instructor clearly hears your comment that "the last lecture was a total waste of time" but says nothing.

Thinking Critically About Excuses.

Can you identify specific situations in which excuses would be inappropriate? What effect does repeated excuse making have on a romantic relationship? Do you have stereotypes of people who consistently make excuses for just about everything they do?

Web Explorations

Companion Website

Visit the Companion Website at www.pearsoned.ca/devito for student resources related to this chapter, including self-grading quizzes, additional skill-building exercises, and links to other online resources.

Research Navigator

Explore our research resources at www.researchnavigator.com:

- Find and read an article on conversation management, conversational effectiveness, or communicating online. On the basis of this article, what can you add to the discussion presented here?

- Investigate one of the key terms discussed in this chapter (for example, conversation, disclaimer, excuse, conversational turns, opening lines, conversational maxims, dialogue, monologue, empathy, flexibility, mindfulness). What additional insights can you provide?

- Try finding answers to one of the following questions or design a research study to answer it.

  1. How are people who monologue perceived? How are people who dialogue perceived?
  2. Do men and women engage in conversation for the same purposes?
  3. Do happy and unhappy couples use the same kinds of excuses?
  4. How are people communicating differently using technology?

Chapter 9

Interpersonal Communication and Culture

Chapter Topics

This chapter discusses culture and intercultural communication and offers suggestions for improving your own intercultural communication.

Culture and Intercultural Communication

How Cultures Differ

Improving Intercultural Communication

Chapter Skills

After completing this chapter, you should be able to:

- send and receive messages, recognizing the influence of cultural factors.

- communicate, recognizing that cultures differ in important ways and that these differences impact on interpersonal communication.

- follow the guidelines for intercultural communication.

The culture of the Snaidanac is still very poorly understood. They are a North American group living in the territory between the Inuit of the north and the American Plains' Sioux. Little is known of their origin, although tradition states that they came from the east. According to Snaidanac mythology, their nation was founded by the cultural hero Jon-mac, who is otherwise known as the originator of an attempt to connect several tribes by magical iron rods placed end to end. Legend has it that Jon-mac (pronounced yon-mic) was also famous for his extensive use of organic medicines which often made him physically sick.

A great deal of the Snaidanac's day is spent in ritual and ceremony. The centre of this activity involves the human body; its appearance and health is vitally important for these people. While this is not unusual, the ceremony and philosophy concerning the body are unique.

The fundamental belief behind their whole system of living appears to be that the human body is ugly and that its natural tendency is to decay and disease. The only hope to avoid decay and disease is religious ritual and ceremony. Every household has one or more shrines for this ritual and ceremony. Powerful people in the society have several shrines in their houses.

The strange rituals of the shrine are not shared by the family together, but are private and secret. The rituals are normally only discussed with children when they are young and being initiated into these mysteries. I was able, however, to talk with the natives and learn something of their shrines and the rituals done around them.

The most important place in the shrine is a box or chest which is built into the wall. In this chest, the native keeps his important charms and magical potions. These charms are bought from special religious people, something like wizards. The most important of these wizards are the medicine men. They do not provide the magic potions or charms to the everyday native, however. They write down the ingredients in an ancient and secret language. The native must take this to an herbalist, very wise in plants and herbs. It is he who, for a gift, supplies the charm.

Beneath the charm-box is a small font or basin. Each day every member of the family, one after the other, enters the shrine room, bows his head before the charm-box, mixes different sorts of holy water in the font, and then proceeds with a brief rite similar to the Christian baptism. The holy waters come from the Water Temple of the community, where the priests hold elaborate ceremonies to make the liquid ritually pure.

Below the medicine men in prestige are specialists who, translated, could best be called "holy-mouth-men." The Snaidanac have a supernatural horror of and fascination with the mouth. It influences all the social relationships of these natives. Were it not for the rituals of the mouth, they believe their teeth would fall out, their gums bleed, the jaws shrink, their friends desert them, and their lovers reject them.

The daily body ritual performed by everyone includes a mouth-rite. Despite the fact that these people are so careful about care of the mouth, this rite strikes the uninitiated stranger as revolting. It was reported to me that the ritual consists of inserting a small bundle of hog hairs into the mouth, along with certain magical powders, and then moving the bundles in a highly formalized series of gestures....

Source: Snaidanac concept developed by Horace Miner. Reproduced by permission of the American Anthropological Association from *American Anthropologist, 58:3, June 1956.* Not for further reproduction.

From these observations of anthropologist Horace Miner (1956), you might conclude that the Snaidanac are a truly strange people. Look more carefully, however, and you will see that *we* are the Snaidanac and the rituals are our own: *Snaidanac* is *Canadians* spelled backwards. This excerpt brings into focus the fact that cultural customs (our own and those of others) are not necessarily logical or natural. Rather, they are better viewed as useful or not useful to the members of that particular culture. The excerpt is an appropriate reminder against ethnocentrism—the tendency to think that your culture's customs are right and the customs of others are wrong. It also awakens our consciousness, our mindful state, to our own customs and values.

CULTURE AND INTERCULTURAL COMMUNICATION

The word *culture,* you'll recall from Chapter 1, refers to the lifestyle of a group of people, their values, beliefs, artifacts, ways of behaving, and ways of communicating. Culture includes all that members of a social group have produced and developed— their language, ways of thinking, art, laws, and religion—and that is transmitted from one generation to another through a process known as **enculturation**. You learn the values of your culture (that is, you become enculturated) through the teachings of your parents, peer groups, schools, religious institutions, government agencies, and media. When discussing the learned nature of culture, Hall (1976) explains that

STUDY TIP

Compare and contrast the notions of enculturation and acculturation.

Interpersonal Communication and Culture

Culture—the lifestyle of a group of people:

- values
- beliefs
- artifacts
- ways of behaving
- ways to communicate
- language
- ways of thinking
- art
- laws
- religion

everything people do and are is modified by this cultural learning, which gradually sinks below the surface of the mind to appear as innate. Thus, one's own culture appears natural and right and as the only way to act.

Through enculturation, you develop an ethnic identity, a commitment to the beliefs and philosophies of your culture (Chung & Ting-Toomey, 1999). This can cause you to compare other cultures and to judge them on the basis of your own culture; in other words, to be ethnocentric.

Acculturation refers to the processes by which a person's culture is modified through direct contact with or exposure to another culture, through, say, the mass media (Kim, 1988). For example, when immigrants settle in the host culture, their own culture becomes influenced by the host culture. Gradually, the values, ways of behaving, and beliefs of the host culture become more and more a part of the immigrants' culture. At the same time, of course, the host culture changes, too. Generally, however, the culture of the immigrant changes more.

The acceptance of the new culture depends on several factors (Kim, 1988). Immigrants who come from cultures similar to the host culture will become acculturated more easily. Similarly, those who are younger and better educated become acculturated more quickly than do older and less educated persons. Personality factors are also relevant. People who are risk-takers and open-minded, for example, have greater acculturation potential. Also, people who are familiar with the host culture before immigration—whether through interpersonal contact or mass media exposure—will be acculturated more readily.

Canada is unique, however, in that it is guided by its focus on multiculturalism—an acceptance and understanding of all the different cultural groups in a community. And yet Canadians seem to have difficulty describing a Canadian culture or a Canadian identity. We often describe it in terms of what Canadians are not—we are not Americans, for example; and we are not aggressive. Bibby (1990) contends that Americans have created a creed that binds, a commitment to ties of church, family, school, and community, and individualism with a pronounced group context. Canadians, on the other hand, don't seem to have an ideology of Canadianism. While Americans have heroes, Canadians often ignore their historical record and almost exclusively adopt the heroes of other nations.

And yet Canadians are generally proud of their "mosaic" concept of society, as opposed to the American "melting pot" version. Bibby (1990) maintains that what is

> I am not an Athenian or a Greek, but a citizen of the world.
>
> —Socrates

What part does intercultural communication play in your personal, social, and professional life? Has this changed in the last five years? Is it likely to change in the next five years?

holding our country together is not loyalty to anything in particular but rather a tenuous agreement to coexist. As a result, Canadians have become "champions of choice" (Bibby, 1990). We seem so interested in and willing to adopt the foods, clothing, books, music, and activities of other countries that we find it hard to remember what might be distinctly Canadian. And maybe this is exactly what is Canadian—the multicultural component of our society.

Intercultural communication, then, refers to communication that takes place between people of different cultures, and it is greatly influenced by both enculturation and acculturation processes. **Barriers to intercultural communication** often exist between people who have different cultural beliefs, values, or ways of behaving.

Visit one of the websites for Canadian census data (for example, www.statcan.ca). What interesting cultural information can you find that would be of value to someone learning the skills of interpersonal communication?

Note, too, that you send messages from your specific and unique cultural context. Your context influences what you say and how you say it. Culture influences every aspect of your communication experience and, of course, you receive messages through the filters imposed by a unique culture. Cultural filters, like filters on a camera, colour the messages you receive. They also influence what you receive and how you receive it. Cultures differ in their tendencies to trust different sources of messages. Some cultures would place their trust in a religious leader, others in an elder, and still others in the television reporter.

The term "intercultural" is used broadly to refer to all forms of communication among persons from different groups as well as to the more narrowly defined area of communication between different cultures. The following types of communication may all be considered intercultural and, more important, subject to the same principles of effective communication identified in this chapter.

When you have to ask directions, you're confessing, in some way, your ignorance and your inability to control the situation by yourself. Men, according to Deborah Tannen (1990, 1994b), are especially reluctant to ask for directions because they want to maintain control; by asking for directions, they lose that control. Do you find that men are more reluctant to ask for directions? Do you agree with Tannen's explanation?

- Communication between cultures—for example, between Chinese and Portuguese, or between French and Norwegian.
- Communication between ethnic groups (sometimes called *interethnic communication*)—for example, between Chinese Canadians and indigenous Canadians.
- Communication between religions—for example, between Roman Catholics and Anglicans, or between Muslims and Jews.
- Communication between nations (sometimes called *international communication*)—for example, between Canada and Argentina, or between China and Italy.
- Communication between smaller cultures existing within the larger culture—for example, between doctors and patients, or between research scientists and the general public.

In-Class Notes

Intercultural Communication— Communication Between

- cultures
- ethnic groups
- religions
- nations
- small cultures
- small groups
- genders

_____

_____

_____

_____

_____

_____

_____

_____

TABLE 9.1	Intercultural Value Conflict Areas

We generally find that most difficulties revolve around different assumptions concerning the following areas.

NORTH AMERICAN VALUES	CONTRAST TO NORTH AMERICAN VALUES
I. Individual versus Family	
(a) Individual perceived as a separate entity;	(a) Individual perceived in context of his or her family;
(b) Individual responsibility is most important;	(b) Involvement and dependence on family is encouraged;
(c) Decisions must involve the individual as much as possible.	(c) Decisions must involve the older respected members of the family.
II. Acceptance of Others	
(a) North Americans relate to others in terms of their roles;	(a) Individuals from other cultures react to other people in terms of the whole person, not the role;
(b) North Americans don't need to like or agree with someone to avail themselves of his or her services, e.g., student/teacher.	(b) Individuals from contrast cultures tend to accept or reject others completely and have difficulty working with those who are unacceptable.
III. Social Relations	
(a) Differences in status, etc., are minimized to make others feel comfortable;	(a) Differences in status and hierarchical rank are noted and stressed;
(b) A direct informal style of communicating is also used to achieve the same result.	(b) Communication follows a predictable, formal series of steps that make others feel more comfortable.
IV. Progress versus Fate	
(a) North Americans believe humans are rational and can construct machines and develop techniques to solve problems.	(a) Humans are perceived by many cultures in a fatalistic manner and such things as disease and suffering are accepted more easily.
V. Time	
(a) Time is perceived in terms of clock time (supper is at 5:30 p.m.);	(a) Time is perceived in terms of the right time to do something (supper is when you eat);
(b) Time moves quickly from past to present to future; one must keep up with it, use it to change and master one's environment.	(b) Time moves slowly; humans must integrate themselves with the environment and adapt to it, rather than change it.

Source: Adapted from Michael J. Miner and M. Kim Harker, International Briefing Associates. Ottawa, ON.

- Communication between a smaller culture and the dominant culture—for example, between homosexuals and heterosexuals, or between senior citizens and the not-yet seniors.
- Communication between genders—between men and women. Some researchers would consider intergender communication as a separate area and only a part of intercultural communication when the two people are also from different races or nationalities. But, because gender roles are largely learned through culture, it seems useful to consider male–female communication as intercultural (Tannen, 1994b).

Regardless of your own cultural background, you will surely come into close contact with people from a variety of other cultures—people who speak different languages, eat different foods, practise different religions, and approach work and relationships in very different ways. It doesn't matter whether you're a long time resident or a newly arrived immigrant. You are—or soon will be—living, going to school, working, and forming relationships with people who are from very different cultures. Your day-to-day experiences are sure to become increasingly intercultural. See Table 9.1 for a list of possible conflicts you may encounter.

"Because my genetic programming *prevents* me from stopping to ask directions—*that's* why!"

© The New Yorker Collection 1991 Donald Reilly from cartoonbank.com. All Rights Reserved.

HOW CULTURES DIFFER

Cultures differ in terms of their (1) orientation (whether individualistic or collectivist); (2) context (whether high or low); and (3) masculinity–femininity. Each of these dimensions of difference has a significant impact on interpersonal communication (Hofstede, 1997; Hall & Hall, 1987; Gudykunst, 1991). Cultures also differ in their characteristic attitude toward uncertainty, a topic discussed in Chapter 3.

Create a chart which summarizes the three dimensions along which cultures differ, and identify an example of a culture at the extremes of each of the three dimensions.

Visit one of the numerous travel websites (for example, www.lonelyplanet.com and www.travel.epicurious.com). What can you learn about intercultural communication from such sources?

Does the individualistic or collectivist nature of one's culture influence success in university? How would you go about researching this question?

Individualist and Collectivist Cultures

Before reading about individualism versus collectivism, take the self-test on page 199 called "How Individualistic Are You?" to see where you and your own culture stand on this concept.

The distinction between **individualistic** and **collectivist** cultures revolves around the extent to which the individual's goals or the group's goals are given greater importance. Individual and collective tendencies are not mutually exclusive; this is not an all-or-none orientation but rather one of emphasis. Thus, you may, for example, compete with other members of your basketball team for most baskets or the most-valuable-player award. In a game, however, you act in a way that will benefit the group. In actual practice, both individualistic and collectivist tendencies will help you and your team each achieve your goals. Even so, these tendencies may conflict; for example, do you shoot for the basket and try to raise your own individual score or do you pass the ball to another player who is better positioned to score the basket and thus benefit your team?

In an individualistic culture, you're responsible for yourself and perhaps your immediate family; in a collectivist culture you're responsible for the entire group. Success in an individualistic culture is measured by the extent to which you surpass other members of your group; you would take pride in standing out from the crowd. And your heroes—in the media, for example—are likely to be those who are unique and who stand apart. In a collectivist culture, success is measured by your contribution to the achievements of the group as a whole; you would take pride in your similarity to other members of your group. Your heroes, in contrast, are more likely to be team players who do not stand out from the rest of the group's members.

In an individualistic culture you're responsible to your own conscience, and responsibility is largely an individual matter. In a collectivist culture you're responsible to the rules of the social group, and responsibility for an accomplishment or a failure is shared by all members. Competition is promoted in individualistic cultures, while cooperation is promoted in collectivist cultures.

Distinctions between in-group members and out-group members are extremely important in collectivist cultures. In individualist cultures, where a person's individuality is prized, the distinction is likely to be less important.

What does this photograph tell you about Canadian culture?

High- and Low-Context Cultures

In a **high-context culture**, much of the information in communication is in the context or in the person—for example, information shared through previous communications, through assumptions about each other, and through shared experiences. The information is not explicitly stated in the verbal message. In a **low-context culture**, most information is explicitly stated in verbal messages, or, in formal transactions, in written (contract) form.

How Individualistic Are You?

Instructions: Respond to each of the following statements in terms of how true they are of your behaviour and thinking: 1 = almost always true, 2 = more often true than false, 3 = true about half the time and false about half the time, 4 = more often false than true, 5 = almost always false.

_____ ❶ My own goals rather than the goals of my group (for example, my extended family, my organization) are more important.

_____ ❷ I feel responsible for myself and to my own conscience rather than for the entire group and to the group's values and rules.

_____ ❸ Success depends on my contribution to the group effort and the group's success rather than my own individual success or surpassing others.

_____ ❹ I make a clear distinction between who is the leader and who are the followers, and similarly make a clear distinction between members of my own cultural group and outsiders.

_____ ❺ In business transactions, personal relationships are extremely important, and so I would spend considerable time getting to know people with whom I do business.

_____ ❻ In my communications, I prefer a direct and explicit communication style; I believe in "telling it like it is," even if it hurts.

HOW DID YOU DO?

To compute your individualist–collectivist score, follow these steps:

1. Reverse the scores for items 3 and 5. That is, if your response was 1, reverse it to a 5; if your response was 2, reverse it to a 4; 3, keep it as 3; 4, reverse it to a 2; 5, reverse it to 1.

2. Add your scores for all six items, being sure to use the reverse scores for items 3 and 5 in your calculations. Your score should be between 6 (indicating a highly individualist orientation) to 30 (indicating a highly collectivist orientation).

3. Position your score on the following scale:

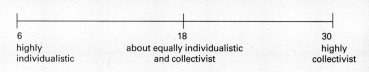

6	18	30
highly individualistic	about equally individualistic and collectivist	highly collectivist

WHAT WILL YOU DO?

Does this scale and score accurately measure the way in which you see yourself on this dimension? Is this orientation going to help you achieve your personal and professional goals? Might it hinder you?

To appreciate the distinction between high and low context, consider giving directions ("Where's the post office?") to someone who knows the neighbourhood and to a newcomer to your city. To someone who knows the neighbourhood (a high-context situation), you can assume the person knows the local landmarks, so you can give directions such as "next to the laundromat on Main Street" or "at the corner of Albany and Elm." To the newcomer (a low-context situation), you cannot assume the person shares any of the information you have, so you would have to use only those directions that even a stranger would understand; for example, "Make a left at the next stop sign" or "Go two blocks and then turn right."

High-context cultures are also collectivist cultures. These cultures (Japanese, Arabic, Aboriginal, Thai, Korean, and Mexican are examples) place great emphasis on personal relationships and oral agreements (Victor, 1992). Low-context cultures, on the other hand, are individualistic cultures. These cultures (German, Swedish, Norwegian, and Canadian are examples) place less emphasis on personal relationships and more emphasis on the written, explicit explanation, and, for example, on the written contracts in business transactions.

Members of high-context cultures spend a lot of time getting to know each other before any important transactions take place. Because of this prior personal knowledge, a great deal of information is shared and therefore does not have to be explicitly stated. Members of low-context cultures spend less time getting to know each other

How do you, your family, and your friends view interethnic friendships? Interethnic romantic relationships? Are there certain interethnic relationships that are "approved" and others that are "not approved"?

and therefore do not have that shared knowledge. As a result, everything has to be stated explicitly. High-context societies, for example, rely more on nonverbal cues in reducing uncertainty (Sanders et al., 1991).

When this simple difference is not taken into account, misunderstandings can easily result. For example, the directness and explicitness characteristic of the low-context culture may prove insulting, insensitive, or unnecessary to members of the high-context culture. Conversely, to members of a low-context culture, someone from a high-context culture may appear vague, underhanded, or dishonest in his or her reluctance to be explicit or engage in communication that a low-context member would consider open and direct.

Another frequent difference and source of misunderstanding between high- and low-context cultures is face-saving (Hall & Hall, 1987). People in high-context cultures place a great deal more emphasis on face-saving. For example, they are more likely to avoid argument for fear of causing others to lose face, whereas people in low-context cultures (with their individualistic orientation) will use argument to win a point. Similarly, in high-context cultures, criticism should take place only in private so that the person who is the object of criticism can save face. Low-context cultures may not make this public–private distinction.

Members of high-context cultures are reluctant to say No for fear of offending and causing the person to lose face. So, it's necessary to understand when a high-context individual's yes means yes and when it means no. The difference is not in the words themselves but in the way they are used. It's easy to see how the low-context individual may interpret this reluctance to be direct—to say No when you mean No—as a weakness or as an unwillingness to confront reality.

Members of high-context cultures are also reluctant to question the judgments of their superiors. For example, if a product was being manufactured with a defect, workers might be reluctant to communicate this back to management (Gross et al., 1987). Similarly, workers may detect problems in procedures proposed by management but never communicate their concerns back to management. Knowledge of this tendency

In-Class Notes

High and Low Context

High Context

Communication is in the context of the person:

- previous communication
- assumptions
- shared experiences

Low Context

Information is explicitly stated:

- verbally
- in written form

_____

_____

_____

_____

_____

_____

_____

_____

_____

would alert a low-context management to look more deeply into the absence of communication. Table 9.2 presents a summary of these differences as they relate to interpersonal communication.

Masculine and Feminine Cultures

Cultures differ in the extent to which gender roles are distinct or overlap (Hofstede, 1997). A **masculine culture** typically views men as assertive, oriented to material success, and strong; people in such a culture tend to see women as modest, focused on the quality of life, and tender. In a **feminine culture** both men and women are supposed to be modest, oriented to maintaining the quality of life, and tender. On the basis of Hofstede's research on 53 countries, the 10 countries with the highest masculinity score (from the highest) are Japan, Austria, Venezuela, Italy, Switzerland, Mexico, Ireland, Jamaica, Great Britain, and Germany. The 10 countries with the highest femininity score (from the highest) are Sweden, Norway, Netherlands, Denmark, Costa Rica, Yugoslavia, Finland, Chile, Portugal, and Thailand.

In masculine cultures, the emphasis on material success is seen in the importance that students place on marks. Students in such cultures are conditioned to strive to be the best, and school failure is shameful and extremely significant. Students from more feminine cultures place greater emphasis on the quality of life and give much less importance to such issues as marks. Students in these cultures are content to be average, and failing in school is unpleasant but nothing serious (Hofstede, 1997).

The masculine culture socializes its children to be assertive, ambitious, and competitive. A masculine organization emphasizes the bottom line and rewards its workers on the basis of their contribution to the organization. The feminine culture socializes its children to be modest and to emphasize close interpersonal relationships. A feminine organization is more likely to emphasize worker satisfaction and to reward its workers on the basis of need; an employee with a large family, for example, may get raises that a single person would not get even if the single person contributed more to the organization.

Masculine cultures are more likely to confront conflicts directly and to competitively fight out any differences; they are more likely to emphasize win–lose conflict strategies. Feminine cultures are more likely to emphasize compromise and negotiation; they are more likely to emphasize win–win solutions to conflicts.

> ❝ We hold these truths to be self-evident: that all men and women are created equal. ❞
>
> —Elizabeth Cady Stanton

TABLE 9.2	Some Individualistic and Collectivist Culture Differences

This table, based on the work of Hofstede (1997), Hall and Hall (1987; Hall, 1983) and on interpretations by Gudykunst (1991) and Victor (1992), parallels the self-test presented on page 199. As you read through the table, consider which statements you agree with, which you disagree with, and how these beliefs influence your communications. Can you identify additional differences between individualistic and collectivist cultures?

INDIVIDUALISTIC (LOW-CONTEXT) CULTURES	COLLECTIVIST (HIGH-CONTEXT) CULTURES
Your goals are most important.	The group's goals are most important.
You're responsible for yourself and to your own conscience.	You're responsible for the entire group and to the group's values and rules.
Success depends on your surpassing others; competition is emphasized.	Success depends on your contribution to the group; cooperation is emphasized.
Clear distinction is made between leaders and members.	Little distinction is made between leaders and members; leadership is normally shared.
Personal relationships are less important; hence, little time is spent getting to know each other in meetings.	Personal relationships are extremely important; hence, much time is spent getting to know each other in meetings.
Directness is valued; face-saving is seldom considered.	Indirectness is valued; face-saving is a major consideration.

Conceptions of masculinity and femininity change over time and as circumstances change. For example, Haddad and Lam (1988) conducted interviews with over 100 new Canadian fathers from nine different national or ethnic backgrounds. Only a small proportion of these men (17 percent) upheld their traditional view of the role of the father after being in Canada for some time. The other participants in the study adapted their beliefs, either for pragmatic reasons or in order to maximize the well-being of their family.

IMPROVING INTERCULTURAL COMMUNICATION

Murphy's Law ("If anything can go wrong, it will") is especially applicable to intercultural communication. Of course, intercultural communication is subject to all the same barriers and problems as the other forms of communication discussed throughout this text. Here, however, are some suggestions designed to counteract the barriers that are unique to intercultural communication (Barna, 1997; Ruben, 1985; Spitzberg, 1991).

Recognize and Reduce Your Ethnocentrism

Before reading this section, take the "How Ethnocentric Are You" test on page 203. **Ethnocentrism**, one of the biggest obstacles to intercultural communication, is the tendency to see others and their behaviours through your own cultural filters, often as distortions of your own behaviours. It's the tendency to evaluate the values, beliefs, and behaviours of your own culture as more positive, superior, logical, and natural than those of other cultures. To achieve effective interpersonal communication, you need to see both yourself and others as different, but neither as inferior or superior—not a very easily accomplished task.

We are all ethnocentric to some degree; however, ethnocentrism exists on a continuum. People are not either completely ethnocentric or not at all ethnocentric; rather, most are somewhere between these polar opposites. Most important for our purposes is that you become aware that your degree of ethnocentrism will influence your interpersonal (intercultural) communications.

Be Mindful

Being mindful rather than mindless (a distinction considered in Chapter 8) is generally helpful in intercultural communication situations (Hajek & Giles, 2003). When you're in a mindless state, you behave with assumptions that would not normally pass intellectual scrutiny. For example, you know that cancer is not contagious and yet you may avoid touching cancer patients. You know that people who cannot see do not have hearing problems and yet you may use a louder voice when talking to people without sight. When the discrepancies between evidence and behaviours are pointed out and your mindful state is awakened, you quickly realize that these behaviours are not logical or realistic.

When you deal with people from other cultures, you're often in a mindless state and therefore function irrationally in many ways. When your mindful state is awakened, as it is in textbook discussions such as this one, you may then resort to a more critical thinking mode, and recognize, for example, that other people and other cultural systems are different but not inferior or superior. Thus, these suggestions for increasing intercultural communication effectiveness may appear logical (even obvious) to your mindful state but are probably frequently ignored in your mindless state.

How would you explain ethnocentrism? Can you give an example of your own ethnocentrism? Are your friends and relatives ethnocentric? How does this manifest itself in everyday interpersonal communications?

"I've never trusted cows."

© The New Yorker Collection 1997 Warren Miller from cartoonbank.com. All Rights Reserved.

Test Yourself

How Ethnocentric Are You?

Here are 18 statements representing your beliefs about your culture. For each statement indicate how much you agree or disagree, using the following scale: strongly agree = 5, agree = 4, neither agree nor disagree = 3, disagree = 2, and strongly disagree = 1.

_____ ① Most cultures are backward compared to my culture.

_____ ② My culture should be the role model for other cultures.

_____ ③ Lifestyles in other cultures are just as valid as those in my culture.

_____ ④ Other cultures should try to be like my culture.

_____ ⑤ I'm not interested in the values and customs of other cultures.

_____ ⑥ People in my culture could learn a lot from people in other cultures.

_____ ⑦ Most people from other cultures just don't know what's good for them.

_____ ⑧ I have little respect for the values and customs of other cultures.

_____ ⑨ Most people would be happier if they lived like people in my culture.

_____ ⑩ People in my culture have just about the best lifestyle anywhere.

_____ ⑪ Lifestyles in other cultures are not as valid as those in my culture.

_____ ⑫ I'm very interested in the values and customs of other cultures.

_____ ⑬ I respect the values and customs of other cultures.

_____ ⑭ I do not cooperate with people who are different.

_____ ⑮ I do not trust people who are different.

_____ ⑯ I dislike interacting with people from different cultures.

_____ ⑰ Other cultures are smart to look up to my culture.

_____ ⑱ People from other cultures act strange and unusual when they come into my culture.

HOW DID YOU DO?

This test was presented to give you the opportunity to examine some of your own cultural beliefs, particularly those cultural beliefs that contribute to ethnocentrism. The person low in ethnocentrism would have high scores (4s and 5s) for items 3, 6, 12, and 13, and low scores (1s and 2s) for all the others. The person high in ethnocentrism would have low scores for items 3, 6, 12, and 13, and high scores for all the others.

WHAT WILL YOU DO?

Use this test to bring your own cultural beliefs to consciousness so you can examine them logically and objectively. Ask yourself if your beliefs are productive and will help you achieve your professional and social goals, or if they're counterproductive and will actually hinder your achieving your goals.

Source: Adapted from James W. Neuliep & James C. McCroskey (1997). The development of a U.S. and generalized ethnocentrism scale, *Communication Research Reports*, 14, 393.

In-Class Notes

Ethnocentrism

We all tend to see others and their behaviours through our own cultural filters and think our culture is better than other cultures in every way.

_____

_____

_____

_____

_____

_____

_____

_____

The characteristics of conversational effectiveness (discussed in detail in Chapter 8) are especially useful in intercultural communication, though caution should be exercised since there are likely to be important cultural differences in the way these characteristics are expected to be used. So, generally:

1. *Be open* to differences among people. Be especially open to different values, beliefs, and attitudes, as well as ways of behaving. Cultural differences may help to explain differences in openness and in responsiveness to openness.

2. *Empathize* with the other person. Try to see the world from this different perspective. Use facial expressions, an attentive and interested body posture, and understanding and agreement responses to communicate your empathy.

3. *Communicate positiveness* to others; it helps put the other person at ease. However, the appropriateness of positive statements about the self will vary greatly with the culture. For example, some cultures expect speakers to use self-denigrating comments and to minimize their own successes and abilities. Other cultures expect success and ability to be acknowledged openly and without embarrassment.

4. *Use immediacy* to unite yourself with others and to surmount differences. Communicate a sense of togetherness to counteract obvious intercultural differences, but realize that members of some cultures may prefer to maintain greater interpersonal and psychological distance from others.

5. *Be sensitive to the differences in turn-taking*. Many North Americans, especially those from large urban centres, have the habit of interrupting or of completing the other person's sentences. Some cultures consider this especially rude.

6. *Communicate expressiveness*. When differences among people are great, some feel uneasy and unsure of themselves. Counteract this by communicating genuine involvement in the interaction. Recognize, however, that some cultures may frown on too much expressiveness. So don't assume that the absence of expressiveness shows an unwillingness to participate in conversation; it may indicate just a difference in the way in which members of different cultures reveal their feelings.

7. *Be other-oriented,* by focusing your attention and the conversation on the other person. Use the techniques already considered to show other-orientation, such as active listening, asking questions, and maintaining eye contact (see Chapter 8). Some cultures, however, may find these techniques too intrusive. So, look carefully for feedback that comments on your own degree of other-orientation.

THEN AND NOW

Recall a recent intercultural interaction that did not go as well as it might have. If you were having the same conversation today, what could you do to make it more effective?

Face Fears

Another factor that stands in the way of effective intercultural communication is fear (Stephan & Stephan, 1985; Gudykunst, 1991). For example, you may fear for your self-esteem. You may become anxious about your ability to control the intercultural situation or you may worry about your own level of discomfort. You may fear that you will be taken advantage of by a member of this other culture. Depending upon your own stereotypes, you may fear being lied to, financially duped, or made fun of. You may fear that members of this other group will react to you negatively. Or, conversely, you may fear negative reactions from members of your own group. These fears can easily create sufficient anxiety to make you avoid holding effective intercultural communications.

> I was raised to believe that excellence is the best deterrent to racism or sexism. And that's how I operate my life.
>
> —Oprah Winfrey

Avoid Overattribution

You'll recall from Chapter 3 that overattribution is the tendency to attribute too much of a person's behaviour or attitudes to one of that person's characteristics: "She thinks that way because she's a woman"; "He believes that because he was raised a Catholic." In intercultural communication situations, you see overattribution in two ways. First, it's the tendency to see too much of what a person believes or does as being caused by the person's cultural identification. Second, it's the tendency to see a person as a spokesperson for that particular culture just because she is a member. Therefore, be careful not to assume that everyone from India is Hindu and a vegetarian, or that all students of Chinese origin are good in math. As demonstrated in the discussion of perception in Chapter 3, people's ways of thinking and ways of behaving are influenced by a wide variety of factors; culture is just one of those factors.

Do you agree with the assumption that everyone is ethnocentric to some degree? If so, where would you place yourself on the ethnocentric continuum when the "other" is a person of the opposite sex? A member of a different affectional orientation? A member of a different race? A member of a different religion?

All communication interactions involve uncertainty and ambiguity. Not surprisingly, this uncertainty and ambiguity is greater when there are wide cultural differences (Berger & Bradac, 1982; Gudykunst, 1989, 1993). Because of this, in intercultural communication it takes more time and effort to reduce uncertainty and thus to communicate meaningfully. Reducing your uncertainty about another person is worth the effort, however: it not only will make your communication more effective but it will also increase your liking for the person (Douglas, 1994). Techniques such as active listening (Chapter 4) and perception checking (Chapter 3) help you check the accuracy of your perceptions and allow you to revise and amend any incorrect perceptions. Also, being specific reduces ambiguity and the chances of misunderstandings; misunderstanding is a lot more likely if you talk about "neglect" (a highly abstract concept) than if you refer to "forgetting my last birthday" (a specific event).

Finally, seeking feedback helps you correct any possible misconceptions almost immediately. Seek feedback on whether you're making yourself clear ("Does that make sense?" or "Do you see where to put the widget?"). Similarly, seek feedback to make sure you understand what the other person is saying ("Do you mean that you'll never speak with them again? Do you mean that literally?").

Recognize Differences

To communicate interculturally, you need to recognize the differences between yourself and people who are culturally different, the differences that exist within the culturally different group, and the numerous differences in meaning that arise from cultural differences.

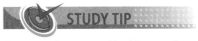

Seek out a classmate or friend from another culture. Discuss the similarities and differences between your cultures.

Differences Between Yourself and Culturally Different People   When you assume that all people are similar and ignore the differences between yourself and those who are culturally different from you, your intercultural efforts are likely to fail. This is especially true with values, attitudes, and beliefs. It's easy to see and accept different hairstyles, clothing, and foods, but when it comes to values and beliefs, it's easier to assume (mindlessly) that deep down we're all similar. We aren't. When you assume similarities and ignore differences, you may implicitly communicate to others that you feel your ways are the right ways and their ways are the wrong ways. The result is confusion and misunderstanding on both sides.

Differences Within the Culturally Different Group   Be mindful of the differences within any cultural group. Just as we know that all Canadians are not alike, neither are all Jamaicans, Koreans, or Mexicans. Within each culture there are many smaller cultures. These smaller cultures differ from each other and from the majority culture. Further, members of one smaller culture may share a great deal with members of that same smaller culture in another part of the world. For example, farmers in Saskatchewan may have more in common with farmers in Borneo than with bankers in Toronto. All will be concerned with and knowledgeable about weather conditions and their effects on crop growth, with crop rotation techniques, and soil composition. Of course, these farmers will also have drastically different views on such issues as government subsidies, trade regulations, and sales techniques.

Recognize Meaning Differences in Verbal and Nonverbal Messages

In Chapter 5 we noted that meaning does not exist in the words we use; rather, it exists in the person using the words. This principle is especially important in intercultural communication. Consider the differences in meaning that might exist for the word "woman" to a Canadian and an Iranian. What about "religion" to a Christian fundamentalist and to an atheist; or "lunch" to a Chinese rice farmer and a Bay Street executive? Or think about the meanings of the terms "security," "future," and "family" to a Vancouver college student and a homeless teenager in Toronto.

There are some distinctive groups in this photograph. Has anyone ever assumed something about you (because you were a member of a particular culture) that was not true? Have you ever been asked to speak on behalf of "your" group? Did you find this disturbing?

When it comes to nonverbal messages, the potential differences are even greater. Thus, the over-the-head clasped hands that signify victory to a North American may signify friendship to a Russian. To someone from Britain, holding up two fingers to make a V signifies victory. To certain South Americans, however, it's an obscene gesture that corresponds to our extended

---

Listen to This   Listening Without Sexist, Racist, or Heterosexist Attitudes

Just as sexist, racist, and heterosexist attitudes will influence your language, they also influence your listening. In biased listening, you hear what the speaker is saying filtered through your stereotypes. You assume unfairly that what the speaker is saying is necessarily influenced by the speaker's gender, ethnicity, or affectional orientation.

Sexist, racist, and heterosexist listening occur in a wide variety of situations. For example, when you dismiss a valid argument or attribute validity to an invalid argument, when you refuse to give someone a fair hearing, or when you give less credibility (or more credibility) to a speaker because the speaker is of a particular ethnicity, gender, or affectional orientation, you're practising sexist, racist, or heterosexist listening. Put differently, sexist, racist, or heterosexist listening occurs when you listen differently to a person because of his or her gender, ethnicity, or affectional orientation, despite the fact that these characteristics are irrelevant to the communication.

But there are many instances where these characteristics are relevant and pertinent to your evaluation of the message.

For example, the gender of the speaker talking about pregnancy, fathering a child, birth control, or surrogate fatherhood is, most would agree, probably relevant to the message. On such topics, it is not sexist listening to hear the topic through the gender of the speaker. But it is sexist listening to assume that only one gender has anything to say that's worth hearing, or that what one gender says can be discounted without a fair hearing. The same is true when stereotypes about a person's ethnicity or affectional orientation affect your listening.

SUGGESTIONS?

Chloe, a good friend of yours and a new trainee at the company you work for, has been assigned to a supervisor of a different ethnicity. Chloe confides in you that she just can't get herself to work with this person; she admits she is just too prejudiced to appreciate anything this supervisor says or does. What listening advice would you give Chloe?

middle finger. Tapping the side of your nose will signify that you and the other person are in on a secret if you're in England or Scotland, but that the other person is nosy if you're in Wales. A friendly wave of the hand is insulting in Greece, where the wave of friendship must show the back rather than the front of the hand.

Are such statements as "Columbus discovered America in 1492" and "All Canadians are immigrants" ethnocentric? If so, how would you rephrase them so that they represent a more multicultural perspective?

Thinking Critically About A Few Choice Words

Pamela Levi is beautiful. She is nineteen years old and her hair tumbles down her shoulders to waist length. She fidgets, smiles, shrugs. Every now and then she sweeps back her hair and laughs. It makes it hard to conduct an interview. I keep losing my train of thought.

Pamela is a Micmac dancer featured in a musical production called *Spirit of a Nation*.

"How do you feel when you dance? What goes through your mind?"

"I feel proud," she says. "Proud to be an Indian."

I sit smiling at her for a few moments until she says, "I think your tape stopped."

Oh. I hit eject, flip over the mini-cassette and press record. "Sorry. Now then, you were saying that when you dance you feel proud to be a Native Canadian."

But that is not what she said. She gives me a puzzled and slightly annoyed look. "I said, I feel proud to be an *Indian*."

Later, I play the tape back, both sides, and discover that she is right. I also discover that during the entire interview I have twisted and contorted my syntax to avoid using the word Indian at all. I say "Native North American." I say "Aboriginal." I say "People of the First Nations." But nowhere do I say, simply, "Indian."

Words, like ideas, can fall out of fashion. Others become tainted. The error made by the Politically Correct movement was in trying to hurry the process along. It isn't something that can be dictated by committee; it just happens. For a long time, the word *squaw* was used simply to mean any Native woman. Today it has a crude, offensive sound to it.

What of the word *Indian* itself? For one thing, it isn't accurate. Columbus was convinced to his dying day that he had reached Asia and that the people he had encountered were honest-to-God Indians. That doesn't necessarily make the word an insult. After all, the name Canada itself is a case of mistaken identity (derived from a Native word for "village"), but no one would find the term *Canadian* demeaning.

I decided to call Gary Abbott.

I met Gary the same way I met Pamela, through the musical theatre of *Spirit of a Nation*. Gary is a member of the Thompson Nation of British Columbia. He is president of NAPA (the North American Pow-Wow Association) and has been a pow-wow dancer since the age of two. He specializes in the Hoop Dance, an intricate ritual involving twenty-nine sep-

arate hoops, which he pulls in and around his body to reveal woven moons, wombs and animal shapes.

Gary is very much aware of the nuance of words. When I referred to the various, spectacular costumes he wears during his dances, he said, "They aren't costumes. The correct term is regalia." I also notice, when I replay my interviews with Gary, that he avoids the word Indian as well. He refers instead to Natives and non-Natives...

What began as a minor semantic quest had taken a new turn. We were no longer talking about mere labels; we were talking about identity. This is what I had been chasing…, my own definition of self, that tenuous connection between the abstract and the specific, between a concept—*Canadian*—and the concrete—*me*.

We are defined by multiple layers, beginning with Canadian and working our way down, peeling the onion—and at the core?

"Are you an Indian?"

It's a stupid question. Of course Gary is an Indian. I rephrase the question. "Is the word Indian offensive?"

He thinks a moment. "It isn't offensive. But it is outdated. We aren't Indians. We are Native Canadians. The proper term is First Nations."

So I called my sister.

Darla is my youngest sister—the Quiet Ferguson, they call her—and she is Cree.

"Is the word Indian offensive?" I ask her.

"No."

I wait, but that's it. "Come on, help me out here. I'm trying to write a book. Give me something pithy and insightful."

She sighs. Darla is a very practical-minded woman and such hairsplitting annoys her.

"Well," she says, "it's like anything. It depends on how it's used. I don't find it offensive, but there are some people who will take offence at anything. I suppose Native sounds better, but most Indians don't really care." Then, as an afterthought. "The volleyball team I play with is called the Hobbema Indians. I helped pick the name."

Words are empty vessels. They take on whatever meaning we give them, good or bad. The single, multisyllable word *Canadian* carries enough weight and context to fill an entire book. The word *Indian* is even more complex, more ambiguous, more problematic.

Will *Indian* ever become socially taboo? Perhaps. But somehow I doubt it. For one thing, the Politically Correct Wave seems to have peaked. For another, the Indians themselves don't seem overly concerned. But most importantly, Pamela Levi of Big Cove, New Brunswick, is proud. Proud to be a dancer. Proud to be an Indian. But above all, proud of herself.

In the end, words fail us.

Jimmy Cardinal, raconteur and general ne'er-do-well from my home town, put it best. "Personally," he says, "I prefer to call myself a First Nations Aboriginal North American Native Indigenous Canadian Person. But it doesn't fit on the forms."

EXAMPLES?

Have you ever been concerned about offending someone by using the wrong word? Does the offence to another come in the choice of word or in the tone of voice in which it is delivered? What can you say or do if you're not sure what words to use? Do you think that politically correct language supports meaningful communication or restricts it?

Source: Will Ferguson. *Why I Hate Canadians* (Vancouver: Douglas and McIntyre), 1997.

Adjust Your Communication

Intercultural communication (in fact, all interpersonal communication) takes place only to the extent that you and the person you're trying to communicate with share the same system of symbols. Your interaction will be hindered to the extent that your language and nonverbal systems differ. Therefore, it's important to adjust your communication to compensate for cultural differences.

This principle takes on particular relevance when you realize that even within a given culture, no two persons share identical symbol systems. Parents and children, for example, not only have different vocabularies but also—even more important—associate different meanings with some of the terms they both use. People in close relationships realize that learning the other person's signals takes a long time, and often great patience. If you want to understand what another person means—by smiling, by saying "I love you," by arguing about trivial matters, by self-deprecating comments—you have to learn the person's system of signals.

In the same way, part of the art of intercultural communication is learning the other culture's signals, how they're used, and what they mean. Furthermore, you have to share your own system of signals with others so that they can better understand you. Although some people may know what you mean by your silence or by your avoidance of eye contact, others may not. You cannot expect others to decode your behaviours accurately without help.

Adjusting your communication is especially important in intercultural situations, largely because people from different cultures use different signals—or sometimes use the same signals to signify quite different things. For example, focused eye contact means honesty and openness for most Canadians. But in Japan and in First Nations cultures, that same behaviour may signify arrogance or disrespect, particularly when engaged in by a youngster with someone older.

Communication accommodation theory holds that speakers will adjust or accommodate to the communication style of their listeners in order to interact more pleasantly and efficiently (Giles et al., 1987). As you adjust your messages, recognize that each culture has its own rules and customs for communication (Barna, 1997; Ruben, 1985; Spitzberg, 1991). These rules identify what is appropriate and what is inappropriate. Thus, in Canadian culture you might call a person you wished to date three or four days in advance. In certain Asian cultures you might call the person's parents weeks or even months in advance. In Canadian culture you say, as a generally friendly gesture—and not necessarily as a specific invitation—"Come over and pay us a visit sometime." In some cultures, such a comment is sufficient to prompt the listeners to actually visit at their convenience.

> " The first need of a free people is to be able to define their own terms and have those terms recognized by their oppressors. "
>
> —Stokely Carmichael

STUDY TIP

Tell a story to a classmate or friend that describes a time in your life when you experienced culture shock.

Recognize Culture Shock

Culture shock is the psychological reaction you experience upon entering a culture very different from your own (Furnham & Bochner, 1986). Culture shock is normal;

most people experience it at some point in their lives when they go away to university, travel, or move to a new city or country. The experience can be unpleasant and frustrating and can sometimes lead to a permanently negative attitude toward the new culture. Understanding that culture shock is normal will help lessen any potential negative implications. (One obvious way to prevent at least some culture shock is to learn as much as you can about the different culture before encountering it. Numerous websites provide information on a wide variety of cultures; one useful site is www.worldbiz.com. Or you can just use your favourite search engine to call up websites on the specific culture you're interested in.)

A commonly encountered case of culture shock occurs with international students. If you're an international student, can you describe your culture shock experiences? If you're not an international student, can you visualize the culture shock you might experience if you were to study in another culture?

Part of culture shock results from your feelings of alienation, conspicuousness, and difference from everyone else. When you lack knowledge of the rules and customs of the new society, you cannot communicate effectively. You're apt to blunder frequently and seriously. In your culture shock, you may not know some very basic things:

- how to ask someone for a favour or pay someone a compliment
- how to extend or accept an invitation for dinner
- how early or how late to arrive for an appointment or how long to stay
- how to distinguish seriousness from playfulness, and politeness from indifference
- how to dress for an informal, formal, or business function
- how to order a meal in a restaurant or how to summon a waiter

Culture shock occurs in four general stages, which can apply to a wide variety of encounters with the new and different (Oberg, 1960).

> **"** Prejudice is a raft onto which the shipwrecked mind clambers and paddles to safety. **"**
>
> —Ben Hecht

In-Class Notes

Recognize That Culture Shock Is Normal

Stages of Culture Shock:

- honeymoon
- crisis
- recovery
- adjustment

_____

_____

_____

_____

_____

_____

_____

Stage One: The Honeymoon At first you experience fascination, even enchantment, with the new culture and its people. You finally have your own apartment. You're your own boss—finally, on your own! Among people who are culturally different, the early (and superficial) relationships of this stage are characterized by cordiality and friendship. Many tourists remain at this stage because their stay in foreign countries is so brief.

Stage Two: The Crisis In the crisis stage, the differences between your own culture and the new one create problems. If you've just moved to your own apartment, for example, you no longer find dinner ready for you unless you make it yourself. Your clothes aren't washed or ironed unless you do it yourself. Feelings of frustration and inadequacy come to the fore. This is the stage during which you experience the actual shock of the new culture. In one study of foreign students from over 100 different countries and studying in 11 different countries, 25 percent of the students were found to have experienced depression (Klineberg & Hull, 1979).

Stage Three: The Recovery During the recovery period, you gain the skills necessary to function effectively. You learn how to shop, cook, and plan a meal. You find a local laundry and figure you'll learn how to iron later. You learn the language and ways of the new culture. Your feelings of inadequacy subside.

Stage Four: The Adjustment At the final stage, you adjust to and come to enjoy the new culture and the new experiences. You may still experience periodic difficulties and strains, but on the whole, the experience is pleasant. Actually, you're now a pretty decent cook. You're even coming to enjoy it. You're making a good salary, so why learn to iron?

Time spent in a foreign country is not in itself sufficient for the development of positive attitudes; in fact, negative attitudes seem to develop over time. Rather, friendships with nationals are crucial for satisfaction with the new culture. Maintaining contacts only with other expatriates or sojourners is not sufficient (Torbiorn, 1982).

People may also experience culture shock when they return to their original culture after living in a foreign culture—a kind of reverse culture shock (Jandt, 2000). Consider, for example, members of the Canadian Armed Forces who serve overseas for extended periods of time or who serve tours of duty as peacekeepers in war-torn countries. Upon returning to their bases in Cold Lake or Moose Jaw, they too may experience culture shock. Students who live and study abroad and then return home may also experience culture shock. In these cases, however, the recovery period is shorter and the sense of inadequacy and frustration is less.

Summary of Concepts and Skills

In this chapter we explored culture and intercultural communication, the ways in which cultures differ, and suggestions for improving intercultural communication.

1. A culture is the specialized lifestyle of a group of people. It consists of their values, beliefs, artifacts, ways of behaving, and ways of communicating. Each generation transmits its culture to the next generation through a process of enculturation. Acculturation is the processes by which your culture is modified through direct contact with or exposure to another culture.

2. Intercultural communication encompasses a broad range of communication. It includes at least the following: communication between cultures, between races, between ethnic groups, between religions, and between nations.

3. Cultures differ in the degree to which they teach individualist or collectivist orientations.

4. High-context cultures are those in which much of the information is in the context or in the person's nonverbals; low-context cultures are those in which most of the information is explicitly stated in the message.

5. Cultures differ in the degree to which gender roles are distinct or overlap. In a masculine culture men are viewed as assertive, oriented to material success, and strong; women are viewed as modest, focused on the quality of life, and tender.

6. Intercultural communication can be made more effective by, for example, reducing ethnocentrism, communicating mindfully, facing fears, recognizing cultural differences between yourself and others, recognizing cultural differences within any group, recognizing meaning differences, not violating cultural rules and customs, and not evaluating differences negatively.

Check Your Ability

Check your ability to apply the skills discussed in this chapter, using a rating scale such as the following: 1 = almost always, 2 = often, 3 = sometimes, 4 = rarely, and 5 = almost never.

____ ❶ Communicate with an understanding of the role of culture and how it influences the messages sent and the messages received.

____ ❷ Appreciate the communication differences in individualistic and collectivist cultures and adjust communications accordingly.

____ ❸ Respond to intercultural communications in light of high- and low-context differences.

____ ❹ Respond to intercultural communications in light of differences in masculinity and femininity.

____ ❺ Recognize and try to combat ethnocentric thinking.

____ ❻ Be mindful of the intercultural communication process.

____ ❼ Communicate in intercultural situations, recognizing potential differences between yourself and the culturally different.

____ ❽ Communicate in intercultural situations, recognizing the differences within any cultural group.

____ ❾ Communicate in intercultural situations, recognizing the possible differences within any cultural group.

____ ❿ Communicate in intercultural situations, recognizing the possible differences in cultural rules and customs.

____ ⓫ Communicate in intercultural situations without evaluating differences negatively.

____ ⓬ Communicate interculturally with appropriate degrees of openness, empathy, positiveness, immediacy, interaction management, expressiveness, and other-orientation.

After completing this self-test, check your answers against the Answer Key at the back of the book.

Multiple Choice Questions *Choose the BEST answer.*

1. Which of the following is NOT true about culture?
   a. It is reinvented with each new generation.
   b. It consists of beliefs and values.
   c. It includes a group's art and laws.
   d. It is learned.

2. The tendency to see and sometimes distort your perceptions through your culture is called
   a. ethnocentrism.
   b. acculturation.
   c. enculturation.
   d. egocentrism.

3. Examples of intercultural communication
   a. include faculty and administration.
   b. include men and women.
   c. include Romans and Greeks.
   d. include all of the above.

4. Which of the following is the least ethnocentric?
   a. racial disparagement
   b. cultural sensitivity
   c. indifference
   d. equality

5. All are stages of culture shock EXCEPT
   a. crisis.
   b. recovery.
   c. discovery.
   d. honeymoon.

6. High-context cultures are those in which
   a. nonverbals are of little importance.
   b. nonverbals are of greater importance.
   c. verbals are of greater importance.
   d. all of the above.

7. Low-context cultures are those in which
   a. verbals are of great importance.
   b. nonverbals are of greater importance.
   c. verbals are of little importance.
   d. none of the above.

8. In a highly masculine culture
   a. grown men cry publicly without shame.
   b. men are passive.
   c. men are assertive.
   d. women are aggressive.

9. Intercultural communication can be made more effective by
   a. reducing ethnocentrism.
   b. facing fears.
   c. not violating cultural rules and customs.
   d. all of the above.

10. In the adjustment stage of culture shock, you
    a. experience ethnocentrism more acutely.
    b. experience a greater enjoyment of the new culture.
    c. have lost your ability to adjust.
    d. none of the above.

True–False Questions *Write a T or F in the blank next to the statement.*

1. _____ Communication between races is considered intercultural.

2. _____ Communication between genders is not intercultural.

3. _____ In an individualist culture, you are responsible for all individuals.

4. _____ In a collectivist culture, you are responsible for the whole group.

5. _____ High-context cultures are also collectivist cultures.

6. _____ In a masculine culture, men are passive.

7. _____ In feminine culture, both genders behave modestly.

8. _____ Ethnocentrism is a great asset to effective communication.

9. _____ You should be mindful rather than mindless in intercultural communication.

10. _____ Teaching culture between generations is called enculturation.

Vocabulary Quiz
The Language of Intercultural Communication

Match the terms of intercultural communication with their definitions. Record the number of the definition next to the appropriate term.

a. _____ high-context cultures

b. _____ acculturation

c. _____ intercultural communication

d. _____ low-context cultures

e. _____ ethnocentrism

f. _____ culture

g. _____ mindfulness

h. _____ enculturation

i. _____ individualist cultures

j. _____ collectivist cultures

1. A culture in which most information is explicitly stated in the verbal message.

2. The specialized lifestyle of a group of people—consisting of their values, beliefs, artifacts, ways of behaving, and ways of communicating—passed on from one generation to the next.

3. The process by which culture is transmitted from one generation to another by, for example, parents, peer groups, and schools.

4. Communication that takes place between people of different cultures or who have different cultural beliefs, values, or ways of behaving.

5. The process through which a person's culture is modified through contact with another culture.

6. The tendency to evaluate other cultures negatively and our own culture positively.

7. That mental state in which we are aware of the logic that governs behaviours.

8. Cultures that emphasize competition, individual success, and responsibility largely to oneself.

9. A culture in which much of the information in communication is in the context or the person and is not made explicit in the verbal message.

10. Cultures that emphasize the member's responsibility to the entire group rather than just to himself or herself.

Skill Building Exercises

9.1 The Source of Your Cultural Beliefs

This exercise is designed to increase your awareness of your cultural beliefs and how you got them. For each of the categories or beliefs noted below, try to answer these six questions:

- *What* were you taught? Phrase it as specifically as possible; for example, "I was taught to believe that...."
- *Who* taught you? Parents? Teachers? Television? Peers? Coaches?
- *How* were you taught? By example? By explicit teaching?
- *When* were you taught this? As a child? As a high school student? As an adult?
- *Where* were you taught this? In your home? Around the dinner table? At school? On the playground?
- *Why* do you suppose you were taught this? What motives led your parents, teachers, peers, or other sources to teach you this belief?

Beliefs

1. The nature of God (for example, the existence of God, organized religion, atheism, an afterlife).

2. The importance of family (respect for elders, interconnectedness, responsibilities to other family members).

3. The meaning of and means to success (the qualities that make for success, financial and relational "success").

4. The rules for sexual appropriateness (sex outside of committed relationships, same-sex, and opposite-sex relationships).

5. The role of education (the role of education in defining success, the obligation to becoming educated, education as a tool for earning a living).

6. Male–female differences (recognizing differences, feminism).

7. Intercultural interactions (friendship and romance with those of other religions, races, nationalities; importance of in-group versus out-group).

8. The importance of money (an amount that's realistic or desirable; acquisition at what price; money and professional goals; relative importance compared with relationships, job satisfaction).

9. The meaning of life (major goal in life, this life versus an afterlife).

10. Time (the importance of being on time; the value of time; wasting time; adherence to the social timetable of your peers—doing what they do at about the same age).

Thinking Critically About Beliefs and Interpersonal Communication.

In which one way did each of your cultural beliefs influence your interpersonal communication style? If you have the opportunity for interaction in small groups, a good way to gain added insight into cultural beliefs is for each person to select one belief, talk about how he or she answered each of the six questions, and comment on how the belief influences the person's way of communicating interpersonally. If the principles for effective interpersonal and intercultural communication (Chapters 8 and 9) are followed, this simple interchange should result in formidable interpersonal and intercultural insight.

9.2 How Do You Talk? As a Woman? As a Man?

Consider how you would respond in each of these situations if you were a typical woman and if you were a typical man.

1. A supervisor criticizes your poorly written report and says that it must be redone.

2. An associate at work tells you she may be HIV-positive and is awaiting the results of her blood tests.

3. You see two neighbourhood preteens fighting in your street; no other adults are around, and you worry that the children may get hurt.

4. An elderly member of your family tells you that he has to go into a nursing home.

5. A colleague confides that she was sexually harassed and doesn't know what to do.

6. You're fed up with neighbours who act decidedly unneighbourly—playing the television at extremely high volume, asking you to watch their two young children while they shop, and borrowing things they rarely remember to return.

Thinking Critically About Woman and Man Talk.

Using your responses and those of others, compile profiles of the following:

a. the typical woman as seen by women

b. the typical woman as seen by men

c. the typical man as seen by men

d. the typical man as seen by women

Consider the sources of the profiles. For example, were the profiles drawn on the basis of actual experience? Popular stereotypes in the media? Evidence from research studies? How do these perceptions of the way women and men talk influence actual communication between women and men?

9.3 Confronting Intercultural Difficulties

How might you deal with the obstacles to intercultural understanding and communication in each of the following scenarios?

1. Your friend makes fun of Radha, who comes to class in her native African dress. You feel you want to object to this.

2. Craig and Louise are an interracial couple. Craig's family treat him fairly well but virtually ignore Louise. They never invite Craig and Louise as a couple to come to dinner or to partake in any of the family affairs. The couple decide that they should confront Craig's family.

3. Malcolm is a close friend and is really an open-minded person. But he has the habit of referring to members of other racial and ethnic groups with the most derogatory language. You decide to tell him that you object to this way of talking.

4. Tom, a good friend of yours, wants to ask Himani out for a date. Both you and Tom know that Himani is a lesbian and will refuse the date, yet Tom says he's going to have some fun and ask her anyway—just to give her a hard time. You think this is wrong and want to tell Tom you think so.

5. Your parents persist in holding stereotypes about other religious, racial, and ethnic groups. These stereotypes come up in all sorts of conversations. You're really embarrassed by these attitudes and feel you must tell your parents how incorrect you think these stereotypes are.

6. Lenny, a colleague at work, recently underwent a religious conversion. He now persists in trying to get everyone else—yourself included—to do the same. Every day he tells you why you should convert, gives you literature to read, and otherwise persists in proselytizing to you. You decide to tell him that you find this behaviour offensive.

Thinking Critically About Intercultural Difficulties.

Why is it so difficult to call to the attention of friends or family their intercultural communication shortcomings? Of all the intercultural problems discussed in this chapter, with which do you have the greatest difficulty? Are these difficulties the result of attitudes and beliefs you hold? Of habit? Of custom?

Web Explorations

Companion Website

Visit the Companion Website at www.pearsoned.ca/devito for student resources related to this chapter, including self-grading quizzes, additional skill-building exercises, and links to other online resources.

Research Navigator

Explore our research resources at www.researchnavigator.com:

- Find and read an article on the nature of culture, cultural differences, or intercultural communication. On the basis of this article, what can you add to the discussion presented here?

- Investigate one of the key terms discussed in this chapter (for example, culture, masculine and feminine cultures, individualist and collectivist orientations, high- and low-context cultures, uncertainty reduction, culture shock, or intercultural communication). What additional insights can you provide?

- Try finding answers to one of the following questions, or design a research study to answer it.

  1. How do cultures differ in their ways of communicating?

  2. What are some of the culturally influenced communication differences between men and women?

  3. How do Canadians view the impact and effectiveness of our multicultural policies?

Chapter 10

Interpersonal Communication and Relationships

Chapter Topics

This chapter looks at the nature and stages of interpersonal relationships, the types of relationships you maintain, and how you can communicate more effectively in these relationships.

Relationships and Relationship Stages

Relationship Types

A POSITIVE Approach to Improving Relationship Communication

Chapter Skills

After completing this chapter, you should be able to:

- formulate both verbal and nonverbal messages appropriate to the relationship stage.

- communicate appropriately and effectively in varied types of relationships.

- use the POSITIVE approach to relationship improvement.

The story is told that in ancient Greece, a young man named Pythias was condemned to death by the tyrant Dionysius for speaking out against the government. Pythias begged Dionysius to delay his execution until he was able to put his family affairs in order. Dionysius agreed but insisted that someone remain in Pythias's place just in case he didn't come back. Damon, Pythias's friend, volunteered and agreed to be executed if Pythias did not return. Damon was then placed in prison while Pythias travelled home. On the day of the scheduled execution, Pythias was nowhere to be found. Without any anger or animosity toward his friend, Damon prepared to die. But just before the execution could be carried out, Pythias arrived and begged the court's forgiveness for his unavoidable delay; he was ready to be executed and asked that his friend be set free. Dionysius was so impressed that he not only freed Damon but also pardoned Pythias—and asked if he could join the two of them in this extraordinary friendship.

> **" Communication is to a relationship what breathing is to maintaining life. "**
>
> —Virginia Satir

> **" People are more frightened of being lonely than of being hungry, or being deprived of sleep, or of having their sexual needs unfulfilled. "**
>
> —Frieda Fromm Reichman

This is the story of an exceptional relationship. In a way, however, all relationships are exceptional and all tell exceptional stories.

RELATIONSHIPS AND RELATIONSHIP STAGES

Relationships come in many forms, as you'll see throughout this chapter. Central to friendships, romantic relationships, family relationships—and in fact to all kinds of relationships—is communication. In fact, the term **relationship communication** is almost synonymous with interpersonal communication.

Although most relationships are face-to-face interactions, internet relationships also are widespread in Canada and around the world. As the number of internet users increases, commercial services are adding, expanding, and improving their services for computer relationships. Many people are turning to the internet to find a friend or, perhaps just as often, a romantic partner. Some use the internet as their only means of interaction; others use it as a way of beginning a relationship, intending to supplement computer talk later with photographs, phone calls, and face-to-face meetings.

In-Class Notes

Advantages of Interpersonal Relationships

- lessen loneliness
- stimulate ideas
- encourage learning about yourself
- enhance self-esteem
- maximize physical, mental, and social pleasures
- minimize pain

_____

_____

_____

_____

_____

_____

_____

_____

Advantages and Disadvantages of Interpersonal Relationships

Like most things in life, interpersonal relationships have both advantages and disadvantages. A good way to begin the study of interpersonal relationships is to examine your own relationships (past, present, or those you look forward to) by taking the accompanying self-test. The test highlights the advantages and disadvantages of relationships.

Test Yourself

What Do Your Relationships Do for You?

For this test you may focus on your own relationships in general (friendship, romantic, family, and work); on one particular relationship (say, with your life partner, child, or best friend); or on one type of relationship (say, friendship). Respond to the statements below by indicating the extent to which your relationship(s) serve each function. Use a 10-point scale, with 1 indicating "never," 10 indicating "always," and the numbers in between indicating levels between these extremes.

_____ **1** My relationships help to lessen my loneliness.

_____ **2** My relationships put uncomfortable pressure on me to expose my vulnerabilities.

_____ **3** My relationships help me to secure stimulation (intellectual, physical, and emotional).

_____ **4** My relationships increase my obligations.

_____ **5** My relationships help me gain in self-knowledge and in self-esteem.

_____ **6** My relationships prevent me from developing other relationships.

_____ **7** My relationships help enhance my physical and emotional health.

_____ **8** My relationships scare me because they may be difficult to dissolve.

_____ **9** My relationships maximize my pleasures and minimize my pains.

_____ **10** My relationships hurt me.

HOW DID YOU DO?

Your responses to these statements should give you some idea of how strongly your relationships serve positive or negative functions.

The odd-numbered statements (1, 3, 5, 7, and 9) reflect what most people would consider advantages of interpersonal relationships—relationships help to lessen loneliness (Rokach, 1998; Rokach & Brock, 1995). They make you feel that someone cares, that someone likes you, that someone will protect you, and that someone ultimately will love you. For instance, regarding item 3, just as plants are heliotropic and orient themselves to light, humans are stimulotropic and orient themselves to sources of stimulation (M. Davis, 1973). Human contact is one of the best ways to secure intellectual, physical, and emotional stimulation. Through contact with others (item 5), you learn about yourself and see yourself from different perspectives and in different roles: as a child or parent, as a coworker, as a friend. Healthy interpersonal relationships help enhance self-esteem and self-worth. Research consistently shows that interpersonal relationships contribute significantly to physical and emotional health (item 7) (Rosen, 1998; Goleman, 1995a; Rosengren et al., 1993; Pennebacker, 1991) and to personal happiness (Berscheid & Reis, 1998). Without close interpersonal relationships you're more likely to become depressed, and depression contributes significantly to physical illness. Isolation, in fact, correlates as closely with mortality as do high blood pressure, high cholesterol, obesity, smoking, or lack of physical exercise (Goleman, 1995a).

Above all, interpersonal relationships tend to maximize pleasure and minimize pain (item 9). Good friends, for example, will make you feel even better at times of good fortune and hurt less in the face of hardships.

The even-numbered statements (2, 4, 6, 8, and 10) suggest what most people consider disadvantages of interpersonal relationships. Close relationships put pressure on you to reveal yourself and to expose your vulnerabilities (item 2). This is generally worthwhile in the context of a supporting and caring relationship, but if the relationship deteriorates, these weaknesses can be used against you. Close relationships increase your obligations (item 4), sometimes to a great extent. Although you enter relationships in order to spend more time with special people, you also incur time (and perhaps financial) obligations with which you may not be happy. Close relationships can limit other relationships (item 6). Sometimes this kind of close relationship involves someone you like but your partner can't stand. More often, however, it's simply a matter of time and energy: You have less to give to other and less intimate relationships. The closer your relationship, the more emotionally difficult it is to dissolve (item 8). A deteriorating relationship can cause distress or depression. In some cultures, religious pressures may prevent unhappily married couples from separating. And if a lot of money is at stake, the end of a relationship can involve a huge financial blow (item 10).

One way to use this self-test is to consider how you might lessen the disadvantages of your interpersonal relationships, at least those disadvantages that you indicate are always or almost always present in your relationships. Consider, for example, if your own behaviours are contributing to the disadvantages. For example, do you bury yourself in one or two relationships and discourage the development of others? At the same time, consider how you can maximize the advantages that your relationships currently offer.

In-Class Notes

Disadvantages of Interpersonal Relationships

- They can expose weaknesses.
- The can involve obligations of time, money, emotion, and behaviour.
- They can impact on other relationships.
- They can be difficult to terminate.
- They can involve the potential for hurt.

You're no doubt attracted to some people and not attracted to others. In a similar way, some people are attracted to you and some people are not. If you're like most people, you're attracted to others on the basis of four major factors: attractiveness (physical appearance and personality); similarity in interests, especially in attitudes; proximity (simple physical closeness, as when you live in the same neighbourhood, attend the same classes, or work together); and reinforcement (the person gives you rewards). Do these factors account for your own attraction to others? If not, what additional factors might influence attraction?

Cultural Influences on Interpersonal Relationships

Cultural factors play important roles in the formation of relationships. In most of North America, interpersonal friendships are drawn from a relatively large pool. Out of all the people you come into regular contact with, you choose relatively few as friends. In rural areas and in small villages throughout the world, however, people have very few choices. The two or three other children your age become your friends; there's no real choice, because these are the only possible friends you could make. In some cultures, children's friends are primarily members of their extended family.

Most cultures assume that relationships should be permanent or at least long lasting. Consequently, it's assumed that people want to keep relationships together and will exert considerable energy to maintain relationships. Because of this bias, there is little research that has studied how to move effortlessly from one intimate relationship to another, or that advises you how to do this more effectively and efficiently.

Culture influences heterosexual relationships by assigning different roles to men and women. In North

America, men and women are supposed to be equal—at least, that's the stated ideal. As a result, both men and women can initiate relationships and both can dissolve them. Both men and women are expected to derive satisfaction from their interpersonal relationships, and when that satisfaction isn't present, either partner may seek to exit the relationship. However, in many Middle Eastern countries, for example, only the man has the right to dissolve a marriage without giving reasons. And in Jordan, it was only recently (May 2002) that the first wife was granted a divorce; before this only husbands could obtain divorces (*New York Times,* May 15, 2002, p. A6).

In some cultures, gay and lesbian relationships are accepted, and in others they are condemned. In Canada, same-sex marriage is legal in some provinces, and federal legislation was passed to approve same-sex marriage. However, this legislation remains highly contested, and the current Conservative government proposes to review it. In some parts of the United States, formally registered "domestic partnerships" grant gay men, lesbians, and (in some cases) unmarried heterosexuals rights that were formerly reserved only for married couples—such as health insurance benefits and one partner's right to make decisions when the other is incapacitated. In Norway, Sweden, and Denmark, same-sex relationship partners have the same rights as married partners.

Influences of Technology on Interpersonal Relationships

As discussed in Chapter 8, computer mediated communication (CMC) is used intensely for interpersonal communication. In fact, evidence suggests that interpersonal communication is an important use of the internet, if not *the most* important use (Cummings et al., 2002). What is less clear is the impact of CMC on the quality of social relationships.

Recent studies have shown that adolescents, for example, use CMC to maintain social relationships with family and friends that were initially developed face-to-face, and also to create new relationships completely online (Mesch & Talmud, 2006). Mesch and Talmud (2006) argue that the quality of social relationships depends upon the length of the relationship and on the topics and activities that are shared. Therefore, because friendships that originate online have usually existed for a shorter period of time and the friends are involved in fewer joint interests and activities, these online friendships are perceived to be less close and supportive.

In addition to potentially having the same advantages and disadvantages of offline interpersonal relationships, as discussed above, conflicting evidence exists about the potential quality of a fully online relationship. Some research suggests that online relationships can be meaningful and deep (Parks & Floyd, as cited in Cummings et al., 2002); however, some data also suggests that people don't value their online relationships to the same degree that they value their face-to-face ones (Parks & Roberts, as cited in Cummings et al., 2002). As well, time spent online reduces the amount of time spent with family and friends and has been shown to diminish social involvement and psychological well-being (Cummings et al., 2002). It would seem that the key issue to determining the effect of CMC on interpersonal relationships is whether CMC is used to supplement communication with friends and family or whether it is used as a substitute for face-to-face communication.

Cummings et al. (2002) conducted a study of university students in the Eastern U.S. who used email extensively. They wanted to determine the students' perceptions of the usefulness of face-to-face conversations, phone, and email for schoolwork, information, and relationship purposes. The 39 students evaluated each communication during 259 communication episodes. The results indicated that the use of the internet was an inferior way to maintain an interpersonal relationship, behind either the phone or in person. However, email was found to be as useful as the phone and face-to-face communication for completing schoolwork, and even better for exchanging information.

Online relationships have some advantages over offline relationships. For example, in some face-to-face relationships, physical appearance outweighs

Alright, I'll admit it... when I was in high school, I was one of those geeky kids with a small circle of fellow social outcasts as friends. In that most charming of high school traditions, one simply didn't talk with someone not in your clique; as a result, I left high school knowing perhaps ten people. I can only imagine how my teenage years would have been different—but probably no less misspent—had there been online social networking systems like Friendster or orkut. I would have had an instant network of friends, all of whom would surely have been my friend too!
(Bates, 2004)

 **STUDY TIP**

Cummings, Butler, & Kraut assert that "online relationships are less valuable than offline ones." Debate this notion with a classmate or friend.

personality; CMC allows the person's inner qualities to be shared without the physical distractions. CMC is a boon to those who are shut-ins or very shy, or for whom meeting others in a more traditional way is difficult. Another obvious advantage is that the number of people you can meet online is vast compared to the number you can meet in person. This increases the opportunity to meet people with whom you may share common interests.

However, online relationships also have their own unique disadvantages. CMC allows people to present a false self with little chance of detection. For example, minors may present themselves as adults, and adults may present themselves as children for illicit and illegal sexual communications. Similarly, a CMC partner can present herself as rich, mature, or serious and committed when none of these characteristics hold true.

Increasingly, it seems that young people prefer to communicate with one another using CMC, a preference that has been called *hyperpersonal communication* (Tidwell & Walther, 2002). Tidwell and Walther (2002) consider three elements of interpersonal conversation that are impacted through these new media: idealized perception, selective self-perception, and reduced cues.

Idealized perception can occur with the limited information that is often provided in CMC conversations, when users may come to perceive the other as the "perfect person." In the process of *selective self-perception*, what is presented can be the idealized person, what one wants the other to think, without having to address characteristics of the physical self such as age, gender, or appearance. Because users of CMC can't see each other and can't hear the other's voice (including expressions, tone, accent, and so on), they must rely solely on the *reduced verbal cues* provided (Tidwell & Walther, 2002), which may lead to a false impression of who the other really is.

While CMC may encourage, permit, or help to develop interpersonal relationships, McQuillen (2003) cautions that CMC relationships could be compared to interactions at a costume party. Party-goers become the characters represented by the costumes they are wearing because they can choose what to disclose to others through what they present to others. If what one communication partner chooses to present to the other is more a function of perception than of reality, the relationship may be disconfirming. Some research has found that, in seeking relationships online, you may become more discriminating, less forgiving of minor imperfections, and less willing to work out differences because the field of available people is so vast (Cohen, 2001).

Stages of Interpersonal Relationships

The six-stage model shown in Figure 10.1 describes the significant stages you may go through in developing (and perhaps dissolving) a relationship as you try to achieve your relationship goals. The stages seem standard, and they apply to all relationships, whether of friendship or love. The six stages are *contact, involvement, intimacy and risk, deterioration, repair,* and *dissolution*. Each stage can be divided into an initial and a final phase.

Contact   At the **contact** stage there is first *perceptual contact*—you see what the person looks like, you hear what the person sounds like, you may even smell the person. From this you get a physical picture: sex, approximate age, height, and so on. After this perception there is usually *interactional contact.* Here the interaction is superficial and impersonal. This is the stage of "Hello, my name is Joe"—the stage at which you exchange basic information that needs to come before any more intense involvement. This interactional contact may also be nonverbal, as in, for example, exchanging smiles, concentrating your focus on one person, or decreasing the physical distance between the two of you.

This is the stage at which you initiate interaction ("May I join you?") and engage in invitational communication ("May I buy you a drink?"). According to some researchers, it's at this contact stage—within the first four minutes of initial interaction—that you decide if you want to pursue the relationship (Zunin & Zunin, 1972).

Physical appearance is especially important in the initial development of **attraction** because it's most readily available to sensory inspection. Yet through both verbal and nonverbal behaviours, qualities such as friendliness, warmth, openness, and dynamism are also revealed at the contact stage.

Involvement   At the **involvement** stage, a sense of mutuality, of being connected, develops. During this stage you experiment and try to learn more about the other person. At the initial phase of involvement a kind of preliminary *testing* goes on. You want to see if your initial judgment—made perhaps at the contact stage—proves reasonable. So you may ask questions such as "Where do you work?" "What are you majoring in?"

If you're committed to getting to know the person even better, you continue your involvement by *intensifying* your interaction. Here you not only try to get to know the other person better but also begin to reveal yourself. It's at this stage that you begin to share your feelings and your emotions. If this is to be a romantic relationship, you might date. If it's to be a friendship, you might share in activities related to mutual interests—go to the movies or to some sports event together.

Throughout the relationship process, but especially during the involvement and early stages of intimacy, partners continue testing each other. For example, you might ask your partner directly how he or she feels; or you might disclose your own feelings on the assumption that your partner will also self-disclose; or you might joke about a shared future together, touch more intimately, or hint that you're serious about the relationship; or you might question mutual friends as to your partner's feelings (Bell & Buerkel-Rothfuss, 1990; Baxter & Wilmot, 1984).

> " Laughter is not at all a bad beginning for a friendship. "
>
> —Oscar Wilde

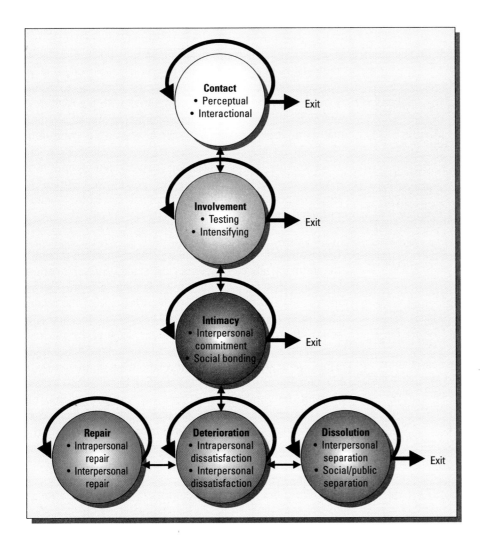

Figure 10.1

The Six Stages of Relationships
This is a general model, but can you identify other stages that would further explain what goes on in relationships? Can you provide a specific example, from literature or from your own experience, that would illustrate some or all of these stages?

Intimacy and Risk   To some people, relational intimacy seems extremely risky. To others it involves only low risk. Consider your own view of relationship risk by responding to the following questions:

- Is it dangerous to get really close to people?
- Are you afraid to get really close to someone because you might get hurt?
- Do you find it difficult to trust other people?
- Do you believe that the most important thing to consider in a relationship is whether you might get hurt?

People who answer Yes to these and similar questions see intimacy as involving considerable risk (Pilkington & Richardson, 1988). Such people have fewer close friends, are less likely to have romantic relationships, have less trust in others, have lower levels of dating assertiveness, have lower self-esteem, are more possessive and jealous, and are generally less sociable and extroverted than those who see intimacy as involving little risk (Pilkington & Woods, 1999).

One way to define *intimacy* is as the feeling that you can be honest and open when talking about yourself; you can express thoughts and feelings that you don't reveal in other relationships (Mackey et al., 2000). At the **intimacy** stage, you commit yourself still further to the other person and, in fact, establish a kind of relationship in which this individual becomes your best or closest friend, lover, or companion. Usually the intimacy stage divides itself quite neatly into two phases: an *interpersonal commitment* phase in which you commit yourselves to each other in a kind of private way, and a *social bonding* phase in which the commitment is made public—perhaps to family and friends, perhaps to the public at large through formal marriage. Here the two of you become a unit, a pair. Commitment may take many forms: an engagement or a marriage, a commitment to help the person or to be with the person, or a commitment to reveal your deepest secrets. It may consist of living together or agreeing to become lovers. The type of commitment varies with the relationship and with the individuals. The important characteristic is that the commitment made is a special one; it's a commitment that you do not make lightly or to everyone. Each of us reserves this level of intimacy for very few people at any given time—sometimes just one person; sometimes two, three, or perhaps four. Rarely do people have more than four intimates, except in a family situation.

In an interesting study on love, men and women from different cultures were asked the following question: "If a man (woman) had all the other qualities you desired, would you marry this person if you were not in love with him (her)?" How would you answer this question? Results varied greatly from one culture to another (Levine et al., 1994). For example, 50.4 percent of the respondents from Pakistan said Yes, 49 percent of those from India said Yes, and 18.8 percent from Thailand said Yes. At the other extreme were those from Japan (only 2.3 percent said Yes), the United States (only 3.5 percent said Yes), and Brazil (only 4.3 percent said Yes).

Deterioration   Although many relationships remain at the intimacy stage, some enter the stage of **deterioration**—the stage that focuses on the weakening of bonds between the parties and that represents the downside of the relationship progression. Relationships deteriorate for many reasons. When the reasons for coming together are no longer present or change drastically, relationships may deteriorate. Thus, for example, when your relationship no longer lessens your loneliness or provides stimulation or self-knowledge, or when it fails to increase your self-esteem or maximize pleasures and minimize pain, it may be in the process of deteriorating. Among the other reasons for deterioration are third-party relationships, sexual dissatisfaction, dissatisfaction with work, or financial difficulties (Blumstein & Schwartz, 1983).

During the process of deterioration, communication patterns change drastically. These patterns are in part a response to the deterioration; you communicate as you do because of the way you feel your relationship is deteriorating. However, the way you communicate (or fail to communicate) also influences the fate of your relationship. During the deterioration stage you may, for example, increasingly withdraw, talk and listen less, and self-disclose less.

Repair The first phase of **repair** is *intrapersonal repair*, in which you analyze what went wrong and consider ways of solving your relational difficulties. At this stage you may consider changing your behaviours or perhaps changing your expectations of your partner. You may also weigh the rewards of your relationship as it is now against the rewards you could anticipate if your relationship ended.

If you decide that you want to repair your relationship, you may discuss this with your partner at the *interpersonal repair* level. Here you may talk about the problems in the relationship, the corrections you would want to see, and perhaps what you would be willing to do and what you would want your partner to do. This is the stage of negotiating new agreements, new behaviours. You and your partner may try to solve your problems yourselves, seek the advice of friends or family, or perhaps enter professional counselling.

You can look at the strategies for repairing a relationship in terms of the following six suggestions (see Figure 10.2). The first letters of each conveniently combine to spell out the word *repair*, a useful reminder that repair is not a one-step but a multi-step process: Recognize the problem, Engage in productive conflict resolution, Pose possible solutions, Affirm each other, Integrate solutions into normal behaviour, and Risk.

- *Recognize* the problem. What, in concrete terms, is wrong with your present relationship? What changes would be needed to make it better—again, in specific terms?

- *Engage* in productive conflict resolution. Interpersonal conflict is an inevitable part of relationship life. It's not so much the conflict that causes relationship difficulties as the way in which the conflict is approached (Chapter 11).

- *Pose* possible solutions. Ideally, each person will ask, "What can we do to resolve the difficulty that will allow both of us to get what we want?"

- *Affirm* each other. For example, happily married couples communicate more agreement, approval, and positive affect than do unhappily married couples (Dindia & Fitzpatrick, 1985).

- *Integrate* solutions into normal behaviour. Make the solutions a part of your normal behaviour.

- *Risk.* Risk giving favours without any certainty of reciprocity. Risk rejection by making the first move to make up or say you're sorry. Be willing to change, to adapt, to take on new tasks and responsibilities.

One way to improve communication during difficult times is to ask your partner to initiate positive behaviours rather than to stop negative behaviours. In keeping with this idea, suggest alternatives to the following comments: (1) I hate it when you ignore me at business functions. (2) I can't stand going to these cheap restaurants; when are you going to start spending a few bucks? (3) Stop being so negative; you criticize everything and everyone.

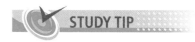
STUDY TIP

Reflecting on a relationship that has ended, analyze where the Relationship Repair Wheel "went off the rails."

How would you distinguish between repair designed to *maintain* a relationship ("preventive maintenance," to keep the relationship satisfying and functioning smoothly) and repair designed to *reverse deterioration* ("corrective maintenance," to fix something that is broken or not functioning properly) (Davis, 1973)? Do these two kinds of repair rely on different strategies?

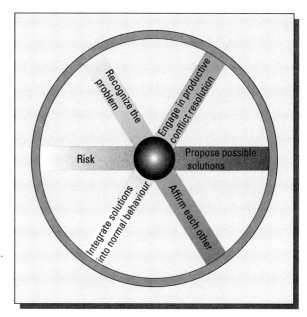

Figure 10.2

The Relationship Repair Wheel
The wheel seems an apt metaphor for the repair process: The specific repair strategies—the spokes—all work together in a constant process. The wheel is difficult to get started, but once in motion the process becomes easier. And, of course, it's easier to start when two people are pushing. How would you describe the repair process?

Relationship Repair: General Strategies

- **R**ecognize the problem.
- **E**ngage in productive conflict resolution.
- **P**ose possible solutions.
- **A**ffirm each other.
- **I**ntegrate solutions into normal behaviour.
- **R**isk change and rejection.

_____

_____

_____

_____

_____

_____

_____

_____

STUDY TIP

Create a chart summarizing the suggestions provided in your text for dealing with relationship dissolution.

❝ After all, my erstwhile dear,
My no longer cherished,
Need we say it was not love,
Just because it perished? ❞

—Edna St. Vincent Millay

Dissolution   The **dissolution** stage is the cutting of the bonds tying you together. At first it usually takes the form of *interpersonal separation,* in which you may not see each other anymore. If this separation period proves workable and if the original relationship is not repaired, you may enter the phase of *social* or *public separation.* Avoidance of each other and a return to being "single" are among the primary identifiable features of dissolution. In some cases, however, the former partners change the definition of their relationship; for example, ex-lovers become friends, or ex-friends become "just" business partners.

This final "goodbye" phase of dissolution is the point at which you become an ex-lover or ex-friend. In some cases, this is a stage of relief and relaxation; finally it's over. In other cases this is a stage of anxiety and frustration, of guilt and regret, of resentment over time ill spent and now lost.

No matter how friendly the breakup, there is likely to be some emotional difficulty. Here are some suggestions for dealing with this.

Break the Loneliness–Depression Cycle.   First, realize that your feelings of loneliness and depression are not insignificant (Rubenstein & Shaver, 1982). Keep in mind that recent research shows that both men and women get depressed when their relationships deteriorate (Spangler & Burns, 2000) and that men are more likely than women to commit suicide as a result of relationship breakups (Kposow, 2000). Avoid *sad passivity,* a state where you feel sorry for yourself, sit alone, and perhaps cry. This may actually make you feel worse. Instead, try to engage in *active solitude* (exercise, write, study, play computer games) and seek *distraction* (do things to put loneliness out of your mind; for example, take a long drive or shop). The most effective way to deal with loneliness is through *social action,* especially through helping people in need.

Take Time Out.   Take some time for yourself. Renew your relationship with yourself. If you were in a long-term relationship, you probably saw yourself as part of a team, as one of a pair. Get to know yourself as a unique individual, standing alone now but fully capable of entering a meaningful relationship in the future.

Bolster Self-Esteem.   If your relationship failed, you may experience a lowering of self-esteem. Positive and successful experiences are most helpful in building

Six Stages in Relationships

Contact
- Hello, how are you?
- May I join you?

Involvement
- I'd like to know you better.
- Is your paper finished?

Intimacy
- I care about you.
- Will you marry me?

Deterioration
- We aren't joined at the hip, you know.
- You never talk to me now.

Repair
- I'm concerned about us.
- I'm willing to try. Are you?

Dissolution
- It's all over.
- I gave it everything I had.

---

self-esteem. As in dealing with loneliness, helping others is one of the best ways to raise your own self-esteem. Engage in activities that you enjoy, that you do well, and that are likely to result in success.

Seek the Support of Others. Support from others is an effective antidote to the discomfort and unhappiness that occurs when a relationship ends. Avail yourself of your friends' and family's support. Seek out people who are positive and nurturing; avoid negative individuals who will paint the world in even darker tones. Also, make the distinction between seeking support and seeking advice. If you feel you need advice, seek out a professional.

Avoid Repeating Negative Patterns. Many people enter second and third relationships with the same blinders and unrealistic expectations with which they entered earlier relationships. Ask yourself at the start of a new relationship if you're entering a relationship modelled on the previous one. If the answer is Yes, be especially careful that you do not repeat the problems. At the same time, avoid becoming a prophet of doom. Do not see in every new relationship vestiges of the old. Do not jump at the first conflict and say, "Here it goes again." Treat the new relationship as the unique relationship it is. Use past relationships and experiences as guides, not filters.

Movement Among the Stages Movement among and within relationship stages is depicted in Figure 10.1 (page 223) by the different types of arrows. The *exit* arrows show that each stage offers the opportunity to exit the relationship. After saying hello, you can say goodbye and exit. The vertical or *movement* arrows going to the next stage and back again represent the fact that you can move to another stage—either to one that is more intense (say, from involvement to intimacy) or to one that is less intense (say, from intimacy to deterioration). The *self-reflexive* arrows—the arrows that return to the beginning of the same level or stage—signify that any relationship may become stabilized at any point. You may, for example, continue to maintain a relationship at the intimate level without its deteriorating or going back to a less intense stage of involvement. Or you may remain at the "Hello, how are you?" stage—the contact stage—without getting further involved.

Within each relationship and within each relationship stage, there are dynamic tensions between opposing desires. The assumption made by **relational dialectics theory** is that all relationships can be defined by a series of opposites. For example, some research has found three such pairs of opposites (Baxter, 1988, 1990; Baxter & Simon, 1993):

> Do any of your relationships involve tension between such opposites as autonomy–connection, novelty–predictability, and closedness–openness? How are these tensions dealt with and reconciled?

- The tension between *autonomy* and *connection* has to do with your desire to remain an individual but also to be intimately connected to another person and to a relationship.
- The tension between *novelty* and *predictability* focuses on your desires for newness and adventure on the one hand, and for sameness and comfort on the other.
- The tension between *closedness* and *openness* relates to your desires to be in an exclusive relationship and, at the other extreme, to be in a relationship that is open to different people.

Research indicates that the closedness–openness tension is more in evidence during the early stages of relationship development. Autonomy–connection tension, and novelty–predictability tension are more frequent as the relationship progresses (Baxter, 1988, 1990; Baxter & Simon, 1993).

Listen to This | Listening to Stage Talk

Learning to listen for stage-talk messages—messages expressing a desire to move the relationship in a particular way or to maintain it at a particular stage—will help you understand and manage your own interpersonal relationships, whether business or personal. Over the next few days listen carefully to all stage-talk messages. Listen to messages referring to your own relationships as well as to messages that friends or coworkers disclose about their relationships. Collect these messages and classify them into the following categories:

1. *Contact messages* express a desire for contact: "Hi, my name is Joe."

2. *Closeness messages* express a desire for increased closeness, involvement, or intimacy: "I'd like to see you more often."

3. *Maintenance messages* express a desire to stabilize the relationship at one stage: "Let's stay friends for now. I'm afraid to get more involved at this point in my life."

4. *Distancing messages* express a person's desire to distance himself or herself from a relationship: "I think we should spend a few weeks apart."

5. *Repair messages* express a desire to repair the relationship: "Can we discuss this issue again, this time in a more constructive way? I didn't mean to hurt your feelings."

6. *Dissolution messages* express a desire to break up or dissolve the existing relationship: "Look, it's just not working out as we planned; let's each go our own way."

SUGGESTIONS?

Grace has been dating Thomas for the past few months and admits that she really can't tell if Tom wants the relationship to become more intimate or more distant. And Tom admits that he has difficulty reading Grace's stage talk. What specific advice would you give both Grace and Tom to help them read each other's stage talk?

RELATIONSHIP TYPES

In this section we look at friendship, love, and family relationships, and their various types. Workplace relationships will be discussed in detail in Chapter 12.

Friendship

Friendship is an interpersonal relationship between two people and is mutually productive and characterized by mutual positive regard.

Friendship is an interpersonal relationship; communication interactions must have taken place between the people. Further, the interpersonal relationship involves a "personalistic focus" (Wright, 1978, 1984). That is, friends react to each other as complete persons; as unique, genuine, and irreplaceable individuals.

Friendships must be mutually productive; by definition, they cannot be destructive to either person. Once destructiveness enters into a relationship, it can no longer be characterized as friendship. Love relationships, marriage relationships, parent–child relationships, and just about any other possible relationship can be either destructive or productive. But friendship must enhance the potential of each person and can only be productive.

Friendships are characterized by mutual positive regard. Liking people is essential if we are to call them friends. Three major characteristics of friendship—trust, emotional support, and sharing of interests (Blieszner & Adams, 1992)—testify to this positive regard.

The closer friends are, the more *interdependent* they become; that is, when friends are especially close, the actions of one will impact more significantly on the other than they would if the friends were just casual acquaintances. At the same time, however, the closer friends are, the more *independent* they are of, for example, the attitudes and behaviours of others. Also, they're less influenced by the societal rules that govern more casual relationships. In other words, close friends are likely to make up their own rules for interacting with each other; they decide what they will talk about and when, what they can and can't say to each other without offending, and when and for what reasons one friend can call the other, and so on.

Friends serve a variety of needs; as your needs change, the qualities you look for in friendships also change. In many instances, old friends are dropped from your close circle to be replaced by new friends who better meet new needs. For example, as your own experience is likely to confirm, friendships serve such needs as *utility* (friends may have special talents, skills, or resources that prove useful to you); *affirmation* (friends may affirm your personal values); *ego support* (friends help you to view yourself as a worthy and competent individual); *stimulation* (friends introduce you to new ideas and new ways of seeing the world); and *security* (friends do nothing to hurt you or to emphasize your inadequacies or weaknesses) (Wright, 1978, 1984).

Types of Friendships Not all friendships are the same. But how do they differ? One way of answering this question is by distinguishing among the three major types of friendship: reciprocity, receptivity, and association (Reisman 1979, 1981).

Social penetration theory describes relationships in terms of the number of topics that people talk about and the degree of "personalness" of these topics (Altman & Taylor, 1973). The breadth of a relationship has to do with the number of topics you and your partner talk about. The depth of a relationship relates to the degree to which friends penetrate each other's inner personality—the core of each person's individuality—in communication. How would you describe the breadth and depth of your close and your casual friendships?

The friendship of *reciprocity* is the ideal type, characterized by loyalty, self-sacrifice, mutual affection, and generosity. A friendship of reciprocity is based on equality: Each individual shares equally in giving and receiving the benefits and rewards of the relationship.

In the friendship of *receptivity*, in contrast, there is an imbalance in giving and receiving; one person is the primary giver and one the primary receiver.

This imbalance, however, is a positive one, because each person gains something from the relationship. The different needs of both the person who receives and the person who gives are satisfied. This is the friendship that may develop between a teacher and a student or between a doctor and a patient. In fact, a difference in status is essential for the friendship of receptivity to develop.

The friendship of *association* is a transitory one. It might be described as a friendly relationship rather than a true friendship. Associative friendships are the kind we often have with classmates, neighbours, or coworkers. There is no great loyalty, no great trust, no great giving or receiving. The association is cordial but not intense.

With a classmate of the opposite sex, discuss the similarities and differences in your expectations of friendship.

Cultural and Gender Differences in Friendship Your friendships and the way you look at friendships will be influenced by your culture and your gender. In Canada, you can be friends with someone and yet never really be expected to go much out of your way for this person. Many Middle Easterners, Asians, and Latin Americans, on the other hand, would consider the willingness to go significantly out of their way an absolute essential ingredient in friendship: If you're not willing to sacrifice for your friend, then this person is really not your friend (Dresser, 1996). The vignette that opened this chapter is a perfect example of this kind of friendship.

Generally, friendships are closer in collectivist cultures than in individualistic cultures (see Chapter 9). In their emphasis on the group and on cooperating, collectivist cultures foster the development of close friendship bonds. Members of collectivist cultures are expected to help others in the group. When you help or do things for someone else, you increase your own attraction to—and attractiveness to—the person, and this is certainly a good start for a friendship. And of course the culture continues to reward these close associations. Members of individualistic cultures, on the other hand, are expected to look out for number one. Consequently, they're more likely to compete and to try to do better than one another—conditions that don't support (generally at least) the development of friendships. You should realize that these opposing characteristics are extremes; most people have both collectivist and individualistic values but have them to different degrees. That is what we are talking about here—differences in degree of collectivist and individualistic orientations.

Generally, women rate higher on the relational functions of friendship than do men (Fritz, 1997). Perhaps the best-documented finding, already noted in our discussion of self-disclosure in Chapter 2, is that women self-disclose more than men do (e.g., Dolgin, Meyer, & Schwartz, 1991). This difference holds true throughout male and female friendships: Male friends self-disclose less often and with less intimate details than female friends do. Men generally don't view intimacy as a necessary quality of their friendships (Hart, 1990).

Women engage in significantly more affectional behaviours with their friends than do males (Hays, 1989). This difference, Hays notes, may account for the greater difficulty men experience in beginning and maintaining close friendships. Women engage in more casual communication; they also share greater intimacy and more confidences with their friends than do men. Communication, in all its forms and functions, seems a much more important dimension of women's friendships.

Men's friendships are often built around shared activities—attending a ball game, playing cards, working on a project at the office. Women's friendships, on the other hand, are built more around sharing feelings, support, and "personalism." One study found that similarity in status, willingness to protect one's friend in uncomfortable situations, academic major, and even proficiency in playing Password were significantly related to the relationship closeness of male–male friends but not of female–female or female–male friends (Griffin & Sparks, 1990). Perhaps similarity is a criterion for male friendships but not for female or mixed-sex friendships. How do you see the changes in gender differences? Do you see the differences between men and women increasing or decreasing? What do you see as the major difference between men and women in their attitudes and beliefs about friendship? About family relationships?

The ways in which men and women develop and maintain their friendships will undoubtedly change considerably—as will all gender-related variables—in the coming years. Perhaps there will be further differentiation, or perhaps an increase in similarities. In the meantime, given the present state of research in gender differences, we must be careful to neither exaggerate differences nor treat small differences as if they were highly significant. We need to avoid stereotyping and stressing opposites, while neglecting the huge number of similarities between men and women (Wright, 1988; Deaux & LaFrance, 1998).

> " We love because it's the only true adventure. "
>
> —Nikki Giovanni

Online Social Relationships

One of the prominent features of CMC is its ability to help build and support large social collectives of communities. Electronic or virtual communities are often described as "groups where relationships form, and whose members provide each other with companionship, information, and social support" (Cummings et al., 2002).

Interestingly, the gender rules that apply to face-to-face conversations tend to hold true in CMC social networks. An individual reacts to another person based on the perceived gender of the other. For example, studies have found that chatrooms that are predominantly male involve more oppositional interaction, whereas predominantly female chatrooms involve more cooperation or aligned communication. (Soukup, 1999). Individuals often use mixed chatrooms to screen others in public, searching for common interests; and to screen for appropriate interactional partners, after which the conversation could move to the more private arena of cellphone text messaging (Soukup, 1999).

Cellphone text messaging and computer instant messaging (IM) capacities are radically altering the way people flirt, make propositions to each other, or even end relationships (Srivastava, 2005). For example, networks are flooded on Valentine's Day with text messages and virtual cards.

Cellphone companies have capitalized on this unexpected use of IM. Srivastava (2005) offers the following examples:

- In 2003, Australia's Virgin Mobile company introduced a 53-page user guide named "The Joy of Text," for users who wanted to increase their dose of "textual intercourse."
- "Flirtfests" are arranged by a number of companies and allow people to flirt with strangers using IM, by way of assigned ID numbers.
- Bars and pubs run "text and flirt" games where messages are exchanged on large central screens located around the bar.

Other wireless companies have launched matchmaking services that allow real-time interaction and access to photographs of potential dates. Other services offer users the possibility of finding mates for life within minutes—using their mobile phones (Srivastava, 2005).

Family Relationships

If you had to define the word *family*, you might first be inclined to say that a family consists of parents and one or more children. When pressed, you might add that some families also consist of other relatives: brothers and sisters, grandparents, aunts and uncles, in-laws, and so on. But, increasingly, other forms of family are becoming common and accepted.

Divorce rate statistics provide significant information about the changing nature of the typical two-parent family. According to Statistics Canada, in 1973, 5.4 percent of divorces involved husbands who had been divorced before. In 2003, this number had dramatically increased to 16.2 percent. Wives involved in multiple divorces showed a slightly lower increase to 15.7 percent in 2003, up from 5.4 percent in 1973. Overall in Canada, there was an increase of 1 percent in the number of divorces between 2001 and 2002, which roughly corresponded to the general increase in population (Statistics Canada). Ontario, Quebec, Prince Edward Island, and Saskatchewan showed slight increases in their overall divorce rate between 2001 and 2002. Surprisingly, Newfoundland and Labrador showed a major decrease of 21.4 percent in the number of divorces during the same time. Statistics in Canada show that the peak divorce rate occurs after three years of marriage, when 26.2 out of every 1000 marriages will fail. After that crucial time, the risk of divorce decreases slightly with each year. However, 38.3 percent of all marriages in Canada will end in divorce before the thirtieth anniversary.

Data from the government of Canada indicate that an increasing number of children under the age of 18 are living in single-parent families (Statistics Canada). Data from the 2001 Census indicates that, while the overwhelming majority (84.3 percent) of children live in two-parent homes, the number has dropped since 1999, when 85.9 percent of children lived in two-parent homes. Approximately 12.6 percent (down from 13.5 percent in 1999) of children are being raised in female-headed families, while 2.9 percent (a dramatic rise from 0.6 percent in 1999) are being raised in male-headed families. Between 1971 and 2001, lone-parent families increased from 9.4 percent of all families to 15 percent of all families.

Another example of changing family relationships involves partners who are not married but live together in an exclusive relationship. For the most part, these cohabitants live as if they were married: there is an exclusive sexual commitment; there may be children; and financial responsibilities, time, and space are shared. These relationships often mirror traditional marriages, except that in marriage, the union is recognized by a religious body, the state, or both, whereas in a relationship of cohabitants the relationship generally is not recognized this way. In Canada, common-law unions have increased steadily since 1981, especially in Quebec, where the rates rose to 25 percent in 2001, from 8 percent in 1981 (Statistics Canada). In the rest of Canada, common-law unions have increased at a lesser but still steady rate, to 13.7 percent in 2001, up from 6 percent in 1981. In 2001, 530 900 common-law families had at least one child living at home; 261 970 of those families were located in Quebec.

Another example of the changing family is the gay male or lesbian couple who live together and have all the characteristics of a family. Many of these couples have children from previous heterosexual unions, through artificial insemination, or by adoption. Although accurate statistics are difficult to secure, couplehood among gays and lesbians seems more common than the popular media might lead us to believe. Some research has estimated the number of gay and lesbian couples at between 70 and 80 percent of the gay population (itself estimated variously at between 4 percent and 16 percent of the total population, depending on the definitions used and the studies cited). In summarizing these previous studies and their own research, Blumstein and Schwartz (1983) conclude, "'Couplehood,' either as a reality or as an aspiration, is as strong among gay people as it is among heterosexuals."

The communication principles that apply to the traditional nuclear family (the mother-father-child family) also apply to these varied relationships. In the following discussion, the term **primary relationship** denotes the relationship between the two principal parties—the husband and wife or the domestic partners, for example. The term **family** denotes the broader constellation that may include children, relatives, and assorted significant others.

All primary relationships and families have several characteristics that further define this relationship type: defined roles, recognition of responsibilities, shared history and future, shared living space, and established rules for communicating.

For example, primary relationship partners have relatively *defined roles* that each person is expected to play in relation to the other and to the relationship as a whole. Each has acquired the rules of the culture and social group; each knows approximately what his or her obligations, duties, privileges, and responsibilities are. The partners' roles might include wage earner, cook, house cleaner, child care giver, social secretary, home decorator, plumber, carpenter, food shopper, money manager, nurturer, philosopher, comedian, organizer, and so on. At times the roles may be shared, but even then it's generally assumed that one person has primary responsibility for certain tasks and the other person for others.

Family members have a *recognition of responsibilities* to one another; for example, responsibilities to help others financially; to offer comfort when family members are distressed; to take pleasure in family members' pleasures, to feel their pain, to raise their spirits.

Primary relationships have *a shared history and the prospect of a shared future.* For a relationship to become a primary one, there must be some history, some significant past interaction. This interaction enables the members to get to know each other, to understand each other a little better, and ideally to like and even love each other. Similarly, the individuals view the relationship as having a potential future.

All families teach *rules for communicating*; for example, never contradict the family in front of outsiders, or never talk finances with outsiders.

Influences of Technology on Family Relationships Every generation of adults since Plato (who correctly worried that reading would negatively impact oral tradition and memory) has been leery of new technology and how it might affect the younger generation. And every generation of youth has wholeheartedly embraced new technology (whether automobiles, TV, or music) and incorporated the changes into their own lifestyles. However, CMC is expanding faster than any previous new technology, often leaving both adults and youth behind. For example, MySpace, a chatroom especially popular with youth, is growing by about 280 000 members a day and now has more than 78 million members (Kornblum, 2006).

Technology has provided ways for families to be able to stay more closely in touch, whether it is the nuclear family trying to arrange and survive hectic daily schedules, or an extended family communicating across vast distances. Many parents find that technology is shifting the kinds of relationships they can have with their children. Not having to say things face-to-face often makes saying difficult things a bit easier. Sending an email message allows the sender to say everything at once without fear of being interrupted. CMC can also allow those communicating over a screen to step outside of their customary roles of parent or child—becoming disinhibited, seeing each other as human beings, and behaving as they might with their friends rather than with a family member (Kornblum, 2006).

However, technology can also negatively impact how close to each other family members living in the same house can feel if they are too hooked-up to their individual technologies. Even caring for the family pet has been impacted by technology. Srivastava (2005) describes how several cellphone service providers have launched "virtual pet" programs or games which provide a digital representation of a family pet. The real thing can be expensive, a problem when you need to travel, and can produce unwanted mess, hair, and odours. Virtual pet owners can decide when they want to take care of their pet, how much time to spend with it, and when they need to leave it with someone else. Of course, with most of these programs, neglect may cause the death of the virtual pet. On the relationship side of the issue, programs that involve interacting with virtual pets or friends may, in fact, heighten social isolation, particularly among those already suffering from antisocial tendencies (Srivastava, 2005).

Many educators and psychologists are now encouraging parents to help their children reduce their compulsion for technology in order to spend more time in the physical company of family and friends (Wallis, 2006). They challenge parents to lead by example and to slow down and unplug once in a while. However, family psychologist Edward Hallowell (as cited in Wallis, 2006) says that technology itself is not the problem. "The problem is ... that you are not having family dinner, you are not having conversations, you are not debating whether to go out with a boy who wants to have sex on the first date, you are not going on a family ski trip or taking time just to veg. It's not so much that the video game is going to rot your brain, it's what you are not doing that is going to rot your life."

As Wallis (2006) concludes, "Generation M has a lot to teach parents and teachers about what new technology can do. But it's up to grownups to show them what it can't do and that there's life beyond the screen."

Some members of Generation M spend up to 6.5 hours a day using some form of electronic media (Wallis 2006). However, much of this time is spent multitasking—simultaneously attending to additional mediums, such as television, music, and books, while working on the computer. While parents are encouraged to set limits on their children's computer usage, as well as monitor content, are there advantages to these new forms of technology? Can you think of some ways that new technology could be used to enhance communication in relationships?

A POSITIVE APPROACH TO IMPROVING RELATIONSHIP COMMUNICATION

There seems little doubt that effective communication is at the heart of effective interpersonal relationships. Without effective communication, such relationships are likely to be a lot less meaningful and satisfying than they could be. The acronym POSITIVE stands for general principles of effective communication that enhance all interpersonal relationships: positiveness, openness, supportiveness, interest, truthfulness, involvement, value, and equality.

Positiveness

Positiveness in conversation, as discussed in Chapter 8, entails both a positive attitude toward the communication act and the expression of positiveness toward the other person. In relationship effectiveness, positiveness toward the relationship is required, not only toward your partner but also about your partner when interacting with third parties.

> " It is wise to apply the oil of refined politeness to the mechanisms of friendship. "
>
> —Colette

Don't confuse positiveness with perfection. Whether influenced by the media, by a self-commitment to have a relationship better than their parents', or by a mistaken belief that other relationships are a lot better than their own, people sometimes look for and expect perfection. But this quest sets up unrealistic expectations; it is almost sure to result in dissatisfaction and disappointment with existing relationships and, in fact, with any relationship that's likely to come along. Psychologist John DeCecco (1988) puts this search for perfection in perspective when he argues that relationships should be characterized by reasonableness—"*reasonableness* of need and expectation, avoiding the wasteful pursuit of the extravagant fantasy that *every* desire will be fulfilled, so that the relationship does not consume its partners or leave them chronically dissatisfied."

Openness

Openness entails a variety of attitudes and behaviours. It includes a readiness to listen to the other person—whether you want to or not. It means you're open to listening to the anxieties and worries of your partner, even when you honestly believe these are minor issues that will go away in the morning.

Openness entails a willingness to empathize with your partner—to seek to experience the feelings of your partner as your partner feels them, to see the world as your partner sees it. It does not mean that you should simply take on the feelings of your partner or even necessarily agree with them, but that you should understand them as your partner experiences them.

Openness recognizes that, throughout any significant relationship, there will be numerous changes in each of the individuals and in the relationship itself. Because persons in relationships are interconnected, with each having an impact on the other, changes in one person may demand changes in the other person. Your willingness to be responsive to such changes, to be adaptable and flexible, is likely to enhance relationship satisfaction (Noller & Fitzpatrick, 1993). Openness thus entails a willingness to consider new ideas, new ways of seeing your partner and your relationship, and new ways of interacting.

In-Class Notes

A POSITIVE Approach to Improving Interpersonal Relationships

- Positiveness
- Openness
- Supportiveness
- Interest
- Truth
- Involvement
- Value
- Equality

Supportiveness

As will be detailed further in the discussion of conflict in Chapter 11, supportiveness entails a variety of behaviours, such as being descriptive rather than evaluative, focusing on the problem rather than trying to control the other person, acting spontaneously rather than strategically, being empathic, treating the other person as an equal, and recognizing that you don't know everything.

In relationship communication, being supportive also includes encouraging the other person to be the best he can be. It entails empowering your partner by raising his self-esteem, by sharing the skills you have that your partner needs to control his own destiny, and by offering constructive criticism rather than simple but discouraging fault-finding.

Interest

The more interested you are in the other person, the more likely it is that your partner will be interested in you. Developing shared interests—learning new skills or hobbies together, learning to appreciate new music, or even something as simple as going to the movies once a week to share the experience together—may help two people learn about each other's likes and dislikes, values and interests, emotions and motivations. In the process, each of you is likely to become a more interesting person, which contributes further to communication enhancement.

Children (and even pets) are a good example of a joint interest that partners come to experience as a couple. As parents share child-rearing and its accompanying joys and problems, they often grow closer as a couple. Through this experience, they come to know each other better because they see each other in a new set of circumstances.

Truthfulness

Honesty and truthfulness do not mean revealing every thought and every desire you have; everyone has a right to some privacy. As already stressed, in any decision concerning self-disclosure, the possible effects on the relationship should be considered (see Chapter 2). Total self-disclosure, in fact, may not always be effective (Noller & Fitzpatrick, 1993). But effectiveness is not the only consideration that needs to be recognized. Ethical issues should also be considered—specifically, the other person's right to know about behaviours and thoughts that might influence the choices she will make.

The truthful sharing of present feelings helps a great deal in enabling each person to empathize with the other; each comes to understand the other's point of view better when these self-disclosures are made. Truthfulness as a quality of effective relationship communication means that what you do reveal will be an honest reflection of what you feel rather than an attempt to manipulate your partner's feelings to achieve a particular and perhaps selfish goal.

Involvement

Involvement means active participation in the relationship. Simply being there or going through the motions is not sufficient. Relationship involvement calls for active sharing in the other person's life (although not to the point of intrusion); and in the other person's goals. It includes active nurturing of the relationship—taking responsibility for its maintenance, satisfaction, and growth. In conflict resolution, as mentioned in Chapter 11, withdrawal and silence are generally unfair conflict strategies. In contrast, actively listening to your partner's complaints, actively searching for solutions to problems and differences, and actively working to incorporate these solutions into your everyday lives are all part of relationship involvement.

Value

When you fall in love or develop a close friendship, you probably do so, in part at least, because you see **value** and worth in the other person. You're attracted to the person because of some inner qualities you feel this person has. Sometimes this sense of appreciation is lost over the years, and you may eventually come to take the other person for granted—a situation that can seriously damage an interpersonal relationship. So it's often helpful to renew and review your reasons for establishing the relationship in the first place and perhaps to focus on the values that originally brought you together. Very likely these qualities have not changed; what may have changed instead is that they're no longer as salient as they once were. Your task is to bring these values to the forefront again and to learn to appreciate them anew.

Equality

Equality entails sharing power and decision making in conflict resolution, as well as in any significant relationship undertaking. Equity theory claims that you develop and maintain relationships in which your cost–benefit ratio is approximately equal to your partner's (Walster et al., 1978; Messick & Cook, 1983). An equitable relationship is simply one in which each party derives rewards that are proportional to their costs. If you contribute more to the relationship than your partner, then equity requires that you get greater rewards. If you each work equally hard, then equity demands that you each get approximately equal rewards. Conversely, inequity exists in a relationship if you pay more of the costs (for example, if you do more of the unpleasant tasks) but your partner enjoys more of the rewards. Inequity also exists if you and your partner work equally hard but one of you gets more of the rewards.

How equitable are your relationships? Are your equitable relationships more satisfying than your inequitable ones?

Summary of Concepts and Skills

In this chapter we explored aspects and major types of interpersonal relationships, and we considered ways to make relationships more effective and more satisfying.

1. Interpersonal relationships have advantages and disadvantages. Among the advantages are that relationships stimulate you, help you learn about yourself, and generally enhance your self-esteem. Among the disadvantages are that relationships often force you to expose your vulnerabilities, make great demands on your time, and may result in your abandoning other relationships.

2. Typical stages of relationships include contact, involvement, intimacy, deterioration, repair, and dissolution.

3. In contact there is first perceptual contact and then interaction.

4. In involvement there is a testing phase ("Will this be a suitable relationship?") and an intensifying of the interaction. Here a sense of mutuality and connectedness often begins.

5. In intimacy there is an interpersonal commitment and perhaps a social bonding in which the commitment is made public.

6. Some relationships deteriorate, proceeding through a period of intrapersonal dissatisfaction to interpersonal deterioration.

7. When there are difficulties, repair may be initiated. Generally, an intrapersonal repair comes first ("Should I change my behaviour?"); this may be followed by an interpersonal repair, in which you and your partner discuss your problems and seek remedies.

8. If repair fails, the relationship may dissolve, moving first to interpersonal separation and later, perhaps, to public or social separation.

9. Among the major interpersonal relationships are friendship, love, family, and work relationships.

10. Friendship is an interpersonal relationship between two people; it is mutually productive and characterized by mutual positive regard.

11. Family relationships are those existing between two or more people who have defined roles, recognize their responsibilities to one another, have a shared history and a prospect of a shared future, and interact with a shared system of communication rules.

12. A communication enhancement approach to relationship effectiveness can be spelled out with the acronym POSITIVE: **p**ositiveness, **o**penness, **s**upportiveness, **i**nterest, **t**ruth, **i**nvolvement, **v**alue, and **e**quality.

Check Your Ability

Check your ability to apply the skills discussed in this chapter. How often do you do the following? Use a rating scale such as the following: 1 = almost always, 2 = often, 3 = sometimes, 4 = rarely, and 5 = almost never.

_____ ❶ See relationships as serving a variety of functions but not necessarily all at the same time.

_____ ❷ Formulate both verbal and nonverbal messages that are appropriate to the stage of the relationship.

_____ ❸ Establish, maintain, repair, and end a wide variety of relationships with a measure of comfort and control.

_____ ❹ Recognize the cultural influences on all interpersonal relationships.

_____ ❺ Enhance relationship communication by stressing positiveness, openness, supportiveness, interest, truthfulness, involvement, value, and equality.

After completing this self-test, check your answers against the Answer Key at the back of the book.

Multiple Choice Questions *Choose the BEST answer.*

1. An advantage of interpersonal relationships is
   a. you generally enhance your self-esteem.
   b. you can learn about yourself.
   c. it stimulates you physically, mentally, and emotionally.
   d. all of the above.

2. The stages of relationship development include
   a. contact, involvement, and recreation.
   b. contact, involvement, and intimacy.
   c. contact, evolvement, and intimacy.
   d. contracts, involvement, and intimacy.

3. In the testing phase of a relationship
   a. you either pass or fail.
   b. there is no right answer.
   c. the relationship intensifies.
   d. the relationship deteriorates.

4. Social bonding in intimacy involves
   a. appearing together in public.
   b. becoming a "couple" to your friends.
   c. making a public commitment.
   d. all of the above.

5. Interpersonal relationships include
   a. friendships.
   b. love.
   c. family.
   d. all of the above.

6. Friendship is characterized by
   a. mutual positive regard.
   b. mutual bank accounts.
   c. mutual friends.
   d. mutual funds.

7. Family relationships include
   a. defined gender.
   b. defined roles.
   c. defined abs.
   d. all of the above.

8. Which of the following is NOT true of the impact of CMC on interpersonal relationships?
   a. Adolescents create new social relationships completely online.
   b. Time spent online reduces the time spent face-to-face with families and friends.

c. Online relationships are always damaging to face-to-face relationships.
   d. People can present themselves falsely online.

9. Technology
   a. can support large social networks.
   b. can impact the way people meet each other.
   c. can encourage people to be "pickier" about who they meet.
   d. can do all of the above.

10. Idealized perception means
    a. dreaming about the perfect partner.
    b. believing that your partner is the perfect one for you.
    c. presenting yourself online as you would like to be.
    d. believing that you are perfect for your partner.

True–False Questions *Write a T or F in the blank next to the statement.*

1. _____ Interpersonal relationships have disadvantages.

2. _____ You can enhance your self-esteem in a relationship.

3. _____ In contact, there is first perceptual contact, then interaction.

4. _____ Intimacy involves no social bonding whatsoever.

5. _____ If repair fails, the relationship might dissolve.

6. _____ CMC affects the quality and quantity of family relationships.

7. _____ Friendship is characterized by a mutual positive regard.

8. _____ CMC allows family members to keep in contact with one another more easily.

9. _____ A shared history is not important when defining a family.

10. _____ Openness is a part of interpersonal effectiveness.

Vocabulary Quiz
The Language of Interpersonal Relationships

Match the terms dealing with interpersonal relationships with their definitions. Record the number of the definition next to the appropriate term.

a. _____ friendship

b. _____ interpersonal repair

c. _____ family

d. _____ dissolution
e. _____ reciprocity
f. _____ supportiveness
g. _____ equality

1. A type of friendship in which one person is not superior to any other, and which encourages supportiveness.

2. A relationship in which there is a shared history and the prospect of a shared future, recognition of mutual responsibilities, defined roles, and rules for communicating.

3. An interpersonal relationship that is mutually productive and characterized by mutual positive regard.

4. An approach to relationship communication that includes empowering your partner by raising his or her self-esteem while avoiding fault-finding.

5. A quality of relationship effectiveness in which each person profits from the relationship, and cooperation rather than competition defines interactions.

6. A stage in some relationships in which the partners recognize a problem and engage in productive conflict resolution.

7. A stage of some relationships that consists of interpersonal separation and social or public separation.

Skill Building Exercises

10.1 Responding to Problems

Based on what you've read in this chapter, your prior readings, and your own experiences, how would you respond to each of the following "letters" if you were an advice columnist?

Love and Age Difference   I'm in love with an older woman. She's 51 and I'm 22 but very mature; in fact, I'm a lot more mature than she is. I want to get married but she doesn't; she says she doesn't love me, but I know she does. She wants to break up our romance and "become friends." How can I win her over?

22 and Determined

Love and the Best Friend   Chris and I have been best friends for the last 10 years. Chris has fallen in love and is moving to Moose Jaw. I became angry and hurt at the idea of losing my best friend and I said things I shouldn't have. Although we still talk, things aren't the same ever since I opened my big mouth. How can I patch things up?

Big Mouth

Love and Sports   My relationship of the last 20 years has been great—except for one thing: I can't watch sports on television. If I turn on the game Mariko moans and groans until I turn it off. Mariko wants to talk; I want to watch the game. I work hard during the week, and on the weekend I want to watch sports, drink beer, and fall asleep on the couch. This problem has gotten so bad that I'm seriously considering separating. What should I do?

Sports Lover

Love and the Dilemma   I'm 49 and have been dating, fairly steadily, two really great people. Each knows about my relationship with the other, and for a while they went along with it and tolerated what they felt was an unpleasant situation. They now threaten to break up if I don't make a decision. To be perfectly honest, I like both of them a great deal and simply need more time before I can make the decision and choose one as my life mate. How can I get them to stay with the status quo for maybe another year or so?

Simply Undecided

Thinking Critically About Relationship Problems.

What general principles did you follow in offering the advice? What role did communication play in your advice?

10.2 From Culture to Gender

This exercise is designed to help you explore how cultures teach men and women different values and beliefs and how these in turn might influence the ways in which men and women communicate in relationships.

Select one of the areas of belief listed on page 241 and indicate what you think the views of the "typical man" and the "typical woman" on this subject would be. For example: *Men believe that women make more effective parents than men do* or *Women believe that men have a higher commitment to career and desire for success than women do.*

Try to identify one way you think these beliefs influence the typical man's behaviour, the typical woman's behaviour, and the typical male–female interpersonal interaction. For example: *Men's belief that women make better parents leads men to leave parenting behaviours up to women* or *Men's belief that women make better parents leads men to avoid making parenting decisions.*

What evidence can you offer for your beliefs about gender differences and about how these cultural beliefs influence interpersonal communication? You may wish to extend this journey by actually locating evidence bearing on your hypotheses. One way to do this is to access the CD-ROM databases that your school library is likely to have; for example, Proquest Direct, ERIC, Psychlit, or Sociofile.

Search for "gender" and the key word of the proposition; for example, gender + friendship, or gender + money. Try several variations for each combination, such as gender + finances, men + money, or gender differences + finance. Some of the abstracts you find will give you the results of a study. Others will just identify the hypotheses studied, so to find out results, you'll have to consult the original research study.

Beliefs

1. the three most important qualities necessary for developing a romantic relationship

2. the importance of money in a relationship and in defining one's success or achievement

3. the role of politeness in interpersonal relationships

4. the tendency to nurture others

5. effectiveness in parenting

6. the tendency to think emotionally rather than logically

7. the likelihood of becoming hysterical—say, during an argument or when placed in a dangerous situation

8. high commitment to career and desire for success

9. the likelihood of becoming depressed because of real or imagined problems

10. the importance of winning—with friends, loved ones, and business associates

Thinking Critically About Culture and Gender.

On the basis of your analysis and research, would you revise your beliefs? State them with even stronger conviction? Urge caution in accepting such beliefs?

10.3 Giving Repair Advice

Whether expert or novice, each of us gives relationship repair advice, and probably each of us seeks it from time to time, from friends and sometimes from therapists. Here are a few situations that call for repair. Can you use what you've read here (as well as your own experiences, readings, observations, and so on) to explain what is going on in these situations? What repair advice would you give to each of the people in these situations?

Friends and Colleagues Mike and Abdul, friends for 20 years, had a falling-out over the fact that Mike supported another person for promotion over Abdul. Abdul is resentful and feels that Mike should have stood by him; Mike's support would have secured a promotion and raise for Abdul, which Abdul and his large family could surely use. Mike feels that his first obligation was to the company and that he chose the person he felt would be best for the job. Mike also feels that if Abdul can't understand or appreciate his motives, then he no longer cares to be friends. Assuming that both Mike and Abdul want the friendship to continue or will at some later time, what do you suggest Mike do? What do you suggest Abdul do?

Coming Out Tom, a second-year college student, recently came out as gay to his family. Contrary to his every expectation, they went ballistic. His parents want him out of the house, and his two brothers refuse to talk with him. In fact, they now refer to him only in the third person, and when they do speak of him, they use derogatory hate speech. Assuming that all parties will be sorry at some later time if the relationship is not repaired, what would you suggest Tom's mother and father do? What do you suggest Tom's brothers do? What do you suggest Tom do?

Betraying a Confidence Josh and Tanya have been best friends since elementary school and even now, in their twenties, speak every day and rely on each other for emotional and sometimes financial support. Recently, however, Josh betrayed a confidence and told several mutual friends that Tanya had been having emotional problems and had been considering suicide. Tanya found out and no longer wants to maintain the friendship; in fact, Tanya refuses even to talk with Josh. Assuming that the friendship is more good than bad and that both parties will be sorry if they don't patch things up, what do you suggest Josh do? What do you suggest Tanya do?

Thinking Critically About Giving Repair Advice.

Look over the repair advice you've offered and see if there is anything in that advice that could cause difficulties. That is, is there anything in your suggestions that could delay the repair process, make it more difficult, or actually prevent it? An alternative way of looking at this is to consciously try to propose advice that will aggravate the problems identified here and contrast them with your initial suggestions. How do the "good" suggestions and the "bad" suggestions differ?

Web Explorations

Companion Website

Visit the Companion Website at www.pearsoned.ca/devito for student resources related to this chapter, including self-grading quizzes, additional skill-building exercises, and links to other online resources.

Research Navigator

Explore our research resources at www.researchnavigator.com:

- Find and read an article on interpersonal relationships; the stages that relationships go through; or the influence of culture and gender on relationships. On the basis of this article, what can you add to the discussion presented here?

- Investigate one of the key terms discussed in this chapter (forexample, interpersonal relationship, online relationship, relationship development, relationship deterioration, relationship repair, friendship, or family). What additional insights can you provide?

- Try finding answers to one of the following questions, or design a research study to answer it.

1. Do the advantages and disadvantages of relationships change with age?
2. In what ways are online relationships impacting family relationships?
3. What are the pros and cons of online social networks?

Chapter 11

Interpersonal Communication and Conflict

Chapter Topics

This chapter focuses on interpersonal conflict and how to make your own conflict interactions more productive.

The Process of Interpersonal Conflict

A Model for Resolving Conflicts

Ways to Manage Conflict

Chapter Skills

After completing this chapter, you should be able to:

■ recognize the differences between content and relationship conflicts and respond appropriately to each.

■ deal with interpersonal conflicts in a systematic way.

■ use more productive conflict strategies and avoid their unproductive counterparts.

In ancient times, the beautiful woman Mi Tzu-hsia was the favourite of the king of Wei. According to the law of Wei, anyone who rode in the king's carriage without permission would be punished by amputation of the foot. When Mi Tzu-hsia's mother fell ill, she took the king's carriage and went out, and the king only praised her for it. "Such filial devotion!" he said. "For her mother's sake she risked the punishment of amputation!"

Another day she was dallying with the king in the fruit garden. She took a peach, which she found so sweet that instead of finishing it she handed it to the king to taste. "How she loves me," said the king, "forgetting the pleasure of her own taste to share with me!"

But when Mi Tzu-hsia's beauty began to fade, the king's affection cooled. And when she offended the king, he said, "Didn't she once take my carriage without permission? And didn't she once give me a peach that she had already chewed on?"

This folktale—taken from *Chinese Fairy Tales and Fantasies* (Roberts, 1979)—captures our common tendency to evaluate the same behaviour in very different ways, depending on how we feel about the person. This tendency is especially clear in interpersonal conflict, the subject of this chapter. More specifically, in this chapter we consider what interpersonal conflict is, how it can go wrong, and how it can be used to improve your interpersonal relationships.

THE PROCESS OF INTERPERSONAL CONFLICT

❝ It is seldom the fault of one when two argue. **❞**

—Swedish proverb

Tranh wants to go to the movies and Sara wants to stay home. Tranh's insistence on going to the movies interferes with Sara's staying home, and Sara's determination to stay home interferes with Tranh's going to the movies. Randy and Grace have been dating. Randy wants to get married; Grace wants to continue dating. The two of them have opposing goals, and each person interferes with the other's attaining his or her goal.

As experience teaches us, **conflict** can arise over many issues. Some examples:

- goals to be pursued ("We want you to go to college and become a teacher or a doctor, not a dancer.")
- allocation of resources such as money or time ("I want to save the tax refund, not spend it on new furniture.")
- decisions to be made ("I refuse to have the Jeffersons over for dinner.")
- behaviours that are considered appropriate or desirable by one person and inappropriate or undesirable by the other ("I hate it when you dress provocatively.")

Interpersonal conflict refers to a disagreement between or among connected individuals: coworkers, close friends, lovers, or family members. The word "connected" in this definition emphasizes the transactional nature of interpersonal conflict, the fact that each person's position affects the other person. That is, the positions in interpersonal conflicts are to some degree interrelated and incompatible.

The Negatives and Positives of Conflict

Interpersonal conflict, because it often occurs between partners, best friends, siblings, and parent and child, can be especially difficult: we like, care for, and even love the individual with whom we are in disagreement. Yet there are both negative and positive aspects or dimensions to interpersonal conflict, and each of these should be noted.

Negative Aspects Conflict often leads to increased negative regard for the opponent. One reason for this is that many conflicts involve unfair fighting methods and are focused largely on hurting the other person. When one person hurts the other, increased negative feelings are inevitable—even the strongest relationship has limits.

At times, conflict may lead you to close yourself off from the other person. When you hide your true self from an intimate, you prevent meaningful communication from taking place. Because the need for intimacy is so strong, one or both parties may then seek intimacy elsewhere. This often leads to further conflict, mutual hurt, and resentment—qualities that add heavily to the costs carried by the relationship. Meanwhile, rewards may become difficult to exchange. In this situation, the costs increase and the rewards decrease, which often results in relationship deterioration and eventual dissolution.

Positive Aspects   The major value of interpersonal conflict is that it forces you to examine a problem and work toward a potential solution. If productive conflict strategies are used, the relationship may well emerge from the encounter stronger, healthier, and more satisfying than before. And you may emerge stronger, more confident, and better able to stand up for yourself (Bedford, 1996).

Conflict enables each of you to state what you want and—if the conflict is resolved effectively—perhaps to get it. For example, let's say that I want to spend our money on a new car (my old one is unreliable) and you want to spend it on a vacation (you feel the need for a change of pace). By talking about our conflict, we should be able to learn what each really wants—in this case, a reliable car and a break from routine. We may then be able to figure out a way for each of us to get what we want. I might accept a good used car or a less expensive new car, and you might accept a shorter or less expensive vacation. Or we might buy a used car and take an inexpensive motor trip. Each of these solutions will satisfy both of us. They are win–win solutions—each of us gets at least part of what we wanted.

Consider, too, that when you try to resolve conflict within an interpersonal relationship, you're saying in effect that the relationship is worth the effort; otherwise you would walk away from such a conflict. Usually, confronting a conflict indicates commitment and a desire to preserve the relationship.

> Where there is no difference, there is only indifference.
>
> —Louis Nizer

Conflict, Culture, and Gender

As in other areas of interpersonal communication, it helps to view conflict in light of culture and gender. Both exert powerful influences on how conflict is viewed and how it's resolved.

Conflict and Culture   Notice how the following three Canadians responded to the question, "What did you learn about culture from your family?"

- Anna is a member of the Métis nation. Her father is Cree. "When I was a child, the kids would try to get me to fight by calling me a half-breed. 'Make them laugh,' said my father. 'Laughing is stronger than punching.'"

- Hadassah is an immigrant to Canada from Israel. Her grandparents are Holocaust survivors. "Always keep one step ahead of those who would hurt you. Outsmart them. Use your head, not your fists to deal with conflict."

- Dawne's family is of British origin and has been in Canada for several generations. "Conflict? What is that?" she said. "We don't like to even acknowledge that conflict exists."

The types of conflicts that arise depend on the cultural orientation of the individuals involved. For example, in collectivist cultures such as those of Ecuador, Indonesia, and Korea, conflicts are more likely to centre on violating collective or group norms and values. Conversely, in individualistic cultures such as those of Canada, the United States, and Western Europe, conflicts are more likely to occur when individual norms are violated (Ting-Toomey, 1985).

When North American and Chinese students were asked to analyze a conflict episode between a mother and her daughter, they saw it quite differently (Goode, 2000). North American students, for example, were more likely to decide in favour of the mother or the daughter—to see one side as right and one side as wrong. The Chinese students, however, were more likely to see the validity of both sides; both mother and daughter were right, but both were also wrong. This finding is consistent with the Chinese preference for proverbs that contain a contradiction (for example, "Too modest is half boastful")—and North Americans' reactions to these proverbs as "irritating."

The ways in which members of different cultures express conflict also differ. In Japan, for example, it's especially important that you not embarrass the person with whom you are in conflict, especially if the disagreement occurs in public. This face-saving principle prohibits the use of such strategies as personal rejection or verbal aggressiveness. In Canada, men and women, ideally at least, are both expected to express their desires and complaints openly and directly. Many Middle Eastern and Pacific Rim cultures, however, would discourage women from such expressions; rather, a more agreeable and submissive posture would be expected.

Conflict and Gender   Do men and women engage in interpersonal conflict differently? One of the few stereotypes that are supported by research is that of the withdrawing and sometimes aggressive male. Men are more apt to withdraw from a conflict situation than are women. The argument is that this may happen because men become more psychologically and physiologically aroused during conflict (and retain this heightened level of arousal much longer than do women) and so may try to distance themselves and withdraw from the conflict to prevent further arousal (Gottman & Carrere, 1994; Canary et al., 1995; Goleman, 1995b). Women, on the other hand, want to get closer to the conflict; they want to talk about it and resolve it. Even adolescents reveal these differences: in a study of boys and girls aged 11 to 17, boys withdrew more than girls but were more aggressive when they didn't withdraw (Lindeman et al., 1997). Similarly, in a study of offensive language, girls were found to be more easily offended by language than were boys; but boys were more apt to fight when they were offended by the words used (Heasley et al., 1995). In another study, young girls were found to use more prosocial strategies than did boys (Rose & Asher, 1999).

Other research has found that women tend to be more emotional and men more logical when they argue (Schaap et al., 1988; Canary et al., 1995). Women have been defined as conflict "feelers" and men as conflict "thinkers" (Sorenson et al., 1995). Another difference is that women are more apt to reveal their negative feelings than are men (Schaap et al., 1988; Canary et al., 1995).

In an interesting longitudinal study of 2000 Ontario adolescents in grades 5 to 13, researcher Debra Pepler shows that bullying may be related to gender and that children don't grow out of it (as cited in Smyth, 2003). They may begin by bullying children of their own gender but often move to verbal or physical attacks on the opposite sex. Bullying may also lead to sexual harassment and other forms of abuse.

Nevertheless, a close examination of the research reveals that the differences between men and women in interpersonal conflict are a lot less clear in reality than they are in popular stereotypes. Much research fails to find the differences that cartoons, situation comedies, novels, and films portray so readily. For example, several studies dealing with both university students and men and women in business found no significant differences in the way men and women engage in conflict (Wilkins & Andersen, 1991; Canary & Hause, 1993; Canary et al., 1995).

Do you find that men and women are equally likely to argue about relationship issues? Are men and women equally likely to address relationship issues in their attempts at conflict resolution?

Conflict Styles Have Consequences

The way in which you engage in conflict has consequences for the resolution conflict and for the relationship between the conflicting parties. Figure 11.1 identifies five basic styles or ways of engaging

Let's say you're on a jury. Do you (a) keep an open mind until all the evidence is in and then evaluate the facts and render a judgment, or (b) render a judgment early in the trial and then interpret the evidence in light of your judgment? Although we'd all like to think we would render a judgment only after considering all the evidence, research finds that many people make their judgments early and then interpret the evidence through the filter of this judgment (Edwards & Smith, 1996; Kuhn et al., 1994).

A natural tendency is to seek out, evaluate, and interpret information that supports or confirms your own position, your own bias (a confirmation bias). Conversely, you may actively avoid or punch holes in any information that would contradict or disconfirm your position or bias (disconfirmation bias). When acquiring and evaluating information, ask yourself if you're being influenced by either of these biases. Bringing this possibility to consciousness will help you think more critically and more fairly about the information.

EXAMPLES?

Think of examples from your own recent experience. Did your biases get in the way of your making accurate judgments about people or ideas?

---

in conflict and is especially relevant to understanding interpersonal conflicts (Blake & Mouton, 1985). Descriptions of the five styles, plotted along the dimensions of concern for self and concern for the other person, provide insight into the ways people engage in conflict and highlight some of the advantages and disadvantages of each style. As you read through these styles, try to identify your own conflict style as well as the styles of those with whom you have close relationships.

STUDY TIP

Debate the merits of the various conflict styles in the following situations: custody battle, bullying, disagreement with a coworker, telemarketing call, family fight.

Competing: I Win, You Lose   The competitive style involves great concern for your own needs and desires and little for those of others. As long as your needs are met, the conflict has been dealt with successfully (for you). In conflict motivated by competitiveness, you would likely be verbally aggressive and blame the other person.

This style represents an *I win, you lose* philosophy. As you can tell, this style might be appropriate in a courtroom or at a used-car lot, two settings where one person benefits from the other person's losses. But in interpersonal situations this philosophy can easily lead to resentment on the part of the person who loses, a situation that can easily morph into additional conflicts. Further, the fact that you win and the other person loses probably means that the conflict hasn't really been resolved but only concluded (for now).

Avoiding: I Lose, You Lose   Conflict avoiders are relatively unconcerned with their own or with their opponents' needs or desires. They avoid any real communication about the problem, change topics when the problem is brought up, and generally withdraw from the scene both psychologically and physically.

As you can appreciate, the avoiding style does little to resolve any conflicts and may be viewed as an *I lose, you lose* philosophy. Interpersonal problems rarely go away of their own accord; rather, if they exist, they need to be faced and dealt with effectively. Avoidance merely allows the conflict to fester and probably grow, only to resurface in another guise.

Accommodating: I Lose, You Win   In accommodating, you sacrifice your own needs for the needs of the other person(s). Your major purpose is to maintain harmony and peace in the relationship or group. This style may satisfy the opposition, but it does little to meet your own needs, which are unlikely to go away.

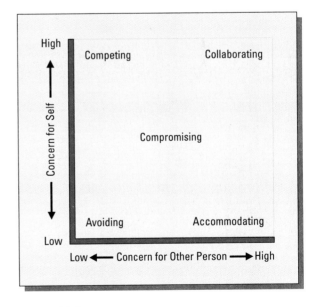

Figure 11.1
Five Conflict Styles
This figure is adapted from Blake and Mouton's (1985) approach to managerial leadership and conflict.

Source: R.R. Blake & J. S. Mouton, *The Managerial Grid III.* Gulf Publishing Company, 1985. Reprinted by permission of Grid International, Inc.

Accommodation represents an *I lose, you win* philosophy. And although this style may make your partner happy (at least on this occasion), it's not likely to be a lasting resolution to an interpersonal conflict. You'll eventually sense unfairness and inequality and may easily come to resent your partner and perhaps even yourself.

Collaborating: I Win, You Win　In collaborating, you address both your own and the other person's needs. This style, often considered the ideal, takes time and a willingness to communicate—and especially to listen to the perspectives and needs of the other person.

Ideally, collaboration enables each person's needs to be met, an *I win, you win* situation. This is obviously the style that, in an ideal world, most people would choose for interpersonal conflict.

Compromising: I Win and Lose, You Win and Lose　The compromising style is in the middle: There's some concern for your own needs and some concern for the other's needs. Compromise is the kind of strategy you might refer to as "meeting each other halfway," "horse trading," or "give and take." This strategy is likely to result in maintaining peace, but there will be a residue of dissatisfaction over the inevitable losses that each side has to endure.

Compromise represents an *I win and lose, you win and lose* philosophy. There are lots of times when you can't both get exactly what you want. You can't both get a new car if the available funds allow for only one. And yet you might each get a better used car than the one you now have. So each of you might win something, though not everything.

Content and Relationship Conflicts

Using concepts developed in Chapter 1, we can distinguish between content conflict and relationship conflict. *Content conflict* centres on objects, events, and persons in the world that are usually, though not always, external to the parties involved in the conflict. Content conflicts have to do with the millions of issues that we argue and fight about every day—the merit of a particular movie, what to watch on television, the fairness of the last examination or job promotion, the way to spend our savings.

> The ultimate test of a relationship is to disagree but to hold hands.
>
> —Alexandra Penney

In-Class Notes

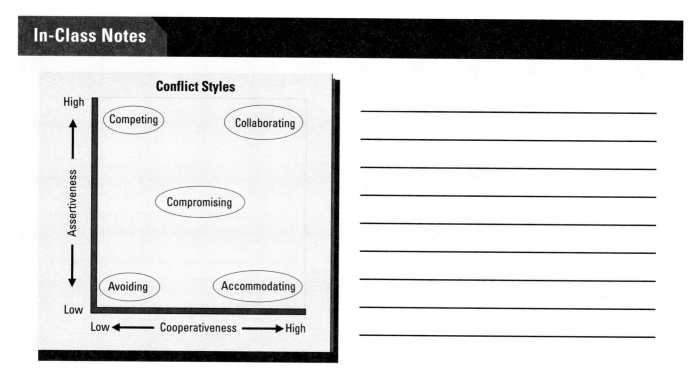

Two Kinds of Conflict

Content: centres on objects, events, and persons external to the parties involved

- what to watch on TV
- how to spend savings
- who to invite over

Relationship: concerned with the relationship between individuals

- who is in charge
- the equality of a relationship
- who has the right to set rules of behaviour

Relationship conflicts are equally numerous and include such examples as a younger brother who refuses to listen to his older brother, two partners who each want an equal say in making vacation plans, and a mother and daughter who each want to have the final word concerning the daughter's lifestyle. Here the conflicts are concerned not so much with some external object as with the relationships between the individuals—with issues such as who is in charge, how equal the members are in a primary relationship, or who has the right to set down rules of behaviour.

Talking Ethics | Libel, Slander, and More

The Canadian Charter of Rights and Freedoms states that everyone has the following fundamental freedoms:

a. freedom of conscience and religion;
b. freedom of thought, belief, opinion, and expression, including freedom of the press and other media of communication;
c. freedom of peaceful assembly; and
d. freedom of association.

But expressions of thought, belief, and opinion are not always free. Some kinds of speech, for example, are unlawful and unethical. It's generally considered unethical (and it's illegal as well) to defame another person—to falsely attack his or her reputation, causing damage to it. When this attack is done in print or in pictures, it's called _libel;_ when done through speech, it's called _slander._

People are becoming increasingly sensitive to and respectful of cultural differences. Whereas a few decades ago it would have been considered quite acceptable to use racist, sexist, or homophobic terms in conversation or to tell jokes at

the expense of various cultural groups, today most Canadians consider these forms of speech inappropriate. Today most Canadians disapprove of speech demeaning another person because of that person's sex, age, race, nationality, affectional orientation, or religion, and most people avoid speaking in cultural stereotypes—fixed images of groups that promote generally negative pictures.

Sexual harassment is unethical, and verbal sexual harassment is a form of speech that is not protected by the Charter of Rights and Freedoms. Also, the courts have ruled that sexual harassment can be undertaken by either sex against either sex.

WHAT WOULD YOU DO?

At the water cooler in the office, you join two of your colleagues only to discover that they're exchanging racist jokes. You don't want to criticize them for fear that you'll become unpopular and these colleagues will make it harder for you to get ahead. At the same time, you don't want to remain silent, for fear it would imply that you're accepting of this type of talk. What would you do in this situation?

In what other ways is face-to-face conflict different from conflict on the net?

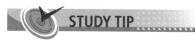

STUDY TIP

With a classmate, role play the five-step model of conflict resolution by applying it to either a personal situation or one you have read about in the media.

Of course, content and relationship dimensions are always easier to separate in a textbook than they are in real life, where many conflicts contain elements of both. For example, you can probably imagine both content and relationship dimensions in each of the content issues mentioned earlier. And yet certain issues seem more one way than the other. For example, intimacy and power issues are largely relational, whereas differences on political and social issues are largely content focused.

Online Conflicts

Just as you experience conflict in face-to-face communication, you can experience the same conflicts online. There are, however, a few conflict situations that are unique to online communication.

Sending commercial messages to those who didn't request them often creates conflict. Junk mail is junk mail; but on the internet, the receiver has to pay with the currency of time—the time it takes to read and delete these unwanted messages.

Spamming often causes conflict. Spamming is sending someone unsolicited email, repeatedly sending the same email, or posting the same message on many bulletin boards, even when the message is irrelevant to the focus of the group. One very practical reason why spamming is frowned upon is that it generally costs people money. And even if the email is free, it takes up valuable time and energy to read something you didn't want in the first place. Another reason, of course, is that spam clogs the system, slowing things down for everyone.

Flaming, especially common in newsgroups, is sending messages that personally attack another user. Flaming frequently leads to flame wars; everyone in the group gets into the act and attacks other users. Generally, flaming and flame wars prevent us from achieving our communication goals, and so are counterproductive.

Listen to This   Listening to Messages in Conflict

Perhaps the most difficult type of listening occurs in the conflict situation; tempers may be running high and you may find yourself being attacked or at least disagreed with. Here are some suggestions for listening more effectively in the conflict situation:

- Act in the role of the listener. Turn off the television, stereo, or computer; face the other person. And think as a listener: Devote your total attention to what the other person is saying.
- Make sure you understand what the person is saying and feeling. One way to make sure, obviously, is to ask questions. Another way is to paraphrase what the other person is saying and ask for confirmation: "You feel that if we pooled our money and didn't have separate savings accounts, this would be a more equitable relationship. Is that the way you feel?"
- Express your support or empathy for what the other person is saying and feeling: "I can understand how you feel. I know I control the finances and that can create a feeling of inequality."

- If appropriate, indicate your agreement: "You're right to be disturbed."
- State your thoughts and feelings on the issue as objectively as you can; if you disagree with what the other person said, then say so: "My problem is that when we did have equal control over the finances, you ran up so many bills that we still haven't recovered from it. And, to be honest with you, I'm worried the same thing will happen again."
- Get ready to listen to the other person's responses to your statement.

SUGGESTIONS?

Your friend is a new teacher at an elementary school. The parents of a student who has been doing very poorly and has created all sorts of discipline problems come to see your friend. They complain that their daughter hates school and isn't learning anything. They want her transferred to another class with another teacher. What listening guidelines would you suggest that your friend try to follow in talking with these parents?

A MODEL FOR RESOLVING CONFLICTS

The model in Figure 11.2 helps explain conflict more fully and at the same time provides guidance for dealing with conflicts effectively. This five-step model is based on the problem-solving technique introduced by John Dewey (1910) and used by most contemporary theorists (e.g., Beebe & Masterson, 2000; Patton et al., 1989). The assumption is that interpersonal conflict is essentially a problem that needs to be solved. This model should not be interpreted as suggesting that there is only one path to conflict resolution. This is just a general way of envisioning the process. Recall a specific conflict that you had recently and try to trace it through the five stages as you read about them.

Before getting to the five stages of conflict, consider a few "before the conflict" suggestions:

- *Try to fight in private.* When you air your conflicts in front of others, you create other problems. You may not be willing to be totally honest when third parties are present; you may feel you have to save face and therefore must win the fight at all costs. You also run the risk of embarrassing your partner in front of others, which will cause resentment and hostility.

- *Make sure you're both relatively free of other problems and ready to deal with the conflict at hand.* The moment your partner comes home after a hard day of work may not be the right time to tackle a conflict.

- *Fight about problems that can be solved.* Fighting about past behaviours or about family members or situations over which you have no control solves nothing; in fact, it's more likely to create additional difficulties. Often such conflicts are really relationship conflicts—concealed attempts at expressing frustration or dissatisfaction.

"Is this a good time to have a big fight?"

© The New Yorker Collection 2002 David Sipress from cartoonbank.com. All rights reserved.

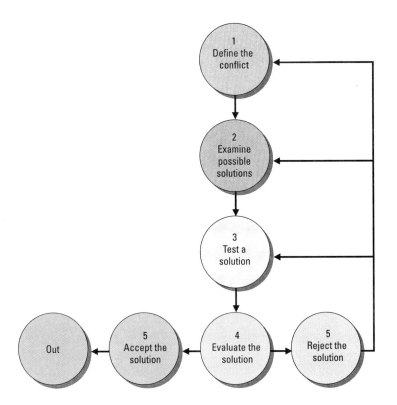

Figure 11.2

The Stages of Conflict Resolution

This model derives from John Dewey's stages of reflective thinking and is a general pattern for understanding and resolving any type of problem.

Define the Conflict

Your first and most essential step is to define the conflict. Here are several techniques to keep in mind:

- *Define both content and relationship issues.* Define the obvious content issues (who should do the dishes, who should take the kids to school) as well as the underlying relationship issues (who has been avoiding household responsibilities, whose time is more valuable).

- *Define the problem in specific terms.* Conflict defined in the abstract is difficult to deal with and resolve. It's one thing for a husband to say that his wife is "cold and unfeeling" and quite another for him to say that she does not call him at the office, kiss him when he comes home, or hold his hand when they're at a party. Specific behaviours can be agreed upon and dealt with, but the abstract "cold and unfeeling" remains elusive.

- *Empathize.* Try to understand the nature of the conflict from the other person's point of view. Why is your partner disturbed that you're not doing the dishes? Why is your neighbour complaining about taking your kids to school? Once you have empathically understood the other person's feelings, validate those feelings when appropriate. If your partner is hurt or angry and you believe such feelings are legitimate and justified, say so: "You have a right to be angry; I shouldn't have said that. I'm sorry. But I still don't want to do what you're asking me." In expressing validation, you're not necessarily expressing agreement; you're merely stating that your partner has feelings that you recognize as legitimate.

- *Avoid mind reading.* Don't try to read the other person's mind. Ask questions to make sure you understand the problem as the other person is experiencing it. Ask directly and simply: "Why are you insisting that I take the dog out now when I have to call three clients before nine o'clock?"

Thinking Critically About   Problems

Critical thinking pioneer Edward de Bono (1987) suggests that in analyzing problems, you put on six "thinking hats." With each hat you look at the problem from a different perspective. Consider this problem: Julia and Raul are in an exclusive relationship and are relatively happy. The problem is that Julia likes to interact with her friends, all of whom Raul dislikes. Here's how looking at this problem with the six hats might work:

- *The fact hat* focuses attention on the facts and figures that bear on the problem. For example, how can Raul learn more about the rewards that Julia gets from her friends? How can Julia find out why Raul doesn't like her friends?

- *The feeling hat* focuses attention on the emotional responses to the problem. How does Raul feel when Julia goes out with friends? How does Julia feel when Raul refuses to meet them?

- *The negative argument hat* asks you to become the devil's advocate. How might this relationship deteriorate if Julia continues seeing her friends without Raul or if Raul resists interacting with Julia's friends?

- *The positive benefits hat* asks you to look at the upside. What are the opportunities that Julia's seeing her friends without Raul might yield? What benefits might Raul and Julia get from this new arrangement?

- *The creative new idea hat* focuses on new ways of looking at the problem. In what other ways can you look at this problem? What other possible solutions might you consider?

- *The control of thinking hat* helps you analyze what you're doing. It asks you to reflect on your own thinking. Have you adequately defined the problem? Are you focusing too much on insignificant issues? Have you given enough attention to possible negative effects?

EXAMPLES?

Recall an example of a problem you had—perhaps a misunderstanding or other interpersonal conflict. Would it have helped if you had analyzed it with each of these six hats?

Let's select an example: a conflict between a couple named Raul and Julia. Their conflict revolves around Raul's not wanting to socialize with Julia's friends. Julia is devoted to her friends, but Raul actively dislikes them. Julia thinks they're wonderful and exciting; Raul thinks they're unpleasant and boring. Let's follow this example through the remaining steps of the conflict-resolution model.

Examine Possible Solutions

The second step in dealing with conflict is to look for possible ways of resolving it. Most conflicts can probably be resolved in a variety of ways. At this stage, try to identify as many solutions as possible.

As noted earlier in the discussion of conflict styles, win–win solutions are the ideal, so look for these whenever possible. Most solutions, of course, will involve costs to one or both parties (after all, someone has to take the dog out), so it's unlikely that solutions to real interpersonal problems are going to involve only rewards for both people. But you can try to seek solutions in which the costs and the rewards will be evenly shared.

Among the solutions that Raul and Julia identify are these:

1. Julia should not interact with her friends any more.
2. Raul should interact with Julia's friends.
3. Julia should see her friends without Raul.

Clearly solutions 1 and 2 are win–lose solutions. In solution 1, Raul wins and Julia loses. In solution 2, Julia wins and Raul loses. Solution 3 has some possibilities. Both might win and neither must necessarily lose. Let's examine this solution more closely by testing it.

STUDY TIP

Apply Edward de Bono's six "thinking hats" approach to a problem you are currently facing.

Test a Solution

Once you have examined all possible solutions, select one and test it out. First test the solution mentally. How does it feel now? How will it feel tomorrow? Are you comfortable with the solution? Will Raul be comfortable when Julia socializes with her friends without him? Some of Julia's friends are attractive unmarried men—is this going to make a difference? Will Julia be comfortable socializing with her

In-Class Notes

A Model of Conflict Resolution

1. Define the conflict:
   - Define both content and relationship issues.
   - Use specific terms.

2. Examine possible solutions:
   - Look for win–win solutions.
   - Weigh the costs and rewards of solutions.
   - Seek solutions in which both share the costs and rewards.

_____

_____

_____

_____

_____

_____

_____

_____

_____

friends without Raul? Will she give people too much to gossip about? Will she feel guilty? Will she enjoy herself without Raul?

Then test the solution in actual practice. How does it work? Give each solution a fair chance. Perhaps Julia might go out once without Raul to try it out. How was it? Did her friends think there was something wrong with her relationship with Raul? Did she feel guilty? Did she enjoy herself? How did Raul feel? Did he feel jealous? Did he feel lonely or abandoned?

Evaluate the Solution

Did the test solution help resolve the conflict? Is the situation better now than it was before the solution was tentatively put into operation? Share your feelings and evaluations of the solution. Use the skills for expressing emotions covered in Chapter 7.

Raul and Julia now need to share their perceptions of this possible solution. Would they be comfortable with this solution on a monthly basis? Is the solution worth the costs that each will pay? Are the costs and the rewards about evenly distributed? Might other solutions be more effective?

Accept or Reject the Solution

If you accept the solution, you're ready to put this solution into more permanent operation. If you decide, on the basis of your evaluation, that this is not the right solution for the conflict, then there are two major alternatives. First, you might test another solution. Perhaps you might now re-examine a runner-up idea or approach. Second, you might go back to the definition of the conflict. As the diagram in Figure 11.2 illustrates, you can re-enter the conflict-resolution process at any of the first three stages.

Let's say that Raul is actually quite happy with the solution. He took the opportunity of his evening alone to visit his brother. The next time Julia goes out with her

---

In-Class Notes

A Model of Conflict Resolution (continued)

3. Test a solution:
   - Test mentally: how does it feel now?
   - How comfortable is it?
   - Test in actual practice: How does it work?

4. Evaluate the solution:
   - Did it resolve the conflict?
   - Is the situation better?
   - Is the solution worth the costs for each?
   - Are rewards about even?

5. Accept or reject the solution:
   - If you accept, put it into operation!
   - If you reject, test another solution or redefine the conflict.

_____

_____

_____

_____

_____

_____

_____

_____

_____

_____

_____

friends, Raul intends to go to wrestling. And Julia feels pretty good about seeing her friends without Raul. She simply explained that occasionally she and Raul socialize separately and that both are comfortable with this.

After a conflict is resolved, it is not necessarily over. Consider a few "after the conflict" suggestions:

- *Learn from the conflict and from the process you went through in trying to resolve it.* For example, can you identify the fight strategies that aggravated the situation? Do you, or does your partner, need a cooling-off period? Can you tell when minor issues are going to escalate into major arguments?

- *Attack your negative feelings.* Often such feelings arise because unfair fight strategies were used (as we'll see in the next section)—for example, blame or verbal aggressiveness. Resolve to avoid such unfair tactics in the future, but at the same time let go of guilt and blame. Don't view yourself, your partner, or your relationship as a failure simply because you have conflicts.

- *Increase the exchange of rewards and cherishing behaviours.* These will show your positive feelings and demonstrate that you're over the conflict and want the relationship to survive.

Recall a recent conflict. Did you follow (at least generally) the five stages identified in this model? If not, can you identify the steps you did follow? How effective was the pattern you did use?

WAYS TO MANAGE CONFLICT

Throughout the process of resolving conflict, try to avoid the common but damaging **unproductive conflict strategies** that can destroy a relationship. At the same time, seek to apply strategies that will help to resolve the conflict and even improve the relationship. The self-test, "Fight Right," on page 256 offers practical suggestions that will complement the following discussion.

Avoidance and Fighting Actively

Avoidance may involve actual physical flight. You may leave the scene of the conflict (walk out of the apartment or go to another part of the office or school), fall asleep, or blast the stereo to drown out all conversation. Avoidance may also take the form of emotional or intellectual avoidance, in which you leave the conflict psychologically by not dealing with any of the arguments or problems raised.

Nonnegotiation is a special type of avoidance. Here you refuse to discuss the conflict or to listen to the other person's argument. At times nonnegotiation takes the form of hammering away at one's own point of view until the other person gives in. We call this technique "steamrolling."

Instead of avoiding the issues, take an active role in your interpersonal conflicts. Involve yourself on both sides of the communication exchange. Be an active participant as a speaker and as a listener; voice your own feelings and listen carefully to the voicing of your opponent's feelings. This is not to say that periodic moratoriums aren't helpful; sometimes they are. But in general, be willing to communicate.

Another part of active fighting involves owning your thoughts and feelings. For example, when you disagree with your partner or find fault with her behaviour, take responsibility for these feelings. Say, for example, "I disagree with..." or "I don't like it when you...." Avoid statements that deny your responsibility; for example, "Everybody thinks you're wrong about..." or "Chris thinks you shouldn't...."

> " The aim of an argument or discussion should not be victory, but progress. "
>
> —Joseph Joubert

Force and Talk

When confronted with conflict, many people prefer not to deal with the issues but rather to force their position on the other person.

"What ever happened to 'Never go to bed angry'?"

© The New Yorker Collection 1999 Victoria Roberts from cartoonbank.com. All Rights Reserved.

Fight Right

Fight Right identifies 11 conflict-resolution behaviours. In order to be able to practise these behaviours consistently, you need to know how well you do with each of them. Once you know how fully you practise each one, you can focus your energies on those that are weak or lacking in your conflict-resolution repertoire.

STEP 1: TAKE THE "CONFLICT-RESOLUTION SURVEY."

Try to recall the typical interactions you have with a particular person when the two of you disagree. Use the survey below to improve your conflict-resolution skills by indicating how you behave with the person you have identified. The more honest you can be on the survey, the more valuable it will be to you.

Conflict-Resolution Survey   5: Almost always   4: Often   3: Sometimes   2: Infrequently   1: Rarely   0: Never

_____ ❶ When I disagree, I am honest about the fact that I disagree, and why.

_____ ❷ When proven wrong, I admit it, rather than deny it or try to cover my tracks.

_____ ❸ In our oral exchanges I let the other person talk first; I don't have to get in my two cents' worth before he or she speaks.

_____ ❹ Before I respond to the other person's assertions, I ask questions or attempt to paraphrase his or her points to make certain I understand what was said.

_____ ❺ I stay calm and rational, being careful not to engage in name-calling or to otherwise say anything I'll regret later.

_____ ❻ When I do allow myself to get angry, I talk about that anger, rather than what the person did to elicit it.

_____ ❼ I am careful to direct my attacks at issues, not personalities. I condemn this person's claims without condemning him or her for making them.

_____ ❽ Even as I may disagree with the person's assertions, I recognize the validity of his or her feelings.

_____ ❾ I direct our attention to *fixing the future* rather than rehashing the past.

_____ ❿ I keep the focus on our comparative needs, *not our opposing positions*, so we can search for creative ways to meet both sets of needs and reach a common ground.

_____ ⓫ I use *we*, *us*, and *our*, rather than *I*, *me*, and *you*, when discussing the issue.

STEP 2: CIRCLE ALL SCORES BELOW A 4.

Are these items more a reflection of your relationship with this particular person or more a reflection of your personal conflict-resolution style? One way to answer this question is to complete the survey for other people in your life with whom you have disagreements. Note which items tend to be scored differently—a reflection of the relationship—and which remain unchanged—your conflict-resolution style. What do these scores suggest you do differently the next time you come into conflict with this person or someone else?

STEP 3: CHOOSE THE NEW CONFLICT RESOLUTION BEHAVIOURS YOU WILL ADOPT.

These recommended improvements in problem-solving skills are keyed by number to the items in the survey.

1. **Honesty.** When you disagree with someone, what is the trigger that brings your disagreement into discussion? Is it because you say something like, "We have a problem"? Or does the discussion begin only after the person notices you acting strangely and calls you on it? Do you admit your disagreement, or do you sulk? When you have something to say but choose not to, you engage in a form of passive–aggressive behaviour. You are being unfair to the other person, to your team, and to yourself.

2. **"I was wrong."** Many people foolishly believe that admitting error is a sign of weakness that will compromise their position in a disagreement. Quite the opposite is true. When you admit to having been wrong about something, you are in the best position to ask other people to reciprocate in some way.... Admitting wrong also happens to be the right thing to do.

3. **Speak second.** In an argument it is foolish to go first and smart to go second for at least four reasons. First, letting other people "get it all out" will help to calm them down and defuse their anger. Second, your willingness to wait is a sign of respect that they will appreciate. Third, by listening carefully to their assertions, you will gain clues to what it will take to persuade them over to your way of thinking. (That's why someone once said, "The second lie always wins.") Finally, and most important,

only after others have emptied themselves of their ideas, emotions, and anger are they likely to pay much attention to yours.

4. **Make sure you understand.** The single greatest cause of interpersonal conflict is little more than misunderstanding. Don't take a chance that miscommunication is at the root of a disagreement you have with someone. Ask clarifying questions before you put your foot into your mouth. When possible encourage the playing of the "paraphrasing game." The first person starts by stating his or her position. The second person must paraphrase to the first person's satisfaction what he or she just said before earning the right to respond. Continue the entire conversation in this manner with permission to talk always tied to a successful paraphrase. You'll be amazed at the results!

5. **Bite your tongue.** A number of years ago, 100 people aged 95 and older were asked the question. "If you could live your life over again, what would you do differently?" The most frequent response they gave was that they would have thought longer before they did and said to others some of the stupid things they did and said.

6. **Talk about your anger.** Much of the advice in the survey is intended to limit your anger. When that advice doesn't work and you lose your temper, start immediately to talk about it. Describe your emotions, your pain, your fear. Only when you have vented completely should you then talk about the incident you got angry about. Never talk about what the person did to make you angry, because that would be a lie. People don't have the ability to make you angry without your full cooperation.

7. **Condemn claims, not claimers.** Attack issues with full force, while letting people escape unscathed. Don't accuse others of a dishonest intent. They'll never see it that way and therefore will conclude that you are malicious. Instead, pinpoint the behaviour or the issue and state what your needs are in regard to it....

8. **Allow for feelings.** All feelings are valid. They are part of our human nature and are not contrived. We should never say something inappropriate like "You have no right to feel that way." Some people have a powerful need to discuss their feelings as a prelude to resolving the conflict into which those feelings are woven. Give them every opportunity to do that even if you don't share that need. You will increase your chances for a win–win outcome.

9. **Fix the future.** Why do we resolve conflict? To prevent more of the same in the future. The ideal posture to take with regard to your antagonists is best described by the question "What can we do to keep this from happening again?" At some point two people in conflict need to stop talking about the behaviour that has contributed to the clash and even stop talking about the feelings that have resulted. One trick for getting the two of you on track to a solution is to invoke the "30-minute rule." It works like this: "Let's agree that for the rest of this discussion neither one of us will talk about anything that happened more than a half hour ago."

10. **Meet needs; don't take positions.** Two people in a disagreement often take opposite positions on an issue. As the debate flares, they harden their stances. This approach leaves little in the way of resolution possibilities other than compromise. A fragile peace is won only after both sides are willing to retreat from their positions to a middle ground that neither side likes, but both realize they must accept. A more satisfying outcome for both parties is possible when they define their differences in terms of needs, not positions. When each person has the opportunity to say, "This is what I want to accomplish by taking this position, or these are the values and beliefs I have that lead me to this conclusion," the two of you can engage in problem solving....

11. **Favour cooperative pronouns.** Pronouns like "I," "me," and "mine" represent the language of a position taker. Pronouns like "we," "our," and "us" encourage collaboration and mutual problem solving.

HOW DID YOU DO?

What did you learn about your own conflict-resolution style when you completed the survey the first time? Did any of your scores change when you completed the survey for other people in your life with whom you have disagreements? What do think that means about your conflict-resolution behaviours?

WHAT WILL YOU DO?

What changes would you like to see in how you manage conflict? Which of the eleven conflict-resolution behaviours do you think you could reasonably adopt and make your own? Why did you choose the ones you chose?

Source: Sam Deep and Lyle Sussman. *Power Tools: 33 Management Inventions You Can Use Today.* © 1998. Reprinted with permission of Basic Books, a member of Perseus Books Group.

The *force* may be emotional (for example, compelling a partner to give in by provoking feelings of guilt or sympathy) or physical. In either case, the issues are avoided and the person who "wins" is the one who exerts the most force. This is the technique of warring nations, quarrelling children, and even some normally sensible and mature adults.

Canadian research on family violence reveals the disturbing fact that over 50 percent of Canadian women over the age of 16 have been victims of violence, and 29 percent of married or previously married women have been assaulted by their husband. Moreover, the majority of acts of violence against women are committed by someone they know. Status of Women Canada conducted a survey in 2000 of 166 police departments representing 53 percent of reported crime. The results of the survey showed that 37 percent of the women were victims of violence by a close friend or acquaintance, 20 percent by a current or past partner, and 11 percent by other family members, including parents. Women were victims of violence by a stranger in 19 percent of reported cases. (Some useful websites to help you explore relationship violence in more detail may be found at www.ccsd.ca, www.cfc-efc.ca, www.hc-sc.gc.ca, www.statcan.ca, and www.swc-cfc.gc.ca.)

The only real alternative to force is talk. Instead of resorting to force, talk and listen. The qualities of openness, empathy, and positiveness, for example, are suitable starting points (see Chapter 8).

Defensiveness and Supportiveness

Although talk is preferred to force, not all talk is equally productive in conflict resolution. One of the best ways to look at destructive versus productive talk is to look at how the style of your communications can create unproductive **defensiveness**—or a productive sense of **supportiveness** (Gibb, 1961). The type of talk that generally proves destructive and sets up defensive reactions in the listener is talk that is evaluative, controlling, strategic, indifferent or neutral, superior, and certain.

Evaluation.   When you evaluate or judge another person or what that person has done, that person is likely to become resentful and defensive and is likely to respond with attempts to defend himself and perhaps, at the same time, to become equally evaluative and judgmental in return. In contrast, when you describe what happened or what you want, it creates no such defensiveness and is generally seen as supportive. The distinction between evaluation and description can be seen in the differences between you-messages and I-messages.

Evaluative You-Messages	**Descriptive I-Messages**
You never reveal your feelings.	I sure would like to hear how you feel about this.
You just don't plan ahead.	I need to know what our schedule for the next few days will be.
You never call me.	I'd enjoy hearing from you more often.

If you put yourself in the role of the listener hearing these statements, you probably can feel the resentment or defensiveness that the evaluative messages (you-messages) would create and the supportiveness from the descriptive messages (I-messages).

Control.   When you try to control the behaviour of the other person, when you order the other person to do this or that, or when you make decisions without mutual discussion and agreement, defensiveness is a likely response. Control messages deny the legitimacy of the person's contributions and in fact deny his importance. They say, in effect, "You don't count; your contributions are meaningless." When, on the other hand, you focus on the problem at hand—and not on controlling the situation

" You cannot shake hands with a clenched fist. **"**

—Indira Gandhi

or getting your own way—defensiveness is much less likely. This problem orientation invites mutual participation and recognizes the significance of each person's contributions.

Strategy. When you use **strategy** and try to get around the other person or the situation through **manipulation**—especially when you conceal your true purposes—that person is likely to resent it and to respond defensively. But when you act openly and with **spontaneity**, you're more likely to create an atmosphere that is equal and honest.

Neutrality. When you demonstrate **neutrality**—in the sense of indifference or a lack of caring for the other person—it's likely to create defensiveness. Neutrality seems to show a lack of interest in the thoughts and feelings of the other person and is especially damaging when intimates are in conflict. This kind of talk says, in effect, "You're not important or deserving of attention and caring." When, on the other hand, you demonstrate empathy, defensiveness is unlikely to occur. Although it can be especially difficult in conflict situations, try to show that you can understand what the other person is going through and that you accept these feelings.

One of the most puzzling findings on violence is that many victims interpret it as a sign of love. For some reason, they see being beaten or verbally abused as a sign that their partner is fully in love with them. Many victims, in fact, accept responsibility for contributing to the violence instead of blaming their partners (Gelles & Cornell, 1985). Why do you think this is so?

Superiority. When you present yourself as superior to the other person, you're in effect putting the other person in an inferior position, and this is likely to be resented. Such **superiority** messages say in effect that the other person is inadequate or somehow second-class. It's a violation of the implicit contract that people in a close relationship have—namely, that each person is equal. The other person may then begin to attack your superiority; the conflict can easily disintegrate into a conflict over who's the boss, with personal attack being the mode of interaction.

Certainty. The person who appears to know it all is likely to be resented, so **certainty** often sets up a defensive climate. After all, there is little room for negotiation or mutual problem solving when one person already has the answer. An attitude of **provisionalism**—"Let's explore this issue together and try to find a solution"—is likely to be much more productive than **closed-mindedness**.

Face-Detracting and Face-Enhancing Strategies

Another dimension of conflict strategies is that of face orientation. **Face-detracting** or **face-attacking** strategies involve treating the other person as incompetent or untrustworthy, as unable or bad (Donohue & Kolt, 1992). Such attacks can vary from mildly embarrassing to the other person to severely damaging to her ego or reputation. When such attacks become extreme they may be similar to verbal aggressiveness—a tactic explained on page 261.

Face-enhancing techniques involve helping the other person maintain a positive image—the image of a person who is competent and trustworthy, able and good. There is some evidence to show that even when you get what you want, say, at bargaining, it's wise to help the other person retain positive face. This makes it less likely that future conflicts will arise (Donohue & Kolt, 1992). Not surprisingly, people are more likely to make an effort to support someone's "face" if they like the person than if they don't (Meyer, 1994).

Generally, collectivist cultures like those of Korea and Japan place greater emphasis on face, especially on maintaining a positive image in public. Face is generally less crucial in individualistic cultures such as Canada's or the United States'. And yet there are many shades to any such broad generalization. For example, in parts of China, whose highly collectivist culture puts great stress on face-saving, criminals are paraded publicly at rallies and humiliated before being put

How important is face-saving to you? What did your culture teach you about the importance of face-saving?

to death (Tyler, 1996). Perhaps the importance of face-saving in China gives this particular punishment a meaning that it could not have in more individualistic cultures.

Confirming the other person's definition of self (Chapter 5), avoiding attack and blame, and using excuses and apologies as appropriate are some generally useful face-enhancing strategies.

Blame and Empathy

> ❝ I never take my own side in a quarrel. ❞
>
> —Robert Frost

Sometimes conflict is caused by one individual's actions. Sometimes it's caused by clearly identifiable outside forces. Most of the time, however, conflict is caused by a wide variety of factors. Any attempt to single out one or two factors for *blame* is sure to fail. Yet a frequently used fight strategy is to blame someone for the situation. Consider, for example, parents who are fighting about their child who is in trouble with the police. Instead of dealing with the problem itself, the parents may blame each other for the child's troubles. Such blaming, of course, does nothing to resolve the problem or to help the child.

Perhaps the best alternative to blame is empathy. Once you have empathically understood your opponent's feelings, validate those feelings as appropriate. If your partner is hurt or angry and you feel that (from the other person's point of view) such feelings are legitimate and justified, say so; say, "You have a right to be angry; I shouldn't have insulted your mother. I'm sorry. But I still don't want to go on vacation with her." Once again, in expressing affirmation and validation you are not necessarily expressing agreement on the issue in conflict; you're merely stating that your partner has feelings that are legitimate and that you recognize them as such. This simple strategy has also been found to reduce verbal aggressiveness (Infante et al., 1996).

Silencers and Facilitating Open Expression

> ❝ Never go to bed mad. Stay up and fight. ❞
>
> —Phyllis Diller

Silencers are a wide variety of unproductive fighting techniques that literally silence the other individual. One frequently used silencer is crying. When a person is unable to deal with a conflict or when winning seems unlikely, he or she may cry and thus silence the other person.

Another silencer is to feign extreme emotionalism—to yell and scream and pretend to be losing control. Still another is to develop some physical reaction—headaches and shortness of breath are probably the most popular. A major problem with such silencers is that we can never be certain that they are mere tactics; they *may* be real physical reactions that we should pay attention to. Regardless of what we do, the conflict remains unexamined and unresolved.

In addition to avoiding silencers, avoid power tactics (raising your voice or threatening physical force) that suppress or inhibit freedom of expression. Such tactics are designed to put the other person down and to subvert real interpersonal equality. Grant other people permission to express themselves freely and openly, to be themselves.

Gunnysacking and Present Focus

A gunnysack is a large bag, usually made of burlap. As a conflict strategy, **gunnysacking** is the unproductive practice of storing up grievances so as to unload them at another time (Bach & Wyden, 1968). The immediate occasion for unloading may be relatively simple (or so it may seem at first); for example, you come home late one night without calling. Instead of arguing about this, the gunnysacker pours out all past grievances: the birthday you forgot, the time you arrived late for dinner, the hotel reservations you forgot to make. As you probably know from experience, gunnysacking often begets gunnysacking. When one person gunnysacks, the other person gunnysacks. The result is that we have two people dumping their stored-up grievances on each other. Frequently the trigger problem never gets addressed. Instead, resentment and hostility escalate.

Focus on the present, on the here and now, rather than on issues that occurred two months ago. Similarly, focus your conflict on the person with whom you're fighting, not on the person's mother, child, or friends.

Fighting Below and Above the Belt

Like fighters in a ring, each of us has a "belt line." When you hit someone below his or her emotional belt line, a tactic called **beltlining**, you can inflict serious injury (Bach & Wyden, 1968). When you hit above the belt, however, the person is able to absorb the blow. With most interpersonal relationships, especially those of long standing, we know where the belt line is. You know, for example, that to hit Maria with the inability to have children is to hit below the belt. You know that to hit Nadim with his failure to get a permanent job is to hit below the belt. Hitting below the belt line causes added problems for all persons involved. Keep blows to areas your opponent can absorb and handle.

Remember that the aim of a relationship conflict is not for you to win and your opponent to lose. Rather, it is to resolve a problem and strengthen the relationship. Keep this ultimate goal always in clear focus, especially when you're angry or hurt.

Have you ever used any of these unproductive conflict strategies? Which unproductive conflict strategy, if any, are you most ashamed of using? Why? Which unproductive conflict strategies, if any, have you used in the last two or three months? What effects—both immediate and long-term—did your use of these strategies have?

Verbal Aggressiveness and Argumentativeness

An especially interesting perspective on conflict is emerging from work on verbal aggressiveness and argumentativeness (Infante & Rancer, 1982; Infante & Wigley, 1986; Infante, 1988). Understanding these two concepts will help you understand some of the reasons things go wrong—and some of the ways in which you can use conflict to actually improve your relationships.

Verbal aggressiveness is a method of winning an argument by inflicting psychological pain, by attacking the other person's self-concept. It is a type of disconfirmation (and the opposite of confirmation) in that it seeks to discredit the opponent's view of himself or herself (see Chapter 5). Atkin et al. (2002) suggest that verbal aggression is widespread in North American society. Further, they suggest that committing and experiencing verbal aggression is reciprocal and that there is a strong relationship between verbal and physical aggression. To explore this tendency further, take the self-test on verbal aggressiveness on page 262.

Contrary to popular usage, **argumentativeness** is a quality to be cultivated rather than avoided. Your argumentativeness is your willingness to argue for a point of view, your tendency to speak your mind on significant issues. It's the mode of

> ❝ People generally quarrel because they cannot argue. ❞
>
> —Gilbert Keith Chesterton

Which of the unproductive methods for dealing with conflict discussed here have you experienced? What effects did these methods have on the conflict and on the relationship? Which unproductive conflict strategy do you think is potentially the most damaging to a relationship? Which would you resent the most?

Test Yourself

How Verbally Aggressive Are You?

Instructions: This scale is designed to measure how people try to win arguments through verbal aggression. For each statement, indicate the extent to which you feel it is true for you. Use the following scale: 1 = almost never true, 2 = rarely true, 3 = occasionally true, 4 = often true, and 5 = almost always true.

_____ **1** I am extremely careful to avoid attacking individuals' intelligence when I attack their ideas.

_____ **2** When individuals are very stubborn, I use insults to soften the stubbornness.

_____ **3** I try very hard to avoid having other people feel bad about themselves when I try to influence them.

_____ **4** When people refuse to do a task I know is important, without good reason, I tell them they are unreasonable.

_____ **5** When people do things I regard as stupid, I try to be extremely gentle with them.

_____ **6** If individuals I am trying to influence really deserve it, I attack their character.

_____ **7** When people behave in ways that are really in very poor taste, I insult them in order to shock them into proper behaviour.

_____ **8** I try to make people feel good about themselves even when their ideas are stupid.

_____ **9** When people simply will not budge on a matter of importance, I lose my temper and say rather strong things to them.

_____ **10** When people criticize my shortcomings, I take it in good humour and do not try to get back at them.

_____ **11** When individuals insult me, I get a lot of pleasure out of really telling them off.

_____ **12** When I dislike individuals greatly, I try not to show it in what I say or how I say it.

_____ **13** I like poking fun at people who do things that are very stupid in order to stimulate their intelligence.

_____ **14** When I attack a person's ideas, I try not to damage their self-concept.

_____ **15** When I try to influence people, I make a great effort not to offend them.

_____ **16** When people do things that are mean or cruel, I attack their character in order to help correct their behaviour.

_____ **17** I refuse to participate in arguments when they involve personal attacks.

_____ **18** When nothing seems to work in trying to influence others, I yell and scream in order to get some movement from them.

_____ **19** When I am not able to refute others' positions, I try to make them feel defensive in order to weaken their positions.

_____ **20** When an argument shifts to personal attacks, I try very hard to change the subject.

HOW DID YOU DO?

To compute your verbal aggressiveness score, follow these steps:

1. Add your scores on items 2, 4, 6, 7, 9, 11, 13, 16, 18, and 19.

2. Add your scores on items 1, 3, 5, 8, 10, 12, 14, 15, 17, and 20.

3. Subtract the sum obtained in step 2 from 60.

4. To compute your verbal aggressiveness score, add the total obtained in step 1 to the result obtained in step 3.

If you scored between 59 and 100, you're high in verbal aggressiveness; if you scored between 39 and 58, you're moderate in verbal aggressiveness; and if you scored between 20 and 38, you're low in verbal aggressiveness. In looking over your responses, make special note of the characteristics identified in the 20 statements that indicate a tendency to act verbally aggressive. Note those inappropriate behaviours that you're especially prone to commit. High agreement (4s or 5s) with statements 2, 4, 6, 7, 9, 11, 13, 16, 18, and 19 and low agreement (1s or 2s) with statements 1, 3, 5, 8, 10, 12, 14, 15, 17, and 20 will help you highlight any significant verbal aggressiveness you might have.

WHAT WILL YOU DO?

Because verbal aggressiveness is likely to seriously reduce interpersonal effectiveness, you probably want to reduce your tendencies to respond aggressively. Review the times when you acted verbally aggressive. What effect did such actions have on your subsequent interaction? What effect did they have on your relationship with the other person? What alternative ways of getting your point across might you have used? Might these have proved more effective? Interestingly, perhaps the most general suggestion for reducing verbal aggressiveness is to increase your argumentativeness.

Source: From "Verbal Aggressiveness" by Dominic Infante and C. J. Wigley, _Communication Monographs, 53,_ 1986. Copyright © 1986 by the Speech Communication Association. Reprinted by permission of the publisher and authors.

How Argumentative Are You?

Instructions: This questionnaire contains statements about ways of dealing with controversial issues. Indicate how often each statement is true for you personally according to the following scale: 1 = almost never true, 2 = rarely true, 3 = occasionally true, 4 = often true, and 5 = almost always true.

_____ ❶ While in an argument, I worry that the person I am arguing with will form a negative impression of me.

_____ ❷ Arguing over controversial issues improves my intelligence.

_____ ❸ I enjoy avoiding arguments.

_____ ❹ I am energetic and enthusiastic when I argue.

_____ ❺ Once I finish an argument, I promise myself that I will not get into another.

_____ ❻ Arguing with a person creates more problems for me than it solves.

_____ ❼ I have a pleasant, good feeling when I win a point in an argument.

_____ ❽ When I finish arguing with someone, I feel nervous and upset.

_____ ❾ I enjoy a good argument over a controversial issue.

_____ ❿ I get an unpleasant feeling when I realize I am about to get into an argument.

_____ ⓫ I enjoy defending my point of view on an issue.

_____ ⓬ I am happy when I keep an argument from happening.

_____ ⓭ I do not like to miss the opportunity to argue a controversial issue.

_____ ⓮ I prefer being with people who rarely disagree with me.

_____ ⓯ I consider an argument an exciting intellectual challenge.

_____ ⓰ I find myself unable to think of effective points during an argument.

_____ ⓱ I feel refreshed and satisfied after an argument on a controversial issue.

_____ ⓲ I have the ability to do well in an argument.

_____ ⓳ I try to avoid getting into arguments.

_____ ⓴ I feel excitement when I expect that a conversation I am in is leading to an argument.

HOW DID YOU DO?

To compute your argumentativeness score, follow these steps:

1. Add your scores on items 2, 4, 7, 9, 11, 13, 15, 17, 18, and 20.

2. Add 60 to the sum obtained in Step 1.

3. Add your scores on items 1, 3, 5, 6, 8, 10, 12, 14, 16, and 19.

4. To compute your argumentativeness score, subtract the total obtained in step 3 from the total obtained in step 2.

The following guidelines will help you interpret your score:

Scores between 73 and 100 indicate high argumentativeness.
Scores between 56 and 72 indicate moderate argumentativeness.
Scores between 20 and 55 indicate low argumentativeness.

WHAT WILL YOU DO?

Infante and Rancer (1982) note that both high and low argumentative people may experience communication difficulties. The high argumentative, for example, may argue needlessly, too often, and too forcefully. The low argumentative, on the other hand, may avoid taking a stand even when it seems necessary. People scoring somewhere in the middle are probably the more interpersonally skilled and adaptable, arguing when it is necessary but avoiding arguments that are needless and repetitive. Does your experience support these observations? What specific actions might you take to improve your argumentativeness?

Source: This scale was developed by Dominic Infante and Andrew Rancer and appears in Dominic Infante and Andrew Rancer, "A Conceptualization and Measure of Argumentativeness," _Journal of Personality Assessment,_ 46 (1982): 72–80.

dealing with disagreements that is the preferred alternative to verbal aggressiveness. Before reading about ways to increase your argumentativeness, take the self-test on argumentativeness above.

The researchers who developed the argumentativeness test note that those who score high in argumentativeness have a strong tendency to state their position on

What one principle from this chapter will most influence your own conflict behaviour?

controversial issues and to argue against the positions of others (Infante & Rancer, 1982). A high scorer sees arguing as exciting, intellectually challenging, and as an opportunity to win a kind of contest. The low scorer sees arguing as unpleasant and unsatisfying. Not surprisingly, this person has little confidence in his ability to argue effectively. The person who scores low in argumentativeness tries to prevent arguments. This person derives satisfaction not from arguing but from avoiding arguments. The moderately argumentative individual possesses some of the qualities of the high argumentative and some of the qualities of the low argumentative.

In-Class Notes

Conflict Management Strategies

Productive:

- fight actively
- talk
- be supportive
- use face-enhancing strategies
- use empathy
- use an open expression
- present focus
- stay above the belt
- don't be argumentative

In-Class Notes

Conflict Management Strategies *(continued)*

Unproductive:
- avoidance
- force
- defensiveness
- face-detracting strategies
- blame
- silencers
- gunnysacking
- hitting below the belt
- aggressiveness

Here are some suggestions for cultivating argumentativeness and for preventing it from degenerating into aggressiveness (Infante, 1988):

- Treat disagreements as objectively as possible. Avoid assuming that because someone takes issue with your position or your interpretation that he or she is attacking you as a person.
- Avoid attacking the other person (rather than the person's arguments) even if this would give you a tactical advantage. Personal attacks will probably backfire at some later time and make your relationship more difficult.
- Avoid interrupting; allow the other person to state his or her position fully before you respond.
- Express interest in the other person's position, attitude, and point of view; reaffirm the other person's sense of competence; compliment the other person as appropriate.
- Avoid presenting your arguments too emotionally. Using an overly loud voice or interjecting vulgar expressions will prove offensive and ineffective.
- Allow the other person to save face; never humiliate the other person.

STUDY TIP

Complete the Chapter 11 crossword puzzle on the textbook website.

What changes would you like to see your relational partners (friends, family members, romantic partners) make in their own verbal aggressiveness and argumentativeness? What might you do to more effectively regulate your own verbal aggressiveness and argumentativeness?

Summary of Concepts and Skills

In this chapter we examined interpersonal conflict. We looked at the distinction between content conflict and relationship conflict and at conflict's positive and negative aspects. We considered a model of conflict resolution and surveyed a variety of unproductive conflict strategies and their more productive counterparts.

1. Interpersonal conflict is disagreement between or among connected individuals. The positions in interpersonal conflicts are to some degree interrelated and incompatible.

2. Content conflict centres on objects, events, and persons in the world that are usually, though not always, external to the parties involved in the conflict. Relationship conflicts are concerned more with the relationships between the individuals, such as who is in charge, the equality of a primary relationship, and who has the right to set down rules of behaviour.

3. Recommendations for before the conflict: Try to fight in private, be sure you're each ready to fight, know what you're fighting about, avoid fighting about problems that cannot be solved. After the conflict: Keep the conflict in perspective, challenge your negative feelings, increase the exchange of rewards.

4. A five-step model is often helpful in resolving conflict: define the conflict, examine possible solutions, test a solution, evaluate the solution, and accept or reject the solution.

5. Unproductive versus productive conflict strategies include avoidance versus fighting actively; force versus talk; face-detracting versus face-enhancing strategies; blame versus empathy; silencing versus facilitating open expression; gunnysacking versus present focus; fighting below versus fighting above the belt; and verbal aggressiveness versus argumentativeness.

6. To cultivate productive argumentativeness, treat disagreements objectively and avoid attacking the other person; reaffirm the other's sense of competence; avoid interrupting; stress equality and similarities; express interest in the other person's position; avoid presenting your arguments too emotionally; and allow the other person to save face.

Check Your Ability

Check your ability to apply the following skills. Use a rating scale such as the following: 1 = almost always, 2 = often, 3 = sometimes, 4 = rarely, and 5 = almost never.

_____ ❶ Recognize the differences between content and relationship conflicts and respond to each accordingly.

_____ ❷ Prepare for conflict and follow it up so that it remains in perspective.

_____ ❸ Deal with interpersonal conflicts via systematic steps, such as definition, examination of possible solutions, testing of a solution, evaluation of the solution, and acceptance or rejection of the solution.

_____ ❹ View problems and solutions from the perspective of facts, feelings, negative arguments, positive benefits, creative new ideas, and control of thinking.

_____ ❺ Use productive interpersonal conflict strategies such as active engagement in the conflict, empathy, facilitating open expression, maintaining present focus, fighting above the belt, and constructive argumentativeness.

_____ ❻ Avoid unproductive conflict strategies such as avoidance, blame, silencers, gunnysacking, beltlining, and verbal aggressiveness.

After completing this self-test, check your answers against the Answer Key at the back of the book.

Multiple Choice Questions *Choose the BEST answer.*

1. Content conflict may centre on
   a. objects external to the relationship.
   b. the equality of a primary relationship.
   c. who is in charge within a relationship.
   d. the gender and the ethnicity of the partners as it affects the relationship.

2. In order to follow the first step of the model of conflict resolution,
   a. focus on only obvious issues.
   b. use general rather than specific terms.
   c. hold to your point of view.
   d. confirm the other person's definition of the problem.

3. Verbal aggressiveness
   a. is equivalent to an intellectual debate.
   b. attempts to win arguments by inflicting psychological pain.
   c. is the same as argumentativeness.
   d. is a type of confirmation.

4. Silencers do NOT include
   a. listening.
   b. crying.
   c. yelling.
   d. interpersonal game-playing.

5. Positive aspects of conflict include
   a. enabling resolution of a problem.
   b. forcing individuals to deal with the problem.
   c. preventing resentments from growing.
   d. all of the above.

6. Myths about conflict include:
   a. If two people in a relationship fight, it means their relationship is a bad one.
   b. Men too often take responsibility for all the problems.
   c. Fighting hurts an interpersonal relationship.
   d. a and c.

7. All of the following are stages of conflict resolution except
   a. defining the conflict.
   b. evaluating the solution.
   c. testing the solution.
   d. rejecting the problem.

8. Which is NOT an example of a conflict management strategy?
   a. avoidance
   b. force and talk
   c. forced hand
   d. defensiveness

9. In a conflict, men are more likely to
   a. withdraw.
   b. become more psychologically aroused.
   c. distance themselves.
   d. all of the above.

10. In a conflict, women are more likely to
    a. withdraw.
    b. get closer.
    c. become verbally aggressive.
    d. be more emotional than men.

True–False Questions *Write a T or F in the blank next to the statement.*

1. _____ When you are trying to resolve conflict, you are willing to work on the relationship.

2. _____ Date rape is a form of relational force.

3. _____ Men and women are different in their conflict styles.

4. _____ Content conflicts centres on the behaviour of others.

5. _____ Relational conflict centres on objects and events.

6. _____ Beltlining is a face-detracting strategy.

7. _____ One value of conflict is that it forces you to examine problems and solutions.

8. _____ You should never fight in private.

9. _____ Fighting about past behaviours effectively focuses the current problem.

10. _____ You should look for win–win solutions.

Vocabulary Quiz
The Language of Conflict

Match the terms dealing with interpersonal conflict with their definitions. Record the number of the definition next to the appropriate term.

a. _____ six-hats technique

b. _____ silencers

c. _____ argumentativeness

d. _____ gunnysacking

e. _____ beltline

f. _____ verbal aggressiveness

g. _____ spamming

h. _____ complaint

i. _____ interpersonal conflict

j. _____ conflict resolution model

1. A disagreement between connected individuals.

2. An unproductive conflict strategy of storing up grievances and holding these in readiness to dump on the person with whom one is in conflict.

3. A person's level of tolerance for absorbing a personal attack.

4. A tendency or willingness to argue for a point of view or speak your mind on significant issues.

5. An expressed dissatisfaction that's a valuable source of feedback.

6. A tendency to try to win arguments by attacking opponents' self-concept.

7. A relatively standard set of procedures for dealing with conflict, consisting of five steps: define the conflict, examine possible solutions, test a solution, evaluate the solution, and accept or reject the solution.

8. Varied ways of looking at a particular issue to give you different perspectives.

9. Sending unsolicited email or repeatedly posting the same message.

10. A group of unproductive conflict strategies that include crying and pretending to be extremely emotional.

Skill Building Exercises

11.1 Dealing with Conflict Starters

The purpose of this exercise is to give you some practice in responding to potential interpersonal conflicts. Use your own conflict experiences as a guide in this exercise. For each "starter": (1) Write an unproductive response—that is, a response that will aggravate the potential conflict. Why do you believe this response will intensify the conflict? (2) Write a productive response—that is, a response that will lessen the potential conflict. Why do you believe this response will help resolve the conflict?

Conflict "Starters"

1. You're late again. You're always late. Your lateness is very inconsiderate of my time and the time of the entire team.

2. I just can't bear another weekend of sitting home watching cartoon shows with the kids. I'm just not going to do that again.

3. Who forgot to phone for reservations?

4. Well, there goes another anniversary—and another anniversary that you forgot.

5. You think I'm fat, don't you?

6. You always complain that I don't participate at meetings, but I do.

7. Did I hear you say your mother knows how to dress?

8. We should have been more available when he needed us. I was always at work.

9. Where's the pepper? Is there no pepper in this house?

10. The Romeros think we should spend our money and start enjoying life.

Thinking Critically About Conflict Starters.

Having read this chapter, ask yourself if your attitudes toward conflict have changed. Will you approach real-life interpersonal conflict with different strategies from now on?

11.2 Generating Win–Win Solutions

Often, people involved in interpersonal conflict fail to consider if there are possible win–win solutions and what they might be. To get into the habit of looking for win–win solutions, consider the following conflict situations, either alone or in groups of five or six. For each situation, try generating as many win–win solutions as possible that you feel the individuals involved in the conflict could reasonably accept. Give yourself two minutes for each case. Write down all the solutions you (or the group) think of; don't censor yourself or any members of the group.

1. Emily and Connor plan to take a two-week vacation in August. Emily wants to go to the shore and relax by the water. Connor wants to go hiking and camping in the mountains.

2. Emily recently got a totally unexpected $3000 bonus. She wants to buy a new computer and printer; Connor wants to have the house painted.

3. Connor hangs around the house in nothing but underwear. Emily really hates this, and they argue about it almost daily.

4. Vicky is 17 and pregnant. She wants her parents to accept her decision to keep the child and not to marry the child's father. Her parents refuse to accept this and have said that she must either have an abortion or marry the child's father.

5. Workers at the local bottling plant want a 20 percent raise to bring their salaries into line with the salaries of workers at other similar plants. Management has repeatedly turned down their requests.

Thinking Critically About Win–Win Solutions.

If possible, share your win–win solutions with other individuals or groups. From this experience it should be clear that win–win solutions exist for most conflict situations but not necessarily all. And, of course, some situations will allow for the easy generation of a lot more win–win solutions than others. Not all conflicts are equal. How might you incorporate win–win strategies into your own conflict management behaviour?

11.3 Increasing Productive Conflict Management

The following brief dialogue was written to illustrate unproductive conflict and to provide a stimulus for the consideration of alternative and more productive methods of conflict management. Identify each unproductive strategy and propose more productive alternatives.

Connor: It's me. Just came in to get my papers for the meeting tonight.

Emily: You're not going to another meeting tonight, are you?

Connor: I told you last month that I had to give this lecture to the new managers on how to use some new research methods. What do you think I've been working on for the past two weeks? If you cared about what I do, you'd have known I was working on this lecture and that it was especially important for it to go well.

Emily: What about shopping? We always do the shopping on Friday night.

Connor: The shopping will have to wait; this lecture is important.

Emily: Shopping is important too, and so are the children, and so is my job, and so is the leak in the basement that's been driving me crazy since last week and that I've asked you to look at every day since then.

Connor: Get off it. We can do the shopping any time. Your job is fine, and the children are fine, and we'll get a plumber just as soon as I get his name from the Johnsons.

Emily: You always do that. You always think only you count, only you matter. Even when we were in school, your classes were the important ones, your papers, your tests were the important ones. Remember when I had that chemistry final and you had to have your history paper typed? We stayed up all night typing *your* paper. I failed chemistry, remember? That's not so good when you're pre-med! I suppose I should thank you that I'm not a doctor? But you got your A in history. It's always been that way. You never give a damn what's important in my life.

Connor: I really don't want to talk about it. I'll only get upset and bomb out with the lecture. Forget it. I don't want to hear any more about it. So just shut up before I do something I should do more often.

Emily: You hit me and I'll call the cops. I'm not putting up with another black eye or another fat lip—never, never again.

Connor: Well, then, just shut up. I just don't want to talk about it any more. Forget it. I have to give the lecture and that's that.

Emily: The children were looking forward to going shopping. Johnny wanted to get a new CD, and Jennifer needed to get a book for school. You promised them.

Connor: I didn't promise anyone anything. You promised them, and now you want me to take the blame. You know, you promise too much. You should only promise what you can deliver, like fidelity. Remember you promised to be faithful? Or did you forget that promise? Why don't you tell the kids about that? Or do they already know? Were they here when you had your sordid affair? Did they see their loving parent loving some stranger?

Emily: I thought we agreed not to talk about that. You know how bad I feel about what happened. And anyway, that was six months ago. What has that got to do with tonight?

Connor: You're the one who brought up promises, not me. You're always bringing up the past. You live in the past.

Emily: Well, at least the kids would have seen me enjoying myself—one enjoyable experience in eight years isn't too much, is it?

Connor: I'm leaving. Don't wait up.

Thinking Critically About Productive Conflict Management.

Can you identify one possible effect that might result from using each of the unproductive conflict strategies illustrated here? How do these effects differ from those that might result from using the more productive strategies? As you read this dialogue, what assumptions did you make about the genders of the characters? On what basis?

Web Explorations

Companion Website

Visit the Companion Website at www.pearsoned.ca/devito for student resources related to this chapter, including self-grading quizzes, additional skill-building exercises, and links to other online resources.

Research Navigator

Explore our research resources at www.researchnavigator.com

■ Find and read an article on conflict, its nature, the stages of conflict resolution, or conflict strategies. On the basis of this article, what can you add to the discussion presented here?

■ Investigate one of the key terms discussed in this chapter (for example, conflict, interpersonal conflict, aggressiveness, argumentativeness, conflict styles, competition and collaboration, and conflict avoidance). What additional insights can you provide?

■ Try finding answers to one of the following questions, or design a research study to answer it.

1. Are men or women more likely to use avoidance (or blame, force, manipulation, ridicule, silencers, beltlining, gunnysacking, or personal rejection) as a conflict strategy?

2. What are some of the advantages research has found (in addition to those discussed here) for argumentativeness as opposed to verbal aggressiveness?

3. How can mediation help in interpersonal conflicts?

Chapter 12

Interpersonal Communication and the Workplace

Chapter Topics

This chapter examines the principles of workplace communication—diversity in the workplace, modes of workplace communications, and interpersonal power in the workplace—and will help you become more effective at work.

Diversity in the Workplace

Workplace Communication

Workplace Relationships

Principles of Power

Chapter Skills

After completing this chapter you should be able to:

- understand the ranges of diversity within the workplace.

- use different modes of workplace communication to become more effective in your place of employment.

- establish positive relationships with peers, supervisors, and people whom you supervise.

Janice is a licensed practical nurse who has recently been promoted to the position of team leader in a long-term care facility. When she called her first team meeting, a health care aide who had worked there for a long time remarked, "You can't tell us what to do, you aren't even a real nurse."

Nazneen has worked in a dynamic software company for the past six months. She recently graduated from a business college and feels that she has many good ideas that would increase the revenues of the company. She has attempted to communicate her ideas to her supervisor, but feels they are not taken seriously. She isn't sure whether she should attempt a meeting with the senior manager because she is afraid to step on the toes of her supervisor.

Charles is employed at the local automobile showroom, where he sells Fords. Although he is a competent salesperson, he often finds himself being used by his coworkers. For example, he is often asked to do errands and menial tasks that other salespeople tend not to do. He is beginning to feel resentful of his coworkers and wonders why he is the only one in the group being treated this way.

All these interpersonal situations occur in a work setting and involve different relationships and interpersonal communication. The first involves the relationship between a team leader and a staff member. The second involves the relationship between a staff member and her supervisor, and the third involves a relationship among peers, or coworkers.

This chapter examines the principles of workplace communication and will help you become more effective in your place of employment. While the principles of communication are similar in both personal and work settings, workplace communication presents a unique set of challenges. Understanding these challenges will better enable you to establish positive relationships with peers, supervisors, and people whom you supervise. Strong workplace communication will lead to career success. As indicated in the box on page 273, verbal and written communication skills rank number 1 among the 10 characteristics employers seek.

DIVERSITY IN THE WORKPLACE

"A diverse workforce is a more productive workforce." Discuss.

Work settings today encompass many kinds of diversity. Organizations have distinct cultures, and so do professional groups. For example, we talk about the culture of the nursing profession, of business culture, and the common traits of accountants. Some of these involve stereotypes and possibly exaggerated characteristics. However, studies have shown that professions have unique characteristics that suit the definition of culture. Secondly, organizations can have very different cultures from each other. You could find two colleges in the same city with very different organizational cultures. One may have a very formal, hierarchical structure and one could be very informal. A professor who moved from a formal to an informal college once remarked, "I worked at one college for 20 years and never so much as exchanged greetings with the president. Then I moved to a less formal institution and found myself having lunch in the staff cafeteria chatting with the president."

Workplaces today have been described as multigenerational, referring to the fact that each generation has unique cultural characteristics. A workplace could well include older baby boomers, Generation "Xers," and young people in their twenties (or the millennium generation). While stereotyping is unhelpful, each generation has been found to differ in values and communication styles. Certainly in Canada today, most workplaces will also include employees from very different cultural backgrounds and with varying levels of ability.

Given this vast diversity in the workplace, how do we manage to be effective communicators? This chapter starts by defining aspects of this diversity, and then looks at some strategies that can be applied and adapted to these contexts. Included are discussions of telephone, electronic, and written communication, as well as networking, mentorship, and teamwork. Finally, leadership and powerful communication are discussed.

Communication is a vital part of our daily lives. While in school, we listen to teachers, read books, write papers, and talk with friends. The workplace is no different. We listen and converse with our supervisors and fellow employees and read and write reports, memos, and other types of correspondence. Experts say that 70 to 80 percent of our working time is spent on some form of communication.

Strong communication skills will lead to career success. In fact, verbal and written communication skills rank number one in the top 10 list of qualities employers seek. Here we will look at ways in which we communicate and how students can improve those skills.

SPEAKING SKILLS

The ability to deliver an effective talk is one of the most valuable skills you can possess. Yet most people are afraid to speak in front of a group. Some panic and their minds go blank, others may get an upset stomach. But, with careful preparation, tips to overcome stage fright and a fair amount of practice, nearly anyone can become a competent speaker.

- *Be prepared.* One way to overcome pre-speech jitters is know what you're talking about. Research your subject area thoroughly until you know your topic inside out. Organize the information, then write one or two summary sentences that clearly define the purpose of your presentation. Next, create an outline to give your speech direction and ensure that you don't leave out key points. Keep in mind that listeners get overwhelmed if you try to tell them too much—two or three main points is usually sufficient. Last, rehearse your presentation several times so you become comfortable with your talk and improve your delivery.
- *Understand your audience.* What do your listeners want to know? How much do they already know about the subject? Once you know your audience, you can better determine what direction your presentation should take.
- *Overcome stage fright.* Channel your nervous energy and get your body involved in what you're saying. Gesture with your hands to reinforce key points, move about a little and take deep breaths to calm your nerves. It also helps to concentrate on just a couple of people instead of the entire group. And remember, your audience wants you to succeed. If they learn something (anything) of value, they will consider their time spent with you worthwhile.

WRITING SKILLS

In school, students are required to write reports, essays, or perhaps an article for the yearbook. Likewise in the workplace you will be expected to write memos, letters, and proposals. Many people just start writing and hope for the best. But, much like speaking, before you begin writing you must first organize your thoughts, understand your intended reader, then clearly define your purpose.

Most writing is done to either persuade describe or explain. But no matter what your purpose, writing should always be

- Concise
- Compelling
- Clear
- Correct

Managers are bombarded with memos, faxes, emails and letters every day and, often, they don't have time to read all of them. If a piece of correspondence doesn't capture their interest quickly, there's a good chance it will not be read. This is especially true with cover letters and résumés. In today's job market, a company may receive up to 300 résumés for a single job opening. To narrow down the selection, some employers put the one-page résumés in one pile, and the two-page résumés go in the trash.

If your writing is clear and simple and you follow these tips, chances are your correspondence will not end up in the basket.

- Understand your intended reader
- Put the most important information at the start of your correspondence
- Don't use big, fancy words
- Keep sentences short
- Use active verbs
- Leave out unrelated information
- Proofread everything you write

THEN AND NOW

Recall a time when you made a presentation in class and felt that you hadn't clearly communicated your ideas. If you were in the same situation today, how would you prepare in order to communicate more effectively?

Source: Career Directions: Communication Skills. Techdirections (64), © 2005.

The Multigenerational Workforce

It is common to speak of the "generation gap" when looking at family dynamics, but only recently has the idea of the generation gap moved to the workplace. Indeed, today there can be as many as four generations working together in one setting. The first of these four groups has been described as "traditionalists," the "silent generation," or the "veterans" (Jennings, 2000)—those people who were born before 1946. The second group, known as baby boomers, were born between 1946 and 1965. The third group, known as Generation Xers or the baby bust, were born between 1966 and 1979.

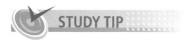

STUDY TIP

Contrast the profile of boomers with the generations that followed them. How might these groups get along in the workplace?

The fourth group, known as the millennials (also referred to as Generation Y or Generation Next), were born after 1980 and are currently just entering the workforce. While any generalization about a group can lead to stereotyping, understanding key characteristics of each generational group can be helpful, since this increased understanding can foster positive and effective communication. It is also important to remember that the descriptions below are based largely on North American research, and these differences in intergenerational workplace communication have been shown to vary between western and non-western countries (McCann & Giles, 2006).

Traditionalists   The traditional generation is characterized by their patriotism (50 percent of men in this generation are veterans), hard work, frugality, and faith in the organizations and institutions of their society. They are described as loyal. They respect discipline, law, and order and tend to be oriented in the past.

Boomers   Boomers were brought up in a more affluent, opportunity-filled world. They are highly competitive, idealistic, and optimistic. They are used to being the centre of attention and look for personal gratification.

Generation Xers   These are the children of the boomers. They tend to be skeptical; they are also resourceful, money-oriented, and independent, and do not like to be micro-managed. They were the generation that experienced the soaring divorce rates and decline in the security of family, in addition to the downsizing of corporations and the general decline in job security. They look for balance and a sense of family. They prefer informality and want to be self-reliant.

The Millennials   The youngest group in the workforce today is the so-called millennials. They have been described as bold, brazen, and "the cockiest in recent history, with an unprecedented sense of entitlement" (McLaren, *The Globe and Mail*, April 16, 2005).

Many were brought up in homes where parents treated children as "equals," which some think has resulted in a generation that has little respect for the wisdom and experience of older people. The self-confidence that seems typical of this generation has been described much like a two-edged sword. On the one hand, their self-confidence, competence (especially in technology), and high expectations bode very well for the millennials. On the other hand, an overestimated sense of self-worth can have negative effects on relationships and lead to unrealistic expectations of one's ability: "In the age of self-esteem, where everybody, not just the best and the brightest, gets gold stars beside their name in school, no one expects to start at the bottom" (McLaren, 2005).

As we can see, there are significant differences between these groups, and each group has its strengths, as well as different needs in workplace relationships. Consider, for example, the different values associated with job changing. Traditionalists tend to view changing jobs as a stigma, and boomers tend to stay in the same job "to make a difference." Generation Xers have been labelled as "job hoppers," and try to get as many skills and experiences on a résumé as possible. The millennials see "job changing as part of normal routine" (*USA Today*, November 7, 2005).

At 24, Craig Kielburger (seen above in an earlier photo with the Dalai Lama) is the poster boy for his generation. As the founder of Free The Children, an international children's charity, Kielburger, nominated three times for the Nobel Peace Prize, is the coauthor of two social studies texts for grades 4 to 8 and of *Me to We*.

This very brief overview of generational differences in the workplace should provide food for thought regarding effective communication. Just consider, for example, if you wanted to express appreciation to a colleague who helped you out, or if you wanted to indicate your dissatisfaction with a particular event at work. What differences might you consider in how you communicate to members of different generations? For example, how formal would you be? Would you use slang? Would you communicate in person or via technology?

THE CULTURE OF THE WORKPLACE

Organizations have distinct cultures (Handy, 1985; Harrison & Carroll, 2006; Davila et al., personal communication). Understanding these cultures can help you communicate more effectively within the work setting. Workplace cultures, like other cultures, revolve around shared values, attitudes, and experiences that validate the culture (Holmes & Marra, 2002). The workplace culture is learned and shared through expectations for behaviour, customs, and ceremonies. Workplaces often have their own jargon, traditions, and stories, which communicate cultural values and provide cues to new employees regarding expected behaviour. Employee recognition ceremonies, sports competitions, fundraisers, and family outings are examples of organizational traditions and ceremonies (Holmes & Marra, 2002).

The culture of organizations has been described in four main categories (Handy, 1985): role culture, achievement culture, power culture, and people culture.

In a **role culture** organization, there is general conformity to expectations, clear regulations and procedures, and clearly defined tasks. Often strategies exist, usually in the form of financial rewards and bonuses, which encourage employees to perform according to expectations. These kinds of strategies are referred to as extrinsic motivation. Many government or civil service offices fit this description. **Power culture** is described as having clear authority, high expectations for loyalty, and measures in place to ensure accountability. Traditional banks are examples of organizations in this category. **Achievement culture** fosters creativity, competition, and independence in its employees. Less formal rules and structures exist, and employees seem to have more intrinsic motivation to perform. Small high-tech start-up companies fit this category. Organizations that have a strong **people culture** emphasize relationships, sharing, and friendship; employees are motivated intrinsically through job satisfaction rather than through external rewards.

What are some differences in the communication styles that fit these different organizational cultures? For example, in a people culture organization, one would probably be more inclined to share personal information and be open about difficulties than in an organization that has a role culture. Communication would likely be more formal in a power culture or role culture organization, and employees would be expected to follow procedures regarding who they talk to, as well as when and how they talk. In organizations that have an achievement culture, competition may be such that employees tend not to share ideas, but communication might tend to be less structured and formal. In a people culture, we would expect communication to be quite open and relaxed, and employees encouraged to share their concerns with their colleagues and supervisors.

Like any other culture, organizational culture is not static. Organizations merge, new employees bring new aspects to organizational culture, and organizational culture often needs to adapt to changing markets and changing needs. The increasing role of women in the workplace is also reshaping business culture (Walsh, 2005). Yet strong organizational cultures are important for the success of organizations, and understanding the culture of the organization will help you become more successful in your communications and interpersonal relationships in the workplace.

STUDY TIP

In a small group, discuss the types of cultures you have been exposed to in the workplace. Of the four organizational cultures, which suits you best? Why?

Consider the culture of the organization that currently employs you, a family member, or a friend. Describe some of its essential features—the beliefs, culture, particular practices, and behaviours that are regarded as appropriate, and those that are not. Based on what you have read in the text, how would you categorize the culture of this organization?

Adapted from Harrison, J. & Carroll, G.R. *Culture and Demography in Organizations*, 2006, Princeton University Press.

The Culture of the Professions

Just as organizations have identifiable cultures, so do many occupational groups such as engineers, teachers, or nurses (Suominen et al., 1997; Rochester, 2002). Professional cultures evolve as societal needs change (Beauschene & Patsdaughter, 2005), and organizations often employ a multidisciplinary workforce. Canadian researchers have shown that, with specialization increasing, professional cultures can actually form barriers to effective communication in the workplace (Hall, 2005). Thus, understanding the culture of the professions involved is important for effective communication within organizations.

Professional culture is not easy to define, but it represents a shared experience that other groups do not have, often reinforced by professional associations (Rochester, 2002). The culture of professions is impacted by the people who make up the profession and by the skills they use in practice. Rochester (2002) describes the engineering profession as practical, problem-solving, and detail-oriented, claiming that the people who enter the profession tend to like to work with things or ideas more than with people. One of the most noticeable differences in occupations is whether they are involved directly in helping or healing people, or whether the occupation is focused on objects or things. While architects and engineers would likely argue that one of the goals of their work is to help people or society, they do so by creating objects (buildings, bridges) rather than by directly helping people. One profession is no less important than the other; however, the type of work seems to be a factor in the culture that has evolved around these groups.

Some professions focus as much on process as they do on outcome. For example, in early childhood education, the goal of each interaction with a child is to enhance and support the child's healthy development. So while the goal and the desired outcome are clear, professionals are generally assessed on the basis of their ongoing interactions with the children. Compare this to architects or engineers, whose work is assessed by the quality of the product they develop. However, it is important not to oversimplify. A performance appraisal of an engineer or an architect would likely include her ability to communicate effectively. In fact, a recent article (Darling & Dannels, 2003) stated that "communication is the life blood" of engineers and recommended much more emphasis on communication training in the curriculum of university engineering programs. Conversely, the requirement that practitioners in health and human service professions evaluate their work on the basis of measurable outcomes is a growing trend in those fields.

Health and human service occupations have been described as the caring professions, and clearly there are similarities between occupations such as nursing, social work, and psychology. The focus on helping, healing, and supporting has led to a strategy of communication with clients, called therapeutic or supportive communication, which is the basis for counselling (Horsfall, 1998). Therapeutic communication includes active listening, reflection of content and feeling, clarifying, paraphrasing, questioning, providing information, and the constructive confrontation of communicative contradictions.

Among the helping professions there are obvious and inevitable differences in communication styles. For example, nurses working in an emergency may tend to emphasize accuracy and speed, and this is often reflected in their verbal and nonverbal communication. Social workers often work with clients in distress. They learn to take time where required, to be patient, and to work with clients on a longer-term basis. This, too, is often reflected in the way they communicate. It is important to note that even within professions, there exist subcultures. For example, articles describing the workplace culture of a special care nursery (Wilson et al., 2005) and an operating theatre (Yamaguchi, 2004) highlight the unique cultures of particular nursing units. These cultural differences in occupations will impact the nature of communication in work settings.

DO

- Approach your patient in a purposeful manner. Always use "Mr.," "Miss," "Mrs.," or another appropriate term to address your patient, and introduce yourself using your first and last names.
- Provide privacy and arrange his environment to eliminate or minimize interruptions.
- Use positive body language, such as sitting at his level, facing him, and leaning forward when he speaks.
- Ask open-ended questions.
- Rephrase or paraphrase what he tells you. Clearly as necessary, help him establish a focus if he rambles or makes vague statements, and ask for additional information and explain why you need it.
- Use verbal and visual indicators, such as nodding and saying yes to show your understanding and acceptance.
- Use touch to silence, when appropriate, as nonverbal signs of attentiveness.
- Keep your patent's sociocultural background in mind to avoid misinterpreting nonverbal behaviour. For example, looking down when you speak may signify respect rather than anxiety or insecurity.

- Toward the end of your conversation, summarize the important points.

DON'T

- Don't use negative body language, such as standing over him, crossing your arms or legs, or appearing distracted.
- Don't block communication by giving unsolicited advice, using approving or disapproving responses, agreeing or disagreeing, changing the subject, providing false reassurance, or responding defensively.

THEN AND NOW

Recall a time when you or a family member met with a health care professional (doctor, nurse, or counsellor). Did you feel that you were being listened to? Did you feel that you were being understood? Did you feel comfortable and safe to disclose information? If so, what behaviours made you feel listened to, understood, and safe? If not, what behaviours prevented this?

Source: Edwina A. McConnell Nursing vol. II, 1998 © Lipincott, Williams & Wilkins.

Diverse Personalities in the Workplace

Diversity is not just about the culture of organizations or professions, or an individual's culture or ability. People are simply different—they have different likes, dislikes, personalities, and temperaments. And while we have some choice in our private lives about who we wish to spend time with, this is not the case at work. Understanding your own learning style, personality, and temperament can help you become more aware of how you affect others in your workplace. Just as important, learning to recognize the characteristics of the people you work with can help you become a more effective communicator.

The study of personality traits has been going on for decades. The terms "introverted" and "extroverted" are attributed to Carl Jung and come from his work almost a century ago. Beginning in the 1940s, Myers and Briggs developed this concept into a widely used personality type test (Martin, 2006). The Myers-Briggs Personality Assessment is based on the assumption that there are 16 basic personality types, all subcategories of introverted (I) and extroverted (E) types.

While the Myers-Briggs test has been thoroughly researched and tested and is used worldwide, numerous other tests are also available. These tests can be useful in assessing yourself, your colleagues, and supervisors, and in using this knowledge to adapt and enhance your communication. For example, new employees often come in to an organization with new ideas and are motivated to share these ideas to benefit the organization. Just as often, employees are disappointed that their ideas are either totally dismissed or simply ignored by those making the decisions. Understanding a bit about the character of the decision makers will help you frame your communication in a way that is more likely to be heard. You would probably use a different approach with a manager who likes having control and power over people than you would with a leader who is more easygoing, warm, and cooperative.

A somewhat simpler and enjoyable test of personalities is based on five personality traits: openness, conscientiousness, extroversion, agreeableness, and negative emotionality. These traits have become the basis of another commonly used personality assessment text, available at www.aboriginemundi.com/personalitytest/.

Cultural Diversity at Work

Chapter 9 examined communication in a multicultural society. Workforce population trends in North America have increased the number and kinds of culturally diverse people who work together (Chao & Moon, 2005). The same understanding and awareness that is required for sensitive, appropriate, and effective intercultural communication applies to work settings as well.

In the business sector, cultural differences lend complexity to interactions and negotiations. The different meanings attributed to business ethics, the interpretation of the right to privacy, the meaning of body language, status, and time, are examples of constructs that, if not understood, interfere greatly with successful business practice (Moon & Williams, 2000). Furthermore, different cultures have different approaches to power, authority, and acceptable public behaviour. Direct confrontation, assertiveness, and expression of warmth are just some of the differences that need to be considered in a multicultural workplace.

Gender and the Workplace

There has been considerable research on differences in communication styles between men and women, and the impact that this has in both personal and professional settings. Most of the research on gender differences in work related communication was conducted with the boomers or Generation Xers—there is little available research on the younger generation at work. It could well be that these differences are diminishing, but to date we can only speculate. Recent research suggests that women managers still face difficulty in being accepted by males in the workplace (Bongiorno & David, 2003), and still face barriers to acceptance in work arenas that were traditionally male (Irizarry, 2004).

Tannen (1990) described how the different communication styles that are related to gender may put women at a disadvantage for being taken seriously at work. For example, women tend to apologize more, not necessarily because they think they did something wrong, but as a way of smoothing out the conversation. Men tend to say "I'm sorry" infrequently, and tend to interpret women's use of apology as a weakness, or as accepting blame for a situation.

Similarly, women tend to use the phrase "thank you" differently from men. For women, "thanks" is often a ritualized way of closing a conversation or an email communication. Men tend to interpret "thank you" as gratitude for something they have done. Women tend to ask for more input than do men. They do that as a way of fostering a sense of collaboration where everyone's opinion is valued. Men tend to see this effort at collaboration as indecisive behaviour—the inability to do things independently.

Men tend to take more oppositional stances than do women; women tend to take these stances as personal attacks. Often, however, the intention is to debate issues or present another view rather than to attack. Humour is reportedly also used differently by men and women, with women tending to use self-putdowns more frequently, and men tending to use teasing and mock hostile attacks (Tannen, 1990).

Diversity in Ability

In every workplace there may be employees with a broad range of abilities. Progressive workplaces are hiring people today who previously may have been considered unemployable. With the proper support for people with disabilities, employees can enjoy the benefits of job satisfaction and a sense of belonging. Furthermore, workplaces that have purposefully provided support to people with developmental disabilities have commented on the benefits to the organization (L'Arche Canada, 2005).

However, communication with employees with disabilities requires thoughtfulness, consideration, and an effort to understand the barriers that these employees may face. For example, Holmes (2003) described the difficulties that people with developmental disabilities may face in participating in small talk at work (so-called water cooler communication). Small talk may not seem complex, but recognizing what is acceptable and what is not—how frequently it can be engaged in, on which occasions, and in which contexts—actually entails sophisticated judgments that may not be easy for workers with developmental disabilities. An employer who wants to foster the success of a worker with a developmental disability will pay attention to managing small talk and to raising awareness of how to include people with disabilities in the formal and informal interactions at work.

Just as employers have an obligation to make accommodations for people with physical disabilities, efforts should be made to accommodate employees with lower levels of cognitive functioning, as specified in the Canadian Human Rights Act. For information on this topic you can visit www.hrma-agrh.gc.ca/ee/ ncfpsd-cnehfpf/duty_to_accomodate_e.asp.

In-Class Notes

Diversity in the Workplace

- may be generational.
- may be influenced by the ability of employees.
- may be influenced by the personality of employees.
- may be influenced by the culture of employees.
- may depend on the professional culture.
- may depend on the organizational culture.

_____
_____
_____
_____
_____
_____
_____
_____

In summary, how can an understanding of these differences help you communicate more effectively at work? First, you can better understand how others may interpret your own communication style. This does not mean that you necessarily have to change your style, but it is important to understand the potential impact of your style. If your natural communication style tends to be very informal, but you work in a role culture organization and report to a manager from the traditionalist generation, you may have to adapt your style. If you are very introverted and don't show excitement readily, you may want to ensure that your coworkers don't perceive your introversion as disinterest. If you are working with people who have developmental disabilities, you may want to ensure that you adapt your language accordingly.

Learning to adapt your communication style to become more effective at work does not change who you are. Consider communication strategies as the palette of an artist: using a richer variety of colours and textures allows for more elaborate and effective expression.

WORKPLACE COMMUNICATION

Telephone Communication

Much communication in the workplace takes place over the phone. Answering the phone is not a difficult physical task, but using it in a businesslike and professional manner is not so straightforward. Being effective, as well as staying calm and controlled, is quite a demanding task. You might like to appraise your own ability by considering the tips outlined in Figure 12.1.

Figure 12.1

Tips for Telephone Communication

1. Be prompt, and answer within three or four rings; callers don't like to be kept waiting.

2. If you are going to be away from your telephone for any length of time, remember to forward your calls in order that the caller doesn't have to be repeatedly transferred.

3. Answer with a smile. It comes across in your voice, making you sound friendly and positive.

4. When you answer, give a verbal handshake, announcing the company name and department, as well as your own name.

5. When making a call, make sure it is a convenient time for the other person to receive it.

6. Show empathy to build an instant relationship with your caller by using a warm, friendly tone of voice.

7. Use open questions to find out facts and information, and closed questions to clarify and check understanding.

8. If you can, answer callers' questions promptly and efficiently. If you can't help, tell them what you can do for them.

9. Use continuity sounds to show the caller that you are listening. For example, "Oh yes," "I see," or "That's right."

10. Make notes, recording all necessary information. It was once said that "a short pencil is far more effective than a long memory."

11. Double check all vital information by reading back, in summary, what you have discussed.

12. Instead of passing callers around from department to department, take the caller's name and telephone number and a brief but comprehensive message, and reassure them that you will pass their message to the appropriate person and have him or her return the call.

13. Give the caller your full attention. Nobody can hold two conversations and retain 100 percent of information from both.

14. Keep focused on the subject at hand, and do not interrupt the caller with pointless questions.

15. Remember that both people engaged in a call have the right to know who they are talking to.

16. End your call on a positive note. Check to see that your caller has asked all the necessary questions and has all the information he or she was asking.

17. "Sign off" properly. Although circumstances vary, this usually means confirming what will happen as a result of the call and thanking the other person for his or her time.

Source: Adapted from Lin Walker. *Telephone Techniques: The Essential Guide to Thinking and Working Smarter.* New York: American Management Association, 1998. © American Management Association.

This work is protected by copyright and it is being used with the permission of *Access Copyright.* Any alteration of its content or further copying in any form whatsoever is strictly prohibited.

COMPUTER MEDIATED COMMUNICATION (CMC) IN THE WORKPLACE

The Changing Workplace Environment

Technology is radically changing the environment of our workplaces, not only in how we conduct business and communicate at work but also from where we can work. Videoconferencing, online collaboration, cellphones, email, Wi-fi, instant messaging, blogs, and the huge numbers of wireless portable technologies are all leading to the creation of virtual teams and even virtual companies. However, while many see technology as a boon to the bottom line, it also poses several risks. The promised paperless office is drowning in paper, and proposed savings are eaten up by the costs of planning, implementing, and continually upgrading labour-saving technology (Grosch, 1994).

Email as Workplace Communication

Email has long been touted as the darling of high-tech communication, but recently it has been losing favour—almost being seen as the new snail mail (Irvine, 2006). Like home mailboxes that are cluttered with advertising and flyers, email inboxes are increasingly saturated with spam, prolonging the job of sorting through new emails to weed out what can be deleted and what should be addressed. People complain that they are often days or even weeks behind in their email. Email is still very useful for sending and receiving attachments, keeping in touch with parents or teachers, informal correspondence, or sending correspondence or a document from one to many. However, many workplaces are turning to instant messaging (IM) or blogs in order to receive an immediate response.

IM is often chosen to facilitate collaboration at a distance and to decrease communications costs. However, according to Cameron and Webster (2005), downsides to IM do exist. Not only is IM less rich than face-to-face communication, many employees see its interruptive and immediate nature during the course of a workday as unfair and distracting.

Blogging, while still a fairly new technology in the workplace, has the potential to become a key business communication tool as email becomes increasingly saturated. Miller (2003) sees two main potential applications for blogs: to be used externally by companies to communicate with potential customers, and internally to distribute information that changes on a regular basis.

For many workplaces now, it's a question of choosing the best communication tool. For example, you might text message during a meeting when you need to be quiet or you might choose to discuss a sensitive issue over the phone so there is no written record. Felling (as cited in Irvine, *Calgary Herald*, July 19, 2006, p. A13), an admitted "serial-texter" and the spokesman for the Centre for Media and Public Affairs in Washington, claims that technology is fast becoming the "ultimate social crutch to avoid personal communication. Don't want to see someone? Then call them. Don't want to call someone? Email them. Don't want to take the trouble of writing sentences? Text them."

Multitasking

All of this new technology in the workplace encourages—or perhaps requires—employees to become experts at multitasking. It's not unusual to see an employee talking on the phone, while reading an email, while checking a calendar entry on a BlackBerry—sometimes with a person waiting at the door of the office for a quick word. The developers of technology often sell their products with the promise of increased efficiency; however, can gadgets really enable one employee to do the work of two?

Psychology professor Hal Pashler (cited in Wallis, 2006) explains that when the brain is asked to multitask, it actually performs the actions sequentially, one task at a time. Sequential processing occurs in the prefrontal cortex of the brain, which is one of the last areas to mature and one of the first to decline with aging. This means that young children and adults over 60 do not multitask well (Wallis, 2006). However, even for younger people, multitasking has its limits. When people try to alternate rapidly between two or more activities, both the time needed to complete the tasks and the errors made go way up.

In fact, researchers are suggesting that multitasking short-circuits attention spans and induces an "air traffic controller-like" stress which can actually increase the time it takes to accomplish tasks by up to 50 percent (Lauer, 2004). Harvard Medical School psychiatrist Edward Hallowell (as cited in Lauer, 2004) describes a new epidemic which he refers to as ADT: attention deficit trait. Constant electronic communication and the immediate demands it makes on employees are diluting performance and increasing irritability. Thus, those who used to be well organized and efficient are increasingly becoming disorganized underachievers.

This phenomenon is leading many concerned workplaces to order a technology vacation for its workers every so often, perhaps an afternoon a week without using any technological devices—no email, no IM, no BlackBerry, no voicemail. Amtrak trains have a "quiet" car and some young people are hosting cellphone-free and no-IM parties. Hopefully, these vacations will allow people to give their brains the rest and recovery time they need to process and consolidate information—as well as people time to enjoy one another's company and have face-to-face conversation.

Technology Confrontations

Previous chapters have explained that CMC is often used as a way for people to resolve personal conflicts, to say things to one another that might not be possible or comfortable to say face-to-face. The workplace is no different. However, a recent survey by VitalSmarts (as cited in Grenny, 2005) found that 87 percent of those polled indicated that email, voicemail, or text messages may actually amplify a workplace conflict. Furthermore, 89 percent of those polled say that CMC actually gets in the way of good workplace communication. This is especially true when news is bad or sensitive, when negative feedback is being delivered, or when differing opinions are involved and nonverbal signals are important in accurately deciphering the message.

Now that CMC is in such wide use, many corporations are formulating policies that prevent inappropriate use and reduce exposure to liability (Sipior & Ward, 1999). Such policies include restricting email use to business only, prohibiting inappropriate language and conduct, and reserving the right to monitor communication. However, as companies begin to institute surveillance and monitor the work of their employees—specifically the use of email, listservs, and the World Wide Web—concerns increase about the violation of employees' right to privacy (Miller & Weckert, 2000).

Written Communication in the Workplace

With the growing use of electronic communication, it's easy to forget that messages written on paper still have an important function in many workplaces. As with other nonverbal messages, the layout and general appearance of a letter or memo communicate an impression before any words have been read. The very fact that someone has taken the time to format a letter and send it in the mail, rather than send a quick email, is a message in itself. There are many guides available for formal business letters (e.g., look at www.usingenglish.com/articles/letter-writing.html).

Written communication extends the opportunity to plan and review the information being sent before it reaches the receiver. Read and review memos and letters carefully, correct any grammar or spelling errors, and ensure that the format is impressive before sending the communication because, as with verbal communication, written communication is irreversible. So take some time before sending a written communication, to ensure that the message sent reflects the message you intend.

Negative Workplace Communication

Negative communication can take place in any context. In the workplace, the effect of negative communication can lead to a decline in staff morale, a decline in productivity, and a decline in service. Four notable kinds of negative communication are rumours, gossip, anonymous communication, and outright lying.

Rumours   Rumours have been defined as "public communications that reflect private hypotheses," or as attempts to make sense of unclear or uncertain situations (Rosnow, 1988). Consider the following event. Dania, who had worked in the office for six years, suddenly did not show up to work and did not let anyone know she wasn't coming. Several days later, an email welcoming her replacement went out to all employees. No official reason was given for Dania's termination of employment, and so rumours started to circulate: "She was caught stealing company property" and "She is suffering from a sudden illness." Then people started to talk and provide rationale for each hypothesis. "She has been acting rather secretive lately" or "She hasn't really looked well for a while." Both rumours were an attempt to find explanations where there was a vacuum of information from a reliable source.

Rumours may, in fact, be true. Often they are not, though there may be a grain of truth in a rumour. Essentially, a rumour is information that is disseminated without official verification. The potential of rumours to damage the workplace and individuals is very real (Difonzo et al., 1994; Robertson, 2005). Not surprisingly, negative rumours tend to be more prevalent than positive rumours in work settings (Bordia et al., 2003). In a workplace setting, rumours tend to proliferate when anxieties and uncertainties prevail. For example, if a company is downsizing, a merger is expected, or a change in leadership occurs, rumours will likely circulate until (and even after) the facts are known.

Although it is impossible to prevent or stop rumours in the workplace, managers and leaders can take steps to avoid the initiation and spread of rumours.

Gossip   Gossip and rumour are closely related. Gossip can often be detected by examining the motive of the person spreading it. For example, private but true information about a coworker often takes the form of gossip. Gossip has been defined as "small talk about personal affairs and peoples' activities with or without a known basis in fact" (Rosnow & Fine, 1976). Similarly, if private information about a coworker is disseminated without her knowledge or consent, this too can be seen as gossip.

Negative gossip can empower the gossiper and disempower the person being gossiped about (Kurland & Pelled, 2000), although gossip can also backfire and harm the gossiper.

Gossip, like rumour, has been referred to as "grapevine communication." One study (Baker & Jones, 1996) highlighted the fact that although many organization leaders say they prefer direct means of communicating, employees often depend on the grapevine within organizations to receive and deliver information.

There is no simple solution to gossip in the workplace. Sometimes it is easiest just to ignore it. But if gossip is hurtful, damaging, and persistent, action needs to be taken. Many of the strategies for preventing rumours apply to gossip as well. It may be helpful to consider the gossiper as a sort of bully or harasser. In that context, the victim needs to be protected from gossip at his workplace as he would from any form of harassment.

Anonymous Communication in the Workplace   In many organizations, a tradition of opposing or ignoring anonymous communication exists. For example, accusations against supervisors or coworkers are often not seen as legitimate unless the source is known. But in reality the issue is not that simple. The old-fashioned Suggestion Box, replaced today by a variety of new communication technologies, gives workers more opportunity to communicate ideas and concerns without identifying themselves. Anonymity allows people in an organization to say what they think, communicate about sensitive topics, and generally interact more openly (Scott & Rains, 2005).

Under what circumstances is anonymous communication acceptable or even preferred? Most colleges and universities distribute anonymous questionnaires in order for students to evaluate their instructors. This seems fair since students may fear retribution if they negatively evaluate an instructor. Similarly, organizations may introduce an anonymous questionnaire to receive feedback on a manager or supervisor. It is difficult to avoid the conclusion that the greater the power differentiation, and the greater the lack of security and trust between people in an organization, the more likely it is that they will prefer anonymous communication. However, the solution to a worker's dissatisfaction often lies in direct communication between the worker and her supervisor. This solution is not possible when communication is anonymous.

Scott and Rains (2005) conclude that anonymous communication can be most effective when it is part of organizational surveys or assessments. Anonymous communication may allow workers who feel powerless to express views that may, in fact, benefit the organization. Organizations that use anonymous communication need to provide clear guidelines to employees regarding appropriate and inappropriate uses of anonymous communication. Clearly, the spread of rumours and gossip through anonymous communication should be considered unacceptable.

Untruthful Communication   An article in *Maclean's* magazine (Righton, 2006) began with the following sentence: "Prospective employers take note: In the business world, honesty is rarely the best policy." Simply put, lying seems to be so inherent in our workplaces (as in other realms of life) that those who don't lie are often disadvantaged. We are reminded (Righton, 2006) that most people lie an average of six times a day, from "real whoppers to slight obfuscations, omissions, false compliments and exaggerations," and often these lies are considered essential for getting ahead in the workplace. Typical lies include falsifying a résumé and taking credit for someone else's work to get a promotion.

People generally discriminate between lies that are harmless and used to smooth over social situations, and those that are hurtful, damaging, or callous. Thus, a mildly untruthful response—"Fine, thank you" to the question, "How are you today?" when you really aren't fine—seems to be acceptable. Falsifying information that would impact a person's decision (e.g., accident details on a used car that is for sale) is seen by many as unacceptable.

While the trend in business seems to be that lying is not always serious, and focuses on the "serious" lies such as cheating, stealing, or telling callous lies about coworkers, we may want to consider another approach. We know that the common cold is very prevalent and is usually not fatal. Yet workplaces today are recognizing that measures can be taken to prevent its spread. They install automatic taps, doors that open with a foot pedal, and air filters to reduce contamination, and put up signs reminding people to wash their hands. We could take a similar approach to workplace lying. Although usually not fatal, it is also usually not healthy. We can encourage truthful communication by modelling it, by reminding people of its value, and by being careful not to disadvantage the truthful communicator.

Negative Workplace Communication

- rumours, gossip
- anonymous communication
- untruthful communication

WORKPLACE RELATIONSHIPS

Workplace relationships are becoming more and more important as more of our time is spent in work situations, whether face-to-face in the traditional office or online. Let's look at several kinds of workplace relationships: mentoring, networking, and working in teams.

Mentoring Relationships

In a **mentoring relationship,** an experienced individual helps train a person who is less experienced. An accomplished teacher, for example, might mentor a young teacher who is newly arrived in a school or who has never taught before. The mentor guides the new person through the ropes, teaches the strategies and techniques for success, and otherwise communicates his accumulated knowledge and experience to the mentored.

The mentoring relationship provides an ideal learning environment. It's usually a supportive and trusting one-on-one relationship between expert and novice. There's a mutual and open sharing of information and thoughts about the job. The relationship enables the novice to try out new skills under the guidance of an expert, to ask questions, and to obtain the feedback so necessary to the acquisition of complex skills. Mentoring is perhaps best characterized as a relationship in which the experienced and powerful mentor empowers the novice, giving the novice the tools and techniques for gaining the same power the mentor now holds. Few mentoring relationships have as much potential for personal growth as the relationship between a manager and an employee (Brown, 2003).

At the same time, the mentor benefits from clarifying his or her thoughts, from seeing the job from the perspective of a newcomer, and from considering and formulating answers to a variety of questions. Just as a teacher learns from teaching, a mentor learns from mentoring.

Networking Relationships

Networking is often viewed simply as a technique for securing a job, but it's actually a much broader process. **Networking** can be viewed as using other people to help you solve your problems, or at least to offer insights that bear on your problems—for example, how to publish your manuscript, where to look for low-cost auto insurance, or how to defrag your hard drive.

Networking comes in at least two forms: informal and formal. Informal networking is what we do every day when we find ourselves in a new situation or unable to answer questions. Thus, for example, in a new job or location, you might ask someone about the best place to eat or shop for clothes, or you might ask more experienced workers how to perform certain tasks or whom to avoid or approach when you have questions. Formal networking is the same thing, except that it's a lot more systematic and strategic. It's establishing connections with people who can help you—who can answer questions, help you at your job, and help you get promoted or accomplish any task you want to accomplish.

Working in Teams

Much workplace communication today takes place in teams. Team approaches to planning, problem solving, and getting the work done seem to be gaining recognition and popularity in organizations. Two main premises apply to teamwork: "Several heads are better than one" and "The sum is greater than all its parts." Teams develop over time as people work together, and the stages of team development are often described (MacMillan, 2001) as:

- forming (becoming oriented).
- storming (struggling over purpose and goals).
- norming (resolving concerns, building trust).
- performing (working productively towards shared goals).
- transforming (bringing about change, celebrating accomplishments).

Team members play different functions. Some members play a significant role in keeping spirits up and providing emotional support, some play devil's advocate by challenging views and sometimes seeming negative, while others may play the more instrumental role of actually getting the tasks done. Most teams have a designated leader, but often, different members of the team take on leadership roles at various times.

Skills Toolbox | Ways to Network Effectively

Here are a few suggestions for networking more effectively:

1. Begin by networking with people you already know. If you review the list of your friends, relatives, and acquaintances, you'll probably find that you know a lot of people with specialized knowledge who can help you in a variety of ways. With email addresses readily available, it's now quite common to email individuals who have particular expertise in order to ask them questions.
2. Consider developing files containing the names of people you can contact. For example, if you're a freelance artist, come up with a list of people who might be in a position to offer you work. Authors, editors, art directors, administrative assistants, people in advertising, and a host of others might eventually provide useful leads, and can often simplify your search for freelance work.

3. Take an active part in locating and establishing networking connections. Be proactive; initiate contacts rather than waiting for them to come to you. But don't overdo it; you don't want to rely on other people to do work you can easily do yourself. If you're respectful of their time and expertise, most people will respond to your networking attempts positively. Following up your requests with thank-you notes, for example, will help you establish networks that can be productive ongoing relationships rather than one-shot affairs.

THEN AND NOW

Have you ever needed information others had, but been unable to secure it? What might you have done to get the information? What would you do now if you needed that same information?

General guidelines for effective communication are equally applicable to a team setting, but given that teams often have specific tasks and timelines in which to achieve these tasks, some features of effective communication stand out. Useful tips can be found at www.effectivemeetings.com/teams/teamwork/effective.asp. They include:

- Communicate, communicate, communicate.
- Listen actively.
- Don't blame others.
- Support group members' ideas.
- Get involved.
- No bragging.
- Be positive.

In addition, it is vital to be sensitive to the diversity issues described earlier in this chapter—gender, culture, ability, organizational culture, and professional culture. The team can be seen as a micro-organization within an organization, and therefore all these factors come into play.

LEADERSHIP IN THE WORKPLACE: BEING A POWERFUL COMMUNICATOR

If you go back to the opening vignette of this chapter, you will see that the licensed practical nurse was frustrated because she wasn't being heard by the people she is supposed to be leading. Leadership in the workplace is a rapidly growing concept, and numerous books, articles, and courses now define leadership and provide advice on how to be effective as a leader. Both formal and informal leadership roles exist in organizations. Leaders can be managers or CEOs or have other titles that give them the power to make decisions and influence people. Formal leaders may have responsibilities for a range of domains, from multi-site industries to small departments within an organization. However, informal leaders may sometimes also be influential in organizations. These informal leaders are people without official titles or offices, but who are respected because of personal wisdom or a willingness to share (Anderson, 1997). Informal leaders are often role models who take on mentoring roles with colleagues.

So what is the essence of leadership, whether it's formal or informal? Leadership really is about being able to affect and influence others and bring about change. In short, leaders have the power to influence others, whether through force or through more acceptable means such as modelling, persuasion, and developing a common vision and goals.

The most respected kind of leader is referred to as "the transformational leader" (Bass & Avolio, 1990), and is empathic rather than confrontational. The transformational leader shares power with others and values collaboration. Usually the transformational leader becomes a source of inspiration to others, considers others' needs, and stimulates them to look at the world from new perspectives. The transformational leader has the trust of those who work with him (Bass & Avolio, 1990).

❝ A leader is the one who climbs the tallest tree, surveys the entire situation, and yells 'wrong jungle'. Leaders provide a vision and a compass. ❞

—Stephen R. Covey,
The 7 Habits of Highly Effective People. Fireside, N.Y. 1989

Leadership and Power

Sometimes we think of power negatively—as if it connotes the use of power to dominate others. In fact, good leaders influence others through powerful communication. Good leaders share power and empower others. Understanding how to communicate powerfully in the workplace will help make you a better member of the team and the organization, as well as a better leader.

The next section examines the principles of power and focuses especially on how you can increase your own interpersonal power in the workplace.

PRINCIPLES OF POWER

Interpersonal power is what enables the individual with power to influence the behaviours of others, and is governed by a few important principles. These principles spell out the basic characteristics of power. They help explain how power works interpersonally and how you may more effectively deal with power.

Power Varies from Person to Person

Some people are born with assets that empower them, but anyone can increase his or her interpersonal power. You can, for example, learn the principles of effective communication and increase your power to persuade.

Confidence communicates power. One of the clearest ways you can communicate power is by demonstrating confidence through your verbal and nonverbal behaviours. The confident communicator is relaxed (rather than rigid); flexible in voice and body (rather than locked into one or two ranges of voice or body movement); and controlled (rather than shaky or awkward). A relaxed posture, researchers find, communicates a sense of control, status, and power. Tenseness, rigidity, and apparent discomfort, on the other hand, signal a lack of self-control (Spitzberg & Hecht, 1984), which in turn signals a general inability to control other people or the environment.

Here are a few additional suggestions for communicating confidence:

- Take the initiative in introducing yourself to others and in introducing topics of conversation; try not to wait for others to act first. When you react, rather than act, you're more likely to communicate a lack of confidence and control over the situation.

- Use open-ended questions to involve the other person in the interaction (as opposed to questions that merely ask for a Yes or No answer). Follow up these questions with appropriate comments or additional questions.

- Use you-statements. These are statements that directly address the other person—they are not accusatory, but instead signal a direct and personalized focus on the other person, such as "Do you agree?" or "How do you feel about that?"

- Avoid various forms of powerless language, such as statements that express a lack of conviction or that are self-critical. Starting a communication with "I may be wrong but … " is an example of powerless language.

Power Is a Part of All Interpersonal Messages

Chapter 1 introduced the key principle that it is impossible to *not* communicate. By the same token, you cannot communicate without making some implicit comment on your power or lack of it. When interacting, therefore, recognize that on the basis of your verbal and nonverbal messages, people will assess your power—along with your competence, trustworthiness, honesty, openness, and so on.

The ways in which people communicate powerfulness and powerlessness through speech have received lots of research attention (Molloy, 1981; Kleinke, 1986; Johnson, 1987; Dillard & Marshall, 2003). Generally, research finds that men use more powerful language forms than do women (Lakoff, 1975; Timmerman, 2002). Listed on the following page are the major characteristics of powerless speech. As you consider this list, think of your own speech. Do you avoid the following speech behaviours?

> " Self-confidence is the first requisite to great undertakings. "
>
> —Samuel Johnson

STUDY TIP

Record yourself making a short presentation. Analyze the result, looking for evidence of powerless speech behaviours.

- *Hesitation* makes you sound unprepared and uncertain. Example: "I … er … want to say that … ah … this one is … er … the best, you know?"

- Too many intensifiers make your speech monotonous and don't allow you to stress what you do want to emphasize. Example: "Really, this was the greatest; it was truly phenomenal."

- *Disqualifiers* signal a lack of competence and a feeling of uncertainty. Examples: "I didn't read the entire article, but..." or "I didn't actually see the accident, but...."

- *Tag questions* ask for another's agreement and therefore may signal your need for agreement—and your own uncertainty. Examples: "That was a great movie, wasn't it?" or "She's brilliant, don't you think?"

- *Self-critical statements* signal a lack of confidence and may make public your own inadequacies. Examples: "I'm not very good at this" or "This is my first public speech."

- *Slang and vulgar language* suggest low social class and hence little power. Examples: "@*+#?$!!" or "No problem!"

Skills Toolbox | 6 Ways to Exert Power

Work relationships differ in the types of power that people use and to which they respond. Differences in amounts and types of power influence who makes important decisions, who will prevail in an argument, and who will control finances. It's useful to distinguish among six types of power: legitimate, referent, reward, coercive, expert, and information or persuasion power (French & Raven, 1968; Raven et al., 1975).

1. You hold *legitimate power* when others believe that by virtue of your position, you have a right to influence or control their behaviours. Your legitimate power derives from the role you occupy; for example, employers, judges, managers, and police officers have legitimate power by virtue of their roles. *Relate your persuasive arguments and appeals to your own role and credibility.*

2. You have *referent power* when others wish to be like you. Referent power holders are often attractive, have considerable prestige, and are well liked and well respected. For example, you might have referent power over a younger brother who wants to be like you. *Demonstrate qualities that are admired by those you wish to influence.*

3. You have *reward power* when you control the rewards that others want. Rewards may be material (for example, money, a promotion, jewellery) or social (for example, love, friendship, respect). *Make rewards contingent on compliance, and follow through and reward those who comply with your requests.*

4. You have *coercive power* when you have the ability to administer punishments to or remove rewards from others if they do not do as you wish. Usually, people who have reward power also have coercive power. *Make clear the negative consequences that are likely to follow noncompliance. But be careful; coercive power may reduce your other power bases and have a negative impact, as when wielded by supervisors in business settings* (Richmond et al., 1984; Kearney et al., 1984, 1985).

5. You have *expert power* when others see you as possessing important expertise or knowledge. For example, judges have expert power in legal matters and doctors have expert power in medical matters. *Cultivate your own expertise, and connect your persuasive appeals to this expertise.*

6. You have *information* or *persuasion power* when others see you as having the ability to communicate logically and persuasively. *Increase your communication competence; this book's major function, of course, is to explain ways for you to accomplish this.*

THEN AND NOW

Can you recall a situation in which you tried to influence another person but failed? To what do you attribute the failure? If this same situation occurred today, what might you do differently to increase your chances for having influence?

Nonverbal Communication of Power Just as you communicate your power (or lack of power) verbally, you also communicate it nonverbally—for example, through the things you wear and own. Truly powerful people have no time for new trends that come and go every six months. Further, they don't wear or have anything cheap because they have money to buy the real thing.

Six Types of Power

- Legitimate: Increase your credibility in your role.
- Referent: Demonstrate qualities admired by those you wish to influence.
- Reward: Make rewards contingent on compliance and follow-through.
- Coercive: Make negative consequences clear. Be careful.
- Expert: Cultivate your own expertise. Connect appeals to this expertise.
- Information/persuasion: Increase your communication competence.

_____
_____
_____
_____
_____
_____
_____
_____
_____
_____

Nonverbal communication takes on a key role in the workplace environment. The norms for nonverbal communication will be impacted by all the factors reviewed at the beginning of this chapter relating to diversity. Dress code norms, for example, may be challenged by younger workers who may emphasize casual attire, tattoos, or body piercing.

Touching, which is a major aspect of nonverbal communication, can also be an expression of power. Touching takes on great complexity in workplace settings. The interpretation of touching is strongly impacted by one's own culture, gender, and the culture of the profession. It is probably better to err on the side of caution and avoid touching, hugging, or patting on the back, unless you are certain that it will be interpreted as you intended.

Skills Toolbox   6 Ways to Nonverbal Power at Work

Your nonverbal communication skills greatly influence the interpersonal power you're seen to have on the job and just about anywhere else. Here are some suggestions for communicating power nonverbally (Lewis, 1989; Burgoon et al., 1995):

1. Other things being equal, dress relatively conservatively if you want to influence others; conservative clothing is associated with power and status. This is doubly true if you're working at a generally conservative office or if you're responsible for meeting clients.

2. Use facial expressions and gestures as appropriate; these help you express your concern for the other person and for the interaction.

3. When you break eye contact, direct your gaze downward; otherwise you'll signal a lack of interest in the other person.

4. Use consistent packaging; that is, be especially careful that your verbal and nonverbal messages don't contradict each other—the principle of congruence.

5. To communicate dominance with your handshake, exert more pressure than usual and hold the grip a bit longer than normal.

6. Walk slowly and deliberately. To appear hurried is to appear to be without power, as if you were rushing to meet the expectations of a supervisor who had power over you.

THEN AND NOW

Can you think of a time when you didn't follow one or more of these suggestions? What was the situation? What happened? Which one of these suggestions would you like to work on now to improve your communication power?

Nonverbal behaviour can convey a lack of power, as when someone fidgets and engages in a lot of self-touching movements at a meeting, indicating discomfort. A powerful person may be bored but will not appear uncomfortable or ill at ease.

Territory also reflects a person's power. It's difficult for the junior executive who operates out of a cubbyhole in the basement of some huge office complex to appear powerful with an old metal desk and beat-up filing cabinet. Often, however, you're more in control of your space than you may realize. Clutter can signify a lack of power—and can easily be eliminated to communicate a more powerful image.

But perhaps the most important part of communicating power is demonstrating your knowledge, your preparation, and your organization in relation to whatever you're doing. If you can exhibit control over your own responsibilities, people generally conclude that you can and do also exhibit control over other aspects of life.

Research finds that men are generally perceived to have higher levels of expert and legitimate power than women and that women are generally perceived to have higher levels of referent power than men.

Empowering Others   While it is important to understand and learn the strategies that will enhance your own power, remember that empowering others is just as important. We usually find that people who feel confident of their own power make more efforts to help others feel empowered. Empowering others is certainly a characteristic of effective leaders, but it is also part of collegial relationships at work.

Power Follows the Principle of Less Interest

In any interpersonal relationship, the person who holds the greater power is less interested in and less dependent on the rewards and punishments controlled by the other person. The more you need a relationship, the less power you have in it. The less you need a relationship, the greater your power. In a situation where there is a shortage of workers for the labour market, workers have more power to negotiate working conditions and salaries than when there are more than enough workers.

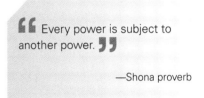

Every power is subject to another power.

—Shona proverb

Power Has a Cultural Dimension

As discussed throughout this text, culture in its many forms can impact communication. The culture of the organization or the profession affects power. For example, the power of a doctor is quite different from that of a nurse, the power of an engineer is different from that of a draftsperson, and the power of a supervisor is different from that of a receptionist. Ethnic diversity also presents different dimensions of power. For those from collectivist cultures, the power resides in the success of the group as a whole, whereas individualistic cultures seek individual accomplishment and power. So an employee from a collectivist culture may struggle with the power orientation of an individualistic colleague or supervisor. Unfortunately, recent immigrants frequently suffer from a lack of understanding and acceptance of their foreign qualifications and may find themselves in a position of disempowerment (unemployment or underemployment), even though they have the abilities and skills to do the job.

Power Is Frequently Used Unfairly

Although it would be nice if power were always wielded for the good of all, it's often used selfishly and unfairly in the workplace. We see unethical uses of power in interpersonal relationships more frequently than we would wish. Here are two serious examples of unethical use of power: sexual harassment and the use of power plays.

Sexual Harassment Harassment of any kind, particularly sexual harassment, is an extreme form of abuse of power. Sexual harassment violates Canadian law (see www.lois.justice.gc.ca/en/L-2/index.html) and the Canadian Human Rights Act. There are two general categories of sexual harassment. In one, employment opportunities (as in hiring and promotion) are made dependent on the granting of sexual favours. Reprisals and various negative consequences can result from the failure to grant such sexual favours.

The other category is hostile environment harassment, which is broader and includes all sexual behaviours (verbal and nonverbal) that make a worker uncomfortable. Putting sexually explicit pictures on the bulletin board, using sexually explicit screen savers, telling sexual jokes and stories, and using sexual and demeaning language or gestures all constitute hostile environment harassment.

If you are trying to determine whether behaviour constitutes sexual harassment, the following questions will help you assess your own situation objectively rather than emotionally (VanHyning, 1993):

1. Is it real? Does this behaviour have the meaning it seems to have?

2. Is it job related? Does this behaviour have something to do with or will it influence the way you do your job?

3. Did you reject this behaviour? Did you make your rejection of unwanted messages clear to the other person?

4. Have these unwanted messages persisted? Is there a pattern, a consistency to these messages?

If you answer Yes to all four questions, then the behaviour is likely to constitute sexual harassment (VanHyning, 1993).

Although most cases brought to public attention are committed by men against women, women may also harass men. Anyone in an organization can be guilty of sexual harassment, although most cases of harassment involve people in authority who harass subordinates. Sexual harassment is not limited to business organizations but can and does occur in schools, in hospitals, and in social, religious, and political organizations.

Power Plays Power plays are patterns of communication (not isolated instances) that take unfair advantage of another person (Steiner, 1981). These are less obvious abuses of power that can be disempowering to others. When someone constantly

---

In-Class Notes

Power Principles

- Power varies from person to person.
- Power is a part of all interpersonal messages.
- Power follows the principle of less interest.
- Power has a cultural dimension.
- Power is frequently used unfairly.

_____

_____

_____

_____

_____

_____

_____

_____

ignores you or what you say, you can feel disempowerment. When someone constantly reminds you that you "owe them" for a past favour, they are exerting unfair power. Or if someone constantly turns everything into a joke, this can be an attempt to take your power away.

When you feel trapped in a power play, try the following:

- *Express your feelings.* Tell the person that you're angry, annoyed, or disturbed by her behaviour.
- *Describe the behaviour to which you object.* Tell the person—in language that describes rather than evaluates—the specific behaviour you object to, for example, reading your mail, coming into your room without knocking, persisting in trying to hug you.
- *State a cooperative response you both can live with comfortably.* Tell the person—in a cooperative tone—what you want; for example, "I want you to knock before coming into my office."

INTRAPERSONAL POWER: SELF-ESTEEM

How much do you like yourself? How valuable a person do you think you are? How competent do you think you are? The answers to these questions will reflect your **self-esteem**, the value that you place on yourself.

Success breeds success. When you feel good about yourself—about who you are and what you're capable of doing—you will perform better. When you think like a success, you're more likely to act like a success. When you think you're a failure, you're more likely to act like a failure. Increasing self-esteem will, therefore, help you function more effectively in interpersonal relationships and in careers. Here are a few suggestions for increasing self-esteem. Recognize, though, that too much self-esteem can be detrimental and can become arrogance (e.g., Baumeister et al., 2000; Hewitt, 1998), especially if based on an unrealistic appraisal of yourself (Bower, 2001).

> **"** Low self-esteem is like driving through life with your hand-brake on. **"**
>
> —Maxwell Maltz

Attack Self-Destructive Beliefs

Actively challenge those beliefs you have about yourself that you find are unproductive or that make it more difficult for you to achieve your goals. Examples of unproductive beliefs are the feeling that you have to succeed in everything you do and believing that you have to be loved by everyone. Replace these self-destructive beliefs with more productive ones, such as "I succeed in many things; I don't have to succeed in everything" and "It would be nice to be loved by everyone, but it isn't necessary to my well-being or my happiness."

Seek Out Positive People

Some people criticize and find fault with just about everything. Others are positive and optimistic—they reward us, they stroke us, they make us feel good about ourselves. To enhance your self-esteem, seek out these people. At the same time, avoid negative people, those who don't make you feel good about yourself.

Secure Affirmation

Remind yourself of your successes. Focus on your good deeds, your positive qualities, strengths, and virtues, and keep your last positive performance appraisal in your desk so you can refer to it occasionally.

"So, when he says, 'What a good boy am I,' Jack is really reinforcing his self-esteem."

© The New Yorker Collection 1993 Mike Twohy from cartoonbank.com. All rights reserved.

> **Most powerful is he who has himself in his own power.**
>
> —Seneca

Affirm yourself by trying to honestly appraise your strengths, and then focus on them. For example, you could affirm yourself by stating:

- I am a reliable employee.
- I have made positive contributions to the sales campaign.
- I helped most of my clients find employment.

Work on Projects That Will Result in Success

Try consciously to select projects that will result in success. Each success will help build self-esteem and make the next success a little easier.

When a project does fail, recognize that this does not mean that you're a failure. Everyone fails somewhere along the line. Failure is something that happens—it's not necessarily something you have created and it's not something inside you. Further, your failing once does not mean that you will fail the next time. So put failure in perspective. Do not make it an excuse for not trying again.

INTERPERSONAL POWER: ASSERTIVENESS

> **The basic difference between being assertive and being aggressive is how our words and behaviors affect the rights and well-being of others.**
>
> —Sharon Anthony Bower

If you disagree with other people in a group, do you speak your mind? Do you allow others to take advantage of you because you're reluctant to say what you want? Do you feel uncomfortable when you have to state your opinion in a group? Questions such as these revolve around your degree of **assertiveness.**

Non-assertive, Aggressive, and Assertive Messages

Assertive Messages Assertive behaviour—behaviour that enables you to act in your own best interests *without* denying or infringing on the rights of others—is the generally desired alternative to non-assertiveness or aggressiveness. Assertive people operate with an "I win, you win" philosophy; they assume that both people can gain something from an interpersonal interaction, even from a confrontation.

In-Class Notes

- Non-assertive people fail to assert their rights—"You win, I lose."
- Assertive people act in their own best interests—"I win, you win."
- Aggressive people think little of others—"I win, you lose."

_____
_____
_____
_____
_____
_____
_____
_____

Principles for Increasing Assertive Communication

- Analyze assertive communication.
- Rehearse assertive communication.
- Do it! Communicate assertively.

_____

_____

_____

_____

_____

_____

_____

_____

_____

Assertive people are willing to assert their own rights. Unlike their aggressive counterparts, however, they do not hurt others in the process. Assertive people speak their minds and welcome others' doing likewise. In addition to identifying some specific assertive behaviours, we can further understand the nature of assertive communication by distinguishing it from non-assertiveness and aggressiveness (Alberti, 1977).

Assertive messages contrast with aggressive messages (as discussed in Chapter 11), which are hurtful or disrespectful to others, or with non-assertive messages, in which one's own rights are not asserted. This can result in a "you win, I lose" situation (Lloyd, 2001).

Communicate Assertively Communicating assertively is naturally the most difficult step, but obviously the most important. Here's a generally effective pattern to follow:

- Describe the problem; don't evaluate or judge it. "We're all working on this advertising project together. You're missing half our meetings, and you still haven't produced your first report."
- State how this problem affects you. Be sure to use I-messages and to avoid messages that accuse or blame the other person. "Our jobs depend on the success of this project and I don't think it's fair that I have to do extra work to make up for what you're not doing."
- Propose solutions that are workable and that allow the person to save face. "If you can get your report to the group by Tuesday, we'll still be able to meet our deadline. And I could give you a call an hour before the meetings to remind you."
- Confirm understanding. "Is it clear that we just can't produce this project if you're not going to pull your own weight? Will you have the report to us by Tuesday?"

Summary of Concepts and Skills

This chapter explored different aspects of workplace communication. Diversity in the workplace and its many aspects were discussed, and suggestions were given for improving communication based on acknowledging diversity. Negative communication patterns such as rumours, gossip, and untruthful communication were analyzed. The chapter also described interpersonal power in terms of personal power, self-esteem and assertiveness, as well as issues such as sexual harassment and power plays.

1. Workplace settings today are complex and diverse. Understanding the diversity of the workplace will help us become more effective communicators. This diversity includes a multigenerational workforce and staff from diverse cultures, with different abilities and temperaments.

2. Organizations have their own culture, and often include different subcultures. Similarly, occupational groups and professions usually have marked cultures.

3. Electronic and written communication are important aspects of workforce communication.

4. Positive communication and work can take place in teams, in mentoring relationships, and through networks.

5. Understanding the sources and reasons for negative communication in the workplace, such as gossip, rumours and untruthfulness, can help deal with these issues.

6. Interpersonal power is the ability of one person to influence or control the behaviour of another person. Five principles govern power in interpersonal relationships: power varies from person to person, power is a part of all interpersonal messages, power follows the principle of least interest, power has a cultural dimension, and power is often used unfairly.

7. Power plays are patterns of communication that take unfair advantage of another person. An effective management strategy for dealing with power plays cooperatively consists of three parts: stating your feelings, describing the behaviour you have difficulty with, and stating a cooperative response.

8. Self-esteem is the way you see yourself, the value you place on yourself. Assertiveness is an important aspect of self-esteem. Assertive people stand up for their rights without denying or infringing upon the rights of others. To increase your assertiveness, analyze assertive messages, and rehearse them before you try them out.

Check Your Ability

Check your ability to apply these skills. Use a rating scale such as the following: 1 = almost always, 2 = often, 3 = sometimes, 4 = rarely, and 5 = almost never.

_____ ❶ I recognize the existing diversity in my own workplace.

_____ ❷ I adapt my communication to the diversity in my workplace.

_____ ❸ I understand the culture of my organization.

_____ ❹ I practise effective workplace communication—verbal, nonverbal, electronic, and written.

_____ ❺ I engage in self-affirmation.

_____ ❻ I manage power through verbal and nonverbal messages.

_____ ❼ I avoid behaviours that could be interpreted as sexually harassing.

_____ ❽ I respond to power plays with appropriate strategies.

_____ ❾ I communicate assertively when it's appropriate to the situation.

After completing this self-test, check your answers against the Answer Key at the back of the book.

Multiple Choice Questions *Choose the BEST answer.*

1. Which of the following generations can be seen in the workplace?
   a. traditionalists
   b. boomers
   c. Xers
   d. millennials
   e. all of the above

2. Which is *not* true of millennials?
   a. They have self-confidence.
   b. They are usually very competent.
   c. They tend to disregard the experience and wisdom of others.
   d. They do not have a sense of entitlement.

3. Gossip at workplaces can
   a. be private but true information about a person.
   b. be information that is disseminated without consent.
   c. empower the gossiper and disempower the person gossiped about.
   d. be all of the above.

4. Anonymous communication in the workplace
   a. can empower people to express views.
   b. should never be allowed.
   c. is usually false.
   d. is always a positive strategy.

5. The culture of an organization
   a. can be understood by looking at artifacts such as stories, legends, rituals, and ceremonies.
   b. never changes.
   c. always impedes change.
   d. is easy to recognize.

6. Which of the following statements is false?
   a. Communication skills are not important for engineers.
   b. Professionals often use therapeutic communication.
   c. Engineers are more likely to be assessed for product than process.
   d. The ongoing interaction of early childhood professionals with children is a key aspect of their profession.

7. Which is true of interpersonal communication in the workplace?
   a. Power is not an important aspect of communication.
   b. Within every communication there is an element of power.

   c. Power is only reflected when people of different backgrounds communicate.
   d. Power increases as people work longer at their jobs.

8. A power play in the workplace is
   a. an unfair use of power.
   b. an exercise strategy during breaks.
   c. a strategy to gain influence over coworkers.
   d. a forceful response to sexual harassment.

9. Assertiveness
   a. is one form of aggressive communication.
   b. is one form of a power play.
   c. can help you communicate more effectively.
   d. should not be practised in the workplace.

10. Empowering others in the workplace
    a. should be avoided at all costs.
    b. should only be tried in intergenerational conflicts.
    c. is a good response to power plays.
    d. should be used to increase coworker collaboration.

True–False Questions *Write T or F in the blank next to the statement.*

1. _____ Generation Xers are skeptical and resourceful.

2. _____ Diversity in the workplace decreases as people conform and adapt.

3. _____ Formal communication is more common in role culture than in achievement culture.

4. _____ Written communication is losing its importance in the workplace.

5. _____ Business professionals often use a strategy called therapeutic communication.

6. _____ Email communication is well on the way to providing paper free workplaces.

7. _____ Rumours are never true.

8. _____ Networking is a good strategy to solve problems at work.

9. _____ Sexual harassment at work can sometimes be blamed on the victim.

10. _____ Assertiveness in the workplace will not help you communicate more effectively.

Vocabulary Quiz
The Language of Power

Match the terms of power with their definitions. Record the number of the definition next to the appropriate term.

a. ___ self-esteem

b. ___ power

c. ___ assertive communication

d. ___ tag questions, disqualifiers, and hesitations

e. ___ non-assertive communication

f. ___ coercive power

g. ___ compliance-gaining strategies

h. ___ legitimate power

i. ___ referent power

j. ___ cooperative management strategy for power plays

1. A willingness to speak out for your rights, but with respect for others.

2. Power held by virtue of your position or role.

3. Stating your feelings, describing the behaviour you object to, and stating a response both you and the other person will find acceptable.

4. Often perceived as signs of powerlessness.

5. The value you place on yourself.

6. Tactics that influence people to do what you want them to do.

7. When others wish to be like you.

8. An unwillingness to speak out for your rights.

9. Having the ability to administer punishment or remove rewards.

10. The ability to control the behaviour of another person.

Skill Building Exercises

12.1 Rewriting Unrealistic Beliefs

1. Here are five unrealistic beliefs that can get you into trouble and lower your self-esteem (Butler, 1981). For each belief, create a rewritten version that is more realistic and productive.

   a. The belief that you must *be perfect* impels you to try performing at unrealistically high levels, believing that anything short of perfection is unacceptable and that you're to blame for anything less than perfection.

   b. The belief that you must *hurry up* compels you to do things quickly, or to do more than can be reasonably expected in any given amount of time.

   c. The belief that you must *be strong* tells you that weakness and vulnerable emotions like sadness, compassion, or loneliness are wrong.

   d. The belief that you must *please others* leads you to seek approval from others. Pleasing yourself is secondary; in fact self-pleasure comes from pleasing others.

   e. The belief that you must always *try harder* leads you to take on tasks that would be impossible for any normal person to handle; yet you take them on.

   These beliefs are unrealistic and unproductive because they set goals and expectations that you cannot fulfill—a situation that is not very helpful to building self-esteem.

2. In each of the following dyads (pairs), there is a power difference. One person is significantly richer, of higher status, more educated, or more attractive than the other. How might the power differences create communication difficulties when the individuals are engaged (1) in informal conversation and (2) in romantic encounters?

   - a young nurse and the chief of surgery at a prestigious hospital
   - an uneducated parent and the high school principal
   - two coworkers, one extremely attractive and one extremely unattractive

12.2 Practising Assertiveness

For one of the following situations, write an assertive response:

Lending money: A coworker borrows $30 and promises to pay you back tomorrow. But tomorrow passes, as do 20 other tomorrows, and there is still no sign of the money. You know that your friend has not forgotten about the debt, and you also know that the person has more than enough money to pay you back.

Coworker favours: A coworker repeatedly asks you to mind her telephone while she runs some errand or another. You don't mind helping out in an emergency, but this occurs almost every day. You feel you're being taken advantage of and simply do not want to do this anymore.

12.3 Empowering Others

Here are two situations in which you might wish to empower the individuals involved. For each situation, write a response that would empower the other person, using such strategies as (1) raising the other person's self-esteem, (2) listening actively and supportively, (3) being open, positive, and empathic, and (4) avoiding verbal aggressiveness or any unfair conflict strategies.

1. You're supervising four college interns, three men and one woman, who are redesigning your company's website. The men are extremely supportive of one another

and regularly contribute ideas. Although equally competent, the woman doesn't contribute; she seems to lack confidence. But the objective of this redesign is to increase the number of female visitors, so you really need her input and want to empower her. What do you say?

2. You are a teacher in an early intervention program. You have a new assistant who is a recent immigrant. She appears to have a great deal to offer the culturally diverse children in your program but she is still unsure of her English. She tends to wait for direction before doing anything, and you really need her to begin to work independently with the children. What do you do and say?

Empowering others enables you to help others but also to benefit yourself. Empowered partners and colleagues, for example, are likely to be happier, a lot less prone to violence or verbal abuse, and more satisfied with the relationship than those lacking in power.

12.4 Sexual Harassment

What can you do about sexual harassment? If you encounter sexual harassment, consider these suggestions

recommended by workers in the field (Petrocelli & Repa, 1992; Bravo & Cassedy, 1992; Rubenstein, 1993):

1. Talk to the harasser. Tell this person, assertively, that you do not welcome the behaviour and that you find it offensive. Simply informing the harasser how you feel may be sufficient.

2. Collect evidence—perhaps corroboration from others who have experienced similar harassment at the hands of the same individual and perhaps a log of the offensive behaviours.

3. Use appropriate channels within the organization. Most organizations have established channels to deal with such grievances. In most cases this step will eliminate any further harassment.

4. If necessary, file a complaint with an organization or governmental agency, or perhaps take legal action.

Web Explorations

Companion Website

Visit the Companion Website at www.pearsoned.ca/devito for student resources related to this chapter, including self-grading quizzes, additional skill-building exercises, and links to other online resources.

Research Navigator

Explore our research resources at www.researchnavigator.com

■ Find and read an article on a principle or type of power, the different ways of communicating power, or how to

empower others. On the basis of this article, what can you add to the discussion presented here?

■ Investigate one of the key terms discussed in this chapter (for example, diversity in the workplace, power, power plays, empowerment, and sexual harassment). What additional insights can you provide?

■ Try finding answers to one of the following questions, or design a research study to answer it.

1. What types of power work best in the workplace?

2. Which strategies work best for improving communication in a diverse workplace?

3. Do women and men differ in assertiveness?

Glossary of Interpersonal Communication Concepts and Skills

Listed here are definitions of the technical terms of interpersonal communication—the words that are peculiar or unique to this discipline—and, where appropriate, the corresponding skills. These definitions and statements of skills should make new or difficult terms a bit easier to understand and should help to place each skill in context. The statements of skills appear in italics. All boldface terms within the definitions appear as separate entries in the glossary.

Acculturation. The process by which a person's culture is modified or changed through contact with or exposure to another culture.

Achievement culture. A workplace culture that fosters creativity, competition, and independence, with fewer formalities, rules, and structures.

Active listening. A process of putting together into some meaningful whole the listener's understanding of the speaker's total message—the verbal and the nonverbal, the content and the feelings. *Listen actively by paraphrasing the speaker's meanings, expressing an understanding of the speaker's feelings, and asking questions to enable you to check the accuracy of your understanding of the speaker. Express acceptance of the speaker's feelings, and encourage the speaker to further explore his feelings and thoughts, and thereby increase meaningful sharing.*

Adaptors. Nonverbal behaviours that, when engaged in either in private or in public without being seen, serve some kind of need and occur in their entirety—for example, scratching one's head until the itch is relieved. *Avoid adaptors that interfere with effective communication and reveal your discomfort or anxiety.*

Adjustment (principle of). The principle of verbal interaction that claims that communication may take place only to the extent that the parties communicating share the same system of signals. *Expand the common areas betwen you and significant others; learn each other's system of communication signals and meanings in order to increase understanding and interpersonal communication effectiveness.*

Affect displays. Nonverbal movements, mostly of the facial area, that convey emotional meaning—for example, anger, fear, and surprise.

Affirmation. The communication of support and approval. *Use affirmation to express your supportiveness and to raise esteem.*

Ageism. Discrimination based on age, usually against older people.

Alter-adaptors. Body movements you make in response to your current interactions, such as crossing your arms over your chest when someone unpleasant approaches, or moving closer to someone you like.

Altercasting. Placing the listener in a specific role for a specific purpose and asking that the listener approach the question or problem from the perspective of this specific role.

Apprehension. *See* **communication apprehension.**

Argumentativeness. A willingness to argue for a point of view, to speak one's mind. *Cultivate your argumentativeness, your willingness to argue for what you believe by, for example, treating disagreements as objectively as possible, reaffirming the other, stressing equality, expressing interest in the other's position, and allowing the other person to save face.* Distinguished from **verbal aggressiveness.**

Assertiveness. A willingness to stand up for one's rights but with respect for the rights of others. *Increase assertiveness (if desired) by analyzing the assertive and nonassertive behaviours of others, analyzing your own behaviours in terms of assertiveness, recording your behaviours, rehearsing assertive behaviours, and acting assertively in appropriate situations. Secure feedback from others for further guidance in increasing assertiveness.*

Attitude. A predisposition to respond for or against an object, person, or position.

Attraction. The state or process by which one individual is drawn to another, by having a highly positive evaluation of that other person.

Attractiveness. The degree to which one is perceived to be physically attractive and to possess a pleasing personality.

Attribution theory. A theory concerned with the processes involved in attributing causation or motivation to a person's behaviour. *In attempting to identify the motivation for behaviours, examine consensus, consistency, distinctiveness, and controllability. Generally, low consensus, high consistency, low distinctiveness, and high controllability identify internally motivated behaviour; high consensus, low consistency, high distinctiveness, and low controllability identify externally motivated behaviour.*

Avoidance. An unproductive **conflict** strategy in which a person takes mental or physical flight from the actual conflict.

Baby boomers. The generation born after the Second World War, characterized as competitive, idealistic, searching for self-gratification.

Backchannelling cues. A technique used to communicate various meanings back to the speaker without assuming the role of the speaker.

Barriers to intercultural communication. Those factors (physical or psychological) that prevent or hinder effective communication. *Avoid the major barriers to intercultural communication: ignoring differences between yourself and the culturally different, ignoring differences among the culturally different, ignoring differences in meaning, violating cultural rules and customs, and evaluating differences negatively.*

Belief. Confidence in the existence or truth of something; conviction. *Weigh both verbal and nonverbal messages before making believability judgments; increase your own sensitivity to nonverbal (and verbal) deception cues—for example, too little movement, long pauses, slow speech, increased speech errors, mouth guard, nose touching, eye rubbing, or the use of few words, especially monosyllabic answers. Use such cues to formulate hypotheses rather than conclusions concerning deception.*

Beltlining. An unproductive **conflict** strategy in which one hits at the level at which the other person cannot withstand the blow. *Avoid beltlining.*

Blame. An unproductive **conflict** strategy in which we attribute the cause of the conflict to the other person, or devote our energies to discovering who is the cause and avoid talking about the issues causing the conflict. *Avoid using blame to win an argument, especially with those with whom you are in close relationships.*

Breadth. The number of topics about which individuals in a relationship communicate.

Certainty. An attitude of closed-mindedness that creates a defensiveness among communication participants; opposed to **provisionalism.**

Channel. The vehicle or medium through which signals are sent.

Chronemics. The study of the communicative nature of time—the way you treat time and use it to communicate. Two general areas of chronemics are cultural and psychological time.

Closed-mindedness. An unwillingness to receive certain communication messages.

Code. A set of symbols used to translate a message from one form to another.

Cognitive labelling theory. A theory of emotions that holds that your emotional feelings begin with the occurrence or an event; then you respond physiologically; then you interpret the arousal (in effect, you decide what it is you're feeling); and then you experience (give a name to) the emotion.

Collectivist culture. A culture in which the group's goals rather than the individual's are given greater importance and where, for example, benevolence, tradition, and con-formity are given special emphasis; opposed to **individualistic culture**.

Colour communication. Use of colours (in clothing and in room decor, for example) to convey desired meanings.

Communication. (1) The process or act of communicating; (2) the actual message or messages sent and received; (3) the study of the processes involved in the sending and receiving of messages. (The term **communicology** is suggested for the third definition.)

Communication apprehension. Fear or anxiety over communicating; "trait apprehension" refers to fear of communication generally, regardless of the specific situation; "state apprehension" refers to fear that is specific to a given communication situation. *Manage your own communication apprehension by acquiring the necessary communication skills and experiences, focusing on success, reducing unpredictability by, for example, familiarizing yourself with the communication situations important to you, and putting communication apprehension in perspective. In cases of extreme communication apprehension, seek professional help.*

Communication network. A virtual network that is established through the use of electronic media such as cellphones.

Competence. "Language competence" is a speaker's ability to use the language; it is a knowledge of the elements and rules of the language. "Communication competence" refers to a knowledge of the elements, principles, and skills of communication and the ability to use these resources for greater communication effectiveness.

Compliance-gaining strategies. Behaviours that are directed toward gaining the agreement of others; behaviours designed to persuade others to do as we wish. *Use the various compliance-gaining strategies to increase your own persuasive power.*

Compliance-resisting strategies. Behaviours directed at resisting the persuasive attempts of others. *Use such strategies as identity management, nonnegotiation, negotiation, and justification as appropriate in resisting compliance.*

Computer Mediated Communications (CMC). The process of conducting conversations with others in a technologically enhanced way (e.g., by computer, email, chatrooms, text messaging).

Confidence. A quality of interpersonal effectiveness; a comfortable, at-ease feeling in interpersonal communication situations. *Communicate a feeling of being comfortable and at ease with the interaction through appropriate verbal and nonverbal signals.*

Confirmation. A communication pattern that acknowledges another person's presence and also indicates an acceptance of this person, this person's definition of self, and the relationship as defined or viewed by this other person; opposed to **disconfirmation**. *Avoid those verbal and nonverbal behaviours that disconfirm another* *person. Substitute confirming behaviours, behaviours that acknowledge the presence and the contributions of the other person.*

Conflict. An extreme form of competition in which a person attempts to bring a rival to surrender; a situation in which one person's behaviours are directed at preventing something or at interfering with or harming another individual. *See also* **interpersonal conflict.**

Connotation. The feeling or emotional aspect of meaning, generally viewed as consisting of the evaluative (for example, good–bad), potency (strong–weak), and activity (fast–slow) dimensions; the associations of a term. *See also* **denotation.**

Consistency. A perceptual process that influences us to maintain balance among our perceptions; a process that makes us tend to see what we expect to see and to be uncomfortable when our perceptions run contrary to our expectations. *Recognize the human tendency to seek and to see consistency even where it doesn't exist—to see our friends as all positive and our enemies as all negative, for example.*

Contact. The first stage in **relationship development** consisting of "perceptual contact" (you see or hear the person) and "interactional contact" (you talk with the person).

Content and relationship dimensions. A principle of communication that messages refer both to content (the world external to both speaker and listener) and to the relationship existing between the individuals who are interacting.

Context of communication. The physical, psychological, social, and temporal environment in which communication takes place. *Assess the context in which messages are communicated and interpret that communication behaviour accordingly; avoid seeing messages as independent of context.*

Conversation. Two-person communication usually possessing an opening, **feedforward**, a business stage, **feedback**, and a closing.

Conversational management. Responding to conversational turn cues from the other person, and using conversational cues to signal one's own desire to exchange (or maintain) speaker or listener roles.

Conversational rules. Principles that are followed in conversation to ensure that the goal of the conversation is achieved. *Discover, try not to violate, and, if appropriate, follow the conversational maxims of the culture in which you are communicating.*

Conversation processes. Using the general five-step process in conversation, and avoiding the several barriers that can be created when the normal process is distorted.

Conversational privacy. A challenge faced by speakers and bystanders when conversations using cellphones and various connecting devices are held in public places.

Conversational turns. The process of passing the speaker and listener roles during conversation. *Become sensitive to and respond appropriately to conversational turn cues, such as turn-maintaining, turn-yielding, turn-requesting, and turn-denying cues.*

Cooperation. An interpersonal process by which individuals work together for a common end; the pooling of efforts to produce a mutually desired outcome.

Critical thinking. The process of logically evaluating reasons and evidence, and reaching a judgment on the basis of this analysis.

Cultural display. Signs that communicate one's cultural identification, such as clothing or religious jewellery.

Cultural display rules. Rules that identify what are and what are not appropriate forms of expression for members of the culture.

Cultural rules. Rules that are specific to a given culture. *Respond to messages according to the cultural rules of the sender; in order to prevent misinterpretation of the intended meanings, avoid interpreting the messages of others exclusively through the perspective of your own culture.*

Cultural time. The meanings given to time communication by a particular culture.

Culture shock. The psychological reaction you experience upon entering a culture very different from your own.

Cyberbullying. Using electronic messaging to ostracize, threaten, and harass an individual.

Decoder. Something that takes a message in one form (for example, sound waves) and translates it into another form (for example, nerve impulses) from which meaning can be formulated (for example, in vocal-auditory communication). In human communication, the decoder is the auditory mechanism; in electronic communication, the decoder is, for example, the telephone earpiece. Decoding is the process of extracting a message from a code—for example, translating speech sounds into nerve impulses. *See also* **encoder.**

Defensiveness. The attitude of an individual or an atmosphere in a group characterized by threats, fear, and domination; messages evidencing evaluation, control, strategy, neutrality, superiority, and certainty are assumed to lead to defensiveness; opposed to **supportiveness.**

Denial. One of the obstacles to the expression of emotion; the process by which we deny our emotions to ourselves or to others.

Denotation. Referential meaning; the objective or descriptive meaning of a word. *See also* **connotation.**

Depth. The degree to which the inner personality—the inner core of an individual—is penetrated in interpersonal interaction.

Deterioration. The stage of a relationship during which the connecting bonds between the partners weaken and the partners begin drifting apart.

Dialogue. A two-way interaction in which each person is speaker and listener, sender and receiver, and in which there is deep concern for the other person and for the relationship between the two people.

Direct speech. Speech in which the speaker's intentions are stated clearly and directly. *Use direct requests and responses (1) to encourage compromise, (2) to acknowledge responsibility for your own feelings and desires, and (3) to state your own desires honestly so as to encourage honesty, openness, and supportiveness in others.*

Disclaimer. Statement that asks the listener to receive what the speaker says as intended without its reflecting negatively on the image of the speaker. *Avoid using disclaimers that may not be accepted by your listeners (they may raise the very doubts you wish to put to rest), but do use disclaimers when you think your future messages might offend your listeners.*

Disconfirmation. The process by which one ignores or denies the right of the individual even to define himself or herself; opposed to **confirmation.**

Dissolution. The termination or end of an interpersonal relationship. *If the relationship ends, (1) break the loneliness–depression cycle; (2) take time out to get to know yourself as an individual; (3) bolster your self-esteem; (4) remove or avoid symbols that may remind you of your past relationship and make you uncomfortable; (5) seek the support of friends and relatives; and (6) avoid repeating negative patterns.*

Downward communication. Communication sent from the higher levels of a hierarchy to the lower levels—for example, messages sent by managers to workers, or from deans to faculty members.

Dyadic effect. The tendency for the behaviours of one person to stimulate behaviours in the other; usually used to refer to the tendency of one person's self-disclosures to prompt the other to self-disclose. *Be responsive to the dyadic effect; if it's not operating (when you think it should be), ask yourself why.*

Effect. The outcome or consequence of an action or behaviour; communication is assumed always to have some effect.

Emblems. Nonverbal behaviours that directly translate words or phrases—for example, the signs for "okay" and "peace."

Emotion. The feelings we have, such as guilt, anger, or sorrow.

Emotional communication. The expression of feelings—for example, our feelings of guilt, happiness, or sorrow. *Before expressing your emotions, understand them, decide whether you wish to express them, and assess your communication options. In expressing your emotions, describe your feelings as accurately as possible, identify the reasons for them, anchor your feelings and their expression to the present time, and own your feelings.*

Emotional contagion. The transferral of emotions from one person to another, analogous to the transmission of a contagious disease from one person to another.

Empathy. The sharing of another person's feeling; feeling or perceiving something as another person does. *Increase empathic understanding for your primary partner by sharing experiences, role playing, and seeing the world from his perspective. Empathize with others, and express this empathic understanding verbally and nonverbally.*

Encoder. Something that takes a message in one form (for example, nerve impulses) and translates it into another form (for example, sound waves). In human communication, the encoder is the speaking mechanism; in electronic communication, the encoder is, for example, the telephone mouthpiece. Encoding is the process of putting a message into a code—for example, translating nerve impulses into speech sounds. *See also* **decoder.**

Enculturation. The process by which culture is transmitted from one generation to another.

Equality. An attitude that recognizes that each individual in a communication interaction is equal, that no one is superior to any other; encourages supportiveness; opposed to **superiority.** *Talk neither down nor up to others but communicate as an equal to increase interpersonal satisfaction and efficiency; share the speaking and the listening; recognize that all parties in communication have something to contribute.*

Ethics. The branch of philosophy that deals with the rightness or wrongness of actions; the study of moral values.

Ethnocentrism. The tendency to see others and their behaviours through our own cultural filters, often as distortions of our own behaviours; the tendency to evaluate the values and beliefs of one's own culture more positively than those of another culture.

Evaluation. A process whereby a value is placed on some person, object, or event. *Avoid premature evaluation; amass evidence before making evaluations, especially of other people.*

Excuse. An explanation designed to lessen the negative consequences of something done or said. *Avoid excessive excuse-making. Too many excuses may backfire and create image problems for the excuse-maker.*

Expressiveness. A quality of interpersonal effectiveness; genuine involvement in speaking and listening, conveyed verbally and nonverbally. *Communicate involvement and interest in the interaction by providing appropriate feedback, by assuming responsibility for your thoughts and feelings and your role as speaker and listener, and by appropriate expressiveness, variety, and flexibility in voice and bodily action.*

Extensional orientation. A point of view in which primary consideration is given to the world of experience and only secondary consideration is given to labels. *See also* **intensional orientation.**

Face-detracting *or face-attacking* **strategies.** One of the face orientation dimensions of conflict strategies which involves treating the other person as incompetent or untrustworthy, as unable or bad.

Face-enhancing strategies. One of the face orientation dimensions of conflict strategies that involves helping the other person maintain a positive image of a person who is competent and trustworthy, able and good.

Facial feedback hypothesis. The hypothesis or theory that your facial expressions can produce physiological and emotional effects.

Facial management techniques. Techniques used to mask certain emotions and to emphasize others—for example, intensifying your expression of happiness to make a friend feel good about a promotion.

Fact–inference confusion. A misevaluation in which one makes an inference, regards it as a fact, and acts upon it as if it were a fact. *Distinguish facts from inferences; respond to inferences as inferences and not as facts.*

Factual statement. A statement made by the observer after observation and limited to what is observed. *See also* **inferential statement.**

Family. A group of people who consider themselves related and connected to one another and where the actions of one have consequences for others.

Feedback. Information that is given back to the source. Feedback may come from the source's own messages (as when we hear what we are saying) or from the receiver(s) in the form of applause, yawning, puzzled looks, questions, letters to the editor of a newspaper, increased or decreased subscriptions to a magazine, and so forth. *Give clear feedback to others, and respond to others' feedback, either through corrective measures or by continuing current performance, to increase communication efficiency and satisfaction. See also* **feedforward.**

Feedforward. Information that is sent prior to the regular messages telling the listener something about what is to follow. *When appropriate, preface your messages in order to open the channels of communication, to preview the messages to be sent, to disclaim, and to altercast. In your use of feedforward, be brief, use feedforward sparingly, and follow through on your feedforward promises. Also, be sure to respond to the feedforward as well as the content messages of others. See also* **feedback**.

Feminine culture. A culture in which both men and women are encouraged to be modest, tender, and oriented to maintaining the quality of life. Feminine cultures emphasize the quality of life and so socialize their people to be modest and to stress close interpersonal relationships; opposed to **masculine culture.**

Flexibility. The ability to adjust communication strategies on the basis of the unique situation. *Apply the principles of interpersonal communication with flexibility, realizing that each situation calls for somewhat different skills.*

Force. An unproductive **conflict** strategy in which you try to win an argument by physically overpowering the other person either by threat or by actual behaviour. *Avoid it.*

Friendship. An interpersonal relationship between two persons that is mutually productive, established and maintained through perceived mutual free choice, and characterized by mutual positive regard. *Adjust your verbal and nonverbal communication as appropriate to the stages of your various friendships. Learn the rules that govern your friendships; follow them or risk damaging the relationship.*

Fundamental attribution error. The tendency to overvalue and give too much weight to the contribution of internal factors (e.g., the person's personality) and undervalue and give too little weight to the contribution of external factors (i.e., the situation the person is in or the surrounding events).

Gender display rules. Cultural rules that identify what are and are not appropriate forms of expression for men and for women.

Generation Xers. The generation born following the baby boomers, characterized as showing self-reliance, and preferring family and balance in the workplace.

Gossip. Communication about someone not present, some third party, usually about matters that are private to this third party. *Avoid gossip that breaches confidentiality, is known to be false, and is unnecessarily invasive.*

Grapevine. Messages that do not follow any formatted organizational structures; office-related gossip.

Gunnysacking. An unproductive **conflict** strategy of storing up grievances—as if in a gunnysack—and holding them in readiness to dump on the person with whom one is in conflict. *Avoid it.*

Halo effect. The tendency to generalize an individual's virtue or expertise from one area to another.

Haptics. Technical term for the study of touch communication.

Heterosexist language. Language that assumes all people are heterosexual, thereby denigrating lesbians and gay men.

High-context culture. A culture in which much of the information in communication is in the context or in the person, rather than explicitly coded in the verbal messages; opposed to **low-context culture**. **Collectivist cultures** are generally high-context.

I-messages. Messages in which the speaker accepts responsibility for personal thoughts and behaviours; messages in which the speaker's point of view is stated explicitly; opposed to **you-messages.** *Generally, I-messages are more effective than you-messages.*

Identity management. A tactic used to resist a request by trying to manipulate the image of the person making the request.

Illustrators. Nonverbal behaviours that accompany and illustrate verbal messages—for example, upward movements that accompany the verbalization "It's up there."

Immediacy. A quality of interpersonal effectiveness; a sense of contact and togetherness; a feeling of interest and liking for the other person. *Communicate immediacy through appropriate word choice, feedback, eye contact, body posture, and physical closeness.*

Implicit personality theory. A theory of personality that we maintain, with rules about what characteristics go with what other characteristics, and through which we perceive others. *Be conscious of your implicit personality theories; avoid drawing firm conclusions about other people on the basis of these theories.*

Inclusion (principle of). The principle of verbal interaction that holds that all members should be part of (included in) the interaction.

Index. An **extensional device** used to emphasize the notion of nonidentity (no two things are the same) and symbolized by a subscript—for example, politician$_{1 \text{ [Smith]}}$ is not politician$_{2 \text{ [Jones]}}$.

Indirect speech. Speech that hides the speaker's true intentions; speech in which requests and observations are made indirectly. *Use indirect speech (1) to express a desire without insulting or offending anyone, (2) to ask for compliments in a socially acceptable manner, and (3) to disagree without being disagreeable.*

Indiscrimination. A misevaluation caused by categorizing people, events, or objects into a particular class and responding to them only as members of that class; a failure to recognize that each individual is unique; a failure to apply the **index**. *Index your terms and statements to emphasize that each person and event is unique; avoid treating all individuals the same way just because they are covered by the same label or term.*

Individualistic culture. A culture in which the individual's goals and preferences, rather than the group's, are given greater importance; opposed to **collectivist cultures.**

Inevitability. A principle of communication holding that communication cannot be avoided; all behaviour in an interactional setting is communication. *Remember that all behaviour in an interactional situation communicates; seek out nonobvious messages and meanings.*

Inferential statement. A statement that can be made by anyone, that is not limited to what is observed, and that can be made at any time. *See also* **factual statement.**

Informal time terms. Terms that are approximate rather than exact, for example, "soon," "early," and "in a while." *Recognize that informal-time terms are often the cause of interpersonal difficulties. When misunderstanding is likely, use more precise terms.*

Intensional orientation. A point of view in which primary consideration is given to the way things are labelled and only secondary consideration (if any) is given to the world of experience. *See also* **extensional orientation.** *Respond first to things; avoid responding to labels as if they were things; do not let labels distort your perception of the world.*

Interaction management. A quality of interpersonal effectiveness; the control of interaction to the satisfaction of both parties; managing conversational turns, fluency, and message consistency. *Manage the interaction to the satisfaction of both parties by sharing the roles of speaker and listener, avoiding long and awkward silences, and being consistent in your verbal and nonverbal messages.*

Intercultural communication. Communication that takes place between persons of different cultures or persons who have different cultural beliefs, values, or ways of behaving.

Interpersonal communication. Communication between two persons or among a small group of persons and distinguished from public or mass communication; communication of a personal nature and distinguished from impersonal communication; communication between or among connected persons or those involved in a close relationship.

Interpersonal competence. The ability to accomplish one's interpersonal goals; interpersonal communication that is satisfying to both individuals.

Interpersonal conflict. A disagreement between two connected people. *To engage in more productive interpersonal conflict, (1) state your position directly and honestly; (2) react openly to the messages of your opponent; (3) own your thoughts and feelings; (4) address the real issues causing the conflict; (5) listen with and demonstrate empathic understanding; (6) validate the feelings of your interactant; (7) describe the behaviours causing the conflict; (8) express your feelings spontaneously rather than strategically; (9) state your position tentatively; (10) capitalize on agreements; (11) view conflict in positive terms to the extent possible; (12) express positive feelings for the other person; (13) be positive about the prospects of conflict resolution; (14) treat your opponent as an equal, avoiding ridicule or sarcasm; (15) involve yourself in the conflict; play an active role as both sender and receiver; (16) grant the other person permission to express himself or herself freely; and (17) avoid power tactics that may inhibit freedom of expression.*

Interpersonal effectiveness. The ability to accomplish one's interpersonal goals; interpersonal communication that is satisfying to both individuals.

Interpersonal perception. The **perception** of people; the processes through which we interpret and evaluate people and their behaviour.

Intimacy. The closest interpersonal relationship; usually used to denote a close primary relationship.

Intimate distance. The closest proxemic distance, ranging from touching to 46 centimetres. *See also* **proxemics.**

Involvement. The second stage in **relationship development**, in which you advance the relationship first by testing each other and then intensifying your interaction.

Irreversibility. A principle of communication holding that communication cannot be reversed; once something has been communicated, it cannot be uncommunicated. *Avoid saying things (for example, in anger) or making commitments that you may wish to retract (but will not be able to) in order to prevent resentment and ill feeling.*

Johari window. A diagram of the four selves: **open, blind, hidden,** and **unknown.**

Justification. Justifying a refusal by citing possible consequences of compliance or noncompliance.

Language. The rules of syntax, semantics, and phonology by which sentences are created and understood; the term "language" refers to the sentences that can be created in any language, such as English, Bantu, or Italian.

Lateral communication. Communication between equals—manager to manager, worker to worker.

Leave-taking cues. Verbal and nonverbal cues that indicate a desire to terminate a conversation. *Increase your sensitivity to leave-taking cues; pick up on the leave-taking cues of others, and communicate such cues tactfully so as not to insult or offend others.*

Levelling. A process of message distortion in which a message is repeated but the number of details is reduced, some details are omitted entirely, and some details lose their complexity.

Listening. An active process of receiving aural stimuli; this process consists of five stages: receiving, understanding, remembering, evaluating, and responding. *Adjust your listening perspective, as the situation warrants, between active and passive, judgmental and non-judgmental, surface and depth, and empathic and objective listening.*

Low-context culture. A culture in which most of the information in communication is explicitly stated in the verbal messages; opposed to **high-context culture. Individualistic cultures** are usually low-context cultures.

Manipulation. An unproductive **conflict** strategy that avoids open conflict; instead, attempts are made to divert the conflict by being especially charming and getting the other person into a non-combative frame of mind. *Avoid it.*

Manner rule. A principle of **conversation** that holds that speakers cooperate by being clear and by organizing their thoughts into some meaningful and coherent pattern. *Use it.*

Markers. Devices that signify that a certain territory belongs to a particular person. *Become sensitive to the markers (central, boundary, and ear) of others, and learn to use these markers to define your own territories and to communicate your desired impression.*

Masculine culture. A culture in which men are viewed as assertive, strong, and oriented to material success, and women are viewed as modest, tender, and focused on the quality of life. Masculine cultures emphasize success and so socialize people to be assertive, ambitious, and competitive; opposed to **feminine culture.**

Mentoring relationship. A relationship in which an experienced individual helps to train someone who is less experienced; for example, an accomplished teacher might mentor a younger teacher who has never taught before.

Message. Any signal or combination of signals that serves as a **stimulus** for a receiver.

Metacommunication. Communication about communication. *Metacommunicate to ensure understanding of the other person's thoughts and feelings: give clear feedforward, explain feelings as well as thoughts, paraphrase your own complex thoughts, and ask questions.*

Millennials. The generation born after 1980, characterized as having very high self-esteem and confidence, and little respect for the wisdom and experience of previous generations.

Mindfulness and mindlessness. States of relative awareness. In a mindful state, we are aware of the logic and rationality of our behaviours and the logical connections existing among elements. In a mindless state, we are unaware of this logic and rationality. *Apply the principles of interpersonal communication mindfully rather than mindlessly. Increase mindfulness by creating and re-creating categories, being open to new information and points of view, and being careful of relying too heavily on first impressions.*

Model. A representation of an object or process.

Monochronic time orientation. A view of time in which things are done sequentially; one thing is scheduled at a time. Opposed to **polychronic time orientation**.

Monologue. Communication in which one person speaks and the other listens with no real interaction between participants.

Myers-Briggs Personality Assessment. A commonly used assessment for personality traits.

Negative feedback. Feedback that serves a corrective function by informing the source that his or her message is not being received in the way intended. Negative feedback serves to redirect the source's behaviour. Looks of boredom, shouts of disagreement, letters critical of newspaper policy, and teachers' instructions on how better to approach a problem would be examples of negative feedback.

Negotiation. Resisting compliance by offering a compromise or by offering to help in another way.

Networking. Connecting with people who can help you accomplish a goal or help you find information related to your goal; for example, to your search for a job.

Neutrality. A response pattern that lacks personal involvement; encourages defensiveness; opposed to **empathy.**

Noise. Anything that interferes with a person's receiving a message as the source intended the message to be received. Noise is present in a communication system to the extent that the message received is not the message sent. *Combat the effects of physical, semantic, and psychological noise by eliminating or lessening the sources of physical noise, securing agreement on meanings, and interacting with an open mind in order to increase communication accuracy.*

Nonnegotiation. An unproductive **conflict** strategy in which an individual refuses to discuss the conflict or listen to the other person.

Nonverbal communication. Communication without words; for example, communication by means of space, gestures, facial expressions, touching, vocal variation, and silence.

Object-adaptors. Movements that involve your manipulation of some object—for example, punching holes in or drawing on the Styrofoam coffee cup, clicking a ball-point pen, or chewing on a pencil. *Avoid these movements; they generally communicate discomfort and a lack of control over the communication situation.*

Olfactory communication. Communication by smell.

Openness. A quality of interpersonal effectiveness encompassing (1) a willingness to interact openly with others, to self-disclose as appropriate, (2) a willingness to react honestly to incoming stimuli, and (3) a willingness to own one's feelings and thoughts.

Other-orientation. A quality of interpersonal effectiveness involving attentiveness, interest, and concern for the other person. *Convey concern for and interest in the other person by means of empathic responses, appropriate feedback, and attentive listening responses.*

Outing. The process whereby a person's affectional orientation is made public by another person and without the gay man or lesbian's consent.

Overattribution. The tendency to attribute a great deal—or even everything—a person does to one or two characteristics.

Owning feelings. The process by which we take responsibility for our own feelings instead of attributing them to others. *To indicate ownership of your feelings, use I-messages and acknowledge responsibility for your own thoughts and feelings.*

Paralanguage. The vocal (but nonverbal) aspect of speech. Paralanguage consists of voice qualities (for example, pitch range, resonance, tempo), vocal characterizers (laughing or crying, yelling or whispering), vocal qualifiers (intensity, pitch height), and vocal segregates ("uh-uh," meaning "no," or "shhh" meaning "silence"). *Vary paralinguistic elements such as rate, volume, and stress to add variety and emphasis to your communications, and be responsive to the meanings communicated by others' variation of paralanguage features.*

Passive listening. Listening that is attentive and supportive but occurs without talking and without directing the speaker in any nonverbal way; also used negatively to refer to inattentive and uninvolved listening.

Pauses. Silent periods in the normally fluent stream of speech. Pauses are of two major types: filled pauses (interruptions in speech that are filled with such vocalizations as "er" or "um"), and unfilled pauses (silences of unusually long duration).

People culture. A workplace culture that emphasizes relationships, sharing, and friendship.

Perception. The process by which you become aware of objects and events through your senses. *Increase your accuracy in interpersonal perception by looking for a variety of cues that point in the same direction, formulating hypotheses (not conclusions), being especially alert to contradictory cues that may refute your initial hypotheses, avoiding the assumption that others will respond as you would, and being careful not to perceive only the positive in those you like and the negative in those you dislike.*

Personal distance. The second-closest proxemic distance, ranging from 46 centimetres to 1.2 metres. *See also* **proxemics.**

Persuasion. The process of influencing attitudes and behaviour.

Pitch. The highness or lowness of the vocal tone.

Polarization. A form of fallacious reasoning by which only two extremes are considered; also referred to as "black-or-white" and "either–or" thinking, or two-valued orientation. *Use middle terms and qualifiers when describing the world; in order to describe reality more accurately, avoid using terms of polar opposites (black and white, good and bad).*

Polychronic time orientation. A view of time in which several things may be scheduled or engaged in at the same time. Opposed to **monochronic time orientation**.

Positive feedback. Feedback that supports or reinforces the continuation of behaviour along the same lines in which it is already proceeding—for example, applause during a speech encourages the speaker to continue speaking in this way.

Positiveness. A characteristic of effective communication involving positive attitudes toward oneself and toward the interpersonal interaction. Also used to refer to complimenting another and expressing acceptance and approval. *Verbally and nonverbally communicate a positive attitude toward yourself, others, and the situation by using smiles, positive facial and verbal expressions, and attentive gestures, and by eliminating or reducing negative appraisals.*

Power. The ability to influence or control the behaviour of another person; A has power of B when A can influence or control B's behaviour. Power is an inevitable part of interpersonal relationships. *Communicate power through forceful speech; avoidance of weak modifiers and excessive body movement; and demonstration of knowledge,* *preparation, and organization in the matters at hand.*

Power culture. A workplace culture in which authority is clear, where a high degree of loyalty is expected, and measures are in place to ensure accountability.

Power plays. Patterns of communication (not isolated instances) that take unfair advantage of another person. These are less obvious abuses of power that can be disempowering to others.

Primacy and recency. Primacy refers to giving more credence to an event that occurs first; recency refers to giving more credence to an event that occurs last (that is, most recently). *Be aware that a first impression can act as a filter that prevents your perception of another person's perhaps contradictory behaviour, changes in situation, and especially, changes in that person. Recognize the normal tendency for first impressions to leave lasting impressions and to colour both what we see later and the conclusions we draw. Be at your very best in first encounters. Also, take the time and effort to revise your impressions of others on the basis of new information.*

Primary relationship. The relationship between two people that they consider their most (or one of their most) important, such as the relationship between husband and wife or domestic partners.

Principle of cooperation. An implicit agreement between speaker and listener to cooperate in trying to understand what each is communicating.

Process. Ongoing activity; referring to **communication** as a process emphasizes that it is always changing, always in motion.

Provisionalism. An attitude of open-mindedness that leads to the creation of supportiveness; opposed to **certainty.**

Proxemics. The study of the communicative function of space; the study of how people unconsciously structure their space—the distance between people in their interactions, the organization of space in homes and offices, and even the design of cities.

Psychological time. The importance placed on past, present, or future time. *Recognize the significance of your own time orientation to your ultimate success, and make whatever adjustments you think desirable.*

Public distance. The farthest proxemic distance, ranging from 3.7 metres to more than 7.6 metres; see also **proxemics.**

Pygmalion effect. The condition in which you make a prediction of success, act as if it's true, and thereby make it come true. (As an example, acting towards students as if they'll be successful influences them to become successful.) A type of **self-fulfilling prophecy.**

Racist language. Language that denigrates a particular race. *Avoid racist language—any language that demeans or is derogatory toward members of a particular race—so as not to offend or alienate others or reinforce stereotypes.*

Rate. The speed with which we speak, generally measured in words per minute. *Use variations in rate to increase com-*

munication efficiency and persuasiveness as appropriate.

Receiver. Any person or thing that takes in messages. Receivers may be individuals listening to or reading a message, a group of persons hearing a speech, a scattered television audience, or machines that store information.

Regulators. Nonverbal behaviours that regulate, monitor, or control the communications of another person.

Rejection. A response to an individual that acknowledges another person but expresses disagreement; opposed to **confirmation** and **disconfirmation**.

Relation rule. A principle of **conversation** that holds that speakers cooperate by talking about what is relevant to the conversation and by not talking about what is not relevant.

Relational dialectics theory. A theory that describes relationships between a series of opposites representing competing desires or motivations, such as the desire for autonomy and the desire to belong to someone, for novelty and predictability, and for closedness and openness.

Relationship communication. Communication between or among intimates or those in close relationships; used by some theorists as synonymous with interpersonal communication.

Relationship message. Messages that comment on the relationship between the speakers rather than on matters external to them. *Recognize and respond to relationship as well as content messages in order to ensure a more complete understanding of the messages intended.*

Repair. A relationship stage in which one or both parties seek to improve the relationship. *Relationship repair may be accomplished by recognizing the problem, engaging in productive conflict resolution, posing possible solutions, affirming each other, integrating solutions into everyday behaviour, and taking relational risks. See also* **maintenance.**

Role culture. A workplace culture wherein there is general conformity to expectations, clear regulations and procedures, and clearly defined tasks.

Schemata. Ways of organizing perceptions; mental templates or structures that help us organize the millions of items of information that we come into contact with every day as well as those we already have in our memory. Schemata include general ideas about people (Pat and Chris, Japanese, Baptists); ourselves (our qualities, abilities, or liabilities); and social roles (the qualities of police officers, professors, or multimillionaire CEOs). Singular: schema.

Script. A type of schema; an organized body of information about some action, event, or procedure. A script is a general idea of how some event should play out or unfold; the rules governing events and their sequence.

Selective exposure. The tendency of listeners to actively seek out information that supports their opinions and to actively avoid information that contradicts their existing opinions, beliefs, attitudes, and values.

Self-acceptance. Being satisfied with ourselves, our virtues and vices, and our abilities and limitations.

Self-adaptors. Movements that usually satisfy a physical need, especially to make us more comfortable—for example, scratching our head to relieve an itch, moistening our lips because they feel dry, or pushing our hair out of our eyes. *Because these often communicate nervousness or discomfort, they are best avoided.*

Self-awareness. The degree to which you know yourself. *Increase self-awareness by asking yourself about yourself and listening to others; actively seek information about yourself from others by carefully observing their interactions with you and by asking relevant questions. See yourself from different perspectives (see your different selves), and increase your open self.*

Self-concept. Your self-image, the view you have of who you are.

Self-disclosure. The process of revealing something about yourself to another, usually used to refer to information that would normally be kept hidden. *Self-disclose to improve the relationship, when the context and the relationship are appropriate for the self- disclosure, when there is an opportunity for open and honest responses, when the self-disclosure will be clear and direct, when there are appropriate reciprocal disclosures, and when you have examined and are willing to risk the possible burdens that self-disclosure might entail. Self-disclose selectively; regulate your self-disclosures as appropriate to the context, topic, audience, and potential rewards and risks to secure the maximum advantage and reduce the possibility of negative effects.*

Self-esteem. The value we place on ourselves; our self-evaluations; usually used to refer to the positive value we place on ourselves. *Increase your self-esteem by attacking destructive beliefs, engaging in self-affirmation, seeking out nourishing people, and working on projects that will result in success.*

Self-fulfilling prophecy. The situation in which making a prediction tends to cause it to come true. For example: expecting a class to be boring and then fulfilling this expectation by perceiving it as boring; expecting a person to be hostile, acting in a hostile manner toward this person, and in doing so, eliciting hostile behaviour from the person—thus confirming your prophecy that the person is hostile. *Avoid fulfilling your own negative prophecies and seeing only what you want to see. Be especially careful to examine your perceptions when they conform too closely to your expectations; check to make sure that you are seeing what exists in real life, not just in your expectations or predictions.*

Self-serving bias. A bias that operates in the self-attribution process and leads us to take credit for the positive consequences and to deny responsibility for the negative consequences of our behaviours. *In examining the causes of your own behaviour, beware of the tendency to attribute negative behaviours to external factors and positive behaviours to internal factors. In self-examinations, ask whether and how the self-serving bias might be operating.*

Sexist language. Language derogatory to one sex, generally women. *Whether man or woman, avoid sexist language—for example, terms that presume maleness as the norm ("policeman" or "mailman").*

Shyness. The condition of discomfort and uneasiness in interpersonal situations.

Signal-to-noise ration. A measure of what is meaningful (signal) to what is interference (noise).

Silence. The absence of vocal communication; often misunderstood to refer to the absence of any and all communication. *Use silence to communicate feelings or to prevent communication about certain topics. Interpret silences of others through their culturally determined rules rather than your own.*

Silencers. A tactic (such as crying) that silences one's opponent—an unproductive **conflict** strategy.

Social comparison. The processes by which you compare aspects of yourself (for example, your abilities, opinions, and values) with those of others, and then assess and evaluate yourself on the basis of the comparison; one of the sources of self-concept.

Social distance. The third proxemic distance, ranging from 1.2 metres to 3.7 metres; the distance at which business is usually conducted. *See also* **proxemics.**

Source. Any person or thing that creates messages; for example, an individual speaking, writing, or gesturing, or a computer solving a problem.

Speech. Messages conveyed via a vocal-auditory channel.

Spontaneity. The communication pattern in which one verbalizes what one is thinking without attempting to develop strategies for control; encourages **supportiveness;** opposed to **strategy.**

Static evaluation. An orientation that fails to recognize that the world is characterized by constant change; an attitude that sees people and events as fixed rather than as constantly changing. *Date your statements to emphasize constant change; avoid the tendency to think of and describe things as static and unchanging.*

Status. The relative level one occupies in a hierarchy; status always involves a comparison, and thus one's status is only relative to the status of another. In our culture, occupation, financial position, age, and educational level are significant determinants of status.

Stereotype. In communication, a fixed impression of a group of people through which we then perceive specific individuals; stereotypes are most often negative ("Those people" are stupid, uneducated, and dirty) but may also be positive ("Those people" are scientific, industrious, and helpful). *Avoid stereotyping others; instead, see and respond to each individual as a unique individual.*

Stimulus. Any external or internal change that impinges on or arouses an organism.

Strategy. The use of some plan to control other members in a communication interaction; a strategy guides your own communications; encourages **defensiveness;** opposed to **spontaneity.**

Superiority. A point of view or attitude that assumes that others are not equal to you; encourages **defensiveness;** opposed to **equality.**

Supportiveness. The attitude of an individual or in a group atmosphere that is characterized by openness, absence of fear, and a genuine feeling of equality. *Exhibit supportiveness to others by being descriptive rather than evaluative, spontaneous rather than strategic, and provisional rather than certain;* opposed to **defensiveness.**

Taboo. Forbidden; culturally censored. Taboo language is language that is frowned upon by "polite society." Topics and specific words may be considered taboo—for example, death, sex, certain forms of illness, and various words denoting sexual activities and excretory functions. *Avoid taboo expressions so that others do not make negative evaluations; substitute more socially acceptable expressions or euphemisms where and when appropriate.*

Tactile communication. Communication by touch; communication received by the skin. *Use touch when appropriate to express positive affect, playfulness, control, and ritualistic meanings, and to serve task-related functions; avoid touching that may be unwelcome.*

Temporal communication. The messages conveyed by your time orientation and treatment of time. *Interpret time cues from the point of view of the other's culture rather than your own.*

Territoriality. A possessive or ownership reaction to an area of space or to particular objects. *Establish and maintain territory nonverbally by marking or otherwise indicating temporary or permanent ownership. Become sensitive to the territorial behaviour of others.*

Touch. Use touch when appropriate to express positive affect, playfulness, control, and ritualistic meanings, and to serve task-related functions.

Touch avoidance. The tendency to avoid touching and being touched by others. *Recognize that some people may prefer to avoid touching and being touched. Avoid drawing too many conclusions about people from the way they treat interpersonal touching.*

Transactional view. The view that communication is an ongoing process in which all elements are interdependent and influence one another.

Transformational leader. The transformational leader shares power with others, values collaboration, is a source of inspiration to others, and has the trust of those who work with her.

Turn-denying cues. Conversational turn-taking cues which indicate your reluctance to assume the role of speaker.

Turn-maintaining cues. Conversational turn-taking cues which enable you to maintain the role of speaker.

Turn-requesting cues. Conversational turn-taking cues which tell the speaker that you would like to take a turn as speaker.

Turn-yielding cues. Conversational turn-taking cues which tell the listener that you're finished and wish to exchange the role of speaker for the role of listener.

Unproductive conflict strategies. Ways of engaging in conflict that generally prove counterproductive; for example, avoidance, force, blame, silencers, gunnysacking, manipulation, personal rejection, and fighting below the belt.

Upward communication. Communication sent from the lower levels of a hierarchy to the upper levels—for example, line worker to manager, faculty member to dean.

Value. Relative worth of an object; a quality that makes something desirable or undesirable; ideals or customs about which we have emotional responses, whether positive or negative.

Verbal aggressiveness. A method of winning an argument by attacking the other person's **self-concept.** Avoid inflicting psychological pain on the other person to win an argument.

Voice qualities. Aspects of **paralanguage**—specifically, pitch range, vocal lip control, glottis control, pitch control, articulation control, rhythm control, resonance, and tempo.

Volume. The relative loudness of the voice.

You-messages. Messages in which the speaker denies responsibility for his or her own thoughts and behaviours; messages that attribute the speaker's **perception** to another person; messages of **blame**; opposed to **I-messages.**

References

Abrams, Jessica, O'Conner, Joan, & Giles, Howard. (2002). Identity and intergroup communication. In William B. Gudykunst, & Bella Mody (Eds.), *Handbook of international and intercultural communication* (2nd ed., pp. 225–240). Thousand Oaks, CA: Sage.

Acor, A.A. (2001). Employers' perceptions of persons with body art and an experimental test regarding eyebrow piercing. *Dissertation Abstracts International: Section B. The Sciences and Engineering, 61,* 3885.

Adams, Dennis M., & Hamm, Mary E. (1991). *Cooperative learning: Critical thinking and collaboration across the curriculum.* Springfield, IL: Charles C. Thomas.

Adria, Marco. (2003). Arms to communications: Idealist and pragmatic strains of Canadian thought on technology and nationalism. *Canadian Journal of Communication, 28,* 167–184.

Adrianson, L. (2001). Gender and computer-mediated communication: Group processes in problem solving. *Computers in Human Behavior, 17,* 71–94.

Albas, Daniel C., McCluskey, Ken W., & Albas, Cheryl A. (1976, December). Perception of the emotional content of speech: A comparison of two Canadian groups. *Journal of Cross-Cultural Psychology, 7,* 481–490.

Albert, Rosita, & Nelson, Gayle L. (1993, Winter). Hispanic/Anglo American differences in attributions to paralinguistic behavior. *International Journal of Intercultural Relations, 17,* 19–40.

Alberti, Robert (Ed.). (1977). *Assertiveness: Innovations, applications, issues.* San Luis Obispo, CA: Impact.

Alessandra, Tony. (1986). How to listen effectively. *Speaking of Success* (videotape series). San Diego, CA: Levitz Sommer Productions.

Altman, Irwin, & Taylor, Dalmas. (1973). *Social penetration: The development of interpersonal relationships.* New York: Holt, Rinehart & Winston.

Andersen, Peter. (1991). Explaining intercultural differences in nonverbal communication. In Larry A. Samovar, & Richard E. Porter (Eds.), *Intercultural communication: A reader* (6th ed., pp. 286–296). Belmont, CA: Wadsworth.

Anderson, M. (1997). *Nursing leadership, management, and professional practice for the LPN/LVN.* Philadelphia: FA Davis Co.

Anderson, Peter A. et al. (2002). Nonverbal communication across cultures. In William B. Gundykunst, & Bella Mody (Eds.), *Handbook of international and intercultural communication* (2nd ed., pp. 89–106). Thousand Oaks, CA: Sage.

Andersen, Peter A., & Leibowitz, Ken. (1978). The development and nature of the construct touch avoidance. *Environmental Psychology and Nonverbal Behavior, 3,* 89–106.

Anderson, Claire J., & Fisher, Caroline. (1991, August). Male-female relationships in the workplace: Perceived motivations in office romance. *Sex Roles, 25,* 163–180.

Argyle, M., & Ingham, R. (1972). Gaze, mutual gaze and distance. *Semiotica, 1,* 32–49.

Argyle, Michael. (1988). *Bodily communication* (2nd ed.). New York: Methuen.

Argyle, Michael, & Henderson, Monika. (1985). *The anatomy of relationships: And the rules and skills needed to manage them successfully.* London: Heinemann.

Aronson, Elliot, Wilson, Timothy D., & Akert, Robin M. (1994). *Social psychology: The heart and the mind* (2nd ed.). New York: HarperCollins.

Asch, Solomon. (1946). Forming impressions of personality. *Journal of Abnormal and Social Psychology, 41,* 258–290.

Ashcraft, Mark H. (1998). *Fundamentals of cognition.* New York: Longman.

Atkin, C. et al. (2002). Correlates of verbally aggressive communication in adolescents. *Journal of Applied Communication Research, 3,* 251–269.

Aune, Krystyna-Strzyzewski, Buller, David B., & Aune, R. Kelly. (1996, September). Display rule development in romantic relationships: Emotion management and perceived appropriateness of emotions across relationship stages. *Human Communication Research, 23,* 115–145.

Aune, R. Kelly, & Kikuchi, Toshiyuki. (1993, September). Effects of language intensity similarity on perceptions of credibility, relational attributions, and persuasion. *Journal of Language and Social Psychology, 12,* 224–238.

Authier, J., & Gustafson, K. (1982). *Microtraining: Focusing on specific skills.* In E. K. Marshall, P. D. Kurtz, & Associates (Eds.), *Interpersonal helping skills: A guide to training methods, programs, and resources* (pp. 93–130). San Francisco: Jossey-Bass.

Axtell, Roger. (1993). *Do's and taboos around the world* (3rd ed.). New York: Wiley.

Axtell, Roger E. (1990). *Do's and taboos of hosting international visitors.* New York: Wiley.

Ayres, Joe, & Hopf, Tim. (1993). *Coping with speech anxiety.* Norwood, NJ: Ablex.

Ayres, Joe, & Hopf, Tim. (1995, Fall). An assessment of the role of communication apprehension in communicating with the terminally ill. *Communication Research Reports, 12*, 227–234.

Azzam, A. (2006). A generation immersed in media. *Educational Leadership (63),* 7.

Bach, George R., & Wyden, Peter. (1968). *The intimacy enemy.* New York: Avon.

Bachman, David L. et al. (2000, October). Caregiver attitudes about patients told they have Alzheimer's disease after truth disclosure. *Journal of Clinical Geropsychology, 6,* 309–313.

Baker, J.S., & Jones, M.A. (1996). The poison grapevine: how destructive are gossip and rumour in the workplace? *Human Resource Development Quarterly, 7,* 75–86.

Balswick, J. O., & Peck, C. (1971). The inexpressive male: A tragedy of American society? *The Family Coordinator, 20,* 363–368.

Barbato, Carole A., & Perse, Elizabeth M. (1992, August). Interpersonal communication motives and the life position of elders. *Communication Research, 19,* 516–531.

Barker, Larry et al. (1980). An investigation of proportional time spent in various communication activities by college students. *Journal of Applied Communication Research, 8,* 101–109.

Barker, Larry L., & Gaut, Deborah A. (1996). *Communication* (7th ed.). Boston: Allyn & Bacon.

Barna, L.M. (1997). Stumbling blocks in intercultural communication. In L. A. Samovar & R.E. Porter (Eds.), *Intercultural communication: A reader* (7th ed., pp. 337–346). Belmont, CA: Wadsworth.

Barna, LaRay M. (1985). Stumbling blocks in intercultural communication. In Larry A. Samovar, & Richard E. Porter (Eds.), *Intercultural communication: A reader* (4th ed., pp. 330–338). Belmont, CA: Wadsworth.

Barnlund, Dean C. (1970). A transactional model of communication. In J. Akin, A. Goldberg, G. Myers, & J. Stewart (Eds.), *Language behavior: A book of readings in communication.* The Hague: Mouton.

Barnlund, Dean. (1989). *Communicative styles of Japanese and Americans: Images and realities.* Belmont, CA: Wadsworth.

Barta, Patrick. (1999, December 16). Sex differences in the inferior parietal lobe. *Cerebral Cortex.* www.wired.com/news/technology/0,1282,33033,00.html.

Bass, B.M., & Avolio, B.J. (1990). The implications of transactional and transformational leadership for individuals, teams and organizational development. *Research in Organization Change and Development, 4,* 231–272.

Bates, M. E. (2004). It's not who you know, it's who's linked to you. *EContent (27)* 11. Academic Search Premier.

Basso, K. H. (1972). To give up on words: Silence in Apache culture. In Pier Paolo Giglioli (Ed.), *Language and social context.* New York: Penguin.

Baumeister, R.F., Bushman, B.J., & Campbell, W.K. (2000, February). Self-esteem, narcissism, and aggression: Does violence result from low self-esteem or from threatened egotism? *Current Directions in Psychological Science, 9,* 26–29.

Baxter, Leslie A. (1988). A dialectical perspective on communication strategies in relationship development. In Steve W. Duck (Ed.), *Handbook of Personal Relationships.* New York: Wiley.

Baxter, Leslie A. (1990, February). Dialectical contradictions in relationship development. *Journal of Social and Personal Relationships, 7,* 69–88.

Baxter, Leslie A., & Simon, Eric P. (1993, May). Relationship maintenance strategies and dialectical contradictions in personal relationships. *Journal of Social and Personal Relationships, 10,* 225–242.

Baxter, Leslie A., & Wilmot, W.W. (1984). "Secret tests": Social strategies for acquiring information about the state of the relationship. *Human Communication Research, 11,* 171–201.

Beach, Wayne A. (1990–1991). Avoiding ownership for alleged wrongdoings. *Research on Language and Social Interaction, 24,* 1–36.

Beatty, Michael J. (1988). Situational and predispositional correlates of public speaking anxiety. *Communication Education, 37:* 28–39.

Beauchesne, M.A., & Patsdaughter, C.A. (2005). Primary care for the underserved conference: The evolution of an emerging professional culture. *Journal of Cultural Diversity, 12,* 77-88.

Beck, A. T. (1988). *Love is never enough.* New York: Harper & Row.

Bedford, Victoria Hilkevitch. (1996). Relationships between adult siblings. In Ann Elisabeth Auhagen, & Maria von Salisch (Eds.), *The diversity of human relationships* (pp. 120–140). New York: Cambridge University Press.

Beebe, Steven A. et al. (2000). *Interpersonal communication: Relating to others* (2nd Canadian ed.). Scarborough: Allyn & Bacon.

Beebe, Steven A., & Masterson, John T. (2000). *Communicating in small groups: Principles and practices* (6th ed.). New York: Longman.

Behzadi, Kavous G. (1994, September). Interpersonal conflict and emotions in an Iranian cultural practice: *Qahr and Ashti. Culture, Medicine, and Psychiatry, 18,* 321–359.

Beier, Ernst. (1974). How we send emotional messages. *Psychology Today, 8,* 53–56.

Bell, Robert A., & Buerkel-Rothfuss, N.L. (1990). S(he) loves me, s(he) loves me not: Predictors of relational information-seeking in courtship and beyond. *Communication Quarterly, 38,* 64–82.

Berg, John H., & Archer, Richard L. (1983). The disclosure-liking relationship. *Human Communication Research, 10,* 269–281.

Berger, Charles R., & Bradac, James J. (1982). *Language and social knowledge: Uncertainty in interpersonal relations.* London: Edward Arnold.

Berger, Charles R., & Calabrese, Richard J. (1975, Winter). Some explorations in initial interaction and beyond: Toward a theory of interpersonal communication. *Human Communication Research, 1,* 99–112.

Bernstein, W. M., Stephan, W. G., & Davis, M. H. (1979). Explaining attributions for achievement: A path analytic approach. *Journal of Personality and Social Psychology, 37,* 1810–1821.

Berscheid, E., & Reis, H. T. (1998). Attraction and close relationships. In D. Gilbert, S. Fiske, & G. Lindzey (Eds.), *The handbook of social psychology* (4th ed., Vol. 2, pp. 193–281). New York: W. H. Freeman.

Bibby, R. (1990). *Mosaic madness: The poverty and potential of life in Canada.* Toronto: Stoddart.

Bierhoff, Hans W., & Klein, Renate. (1991, March). Dimensionen der Liebe: Entwicklung einer Deutschsprachigen Skala zur Erfassung von Liebesstilen. *Zeitschrift für Differentielle und Diagnostische Psychologie, 12,* 53–71.

Birdwhistell, Ray L. (1970). *Kinesics and context: Essays on body motion communication.* New York: Ballantine Books.

Bishop, Jerry E. (1993, April 7). New research suggests that romance begins by falling nose over heels in love. *Wall Street Journal,* B1.

Blake, R.R., & Mouton, J.S. (1985). *The managerial grid III* (3rd ed.). Houston, TX: Gulf Publishing.

Blieszner, Rosemary, & Adams, Rebecca G. (1992). *Adult friendship.* Thousand Oaks, CA: Sage.

Blood, Robert O., Jr. (1973). Resolving family conflicts. In Fred E. Jandt (Ed.), *Conflict resolution through communication.* New York: Harper & Row.

Blumstein, Philip, & Schwartz, Pepper. (1983). *American couples: Money, work, sex.* New York: Morrow.

Bochner, Arthur. (1978). On taking ourselves seriously: An analysis of some persistent problems and promising directions in interpersonal research. *Human Communication Research, 4,* 179–191.

Bochner, Arthur. (1984). The functions of human communication in interpersonal bonding. In Carroll C. Arnold & John Waite Bowers (Eds.), *Handbook of rhetorical and communication theory.* Boston: Allyn & Bacon.

Bochner, Arthur, & Kelly, Clifford. (1974). Interpersonal competence: Rationale, philosophy, and implementation of a conceptual framework. *Communication Education, 23,* 279–301.

Bochner, Arthur P., & Yerby, Janet. (1977). Factors affecting instruction in interpersonal competence. *Communication Education, 26,* 91–103.

Bochner, Stephen, & Hesketh, Beryl. (1994, June). Power distance, individualism/collectivism, and job-related attitudes in a culturally diverse work group. *Journal of Cross-Cultural Psychology, 25,* 233–257.

Bok, Sissela. (1978). *Lying: Moral choice in public and private life.* New York: Pantheon.

Bok, Sissela. (1983). *Secrets.* New York: Vintage Books.

Bommelje, R., Houston, J.M., & Smither, R. (2003). Personality characteristics of effective listeners: A five factor perspective. *International Journal of Listening, 17,* 32–46.

Bongiorno, R., & David, B. (2003). Gender and the categorization of powerful others. *Australian Journal of Psychology, 55,* 34.

Borden, George A. (1991). *Cultural orientation: An approach to understanding intercultural communication.* Englewood Cliffs, NJ: Prentice-Hall.

Bosmajian, Haig. (1974). *The language of oppression.* Washington, DC: Public Affairs Press.

Bourque, Nicole. (2001). Eating your words: Communicating with food in the Ecuadorian Andes. In Joy Hendry, & C.W. Watson, *An anthropology of indirect communication.* New York: Routledge.

Bower, B. (2001). Self-illusions come back to bite students. *Science News, 159,* 148.

Bransford, John D., Sherwood, Robert D., & Sturdevant, Tom. (1987). Teaching thinking and problem solving. In Joan Boykoff Baron & Robert J. Sternberg (Eds.), *Teaching thinking skills: Theory and practice,* pp. 162–181. New York: W. H. Freeman.

Bravo, Ellen, & Cassedy, Ellen. (1992). *The 9 to 5 guide to combating sexual harassment.* New York: Wiley.

Bresnahan, Mary I., & Cai, Deborah H. (1996, March/April). Gender and aggression in the recognition of interruption. *Discourse Processes, 21,* 171–189.

Bridges, Carl R. (1996, July). The characteristics of career achievement perceived by African American college administrators. *Journal of Black Studies, 26,* 748–767.

Briton, Nancy J., & Hall, Judith A. (1995, January). Beliefs about female and male nonverbal communication. *Sex Roles, 32,* 79–90.

Brody, Jane E. (1991, April 28). How to foster self-esteem. *New York Times Magazine,* 26–27.

Brody, Jane E. (1994, March 21). Notions of beauty transcend culture, new study suggests. *The New York Times,* p. A14.

Brody, Leslie R. (1985, June). Gender differences in emotional development: A review of theories and research. *Journal of Personality, 53,* 102–149.

Brown, A. (2003). Developing a productive, respectful manager–employee relationship. *Canadian HR Reporter, 7,* 10.

Brown, P. (1980). How and why are women more polite: Some evidence from a Mayan community. In S. McConnell-Ginet, R. Borker, & M. Furman (Eds.),

Women and language in literature and society (pp. 111–136). New York: Praeger.

Brown, Penelope, & Levinson, S.C. (1987). *Politeness: Some universals of language usage.* Cambridge, UK: Cambridge University Press.

Brownell, Judi. (1987). Listening: The toughest management skill. *Cornell Hotel and Restaurant Administration Quarterly, 27,* 64–71.

Brownell, J. (2002). *Listening: attitudes, principles, and skills* (2nd ed.). Boston: Allyn & Bacon.

Bruneau, Tom. (1985). The time dimension in intercultural communication. In Larry A. Samovar & Richard E. Porter (Eds.), *Intercultural communication: A reader* (4th ed., pp. 280–289). Belmont, CA: Wadsworth.

Bruneau, Tom. (1990). Chronemics: The study of time in human interaction. In Joseph A. DeVito, & Michael L. Hecht (Eds.), *The nonverbal communication reader* (pp. 301–311). Prospect Heights, IL: Waveland Press.

Buber, M. (1958). *I and thou* (2nd ed.). New York: Scribners.

Buck, Ross, & VanLear, C. Arthur (2002). Verbal and nonverbal communication: Distinguishing symbolic, spontaneous and pseudo-spontaneous nonverbal behavior. *Journal of Communication, 52,* 522–541.

Bull, R., & Ramsey, N. (1988). *The social psychology of facial appearance.* New York: Springer.

Buller, David B., & Aune, R. Kelly. (1992, Winter). The effects of speech rate similarity on compliance: Application of communication accommodation theory. *Western Journal of Communication, 56,* 37–53.

Buller, David B. et al. (1992, December). Social perceptions as mediators of the effect of speech rate similarity on compliance. *Human Communication Research, 19,* 286–311.

Burgoon, J.K., & Bacue, A.E. (2003). Nonverbal communication skills. In J.O. Greene & B.R. Burleson (Eds.), *Handbook of communication and social interaction skills* (pp. 179–220). Mahwah, NJ: Erlbaum.

Burgoon, J.K., Berger, C.R., & Waldron, V.R. (2000). Mindfulness and interpersonal communication. *Journal of Social Issues, 56,* 105–127.

Burgoon, J.K., & Hoobler, G.D. (2002). Nonverbal signals. In M.L. Knapp & J.A. Daly (Eds.). *Handbook of interpersonal communication* (3rd ed., pp. 240–299). Thousand Oaks, CA: Sage.

Burgoon, Judee K., Buller, David B., & Woodall, W. Gill. (1995). *Nonverbal communication: The unspoken dialogue* (2nd ed.). New York: McGraw-Hill.

Burleson, B.R. (2003). Emotional support skills. In J.O. Greene & B.R. Burleson (Eds.), *Handbook of communication and social interaction skills* (pp. 551–594). Mahwah, NJ: Erlbaum.

Burleson, Brant B., & Mortenson, Steven R. (2003). Explaining cultural differences in evaluation of emotional support behavior: Explaining the mediating

influence of value system and interaction goals. *Communication Research, 30,* 113–146.

Byers, E. Sandra, & Demmons, Stephanie. (1999, May). Sexual satisfaction and sexual self-disclosure within dating relationships. *Journal of Sex Research, 36,* 180–189.

Cameron, A., & Webster, J. (2005). Unintended consequences of emerging communication technologies: Instant messaging in the workplace. *Computers in Human Behaviour (21),* 1, pp. 85–103.

Canary, D.J., & Hause, K. (1993). Is there any reason to research sex differences in communication? *Communication Quarterly, 41,* 129–144.

Canary, Daniel, Cupach, William R., & Messman, Susan J. (1995). *Relationship conflict.* Thousand Oaks, CA: Sage.

Cappella, Joseph N. (1993, March–June). The facial feedback hypothesis in human interaction: Review and speculation. *Journal of Language and Social Psychology, 12,* 13–29.

Carli, Linda L. (1999, Spring). Gender, interpersonal power, and social influence. *Journal of Social Issues, 55,* 81–99.

Carroll, D. W. (1994). *Psychology of language.* (2nd ed.). Pacific Grove, CA: Brooks/Cole.

Cate, R. et al. (1982). Premarital abuse: A social psychological perspective. *Journal of Family Issues, 3,* 79–90.

Challenges facing workers in the future. (August, 1999). *Human Relations Focus, 76,* 6.

Chamberlain, L. (2005). Using Feng Shui in offices and stores. *New York Times,* July 10, p.11.

Chang, Hui-Ching, & Holt, G. Richard. (1996, Winter). The changing Chinese interpersonal world: Popular themes in interpersonal communication books in modern Taiwan. *Communication Quarterly, 44,* 85–106.

Chao, G.T., & Moon, H. The cultural mosaic: a metatheory for understanding the complexity of culture. *Journal of Applied Psychology,* 90(6):1128–1140.

Chen, Guo-Ming. (1992). Differences in self-disclosure patterns among Americans versus Chinese: A comparative study. Paper presented at the annual meeting of the Eastern Communication Association, Portland, ME.

Chen, Ling. (1993, Summer). Chinese and North Americans: An epistemological exploration of intercultural communication. *Howard Journal of Communications, 4,* 342–357.

Cherulnik, Paul D. (1979, August). Sex differences in the expression of emotion in a structured social encounter. *Sex Roles, 5,* 413–424.

Chin, Peggy Evan, & McConnell, Allen (2003). Do racial minorities respond in the same way to mainstream beauty standards? Social comparison processes in Asian, black and white women. *Self and Identity, 2,* 153–168.

Chin, P.P., & McConnell A.R. (2000). Stigma and self-protective strategies: social comparison and self-esteem in Asian, Black and White women. Paper presented at the 72nd Annual Meeting of the Midwestern Psychological Association, Chicago, IL.

Chiou, W.B., & Wan, C.S. (2006). Sexual self-disclosure in cyberspace among Taiwanese adolescents: Gender differences and the interplay of cyberspace and real life. *CyberPsychology & Behavior, 9,* 46–53.

Christie, Richard. (1970). Scale construction. In R. Christie, & F.L. Geis (Eds.), *Studies in Machiavellianism* (pp. 35–52). New York: Academic Press.

Chung, L.C., & Ting-Toomey, S. (1999, Spring). Ethnic identity and relational expectations among Asian Americans. *Communication Research Reports, 16,* 157–166.

Clement, Donald A., & Frandsen, Kenneth D. (1976). On conceptual and empirical treatments of feedback in human communication. *Communication Monographs, 43,* 11–28.

Coates, J., & Cameron, D. (1989). *Women, men, and language: Studies in language and linguistics.* London: Longman.

Coats, Erik J., & Feldman, Robert S. (1996, October). Gender differences in nonverbal correlates of social status. *Personality and Social Psychology Bulletin, 22,* 1014–1022.

Cohen, Joyce. (2001, January 18). On the Internet, love really is blind. *The New York Times,* pp. G1, G9.

Coleman, P. (2002). *How to say it for couples: Communicating with tenderness, openness, and honesty.* Paramus, NJ: Prentice-Hall.

Collier, Mary Jane. (1991). Conflict competence within African, Mexican, and Anglo American friendships. In Stella Ting-Toomey, & Felipe Korzenny (Eds.), *Cross-cultural interpersonal communication* (pp. 132–154). Newbury Park, CA: Sage.

Collins, Nancy L., & Miller, Lynn Carol. (1994, November). Self-disclosure and liking: A meta-analytic review. *Psychological Bulletin, 116,* 457–475.

Conference Board of Canada. (2003). www.conference-board.ca.

Cooley, Charles Horton. (1922). *Human nature and the social order* (rev. ed.). New York: Scribners.

Coon, Christine A., & Schwanenflugel, Paula J. (1996, July/August). Evaluation of interruption behavior by naive encoders. *Discourse Processes, 22,* 1–24.

Crocker, Jennifer. (2002). The contingencies of self-worth: Implications for self-regulation and psychological vulnerability. *Self and Identity, 1,* 143–150.

Cummings, J., Butler, B., & Kraut, R. (2002). The quality of online social relationships. *Communications of the ACM (45),* 7, pp. 103–108.

Darling A.L., & Dannels, D.P. (2003). Practicing engineers talk about the importance of talk: A report on the role of oral communication in the workplace. *Communication Education, 52,* 1–16.

D'Augelli, Anthony R. (1992, September). Lesbian and gay male undergraduates' experiences of harassment and fear on campus. *Journal of Interpersonal Violence, 7,* 383–395.

Davila, A. Culture in organizations of the computer industry: insights from Latin America. Unpublished personal correspondence.

Davis, Murray S. (1973). *Intimate relations.* New York: Free Press.

Davis, Ossie. (1973). The English language is my enemy. In Joseph A. DeVito (Ed.), *Language: Concepts and processes* (pp. 164–170). Englewood Cliffs, NJ: Prentice-Hall.

Deal, James E., & Wampler, Karen Smith. (1986). Dating violence: The primacy of previous experience. *Journal of Social and Personal Relationships, 3,* 457–471.

Deaux, K., & LaFrance, M. (1998). Gender. In D. Gilbert, S. Fiske, & G. Lindzey (Eds.), *The Handbook of Social Psychology, Vol. 1.* (4th ed., pp. 788–828). New York: Freeman.

de Bono, Edward. (1987). *The six thinking hats.* New York: Penguin.

DeCecco, John. (1988). Obligation versus aspiration. In John DeCecco (Ed.), *Gay relationships.* New York: Harrington Park Press.

DePaulo, Bella M. (1992). Nonverbal behavior and self-presentation. *Psychological Bulletin, 111,* 203–212.

Derlega, Valerian J. et al. (1987). Self-disclosure and relationship development: An attributional analysis. In Michael E. Roloff & Gerald R. Miller (Eds.), *Interpersonal processes: New directions in communication research* (pp. 172–187). Newbury Park, CA: Sage.

Derlega, V.J. et al. (1985). Gender effects in an initial encounter: A case where men exceed women in disclosure. *Journal of Social and Personal Relationships, 2,* 25–44.

Derwig, Tracey, & Munro, Murray J. (2001). What speaking rates do non-native speakers prefer? *Applied Linguistics, 22,* 324–334.

DeTurck, Mark A. (1987). When communication fails: Physical aggression as a compliance-gaining strategy. *Communication Monographs, 54,* 106–112.

DeVito, Joseph A. (1996). *Brainstorms: How to think more creatively about communication (or about anything else).* New York: Longman.

DeVito, Joseph A., & Hecht, Michael L. (Eds.). (1990). *The nonverbal communication reader.* Prospect Heights, IL: Waveland Press.

Dewey, John. (1910). *How we think.* Boston: Heath.

Dickinson, A. (1999, November 6). Assertiveness creates healthy mentality. *Chatham Daily News,* p. 11.

Difonzo, N., Bordia, P., & Rosnow, R.L. (1994). Reining in rumors. *Organizational Dynamics, 23,* 47–62.

Dillard, J.P., & Marshall, L.J. (2003). Persuasion as a social skill. In J.O. Greene & B.R. Burleson (Eds.), *Handbook of communication and social interaction skills* (pp. 479–514). Mahwah, NJ: Erlbaum.

Dindia, Kathryn. (2000). Sex differences in self-disclosure and self-disclosure and liking: Three meta-analyses reviewed. In Sandra Petronio (Ed.), *Balancing the secrets of private disclosures* (pp. 21–36). Mahwah, NJ: Lawrence Erlbaum Associates.

Dindia, Kathryn, & Fitzpatrick, Mary Anne. (1985). Marital communication: Three approaches compared. In Steve Duck & Daniel Perlman (Eds.), *Understanding personal relationships: An interdisciplinary approach* (pp. 137–158). Thousand Oaks, CA: Sage.

Dion, K., Berscheid, E., & Walster, E. (1972). What is beautiful is good. *Journal of Personality and Social Psychology, 24,* 285–290.

Dion, Karen K., & Dion, Kenneth L. (1993a, Fall). Individualistic and collectivist perspectives on gender and the cultural context of love and intimacy. *Journal of Social Issues, 49,* 53–69.

Dion, Kenneth L., & Dion, Karen K. (1993b, December). Gender and ethnocultural comparisons in styles of love. *Psychology of Women Quarterly, 17,* 464–473.

Dittman, David A. (1997, December). Reexamining curriculum. *The Cornell Hotel and Restaurant Administration Quarterly, 38,* 3.

Dolgin, Kim Gale, & Lindsay, Kristen Renee. (1999, September). Disclosure between college students and their siblings. *Journal of Family Psychology, 13,* 393–400.

Dolgin, Kim G., Meyer, Leslie, & Schwartz, Janet. (1991, September). Effects of gender, target's gender, topic, and self-esteem on disclosure to best and middling friends. *Sex Roles, 25,* 311–329.

Donohue, William A., & Kolt, Robert. (1992). *Managing interpersonal conflict.* Thousand Oaks, CA: Sage.

Douglas, W. (1994). The acquaintanceship process: An examination of uncertainty, information seeking, and social attraction during initial conversation. *Communication Research, 21,* 154–176.

Dovidio, J.F. et al. (2002). Why can't we just get along? Interpersonal biases and interracial distrust. *Cultural Diversity and Ethnic Minority Psychology, 8,* 88–102.

Drass, Kriss A. (1986, December). The effect of gender identity on conversation. *Social Psychology Quarterly, 49,* 294–301.

Dresser, Norine. (1996). *Multicultural manners: New rules of etiquette for a changing society.* New York: Wiley.

Drews, D.R., Allison, C.K., & Probst, J.R. (2000). Behavioral and self-concept differences in tattooed and non-tattooed college students. *Psychological Reports, 86,* 475–481.

Dreyfuss, Henry. (1971). *Symbol sourcebook.* New York: McGraw-Hill.

Duncan, S.D., Jr. (1972). Some signals and rules for taking speaking turns in conversation. *Journal of Personality and Social Psychology, 23,* 283–292.

Eden, Dov. (1992, Winter). Leadership and expectations: Pygmalion effects and other self-fulfilling prophecies in organizations. *Leadership Quarterly, 3,* 271–305.

Eder, D., & Enke, J.L. (1991). The structure of gossip: Opportunities and constraints on collective expression among adolescents. *American Sociological Review, 56,* 494–508.

Edwards, K., & Smith, E. (1996). A disconfirmation bias in the evaluation of arguments. *Journal of Personality and Social Psychology, 71,* 5–24.

Ehrenhaus, Peter. (1988, March). Silence and symbolic expression. *Communication Monographs, 55,* 41–57.

Ehrlich, Larry G. (2000). *Fatal words and friendly faces: Interpersonal communication in the twenty-first century.* New York: University Press of America Inc.

Einstein, E. (1995). Success or sabotage: Which self-fulfilling prophecy will the stepfamily create? In D.K. Huntley (Ed.), *Understanding stepfamilies: Implications for assessment and treatment.* Alexandria, VA: American Counseling Association.

Ekman, Paul. (1985a). Communication through nonverbal behavior: A source of information about an interpersonal relationship. In S.S. Tomkins & C.E. Izard (Eds.), *Affect, cognition and personality.* New York: Springer.

Ekman, Paul. (1985b). *Telling lies: Clues to deceit in the marketplace, politics, and marriage.* New York: Norton.

Ekman, Paul, & Friesen, Wallace V. (1969). The repertoire of nonverbal behavior: Categories, origins, usage, and coding. *Semiotica, 1,* 49–98.

Ekman, Paul, Friesen, Wallace V., & Ellsworth, Phoebe. (1972). *Emotion in the human face: Guidelines for research and an integration of findings.* New York: Pergamon Press.

Elfenbein, H.A., & Ambady, N. (2002). Is there an in-group advantage in emotion recognition? *Psychological Bulletin, 128,* 243–249.

Ellis, Albert. (1988). *How to stubbornly refuse to make yourself miserable about anything, yes, anything.* Secaucus, NJ: Lyle Stuart.

Ellis, Albert, & Harper, Robert A. (1975). *A new guide to rational living.* Hollywood, CA: Wilshire Books.

Elmes, Michael B., & Gemmill, Gary. (1990, February). The psychodynamics of mindlessness and dissent in small groups. *Small Group Research, 21,* 28–44.

Emanuel, E.J., Fairclough, D.L, Slutsman, J., & Emanuel, L.L. (2000, March 21). Understanding economic and other burdens of terminal illness: The experience of patients and their caregivers. *Annals of Internal Medicine, 132,* 451–459.

Ennis, Robert H. (1987). A taxonomy of critical thinking dispositions and abilities. In Joan Boykoff Baron, & Robert J. Sternberg (Eds.), *Teaching thinking skills: Theory and practice* (pp. 9–26). New York: W. H. Freeman.

Epstein, N., Pretzer, J.L., & Fleming, B. (1987). The role of cognitive appraisal in self-reports of marital communication. *Behavior Therapy, 18,* 51–69.

Eriksen, John, & Lindsay, Jo. (1999). Unmarried cohabitation and family policy: Norway and Australia compared. *Comparative Social Research, 18,* 79–103.

Exline, R.V., Ellyson, S.L., & Long, B. (1975). Visual behavior as an aspect of power role relationships. In P. Pliner, L. Krames, & T. Alloway (Eds.), *Nonverbal communication of aggression.* New York: Plenum.

Feldstein, Stanley, Dohm, Faith-Anne, & Crown, Cynthia L. (2001). Gender and speech rate in the perception of competence and social attractiveness. *Journal of Social Psychology, 141,* 785–806.

Fesko, S.L. (2001, November). Disclosure of HIV status in the workplace: Considerations and strategies. *Health and Social Work, 26,* 235–244.

Festinger, Leon. (1954). A theory of social comparison processes. *Human Relationships, 7,* 117–140.

Field, R.H.G. (1989, March). The self-fulfilling prophecy leader: Achieving the Metharme effect. *Journal of Management Studies, 26,* 151–175.

Fischer, Agneta H. (1993). Sex differences in emotionality: fact or stereotype? *Feminism and Psychology, 3,* 303–318.

Folger, Joseph P., Poole, Marshall Scott, & Stutman, Randall K. (1997). *Working through conflict: A communication perspective* (3rd ed.). Boston: Allyn & Bacon.

Forbes, G.B. (2001). College students with tattoos and piercings: Motives, family experiences, personality factors, and perceptions by others. *Psychological Reports, 89,* 774–786.

Franklin, C.W., & Mizell, C.A. (1995). Some factors influencing success among African-American men: A preliminary study. *Journal of Men's Studies, 3,* 191–204.

Fraser, Bruce. (1990, April). Perspectives on politeness. *Journal of Pragmatics, 14,* 219–236.

Fratiglioni, L. et al. (2000, April 15). Influence of social network on occurrence of dementia: A community-based longitudinal study. *Lancet, 355,* 1315–1319.

French, J.R.P., Jr., & Raven, B. (1968). The bases of social power. In Dorwin Cartwright & Alvin Zander (Eds.), *Group dynamics: Research and theory* (3rd ed., pp. 259–269). New York: Harper & Row.

Friedman, Joel, Boumil, Marcia Mobilia, & Taylor, Barbara Ewert. (1992). *Sexual harassment.* Deerfield Beach, FL: Health Communications.

Fritz, J. (1997). Men's and women's organizational peer relationships: A comparison. *The Journal of Business Communication, 1,* 27–47.

Frost, Catherine. (2003). How Prometheus is bound: Applying the Innis Method of communication to the internet. *Canadian Journal of Communication, 28,* 9–24.

Fuller, Linda K. (1995). *Media-mediated relationships: Straight and gay, mainstream and alternative perspectives.* New York: Harrington Park Press.

Furlow, F. Bryant. (1996, March/April). The smell of love. *Psychology Today, 29,* 38–45.

Furnham, Adrian, & Bochner, Stephen. (1986). *Culture shock: Psychological reactions to unfamiliar environments.* New York: Methuen.

Gable, Myron, Hollon, Charles, & Dangello, Frank. (1992, May). Managerial structuring of work as a moderator of the Machiavellianism and job performance relationship. *Journal of Psychology, 126,* 317–325.

Galvin, Kathleen, & Brommel, Bernard J. (2000). *Family communication: Cohesion and change* (5th ed.). Boston: Allyn & Bacon.

Gelles, R., & Cornell, C. (1985). *Intimate violence in families.* Newbury Park, CA: Sage.

Gibb, J. (1961). Defensive communication. *Journal of Communication, 11,* 141–148.

Giles, Howard et al. (1987). Speech accommodation theory: The first decade and beyond. In Margaret L. McLaughlin (Ed.), *Communication yearbook 10* (pp. 13–48). Thousand Oaks, CA: Sage.

Gillis, C. (2006). Cyberbullying is on the rise: Who can stop it?, *Maclean's (119),* 2.

Glucksberg, Sam, & Danks, Joseph H. (1975). *Experimental psycholinguistics: An introduction.* Hillsdale, NJ: Erlbaum.

Goffman, Erving. (1967). *Interaction ritual: Essays on face-to-face behavior.* New York: Pantheon.

Goldin-Meadow, S. et al. (2001). Gesture-psychological aspects. *Psychological Science, 12,* 516–522.

Goldsmith, M. (2003). Feed forward. *Executive Excellence, 2,* 15.

Goleman, Daniel. (1995a). *Emotional intelligence.* New York: Bantam.

Goleman, Daniel. (1995b, February 14). For man and beast, language of love shares many traits. *The New York Times,* pp. C1, C9.

Gonzalez, Alexander, & Zimbardo, Philip G. (1985). Time in perspective. *Psychology Today, 19,* 20–26. Reprinted in DeVito & Hecht (1990).

Goode, Erica. (2000, August 8). How culture molds habits of thought. *The New York Times,* pp. F1, F8.

Goodwin, Robin, & Lee, Iona. (1994, September). Taboo topics among Chinese and English friends: A cross-cultural comparison. *Journal of Cross-Cultural Psychology, 25,* 325–338.

Gordon, Thomas. (1975). *P.E.T.: Parent effectiveness training.* New York: New American Library.

Gottman, John M., & Carrere, S. (1994). Why can't men and women get along? Developmental roots and marital inequities. In D.J. Canary & Laura Stafford (Eds.), *Communication and relational maintenance* (pp. 203–229). San Diego, CA: Academic Press.

Gould, Stephen Jay. (1995, June 7). No more "wretched refuse." *The New York Times,* p. A27.

Government of Canada. The atlas of Canada: Families with children living at home. Retrieved September 21, 2003, from http://atlas.gc.ca/site/english/maps/people and society.

Graham, E.E. (1994). Interpersonal communication motives scale. In R.B. Rubin, P. Palmgreen, & H.E. Sypher (Eds.), *Communication research measures: A sourcebook* (pp. 211–216). New York: Guilford.

Graham, E.E., Barbato, C.A., & Perse, E.M. (1993). The interpersonal communication motives model. *Communication Quarterly, 41,* 172–186.

Graham, Jean Ann, & Argyle, Michael. (1975, December). The effects of different patterns of gaze, combined with different facial expressions, on impression formation. *Journal of Movement Studies, 1,* 178–182.

Graham, Jean Ann, Bitti, Pio Ricci, & Argyle, Michael. (1975, June). A cross-cultural study of the communication of emotion by facial and gestural cues. *Journal of Human Movement Studies, 1,* 68–77.

Grandey, Alicia A. (2000, January). Emotion regulation in the workplace: A new way to conceptualize emotional labor. *Journal of Occupational Health and Psychology, 5,* 95–110.

Gray, S., & Heatherington, L. (2003). The importance of social context in the facilitation of emotional expression in men. *Journal of Social and Clinical Psychology, 3,* 294.

Greif, Esther Blank. (1980). Sex differences in parent–child conversations. *Women's Studies International Quarterly, 3,* 253–258.

Grenny, J. (2005). Talking hi-tech at work. *T+D(59),* 11, pp.14–14.

Grice, H.P. (1975). Logic and conversation. In P. Cole, & J.L. Morgan (Eds.), *Syntax and semantics*: Vol. 3. Speech acts (pp. 41–58). New York: Seminar Press.

Griffin, Em, & Sparks, Glenn G. (1990). Friends forever: A longitudinal exploration of intimacy in same-sex friends and platonic pairs. *Journal of Social and Personal Relationships, 7,* 29–46.

Grosch, H. (1994). Dehumanizing the workplace. *Communications of the ACM (37),* 11, pp.122–122.

Gross, Ronald. (1991). *Peak learning.* Los Angeles: Jeremy P. Tarcher.

Gross, T., Turner, E., & Cederholm, L. (1987, June). Building teams for global operation. *Management Review,* 32–36.

Gu, Yueguo. (1990, April). Polite phenomena in modern Chinese. *Journal of Pragmatics, 14,* 237–257.

Gudykunst, W., & Nishida, T. (1984). Individual and cultural influence on uncertainty reduction. *Communication Monographs, 51,* 23–36.

Gudykunst, W. B. (1989). Culture and the development of interpersonal relationships. In J.A. Anderson (Ed.), *Communication yearbook 12* (pp. 315–354). Thousand Oaks, CA: Sage.

Gudykunst, W. B. (1991). Bridging differences: Effective intergroup communication. Newbury Park, CA: Sage.

Gudykunst, W. B. (1993). Toward a theory of effective interpersonal and intergroup communication: An anxiety/ uncertainty management (AUM) perspective. In R.L. Wiseman (Ed.), *Intercultural communication competence.* Thousand Oaks, CA: Sage.

Gudykunst, W., Yang, S., & Nishida, T. (1985). A cross-cultural test of uncertainty reduction theory: Comparisons of acquaintance, friend, and dating relationships in Japan, Korea, and the United States. *Human Communication Research, 11,* 407–454.

Gudykunst, W. B. (2002). Intercultural communication theories. In William B. Gudykunst & Bella Mody (Eds.), *International and intercultural communication* (2nd ed., pp. 183–206).

Gudykunst, W. B. (1994). *Bridging differences: Effective intergroup communication* (2nd ed.). Thousand Oaks, CA: Sage.

Gudykunst, W. B. (Ed.). (1983). *Intercultural communication theory: Current perspectives.* Newbury Park, CA: Sage.

Guimond, S. et al. (2006). Social comparison, self-stereotyping, and gender differences in self-construals. *Journal of Personality and Social Psychology, 90,* 221–242.

Haar, Birgit Friederike, & Krahe, Barbara. (1999, November). Strategies for resolving interpersonal conflicts in adolescence: A German–Indonesian comparison. *Journal of Cross Cultural Psychology, 30,* 667–683.

Haddad, T., & Lam, L. (1988). Canadian families: Men's involvement in family work: A case study of immigrant men in Toronto. *International Journal of Comparative Sociology, (XXIX) 3–4,* 269–281.

Haddock, P. (2003). Communicating personal power. *The American Salesman, 6,* 30.

Hajek, C., & Giles, H. (2003). New directions in intercultural communication competence: The process model. In J.O. Greene & B.R. Burleson (Eds.), *Handbook of communication and social interaction skills* (pp. 935–957). Mahwah, NJ: Erlbaum.

Hall, Edward T. (1959). *The silent language.* Garden City, NY: Doubleday.

Hall, Edward T. (1966). *The hidden dimension.* Garden City, NY: Doubleday.

Hall, Edward T. (1976). *Beyond culture.* Garden City, NY: Doubleday.

Hall, Edward T. (1983). *The dance of life: The other dimension of time.* New York: Doubleday.

Hall, Edward T., & Hall, Mildred Reed. (1971, June). The sounds of silence. *Playboy,* pp. 139–140, 204, 206.

Hall, Edward T., & Hall, Mildred Reed. (1987). *Hidden differences: Doing business with the Japanese.* New York: Doubleday.

Hall, J.A. (1998). How big are nonverbal sex differences?

The case of smiling and sensitivity to nonverbal cues. In D.J. Canary & K. Dindia (Eds.) *Sex differences and similarities in communication: Critical essays and empirical investigations of sex and gender in interaction* (pp. 155–178). Mahwah, NJ: Erlbaum.

Hall, Joan Kelly. (1993). Tengo una bomba: The paralinguistic and linguistic conventions of the oral practice chismeando. *Research on Language and Social Interaction, 26,* 55–83.

Hall, Judith A. (1984). *Nonverbal sex differences.* Baltimore: Johns Hopkins University Press.

Hall, Judith A. (1996, Spring). Touch, status, and gender at professional meetings. *Journal of Nonverbal Behavior, 20,* 23–44.

Hall, P. (2005). Interprofessional teamwork: Professional cultures as barriers. *Journal of Interprofessional Care,* Supplement 1, 188–196.

Hanke, B. (2005). Connected, or what it means to live in a network society. *Canadian Journal of Communication, 30,* 160–162.

Handy, C.B. (1985). *Understanding organizations* (3rd ed.). Harmondsworth: Penguin Books.

Haney, William (1973). *Communication and organizational behavior: Text and cases* (3rd ed.). Homewood, IL: Irwin.

Harkin, J. (2003). *Mobilisation: The growing public interest in mobile technology.* O2 and Demos.

Harris, Judy. (1995, March). Educational telecomputing projects: Interpersonal exchanges. *Computing Teacher, 22,* 60–64.

Harris, Thomas E. (2002). *Applied organizational communication: Principles and pragmatics for future practice.* Mahwah, NJ: Lawrence Erlbaum Associates.

Harrison J.R., & Carroll, G.R. (2006). *Culture and demography in organizations.* Princeton University Press.

Hart, Fiona. (1990, September/December). The construction of masculinity in men's friendships: Misogyny, heterosexism and homophobia. *Resources for Feminist Research, 19,* 60–67.

Hart, R.P., Carlson, R.E., & Eadie, W.F. (1980). Attitudes toward communication and the assessment of rhetorical sensitivity. *Communication Monographs, 47,* 1–22.

Hatfield, Elaine, & Rapson, Richard L. (1992). Similarity and attraction in close relationships. *Communication Monographs, 59,* 209–212.

Hatfield, Elaine, & Rapson, Richard L. (1996). *Love and sex: Cross-cultural perspectives.* Boston: Allyn & Bacon.

Havlena, William J., Holbrook, Morris B., & Lehmann, Donald R. (1989, Summer). Assessing the validity of emotional typologies. *Psychology and Marketing, 6,* 97–112.

Hayakawa, S.I., & Hayakawa, A.R. (1989) *Language in thought and action* (5th ed.). New York: Harcourt Brace Jovanovich.

Hays, Robert B. (1989). The day-to-day functioning of close versus casual friendships. *Journal of Social and Personal Relationships, 6,* 21–37.

Heasley, John B., Babbitt, Charles E., & Burbach, Harold J. (1995, Fall). Gender differences in college students' perceptions of "fighting words." *Sociological Viewpoints, 11,* 30–40.

Hecht, Michael. (1978a). The conceptualization and measurement of interpersonal communication satisfaction. *Human Communication Research, 4,* 253–264.

Hecht, Michael. (1978b). Toward a conceptualization of communication satisfaction. *Quarterly Journal of Speech, 64,* 47–62.

Hecht, Michael L., Collier, Mary Jane, & Ribeau, Sidney. (1993). *African American communication: Ethnic identity and cultural interpretation.* Thousand Oaks, CA: Sage.

Hendrick, Clyde, & Hendrick, Susan. (1990). A relationship-specific version of the love attitudes scale. In J.W. Heulip (Ed.), *Handbook of replication research in the behavioral and social sciences* [special issue]. *Journal of Social Behavior and Personality, 5,* 239–254.

Hendrick, Clyde et al. (1984). Do men and women love differently? *Journal of Social and Personal Relationships, 1,* 177–195.

Hess, Eckhard H. (1975). *The tell-tale eye.* New York: Van Nostrand Reinhold.

Hess, Ursula et al. (1992, May). The facilitative effect of facial expression on the self-generation of emotion. *International Journal of Psychophysiology, 12,* 251–265.

Hewitt, J.P. (1998). *The myth of self-esteem: Finding happiness and solving problems in America.* New York: St. Martin's Press.

Hewitt, John, & Stokes, Randall. (1975). Disclaimers. *American Sociological Review, 40,* 1–11.

Hickson, Mark L., & Stacks, Don W. (1993). *NVC: Nonverbal communication: Studies and applications* (3rd ed.). Dubuque, IA: William C. Brown.

Hofstede, Geert. (1997). *Cultures and organizations: Software of the mind.* New York: McGraw-Hill.

Hoft, Nancy L. (1995). *International technical communication: How to export information about high technology.* New York: Wiley.

Hogg, Michael. (2002). *Handbook of social psychology.* London: Sage.

Holland, Carol A., & Fletcher, Janet. (2000). The effect of speech rate at natural borders on older adults' memory for auditorially presented stories. *Australian Journal of Psychology, 52,* 149–154.

Holmes, J. (2003). Small talk at work: potential problems for workers with an intellectual disability. *Research on Language and Social Interaction, 36,* 65–84.

Holmes, J., & Marra, M. (2002). Having a laugh at work: how humour contributes to workplace culture. *Journal of Pragmatics,* 34:1683–1710.

Holmes, Janet. (1986). Compliments and compliment responses in New Zealand English. *Anthropological Linguistic, 28,* 485–508.

Holmes, Janet. (1995). *Women, men and politeness.* New York: Longman.

Horenstein Diaz-Peralta V., & Downey, J.L. (2003). A cross-cultural investigation of self-disclosure. *North American Journal of Psychology, 5,* 373–386.

Horsfall, J. (1998). Structural impediments to effective communication. *Australian and New Zealand Journal of Mental Health Nursing, 7,* 74–80.

Horton, Robert S. (2003). Similarity and attractiveness in social perception: Differentiating between biases for the self and the beautiful. *Self and Identity, 2,* 137–153.

Hunter, D., Gambell, T., & Randhawa, B. (2005). Gender gaps in group listening and speaking: Issues in social constructivist approaches to teaching and learning. *Educational Review, 57,* 329–355.

Hupka, R. (1981). Cultural determinants of jealousy. *Alter-native Lifestyles, 4,* 310–356.

Hurston, C., & Wilson, G. (1978). Body talk—The unspoken language. *Management World, 7,* 14.

Ikemi, Akira, & Kubota, Shinya. (1996, Winter). Humanistic psychology in Japanese corporations: Listening and the small steps of change. *Journal of Humanistic Psychology, 36,* 104–121.

Imhof, Margaret. (2002). The eye of the beholder: Children's perception of good and poor listening behavior. *International Journal of Listening, 16,* 40–57.

Imhof, M. (2004). Who are we as we listen? Individual listening profiles in varying contexts. *International Journal of Listening, 18,* 36–45.

Infante, Dominic A. (1988). *Arguing constructively.* Prospect Heights, IL: Waveland Press.

Infante, Dominic A., & Rancer, Andrew S. (1982). A conceptualization and measure of argumentativeness. *Journal of Personality Assessment, 46,* 72–80.

Infante, Dominic A., Rancer, Andrew S., & Jordan, Felecia F. (1996, March). Affirming and nonaffirming style, dyad sex, and the perception of argumentation and verbal aggression in an interpersonal dispute. *Human Communication Research, 22,* 315–334.

Infante, Dominic A. et al. (1990, Fall). Verbal aggression in violent and nonviolent marital disputes. *Communication Quarterly, 38,* 361–371.

Infante, Dominic A., & Wigley, C.J. (1986). Verbal aggressiveness: An interpersonal model and measure. *Communication Monographs, 53,* 61–69.

Insel, Paul M., & Jacobson, Lenore F. (Eds.) (1975). *What do you expect? An inquiry into self-fulfilling prophecies.* Menlo Park, CA: Cummings.

Irizarry, C.A. (2004). Face and the female professional: A thematic analysis of face-threatening communication in the workplace. *Qualitative Research Reports in Communication, 5,* 15–21.

Irvine, M. (2006). Instant, text messaging takeover. *Calgary Herald.* July 19, 2006, pp. A13.

Jackson, Linda A., & Ervin, Kelly S. (1992, August). Height stereotypes of women and men: The liabilities of shortness for both sexes. *Journal of Social Psychology, 132,* 433–445.

Jacobsen, Thomas. (2003). Kandinsky's questionnaire revisited: Fundamental correspondence of basic colors and forms? *Perceptual & Motor Skills, 95,* 903–913.

Jacobson, D. (1999). Impression formation in cyberspace: online expectations and offline experiences in text-based virtual communities. *Journal of Computer Mediated Communication, 5,* np.

Jaksa, James A., & Pritchard, Michael S. (1994). *Communication ethics: Methods of analysis* (2nd ed.). Belmont, CA: Wadsworth.

Jandt, Fred E. (2000). *Intercultural communication* (3rd ed.). Thousand Oaks, CA: Sage.

Janusik, Laura. (2002). Teaching listening: What do we do? What should we do? *International Journal of Listening, 16,* 5–40.

Jaworski, Adam. (1993). *The power of silence: Social and pragmatic perspectives.* Thousand Oaks, CA: Sage.

Johannesen, Richard L. (1974, Winter). The functions of silence: A plea for communication research. *Western Speech, 38,* 25–35.

Johansson, Warren, & Percy, William A. (1994). *Outing: Shattering the conspiracy of silence.* New York: Harrington Park Press.

Johnson, C.E. (1987). An introduction to powerful and powerless talk in the classroom. *Communication Education, 36,* 167–172.

Joiner, Tomas E. (1994). Contagious depression: Existence, specificity to depressed symptoms, and the role of reassurance seeking. *Journal of Personality and Social Psychology, 67,* 287–296.

Joinson, A.N. (2001). Self-disclosure in computer-mediated communication: The role of self-awareness and visual anonymity. *European Journal of Social Psychology, 31,* 177–192.

Jones, Edward E. et al. (1984). *Social stigma: The psychology of marked relationships.* New York: W.H. Freeman.

Jones, Stanley, & Yarbrough, A. Elaine. (1985). A naturalistic study of the meanings of touch. *Communication Monographs, 52,* 19–56. (A version of this paper appears in DeVito & Hecht, 1990.)

Jones, Stanley E. (1999). Contact codes: Proxemics and hepatics. In Laura K. Guerrero, & Joseph A. DeVito (Eds.), *The nonverbal communication reader: Classic and contemporary readings* (2nd ed., pp. 175–123).

Jourard, Sidney M. (1968). *Disclosing man to himself.* New York: Van Nostrand Reinhold.

Jourard, Sidney M. (1971). *Self-disclosure.* New York: Wiley.

Kagan, Jerome. (2002). *Surprise, uncertainty and mental structures.* Cambridge, Mass.: Harvard University Press.

Kanner, Bernice. (1989, April 3). Color schemes. *New York,* pp. 22–23.

Kaya, Naz, & Weber, Margaret J. (2003). Territorial behavior in residence halls: A cross-culture study. *Environment & Behavior, 35,* 400–414.

Kearney, P. et al. (1984). Power in the classroom IV: Alternatives to discipline. In R. N. Bostrom (Ed.), *Communication yearbook 8* (pp. 724–746). Thousand Oaks, CA: Sage.

Kearney, P. et al. (1985). Power in the classroom III: Teacher communication techniques and messages. *Communication Education, 34,* 19–28.

Keenan, Elinor Ochs. (1976, April). The universality of conversational postulates. *Language in Society, 5,* 67–80.

Kennedy, C.W., & Camden, C.T. (1988). A new look at interruptions. *Western Journal of Speech Communication, 47,* 45–58.

Keren, M. (2004). Blogging and the politics of melancholy. *Canadian Journal of Communication, 29,* 5–23.

Keyes, Ralph. (1980). *The height of your life.* New York: Warner Books.

Kiesler, Sara, & Sproull, Lee. (1992, June). Group decision making and communication technology. [Special issue: Group Decision Making], *Organizational Behavior and Human Decision Processes, 52,* 96–123.

Kiewitz, C. et al. (1997). Cultural differences in listening style preferences: A comparison of adults in Germany, Israel, and the United States. *International Journal of Public Opinion Research, 9,* 233–247.

Kim, Heejung S., & Markus, Hazel Rose (2002). Freedom of speech and freedom of silence: An analysis of talking as a cultural practice. In Richard A. Shwede, & Martha Minow (Eds.), *Engaging cultural differences: The multicultural challenge in liberal democracies* (pp. 432–452). New York: Sage.

Kim, Young Yun. (1988). Communication and acculturation. In Larry A. Samovar, & Richard E. Porter (Eds.), *Intercultural communication: A reader* (5th ed., pp. 344–354). Belmont, CA: Wadsworth.

Kim, Young Yun. (1991). Intercultural communication competence. In Stella Ting-Toomey, & Felipe Korzenny (Eds.), *Cross-cultural interpersonal communication* (pp. 259–275). Newbury Park, CA: Sage.

King, Robert, & DiMichael, Eleanor. (1992). *Voice and diction.* Prospect Heights, IL: Waveland Press.

Kito, M. (2005). Self-disclosure in romantic relationships and friendships among American and Japanese college students. *Journal of Social Psychology, 145,* 127–140.

Kleinfield, N.R. (1992, October 25). The smell of money. *The New York Times,* pp. C1, C8.

Kleinke, Chris L. (1986). *Meeting and understanding people.* New York: W.H. Freeman.

Kleinman, S. (2002). Why sexist language matters. *Qualitative Sociology, 25,* 299–304.

Klineberg, O., & Hull, W.F. (1979). *At a foreign university: An international study of adaptation and coping.* New York: Praeger.

Knapp, Mark L., & Hall, Judith. (1996). *Nonverbal behavior in human interaction.* (3rd ed.). New York: Holt, Rinehart, & Winston.

Knapp, Mark et al. (1973). The rhetoric of goodbye: Verbal and nonverbal correlates of human leave-taking. *Speech Monographs, 40,* 182–198.

Knapp, Mark L., & Vangelisti, Anita. (2000). *Interpersonal communication and human relationships* (4th ed.). Boston: Allyn & Bacon.

Knobloch, S. et al. (2003). Imagery effects on the selective reading of internet newsmagazines. *Communication Research,* 30(1), 3–29.

Koberg, Don, & Bagnall, Jim. (1976a). *The universal traveler.* Los Altos, CA: William Kaufmann.

Koberg, Don, & Bagnall, Jim. (1976b). *Values tech: A portable school for discovering and developing decision-making skills for self-enhancing potentials.* Los Altos, CA: William Kaufmann.

Kochman, Thomas. (1981). *Black and white: Styles in conflict.* Chicago: University of Chicago Press.

Komarovsky, M. (1964). *Blue-collar marriage.* New York: Random House.

Korda, M. (1975). *Power! How to get it, how to use it.* New York: Ballantine.

Kornblum, J. (2006). Parents are tech-savvier. *USA Today,* May 18, 2006, p. 13d.

Korzybski, A. (1933). *Science and sanity.* Lakeville, CT: The International Non-Aristotelian Library.

Kposow, Augustine J. (2000, April). Marital status and suicide in the National Longitudinal Mortality Study. *Journal of Epidemiology and Community Health, 54,* 254–261.

Kramarae, Cheris. (1974a). Folklinguistics. *Psychology Today, 8,* 82–85.

Kramarae, Cheris. (1974b). Stereotypes of women's speech: The word from cartoons. *Journal of Popular Culture 8,* 624–630.

Kramarae, Cheris. (1977). Perceptions of female and male speech. *Language and speech, 20,* 151–161.

Kramarae, Cheris. (1981). *Women and men speaking.* Rowley, MA: Newbury House.

Krivonos, Paul D., & Knapp, Mark L. (1975). Initiating communication: What do you say when you say hello? *Central States Speech Journal, 26,* 115–125.

Kuhn, D., Weinstock, M., & Flaton, R. (1994). How well do jurors reason? Competence dimensions of individual variation in a juror reasoning task. *Psychological Science, 5,* 289–296.

Kurdek, Lawrence A. (1994, November). Areas of conflict for gay, lesbian, and heterosexual couples: What couples argue about influences relationship satisfaction. *Journal of Marriage and the Family, 56*, 923–934.

Kurland, N.B., & Pelled, L.H. (2000). Passing the word: toward a model of gossip and power in the workplace. *Academy of Management Review, 25*, 428–439.

Labott, Susan M. et al. (1991, September/November). Social reactions to the expression of emotion. *Cognition and Emotion, 5*, 397–417.

LaFrance, Marie. (2002). Smile boycotts and other body politics. *Feminism and Psychology, 12*, 319–323.

Laing, Milli. (1993, Spring). Gossip: Does it play a role in the socialization of nurses. *Journal of Nursing Scholarship, 25*, 37–43.

Laing, Ronald D., Phillipson, H., & Lee, A. Russell. (1966). *Interpersonal perception*. New York: Springer.

Lakoff, R. (1975). *Language and women's place*. New York: Harper & Row.

Langer, Ellen J. (1989). *Mindfulness*. Reading, MA: Addison-Wesley.

Lanzetta, J.T., Cartwright-Smith, J., & Kleck, R.E. (1976). Effects of nonverbal dissimulations on emotional experience and autonomic arousal. *Journal of Personality and Social Psychology, 33*, 354–370.

L'Arche Canada. (2005). More than Inclusion. www.larche.ca.

Larsen, Randy J., Kasimatis, Margaret, & Frey, Kurt. (1992, September). Facilitating the furrowed brow: An unobtrusive test of the facial feedback hypothesis applied to unpleasant affect. *Cognition and Emotion, 6*, 321–338.

Larson, Charles U. (1998). *Persuasion: Reception and responsibility* (8th ed.). Belmont, CA: Wadsworth.

Lauer, C. (2004). Cross with wireless. *Modern Healthcare (34)*, 51, pp. 20–20.

Lea, Martin, & Spears, Russell. (1995). Love at first byte? Building personal relationships over computer networks. In Julia T. Wood, & Steve Duck (Eds.), *Under-studied relationships: Off the beaten track* (pp. 197–233). Thousand Oaks, CA: Sage.

Leaper, Campbell et al. (1995). Self-disclosure and listener verbal support in same-gender and cross-gender friends' conversations. *Sex Roles, 33*, 387–404.

Leaper, Campbell, & Holliday, Heithre. (1995, September). Gossip in same-gender and cross-gender friends' conversations. *Personal Relationships, 2*, 237–246.

Leathers, Dale G. (1997). *Successful nonverbal communication: Principles and applications* (2nd ed.). New York: Macmillan.

Lee, Fiona. (1993, July). Being polite and keeping mum: How bad news is communicated in organizational hierarchies. *Journal of Applied Social Psychology, 23*, 1124–1149.

Lee, John Alan. (1976). *The colors of love*. New York: Bantam.

Lee, Karen. (2000, November 1). Information overload threatens employee productivity. *Employee Benefit News*, Securities Data Publishing, p. 1.

Leon, Joseph J. et al. (1994, February). Love styles among university students in Mexico. *Psychological Reports, 74*, 307–310.

Leung, Kwok. (1988, March). Some determinants of conflict avoidance. *Journal of Cross-Cultural Psychology, 19*, 125–136.

Lever, Janet. (1995, August 22). The 1995 advocate survey of sexuality and relationships: The women, lesbian sex survey. *The Advocate, 687/688*, 22–30.

Levesque, M.J., Nave, C.S., & Lowe, C.A. (2006). Towards an understanding of gender differences in sexual interest. *Psychology of Women Quarterly, 30*, 150–158.

Levine, D. (2000). Virtual attraction: What rocks your boat. *CyberPsychology and Behavior, 3*, 565–573.

LeVine, R., & Bartlett, K. (1984). Pace of life, punctuality, and coronary heart disease in six countries. *Journal of Cross-Cultural Psychology, 15*, 233–255.

LeVine, R. et al. (1994). Love and marriage in eleven cultures. Unpublished manuscript. California State University, Fresno. Cited in Hatfield & Rapson (1996).

Lewin, Catharina, & Herlitz, Agneta. (2002). Sex differences in face recognition—women's faces make the difference. *Brain & Cognition, 50*, 121–128.

Lewis, David. (1989). *The secret language of success*. New York: Carroll & Graf.

Lindeman, Marjaana, Harakka, Tuija, & Keltikangas-Jarvinen, Liisa. (1997, June). Age and gender differences in adolescents' reactions to conflict situations: Aggression, prosociality, and withdrawal. *Journal of Youth and Adolescence, 26*, 339–351.

Lister, Larry. (1991, June). Men and grief: A review of research. *Smith College Studies in Social Work, 61*, 220–235.

Lloyd, S. R. (2001). *Developing positive assertiveness* (3rd ed.). Menlo Park, CA: Crisp Publications.

Lock, C. (2004). Deception detection. *Science News, 166*, 72–73.

Lustig, Myron W., & Koester, Jolene. (1999). *Intercultural competence: Interpersonal communication across cultures* (3rd ed.). New York: HarperCollins.

Ma, Karen. (1996). *The modern Madame Butterfly: Fantasy and reality in Japanese cross-cultural relationships*. Rutland, VT: Charles E. Tuttle.

Ma, Ringo. (1992, Summer). The role of unofficial intermediaries in interpersonal conflicts in the Chinese culture. *Communication Quarterly, 40*, 269–278.

Macgeorge, Erina L. et al. (2003). Skill deficit or differential motivation? Testing alternative explanations for gender differences in providing emotional support. *Communication Research, 3*, 272–303.

Mackey, R.A., Diemer, M.A., & O'Brien, B.A. (2000). Psychological intimacy in the lasting relationships of heterosexual and same-gender couples. *Sex Roles, 43,* 201–227.

MacLachlan, James. (1979). What people really think of fast talkers. *Psychology Today, 13,* 113–117.

Macmillan, P. (2001). *The performance factor: Unlocking the secrets of teamwork.* Broadman and Holman.

Maggio, Rosalie. (1997). *Talking about people: A guide to fair and accurate language.* Phoenix, AZ: Oryx Press.

Malandro, Loretta A., Barker, Larry, & Barker, Deborah Ann. (1989). *Nonverbal communication* (2nd ed.). New York: Random House.

Manes, Joan, & Wolfson, Nessa. (1981). The compliment formula. In Florian Coulmas (Ed.), *Conversational routine* (pp. 115–132). The Hague: Mouton.

Manniche, Erik. (1991). Marriage and non-marriage cohabitation in Denmark. *Family Reports, 20,* 9–35.

Mao, LuMing Robert. (1994, May). Beyond politeness theory: "Face" revisited and renewed. *Journal of Pragmatics, 21,* 451–486.

Marshall, Evan. (1983). *Eye language: Understanding the eloquent eye.* New York: New Trend.

Marshall, Linda L., & Rose, Patricia. (1987). Gender, stress and violence in the adult relationships of a sample of college students. *Journal of Social and Personal Relationships, 4,* 299–316.

Martin, C. (2006). The sixteen types at a glance. Centre for Applications of Psychological Types. http:// www. capt.org/mbti-assessment/type-descriptions.htm.

Martin, G.N. (1998). Human encephalographic (EEG) response to olfactory stimulation: Two experiments using the aroma of food. *International Journal of Psychophysiology, 30,* 287–302.

Martin, Matthew M., & Anderson, Carolyn M. (1995, Spring). Roommate similarity: Are roommates who are similar in their communication traits more satisfied? *Communication Research Reports, 12,* 46–52.

Martin, Matthew M., Anderson, Carolyn M., & Mottet, Timothy P. (1999, May). Perceived understanding and self-disclosure in the stepparent-stepchild relationship. *Journal of Psychology, 133,* 281–290.

Marwell, G., & Schmitt, D. R. (1967). Dimensions of compliance-gaining behavior: An empirical analysis. *Sociometry, 39,* 350–364.

Mathews, A., & Mackintosh, B. (2000). Induced emotional interpretation bias and anxiety. *Journal of Abnormal Psychology, 4,* 602.

Matsumoto, David. (1991, Winter). Cultural influences on facial expressions of emotion. *Southern Communication Journal, 56,* 128–137.

Matsumoto, David. (1994). *People: Psychology from a cultural perspective.* Pacific Grove, CA: Brooks/Cole.

Matsumoto, D. (1996). *Culture and psychology.* Pacific Grove, CA: Brooks/Cole.

Matsumoto, David, & Kudoh, T. (1993). American-Japanese cultural differences in attributions of personality based on smiles. *Journal of Nonverbal Behavior, 17,* 231–243.

McBroom, William H., & Reed, Fred W. (1992, June). Toward a reconceptualization of attitude-behavior consistency. *Social Psychology Quarterly, 55* [Special issue. Theoretical Advances in Social Psychology], 205–216.

McCann, R.M., & Giles, H. (2006). Communicating with people of different ages in the workplace: Thai and American data. *Human Communication Research* 32(1): 74–108.

McCarthy, Michael J. (1991). *Mastering the information age.* Los Angeles: Jeremy P. Tarcher.

McConatha, Jasmin-Tahmaseb, Lightner, Eileen, & Deaner, Stephanie L. (1994, September). Culture, age, and gender as variables in the expression of emotions. *Journal of Social Behavior and Personality, 9,* 481–488.

McCroskey, James C. (1997). *Introduction to rhetorical communication* (7th ed.). Englewood Cliffs, NJ: Prentice-Hall.

McCroskey, James C. (1998). *Why we communicate the ways we do: A communibiological perspective.* Boston, MA: Allyn & Bacon.

McCroskey, James C., Booth-Butterfield, S., & Payne, S.K. (1989). The impact of communication apprehension on college student retention and success. *Communication Quarterly, 37,* 100–107.

McCroskey, James C., & Wheeless, Lawrence. (1976). *Introduction to human communication.* Boston: Allyn & Bacon.

McGill, Michael E. (1985). *The McGill report on male intimacy.* New York: Harper & Row.

McLaughlin, Margaret L. (1984). *Conversation: How talk is organized.* Newbury Park, CA: Sage.

McLoyd, Vonnie, & Wilson, Leon. (1992, August). Telling them like it is: The role of economic and environmental factors in single mothers' discussions with their children. *American Journal of Community Psychology, 20,* 419–444.

McMahan, Elizabeth, & Day, Susan. (1984). *The writer's rhetoric and handbook* (2nd ed.). New York: McGraw-Hill.

McNamee, S., & Gergen, K. J. (Eds.). (1999). *Relational responsibility: Resources for sustainable dialogue.* Thousand Oaks, CA: Sage.

McNatt, D.B. (2001). Ancient Pygmalion joins contemporary management: A meta-analysis of the result. *Journal of Applied Psychology, 85,* 314–322.

McQuillen, J. (2003). The influence of technology on the initiation of interpersonal relationships. *Education (123)* 3. Academic Search Premier.

Mendoza, Louis. (1995). *Ethos, ethnicity, and the electronic classroom: A study in contrasting educational environments.* Paper presented at the 46th annual meeting of the

Conferences on College Composition and Communication, Washington, DC.

Merton, Robert K. (1957). *Social theory and social structure.* New York: Free Press.

Mesch, G., & Talmud, I. (2006). The quality of online and offline social relationships: The role of multiplexity and duration of social relationships. *Information Society (22)*, 3, pp. 137–148.

Messick, R.M., & Cook, K.S. (Eds.). (1983). *Equity theory: Psychological and sociological perspectives.* New York: Praeger.

Messmer, Max. (1999, August). Skills for a new millennium: Accounting and financial professionals. *Strategic Finance Magazine,* 10ff.

Metts, Sandra. (1989, May). An exploratory investigation of deception in close relationships. *Journal of Social and Personal Relationships, 6,* 159–179.

Metts, S., & Planalp, S. (2002). Emotional communication. In M.L. Knapp & J.A. Daly (Eds.) (pp. 339–373) *Handbook of interpersonal communication* (3rd ed.), Thousand Oaks, CA: Sage.

Meyer, Janet R. (1994, Spring). Effect of situational features on the likelihood of addressing face needs in requests. *Southern Communication Journal, 59,* 240–254.

Michalko, Michael. (1991). *Thinkertoys: A handbook of business creativity for the 90s.* Berkeley, CA: Ten Speed Press.

Midooka, Kiyoski. (1990, October). Characteristics of Japanese-style communication. *Media Culture and Society, 12,* 47–489.

Miller, Gerald R., & Parks, Malcolm R. (1982). Communication in dissolving relationships. In Steve Duck (Ed.), *Personal relationships: Vol. 4. Dissolving personal relationships* (pp. 127–154). New York: Academic Press.

Miller, LaRonda R. (1997, December). Better ways to think and communicate. *Association Management, 49,* 71–73.

Miller, Mark J., & Wilcox, Charles T. (1986). Measuring perceived hassles and uplifts among the elderly. *Journal of Human Behavior and Learning, 3,* 38–46.

Miller, R. (2003). Blogging for business. *EContent (26),* 10, pp. 30–34.

Miller, S., & Weckert, J. (2000). Privacy, the workplace, and the internet. *Journal of Business Ethics (28),* 3, pp. 255–265.

Miller, Sally Downham. (1999). *Mourning and dancing: A memoir of grief and recovery.* Deerfield Beach, FL: Health Communications.

Miner, Horace. (1956). Body ritual among the Nacirema. *American Anthropologist, 58,* 503–507.

Mir, Montserrat. (1993). *Direct requests can also be polite.* Paper presented at the annual meeting of the International Conference on Pragmatics and Language Learning, Champaign, IL.

Moghaddam, Fathali M., Taylor, Donald M., & Wright, Stephen C. (1993). *Social psychology in cross-cultural perspective.* New York: W. H. Freeman.

Mohr, C.D., & Kenny, D.A. (2006). The how and why of disagreement among perceivers: an exploration of person models. *Journal of Experimental Psychology, 42,* 337–349.

Molloy, John. (1977). *The woman's dress for success book.* Chicago: Follett.

Montagu, Ashley. (1971). *Touching: The human significance of the skin.* New York: Harper & Row.

Moon, Dreama G. (1966, Winter). Concepts of "culture": Implications for intercultural communication research. *Communication Quarterly, 44,* 70–84.

Moon, H., & Williams, P. (2000). Managing cross cultural business ethics. *Journal of Business Ethics, 27,* 105–115.

Moore, A. et al. (1996). College teacher immediacy and student ratings of instruction. *Communication Education, 45,* 29–39.

Morris, Desmond. (1977). *Manwatching: A field guide to human behavior.* New York: Abrams.

Morrow, Gregory D., Clark, Eddie M., & Brock, Karla F. (1995, August). Individual and partner love styles: Implications for the quality of romantic involvements. *Journal of Social and Personal Relationships, 12,* 363–387.

Murstein, Bernard I., Merighi, Joseph R., & Vyse, Stuart A. (1991, Spring). Love styles in the United States and France: A cross-cultural comparison. *Journal of Social and Clinical Psychology, 10,* 37–46.

Naifeh, Steven, & Smith, Gregory White. (1984). *Why can't men open up? Overcoming men's fear of intimacy.* New York: Clarkson N. Potter.

Nelson, Adie, & Robinson, Barrie R. (2002). *Gender in Canada.* Toronto: Prentice Hall.

Neugarten, Bernice. (1979). Time, age, and the life cycle. *American Journal of Psychiatry, 136,* 887–894.

Nichols, Michael P. (1995). *The lost art of listening: How learning to listen can improve relationships.* New York: Guilford Press.

Nichols, Ralph. (1961). Do we know how to listen? Practical helps in a modern age. *Communication Education, 10,* 118–124.

Nichols, Ralph, & Stevens, Leonard. (1957). *Are you listening?* New York: McGraw-Hill.

Nickerson, Raymond S. (1987). Why teach thinking? In Joan Boykoff Baron & Robert J. Sternberg (Eds.), *Teaching thinking skills: Theory and practice* (pp. 27–37). New York: W. H. Freeman.

Noble, Barbara Presley. (1994, August 14). The gender wars: Talking peace. *The New York Times,* p. 21.

Noller, Patricia. (1982). Couple communication and marital satisfaction. *Australian Journal of Sex, Marriage, and Family, 3,* 69–75.

Noller, Patricia, & Fitzpatrick, Mary Anne. (1993). *Communication in family relationships.* Englewood Cliffs, NJ: Prentice-Hall.

Nordhaus-Bike, Anne M. (1999, August). Learning to lead. *Hospitals & Health Networks, 73,* 28ff.

Norton, Robert, & Warnick, Barbara. (1976). Assertiveness as a communication construct. *Human Communication Research, 3,* 62–66.

Notarius, Clifford I., & Herrick, Lisa R. (1988). Listener response strategies to a distressed other. *Journal of Social and Personal Relationships, 5,* 97–108.

Oatley, Keith, & Duncan, Elaine. (1994). The experience of emotions in everyday life. *Cognition and Emotion, 8,* 369–381.

Ober, C. et al. (1997). *American Journal of Human Genetics, 61,* 494–496.

Oberg, K. (1960). Cultural shock: Adjustment to new cultural environments. *Practical Anthropology, 7,* 177–182.

O'Hair, D., Cody, M.J., & McLaughlin, M.L. (1981). Prepared lies, spontaneous lies, Machiavellianism, and nonverbal communication. *Human Communication Research, 7,* 325–339.

Olaniran, Bolanle A. (1994, February). Group performance in computer-mediated and face-to-face communication media. *Management Communication Quarterly, 7,* 256–281.

Ong, C.S., & Lai, J.Y. (2006). Gender differences in perceptions and relationships among dominants of e-learning acceptance. *Computers in Human Behaviour, 22,* 816–829.

Otaki, Midori et al. (1986). Maternal and infant behavior in Japan and America. *Journal of Cross-Cultural Psychology, 17,* 251–268.

Parker, Rhonda G., & Parrott, Roxanne. (1995). Patterns of self-disclosure across social support networks: Elderly, middle-aged, and young adults. *International Journal of Aging and Human Development, 41,* 281–297.

Patton, Bobby R., Giffin, Kim, & Patton, Eleanor Nyquist. (1989). *Decision-making group interaction* (3rd ed.). New York: HarperCollins.

Pearson, J.C. et al. (2003). *Human communication.* New York: McGraw Hill.

Pearson, Judy C., West, Richard, & Turner, Lynn H. (1995). *Gender and communication* (3rd ed.). Dubuque, IA: William C. Brown.

Pearson, J.C., & Spitzberg, B.H. (1990). *Interpersonal communication: Concepts, components, and contexts* (2nd ed.). Dubuque, IA: William C. Brown.

Pease, Allan, & Pease, Barbara (2006). *The definitive book of body language, the hidden meaning behind people's gestures and expressions.* Bantam.

Penfield, Joyce (Ed.). (1987). *Women and language in transition.* Albany: State University of New York Press.

Pennebacker, James W. (1991). *Opening up: The healing power of confiding in others.* New York: Avon.

Peterson, Candida C. (1996). The ticking of the social clock: Adults' beliefs about the timing of transition events. *International Journal of Aging and Human Development, 42,* 189–203.

Petrocelli, William, & Repa, Barbara Kate. (1992). *Sexual harassment on the job.* Berkeley, CA: Nolo Press.

Phlegar, Phyllis. (1995). *Love online: A practical guide to digital dating.* Reading, MA: Addison-Wesley.

Pilkington, C.J., & Richardson, D.R. (1988). Perceptions of risk in intimacy. *Journal of Social and Personal Relationships, 5,* 503–508.

Pilkington, C.J., & Woods, S.P. (1999). Risk in intimacy as a chronically accessible schema. *Journal of Social and Personal Relationships, 16,* 249–263.

Pilkington, Neil W., & D'Augelli, Anthony R. (1995, January). Victimization of lesbian, gay, and bisexual youth in community settings. *Journal of Community Psychology, 23,* 34–56.

Piot, Charles D. (1993, June). Secrecy, ambiguity, and the everyday in Kabre culture. *American Anthropologist, 95,* 353–370.

Pittenger, R.E., Hockett, C.F., & Danehy, J.J. (1960). *The first five minutes.* Ithaca, NY: Paul Martineau.

Plant, A., Hyde, J., & Devine, P. (2000). The gender stereotyping of emotions. *Psychology of Women Quarterly, 1,* 81.

Plutchik, Robert. (1980). *Emotion: A psycho-evolutionary synthesis.* New York: Harper & Row.

Porter, R.H., & Moore, J.D. (1981). Human kin recognition by olfactory cues. *Physiology and Behavior, 27,* 493–495.

Proctor, Russell F. (1991). *An exploratory analysis of responses to owned messages in interpersonal communication.* Unpublished doctoral dissertation, Bowling Green State University, Ohio.

Raney, Rebecca Fairley. (2000, May 11). Study finds Internet of social benefit to users. *The New York Times,* p. G7.

Rankin, Paul. (1929). *Listening ability.* Proceedings of the Ohio State Educational Conference's ninth annual session.

Raven, R., Centers, C., & Rodrigues, A. (1975). The bases of conjugal power. In R.E. Cromwell, & D.H. Olson (Eds.), *Power in families* (pp. 217–234). New York: Halsted Press.

Rector, M., & Neiva, E. (1996). Communication and personal relationships in Brazil. In W. B. Gudykunst, S. Ting-Toomey, & T. Nishida (Eds.), *Communication in personal relationships across cultures* (pp. 156–173). Thousand Oaks, CA: Sage.

Reed, Mark D. (1993, Fall). Sudden death and bereavement outcomes: The impact of resources on grief, symptomatology and detachment. *Suicide and Life-Threatening Behavior, 23,* 204–220.

Reisman, John. (1979). *Anatomy of friendship.* Lexington, MA: Lewis.

Reisman, John M. (1981). Adult friendships. In Steve Duck, & Robin Gilmour (Eds.), *Personal relationships: Vol. 2: Developing personal relationships* (pp. 205–230). New York: Academic Press.

Renner, M. (1993, May 3). Assert yourself to a more satisfying career. *The Gazetteer,* p. C6.

Rheingold, H. (2002). *Smartmobs: The next social revolution.* Cambridge, MA: Persons Publishing.

Rich, Andrea L. (1974). *Interracial communication.* New York: Harper & Row.

Richmond, Virginia P. et al. (1984). Power strategies in organizations: Communication techniques and messages. *Human Communication Research, 11,* 85–108.

Richmond, Virginia P., & McCroskey, James C. (1996). *Communication: Apprehension, avoidance, and effectiveness* (4th ed.). Scottsdale, AZ: Gorsuch Scarisbrick.

Riggio, Ronald E. (1987). *The charisma quotient.* New York: Dodd, Mead.

Righton, B. (2006). Hey, boss, your pants are on fire. *Maclean's,* June 5, p. 42.

Robbins, Stephen P., & Hunsaker, Phillip L. (2003). *Training in interpersonal skills: Tips for managing people at work* (3rd ed.). New Jersey: Prentice Hall.

Roberts, Carlos A., & Aruguete, Mara S. (2000, February). Task and socioemotional behaviors of physicans: A test of reciprocity and social interaction theories in analogue physician-patient encounters. *Social Science and Medicine, 50,* 309–315.

Roberts, Moss (Ed. and Trans., with the assistance of C.N. Tay.). (1979). *Chinese fairy tales and fantasies.* New York: Pantheon.

Robertson, R.G. (2005). Rumours: constructive or corrosive. *Journal of Medical Ethics, 31,* 540–541.

Rochester, J. (2002). Becoming a professional—education is only the beginning. IEEE-USA *Today's Engineering Online,* www.todaysengineer.org/archives/te_archives/feb02/tel.asp.

Rokach, A. (1998). The relation of cultural background to the causes of loneliness. *Journal of Social and Clinical Psychology, 17,* 75–88.

Rokach, A., & Brock, H. (1995). The effects of gender, marital status, and the chronicity and immediacy of loneliness. *Journal of Social Behavior and Personality, 19,* 833–848.

Roger, Derek, & Nesshoever, Willfried. (1987, September). Individual differences in dyadic conversational strategies: A further study. *British Journal of Social Psychology, 26,* 247–255.

Rogers, Carl, & Farson, Richard. (1981). Active listening. In Joseph A. DeVito (Ed.), *Communication: Concepts and processes* (3rd ed., pp. 137–147). Englewood Cliffs, NJ: Prentice-Hall.

Rose, Amanda J., & Asher, Steven R. (1999, January). Children's goals and strategies in response to conflicts within a friendship. *Developmental Psychology, 35,* 69–79.

Rosen, Emanuel. (1998, October). Think like a shrink. *Psychology Today,* 54–59.

Rosenfeld, Lawrence. (1979). Self-disclosure avoidance: Why I am afraid to tell you who I am. *Communication Monographs, 46,* 63–74.

Rosengren, A. et al. (1993, October 19). Stressful life events, social support, and mortality in men born in 1933. *British Medical Journal.* Cited in Goleman (1995a).

Rosenthal, Robert, & Jacobson, L. (1968). *Pygmalion in the classroom.* New York: Holt, Rinehart and Winston.

Rosnow, R.L. (1988). Rumor as communication: A contextualist approach. *Journal of Communication, 38,* 12–28.

Rosnow, R.L., & Fine, G.A. (1976). *Rumor and gossip: The social psychology of hearsay.* New York: Elsevier.

Rosnow, Ralph L. (1977, Winter). Gossip and marketplace psychology. *Journal of Communication, 27,* 158–163.

Ross, J.L. (1995). Conversational pitchbacks: Helping couples bat 1000 in the game of communications. *Journal of Family Psychotherapy, 6,* 83–86.

Rowland-Morin, P.A., & Carroll, J.G. (1990). Verbal communication skills and patient satisfaction: A study of doctor–patient interviews. *Evaluation and the Health Professions, 13,* 168–185.

Ruben, Brent D. (1985). Human communication and cross-cultural effectiveness. In Larry A. Samovar, & Richard E. Porter (Eds.), *Intercultural communication: A reader* (4th ed., pp. 338–346). Belmont, CA: Wadsworth.

Rubenstein, Carin. (1993, June 10). Fighting sexual harassment in schools. *The New York Times,* p. C8.

Rubenstein, Carin, & Shaver, Philip. (1982). *In search of intimacy.* New York: Delacorte.

Rubin, D.L., Yang, H., & Porte, M. (2000). A comparison of self-reported self-disclosure among Chinese and North Americans. In S. Petronio (Ed.), *Balancing the secrets of private disclosure* (pp. 215–230). Mahwah, NJ: Lawrence Erlbaum.

Rubin, Rebecca B., Fernandez-Collado, C., & Hernandez-Sampieri, R. (1992). A cross-cultural examination of interpersonal communication motives in Mexico and the United States. *International Journal of Intercultural Relations, 16,* 145–157.

Rubin, Rebecca B., & Martin, M.M. (1994). Development of a measure of interpersonal communication competence. *Communication Research Reports, 11,* 33–44.

Rubin, Rebecca B., Perse, Elizabeth M., & Barbato, Carole A. (1988). Conceptualization and measurement of interpersonal communication motives. *Human Communication Research, 14,* 602–628.

Rubin, Rebecca B., & Rubin, Alan M. (1992). Antecedents of interpersonal communication motivation. *Communication Quarterly, 40,* 315–317.

Rubin, Zick. (1973). *Liking and loving: An invitation to social psychology.* New York: Holt, Rinehart & Winston.

Rundquist, Suellen. (1992, November). Indirectness: A gender study of flaunting Grice's maxims. *Journal of Pragmatics, 18,* 431–449.

Saboonchi F., Lundh, L.G., & Ost, L.G. (1999). Perfectionism and self-consciousness in social phobia and panic disorder with agoraphobia. *Behaviour Research and Therapy, 37 (9),* 799–808.

Sadker, Myra Pollac, & Sadker, D.C. (1994). *Failing at fairness: How American schools cheat girls.* New York: Scribner.

Sadr, Javid, Jarudi, Izzat, & Sinha, Pawan. (2003). The role of eyebrows in face recognition. *Perception, 32,* 285–293.

Salamensky, S.I. (2001). Dangerous talk: Phenomenology, performativity, cultural crisis. In Author (Ed.), *Talk, talk, talk: The cultural life of everyday conversation* (pp. 16–35). New York: Routledge.

Salekin, Randall T. et al. (1995, Spring). Influencing jurors' perceptions of guilt: Expression of emotionality during testimony. *Behavioral Sciences and the Law, 13,* 293–305.

Samovar, Larry A., & Porter, Richard E. (Eds.). (1991). *Communication between cultures.* Belmont, CA: Wadsworth.

Sanders, Judith A., Wiseman, Richard L., & Matz, S. Irene. (1991). Uncertainty reduction in acquaintance relationships in Ghana and the United States. In Stella Ting-Toomey & Felipe Korzenny (Eds.), *Cross-cultural interpersonal* (pp. 79–98). Thousand Oaks, CA: Sage.

Sarwer, David B. et al. (1993, June). Sexual aggression and love styles: An exploratory study. *Archives of Sexual Behavior, 22,* 265–275.

Saunders, Carol S., Robey, Daniel, & Vaverek, Kelly A. (1994, June). The persistence of status differentials in computer conferencing. *Human Communication Research, 20,* 443–472.

Scandura, T. (1992). Mentorship and career mobility: An empirical investigation. *Journal of Organizational Behavior, 13,* 169–174.

Schaap, C., Buunk, B., & Kerkstra, A. (1988). Marital conflict resolution. In Patricia Noller & Mary Anne Fitzpatrick (Eds.), *Perspectives on marital interaction* (pp. 203–244). Philadelphia: Multilingual Matters.

Schachter, Stanley. (1964). The interaction of cognitive and physiological determinants of emotional state. In Leonard Berkowitz (Ed.), *Advances in experimental social psychology* (Vol. 1). New York: Academic Press.

Scheetz, L. Patrick. (1995). *Recruiting trends 1995–1996: A study of 527 businesses, industries, and governmental agencies employing new college graduates.* East Lansing, MI: Collegiate Employment Research Institute, Michigan State University.

Scherer, K.R. (1986). Vocal affect expression. *Psychological Bulletin, 99,* 143–165.

Schmidt, Tracy O., & Cornelius, Randolph R. (1987). Self-disclosure in everyday life. *Journal of Social and Personal Relationships, 4,* 365–373.

Scholl, J.C., & O'Hair, D. (2005). Uncovering beliefs about deceptive communication. *Communication Quarterly, 53,* 377–399.

Schwartz, Marilyn, & The Task Force on Bias-Free Language of the Association of American University Presses. (1995). *Guidelines for bias-free writing.* Bloomington: Indiana University Press.

Scott, C.R., & Rains, S.A. (2005). Anonymous communication in organizations. *Management Communication Quarterly, 19,* 157–197.

Shafer, K. (1993). Talk in the middle: Two conversational skills for friendship. *English Journal, 1,* 53.

Shaffer, David R., Pegalis, Linda J., & Bazzini, Doris G. (1996, May). When boy meets girl (revisited): Gender, gender role orientation, and prospect of future interaction as determinants of self-disclosure among same- and opposite-sex acquaintances. *Personality and Social Psychology Bulletin, 22,* 495–506.

Shtern, J. (2005). The e-connected world: Risks and opportunities. Canadian *Journal of Communication, 30,* 441–444.

Shuter, Robert. (1990, Spring). The centrality of culture. *Southern Communication Journal, 55,* 237–249.

Siegert, John R., & Stamp, Glen H. (1994, December). "Our first big fight" as a milestone in the development of close relationships. *Communication Monographs, 61,* 345–360.

Signorile, Michelangelo. (1993). *Queer in America: Sex, the media, and the closets of power.* New York: Random House.

Silvia, Paul (2002). Self-awareness and the regulation of emotional intensity. *Self and Identity, 1,* 3–11.

Sipior, J,. & Ward, B. (1999). The dark side of employee email. *Communications of the ACM (42),* 7, pp. 88–95.

Slade, Margot. (1995, February 19). We forgot to write a headline: But it's not our fault. *The New York Times,* p. 5.

Smyth, J. (2003, June 20). Bullying guidelines to go beyond schoolyard. *National Post,* p. A2.

Snyder, C.R. (1984). Excuses, excuses. *Psychology Today, 18,* 50–55.

Snyder, C.R., Higgins, Raymond L., & Stucky, Rita J. (1983). *Excuses: Masquerades in search of grace.* New York: Wiley.

Solomon, G.B. et al. (1996). The self-fulfilling prophecy in college-basketball: Implications for effective coaching. *Journal of Applied Sport Psychology, 8,* 44–59.

Sommers, S. (1984). Reported emotions and conventions of emotionality among college students. *Journal of Personality and Social Psychology, 46,* 207–215.

Sorenson, Paula S., Hawkins, Katherine, & Sorenson, Ritch L. (1995, August). Gender, psychological type and conflict style preferences. *Management Communication Quarterly, 9*, 115–126.

Soukup, C. (1999). The gendered interactional patterns of computer-mediated chatrooms: A critical ethnographic study. *The Information Society (15)*, pp.169–176.

Spangler, Diane L., & Burns, David D. (2000, Winter). Is it true that men are from Mars and women are from Venus? A test of gender differences in dependency and perfectionism. *Journal of Cognitive Psychotherapy, 13*, 339–357.

Spencer, S.J., Fein, S., & Lomore, C.D. (2001). Maintaining one's self-image vis-à-vis others: The role of self-affirmation in the social evaluation of the self. *Motivation and Emotion, 25*, 41–64.

Spitzberg, B.H. (1991). Intercultural communication competence. In L.A. Samovar & R. E. Porter (Eds.), *Intercultural communication: A reader* (pp. 353–365). Belmont, CA: Wadsworth.

Spitzberg, Brian H., & Cupach, William R. (1989). *Handbook of interpersonal competence research*. New York: Springer.

Spitzberg, Brian H., & Hecht, Michael L. (1984). A component model of relational competence. *Human Communication Research, 10,* 575–599.

Sprecher, Susan. (1987). The effects of self-disclosure given and received on affection for an intimate partner and stability of the relationship. *Journal of Social and Personal Relationships, 4,* 115–127.

Sprecher, S., & Hendrick, S.S. (2004). Self-disclosure in intimate relationships: Associations with individual and relationship characteristics over time. *Journal of Social and Clinical Psychology, 6,* 857–877.

Sriram, K., & Shyam, S.S. (2006). The psychological appeal of personalized content in web portals: Does customization affect attitudes and behaviour? *Journal of Communication, 56,* 110–132.

Srivastava, L. (2005). Mobile phones and the evolution of social behaviour. *Behaviour and Information Technology (24)*, 2, 111–129.

Steil, Lyman K., Barker, Larry L., & Watson, Kittie W. (1983). *Effective listening: Key to your success*. Reading, MA: Addison-Wesley.

Steiner, Claude. (1981). *The other side of power*. New York: Grove.

Steinfatt, Thomas M. (1987). Personality and communication: Classic approaches. In James C. McCroskey & John A. Daly (Eds.), *Personality and interpersonal communication* (pp. 42–126). Thousand Oaks, CA: Sage.

Stephan, Cookie White, & Stephan, Walter G. (1992, Winter). Reducing intercultural anxiety through intercultural contact. *International Journal of Intercultural Relations, 16,* 89–106.

Stephan, W., Stephan, C., & De Vargas, M. (1996). Emotional expression in Costa Rica and the United States. *Journal of Cross-Cultural Psychology, 2,* 147–162.

Stephan, Walter G., & Stephan, Cookie White. (1985). Intergroup anxiety. *Journal of Social Issues, 41,* 157–175.

Sternberg, Robert J. (1987). Questions and answers about the nature and teaching of thinking skills. In Joan Boykoff Baron & Robert J. Sternberg (Eds.), *Teaching thinking skills: Theory and practice* (pp. 251–259). New York: W.H. Freeman.

Strecker, Ivo. (1993). Cultural variations in the concept of "face." *Multilingua, 12,* 119–141.

Suominen, T., Kovasin, M., & Ketola, O. (1997). Nursing culture—some viewpoints. *Journal of Advanced Nursing, 25,* 186–190.

Swim, J.K., Mallett, R., & Stangor, C. (2004). Understanding subtle sexism: Detection and use of sexist language. *Sex Roles, 51,* 117–128.

Szapocznik, Jose. (1995, January). Research on disclosure of HIV status: Cultural evolution finds an ally in science. *Health Psychology, 14,* 4–5.

Tae-Seop, Lim. (2002). Language and verbal communication across cultures. In William B. Gudykunst, & Bella Mody (Eds.), *Handbook of international and intercultural communication* (2nd ed., pp. 69–87).

Tannen, Deborah. (1990). *You just don't understand: Women and men in conversation*. New York: Morrow.

Tannen, Deborah. (1994a). *Gender and discourse*. New York: Oxford University Press.

Tannen, Deborah. (1994b). *Talking from 9 to 5*. New York: Morrow.

Tannen, Deborah, & Alatis, James E. (Eds.) (2003). *Language, culture and the real world: Discourse and beyond*. Washington, DC: Georgetown University Press.

Tarnove, Elizabeth J. (1988). *Effects of sexist language on the status and self-concept of women*. Paper presented at the annual meeting of the Association for Education in Journalism and Mass Communication, Portland, OR.

Tate, Marsha, & Allen, Vallerie. (2003). Integrating distinctly Canadian elements into television drama: A formula for success or failure? The *Due South* experience. *Canadian Journal of Communication, 28,* 67–83.

Tetley, Deborah, & Seskul, Tony. (2003, June 15). Council startled by tale, closed ranks around Dar. *Calgary Herald*.

Tidwell, L. & Walther, J. (2002). Computer-Mediated Communication Effects on Disclosure, Impressions, and Interpersonal Evaluations. *Human Communication Research (28)*, 3, p. 317–348.

Timmerman, L.J. (2002). Comparing the production of power in language on the basis of sex. In M. Allen & R.W. Preiss (Eds.), *Interpersonal communication research: Advances through meta-analysis* (pp. 117–88). Mahwah, NJ: Erlbaum.

Ting-Toomey, Stella. (1985). Toward a theory of conflict and culture. *International and Intercultural Communication Annual, 9,* 71–86.

Ting-Toomey, Stella. (1986). Conflict communication styles

in black and white subjective cultures. In Young Yun Kim (Ed.), *Interethnic communication: Current research* (pp. 75–88). Thousand Oaks, CA: Sage.

Titlow, Karen I., Rackoff, Jonathan E., & Emanuel, Ezekiel J. (1999). What will it take to restore patient trust? *Business & Health, 17,* (6A), 61–64.

Torbiorn, I. (1982). *Living abroad.* New York: Wiley.

Trager, George L. (1958). Paralanguage: A first approximation. *Studies in Linguistics, 13,* 1–12.

Trager, George L. (1961). The typology of paralanguage. *Anthropological Linguistics, 3,* 17–21.

Traxler, A.J. (1980). Let's get gerontologized!: Developing a sensitivity to aging. Springfield, IL: Illinois Department of Aging.

Tyler, Patrick E. (1996, July 11). Crime (and punishment) rages anew in China. *The New York Times,* pp. A1, A8.

Tzanne, Angeliki. (2000). *Talking at cross-purposes.* Philadelphia: John Benjamins Publishing Company.

VanHyning, Memory. (1993). *Crossed signals: How to say no to sexual harassment.* Los Angeles: Infotrends Press.

Veenendall, Thomas L., & Feinstein, Marjorie C. (1995). *Let's talk about relationships: Cases in study* (2nd ed.). Prospect Heights, IL: Waveland Press.

Victor, David. (1992). *International business communication.* New York: HarperCollins.

Victor, David A. (2001). A cross-cultural perspective on gender. In Laurie P. Arliss, & Deborah J. Borisoff (Eds.), *Women and men communicating: Challenges and changes* (2nd ed., pp. 65–77). Prospect Heights, IL: Waveland Press Inc.

Vishwanath, A. (2003). Comparing online information effects. A cross-cultural comparison of online information and uncertainty avoidance. *Communication Research, 30,* 579–598.

Wade, Carole, & Tavris, Carol. (1990). *Learning to think critically: The case of close relationships.* New York: HarperCollins.

Wade, Carole, & Tavris, Carol. (1998). *Psychology* (5th ed.). New York: Longman.

Wade, N. (2002, January 22). Scent of a man is linked to a woman's selection. *New York Times,* p. F2.

Wallis, C. (2006). The multitasking generation. *Time Canada (167),* 13.

Walsh, M. (2005). Gendered endeavours: Women and the reshaping of business culture. *Women's History Review, 14,* 181–202.

Walster, E., Walster, G.W., & Berscheid, E. (1978). *Equity: Theory and research.* Boston: Allyn & Bacon.

Watzlawick, Paul. (1977). *How real is real? Confusion, disinformation, communication: An anecdotal introduction to communications theory.* New York: Vintage.

Watzlawick, Paul. (1978). *The language of change: Elements of therapeutic communication.* New York: Basic Books.

Watzlawick, Paul, Beavin, Janet Helmick, & Jackson, Don D. (1967). *Pragmatics of human communication: A study of interactional patterns, pathologies, and paradoxes.* New York: Norton.

Weathers, M.D., Frank, E.M., & Spell, L.A. (2002). Differences in the communication of affect: Members of the same race versus members of a different race. *Journal of Black Psychology, 28,* 66–77.

Weinberg, Harry L. (1959). *Levels of knowing and existence.* New York: Harper & Row.

Weiner, Bernard, Russell, Dan, & Lerman, David. (1979). Affective consequences of causal ascriptions. In J.H. Harvey, W.J. Ickes, & R.F. Kidd (Eds.), *New directions in attribution research* (Vol. 2). Hillsdale, NJ: Erlbaum.

Weinstein, Eugene A., & Deutschberger, Paul. (1963). Some dimensions of altercasting. *Sociometry, 26,* 454–466.

Werrbach, Gail B., Grotevant, Harold D., & Cooper, Catherine R. (1990, October). Gender differences in adolescents' identity development in the domain of sex role concepts. *Sex Roles, 23,* 349–362.

West, Candace, & Zimmerman, Don H. (1977, June). Women's place in everyday talk: Reflections on parent–child interaction. *Social Problems, 24,* 521–529.

Westwood, R.I., Tang, F.F., & Kirkbride, P.S. (1992, Summer). Chinese conflict behavior: Cultural antecedents and behavioral consequences. *Organizational Development Journal, 10,* 13–19.

Wetzel, Patricia J. (1988). Are "powerless" communication strategies the Japanese norm? *Language in Society, 17,* 555–564.

Whalen-Bell, S. (2003). The strategic power of positive language. *Chartered Accountants Journal of New Zealand, 6,* 69.

Wheeless, Lawrence R., & Grotz, Janis. (1977). The measurement of trust and its relationship to self-disclosure. *Human Communication Research, 3,* 250–257.

Wiederman, Michael W., & Hurd, Catherine. (1999, April). Extradyadic involvement during dating. *Journal of Social and Personal Relationships, 16,* 265–274.

Wilkins, B.M., & Andersen, P.A. (1991). Gender differences and similarities in management communication: A meta-analysis. *Management Communication Quarterly, 5,* 6–35.

Wilmot, William W. (1987). *Dyadic communication* (3rd ed.). New York: Random House.

Wilson, V.J., McCormack, B.G., & Ives, G. (2005). Understanding the workplace culture of a special care nursery. *Journal of Advanced Nursing, 50* (1): 27038.

Winquist, Lynn A., Mohr, Cynthia D., & Kenny, David A. (1998, September). The female positivity effect in the perception of others. *Journal of Research in Personality, 32,* 370–388.

Witcher, S. Karene. (1999, August 9–15). Chief executives

in Asia find listening difficult. *Asian Wall Street Journal Weekly, 21,* 11.

Witt, P.L., & Wheeless, L.R. (2001). An experimental study of teachers' verbal and nonverbal immediacy and students' affective and cognitive learning. *Communication Education, 50,* 327–342.

Wolfson, Nessa. (1988). The bulge: A theory of speech behaviour and social distance. In J. Fine (Ed.), *Second language discourse: A textbook of current research.* Norwood, NJ: Ablex.

Won-Doornink, Myong-Jin. (1991). Self-disclosure and reciprocity in South Korean and U.S. male dyads. In Stella Ting-Toomey & Felipe Korzenny (Eds.), *Cross-cultural interpersonal communication* (pp. 116–131). Thousand Oaks, CA: Sage.

Wood, Julia T. (1994). *Gendered lives: Communication, gender, and culture.* Belmont, CA: Wadsworth.

Worthington, Deborah, L. (2001). Exploring juror's listening processes: The effect of listening style preference on juror decision making. *International Journal of Listening, 15,* 20–38.

Wright, John W. (1995). *The universal almanac 1995.* Kansas City, MO: Andrews & McMeel.

Wright, Paul H. (1978). Toward a theory of friendship based on a conception of self. *Human Communication Research, 4,* 196–207.

Wright, Paul H. (1984). Self-referent motivation and the intrinsic quality of friendship. *Journal of Social and Personal Relationships, 1,* 115–130.

Wright, Paul H. (1988). Interpreting research on gender differences in friendship: A case for moderation and a plea for caution. *Journal of Social and Personal Relationships, 5,* 367–373.

Wrighter, Carl. (1972), *I can sell you anything.* New York: Ballantine.

Yamaguchi, S. (2004). Nursing culture of an operating theatre in Italy. *Nursing and Heath Sciences, 6,* 261–269.

Yau-fair Ho, D. et al. (2001). The dialogical self: Converging East–West constructions. *Culture and Psychology, 7,* 393–408.

Yovetich, Nancy A., & Drigotas, Stephen M. (1999, September). Secret transmission: A relative intimacy hypothesis. *Personality and Social Psychology Bulletin, 25,* 1135–1146.

Yun, Hum. (1976). The Korean personality and treatment considerations. *Social Casework, 57,* 173–178.

Zimmerman, Don H., & West, Candace. (1975). Sex roles, interruptions and silences in conversations. In B. Thorne & N. Henley (Eds.), *Language and sex: Differences and dominance.* Rowley, MA: Newbury House.

Zuckerman, M. et al. (1981). Facial, autonomic, and subjective components of emotion: The facial feedback hypothesis versus the externalizer-internalizer distinction. *Journal of Personality and Social Psychology, 41,* 929–944.

Zunin, Leonard M., & Zunin, Natalie B. (1972). *Contact: The first four minutes.* Los Angeles: Nash.

Zunin, Leonard M., & Zunin, Hilary Stanton. (1991). *The art of condolence: What to write, what to say, what to do at a time of loss.* New York: Harper Perennial.

Photo Credits

1: Mark Richards/PhotoEdit
8: Bob Strong/The Image Works
11: Flash! Light/Stock Boston
14: CBC (left); CBC (right)
16: Jake Wright (photo)/Stephen Kroninger (digital art)
20: CP Photo/Fred Chartrand (left); CP Photo/Jonathan Hayeard (right)
27: Paul Thomas/Getty Images
28: © Reuters New Media Inc/CORBIS/Magmaphoto.com
29: Gary Connor/PhotoEdit
33: David Young-Wolff/PhotoEdit
42: David Young-Wolff/PhotoEdit
49: Tony Latham/Getty Images
50: CP Photo/Joe Gararetta (left); CP Photo/Ryan Remiorz (right)
52: AP/Wide World Photos
58: Ian Shaw/Stone
59: Francisco Cruz/SuperStock
71: Ryan McVay/Getty Images
75: Ilene Perlman/Stock Boston
81: Ghislain & Marie David de Lossy/Getty Images
83: Zigy Kaluzny/Stone
91: Robert Nickelsberg/Getty Images
93: Michelle D. Birdwell/PhotoEdit
100: Tobin Grimshaw
101: Bob Daemmrich/Stock Boston
115: Bob Daemmrich/The Image Works
119: Reuters/Peter Morgan (left); CP Photo/Fran Gunn (right)
126: Michael Newman/PhotoEdit
128: James D. Wilson/Woodfin Camp & Associates

131: John Moore/The Image Works
139: Mary Kate Denny/Stone/Getty Images
141: Dick Hemingway
147: Al Harvey/The Slide Farm
150: Zigy Kaluzny/Getty Images
167: John Boykin/PhotoEdit
168: Bill Aron/PhotoEdit
169: Larry Williams/CORBIS
176: Lisa Sakulensky
184: CP Photo/PA (David Cheskin)
193: Bob Handelman/Getty Images
198: CP Photo/Paul Chiasson
200: Chuck Savage/CORBIS
205: Robert Brenner/PhotoEdit
206: SIAL Montréal
209: John Nordel/The Image Works
217: James McLoughlin/Stone
220: Ghislain & Marie David de Lossy/Getty Images
224: Bruce Ayres/Getty Images
229: Mitch Wojnarowicz/The Image Works
234: Amanda Wesson
237: Michael Newman/PhotoEdit
243: Jeff Smith/Getty Images
246: Bruce Ayres/Stone
250: Michael Newman/PhotoEdit
259: Owen Franken/Stock Boston
260: Michael Newman/PhotoEdit
271: Ron Chapple/Getty Images
274: Courtesy of Free the Children, www.freethechildren.com
291: Zigy Kaluzny/Getty Images

Index

risk, and intimacy, 224
ritualistic touching, 127
role culture, 275
rules, organization by, 51
rumours, 283

S

sad passivity, 226
sadness, 145
sassuru, 94
schemata, 51
scripts, 51
security, 229
selective attention, 50
selective exposure, 50
selective self-perception, 222
self-acceptance, 36
self-adaptors, 121
self-affirming statements, 32
self-awareness
    blind self, 31
    four selves, 30–31
    hidden self, 31
    importance of, 30
    increasing, 31–32
    Johari window, 30
    listen to others, 31–32
    open self, 30, 31
    unknown self, 31
self-concept
    cultural teachings, 29
    described, 28
    looking-glass self, 28
    observations, interpretations and evaluations, 30
    others' images of you, 28
    social comparisons, 29
    sources of, 29
self-critical statements, 289
self-denigration, 169
self-destructive beliefs, 294
self-destructive statements, 32
self-disclosure
    active and effective listening, 39
    appropriateness of, 38
    burdens, imposition of, 38
    confidentiality of disclosures, 39–40
    culture and, 33–34
    dangers of, 37
    described, 33
    dyadic effect, 35
    and effective communication, 36
    factors influencing, 33–34
    and gender, 34
    guidelines, 38–40
    listeners, 35
    making self-disclosures, guidelines, 38–39
    motivation for, 38
    outing, 34
    personal risks, 37
    physiological health, 37
    professional risks, 37
    reciprocity of, 38
    relationship risks, 37
    and relationships, 41–42
    responding to self-disclosure, guidelines, 39–40
    rewards of, 35–37
    self-acceptance, 36
    self-test, 36
    support the disclosure, 39
    topic, 35
    who you are, 33
self-esteem, 226–227, 293–294
self-fulfilling prophecy, 56–57
self-serving bias, 60
self-tests
    argumentativeness, 263
    beliefs about interpersonal communication, 3
    communication apprehension, 40–41
    confirmation, 98
    conflict-resolution survey, 256–257
    conversation, 162–163
    emotion, 144–145
    ethnocentrism, 203
    fact *vs.* inference, 107
    individualism, 199
    interpersonal perception, 54–55
    interpersonal relationships, 219–220
    listening, 77
    politeness, 169–170
    self-disclosure, 36
    verbal aggressiveness, 262
senders, 5
sex role stereotyping, 100
sexism, 99–100, 206
sexist language, 99–100
sexual harassment, 249, 292
signals, package of, 13
significant others, 28
silence, 129, 130, 132
silencers, 260–261
silent generation, 274
similarity, 51
six-stage model of interpersonal relationships, 222–228
skills. *See* interpersonal skills
slander, 249
slang, 289
smell messages, 130–131
the Snaidanac, 194
social action, 226
social bonding, 224
social comparisons, 29
social distance, 124
social interaction, 118
social-psychological dimension, 8
social separation, 226
social support, 227
societal rules and customs, 150
source, 5
space decoration, 126–127
space messages, 123–125
spamming, 250